Burning Boy

Burning Boy

The Life and Work of Stephen Crane

Paul Auster

HENRY HOLT AND COMPANY

NEW YORK

Henry Holt and Company
Publishers since 1866
120 Broadway
New York, New York 10271
www.henryholt.com

Henry Holt® and Ⓗ® are registered trademarks of Macmillan Publishing
Group, LLC.

Library of Congress Cataloging-in-Publication Data

Names: Auster, Paul, 1947– author.
Title: Burning boy : the life and work of Stephen Crane / Paul Auster.
Other titles: Life and work of Stephen Crane
Description: First edition. | New York : Henry Holt and Company, 2021. |
Includes bibliographical references and index.
Identifiers: LCCN 2020050244 (print) | LCCN 2020050245 (ebook) |
ISBN 9781250235831 (hardcover) | ISBN 9781250235848 (ebook)
Subjects: LCSH: Crane, Stephen, 1871–1900. | Authors, American—19th
century—Biography.
Classification: LCC PS1449.C85 Z543 2021 (print) | LCC PS1449.C85
(ebook) | DDC 813/.4 [B]—dc23
LC record available at https://lccn.loc.gov/2020050244
LC ebook record available at https://lccn.loc.gov/2020050245

Our books may be purchased in bulk for promotional, educational, or
business use. Please contact your local bookseller or the Macmillan
Corporate and Premium Sales Department at (800) 221-7945, extension 5442,
or by e-mail at MacmillanSpecialMarkets@macmillan.com.

First Edition 2021

Designed by Meryl Sussman Levavi

Printed in the United States of America

1 3 5 7 9 10 8 6 4 2

CONTENTS

✳

Burning Boy

STEVIE

❧❧

I

Born on the Day of the Dead and dead five months before his twenty-ninth birthday, Stephen Crane lived five months and five days into the twentieth century, undone by tuberculosis before he had a chance to drive an automobile or see an airplane, to watch a film projected on a large screen or listen to a radio, a figure from the horse-and-buggy world who missed out on the future that was awaiting his peers, not just the construction of those miraculous machines and inventions but the horrors of the age as well, including the destruction of tens of millions of lives in two world wars. His contemporaries were Henri Matisse (twenty-two months older than he was), Vladimir Lenin (seventeen months older), Marcel Proust (four months older), and such American writers as W. E. B. Du Bois, Theodore Dreiser, Willa Cather, Gertrude Stein, Sherwood Anderson, and Robert Frost, all of whom carried on well into the new century. But Crane's work, which shunned the traditions of nearly everything that had come before him, was so radical for its time that he can be regarded now as the first American modernist, the man most responsible for changing the way we see the world through the lens of the written word.

He took his first breath on Mulberry Place in Newark, New Jersey, the ninth surviving child of the fourteen offspring born to his devout Methodist parents, Jonathan Townley Crane and Mary Helen Peck Crane, and because his father was a minister who traveled from parish to parish in the later years of his long pastoral career, the boy grew up without the standard attachments to place, schools, and friends, moving at age three from Newark to Bloomington (now called South Bound Brook), at age five from Bloomington to Paterson, at age seven leaving Paterson for his father's next post as head of the congregation at Drew Methodist Church in Port Jervis, New York, a town of nine thousand people situated at the tristate juncture of New Jersey, Pennsylvania, and New York, where the Delaware and Neversink Rivers converge, and then, when his sixty-year-old father died suddenly of a heart attack three months after Crane's eighth birthday, the family was compelled to leave the parsonage, with his mother moving to Roseville, New Jersey, an unincorporated community/neighborhood within Newark bordering Bloomfield and East Orange, and the boy and his brother Edmund (older than Crane by fourteen years) going off to live with relatives on a farm in Sussex County, all of them eventually regrouping in Port Jervis to live with another brother, William (older by seventeen years), after which, in 1883, his mother bought a house in the resort town of Asbury Park, New Jersey ("The Summer Mecca of American Methodism"), where the teenage Crane began his career as a writer by composing summer holiday squibs for yet another one of his brothers (Townley, older by eighteen years), who ran a local news agency for the *New York Tribune* and the Associated Press. By then, two more of Crane's siblings had died: In 1884, his twenty-eight-year-old sister Agnes Elizabeth, a schoolteacher and short story writer who had been as much a mother to him as his own mother and had encouraged his interest in books, was killed by meningitis, and, in 1886, his twenty-three-year-old brother Luther was crushed to death when he fell under a moving train while working as a flagman and brakeman on the Erie Railroad. After one disaffected and aborted year as a college student (a single semester at Lafayette followed by another semester at Syracuse, where he played on the baseball team and registered for just one course), Crane headed back south to the twin destinations of Asbury Park and New York City, determined to make his way as a professional writer. He was not yet twenty years old. On September twenty-eighth, just blocks away from where Crane would soon be living in Manhattan, the unread and all but forgotten Herman Melville died. On November tenth, thousands of miles to the east in Marseille, France, Arthur Rimbaud died at the age of thirty-seven. Twenty-seven days after that, Crane's sixty-four-year-old mother died of cancer. The newly orphaned budding writer had only eight and a half more years to live himself, but in that short time he produced one masterpiece of a novel (*The Red Badge of Courage*), two boldly imagined and exquisite novellas (*Maggie: A Girl of the Streets* and *The Monster*), close to three dozen stories of unimpeachable brilliance (among them "The Open Boat" and "The Blue Hotel"), two collections of some of the strangest, most savage poems of the nineteenth century (*The Black Riders* and *War Is Kind*), and more than two hundred pieces of journalism, many of them so good that they stand on equal footing with his literary work. A burning boy of rare precociousness who was blocked from entering the fullness of adulthood, he is America's answer to Keats and Shelley, to Schubert and Mozart, and if he continues to live on as they do, it is because his work has never grown old. One hundred and twenty years after his death, Stephen Crane continues to burn.

2

IT COULD BE THAT I AM EXAGGERATING SOMEWHAT. THAT CRANE continues to burn is not in question, but whether he lives on as brightly as those other too soon extinguished burning boys is less clear. Once upon a time, almost every high school student in America was required to read *The Red Badge of Courage.* I was fifteen when I first encountered the novel in 1962, and it was an explosive, life-altering discovery for me, as it was for most of my classmates (boys and girls alike), but now, for reasons I find difficult to understand, the book seems to have fallen off the required reading lists, which has the double effect of depriving young students of an important literary experience and relegating Crane to the shadows, for if my classmates and I hadn't been exposed to *The Red Badge of Courage*, it is doubtful we would have taken the initiative to look into other works by Crane, the poems, for example (which can cause a sudden, general shock to the system), or the short stories, or the brutal depiction of New York slum life in *Maggie.* My evidence is purely anecdotal, but when I recently asked my thirty-year-old daughter if she had been assigned the book in high school, she said no, which led me to begin an informal survey of her friends, fifteen or twenty young men and women who had gone to high schools in various far-flung parts of the country, asking them the same question I had asked her, and one by one they all said no as well. Even more surprising, only one of my literary acquaintances from non-English-speaking countries has ever heard of Crane, which is also true for the vast majority of my English acquaintances, even though Crane was just as celebrated in England as he was in America during his lifetime. My non-American friends are familiar with Twain, Poe, Hawthorne, Emerson, Whitman, Henry James, and the once neglected Melville and Dickinson, but Crane, who deserves to stand among those gods (in my opinion), is a cipher to them.

That isn't to say that Crane no longer exists. His principal writings are readily available in numerous paperback editions, his collected works, published in ten volumes by the University Press of Virginia in the 1970s, are still in print, there is an excellent gathering of his selected prose and poetry that runs close to fourteen hundred pages from the Library of America, his novels and stories continue to be taught in college courses on American literature, and there is a veritable industry of Stephen Crane scholarship in the academic world. All that is reassuring, but at the same time I feel that Crane is now in the hands of the specialists, the lit majors and PhD candidates and tenured professors, while the invisible army of so-called general readers, that is, people who are not academics or writers themselves, the same people who still take pleasure in reading old standbys such as Melville and Whitman, are no longer reading Crane.

If it had been otherwise, I never would have thought of writing this book.

I come at it not as a specialist or a scholar but as an old writer in awe of a young writer's genius. Having spent the past two years poring over every one of Crane's works, having read through every one of his published letters, having snatched up every piece of biographical information I could put my hands on, I find myself just as fascinated by Crane's frantic, contradictory life as by the work he left us. It was a weird and singular life, full of impulsive risks, an often pulverizing lack of money, and a pigheaded, intractable devotion to his calling as a writer, which flung him from one unlikely and perilous situation to the next—a controversial article written at twenty that disrupted the course of the 1892 presidential campaign, a public battle with the New York Police Department that effectively exiled him from the city in 1896, a shipwreck off the coast of Florida that led to his near drowning in 1897, a common-law marriage to the proprietress of Jacksonville's most elegant bawdy house, the Hotel de Dreme, work as a correspondent during the Spanish-American War in Cuba (where he repeatedly stood in the line of enemy fire), and then his final years in England, where Joseph Conrad was his closest friend and Henry James wept over his early death—and this writer, who is best known as a chronicler of war, embraced many other subjects as well, handling them all with immense skill and originality, from stories about young children and struggling bohemian artists to firsthand accounts of New York opium dens, conditions in a Pennsylvania coal mine, and a devastating drought in Nebraska, and much like Edgar Allan Poe, often mistakenly identified as nothing more than our dark-browed purveyor of horror and mystery when in fact he was a master humorist as well, the somber, pessimistic

Crane could be hilariously funny when he chose to be. And underneath the mountain of his prose, or perhaps on top of it, there are his poems, which few people in or out of the academy have ever known quite what to do with, poems so far from the traditional norms of nineteenth-century verse-making—including the norm-breaking deviations of Whitman and Dickinson—that they scarcely seem to count as poetry at all, and yet they stay in the mind more persistently than most other American poems I can think of, as for example this one, which has continued to haunt me ever since I first read it more than five decades ago:

> In the desert
> I saw a creature, naked, bestial,
> Who, squatting upon the ground,
> Held his heart in his hands,
> And ate of it.
> I said, "Is it good, friend?"
> "It is bitter—bitter," he answered;
> "But I like it
> "Because it is bitter,
> "And because it is my heart."

3

BEFORE TACKLING CRANE HIMSELF, A BRIEF PAUSE TO SURVEY THE American landscape as it looked between 1871 and 1900, to situate our subject in the time and space he inhabited.

Among the new things that entered the world during those years, a partial list would include the following: barbed wire, earmuffs, the grain silo, blue jeans, the jockstrap, the mimeograph machine, the telephone, the dry-cell battery, the phonograph, the cable car, Heinz ketchup, Budweiser beer, the National League of Professional Baseball Clubs, the cash register, the typewriter, the incandescent lightbulb, the carpet sweeper, the Transcontinental Express (New York to San Francisco in 83½ hours), moving pictures, the player piano, the electric iron, the fountain pen, the flexible film roll, the all-purpose fixed-focus camera, the self-powered machine gun, the revolving door, the AC motor and transformer, the paper clip, saltwater taffy, the skyscraper, the slot machine, the drinking straw, the Flexible Flyer sled, the pay telephone, the safety razor, the electric fan, the electric chair, the blowtorch, the Linotype machine, the trolley car, cornflakes, the ceiling fan, color photography, the automatic telephone exchange, the milking machine, Coca-Cola, wireless telegraphy, the dishwasher, the X-ray, basketball, the comic strip, the escalator, the tabulating machine, shredded wheat, the smoke detector, the zipper, the rotary dial telephone, the bottle cap, pinking shears, the mousetrap, medical gloves, volleyball, the voting machine, the vertical filing cabinet, the modern Olympic Games, the Boston Marathon, the portable motion-picture camera, the film projector, remote control, the internal combustion engine, the flyswatter, the thumbtack, and cotton candy.

Between the assassination of Abraham Lincoln and the assassination of William McKinley in September 1901, which led to the presidency of Theodore Roosevelt (Crane's onetime friend and admiring reader, later his unbudgeable foe), the United States lived through a long period of growth, tumult, and moral failure, which transformed it from a backward, isolated country into a world power, but its leaders were mostly inept or corrupt or both, and the two great crimes embedded in the American Experiment— the enslavement of black Africans and the systematic annihilation of the continent's first settlers, an immense array of cultures lumped under the heading *Indians*—were never properly addressed or atoned for, and even though slavery had been abolished, the postwar efforts at Reconstruction dribbled away into nothing by 1877, forcing the black population in the South to live under a new but equally vile system of oppression, misery, exclusion, and intimidation, even to the point of death at the end of ropes knotted by racist vigilantes from the Ku Klux Klan. As for the Indians during those years, they were slaughtered by the United States cavalry (often commanded by generals who had been Civil War heroes), and those who survived were kicked off their land and penned up in government-run reservations, remote tracts of end-of-the-world desolation and despair, the hot, hopeless regions of Hell on Earth. The Battle of Little Bighorn (a.k.a. Custer's Last Stand) was fought in late June 1876, a week before America's one-hundredth-anniversary celebration, and so incensed were the white citizens of the Republic over this defeat at the hands of savages such as Chief Gall, Crazy Horse, and Chief Two Moons that the emboldened army resolved to answer the Indian Question once and for all. They finally accomplished their task by mowing down a crowd of ghost-dancing men, women, and children at Wounded Knee in South Dakota on December 29, 1890, two months after Crane's nineteenth birthday.

Meanwhile, the sparsely populated West was filling up with white settlers, vast numbers of Chinese were crossing the Pacific to find work in California, and the industrialized cities along the East Coast were absorbing millions of immigrants from all parts of Europe, a much-needed source of low-cost labor to toil in the factories, mills, sweatshops, and mines. Conditions were harsh for all of them. Homesteaders on the prairie often faced starvation and had to endure summer temperatures as high as one hundred degrees and winter temperatures that could sink to twenty, thirty, and sometimes forty below zero. Riots broke out in San Francisco, Los Angeles, and Seattle against the Chinese, who had to cope with unrelenting discrimination, bloody physical attacks, and spontaneous lynchings by crazed white mobs. (Anti-Chinese sentiment became so strong that in 1882 Congress passed the Chinese Exclusion Act, which barred Chinese workers from entering the country for the next ten years; in 1892, Congress renewed the act for another ten years.) In the case of the European immigrants, they were squeezed into stinking, airless tenements, too poor to live anywhere but in rough, dangerous slums as they worked for pennies at their twelve-hour-a-day jobs, which were often rough and dangerous as well, with no unions or labor laws to protect them. Such was city life at the bottom of the social ladder: a brave new world in which the Irish, the Germans, the Italians, the Greeks, the Scandinavians, the Hungarians, and the Poles all despised one another, and together as one they all despised the blacks and the Jews.

The rich, however, were very rich, and the richest among them, the so-called robber barons of that so-called Gilded Age, accumulated fortunes running into the hundreds of millions of dollars (the equivalent of untold billions today). Remarkably, most of their names are still familiar to us: J. P. Morgan, Andrew Carnegie, Cornelius Vanderbilt, John D. Rockefeller, Jay Gould, Leland Stanford, and numerous others. They made their money in the railroads, in steel, in oil, in banking, and all of them were clever, single-minded whirlwinds of ambition who crushed their competitors by both legal and illegal means to attain their extraordinary power. It was the era of the trust—a new form of monopoly designed to evade the anti-monopoly laws—which was invented by one of Rockefeller's lawyers (Samuel C. T. Dodd), and once it was put into practice in the oil industry, other industries soon followed, among them copper, steel, tobacco, sugar, rubber, leather, and even farm implements. The Sherman Anti-Trust Act of 1890 was supposed to put a stop to such massive concentrations of wealth, but it was weakly enforced and further undermined by a series of negative Supreme Court decisions. It was true that some of the biggest tycoons and their heirs later turned to philanthropy, but it was also true that Vanderbilt's son William (famous for throwing the most lavish and expensive parties of the time, no doubt among the most lavish and expensive since the fall of the Roman Empire) responded to a question from a reporter about his responsibility to the public by saying, "The public be damned." The railroad-rich Jay Gould, one of the more flamboyant crooks of nineteenth-century capitalism, is reported to have bragged, "I can hire one half of the working class to kill the other half."

Contrary to Gould's assertion, members of the working class were not killing one another so much as being killed by a system designed to extract maximum profits for business owners at the expense of their employees' health, earning power, and safety. The pushback against capitalism had begun in Europe long before the outbreak of the American Civil War, but various forms of that pushback came to the New World with the immigrants—the revolutionary socialism of Marx, the evolutionary socialism of Eduard Bernstein, the subversive doctrines of anarchism (McKinley was murdered by an anarchist, Leon Czolgosz)—and on home ground indigenous opposition groups sprang up as well, some of them both progressive and reactionary at the same time, such as the Populist Party and the Grange, which defended the little man and the farmer against the depredations of big capital but turned their backs on immigrants and (no surprise) black people and Jews, but a number of more forward-looking and inclusive workers' organizations also came into being, among them the Noble Order of the Knights of Labor (founded in 1869), which had seven hundred thousand members at its peak in the 1880s, and the American Federation of Labor (the AF of L), founded by Samuel Gompers in 1886, which fought for an eight-hour workday, the abolition of child labor, better wages, and improved working conditions. Alongside those moderate, practical goals, there were the more strident positions advanced by the Socialists (as embodied in the person of Eugene Debs, who ran for president five times), the Anarchists (notably Alexander Berkman and Emma Goldman, both of whom were eventually deported), and Pennsylvania Coal Country's Molly Maguires, who terrorized the mine owners with their violent guerrilla tactics and were infiltrated and ultimately destroyed by undercover Pinkerton agents (ten were hanged for murder in June 1877). If the latter part of the nineteenth century was the era of the trusts, it was also the era of some of the most prolonged and deadly strikes in American history. The Great Strike of 1877 began in July with a walkout of workers on the Baltimore and Ohio Railroad, then spread to other railroads from New England to the Mississippi and finally across the entire country, which led factory workers and miners to stage sympathy strikes of their own. When violence broke out in Martinsburg, West Virginia, the state militia was called in, but after the militia refused to open fire on the strikers, the secretary of war summoned federal troops to take their place. In Baltimore, nine strikers were killed and several wounded when the state militia fired point-blank into a crowd. Riots ensued, and over the next days fifty more people were killed. In Pittsburgh, the state militia and strikers exchanged gunfire, and then a real fire was set, which burgeoned into a wall of flame that extended over three miles, destroying two thousand freight cars and causing more than ten million dollars' worth of property damage. In Chicago, local police and cavalry attacked an impromptu gathering of strikers and nineteen people were killed. Sympathy strikes continued to grow, and by the end of July forty thousand coal miners had walked off their jobs in Scranton, Pennsylvania. For all their efforts, not much improved for the railroad workers in the wake of these battles, but the Scranton miners managed to win a ten percent wage increase and other concessions from the mine owners. More to the point, the events of 1877 proved to the country that the labor movement was now large enough to have become an omnipresent force in American life.

The litany continues. In 1882: the three-month-long strike of iron and steel workers; the freight handlers strike that disrupted rail transportation for several weeks. 1886: the strike against Jay Gould's Missouri-Pacific railroad system, during which nine thousand strikers shut down five thousand miles of track. That year, more than six hundred thousand workers in various industries went out on strike. In May, an attack on strikebreaking workers at the McCormick Reaper Manufacturing Company in Chicago elicited a response from the police that wound up killing six and wounding a dozen others, which led to the Haymarket Square riots the following afternoon, during which a bomb was thrown, killing seven policemen and wounding fifty. Four anarchists were sentenced to death and four others put in prison, three of them for life. It seems likely that none of the eight was responsible for throwing the bomb, but with newspaper headlines declaring, "TERROR GRIPS THE COUNTRY," it hardly mattered who was responsible or not. Countless other strikes took place over the years that followed, but the biggest and most notorious among them were no doubt the Homestead Strike of 1892 and the Pullman Strike of 1894. The action against Andrew Carnegie's Homestead mill on the Monongahela River in Pennsylvania lasted five months and led to dozens of deaths and hundreds of injuries, an emblematic instance of management's refusal to negotiate with labor, backing up that intransigence by persuading the governor to call in seven thousand members of the state militia. Carnegie's associate Henry Clay Frick (the same Frick who lived in the New York mansion on Fifth Avenue that housed the private art collection which has been open to the public since 1935) was responsible for calling in Pinkerton agents armed with Winchester rifles to attack the strikers, and so hated did he become among those who supported the strike that anarchist Alexander Berkman attempted to assassinate him in his office, shooting Frick twice and stabbing him three times, but the attempt failed, the strike was broken, and Berkman was sentenced to twenty-two years in prison. Thousands lost their jobs. In 1894, a year when three-quarters of a million workers laid down their tools in protest, the Pullman Strike in Chicago was also broken with no tangible results, but for a brief time mayhem ruled, leading to a nationwide boycott that stopped all rail traffic west of Detroit, and the leader of the insurrection, Eugene Debs, although sentenced to six months in prison for defying a federal injunction against interfering with the operation of the U.S. mail, emerged as a hero of the Left. He lived on until 1926 and is perhaps best known today for having said, "While there is a lower class, I am in it, while there is a criminal element, I am of it, and while there is a soul in prison, I am not free."

Not to be forgotten in the midst of these ongoing wars between capital and labor were the ups and downs of the market itself, which crashed twice during the years in question. The Panic of 1873 forced the New York Stock Exchange to close for ten days, and in a depression that lasted for five years, more than ten thousand businesses failed, hundreds of banks shut down, and plans for a second transcontinental railroad line were scrapped. It is doubtful that the two-year-old or even six-year-old Crane was aware of what was happening then, but the Panic of 1893 was a different story. Crane was nearly twenty-two and already living in New York when the largest and deepest of all American depressions struck (surpassed only by the Great Depression of the 1930s), in the throes of the most sustained creative burst of his life (the completion and publication of *Maggie*, the composition of his first book of poems, the preliminary drafts of *George's Mother* and *The Red Badge of Courage*, not to speak of various stories, sketches, and articles), and he suffered along with everyone else in the city, where unemployment oscillated between thirty and thirty-five percent, so poor at times that he had to scrounge for food and was often dressed so shabbily that he felt ashamed to go out in public.

It was also the era of Jane Addams and the settlement house movement, which began in Chicago and spread east and west to more than thirty states, an idealistic yet pragmatic effort to protect the rights of children and ameliorate conditions among the poor. The success of Hull House, the Henry Street Settlement in New York, and scores of other charitable endeavors proved that women could play a significant role in the civic life of the country. Without question, women were still relegated to the margins during those years, but a number of remarkable exceptions should be noted, women like Jane Addams who also managed to make their mark on society: Susan B. Anthony, Elizabeth Cady Stanton, Mary Baker Eddy, Mother Jones, Clara Barton, Madame Blavatsky, the painter Mary Cassatt, and the journalist Nellie Bly (the pen name of Elizabeth Cochran), one of America's first and most intrepid investigative reporters, who famously pretended to be mad in order to gain admittance to an insane asylum, and then, after being released at the request of her employer, Joseph Pulitzer of the *New York World*, exposed the wretched, inhuman treatment she had been subjected to there. She also bested Phileas Fogg's imaginary record of circumnavigating the globe in eighty days (as recounted in Jules Verne's novel) by completing the journey in seventy-two days. But women were also joining together to form large mass movements demanding change of the status quo, among them the National American Woman Suffrage Association and the Woman's Christian Temperance Union (of which Crane's mother was an active member and served as president of three different local chapters). The union finally won its victory with the passage of the Eighteenth Amendment to the Constitution in 1919, ushering in the less than fondly remembered Prohibition Era, but just one year later, after making some small headway on the municipal and state levels, women's suffrage became the law of the land, and the door that had been bolted shut for so many centuries at last began to crack open.

State universities, colleges for women, colleges for black students, private colleges founded by various religious denominations, along with the building of libraries, museums, concert halls, and opera houses radically altered America's intellectual and cultural life, so much so that a number of black and Jewish figures eventually worked their way into prominence: Paul Laurence Dunbar, Booker T. Washington, W. E. B. Du Bois, Louis Brandeis, Abraham Cahan, and Emma Lazarus, to mention just a handful of the most recognizable names. In New York City alone, the years during which Crane lived saw the construction of the Metropolitan Museum of Art, the Brooklyn Bridge, Grand Central Station, the Statue of Liberty, Carnegie Hall, the American Museum of Natural History, the Columbia University campus, and Frederick Law Olmsted's two glorious creations, Central Park in Manhattan and Prospect Park in Brooklyn. They are all still with us today, twenty years into the twenty-first century.

And then there was the West, which would tug at the New Jersey–born Crane all his life. The years of his boyhood were saturated with the dime novels that made legends of the fighting men from the rugged frontier, the same men who evolved into the characters featured in hundreds of films throughout the twentieth century, Wild Bill Hickok, Buffalo Bill Cody, Wyatt Earp, Jesse James, and the boy assassin Billy the Kid, who was gunned down by Pat Garrett in 1881 and continues to sit on his sacred throne as an American Immortal. But the West was more than just a place, it was an idea, a myth, a dream territory that belonged exclusively to the New World with no lingering ties to the European past, the land of the country's future. When Crane traveled west in 1895 to write articles for the Bacheller Syndicate, he had never been anywhere outside of New Jersey, New York, and Pennsylvania, and he fell in love with what he saw. It was his one and only visit to the region, but it stayed with him to the end and inspired some of his most sharply written and memorable stories, "A Man and Some Others," "The Bride Comes to Yellow Sky," and "The Blue Hotel."

As for the American novelists who overlapped with Crane from the early nineties to the turn of the century, only a few of them are still read today. At the top of the list stand Mark Twain, William Dean Howells, and Henry James, all of whom were flourishing during those years and all of whom would come to know Crane, as well as Ambrose Bierce, Kate Chopin, Frank Norris, and Sarah Orne Jewett. In painting, some of the leading members of the Hudson River school were still alive (Thomas Moran, Frederic Edwin Church, and Albert Bierstadt), but a younger generation had already established itself by then, and because Crane's years in New York were spent mostly among artists, not writers, and because he learned as much about writing from looking at art as he did from reading books, the names of those artists bear mentioning: John Singer Sargent, Winslow Homer, Thomas Eakins, James Whistler, and the two eccentric but enduring innovators who worked on past the Gilded Age into the new century, Ralph Albert Blakelock and Albert Pinkham Ryder.

Not least, it was the moment when Samuel S. McClure created the first international news syndicate, which coincided with the birth of large-circulation newspapers. The engine that made this possible was the newly invented Linotype machine, which worked six times faster than the hand-set, letter-by-letter system it replaced and allowed daily papers to publish editions that far exceeded the eight-page limit of the past. In Manhattan, Joseph Pulitzer took charge of the *New York World*, William Randolph Hearst assumed control of the *New York Journal*, and the high-pressure sweepstakes of yellow journalism began, forever changing how Americans interacted with their own universe. After Crane moved to the city in 1891/1892, he worked for all three of those men in a kind of permanent rotation until the year of his death, scratching along on the bits they paid him because he was bent on earning his living as a writer and refused to consider any other sort of work. A noble decision, perhaps, but except for a few periods of relative tranquility, he had a rough time of it until the very end.

The Linotype machine giveth, and the Linotype machine taketh away.

4

HIS PARENTS NAMED HIM STEPHEN AFTER TWO OF HIS CRANE ANCESTORS, a seventeenth-century Stephen Crane who was one of the founding fathers of Elizabethtown, the earliest English settlement in what would become the colony of New Jersey (other seventeenth-century Cranes not named Stephen helped found Newark and Montclair, which was originally known as Cranetown), and an eighteenth-century Stephen Crane who supported the Revolution, served as Speaker of the New Jersey General Assembly, and was a delegate to the Continental Congress in Philadelphia, where he would have been one of the signers of the Declaration of Independence if he had not been called back to New Jersey on urgent political business. In 1780, he was captured by the British and bayoneted to death; not long after, his son Jonathan was also captured by the British and executed for refusing to divulge the position of Washington's army to them. Another one of the second Stephen Crane's sons, William, distinguished himself in the Revolution by commanding a New Jersey regiment and rose to the rank of major general, and his son, also named William, was a naval commander during the War of 1812. As Crane himself wrote to an inquiring journalist from the *Newark Sunday Call* in 1896: "The family is founded deep in Jersey soil (since the birth of Newark), and I am about as much a Jerseyman as you can find."

However far he might have drifted from that Jersey soil, his family was of utmost importance to him, not just the heroic figures from the Crane past but the Cranes from the present as well, for even though he turned against the Methodism of his parents, he never turned against his parents themselves, and he remained in close contact with two of his brothers throughout his adulthood—the same Edmund and William who had taken care of him as a boy. In answer to a request for autobiographical information from journalist John Northern Hilliard in early 1896, Crane starts his half-serious, half-jocular reply by confessing that "I am not much versed in talking about myself" and in the third paragraph makes these few short comments about his parents: "Upon my mother's side, everybody as soon as he could walk, became a Methodist clergyman—of the old ambling-nag, saddle-bag,

Jonathan Townley Crane.
(COURTESY OF SYRACUSE UNIVERSITY)

exhorting kind. My uncle, Jesse T. Peck, D.D., L.L.D., was a bishop in the Methodist Church. My father was also a clergyman of that church, author of numerous works of theology, an editor of various periodicals of the church. He graduated at Princeton. He was a great, fine, simple mind."

Jonathan Townley Crane was born in 1819, the same year as Melville and Whitman, and like his son he was the youngest child in a family of many siblings. Orphaned at thirteen, apprenticed to a Newark trunk-maker as an adolescent, he converted to Methodism at age eighteen and was eventually admitted to Princeton (then called the College of New Jersey), where he excelled at his studies, won a prize in English composition, and was president of one of the two literary societies on campus. He joined the Methodist clergy after graduation and spent the rest of his life in the church, serving in various capacities both administrative and pastoral over the decades, the longest stint being the nine years he spent after his 1848 marriage to Crane's mother in Pennington, New Jersey, where he served as principal of Pennington Seminary, a Methodist-run school for male and female students, and the eight years he spent as presiding elder of the Newark district. Otherwise, he was given short postings of no more than a year or two at assorted churches in northern New Jersey and southern New York State, fathered fourteen children in the process (five of whom did not live beyond infancy or babyhood), wrote numerous articles for the *Methodist Quarterly Review* and the *Christian Advocate*, and published several books, among them *An Essay on Dancing* (1849), *Popular Amusements* (1869), and *Arts of Intoxication: The Aim and the Results* (1870), which attacked not only the frivolous pastime of dancing (as the first title suggests) but other activities such as reading second-rate, sentimental novels, card playing, and drinking. It will come as no surprise, perhaps, that his youngest son did not refrain from indulging in the last two of those vices, rarely if ever drinking to excess but drinking as much or as little as he pleased and developing a lifelong passion for poker, to such a degree that it would be fair to call him a *poker fanatic*. For all that exhorting, however, Crane's father was widely known as a warmhearted, humorous man with a strong social conscience. He supported women's suffrage, had denounced slavery in print long before the Civil War began, and toward the end of his life, after the family moved to Port Jervis in 1878, he and Crane's mother founded two schools to help struggling black residents of the area, the Mission Sunday School for men and the Drew Mission and Industrial School for women and children. His death in 1880 was the first great blow of his son's life. Although Reverend Crane had been in town for just two years, fourteen hundred people turned out for his funeral—more than double the size of his congregation. By all accounts, it was the largest funeral in the history of Port Jervis.

Crane's mother plays a larger role in the story if only because she outlived her husband by almost twelve years, also dying when Crane was young, but not desperately young, not eight years old but twenty, and as her last, unanticipated offspring, her little miracle baby following thirteen other pregnancies, born a full eight years after her previous child, she doted on him in ways his father never did—or could. Mary Helen Peck Crane (1827–1891) grew up in Wilkes-Barre, Pennsylvania, the third child and only girl out of the five children in the Peck family. Her father, Reverend George Peck, started out as an itinerant backwoods Methodist preacher and rose through the ranks of the church to become one of its most important representatives, an author of several books and the editor of the *Methodist Quarterly Review* and the *Christian Advocate*, publications that Crane's father contributed to. All four of her father's brothers were also in the Methodist clergy, including the bishop referred to in her son's

1896 letter, Jesse T. Peck, yet one more prolific writer in the clan and a co-founder of Syracuse University, and two of her brothers went on to become Methodist ministers as well. The entire Peck family was immersed in the waters of religion—including Crane's mother—but it should be pointed out that not one of the seven Crane boys was ever tempted to follow his father, grandfather, or uncles into the Methodist lake.

She was allowed to pursue an education because her father was a staunch defender of equal rights for women, and in her teens she left Pennsylvania to attend the Young Ladies Institute of Brooklyn, then moved on to the Rutgers Female Institute, the first college for women in New York City, where she earned a degree in 1847. The following year, at twenty-one, she married Crane's father and held fast throughout the thirty-two years of their solid if somewhat frenzied union (so many houses occupied and abandoned, so many children living and dead), addressing Jonathan Townley by the affectionate nickname of "Jounty" rather than as "Mr. Crane," which would have been standard wife protocol for the period, and in spite of her gargantuan family responsibilities, she became increasingly active outside the home as well, so active by the time Crane was born that she was at the forefront of various social and religious causes as both a writer and a spokeswoman, traveling throughout the country to deliver her temperance lectures before large crowds, and, in her spare time (one asks: What spare time?), she painted, sculpted much-admired wax figures, and occasionally wrote short stories. In 1885–86, she suffered a nervous breakdown. Out of commission for about six months, she returned to her former activities with full vigor and in one year alone was credited with having written twenty-five columns for a local newspaper and more than one hundred dispatches for the Associated Press and various New York publications.

Helen R. Crane, the eldest daughter of Crane's brother Wilbur, who grew up to become a journalist and had known her uncle well during her childhood, was perhaps the first person ever to report on Crane's feelings about his mother. In a reminiscence published in the *American Mercury* in 1934, she wrote: "His mother's memory was dear to him, he had nothing dearer, and although he never questioned her ways when he was outside the family portals, he did marvel always that such an intellectual woman, a university graduate, and capable of being a regular contributor to magazines and newspapers, could have wrapped herself so completely in the 'vacuous, futile, psalm-singing that passed for worship' in those days."

Nevertheless, if Crane learned nothing else from his parents, their

Mary Helen Peck Crane.
(COURTESY OF SYRACUSE UNIVERSITY)

example taught him that the world was a place in which responsible grown-ups sat at their desks and wrote, that writing was an important if not essential human activity. Or, as his niece put it: "Being a Crane, he was born with printer's ink in his veins."

There is no record of how Crane responded to the deaths of his parents nor a single word in print about his reaction to the deaths of his sister Agnes and his brother Luther. Of his remaining siblings, he had little more than the most tenuous connection with his sister Mary Helen ("Nellie"), a painter born in 1849, and his brother George, a Jersey City post office employee born in 1850, but the four others were all a presence in his life, and their stories are worth telling here, since their divergent fates run the gamut from bourgeois respectability to oddball outlandishness, from material success to grim failure, from sober rectitude to alcoholism, from normal health to confinement in a madhouse.

Wilbur (born in 1859) spent five years at Columbia's College of Physicians and Surgeons and flunked out after failing to pass his courses on anatomy and having his thesis on typhoid fever rejected twice. With a medical career no longer in his future, he returned to home base in Asbury Park and worked for a couple of years at his brother Townley's news agency. In 1888, he scandalized the family by marrying one of his brother William's servants and eventually moved with his wife and four children to Binghamton, New York. He went into a business of some kind there (the sources are obscure on this point), but just as he was beginning to prosper, his wife left him, taking their children with her. Heart-shattered and defeated, he moved to a small town in Georgia and died in 1918, a victim of the Spanish flu pandemic.

Even bleaker is the tale of the eccentric and gifted Townley (pronounced "Toonley"), the man responsible for giving the young Crane his first job as a writer. Born in 1853, he was the wild one in the family, a fractious, subversive boy who often clashed with and insulted his father, but in his adulthood he turned into a first-rate journalist. Secretary of the New York Press Club, a sought-after lecturer, the historian of baseball's National League, an outspoken advocate for women's rights, and founder of his own news agency, he was so assiduous in hunting down stories that he came to be known as the "Shore Fiend." An incorrigible flake who was forever quipping and cracking off-the-wall jokes, he never wore a shirt while at work, hiding his torso under a long coat and sporting a filthy slouch hat on his head. For all his quirks, he was an admired figure, the leading newspaperman of the area, but also a person with a talent for running into some of the foulest bad luck imaginable. He and his wife lost two children, and in 1883, after just five years of marriage, she died of Bright's disease before the age of thirty. He remarried in 1890, and within half a year his second wife suffered a breakdown and wound up in the Trenton asylum, where she died two months later. A third marriage in 1893 ended in divorce. By the turn of the century, Townley had lapsed into severe alcoholism and was subject to periodic fits of violence. He had turned into what one friend called a "physical derelict" and was no longer employable. After moving to upstate New York to live with Wilbur and his wife (the same wife who would soon abandon Wilbur), he was twice committed to the Binghamton Asylum for the Chronic Insane—and died there, penniless, in 1908.

William, just one year younger than Townley, turned into a solid burgher with a law degree and a good nose for business, a leading citizen of Port Jervis known as Judge Crane (after serving a single one-year term as special judge of Orange County), the acknowledged head of the family after the reverend's death in 1880 and a quasi second father to his youngest brother, with all the positives and negatives that term implies. During his years in New York City, Crane would go up to Port Jervis for brief or more extended irregular visits with William and his family, but aside from some sporadic, minimal handouts when Crane was dead broke, the one gift of any true importance William gave him was free run of the Hartwood Club, a nature preserve of thirty-six hundred acres located twelve miles north of town, which William and a group of associates began acquiring in the late 1880s and incorporated in 1893, for even though much of Crane's early writing is grounded in the streets of the city, he was a country boy at heart, and the chance to escape into that wilderness was a great boon to him. For the rest of his life—even after he settled in England—he used Edmund's house in Hartwood, New York, as his permanent address.

Of all the brothers, it was Edmund who was closest to him, the same Edmund whom Crane chose to be his legal guardian after their mother's death in 1891 (he still had one year to go before he officially became an adult), the same Edmund at whose house in Lake View, New Jersey, Crane frequently lived during his early years in the New York area, writing much of the first draft of *The Red Badge of Courage* there in the summer of 1893, and when Edmund left his office job in New York to work as custodian of the Hartwood Club in the spring of 1894 (where he served, according to a letter Crane wrote to his friend Willis Brooks Hawkins, as "postmaster, justice-of-the-peace, ice-man, farmer, millwright, blue stone man, lumberman, station agent on the P.J.M. and N.Y.R.R., and many other things which I now forget"), Crane's subsequent visits to the north were as much about reconnecting with Edmund as riding his horse through the woods. To understand their bond, one has only to read the short letter Crane wrote to his infant nephew from England a few months before his death—upon learning that Edmund's wife, Mary, had given birth to twin boys and that one of them had been named Stephen.

> My dear Stephen: I need not say to you that I welcomed your advent with joy. You and I will struggle on with the name together and do as best we may. In the meantime, I would remind you to grow up, as much as possible, like your gentle kindly lovable father and please do not repeat the vices and mistakes of
> Your devoted uncle,
> Stephen Crane.

5

WHATEVER IS KNOWN ABOUT CRANE'S CHILDHOOD COMES FROM A COU-
ple of photographs and several eyewitness accounts written by relatives and
friends. Nearly all of those texts were composed years after the fact and
therefore are susceptible to the wobbles and deceptions of memory. Whenever someone quotes Crane directly, we have to read the words with suspicion, since most of us would be hard-pressed to rehash verbatim what
someone said to us just five minutes ago, let alone five years ago, or thirty
years ago. This holds true not just of Crane's childhood but of all the other
periods of his life as well, for many people who had known him put their
reminiscences down on paper after his death, but it is doubtful that the
words they attribute to him were the ones he actually spoke. Still, because
Crane never kept a diary, and because his published letters are mostly devoid
of intimate revelations about himself, we must rely on those witnesses, however flawed their memories might be. And yet, flawed or not, that isn't to say
their memories aren't valuable, for in the end they tell us much.

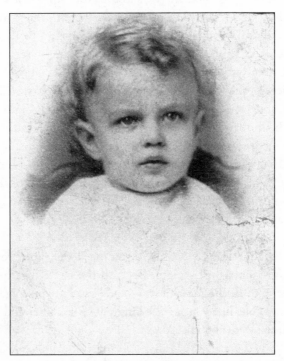

Stephen Crane, circa 1873.
(COURTESY OF SYRACUSE UNIVERSITY)

Crane at the Jersey Shore, circa 1879.
(COURTESY OF THE UNIVERSITY OF VIRGINIA)

The first photograph shows him as an infant of about one and a half looking into the camera with a steady gaze. A curly-headed blond with full lips and somewhat larger than average ears, he was, to use the words his brother Wilbur later wrote about him, "a beautiful baby."

The second photograph is more interesting: Crane at about seven, standing on a pebble beach somewhere along the New Jersey coast, a full-body shot cut off at the toes, dressed in a white sailor suit with short pants hanging down an inch below his knees, a broad straw hat sitting precariously on his head, his left arm draped over the edge of a dinghy, into which his left hand has disappeared, his right arm hanging plumb down his right side, and a look on his face that can be read as either a slight scowl or a reflexive squint against the glare of the sun, but whatever that look is, there is something peeved about it, as if he resented having to stand still for the photo, and from his expression one gathers there are numerous wheels turning around in his head, that this is a boy who has already cultivated an uncommonly rich inner life.

Everyone called him "Stevie," both in and out of the family, an affectionate diminutive that clung to him into adulthood, and when he first learned to talk, he couldn't handle the *s* and dubbed himself "Tevie." In a series of rapidly dashed-off notes for a potential biography that was never written, the female companion of his last years, Cora Taylor (known as Mrs. Crane), added: "One day when 2½ yrs of age someone asked him his name while his eyes fairly danced he said: 'nome Pe-pop-ty' no one ever knew where he got it from; he evidently made it up—"

He seems to have been both robust and sickly, an active child prone to frequent, sometimes alarming illnesses that kept him in and out of school until his health stabilized at around the age of eight, but when he was in good form he played hard at physical games and impressed everyone with his fearlessness. Edmund reports that when the family left Newark for Bloomington, he and his brothers often went swimming in the Raritan River, not just the big boys but the pint-sized Crane as well.

> There was a smooth, sandy bar extending from the south bank across the river, very shallow near shore and growing deeper toward the middle of the river. Stevie would wade around in the shallows watched by one of us. Wading breast deep in the water, he would stretch out his arms and waving his hands, would achieve what he called "fimming." He started to "fim" to Wee-wee, (Willie), my next older brother, who was farther out in the river. As the depth gradually increased the water came up to his chin, then to his mouth, and then his eyes, but he kept steadily on, and, I plucked him out, gasping but unscared, just as his yellow hair was going under. We boys were naturally delighted with his grit.

Elizabeth Crane, the wife of Crane's brother George, remembered her boy brother-in-law as "a vigorous lad . . . passionately fond of outdoor sports, as well as everything pertaining to military affairs. . . . He loved to play at soldiers from his early childhood. Most of his playthings were in the form of toy soldiers, guns and the like. . . . When the boy grew older he learned to play baseball and football. He was a member of a uniformed baseball team in Asbury Park, and proved one of the mainstays of the club, although he was the lightest and youngest member."

In Cora's telegraph-style notes, there is also this: "greatest play as infant boy buttons which he would call soldiers & would maneuver his armies— never picked up buttons after play."

Edmund elaborates: "Indoors he had a military game he played alone with buttons of different colors which to him were soldiers of opposing armies. These he marshalled about the floor operating some system that I, for one, did not understand. This game would occupy him for hours at a time, especially on rainy days."

Edmund also adds that in Asbury Park, Crane had "a trick pony, that he loved devotedly, and whose tricks, learned in some past circus experience, were constantly coming to the surface to Stevie's wonder and delight. The pony had a large B branded upon his shoulder, and we credited the late P. T. Barnum with having been his owner."

As for the little boy's mind, who knows what he was thinking? Edmund asserts that he was "bright and very teachable" and goes on to explain that shortly after Crane learned to talk, "I amused myself by having him pronounce five and six syllable words. After a few laughable failures, he would accomplish a correct pronunciation by spelling the word after me syllable by syllable, resolving them into their sound elements." In the next paragraph of his short memoir, he tells a family anecdote that reveals why he and his siblings looked upon their tyke brother as "a pet and entertainer":

> When he was about three years old, an older brother, Townley, was a cub reporter with one of the Newark dailies . . . and when writing his stories at home would often call on his mother for the correct spelling of a word. Stevie was making weird marks on a paper with a lead pencil one day and in the exact tone of one, absorbed in composition, and coming to the surface only for a moment of needed information, called to his mother, "Ma, how do you spell 'O'?" this happening to be a letter he had just become acquainted with.

Everyone insists that Crane could read fluently by the time he was four.

Nothing is known about his day-to-day conduct in childhood, whether he was a cooperative boy, an obstreperous boy, or a combination of the two, but the available testimony suggests that he was more independent than most small people, an entertaining pet but not a docile one, with a character that tended more toward willfulness than mute submission and, every so often, led to acts of out-and-out mischief. At seven, inspired by a picture that was hanging on a wall in the house (a duck-hunting scene painted by his mother), he shot an arrow straight into the canvas. No word survives on whether he was punished or not.

Religion, of course, was all around him from the moment his life began, the competing strains of Methodism as embodied by his mother's family (harsh) and his father (somewhat less harsh), which meant that he was obliged to attend Sunday school every week, and while it isn't known how often he took part in church services and listened to his father's much-admired sermons, there is no question that the Methodist prayers and hymns he heard throughout his childhood dug their way into the deepest, most internal recesses of his memory. When he was nine or ten, he was given a copy of a book written in 1858 by his great-uncle Bishop Jesse T. Peck, *What Must I Do to Be Saved?*, which the boy surely read, or at least handled and looked at and absorbed to some extent. Crane soon rebelled against the narrowness of his great-uncle's teachings, but he held on to the book for the rest of his life.*

Before long, the stubbornness that would evolve into one of his enduring traits was already beginning to coalesce into what one might call *a code of being*. According to Wilbur, "Stephen's most marked characteristic was his absolute truthfulness. He was in many minor scrapes but no consideration of consequences would induce him to lie out of them, and the imputation that he was a liar, made the imputer *persona non grata* with Stephen forever thereafter." Or, as Helen R. Crane put it in her article for the *American Mercury*, writing about an older version of her uncle: "I can't imagine him lying about anything. In fact, he was the sort of person who would have got a great thrill out of being shot at sunrise and all that kind of thing."

An honest boy, but not always an upright or obedient one, and deep down in his conflicted Methodist heart, a quiet rebel was lurking, who from time to time would transform himself into a daredevil tough. One such episode, as recounted by Post Wheeler, is among the most pertinent stories preserved from Crane's childhood. It comes from the summer of 1878, when Wheeler was about to turn nine and Crane was six and a half. After a lapse of more than a dozen years, they crossed paths again in the early 1890s when they were both working for New York newspapers in Asbury Park, and a solid, lasting friendship developed between them. Wheeler eventually left journalism for a long and successful career in diplomacy, but the memory of his first meeting with Crane never left him,

---

* During his one semester at Syracuse when he was nineteen, Crane told a friend, classmate Frank W. Noxon, that "he thought his indifference to religion exceeded the intrinsic merits and attributed this to a reaction against too much." Notwithstanding that *too much*, Crane took pleasure in attending Sunday night recitals with Noxon at St. Paul's Episcopal Cathedral where, in the words of his friend, "from a rear pew we sang a robust obligate to the music of the boy choir." Liturgical music—along with a love of singing—had been planted in Crane as a boy, and even if Christian dogma now left him cold, the musical trappings of his rejected faith continued to provide him with a zone of inner comfort.

and when he wrote about it as an old man in the 1950s, it still has the ring of truth. Not the precise words they spoke to each other, perhaps, but the gist of it—and the shock of it.

In early July 1878, Crane and his mother left New Jersey to spend a few days in Pennsylvania's Wyoming Valley (not far from where she was born) to listen to a speech delivered by Frances E. Willard, the secretary of the Woman's Christian Temperance Union, and to attend the one-hundredth-anniversary reenactment of the Wyoming Valley Massacre, a Revolutionary War battle during which local settlers were attacked and murdered by a combination of British and Indian forces. That was where he met Wheeler, whose background was remarkably similar to his: a father who was a Methodist minister, a mother who was active in the temperance movement. Wheeler's mother had an appointment with Mrs. Crane at the hotel where he and his parents had spent the night, and the New Jersey woman arrived with her boy in tow.

That was my first meeting with Stevie Crane. He was a pale-faced, blond-headed, hungry-looking boy a bit younger than I, and we struck up an intimacy that was to be renewed when we were in our twenties.

Next day Mrs. Crane and Stevie accompanied us to our town to spend two days as my parents' guests. The day coach was full and we boys were allowed to ride in the "smoker," where Stevie blandly (though with some covert backward glances toward the car which held his mother) lighted a Sweet Caporal cigarette and offered me one. . . . I accepted Stevie's weed and to my surprise was not sick.

The day following . . . was a red-letter day for us, with popcorn, toy balloons, rattan canes, and stick candy, and hawkers selling every conceivable gewgaw. . . .

Yet the peak was to come. Beside the exit gate a fat Pennsylvania Dutchman had set up a keg of beer on an upturned box on which stood a row of glass mugs, with a sign which said: Beer 10 cents. When Stevie took a dime from his pocket and approached it with an air of purpose, my blood chilled. "What are you going to do?" I asked in a hollow undertone. Stevie did not answer. He set down the dime on the box and said, "Gimme one."

I can still see the man's rotund face as he bent down over his keg and surveyed Stevie's diminutive figure. "Hey?" he said.

"I said gimme a beer," said Stevie.

The man's fingers had closed on the eloquent coin. "You gimme a beer or gimme back my dime!" said Stevie in a shrill falsetto.

The man held the mug with a dab of foam in it toward him, but Stevie regarded it with fine scorn. "That ain't half full!" he said indignantly. "You fill it up."

The tap was turned then and Stevie drank it slowly, while I watched in stupefaction. We walked through the gate. "How does it taste?" I asked.

"Taint any better'n ginger ale," he said. "I been saving that dime for it all afternoon."

I was still in a daze when we came to the streetcar. Beer! Right in the crowd, too. . . . "Stevie," I whispered as the driver whipped up the horses and the bells clanged, "how'd you dast do it?"

"Pshaw!" said Stevie. "Beer ain't nothing at all." Then he added, defensively but emphatically. "How was I going to know what it tasted like less'n I tasted it? How you going to know about things at all less'n you *do* em?"

Smoking cigarettes at age six. Drinking beer at age six. It is not uncommon for curious children to try such things when they are still considered too young to try them, but nearly all the curious ones conduct their experiments in secret and, for the most part, at a more advanced age than six. Standard tactics: chancing upon a stray pack of cigarettes lying around the house, pulling one out of the pack, lighting up, and then coughing, turning green, or vomiting—in all cases ending with a vow never to smoke again. Not only did Crane smoke again, he was carrying around a pack of cigarettes in his pocket (where and how did he get it?) and had the temerity to light up in public. As for beer, the opportunities for youthful experimentation are probably more abundant: a bottle sitting in the pantry (back then) or sitting in the refrigerator (now), a half-finished glass your father or uncle or big brother has left on the dining room table, and when no one is looking, you take a swig and either enjoy the taste or find it bitter, but again, Crane took his first sip of beer out in the open, where hundreds of people could see him. And no doubt at the precise moment when his mother and Wheeler's mother were attending a temperance lecture.

I look at the 1879 photograph again, and when I fix my attention on the eyes and what the face seems to be expressing, I see something hidden there, and also, for want of a better word, *defiance*.

If the photograph was indeed taken in 1879 and not 1878, Crane's eyes would also bear the memory of an event he had recently witnessed. At the July Fourth celebration in Port Jervis, the festivities were scheduled to begin with the firing of a cannon. Two veterans from the U.S. Colored

Volunteer Heavy Artillery, Samuel Hasbrouck and Theodore Jarvis, were put in charge of the operation, but something went wrong and the cannon exploded too soon, blasting the two ex-soldiers into the air and then through the air until they landed some distance away. Both were badly injured, and both men's faces were severely burned. Jarvis soon died, but Hasbrouck pulled through—blinded in one eye, his face permanently disfigured, *a man with no face*. Eighteen years later, Crane wrote *The Monster*, the most powerful and complex of his short novels. The central figure in the story is a black man who rushes into a burning house to save his white employer's son. The boy is rescued, but the rescuer's skin is thoroughly scorched by the fire, and thereafter everyone in the town looks upon him as a monster—because he is *a man with no face*.

At least two other episodes from Crane's childhood found their way into his fiction. In August 1879, a year after dazzling Post Wheeler with his smoking and drinking exploits, Crane was bitten by a snake on a family camping trip. His brother Wilbur, the almost-but-not-quite doctor, saved him by performing emergency surgery in the woods. That incident, along with another snake incident from the 1890s, resurfaced in a story aptly entitled "The Snake." More important, one of the best works in Crane's collection of childhood tales ("The Fight," in *Whilomville Stories*, which was going to press when he died) is directly based on something that happened to him as a boy. Again, it is Wilbur who chronicles the event in his memoir from 1900:

> One fight of Stephen's is historic in the family, when as a boy of nine he thrashed the bully of Brooklyn street, Port Jervis, a boy twelve years of age. Mother had recently moved into the neighborhood, and as Stephen was younger and smaller, the bully proceeded to bulldoze him as he bulldozed the other small boys of the neighborhood. Stephen stood it for a while but at some added insult to his boyhood he turned on the bully, and after some preliminary sparring, he tackled him and threw him to the ground, and sat on him until he heard a voice saying, "Let him up Stevie." Stephen then ran home and threw himself on the lounge and cried for several minutes, while the bully's mother, who had been watching the scrap, took her hopeful son home and finished the thrashing that Stephen had begun.

There is one last story that strikes me as significant. The source is anonymous, which means that it might or might not be true, but it carries enough conviction and command of detail to be more believable than not. Transcribed by the artist Corwin Knapp Linson, one of Crane's most loyal friends during his years in New York, and sent to the Crane scholar Melvin H. Schoberlin, it is a short text written by a boyhood neighbor from Asbury Park:

> His mother was small, a bright, round, active woman, bird-like in move-ment, an ardent temperance lecturer. You could not be a temperance worker then and be much at home. His sister Agnes taught public school, a tall, kindly, graceful, brown-eyed woman of magnetic charm, a sweet nature. She mothered the family, but the brood was too much for her. Steve was just out of "knee pants;" small, under-nourished, coming home from school or play, maybe skating on the lake, to find no supper. He would then range the neighborhood for food and companionship, telling tales to the children of the various mothers—mine was one—who often sewed on his buttons.

He was so much younger than his brothers and sisters that he was in effect an only child, much loved by the family but also neglected, with buttons missing from his clothes and a stomach that was often empty, and with so many changes of address during the first years of his life, again and again he found himself in the position of being the lonely newcomer. The earliest surviving literary work written by Crane was composed just after he turned eight. It is an astonishingly good poem for someone that young, but even though its tone is whimsical, there is an ache at the core of it that is finally unsettling.

I'D RATHER HAVE—

Last Christmas they gave me a sweater,
    And a nice warm suit of wool,
But I'd rather be cold and have a dog,
    To watch when I come from school.

Father gave me a bicycle,
    But that isn't much of a treat,
Unless you have a dog at your heels
    Racing away down the street.

They bought me a camping outfit,
    But a bonfire by a log
Is all the outfit I would ask,
    If only I had a dog.

The Crane family house, Asbury Park. The building now serves as the headquarters of the town's historical society. (PHOTOGRAPH BY SPENCER OSTRANDER)

> They seem to think a little dog
>   Is a killer of all earth's joys;
> But oh, that "pesky little dog"
>   Means hours of joy to the boys.

6

DOGS, PONIES, SOLDIERS, BASEBALL, FOOTBALL, CIGARETTES, AND telling stories in exchange for food.

Most people outgrow their childhood interests and occupations, but Crane never did. Every item on that list remained a passion for him until the end.

DOGS. Crane owned several dogs over the years. Toward the end of his life, when he lived in a house with enough space for a private study, he preferred writing with a dog in the room, even though he was often interrupted by having to open and close the door. "A Dark-Brown Dog" is one of his best early stories (1893), "The Black Dog" is one of the first he published (the *New York Tribune,* July 1892), and in his novel *The Third Violet* (written in 1895, released in 1897), a dog named Stanley is one of the principal characters. In that same year, 1897, when Crane was covering the Greco-Turkish War as a correspondent for Hearst's *New York Journal* and McClure's syndicate, he rescued a puppy from the battlefield at Velestino and named him "Velestino, the Journal dog." He and Cora took their new pet with them to England, and when the dog became ill with distemper, all work stopped as the two of them tried to save his life. "For eleven days we fought death for him," Crane wrote to Sylvester Scovel, a fellow correspondent who had been with him in Greece, "thinking nothing of anything but his life. He made a fine manly fight, with only little grateful laps of his tongue on Cora's hands, for he knew that she was trying to help him. . . . We are burying him tomorrow in the rhododendron bed in the garden." Later on, when Crane and Joseph Conrad became close friends, Crane developed a special fondness for Conrad's baby son, Borys, and insisted that his father give him a dog, saying that "he must have a dog, a boy ought to have a dog," and when Conrad failed to deliver the required animal, Crane gave Borys a dog himself. In 1900, the last photograph ever taken of Crane (by Cora) shows him sitting on a bench in front of his house holding his little dog Spongie in his arms.

PONIES. As Crane grew up, the ponies grew into horses and riding became a pleasure that surpassed all others. In a letter sent from Hartwood to Willis Brooks Hawkins in October 1895, he writes: "What can be finer than a fine frosty morning, a runaway horse, and only the still hills to watch. Lord, I do love a crazy horse with just a little pig-skin between him and me." In 1919, Conrad remembered his American friend as a man who "never appeared so happy or so much to advantage as on the back of a horse," and in Crane's 1896 letter to John Northern Hilliard, he ends two pages of remarks about himself and his family by declaring, "My idea of happiness is the saddle of a good-riding horse." For a short spell after the publication of *The Red Badge of Courage*, when Crane finally had some money and no longer had to worry about where his next meal was coming from, the first thing he did was to make arrangements to buy a horse named Peanuts.

Almost inevitably, countless horses also appear in his work. To cite just one example, consider "One Dash—Horses," a story from 1895 set in Mexico and in all likelihood based on a real experience. The American protagonist, Richardson, who fears he is about to be robbed and killed by a bandit, sneaks off in the middle of the night, knowing that his fate rests on how his horse will respond to his commands. "[Richardson's fingers] were shaking so hard that he could hardly buckle the girth. His hands were invisible mittens." But then the horse takes off, and "he felt in his heart the first thrill of confidence. The little animal, unurged and quite tranquil, moving his ears this way and that way with an interest in the scenery, was nevertheless bounding into the eye of the breaking day with the speed of a frightened antelope. Richardson, looking down, saw the long, fine reach of forelimb, as steady as steel machinery."

Three years later, when Crane was in Puerto Rico reporting on the Spanish-American War for Hearst, another *Journal* reporter, Charles Michelson, closely observed how Crane interacted with horses. Writing in 1926, he remembered:

> His horse was always a full partner in Crane's adventures. . . . During the Porto Rico campaign he rode a hammer-headed, spur-scarred, hairy-hoofed white beast hardly bigger than a goat, with all the bad habits that could be grafted on original sin by ignorance and bad treatment. . . . He was always picketed apart from the other horses, for he was both a biter and a kicker, but he and Crane got along like sweethearts. There came the day when we were due to sail for home. . . . I found Crane. His arm was over the bowed neck of the disreputable pony, and the face he turned to me was stained with tears. . . . It sounds maudlin and mawkish in the telling, but somehow it did not appear either that afternoon in Porto Rico.

To complete the picture, it should be noted that Crane's affection for horses extended beyond horses themselves to include their cousins. When he and Linson were commissioned by McClure to go to Pennsylvania in 1894 to gather information for their feature article "In the Depths of a Coal Mine" (Crane as reporter, Linson as illustrator), Crane devoted several paragraphs to the mules who were condemned to work in the ink-black darkness underground. "The stable was like a dungeon. The mules were arranged in solemn rows. They turned their faces toward our lamps. They made their eyes shine wondrously, like lenses. They resembled enormous rats." Crane learns that the mules are often kept in the dark for years on end and then adds: "Usually when brought to the surface, these animals tremble at the earth, radiant in the sunshine. Later, they go almost mad with fantastic joy. The full splendor of the heavens, the grass, the trees, the breeze breaks upon them suddenly." In Mexico the following year, he wrote "How the Donkey Lifted the Hills," a twelve-hundred-word fable that tells how the donkey became man's primary beast of burden. It concludes: "So now, when you see a donkey with a church, a palace, and three villages upon its back, and he goes with infinite slowness, moving but one leg at a time, do not think him lazy. It is his pride."

SOLDIERS. Crane's adolescent ambition was to go to West Point and pursue a career in the military, but his brother William talked him out of it, arguing that it was unlikely there would be a war in his lifetime. Needless to say, that did not prevent Crane from continuing to think about soldiers and war. In addition to *The Red Badge of Courage*, he wrote twenty-four stories on the subject and filed more than sixty dispatches as a war correspondent from Greece, Cuba, and Puerto Rico.

BASEBALL. Another one of Crane's adolescent ambitions was to become a professional baseball player. Small and wiry (about five foot seven and 125 pounds as an adult), he played catcher and hit for a high average, though with little power even by the standards of those deadball times. Elected captain of both his boarding school team and the Syracuse varsity during the one spring he was enrolled there (the youngest team captain in American college baseball), he was generally considered to be an excellent all-around player, in spite of his physical limitations. Mostly catching bare-handed in high school (as reported by classmate Abram Lincoln Travis in 1930), Crane eventually "secured a heavy buckskin glove which he used effectively and so saved much iodine and witch hazel which he had used before." A pitcher on the Syracuse team (Mansfield J. French, writing in 1934) described his battery-mate as

> very quick and active on his feet, his body was slender, his shoulders somewhat drooping, his chest not robust and his knees inclined some- what to knock together. . . . He played ball with a fiendish glee. Usu- ally of a quiet and taciturn mien, on the ball field he was constantly in motion, was free of speech, wantonly profane at times. . . . He was first tried out as a catcher and proved to be, in his ability to hold the ball, the best candidate for that position. His throwing arm was weak, however, and although he threw with his whole body, he was unable to line the ball down to second base in acceptable form . . . The strain upon the liga- ments of his shoulder would, at times, cause him to double up with pain.

Regardless of these throwing problems, another classmate (Clarence Loomis Peaslee, writing in 1896) confidently asserted, "He was the best player of the nine, and one of the best catchers that the University ever had." Crane also "loved talking baseball" (French), and long after he had stopped playing on organized teams, the first thing he would do when he opened the morning paper was turn to the baseball scores. After dumping college and heading off for Asbury Park in the summer of 1891, baseball turned out to be the glue that sealed his first important literary friendship. Hamlin Garland (1860–1940) is mostly forgotten today, but at the time he was considered a promising young advocate of the "new realism," and in a long productive writing life that included works of fiction, autobiography, and criticism, he was so well thought of that twenty years after Crane's death one of his now-forgotten books was awarded the Pulitzer Prize. In August, he came to the Jersey Shore to deliver a lecture on William Dean Howells, and Crane, who was again working for Townley's news agency, covered the event for the *Tribune*. After the article was published the next day, Garland was sufficiently impressed to want to meet the author. The young man from the Dakota Territory and the younger man from the East Coast hit it off during the time Garland spent in the neighborhood, not just because of their shared tastes in literature but because of their common interest in baseball. Garland had been a pitcher, and what better person to discuss the finer points of moundsmanship with than catcher Crane? The two of them therefore discussed baseball as well as books, sometimes discussing books even as they were tossing a ball back and forth, and for the next several years, as Crane struggled to find his footing in New York, Garland stood behind him, in one crucial instance urging Crane to send a copy of the self-published *Maggie* to Howells, which proved to be a significant turn in Crane's life, for even though the rest of the literary world had ignored the book, Howells was impressed by it, and given that he was the leading novelist and critic of the moment, his support meant everything.

FOOTBALL. Information about Crane's early football activities is scant to nonexistent. Aside from his sister-in-law Elizabeth's mention that he played the sport as a boy, I have come across nothing. In the summer of 1893, however, when Crane was working on the first draft of *The Red Badge of Courage* at his brother Edmund's house in Lake View (just outside Paterson), he wrote at night when everyone else was asleep, went to bed around dawn, rose late, and spent the afternoons organizing and coaching a football team for the youngsters in town. Somehow or other, he had caught the football bug that was spreading across the country. Three years later, when he ran into trouble with Theodore Roosevelt and the New York police for defending a falsely accused prostitute in court, he escaped the city on two successive weekends to cover Harvard football games in Cambridge, Massachusetts, the only sports reporting he ever did. Most important: After the publication of *The Red Badge of Courage*, he was asked repeatedly by journalists how someone who had never been in combat or even witnessed a battle could write so vividly about war, and again and again he responded with answers like this one to the *Book Buyer* in April 1896, "I have never been in a battle, of course, and I believe that I got my sense of the rage of conflict on the football field." That could have been true, but then again, it is impossible to tell if he was joking or not.

SMOKING. The six-year-old truant smoker continued to puff away on cigarettes, cigars, pipes, and water pipes for as long as he went on breathing. Smoking was a habit, a compulsion, and a way of life that Crane joyously and recklessly pursued, in spite of weak lungs and an intermittently severe cough. Everyone who knew him remarked on it. "An inveterate smoker of cigarettes," writes his boarding school classmate Travis; "an inveterate cigarette smoker," echoes Lafayette classmate Ernest G. Smith; "his fingers deeply stained with nicotine," says Syracuse teammate French; "smoked constantly," observes New York artist friend Nelson Greene, who adds: "smoked cigars incessantly when he could find them." The ever astute Helen R. Crane writes: "He could not talk unless he was walking up and down the room with his hands stuffed into his pockets and a cigarette balanced on his lips." Another niece, Edna Crane Sidbury, one of William's five daughters, who knew and loved Crane when she was a girl, comments on her uncle's visits to the house in Port Jervis: "My mother . . . was always glad to see him, in spite of the fact that he used to smoke in bed and burned holes in the sheets." Crane might have rejected God, but from boyhood into manhood he never stopped worshipping at the altar of Holy Smoke.

As for TELLING STORIES IN EXCHANGE FOR FOOD, there is no need to elaborate. It would become the story of his life.

7

HIS EARLIEST PIECE OF SURVIVING PROSE FICTION COMES FROM 1885, when Crane was thirteen or, if it was written in November or December, just fourteen. As with the poem about wishing for a dog, it is remarkably good for someone his age, at least as good if not better than most of the things I read as a college writing instructor years ago. "Uncle Jake and the Bell-Handle" covers four and a half pages in the University Press of Virginia edition of Crane's work, and while it is a breezy, humorous, inconsequential story, there is surprising skill in how he constructs his sentences and a quick, observant eye for sensory detail. Uncle Jake is a genial old farmer from an imaginary Somewhere. One day, he decides to go off to the City (where he has been only once before) with his twenty-eight-year-old niece, Sarah, to sell his crop of turnips and stock up on various household supplies. The second paragraph has a sharp, vigorous quality to it, and word by word, in both rhythm and tone, there is no doubt that young Crane is in full control of what he is doing:

> So the next day at sunrise Uncle Jake dressed himself in his best suit
> of black clothes and Sarah arrayed her angular form in her best calico

gown, and put on her cotton mitts and the lilac sun-bonnet with the sun-flowers on it. After surveying his niece with a good deal of pride and some misgivings about city men, whom he thought might be likely to steal such a lovely creature, he kissed his wife good-bye as if he were going to Europe for ten years, clambered upon the high seat, pulled Sarah up beside him as if she had been a bundle of straw, flourished his whip, smiled blandly and confidently upon his wife, the two hired men and a neighbor's-boy, and drove away.

The two of them clatter along a country road with the turnips bouncing around in back, and by the fourth paragraph the landscape begins to shift:

> Soon the houses began to appear closer together, there were more tin-cans and other relics strewn about the road-side, they began to get views of multitudes of back-yards, with washes on lines; grimy, smoky facto-ries; stock yards filled with discordant mobs of beasts; whole trains of freight cars, standing on side tracks; dirty children, homeless dogs and wandering pigs. To Uncle Jake's experienced eye, this denoted that they were entering the city.

Crane's keen attention to physical detail, which would become one of the notable strengths of his later writing, is already in evidence here. To combine "dirty children, homeless dogs and wandering pigs" in a single phrase is a deft and evocative stroke, light-years beyond the bland generalities you would expect to find in the work of a thirteen-year-old author. Of course, not much of anything happens in the story, which ends when Uncle Jake and Sarah are waiting in the parlor of a local hotel before going into the dining room for lunch and the old man pulls on the handle of some brass "scoop or cup" sticking out of the wall at the precise instant when a waiter elsewhere in the hotel makes "a terrific onslaught on a gong." Thinking he has produced this noise by pulling on the brass handle, which must be an alarm of some kind to signal the fire department, the police department, the ambulance corps, or the board of health, the farmer panics and hightails it out of town with his niece. But along the way there are some cunning and insightful touches, fine little bits of writing that sustain interest: the men in front of the beer saloons winking "bleared eyes . . . at the lilac bonnet with the sun-flowers" (Sarah), or the turnip dealer who stiffs Uncle Jake "by lying to him about 'market prices,'" or the livery stable owner who charges him "fifty cents more than he did anyone else, merely on principle," or Uncle Jake telling a store clerk he doesn't know when he'll be back because "his wife, poor critter, had the most astonishing case of plumbago that had been in Green County since '58 when old Bill Williams's wife's second cousin took down with it," or, near the end: "When they arrived at the livery stable, their route from the hotel if it could be mapped out would look like a brain-twisting Chinese puzzle."

He had nothing much to write about yet, but there was no question that he could write, and the way he wrote back then already gives a taste of how he would write in the years to come.

A last thought. Twice in the story, Crane mentions Sarah's age as twenty-eight. Whether this is a conscious or unconscious reference to his sister Agnes or just a random coincidence, it should be remembered she had died the previous year at the same age—twenty-eight. A small sign, perhaps, of how deeply he was still mourning her death. Like Sarah, Agnes had an "angular frame."

8

CRANE ATTENDED THE LOCAL PUBLIC SCHOOLS IN ASBURY PARK AS a young boy, but in the fall of 1885, when he was thirteen going on fourteen (the same year he composed "Uncle Jake and the Bell-Handle"), his mother enrolled him in the school where his father had served as principal from 1849 to 1858, Pennington Seminary. Nothing is known about the time Crane spent there as a student for the next four and a half semesters, but as an institution that specialized in training adolescent boys to become Methodist clergymen, where attendance at two chapel services per day was compulsory and such activities as smoking, drinking, and gambling were forbidden, it is hard to imagine that Crane felt comfortable in his father's old haunts. Whatever he might or might not have felt, the one thing we know for certain is that he quit the school in late November or early December 1887. According to his brother Wilbur's brief memoir, it fell out more or less as follows:

> While at Pennington seminary some hazing was done which one of the professors charged to Stephen. He denied any knowledge of it, and when the professor told him he lied, Stephen went to his room, packed his trunk and went home to Asbury Park where he told his story, adding that "as the Professor called me a liar there was not room in Pennington for us both, so I came home." Nothing would induce him to return to the seminary.

He was sixteen by then, and in his high-minded adolescent willfulness he would not bend or compromise. One supposes that his mother
could have forced him to return to the school, but she either believed
her boy's judgment of the situation or didn't have the heart to challenge
him. Pennington was the place where she had lived for the first nine
years of her marriage, the place where her husband had turned a failing
school into a successful one, and surely she must have been torn by this
unexpected development, but she gave in to her son's wishes and allowed
him to transfer to another school in January, a more expensive school,
as it turned out, which must have put a strain on her limited finances,
even with the twenty-five percent tuition reduction granted to the sons
of ministers.

With his mind now set on West Point and a career in the army, Crane's
next stop landed him in Columbia County, New York, three miles from
the small city of Hudson, at a school that was in fact two schools, or two
schools that had merged into one: Claverack College and Hudson River
Institute, which welcomed both male and female students and offered a
dose of military training to the boys (drilling in uniform), sports of various
kinds (mostly tennis and baseball), an excellent music program (Crane, mad
for music, played the guitar, the flute, the banjo, and the melodeon, sang
tenor, and owned plaster wall plaques of Mozart and Beethoven), and the
opportunity to graduate with the equivalent of two years of college behind
you. As another school founded by the Methodist church, however, it was
governed by the same dreary code of regulations and restrictions that Crane
was already familiar with: compulsory attendance at chapel and no dancing, no smoking, no drinking, and no card playing. Those rules had been
enforced at Pennington, but at Claverack it wasn't hard to break them, and
Crane broke them, broke them again and again, along with nearly everyone
else he knew. As his classmate Harvey Wickham remembered in a 1926
article for the *American Mercury*: "Students . . . roamed as in a terrestrial
paradise like packs of cheerful wolves out of bounds, out of hours and very
much out of hand."

There is one photograph of him from his days at Claverack, probably
taken when he was seventeen: sitting for the camera in his trim, sprightly
tailored cadet's uniform with its high collar, brass buttons, and ornamen-
tal braids. He is looking off to his right. His ears no longer seem big,
his lips are full, and his short hair is pristinely cut, parted on the right
side with a longer shank of impeccably clipped bangs combed down and
across the left side of his forehead. His cheeks and chin are so smooth

Crane as a lieutenant in the Claverack College and
Hudson River Institute Cadet Corps, circa 1889.
(COURTESY OF THE UNIVERSITY OF VIRGINIA)

and unblemished that it is difficult to tell if he has started to shave or, if he has, whether he needs to shave more than once a month. No, he is not and never would be called handsome, but he is a presentable figure, and his eyes exude an attractive warmth, even though he looks rather nervous sitting there in his natty getup, altogether uncomfortable in his own skin. The "beautiful baby" of the past has disappeared, as has the squinting, defiant little boy standing on the beach. The person in this photograph is a raw youth, trapped in that mysterious, transitional country known as "the awkward age."

In March 1896, several months after the publication of *The Red Badge of Courage*, Crane wrote a letter to one of his former classmates, Viola Allen:

> My dear Miss Allen: I am very glad to be able to forward you by this mail a copy of The Red Badge. My years at Claverack are very vivid to me. They were I believe the happiest period of my life although I was not then aware of it. Of course, you were joking when you inferred that I might not remember you. And Anna Roberts! And Eva Lacy! And Jennie Pierce! Alas, Jennie Pierce. You must remember that I was in love with her, madly,

in the headlong way of seventeen. Jennie was clever. With only half an effort she made my life so very miserable.

Men usually refuse to recognize their school-boy dreams. They blush. I dont. The emotion itself was probably higher, finer, than anything of my after-life, and so, often I like to think of it. I was such an ass, such a pure complete ass—it does me good to recollect it.

There were crushes, then, the early excitations, frustrations, and inanities of teenage courtship, along with a ruse to avoid listening to chapel services by volunteering to pump the organ, a vigorous involvement in the school's military program (rising in rank to first lieutenant and then to captain in the two and a half years he spent there, commander of drilling exercises for his battalion, which was awarded top honors during his final semester), a hot and cold student who did well in the subjects he liked and poorly in the ones he didn't, a period of much reading, perhaps more reading than at any other moment of his life, immersion in the classics with a particular fondness for Plutarch and for memorizing poems, a shy, standoffish person who nevertheless made more than a few friends, an adolescent boy who struck the adolescent pose of militant outsider and shunned taking part in the other boys' cruel, adolescent pranks, a hell-bent catcher on the baseball team, a crafty poker player, and, as has already been established, an "inveterate smoker."

His classmate Wickham: "He wanted to be a democrat, and yet a dictator. Hence that contradiction, self-depreciation coupled with arrogance, which has puzzled so many." Another fellow student, Armistead ("Tommie") Borland, confessed in a letter to Melvin H. Schoberlin that "'Steve' was my hero and ideal. . . . I tried to copy him in every way and learned many things, not all for the good of my immortal soul—the rudiments of the great American game of poker and something more than the rudiments of the ways of a man with a maid." A bit further on, Bowland calls Crane a "congenital introvert" and a person "extremely irregular in his habits—a law unto himself, indifferent (!) to the opinion of others who might be critical of him."

A portrait of the burning boy at sixteen, seventeen, and eighteen— which is hardly more than a rough sketch at this point and tells little about the future. Some of the lines in it would eventually fade away, others would grow sharper and more vivid as time went on, but for now he was still just a young kid trying to find a path for himself, yet one more adolescent searcher blundering around in the woods, looking for a way out and into the clear.

9

THOSE WERE THE SUMMERS WHEN HE WORKED FOR HIS BROTHER Townley's news agency in Asbury Park. As a Jersey man myself, who also came into the world by way of Newark, I remember Asbury Park as a prime warm-weather destination for adolescent boys and girls. Once my older friends turned seventeen and had driver's licenses in their pockets, I tagged along with them on a number of Saturday excursions down the Garden State Parkway to visit the ocean, the boardwalk, and the best amusement park within an hour of home, which had everything in it an amusement park should have: a carousel, a fun house, bumper cars, a mirror maze, and New Jersey's most vertiginous, stomach-churning roller coaster. Since I knew nothing about the origins of Asbury Park, I took it for granted that my favorite pleasure town was a for-profit venture devoted exclusively to the demands of the pleasure principle. So it had become by the early 1960s, but in the beginning it was something quite different: not just a summer resort but a bastion of the American Methodist Church.

It started in the 1860s when Methodists discovered the Jersey Shore as a place to pitch their tents and build large open-air wooden shelters ("tabernacles") in which thousands could congregate for communal prayer and worship during the summer. Ocean Grove, the "Queen of Religious Resorts," was established in 1869, and by the following year Methodist convert James A. Bradley, a wealthy brush manufacturer from New York who had visited one of the summer camp meetings there, bought five hundred acres of oceanfront land just to the north and established another town, which he named after America's first Methodist bishop, Francis Asbury. Crane's parents had bought a lot at the Ocean Grove Camp Ground in 1872—which would account for Crane's mother's decision to relocate there after her husband's death—but by the time the family moved to Asbury Park in 1883, the place had been transformed into one of the most thriving and crowded vacation spots along the east coast. Its Methodist principles were still intact (a ban on the sale of alcohol, a Sunday ban on the sale of tobacco), and there was much religious activity in town, but this was an attractive part of the world, and once Founder Bradley had built his gigantic boardwalk and the bungalows, cottages, houses, hotels, and amusement centers had gone up, people less fervent in their religious convictions began vacationing there as well—more than six hundred thousand per year by most reports, including day-trippers, weekenders, and season-long summer residents—and with their arrival came the clandestine beer trucks known as "arks" and the Sunday prescriptions from local doctors for "Tabaci Folium." From mid-June to early September, Asbury Park was a human circus that offered visitors any number of entertainments, distractions, and cultural opportunities: the beach and the ocean first of all, the social pleasures of dressing up in fine clothes and parading along the boardwalk, music recitals and concerts, dances at the grand hotels (commonly referred to as "hops"), courses of instruction on various subjects for both children and adults (everything from art classes to classes in marine biology), and a perpetual round of lectures that featured standard temperance harangues on the same day that talks were given about literary matters (Hamlin Garland on William Dean Howells, for example) and current social issues (reformer Jacob Riis on life in the New York slums). What a town it must have been for a cub reporter to learn his trade, and how enjoyable it is to imagine little Stevie Crane hustling along the boardwalk on his bicycle or lurking in hotel lobbies as he tracks down tidbits and scoops for his big brother Townley, the redoubtable Shore Fiend of local legend.

The summer articles in the *New York Tribune* were unsigned, but hardworking Crane scholars have attributed a number of early pieces to him based on the evidence of the prose, and given the stylistic thumbprint that can be seen as far back as 1885 (in "Uncle Jake and the Bell-Handle") and which would continue to be present in his later writing, there is no reason to doubt their attributions. After a couple of summers of informal work for Townley, Crane was officially put on the staff of his brother's New Jersey Coast News Bureau in the summer of 1890, just after his final semester at Claverack. That was when he renewed his friendship with Post Wheeler, his old childhood smoking buddy, and met another young journalist, Ralph Paine, who also became a friend, and after the three young reporters had finished their work for the day, they tended to hang out together in the evenings. According to Wheeler, Crane's assignments were devoted to chronicling "north Jersey social activities," but slight as his subjects might have been, his writing is seldom dull. A few extracts from the summer of 1890, when he was still just eighteen:

WORKERS AT OCEAN GROVE: Ocean Grove is, beyond all doubt, for the family, of the family and by the family. There are thousands of babies here. The plump and pretty infants swing in hammocks under the trees and upon cottage stoops, shout with glee as they roll and tumble upon the sands of the beach or gaze with supreme disdain upon those who have to walk while they ride in royal state in gay carriages propelled by demure nurse girls wearing coquettish little white caps.

THRONGS AT ASBURY PARK: The city maidens and their gallant attendants have blossomed out in blazer jackets with caps to match which make them look like huge potato bugs.

THE BABIES ON PARADE AT ASBURY PARK: The most unique parade ever known here since the time when Asbury Park was a howling wilderness and the Indians marched in single file through the woods was seen this afternoon on the famous board walk of James A. Bradley, the founder of the town. It was a baby show on wheels. About 200 mothers and nurses wheeled babies in their little carriages . . . from the foot of Wesley Lake up the board walk to the big pavilion at the foot of Fifth-ave., and back again. . . . There were all kinds of babies. The little wagons were decorated with silk and satin flags, streamers and Japanese lanterns. Two Armenians carried a silk hammock hanging from bamboo poles on their shoulders, in which were Armenian twins. Several other carriages contained twins. Only one baby cried. The rest sucked their thumbs in great contentment, or cooed and smiled at the spectators and waved their rattles and other toys when the procession was applauded.

ASBURY PARK: The opening of the Ocean Grove camp-meeting this week has been the means of attracting large crowds to this town, and the good people from all parts of the country have been shocked to find that rum-selling was a thriving business in this supposedly staid prohibition town. . . . The principal offender's place of business was near the main artery of traffic between this town and the Grove, which is only separated from Asbury Park by a small lake a few hundred feet wide. As the poker players rattled the "chips," they could hear the sound from 5,000 throats singing the doxology. . . . On Thursday night, during the heavy storm, there were hops at Ralph's Coleman House, the West End Hotel, the Oriental, Sunset Hall, the Ocean Hotel, Norwood Hall, the Colonnade, the Metropolitan Hotel and other large houses. There were also a number of progressive whist and euchre parties. At some of the houses the guests, while blindfolded, tried to pin tusks on elephants and tails on donkeys made of cloth, or engaged in the festive amusement of hunting the slippery button or firing the bean-bag at each other.

ASBURY PARK'S BIG BOARD WALK: All sorts and conditions of men are to be seen on the board walk. There is the sharp, keen-looking New-York business man, the long and lank Jersey farmer, the dark-skinned sons of India, the self-possessed Chinaman, the black-haired Southerner and the man with the big hat from "the wild and wooly plains" of the West. . . . The stock brokers gather in little groups on the broad plaza and discuss the prospective rise and fall of stocks; the pretty girl, resplendent

in her finest gown, walks up and down within a few feet of the surging billows and chatters away with the college youth, who wears "old
mater's" colors in his blazer jacket and cap, or else sits hand in hand with
her "own dear one" in a pavilion, and they two, "the world forgetting and
by the world forgot," chew gum together in time to the beating of the
waves upon the sandy beach.

The mockery is refreshing, the jabs at bourgeois convention and the
insipid pastimes of the summer crowd give a welcome dose of youthful
cynicism to the articles, and whether the articles themselves qualify as true
reporting or as semifictionalized renderings of personal impressions is less
important than the fact that Crane was taking advantage of the opportunity
he had been given. Not many aspiring writers have brothers who run their
own news agencies, brothers twice their age who can hand out jobs to rank,
untested beginners, and even if Crane wasn't cut out for a steady career in
journalism (*extremely irregular in his habits*), he didn't know that yet, and at
this juncture in his life he seems to have had no other ambition than to work
for newspapers. As far as anyone knows, he wasn't writing fiction then, nor
had he ever expressed a desire to become the next Nathaniel Hawthorne
or Charles Dickens. He had finished the equivalent of high school, he had
returned to the Jersey Shore, and for now it looked as if he was content (perhaps even thrilled) to be doing what he was doing. But this work, trivial as it
may seem in retrospect, proved to be a good training ground for his progress
as a writer, for the only way a person can become a writer is to write, to write
as much and as often as possible, and because of his job, Crane was writing
much and often and quickly to boot, learning as he went along, and how
fortunate for him that he started at such a young age, since it was imperative
that he learn fast, learn fast and well, because it was already 1890, and when
he arrived in Asbury Park that summer, he had only ten years to live.

10

THAT FALL, FOR REASONS THAT MADE NO SENSE, CRANE WENT OFF TO
Lafayette College in Easton, Pennsylvania. Most likely, the decision to go
there was prompted by a suggestion from his brother William. Having talked
Crane out of West Point and a future commission in the army, the Judge
now proposed (with crackpot logic) that he enter the mining-engineering
program at Lafayette because it might turn out to be advantageous to the
family. And why, one asks, would he have thought that? Because whatever
extra income the Cranes earned was derived from a portfolio of stocks they

held in a number of Pennsylvania coal mines. By that reasoning, if they had owned shares in a tin company, William would have counseled his brother to become a metallurgist. No matter that the boy lacked all interest in mining and engineering, that he had barely passed his science and math courses at Claverack—maybe he would learn to enjoy those subjects in time. Not only was Crane being given bad advice, he was still being neglected by his family—not with any malicious intent, but simply because they sometimes forgot he was there. As Helen R. Crane bitterly recounts in her memoir: "His brothers and sisters may be the last persons in the world to note his gifts; if they happen to be many years older, married, and engrossed in their own children, he probably always remains much of an outsider to them." Three paragraphs on, she writes: "It never occurred to them that he was a promising boy: he was merely their younger brother, rather strange and erratic, and a person who, if he mentioned his needs, did so in such a light manner that they did not take him seriously."

Of course, Crane could have stood up and refused, telling William that he wanted to go somewhere else, but he was such an indifferent student, so unengaged in the question of what to study or not, of where to study or not, of why even bother to study or not, that he allowed himself to go along with the plan.

Predictably, the fall semester at Lafayette was a washout. Not a Methodist school this time but a Presbyterian one, with compulsory chapel attendance seven days a week and a fixed curriculum of seven courses with no electives: algebra, Bible study, chemistry, elocution, French, industrial drawing, and theme writing. Crane flunked five of them, receiving a grade of zero in theme writing, which was taught by an engineering professor and required the students to write papers on strictly technical subjects. In spite of cutting most of his classes, he became a member of the Delta Upsilon fraternity, joined both literary societies on campus, and played intramural baseball in preparation for the spring season. That was the good part of what happened to him during the three and a half months he spent there. Otherwise, Lafayette was a madhouse of violent hazing rituals and masculine mayhem, with constant battles between the sophomore and freshman classes, a notoriously out-of-control institution where "fellows . . . raise more hell than any other college in the country," as Crane put it in a letter to an old friend from Claverack. According to Lafayette classmate Ernest G. Smith (writing in 1926), Crane's dormitory room was broken into one night by a bunch of raucous "Sophomore gangsters," who were persuaded to leave only after Crane pointed a loaded revolver at them. No one else witnessed the standoff, and Crane himself never talked about it, but even if Smith got his facts wrong, the fact was that Crane quit the school at the end of the semester.

It was Pennington redux. Once again, her son had said no to a school, and once again it was up to Crane's mother to find him another school, in this case another college. Too bad there is no source to tell us how they wrangled with each other to solve the problem, what pressures they brought to bear on each other over how many hours or days, and how eager or reluctant Crane was to give college another try, for I suspect his heart wasn't in it, and if in the end he went back for another semester, chances are that he did it to please—or appease—his mother. Under the circumstances, Mrs. Crane's solution was probably the best one available on such short notice. Her uncle had taken an active part in the founding of Syracuse University, and because of that family connection, she managed to negotiate a scholarship for her son. She also knew that the place had a good reputation and was untouched by the sort of scandal that had occurred at Lafayette in the fall when another freshman in her son's class had been invaded by a horde of sophomores and had fought off the thugs by cracking one of them on the head with a baseball bat, which had fractured the sophomore's skull. What Mrs. Crane probably didn't know, however, and what her son surely did, was that there were numerous bats at Syracuse as well (for hitting balls, not heads) and that the school had an excellent baseball team.

In Crane's 1896 letter to Hilliard, he concludes his remarks about his parents and then begins another paragraph: "As for myself, I went to Lafayette College but did not graduate. I found mining-engineering not at all to my taste. I preferred base-ball. Later I attended Syracuse University where I attempted to study literature but found base ball again much more to my taste." In an earlier letter to Hilliard (probable date: February 1895), he is somewhat more expansive about his college memories:

> I did little work at school, but confined my abilities, such as they were, to the diamond. Not that I disliked books, but the cut-and-dried cur- riculum of the college did not appeal to me. Humanity was a much more interesting study. When I ought to have been at recitations I was studying faces on the streets, and when I ought to have been studying my next day's lessons, I was watching the trains roll in and out of the Central Station. So, you see, I had, first of all, to recover from college.

We know that he stuck with Syracuse for only five months (early January to early June 1891), but that doesn't mean it was the same kind of washout he had experienced in the fall. On the contrary, it was a time of enormous change for him, of profoundest change, and it served as a bridge between his adolescence and early adulthood, a finishing school that not only finished school for him but prepared him for the next step.

Syracuse was his first city, the first time he inhabited a place that was not a small town or seaside resort, a cold-weather city with a permanent population of around ninety thousand, not large by the metropolitan standards of New York but large enough to encompass a dense mixture of high and low, of wealth and poverty, and when Crane was slacking off from his schoolwork, he wasn't only "studying faces on the streets" but prowling around the rougher parts of town, sitting in on sessions at the police court, drinking five-cent beers at the Music Hall on North Salina Street while he watched the show girls in their skimpy costumes (plunging necklines, skirts above the knees) sing and dance onstage, striking up acquaintances with tramps, winos, and prostitutes, and exploring the brothels on Railroad Street not far from the Central Station. There is ample evidence that he started working on an early draft of *Maggie* that spring, or at least an early incarnation of what was to become *Maggie*, and how could he have conceived of writing a story set in the slums without knowing something of the slums himself? Syracuse offered him his first taste of that world, and he was so stirred by the encounter that he was moved to write about it—not as a piece of journalism but as an extended, multilayered work of fiction.

That first of all and above all else—the birth of *Maggie* and the impulse to write fiction again—but even as a grudging, recalcitrant student, he was working during those months in central New York State as the Syracuse correspondent for the *New York Tribune*, a job given to him by the day editor of the paper, Willis Fletcher Johnson, a graduate of Pennington Seminary and a family friend who knew Crane's writing from the work he had done for Townley in Asbury Park. In the final weeks of his final year as a student, Crane concocted a frivolous and funny little journalistic hoax with Johnson's backing, a bagatelle that bore the headline GREAT BUGS IN ONONDAGA, which was published in both the *Tribune* and the *Syracuse Daily Standard* on June first. Inspired by an earlier report about an infestation of caterpillars that had stopped a train somewhere in Minnesota, the nineteen-year-old correspondent upped the ante and invented a new form of gigantic armored bug that had brought rail traffic to a halt near Syracuse, the seat of Onondaga County.

As the drivers rolled over the insects the things gave up the ghost with a crackling sound like the successive explosions of toy torpedoes.... The bugs became more numerous and the crackling grew to a monotonous din, as though some fire cracker storehouse had been touched off in an hundred places, until in the thick of the multitudinous swarm the engine was brought to a stop. . . . An erudite recluse whose abode is in the neighborhood of the quarries had by this time appeared, for news of the strange occurrence had spread rapidly. His opinion was that the bugs that had blocked the track were the issue of a rare species of lithodome—a rock-boring mollusk—crossed with some kind of predatory insect.

The following day, the joke was prolonged with a mock-serious apology from the paper, likely written by Johnson or by Johnson and Crane together, in which the "state entomologist" was warned that if he wanted to keep his job "he must board a monster of steel and iron, hurry to Syracuse and report on this new bug." The older man and the younger man must have reveled in their little prank. Further proof that Crane was not languishing in some dark funk at Syracuse but was often in high spirits, for how could someone in low spirits find the energy to dig up such a recondite term as *lithodome* (not to be found in any standard dictionary) or to invent such a delicious phrase as *erudite recluse*?

His mother had made arrangements for him to live with her great-aunt, the venerable Widow Peck, longtime spouse of the now departed Bishop Peck, which would further cut down on expenses and ensure that her son was subject to adult supervision, but the experiment lasted only a matter of days, since the Widow was displeased with the boy's behavior, although precisely how or why has never been elucidated. Perhaps it was his smoking, or his *irregular habits*, or his uncombed hair and slovenly approach to dressing, or perhaps they simply didn't get along. Whatever the reason, Crane wound up spending the semester living at the Delta Upsilon fraternity house, where he fell in with a like-minded crowd of smoking renegades and made a number of close friendships that continued for years afterward. The crowd consisted of bright young men who went on to distinguish themselves as lawyers, journalists, doctors, and engineers, but as college undergraduates they shared Crane's contempt for the stultifying strictures of the school's academic and religious program. On top of that, every one of those friends seemed to admire him intensely. Crane's Sunday night recital companion Frank Noxon (future reporter, drama critic, and editor) wrote in 1926: "Crane was brave, physically, morally, and socially. . . . One of [his] characteristics was a haunting solicitude for the comforts and welfare of other people, especially those of narrow opportunity. He thought about it as one thinks about an art or craft, developing a style and inventing original methods." Clarence N. Goodwin (future lawyer) in 1926:

He soon proved himself to be unstudious, brilliant, volatile, entertaining, and giftedly profane. He was at that time in years about 19 and in worldly experience about 87. . . . He had a keen sense of the dramatic and his countenance usually displayed an amusedly satirical, but kindly grin. His keen mind instantly caught the absurd, bizarre, or ridiculous aspect of any incident and he would draw out an account of it in his own entertaining fashion. . . . My recollection of him is that of a boyish smiling young man, kind in heart, keen in mind. He saw into and through the conceits, hypocrisies, weaknesses and selfishness of mankind, but continued to smile with amusement [and] without bitterness.

Frederic M. Lawrence (future doctor and the closest of Crane's Syracuse friends) sometime in the 1920s:

Having thus promptly and fearlessly raised the standard of revolt, Crane settled down to acquire such education as he desired in his own way. Already he was mature in mind. His intellect was indifferent to authority or tradition. It examined any new conception with complete detachment, reached conclusions with utter disregard for accepted beliefs. His room in the chapter house . . . speedily became a citadel for the un-Godly. . . . Crane, often taciturn, never by any means the most loquacious, directed the trends of thought. His own future was determined. He was to be a writer, and by no uncertain implication a great one.

He was scornful of the curriculum, argued contrarian points of view with his professors when he deigned to show up for class, but as Lawrence suggests in his piece (which goes on for many pages), Crane was privately pursuing his education in his own manner, and he read much during those months, including *War and Peace* and *Anna Karenina* (from then on, he would rank Tolstoy as his favorite novelist) as well as Goethe's *Faust* and, even more important, Goethe's *Theory of Colors*, which marked his work forever. It is also known that he inscribed his name in a copy of Keats's collected poems, which he bought at a local bookstore, and that when he wasn't reading books or floating around the city or pursuing girls or listening to music at St. Paul's Cathedral or writing articles, short stories, and an early version of *Maggie*, he was playing baseball.

There is a photograph from that spring of Crane and his teammates sitting and standing together for an outdoor group portrait, nine young men in a motley array of uniforms and partial uniforms and one older man in the rear, undoubtedly the coach. Crane is in the middle of the front row,

Syracuse University baseball team, spring 1891.
Crane is in the middle of the front row. (COURTESY OF SYRACUSE UNIVERSITY)

leaning back in his chair. His small, snub-billed cap is perched so far back on his head that it is hard to decipher, and his hair, which comes across as brown in the photo, not blond, is slightly unkempt. He is wearing a white sweater with a white collared shirt underneath it and traditional baseball pants that come down to his knees, with a pair of black baseball stockings covering the calves of his exceedingly thin legs. The legs are wide open, and because he is leaning back in his chair, he looks relaxed and confident, the very opposite of the self-conscious cadet who had posed for the camera just two or two and a half years earlier. His left hand is resting comfortably in his lap, but somewhat oddly his right arm is up, lying across the front of his body, and his right hand is closed, not quite in a fully clenched fist but in a three-quarters fist, what I would call a loosely clenched fist. It could be that he didn't know where to put that right arm, since he is sitting very close to the player to his right, whose left shoulder is in fact blocking off Crane's right side, so instead of putting his right arm over his neighbor's shoulder, Crane lifted it against his own body, and then, not knowing what to do with the hand, closed it, so he wouldn't block off his own face. Nevertheless, the hand resembles a fist, and while I wouldn't want to impute a symbolic value to that fist or three-quarters fist, it is undeniably a curious touch. Not exactly aggressive or defensive—but poised and ready. The eyes look off into the distance. The expression on the face is neutral, pensive, detached, and the features are calm. Crane seems to have arrived at the threshold of understanding who he is, and he looks ready, ready for anything.

THE PACE OF YOUTH

⚜

I

Mozart composed his first piece of music at five and his first symphony at eight. Chopin, Bizet, Liszt, and Glenn Gould all performed on the piano in public before they were ten. Jascha Heifetz and Yehudi Menuhin made their debuts on the violin at seven. Sammy Davis Jr. could dazzle variety audiences with his tap dancing at four. Picasso was an accomplished painter when he was still in his teens. Bobby Fischer won the United States Chess Championship in his second year as a teen and by the next year had become the youngest grand master in history.

Prodigies. Children kissed by the gods who claim our attention because they can hold their own against the adults in their field. It happens most often in music, sometimes in visual art, and occasionally in the pure, Pythagorean realms of mathematics and chess, but there are no prodigies in the domain of writing. The medium of language is far messier and more intricate than the stark geometries of number and form, and, as opposed to the wunderkinds on their pianos and violins, manual dexterity plays no part in becoming a writer. It takes years of living before one can feel at home in the labyrinthine complexities of language, and therefore writers develop slowly, often struggling into their late twenties and thirties before they manage to produce anything worth the ink in their pens. The poem Crane wrote at eight and the story he turned out at thirteen show immense promise, but they could never be confused with the work of an adult. Thousands of teenagers show promise, but few ever amount to anything, and even the most gifted ones must develop. Mary Shelley, who wrote *Frankenstein* at nineteen, began her journey toward that book as an illiterate child, which was also true of the plays written by the astounding Georg Büchner (medical doctor, scientist, political revolutionary), who reinvented nineteenth-century dramatic literature with *Woyzeck* and *Danton's Death* before his own death at twenty-three, whereas countless musical prodigies can read the notes of the bass and treble clefs long before they have mastered the letters of the Roman alphabet.

Like Mary Shelley and Büchner, Crane developed, developed almost as rapidly as they did, moving at such an accelerated pace that in the five and a half years he spent in and around New York (including the months he spent out west and in Mexico), he progressed from floundering apprentice to ferocious innovator, an artist in full possession of his talents and vision of the world. He did not, however, progress in a straight line. Until he struck out on his own, the little work he had published so far had been mostly of a satirical bent—light, humorous, even sardonic—and he continued writing in that vein after arriving in the New York area, putting in another two summers on the boardwalk at Asbury Park as society beat writer for his brother's news agency and composing sketches and stories about life in the wilds of Sullivan County, New York, most of which were lighthearted in tone as well. At the same time, he was also discovering the world of Manhattan and digging more deeply into the ever deepening *Maggie*, one of the least comic and lighthearted books ever written, a pitiless, hallucinatory rendering of the New York slums that ran so counter to the moral pieties of the age that no publisher would touch it. *At the same time.* It is a phrase worth remembering, for the intensity and volume of Crane's output was made possible only because he was always working on several things *at the same time*, meaning that when he was at work on his novels he was also writing short stories, sketches, and journalism, not just because he had to (out of financial necessity) but because he wanted to, and not just because he wanted to but because he had to (out of financial necessity).

About two-thirds of Crane's best work was written during those five and a half years (from mid-1891 to the end of 1896). He had numerous friends and acquaintances, he fell in love at least three times, he went out to restaurants and theaters when he could afford them, he traveled north to Hartwood and did many other things besides write, but when one considers how much he did write, it scarcely seems credible that he was not holding a pen in his hand twenty-four hours a day every day over the course of those five and a half years. How else to account for the two short novels written during that period (*Maggie: A Girl of the Streets* and

George's Mother), the two longer novels (*The Red Badge of Courage* and *The Third Violet*), the Sullivan County sketches and stories, a collection of poems (*The Black Riders*), the Civil War stories gathered in *The Little Regiment*, and close to a hundred other works of fiction and nonfiction, including his trio of startling "Baby Stories" from 1893—"An Ominous Baby," "A Great Mistake," and "A Dark-Brown Dog"—as well as nearly all of his sketches about New York City, among them the unforgettable "An Experiment in Misery," "The Men in the Storm," "An Eloquence of Grief," "Coney Island's Failing Days," "In a Park Row Restaurant," "The Fire," "Opium's Varied Dreams," and "The Devil's Acre," a dark, powerful meditation on the electric chair at Sing Sing? And all of these books, stories, poems, and sketches with all of their varied approaches and registers were sparking in him *at the same time*—which is to say, the young man had caught fire, and the question to be examined now is what caused that fire to ignite and how someone who claimed that he "began the war with no talent" could have won so many battles with himself and generated such a vast body of sublime and original work.

When Crane left New York at the end of 1896, he was twenty-five years old. He was also famous, unquestionably the most famous young American writer of the period, perhaps the most famous young writer the Republic had ever produced. It was the era of the large-circulation newspaper, and with eighteen daily papers published in New York alone (in addition to nineteen foreign-language dailies), America's celebrity culture had begun, with all the clamor, adulation, and vicious cruelty that are still with us today. The publication of *The Red Badge of Courage* in September 1895 turned Crane into a celebrity. He hadn't sought that fame, but fame had found him and singled him out, and once he was turned into the man of the hour, he was also turned into a target—not just for his opponents in the literary world but for the New York Police Department as well. He had stood up for a fallen woman in court, a known prostitute named Dora Clark (when she wasn't calling herself Ruby Young or Dora Wilkins) who had charged an officer with false arrest, and because Crane had witnessed the scene and knew her charges were justified, he defended her, which led the police to go after him and try to destroy his reputation. Their efforts were largely successful, and for the rest of Crane's life and long after his death, many considered him to be a dangerous, unwholesome person, a whore-mongering dope fiend and a blot on the fabric of society. It wasn't that Crane wanted to leave New York, but after his apartment was ransacked in an undercover raid and he was subjected to continual surveillance and harassment, he had to leave for his own good. He had to run.

2

HIS FIRST SUMMER AS AN EX–COLLEGE MAN STARTED WITH A BRIEF camping trip in Sullivan County and ended with a longer camping trip in Pike County, Pennsylvania. In between, he was back in Asbury Park, where he wrote twelve or thirteen more news items for his brother Townley, all of them in the same spirit as the ones from the previous summer except for the article on Garland's lecture about Howells, which led to Crane's friendship with Garland and, just as important, helped stimulate and crystalize his thinking about what kind of writer he wanted to be, since at that early stage he was still torn between conflicting impulses, on the one hand the tough, lyrical fury of his novella in progress, *Maggie*, and, on the other hand, the small, jocular works he was also writing that summer, the Sullivan County stories and sketches, which he would later disparage as belonging to the "clever school in literature." Nevertheless, the nineteen-year-old Crane was cranking out those tales at a fast and regular clip, and his cleverness paid off, at least in the short run. Willis Fletcher Johnson happened to be spending the summer in Asbury Park, the same man who had employed Crane that spring as Syracuse correspondent for the *New York Tribune* and had acted as his co-conspirator in the Great Bug Hoax, but the two of them hadn't met since Crane's early boyhood, and the bold young man who was also an intensely shy young man hesitated to approach Johnson with his new work. He mentioned it to Townley, however, and when his big brother approached Johnson on his behalf, Johnson said of course, he would be happy to take a look at the kid's writing. Crane showed him a couple of samples, each about two thousand words in length. "They were fantastic and impressionistic fiction pieces," Johnson wrote in 1926. "I was very favorably imprest by them and told him so, and at once accepted them for use in the Sunday supplement of the *Tribune*. They, and a number more, were printed in that newspaper . . . and attracted much flattering attention."

Sullivan County had once been part of the American frontier, a rugged area near the Catskills where white settlers had fought against the local Indians whose land they had usurped and where battles had been fought in the Revolution. (How many people remember that *Last of the Mohicans* is set in New York State?) It was still rugged and largely unsettled territory in the 1890s, but the only battles still being fought were the ones waged between hunters and unarmed wild animals. In June 1891, Crane went there with three of his Port Jervis friends to spend some time in the woods. One of them was his Syracuse classmate Frederic Lawrence (the future doctor), and the other two had been close to him since childhood, Louis Carr and Louis Senger. Lawrence writes about that camping trip in his piece from the 1920s:

> We spent the days wandering into the nearby hills and occupied the daylight hours with pipes, books and conversation. In the evenings, we played cards, still with much conversation. For August we organized a real camp, almost a *de luxe* affair for those days, and spent four weeks in the wilds of Pike County, Pa. As I recall it, our days were devoted mostly to ransacking the shores of the adjacent lakes for logs with which to maintain the night's huge camp fires. The choicest hours were those spent around its blaze, and when the light died down at last, we wrapped ourselves in blankets and slept on the ground like true savages. Crane loved this life, and his health was magnificent. As the month wore on, exposure to the sun gave his skin a copper color almost like that of an American Indian, and it formed a strange contrast to his still light hair. So great was the success of this camp that for several subsequent summers we made similar excursions into Pike County. Between times we made shorter journeys, often into Sullivan County, N.Y., and from our experiences there Crane drew inspiration for his first published stories.

Crane would grow disenchanted with those early efforts, confessing to the *Boston Herald* in 1896 that he wished he had "dropped them into the waste basket," but they nevertheless deserve some attention, not so much for their *cleverness* as for certain flashes in the prose—invigorating sentences that dance and kick on the page—and for the embryonic articulation of ideas and methods that would begin to flower in Crane's work just several months ahead. Of the nineteen Sullivan County pieces, written between the summer of 1891 and early 1892, fourteen were published by Johnson in the *New York Tribune*, one in the *Syracuse University Herald* (for old times' sake?), and one in a bygone incarnation of *Cosmopolitan* (Crane's first appearance in a national magazine). If nothing else, he must have found it encouraging to see so much of his work in print so soon after quitting college—at a time when he was only just beginning to clear his throat.

Eleven are works of fiction and eight fall into the category of sketch, essay, meditation, or whatever term one cares to use for a short work of nonfiction that ambles leisurely around a single subject. Those subjects are clearly delineated by their newspaper headlines, yielding such titles as "The Last Panther," "Sullivan County Bears," "Bear and Panther," and "Hunting

Wild Hogs," which to my non-hunter ears does not sound terribly promising, but once you plunge in and start reading, the words carry you along, and after a couple of paragraphs it no longer matters if you are interested in hunting or not:

> Children going to school were frightened home by wild hogs. Men coming home late at night saw wild hogs. It became a sort of fashion to see wild hogs and turn around and come back. But when the outraged farmers made such a terrific onslaught upon the stern and rock-bound land the wild hogs, it appears, withdrew to Sullivan County. This county may have been formed by a very reckless and distracted giant who, observing a tract of tipped-up and impossible ground, stood off and carelessly pelted trees and boulders at it. Not admiring the results of his labors he set off several earthquakes under it and tried to wreck it. He succeeded beyond his utmost expectations.... In the holes and crevices, valleys and hills, caves and swamps of this uneven country, the big game of the southern part of this State have made their last stand.

Other of the nonfiction pieces provide similar rhetorical flourishes and exaggerations of tone, most especially in "The Way in Sullivan County," a sketch that deals with the nature of exaggeration itself.

> A country famous for its hunters is naturally prolific of its liars. Wherever the wild deer boundeth and the shaggy bear waddleth, there does the liar thrive and multiply. Every man cultivates what taste he has for prevarication lest his neighbors may look down on him. One can buy sawlogs from a native and take his word that the bargain is square, but ask the same man how many deer he has killed in his lifetime and he will paralyze the questioner with a figure that would look better than most of the totals to the subscription lists for monuments to national heroes.

On the next page, Crane pinpoints the precise mental spot where the impulse to tell tall tales is born: "In a shooting country, no man should tell just exactly what he did. He should tell what he would have liked to do or what he expected to do, just as if he accomplished it."

The fictional works in the Sullivan County cycle emerged from Crane's camping experiences with his three friends, and the four characters in these tales are identified throughout as the little man (Carr), the pudgy man (Lawrence), the tall man (Senger), and the quiet man (Crane— although the quiet man is so quiet that he often seems to merge with the little man). They come across as a late-nineteenth-century version of the Marx Brothers or, more accurately because more crudely, a twofold version of Abbott and Costello.*

As with the sketches, the stories are replete with hyperbolic riffs and tall-tale bravura, a pumped-up tone that is then systematically undercut as the action devolves into a string of slapstick discombobulations. In "Four Men in a Cave," the four bumblers climb into a deep and spooky subterranean grotto, looking for an adventure they can turn into a story to tell their friends, and chance upon a crazed hermit at the bottom who insists on playing poker with them—or else. In "The Octopush," the four go off to a pond to fish for pickerel and engage an old-timer referred to as "the individual" to row them out onto the pond in his boat, but once they are deposited on their separate stumps in the middle of the water, the individual gets drunk and leaves them there, stranded, far into the night. Fear overcomes them. "A night wind began to roar and clouds bearing a load of rain appeared in the heavens and threatened their position. The four men shivered and turned up their coat collars. Suddenly it struck each that he was alone, separated from humanity by impassable gulfs." Salvation comes only after the drunken individual begins hallucinating an "octopush" in the darkness and flees to safety with the four others in his boat. "A Ghoul's Accountant" begins eerily and poetically with the four companions sleeping around a fading campfire. "In a wilderness sunlight is noise. Darkness is a great, tremendous silence, accented by small and distant sounds. The music of the wind in the trees is songs of loneliness, hymns of abandonment, and lays of the absence of things congenial and alive." In the third paragraph, "the ghoul" approaches the slumbering men, four "bundles" gathered around the campsite. "His skin was fiercely red and his whiskers infinitely black," and when he looks down on the foursome, he "smiled a smile that curled his lip and showed yellow, disordered teeth." The reader is being set up for a horror tale of the most chilling kind, and after the ghoul rousts the little man from his blankets and forces him to march through the woods,

---

* It is interesting to note that Bud Abbott was born in Asbury Park (where Crane's career began) and that Lou Costello was born in Paterson (where a trial first draft of *Red Badge* was written), but I wouldn't want to make too much of the connection, since America is nothing if not a hodgepodge of multiple, contrasting realms, the global epicenter of unlikely intersections and sumptuous incongruities. In the same spirit, however, it should also be noted that in the generation following Crane's death, the dense forests of Sullivan County were transformed into the Borscht Belt, a vast constellation of hotels and resorts that catered primarily to New York Jews (the Old Testament equivalent of New Testament Asbury Park) and is best remembered today as the breeding ground of a thousand stand-up comics. There was humor in those craggy hills, and Crane was the first to exploit it.

the suspense continues to mount: "The bundles were left far in the rear and the little man stumbled on with the ghoul. Tangled thickets tripped him, saplings buffeted him, and stones turned away from his feet. Blinded and badgered, he began to swear frenziedly. A foam drifted to his mouth, and his eyes glowed with a blue light." They come to a broken-down hovel in the middle of nowhere, and when they step into the chaotic, smashed-up interior, they find a "wild gray man" sitting at a table. The ghoul throws the little man into a chair, and just when it seems that all kinds of grotesque things are about to happen, Crane punctures his vastly inflated balloon with a deft little pinprick of nonsense. Standing by the wild gray man, the ghoul clears his throat and says, "Stranger, how much is thirty-three bushels of pertaters at sixty-four and a half a bushel?" When the little man finally stammers forth the correct answer, the ghoul kicks him out of the house and the story ends. The same combination of terror and nonsense continues through most of the other stories, including "An Explosion of Seven Babies," a madcap fairy tale about a giantess and her seven little children who have eaten flypaper and are about to burst—whether from puking or shitting is not made clear—and when, within minutes of each other, the little man and the pudgy man approach the house because they are lost in the woods, they are given the works by the giantess, who one by one tosses them over the wall of her garden, "A Tent in Agony," which recounts the little man's confrontation with a menacing black bear who gets tangled up in a collapsed tent and runs through the woods "like a white-robed phantom pursued by hornets," and "The Cry of a Huckleberry Pudding," which is a story about a stomach-ache, a stomach-ache pure and simple, and yet the screams emitted by the little man in the darkness of the woods strike panic in the three others because they are unaware that the little man is missing and consequently cannot identify the source of the sound. All of a sudden, the tone shifts:

> The cry of the unknown instantly awoke them to terror. It is mightier than the war-yell of the dreadful, because the dreadful might be definite. But this whoop strikes greater fear from hearts because it tells of formidable mouths and great, grasping claws that live in impossibility. It is the chant of a phantom force which imagination declares invincible, and awful to the sight.

Only one of the stories escapes the comic-spooky and/or spooky-comic oscillations of the others in the series. Just two and a half pages long, "Killing His Bear" stands apart for several reasons—first, because it dispenses with the four blockheads and focuses on just one of them, the little man; second, because it follows a single, concerted action from beginning to end and does not break up into several loosely connected actions; third, because the writing is wholly consistent with Crane's purpose, which is to track a solitary man's thoughts and movements as he tiptoes through the woods with a rifle and hunting dog to vanquish his first bear, that is, to kill his first bear, which by the end assumes the metaphorical weight of vanquishing his first woman; and fourth, because the writing is more robust and precisely articulated than in any of the other stories. Consider these extracts:

> The dying sun created a dim purple and flame-colored tumult on the horizon's edge and then sank until crimson beams struck the trees. As the red rays retreated, armies of shadows stole forward.
>
> A hound, as he nears large game, has the griefs of the world on his shoulders and his baying tells of the approach of death. He is sorry he came.
>
> His rifle-barrel was searching swiftly over the dark shape. Under the fore-shoulder was the place. A chance to pierce the heart, sever an artery or pass through the lungs. The little man saw swirling fur over his gun-barrel. The earth faded to nothing. Only space and the game, the aim and the hunter. Mad emotions, powerful to rock worlds, hurled through the little man, but did not shake his tiniest nerve.
>
> When the rifle cracked it shook his soul to a profound depth. Creation rocked and the bear stumbled.

And then the surprising last paragraph:

> The little man yelled again and sprang forward, waving his hat as if he were leading the cheering of thousands. He ran up and kicked the ribs of the bear. Upon his face was the smile of a successful lover.

What are we to make of the Sullivan County stories and sketches? The nonfiction pieces tend to be solid if unremarkable works, with Crane exploring not only legends of the past but at times also debunking them, as he does in a short essay entitled "The Last of the Mohicans" (Cooper's heroic warrior, Uncas, turns out to be a pathetic, much-pitied character whose only ambition is to "beg, borrow or steal a drink") and in another essay entitled "Not Much of a Hero," which takes on the vaunted legend of Indian fighter Tom Quick by asserting in the last sentence that he was "purely and simply a murderer." As for the stories, the best one can say about them is that they are uneven in quality and rather sophomoric in tone—but that is precisely what Crane would have been if he had remained in college: a sophomore. Aside from the well-executed "Killing His Bear," only "The Mesmeric Mountain" calls for a second look. The little man, on his own again, imagines that a mountain is moving toward him, runs off afraid, stops, is bewildered to discover that the mountain is now standing directly in front of him, attacks the mountain by throwing pebbles at it, then angrily climbs to the top and discovers that the mountain under his feet is "motionless." It is a bizarre, somewhat confused parable, but it announces an image that would come to haunt the poems Crane started writing in 1894, for mountains (where earth meets sky, where man looks for God) crop up incessantly in the pages of *The Black Riders*. Beyond that, for all their flaws and stumbles, the Sullivan County stories contain some vivid bursts of prose and prefigure many of Crane's obsessions and stylistic trademarks: an abundant use of color imagery to express both emotional states and sensory experiences, a gift for unexpected metaphors and jolting similes, an animistic view of the natural world (the trees, stones, and plants in the woods are alive), a dispassionate approach to character that posits the isolation of the individual in the face of an indifferent universe, and a close scrutiny of the metaphysics of fear, the same fear that runs through every paragraph of *The Red Badge of Courage*, which Crane would begin writing just two years later. Still, it isn't difficult to understand why he eventually soured on these early fictions, and if not for his subsequent work, the Sullivan County cycle would have vanished from human memory, in the same way most writings by most writers have vanished since the beginning of time. That said, how not to admire certain bits and pieces of these less than minor works, for example the following paragraph from "The Black Dog," which was written (we must remember) by a nineteen- or twenty-year-old boy who still had no clear idea of where he was headed:

> The phantom dog lay . . . asleep down the roadway against the windward side of an old shanty. The spectre's master had moved to Pike County. But the dog lingered as a friend might linger at the tomb of a friend. His fur was like a suit of old clothes. His jowls hung and flopped, exposing his teeth. Yellow famine was in his eyes. The wind-rocked shanty groaned and muttered, but the dog slept. Suddenly, however, he got up and shambled to the roadway. He cast a long glance from his hungry, despairing

eyes in the direction of the venerable house. The breeze came full to his nostrils. He threw back his head and gave a long, low howl and started intently up the road. Maybe he smelled a dead man.

3

AFTER THE 1891 SUMMER SEASON ENDED IN ASBURY PARK, CRANE moved to his brother Edmund's house just outside Paterson. On September sixteenth, Townley's wife, Anna, cracked up and landed in the Trenton asylum. On the thirtieth, for reasons I find difficult to fathom, Townley joined his mother and three of his brothers—William, Edmund, and Stephen—on an excursion to Hartwood. One asks: How could he have gone off on a camping and fishing trip with his young wife raving in a madhouse more than one hundred miles away, unreachable in the event of another emergency? What could he have been thinking, and what could the family have been thinking by inviting him to join them? Did they see it as an attempt to distract him from his troubles, or were those troubles too overwhelming for him to face? Impossible to know, but the words written by Crane in the Hartwood register upon their arrival suggest that the family was in high spirits: "Shortly after dusk this evening a flock of Cranes flew upon the property of the Association and alighted near the clubhouse. The mother bird had considerable difficulty in keeping her children quiet and making them retire for the night." On October second, he added: "Mother Crane caught seven fine pickerel to her own satisfaction and the astonishment of her brood. The next day she caught three more nice fish in less than an hour."

An eerie disjunction. How to resolve the dread of a young woman's mental and physical breakdown with a cheerful romp through the woods? Was the family just as unhinged as she was, or were they a stoical, unflinching lot who had mastered the art of laughing through their troubles?

Near the end of the month, the *Asbury Park Journal* reported that "Anna Crane has had a second attack of paralysis, and lives in a precarious condition," and two weeks later (November sixteenth) Townley's wife died. On the twenty-eighth, the *Journal* published a short item countering the rumor that Crane's mother had also died (on the twenty-fifth in Paterson): "Mrs. Crane attended a National W.C.T.U. Convention at Boston and took a severe cold. In addition to this a carbuncle on the neck has greatly prostrated her, so that she is in a critical condition. News of the recent death of her daughter-in-law, which reached her after she had been confined to her bed, produced a great depression and distress of mind, which it is hoped good nursing and the best medical skill will in time relieve."They did not relieve, and nine days after that Crane's mother was dead.

Not only do we know nothing about Crane's reaction to that death, but the next six months of his life are more or less a blank as well. Except for a couple of surviving letters in his published correspondence from February 1892 (one sent from Lake View, the other from Port Jervis) and, sometime in May, a brief, water-soaked, fairly miserable jaunt to Sullivan County with his friend Lawrence (who writes that he had seen "little of Crane for several months"), his personal activities are undocumented between the family trip to Hartwood in October and his setting off to Asbury Park at the end of May for another season of summer reporting. Johnson began publishing the Sullivan County pieces in February 1892, meaning that most of them appeared months after they had been composed, with Johnson no doubt fitting them into the Sunday supplement as best he could whenever space was available, which makes it hard to pinpoint when they were written. The same is true of one of Crane's first published pieces about New York City, "The Broken-Down Van," which came out in the *Tribune* on July 10, 1892, but most likely had been written weeks or months earlier, since Crane was in Asbury Park during the summer and didn't start living in New York until October, although another, much shorter item, "Youse Want 'Petey,' Youse Do," which was printed in the *New York Herald* on January 4 (less than a month after his mother's death), could have been written a day or two before it was published. If nothing else, these articles confirm that he was traveling into the city from Edmund's house in Lake View to visit the Jefferson Market Police Court and wander around the slums of the Lower East Side. *Maggie* was surely on his mind, but how far he had advanced with it at that point is not clear. Johnson writes that Crane showed him a version of the manuscript in 1891 (although he undoubtedly meant 1892), which he found "in some respects crude, but powerful and impressive . . . throbbing with vitality," although whatever version that was, it is certain that Crane continued working on the book and didn't begin the final draft until he had settled in New York that fall. None of this matters. What counts is that there is a gap in the story, and the most important gap concerns his mother's death, about which he said nothing—except perhaps in *George's Mother*, which he began writing not long after the publication of *Maggie* in 1893, but that is not an autobiographical work, and one has to tread carefully when it comes to novels and resist the temptation of reading fiction as an unfiltered look into the author's life.

There are four things buried in this gap that are worth exploring, however. The first is a letter to his old boarding school sidekick Armistead "Tommie"

Borland, who was living in Norfolk, Virginia, by then, the same Borland who had worshipped Crane and tried to emulate him during their years at Claverack. Borland's letter has been lost, but he had apparently written to grumble about being starved for female companionship in Virginia—more specifically, white female companionship. From Crane's response:

> So you lack females of the white persuasion, do you? How unfortunate! And how extraordinary! I never thought that the world would come to such a pass that you would lack females. Thomas! You indeed must be in a God forsaken country.
>
>   Just read these next few lines in a whisper:—I—I think black is quite good—if—if its yellow and young.

For now, I want to confine my remarks to the mysteries of sex. The hushed tones concerning *black*, *yellow*, and *young* warrant further attention, but I will put off examining Crane's contradictory and evolving attitudes toward race and ethnic bias until later (pages 227–36). At this early moment in the story, the letter to Borland seems to confirm that the twenty-year-old Crane was no longer a virgin (hardly a surprise), and because there is nothing on record to make us think that he had any black friends or traveled in black social circles, we can assume that the black women he slept with were prostitutes. We know that he slept with white prostitutes as well, but where and when and how his sex life began remains a mystery. As a boy who was already smoking and drinking at six, perhaps his education began earlier than it did for most young men at the time, but for nearly all of them (those from the middle class, at any rate) erotic fulfillment before marriage could be found only with prostitutes, and in American cities of the 1890s prostitutes were everywhere—in the streets, in brothels, and even in the uppermost balconies of theaters, where fornicating couples humped in the darkness as orchestras blared in the pits below. It is not my job to make moral judgments about the evils of women selling their bodies for cash or to delve into the hypocrisies of a social system that tacitly encourages such exchanges. Prostitution was a fact then, it continues to be a fact now, and like it or not we live in a flawed world in which sex is a commodity that can be bought and sold. What I am interested in is understanding who Crane was. Among a multitude of other things, he was a boy who lusted after women and therefore slept with hookers regardless of the color of their skin. Even more, I am interested in understanding Crane's work as a writer, and because prostitution figures heavily in his first extended piece of fiction, it is instructive to know that he was intimately acquainted with his subject. The letter to Borland provides the earliest clue and is doubly helpful because it overlaps with the creation of *Maggie*.

The second and third things are the articles he wrote during that six-month interval. The piece from January concerns two seven-year-old boys and a thirteen-year-old boy who were charged with filching some brushes and a can of corn from a street stand on lower Broadway. A petty crime of little consequence, which Crane duly reports, but what stands out in the short text is his effort to capture the speech of one of the boys, to learn the language of the New York slums and put it down correctly on the page. It is the language spoken by the characters in *Maggie*, and here we see Crane beginning to master it. The dialogue in the Sullivan County stories is unliterary, colloquial, and direct—but nothing quite like this:

> "Yer see," said little Alstrumpt, the leader of the gang, to Justice Diver, "we was doin' notten but playen tag in der street when a blokie wat's called 'Petey' come along and says, 'Hi, fellers, lets go a swipen.' We went wid him—see? Youse wants 'Petey,' youse do. He did der swipen—not me nor de kids."
>
> "Who's Petey?" asked Justice Divver.
>
> "Why he's 'Petey' Larkin, a mug wot lives in Thompson street."

Whenever it might have been written, "The Broken-Down Van" represents a step forward for Crane and is superior to anything he had written so far. About twenty-five hundred words in length, it tells in exacting detail the story of a traffic jam on an unspecified street in lower Manhattan as two large furniture vans pulled by four horses each are rumbling down the narrow thoroughfare when a wheel on the second van falls off, causing an ever mounting number of cars to come to a halt behind it. In other words, as with much of his early work, it is a story about almost nothing—a banal and fleeting episode of city life—but Crane's telling is so energetic, borne along by a flood of such marvelously turned sentences, that one reads on with astonished delight, in the same way one listens to a singer blast forth a well-executed aria in an otherwise mundane opera. The long second paragraph, which includes some of the longest sentences Crane ever wrote, deserves to be presented in full—to show what the rapidly developing young writer was now capable of:

They tossed and pitched and proceeded slowly, and a horse car with a red light came up behind. The car was red, and the bullseye light was red, and the driver's hair was red. He blew his whistle shrilly and slapped the horse's lines impatiently. Then he whistled again. Then he pounded on the red dash board with his car-hook till the red light trembled. Then a car with a green light crept up behind the car with the red light; and the green driver blew his whistle and pounded on his dash board; and the conductor of the red car seized his strap from his position on the rear platform and rang such a rattling tattoo on the gong over the red driver's head that the red driver became frantic and stood up on his toes and puffed out his cheeks as if he were playing the trombone in a German street-band and blew his whistle till an imaginative person could see slivers flying from it, and pounded his red dash board till the metal was dented in and the car-hook was bent. And just as the driver of the newly-come car with a blue light began to blow his whistle and pound his dash board and the green conductor began to ring his bell like a demon which drove the green driver mad and made him rise up and blow and pound as no man ever blew or pounded before, which made the red conductor lose the last vestige of control of himself and cause him to bounce up and down on his bell strap as he grasped it with both hands in a wild, maniacal dance, which of course served to drive uncertain Reason from her tottering throne in the red driver, who dropped his whistle and his hook and began to yell, and ki-yi, and whoop harder than the worst personal devil encountered by the sternest of Scotch Presbyterians ever yelled and ki-yied and whooped on the darkest night after the good man had drunk the most hot Scotch whiskey; just then the left-hand forward wheel on the rear van fell off and the axle went down. The van gave a mighty lurch and then swayed and rolled and rocked and stopped; the red driver applied his brake with a jerk and his horses turned out to keep from being crushed between car and van; the other drivers applied their brakes with a jerk and their horses turned out; the two cliff-dwelling men on the shelf half-way up the front of the stranded van began to shout loudly to their brother cliff-dwellers on the forward van; a girl, six years old, with a pail of beer crossed under the red horses' necks; a boy, eight years old, mounted the red car with the sporting extras of the evening papers; a girl, ten years old, went in front of the van horses with two pails of beer; an unclassified boy poked his finger in the black grease in the hub of the right-hand hind van wheel and began to paint his name on the red landscape on the van's side; a boy with a little head and big ears examined the white rings on the martingales of the van leaders with a view of stealing them in the confusion; a sixteen-year-old girl without any hat and with a roll of half-finished vests under her arm crossed the front platform of the green car. As she stepped up on to the sidewalk a barber from a ten-cent shop said "Ah! there!" and she answered "smarty!" with withering scorn and went down a side street. A few drops of warm summer rain began to fall.

The point of view is that of a camera mounted on a tripod. The position is fixed, and only what enters the frame of the camera is included in the sketch. First the vans and the men who drive them, followed by the horsecars behind the vans, and when the second van breaks down and traffic stalls, children begin to march into and out of the frame, each one introduced by his or her sex and age—girl, boy, girl, six, eight, ten—but just when a pattern seems to have been established, the author breaks it by introducing the next child as an "unclassified boy" and the one after as a boy with a "little head and big ears," in that way keeping the reader off-balance and therefore more alert to what is going on, for there are at least two things going on here at the same time: the visual depiction of whatever can be seen within the frame as well as the rhythmic, highly charged language used by the author to convey the images he is showing us. The language is the heartbeat of the text, and it turns what could have been a dull and limited account of a commonplace event—almost a non-event—into a rollicking piece of work. As the text advances, more and more people crowd into the frame, more and more things keep happening, and more and more traffic piles up, leading to sentences such as this one, which could have been inserted by Samuel Beckett into the pages of *Watt*, written fifty years later: "A car with a white light, a car with a white and red light, a car with a white light and a green bar across it, a car with a blue light and a white circle around it, another car with a red bullseye light and one with a red flat light had come up and stopped." As frantic efforts are made to repair the wheel, we see the ten-cent barber ogle another young woman, who also draws the amorous attentions of a policeman, but the policeman is on duty and must maintain order, since there are more than a hundred people gathered on the sidewalk by now, so he "left the girl . . . and made the truckman give over his warlike movement, much to the disgust of the crowd. Then he punched the suspender man in the back with the end of his club and went back to the girl."

Note that Crane never judges the actions of the people who fall within his view. The larcenous boy who covets the martingales, the lecherous barber who covets the girls, and the over-zealous cop who slugs the suspender man are not subjected to the right-thinking, sermonizing impulses of the period. Crane means to be cool and dispassionate, to keep his distance and not insinuate himself into the actions he is describing, to let the facts speak for themselves. It is a rigorous, third-person stance, and with few exceptions he maintained that stance to the end of his writing life. Combined with the innate lyricism and metaphorical richness of his prose, it produces a curious, destabilizing effect on the reader—a strange effect. In "The Broken-Down Van," he was beginning to discover that strangeness in himself and, in the process, inching ever closer to establishing his style.

The fourth thing did not happen directly to Crane but to his brother William, a most terrible thing that proved what the citizens of a Yankee town like Port Jervis were capable of, dispelling the myth that acts of racial violence were committed only in the South. On June 2, 1892, four days after Crane left for Asbury Park, Robert Lewis, a black man falsely accused of raping a white woman, was pulled from a police wagon and strung up from a maple tree by a mob of two thousand people in front of the Reformed Church in the center of town. William's house was just opposite, and when he heard the shouting voices across the way, he rushed outside and did what he could to stop the lynching, cutting through the crowd and grabbing hold of the rope just as "the body was going up" (*Port Jervis Evening Gazette*). Lewis was still alive at that point, and William had apparently saved him, but the crowd was unstoppable and began crying out in unison, "Hang him," "Hang all the niggers," at which point William was thrust aside and Lewis was strung up again and hanged until he was well and truly dead. William's actions had only delayed the inevitable, but he had acted nobly, with an almost impossible heroism, for not many men would have the courage to do what he did: risk his own life to prevent another man's death by standing up to a frenzied, hate-filled mob. His youngest brother didn't witness the scene, but there is no question that he heard about it and didn't forget what he heard. Five years later, he wrote *The Monster*, which is set in a town modeled on Port Jervis and features a black man as the central character. While there is no outright lynching in the novella, the citizens of Whilomville display an attitude toward justice scarcely different from the one shown by the citizens of Port Jervis on the evening of June 2, 1892. In that same town thirteen years earlier, a black man's face had been burned off his bones by a backfiring cannon. Now there was this.

4

THAT SUMMER IN ASBURY PARK, THE TWENTY-YEAR-OLD CRANE fell in love for the first time, not "in the headlong way of seventeen," as he wrote about one of his boarding school crushes, but in the earnest, passionate way of a young man of twenty in search of a soul mate and companion for the long road ahead. Twenty is not seventeen, but it is still a precariously young age, and however experienced or inexperienced Crane might have been in carnal matters, he was a novice when it came to the protocols of bourgeois courtship, a jittery and awkward suitor, somewhat out of his depth, it would seem, but intense and adoring, a conundrum of tongue-tied reserve and sudden bursts of playfulness. Fortunately for him, his feelings were reciprocated. While nothing came of the romance in the end, Crane's love was not some momentary delusion or summer fling, and he didn't abandon his hope of making Lily Brandon Munroe his wife until 1898, six years after they first met.

She was one year older than he was and already married, but unhappily married and already estranged from her husband, Hersey Munroe, a geologist employed as a topographer by the U.S. Geological Survey who was frequently absent from home because of his work. A young woman born into wealth, she had been educated in England and New York City and was spending the summer at the Lake Avenue Hotel in Asbury Park with her mother-in-law and young sister, Dottie. Townley's office was in the same hotel, and that was where she and Crane met. For the next two months they often went out together in public, riding the carousel at the Hippodrome and walking along the beach and the boardwalk, but what they did together when alone in private is anyone's guess. I assume that a disappointed and frustrated married woman would have been less coy about physical intimacy than a young, unmarried virgin, but that is only a general observation and tells us nothing about this particular case. Sex is the great blank that sits at the heart of nearly all biographies, and because nothing has been uncovered about Crane's erotic appetites (except that he frequented prostitutes, as did millions of other men) nor anything about Lily Brandon Munroe's appetites, one can just as easily imagine that the young Crane stifled his impulses in order to present himself as an honorable gentleman, a man worthy of her love. I somehow doubt it, but that doesn't mean my doubts aren't wrong. Speculation aside, what is known for certain is this: that Crane asked Lily to elope with him and that she weighed her decision carefully before rejecting his offer. What is also known is that both families disapproved of a potential marriage between them.

Most of what has come down to us about that summer was recorded in 1948, fifty-six years after the fact, when Lily was no longer Mrs. Munroe but Mrs. George F. Smillie, a seventy-eight-year-old matron who agreed to be questioned by the bibliographer and scholar Ames Williams about her long-ago affair with Crane. Unfortunately, Williams does not quote her directly but only summarizes her remarks, which puts an even greater distance between the then of 1892 and the now of 1948. The account is necessarily one-sided (based on her memories, told from her point of view), but it appears to be honest, or at least not untruthful as set forth within the limits she has imposed on her story, which is a story that resolutely sticks to the surface of things and does not delve into her innermost feelings. But who can blame her for her reticence? She was an old woman by then, and why would she divulge long-guarded personal secrets to a stranger? It is a decorous account, then, but nevertheless an informative one. Among her memories, as reported by Williams:

> ... not a handsome man, but had remarkable almond-shaped gray eyes ... appeared to be frail ... a hacking cough ... smoked incessantly and usually had a cigarette dangling from his lower lip ... drank very little ... abjectly poor and undernourished ... indifferent to dress ... would use his cuffs for making notes ... was rather prudish ... would comment on the bathing suits worn by the women ... did not care for dancing, although he danced several times with Lily. Lily had a good voice and would attract a group of admirers when she sang; Crane discouraged this practice ... [they] spent happy hours riding the merry-go-round and pulling the rings, going to Day's for ice cream (Crane never ate any and Lily felt guilty about squandering his meager income), walking the board walk and observing people. Steve ... enjoyed watching the surf with Lily ... told her that whenever she saw the ocean she would think of him ... [he] hated the gossiping porch-sitters at the hotels ... and delighted in shocking them. Steve was very much in love with Lily and she with him, but he seemed to have no concrete plans for the future and was melancholy and anxious in that respect ... a troubled spirit seeking happiness which always seemed beyond reach ... he once told her that he would not live long. All he wanted was a few years of real happiness. Crane begged Lily to elope with him and she considered the proposal seriously before declining ...

Much of what she says turns Crane into a haughty, unappealing character, at once priggish (the women's bathing suits), jealous (about her singing in front of others), and morose (brooding over his early death), as if, fifty-six years later, she were still rehearsing the various reasons why she had turned down his proposal, and yet how to reconcile her misgivings with this baldly stated fact: *Steve was very much in love with Lily and she with him*? Why would she fall in love with a glum prude unless he was only occasionally a glum prude and the rest of the time a different, more lovable sort of man? If not, why would she have considered running away with him? Something is missing here, something about who they were together isn't being told, and more than seventy years after she sat down and talked to Williams, with Lily Brandon Munroe Smillie now long dead, whatever that untold story might have been lies buried in her grave.

More verifiable bits from that summer and beyond. Crane got along well with Lily's kid sister, Dottie, in the jesting, genial manner that came naturally to him as an uncle of numerous girls (William alone had five daughters), once betting her a necklace that his brother Townley wouldn't marry for a third time (she won, he lost). On August seventh, about six weeks after meeting Lily, Crane published a humorous sketch in the *New York Tribune* entitled "The Captain," which had nothing to do with the Asbury Park reporting he was engaged in that summer. Undoubtedly inspired by his romance with Lily, the piece is written in the present tense, a rare if not unique tactic for Crane in his fictional work, which only underscores how fully he was living in the present at the time—all filled up with it, in thrall to it. The Captain, "a most marvelous and mysterious wit," is both a member of the village fire department and the skipper of a catboat, which enables him to earn a living by shepherding tourists across the waters of the Sound (not a particular sound, just the Sound). In the sketch, there are four passengers on board that day, a young woman from Baltimore, a young woman from Philadelphia, a young woman from New York, and "'a smart young man' from nowhere." All of the women are Lily in one guise or another. The one from Baltimore (Lily and her husband lived in nearby Washington) speaks "with a soft voice and the slightest Southern accent," and as she looks up and surveys the sky, she asks the Captain if "a squall" is coming (the first sexual innuendo). The one from Philadelphia banters with him about putting out and starting fires (the second innuendo), and when the hair of the one from New York is drenched in a spray of water, she unfastens it and puts it down. As it "tumbles about her shoulders," she asks the Captain how she looks. "Looks like the gypsies that camps in the woods back of our house," he says. "They're wild, you know" (the third wink). Finally, when the Baltimore girl tries her hand at fishing, she gives the Captain a "bewildering smile" and asks him what he thinks she will catch. "'Well,' he answers in a low voice ... 'you might catch some of those men. Ain't any of them heavy enough to break your line.'" Wishful thinking, perhaps, but when Crane wrote this airy little creampuff he hadn't yet been turned down by Lily and still had hope.

It is also known that he gave her copies of a number of his stories along with the manuscript of *Maggie*, that his artist friend David Ericson agreed to paint her portrait but did not finish it for reasons that have never been explained (perhaps Lily had to return to Washington, perhaps Ericson was too busy, perhaps something else), and that Crane was asked to dine at the Brandons' house in the city. Lily's well-heeled businessman father had no interest in allowing his married daughter to entangle herself with a lowlife bohemian vagabond, and when Crane began speaking French at the table, having learned that Mr. Brandon was fluent in several languages, Lily's father cut him down with a blunt, humorless response: "My daughter does not speak French, Mr. Crane."

Either at that dinner or possibly on another visit to the Brandons' house sometime later, Crane was accompanied by his artist friend Corwin K. Linson (known as CK, pronounced "Seek"), who in his invaluable memoir, *My Stephen Crane* (published in 1958 but written years earlier), recounts some moments of conversation in which Crane talks to Lily about his work, with S.C. declaring that "you can't find preaching on any page of *Maggie*! An artist has no business to preach." According to Linson, the conversation touched on many other subjects besides books, for the most part "searching the avenues of young interests," and he found it "refreshing, delightfully revealing." Afterward: "When we were again on the street . . . Steve said nothing for two or three blocks. Then all at once he turned. 'CK! Didn't you like it? I don't know anything finer than the natural talk of a nice girl with brains in her head.'"

There was no question that he was mad about her, to such a degree that at times his ardor provoked the romantic excesses of a besotted, lovesick Werther—or the doomed and pining Michael Furey from James Joyce's "The Dead." One evening in New York, Crane asked Lily to light a candle in her room so he could look up from the street and watch her moving around inside. Lily lit the candle, but then it started to rain, and thinking he must have gone away, she blew it out. He hadn't gone away. He went on standing in the darkness and the rain for many minutes, perhaps for an hour, hoping the candle would be relit, and when he finally left to return home, he was soaked through. He didn't die as Michael Furey did, but he caught a horrendous cold and was sick for days afterward.

Also this: At some point during Lily's involvement with Crane, her husband got wind of what they were up to and destroyed everything connected to Crane in the house, which presumably had been stashed away in some hidden spot—letters, photographs, manuscripts. By some miracle, four of those letters escaped the purge. Four out of how many? one might ask, but at least there are four, which constitute the only scraps of evidence that give Crane's side of the affair.

The letters are often painful to read, embarrassing in their boastfulness and boyish desire to impress her, heartbreaking in their innocent intensity and gushing proclamations of love, marred by confusing shifts of tone and frequent misspellings (Crane was a wretched speller), but for all that achingly sincere and moving, not the work of a rising literary star but of a rejected, inexperienced lover, someone in the impossible position of trying to win back the person who has rejected him without groveling or blaming or begging for another chance.

The first letter comes from April 1893, a month after the publication of *Maggie* and three months after their last meeting. Addressing Lily as "Dearest L.B.," he explains his silence by telling her that "the three months which have passed have been months of very hard work for S. Crane. I was trying to see if I was worthy to have you think of me. . . . Well, at least I've done something. I wrote a book." Rather than say anything about the book, he goes on to list all the brilliant, distinguished men who have admired it (Garland, Howells, B. O. Flower of the *Arena*, Albert Shaw of the *Review of Reviews*, the editor of the *Forum*) and then adds, "So I think I can say that if I 'watch out,' I am almost a success. And 'such a boy, too' they say." Crane is intent on proving to her that he is not the floundering, unmotivated person she thought she had met back in the summer but a spirited young man who has begun his conquest of the world, and if he can conquer the world, surely (by implication) she would be willing to be conquered by him as well. Then, realizing that perhaps he has taken his bragging too far, he backtracks and says, "Any particular vanity in my work is not possible to me. I merely write you these things, to let you know why I was silent for so long." In the next sentence, however, he does another reversal and plunges forward again: "I thought if I could measure myself by the side of some of the great men I could find if I was of enough value to think of you, L.B." One would have expected him to say the opposite—of enough value for you to think of *me*, as he does in the first paragraph—but here he turns the proposition around and questions his own worth as a human being, and if in the end he cannot find himself worthy, he will have lost the right to let Lily enter his mind. Both addled and muddled, he is at such a disadvantage at this point (Lily holds all the cards, and he has nothing but his pride, which, in spite of his bluster, he scarcely seems to believe in anymore) that he has no choice but to sign off with this lame conclusion:

"And I? I have merely thought of you and wondered if you cared that they said these things. Or wether [*sic*] you have forgotten?"

It is not known if Lily replied to this letter or how much or how little they might have corresponded between April 1893 and the winter of '93–'94, the conjectured date of the second of Crane's four surviving letters to her. Around the time of the first one, however, the spring of 1893, when Crane had already begun formulating plans for *The Red Badge of Courage*, he wrote a short story entitled "The Pace of Youth," which is one of the best of his early stories, a work directly tied to Lily and the months they had spent together in Asbury Park, all of it fictionalized and transformed into a modern-day fairy tale of about four thousand words. As opposed to the hesitant and clumsy writing in the first letter, "The Pace of Youth" barrels along with a sparkling confidence, demonstrating yet again, for the thousandth time in literary history, that the man and the artist are not the same person, even though they happen to live in the same body, and that what the man garbles and stumbles over in his daily life can sing and prance in his work.

A quarrelsome old coot named Stinson, proprietor of "Stinson's Mammoth Merry-Go-Round" at an unidentified seaside resort, grows hot under the collar when he catches one of his young employees making eyes at his daughter. The young man's job consists of standing all day on a small raised platform and manipulating a long wooden arm that holds the rings which children slide off as the merry-go-round comes round to the young man's spot (the lucky child who grabs the brass ring gets another ride for free). The young man is stuck up there on his narrow platform all morning and afternoon, unable to move to his left or right, but if he twists his body around into the proper position, he can look down and see Stinson's daughter, Lizzie, selling tickets in the cashier's booth, her face slightly obscured by a sheath of "silvered netting," but not so obscured that it prevents her from looking back at him. The geometrical constraints are pure Crane, the boy trapped on his plank of wood, the girl trapped behind her netting, just as all the characters and objects in "The Broken-Down Van" are trapped within the rectangle of the fixed camera's point of view. The setup also brings to mind some of the contorted manipulations found in the silent comedies of Harold Lloyd and Buster Keaton, and oddly enough, although it was written thirty years before those films were made, much of Crane's story unfolds in the spirit of a silent comedy. The lovers can't talk, they can only make eyes at each other, and the entire drama of their flirtation is enacted in the interplay of their glances.

The silent courtship was conducted over the heads of the crowd who thronged about the bright machine. The swift eloquent glances of the young man went noiselessly and unseen with their message. There had finally become established between the two in this manner a subtle understanding and companionship. They communicated accurately all that they felt. The boy told his love, his reverence, his hope in the changes of the future. The girl told him that she loved him, that she did not love him, that she did not know if she loved him, that she loved him.

It is only in the second half of the story that they manage to exchange a few words on the beach at night. The boy stammers, the girl pouts, but their love is secure, and the next afternoon they run off together, flying away in a carriage "drawn by the eager spirit of a young and modern horse." Stinson chases after them in a hack pulled by an old, plodding nag, and as the lovers disappear into the distance,

> he began to feel impotent. . . . That other vehicle, that was youth, with youth's pace, it was swift-flying with the hope of dreams. He began to comprehend those two children ahead of him, and he knew a sudden and strange awe, because he understood the power of their young blood, the power to fly strongly into the future and feel hope again.

Lizzie (Lily) elopes with her man, and old Stinson ("My daughter does not speak French, Mr. Crane") is left in the dust.

The second letter is more expansive, more revealing, but also more desperate and resigned, since Lily was still trapped in her marriage to Munroe and, to augment Crane's difficulties in luring her back, had recently become the mother of an infant son.

> Your face is a torturing thing, appearing to me always, with the lines and the smile that I love,—before me always the indelible picture of you with it's [*sic*] fragrance of past joys and it's [*sic*] persistent utterance of the present griefs which are to me tragic, because they say they are engraven for life. . . . I conceive those days with you well spent if they cause me years of discontent. It is better to have known you and suffered, than never to have known you. I would not exchange one little detail of memory of you; I would not give up one small remembrance of our companionship. . . . I ask nothing of you in return. Merely that I may tell you I adore you; that you are the shadow and the light of my life;—the whole of it.

Crane then goes on to tell her that he will soon be traveling to Europe (the trip never materialized) and adds, with astonishing restraint, "I have been in town long. I have had a strange life," which skips over the enormous amount of work he had produced in the past year as well as the crushing poverty he had been living in, and in the next sentence of the same paragraph moves on to Dottie: "I have recently heard that Townley is married. For that, I owe Dottie a necklet. I am delighted to think I am in debt to her." After a couple of muted, self-flattering remarks about the support of "the Boston critics and Mr. Howells," which he attributes to the nurturing effect she has had on him, calling himself "the man you have made," he wraps up the letter by asking for a response: "Write to me dearest, for I need it. I may leave sooner for Europe than is now my plan. And in my infinitely lonely life it is better that I should have all the benefits you can say to me."

The third letter is the longest of the four, written several months after the previous one and sent in March or April 1894, almost two years after their summer idyll on the Jersey coast, and by now Crane has apparently given up on his old dream of sharing a possible future with her. The bulk of the letter is about himself, about his struggles and progress as a writer, and for that reason the letter is important, but he doesn't get around to talking about them as a couple until the last ten lines of the seventy-line letter (in published form). Crane wrote next to nothing in the way of literary criticism and commented only rarely on his own work (often contradicting himself from one pronouncement to the next), but his remarks to Lily were among the first he put in writing, and if they don't say much about what he was actually doing then, they give a good idea of what he *thought* he was doing, which in the end is just as valuable.

> My career has been more of a battle than a journey. You know, when I left you, I renounced the clever school in literature. It seemed to me that there must be something more in life than to sit and cudgel one's brains for clever and witty expedients. So I developed all alone a little creed of art which I thought was a good one. Later I discovered that my creed was identical with the one of Howells and Garland and in this way I became involved in the beautiful war between those who say that art is man's substitute for nature and we are the most successful in art when we approach the nearest to nature and truth, and those who say—well, I don't know what they say. They don't, they can't say much. . . . If I had kept to my clever Rudyard-Kipling style, the road

might have been shorter, but ah, it wouldn't be the true road. The two years of fighting have been well-spent. And now I am almost at the end of it. The winter fixes me firmly.

Remember that he was just twenty-two at this point, no longer a nineteen- or twenty-year-old beginner but still embattled, and because he had taken his lumps in the "beautiful war" and was still taking them, he was in a pugnacious mood, a young man struggling for his artistic life, and if he felt that Howells and Garland were his allies, he would cling to them for support, but they knew (even if he didn't) that he was far more daring and radical than either one of them. Crane's friend Post Wheeler concurred with this assessment: "Garland understood that Stevie was blazing a new path through the mawkish and hypocritical jungle of goody-good American letters, though he had not a mind to adopt that trail himself."

As for Lily and the torch Crane still carried for her, this is how he concluded the letter:

> Don't forget me, dear, never, never, never. For you are to me the only woman in life. I am doomed, I suppose, to a lonely existence of futile dreams. It has made me better, it has widened my comprehension of people and my sympathy with whatever they endure. And to it I owe whatever I have achieved and the hope of the future. In truth, this change in my life should prove of some value to me, for, ye gods, I have paid a price for it.
>
> I write to our friend, the ever-loyal Miss Dottie Brandon by this same post—Heaven send her rest. Good-bye, beloved.

It sounds definitive, as if *good-bye* were in fact *farewell*, a graceful, even courtly exit from an untenable situation, a feeling only enhanced by the fourth and final letter—hardly more than a note—sent in July 1895, fifteen or sixteen months after the above farewell, a polite query in which he tells her that a publisher is interested in reprinting his Sullivan County stories, the same works he had renounced for being too "clever" and which, as it happened, were never reprinted in his lifetime, and because "no one in the world has copies of them but you," he asks her if she would mail the pieces to him and then quickly signs off: "Are you coming north this summer? Let me know, when you send the stories. I should like to see you again. Yours as ever, S.C." Such a dry note would appear to have signaled the end of his fascination with her, but it hadn't—or at least not quite.

I have come across one photograph of Lily Brandon Munroe from the

Lily Brandon Munroe and her husband, Hersey Munroe.
(COURTESY OF THE UNIVERSITY OF VIRGINIA)

period when Crane knew her. In its ensemble, it is a strange and enigmatic picture, almost a nonsensical picture, but Lily's part in that ensemble is strange only because it is not strange, which puts it at odds with the rest of the image. She is standing somewhere outside in the woods, tall and erect, with her right arm wrapped around the top rung of a four-rung log fence, holding a dark hat ornamented with flowers or artificial flowers in her right hand and looking off to her left. Her dark dress, which hangs all the way down below her ankles, is an 1890s affair with puffed-up, leg-of-mutton sleeves, a tightly cinched waist, and a V-shaped opening at the top of the bodice that is filled with the upper portion of a white blouse that covers her neck. Her hair appears to be light brown (perhaps blond), and although it is pulled back, there is a fringe of curled bangs adorning her forehead, which adds a playful touch that helps undermine the severity of her costume. It is hard to decipher the details of her face, but it appears to be an attractive face, not a beautiful one, perhaps, but handsome and well formed, and beyond that it is important to note that she is smiling, a great rarity for photos of the period, which suggests that the picture was taken on celluloid with one of Kodak's newly invented fixed-focus box cameras, the precursor of the Brownie, which gave the world the snapshot in 1900. However the photo was taken, Lily's smile is warm and intelligent, a self-possessed smile, the smile of *a nice girl with brains*, and her eyes are lit up and unself-conscious, bold in their frankness. Not strange, then, not the least bit strange, but Lily is not the only figure in the photograph, for there to her right and just below her, sitting on the other side of the fence in a dark three-piece suit, visible only from the waist up, is her husband, Hersey Munroe, propping his left elbow against the third rung of the log fence and shielding his face from the sun with his hand. His eyes are shut, and his thin lips are shut as well, not so firmly as to create a grimace yet shut tight for all that. What is he doing there, and why is he planted on the ground in that awkward, unguarded pose? I suspect it is because he didn't understand that he was in the picture. It was to be Lily's portrait, and she is fully ready for it, fully aware that the camera's eye is on her, and because her husband imagines he has ducked out of sight, he is confident that the eye can't see him. But it does, and what it shows is a man who looks as if he doesn't want to be where he is, a man who is with his wife but doesn't want to be with her, who has parked himself on the other side of the fence in order to separate himself from her, who is sitting while she is standing, who is grim-faced while she is smiling, and who has put his hand against his head not only to shield his face from the sun but because his head hurts, because everything hurts. No doubt the picture is a mistake, but if it was meant to be a portrait of Lily, then why wasn't Munroe cropped out of it? The unedited version captures a single, oddly disjointed moment in time, but time stands still only in photographs, and because the future that followed from that day is now long past and we know how the story ended, the picture can also be read as the portrait of a marriage in trouble. I study it again. The young Lily Brandon Munroe looks self-assured and happy. The somewhat older Hersey Munroe looks annihilated. The picture bears no date, but the record tells us they were married in 1891. By the end of the century, they were divorced.

In the spring of 1898, Crane returned to America after spending ten months in England as the common-law husband of Cora Taylor. He was on his way to Cuba to cover the Spanish-American War for Pulitzer's *World*, and in the past three years he had seen Lily only twice, once in early 1895, to say good-bye to her before he traveled out west on his reporting expedition for the Bacheller Syndicate, and again in early 1897, during a short visit to New York after his near drowning off the coast of Florida. Although it has never been fully confirmed, there are reasons to believe that he stopped in Washington on his way south toward Cuba to see Lily again and propose to her one last time. They met on neutral ground at the Library of Congress, the least private place in the city, and in that enormous sanctuary of books she said no to him for the last time. He never saw her again, but according to Ames Williams, Crane wrote her at least one letter from Cuba, which could have meant two or three letters, perhaps even several letters. Lily Brandon was the first and most enduring love of his life, and after their summer romance in 1892, he could never break free from the spell of those months and went on longing for her until the end.

One year after his death, Lily married for the second time.

In 1948, she told Williams that she had never put on a bathing suit or gone swimming and that still, after fifty-six years, whenever she saw the ocean she thought of Crane.

5

ONE AUGUST AFTERNOON DURING THAT EVENTFUL SUMMER OF 1892, Crane was sitting on the beach with a fellow junior reporter, Arthur Oliver, who had been a classmate of his at Lafayette. As Oliver later wrote in a 1931 article, "Jersey Memories—Stephen Crane," he was struggling with his work and felt blocked, unable to express himself as vividly as he wanted to.

> "Somehow I can't get down to the real thing," I said. "I know I have something unusual to tell, but I get all tangled up with different notions of how it ought to be told."
>
> "Stevie" scooped up a handful of sand and tossed it to the brisk sea breeze.
>
> "Treat your notions like that," he said. "Forget what you think about it and tell how you feel about it. Make the other fellow realize you are just as human as he is. That's the big secret of story-telling. Away with literary cads and cannons. Be yourself!"

More and more that summer, Crane was learning how to be himself, and the dispatches he wrote during those months attained a new level of concision, zestful irony, and stylistic accomplishment. He was still writing about nothing at all, but his keen eye and sharp pen managed to turn that nothing into something more pointed than mere seaside chat. The wonder is that the editors of the *Tribune* allowed him to get away with it, for many of Crane's satirical darts were thrown at the very people who were no doubt reading the *Tribune*.

> From ON THE BOARDWALK: The average summer guest here is a rather portly man, with a good watch-chain and a business suit of clothes, a wife and about three children. He stands in his two shoes with American self-reliance and, playing casually with his watch-chain, looks at the world with a clear eye. He submits to the arrogant prices of some of the hotel proprietors with a calm indifference; he will pay fancy prices for things with a great unconcern. However, deliberately and baldly attempt to beat him out of fifteen cents and he will put his hands in his pockets, spread his legs apart and wrangle, in a loud voice, until sundown. All day he lies in the sand or sits on the beach, reading papers and smoking cigars, while his blessed babies are dabbling around throwing sand down his back and emptying their little pails of sea-water in his boots. In the evening he puts on his best and takes his wife and the "girls" down to the boardwalk. He enjoys himself in a very mild way and dribbles out a lot of money under the impression that he is proceeding cheaply.

Later on in the same article, Crane even goes after "Founder" James A. Bradley and his penchant for posting cautionary signs everywhere around town:

> He also shows genius of an advanced type and the qualities of authorship in his work. . . . For instance: "Modesty of apparel is as becoming to a lady in a bathing suit as to a lady dressed in silks and satins." There are some very sweet thoughts in that declaration. It is really a beautiful expression of sentiment. It is modest and delicate. Its author merely insinuates. There is nothing to shake vibratory senses in such gentle phraseology. Supposing he had said: "Don't go in the water attired merely in a tranquil smile," or "Do not appear on the beach when only enwrapped in reverie." A thoughtless man might have been guilty of some such unnecessary uncouthness. But to "Founder" Bradley it would be impossible. He is not merely a man. He is an artist.

He managed to get away with it for most of the summer, and then the great blue sky over the Jersey Shore came tumbling down on top of him. Not only did he lose his job at the *Tribune*, but the first three paragraphs of his article "Parades and Entertainments," published on Sunday, August twenty-first, caused such a maelstrom of rebukes and counter-rebukes that the controversy disrupted the 1892 presidential election campaign and possibly affected its outcome. The small, taciturn, undemonstrative S.C. had a strange talent for stirring up trouble around him, not by volition or design but by circumstances and bad luck, and now that he was receiving his first stabs of public criticism, he had no idea how to defend himself against the attack.

Manifold contingent factors were at play in producing such a mighty uproar. First: Whitelaw Reid, the owner of the *Tribune*, had left his post as ambassador to France to join the Republican ticket as Benjamin Harrison's vice presidential running mate. Second: Two large and murderous strikes begun in April and July had turned labor against the Republican administration—the silver miners' walkout in Coeur d'Alene, Idaho, and the Homestead debacle in Pennsylvania—and the Republicans were doing their best to alter the perception that their party was opposed to the interests of labor. Third: A right-wing, nativist workers' organization called the Junior Order of United American Mechanics (JOUAM) was planning to hold its annual parade through the streets of Asbury Park on August seventeenth. Fourth: Townley had covered the parade in 1890 and 1891, but on this particular Wednesday in 1892, he decided to leave town and go on a five-day fishing trip. Fifth: He handed over the assignment to his brother and asked another newsman, Billy Devereaux, to check Crane's article and make sure it passed muster. Devereaux found the short piece provocative and funny and wired it to the paper's office in New York, convinced that the stodgy editors would refuse to run it. Sixth: The *Tribune* building was undergoing renovations. The editorial offices were in disarray, and consequently the left hand had lost track of the right hand and the right hand had lost track of the left. The article sailed through the breach and was published the following morning.

These are the paragraphs that caused the commotion:

> The parade of the Junior Order of United American Mechanics here on Wednesday afternoon was a deeply impressive one to some persons. There were hundreds of members of the order, and they wound through the streets to the music of enough brass bands to make furious discords. It probably was the most awkward, ungainly, uncut and uncarved procession that ever raised clouds of dust on sun-beaten streets. Nevertheless, the spectacle of an Asbury Park crowd confronting such an aggregation was an interesting sight to a few people.

Asbury Park creates nothing. It does not make; it merely amuses. There is a factory where nightshirts are manufactured, but it is some miles from town. This is a resort of wealth and leisure, of women and considerable wine. The throng along the line of march was composed of summer gowns, lace parasols, tennis trousers, straw hats and indifferent smiles. The procession was composed of men, bronzed, slope-shouldered, uncouth, and begrimed with dust. Their clothes fitted them illy, for the most part, and they had no ideas of marching. They merely plodded along, not seeming quite to understand, stolid, unconcerned and, in a certain sense, dignified—a pace and bearing emblematic of their lives. They smiled occasionally and from time to time greeted friends in the crowd on the sidewalk. Such an assemblage of the spraddle-legged men of the middle class, whose hands were bent and shoulders stooped from delving and constructing, had never appeared to an Asbury Park summer crowd, and the latter was vaguely amused.

The bona fide Asbury Parker is a man to whom a dollar, when held close to his eye, often shuts out any impression he may have had that other people possess rights. He is apt to consider that men and women, especially city men and women, were created to be mulcted by him. Hence the tan-colored, sun-beaten honesty in the faces of the members of the Junior Order of United American Mechanics is expected to have a very staggering effect upon them. The visitors were men who possessed principles.

The prize-winning drill captain at his fondly remembered boarding school could not help feeling offended by the sloppiness of the mechanics, but the true brunt of his splenetic outburst was Asbury Park itself, and his most savage comments were aimed at the condescension shown by the moneyed vacationers toward the ragtag mechanics who, when all was said and done, deserved praise for having "principles." Ironically, the sale of newspapers was prohibited in Asbury Park on Sundays, and so the crowd of well-dressed onlookers did not get to see themselves ridiculed in print. But JOUAM took offense, and in a letter to the *Tribune* published on August twenty-third they objected to the "uncalled-for and un-American criticism" of their organization. In their own defense they wrote, "Our main objects are to restrict immigration . . . [and to] demand that the Holy Bible be read in our public schools, not to teach sectarianism but to inculcate its teachings. We are bound together to protect Americans in business and shield them from the depressing effect of foreign competition."

The next day, the *Tribune* published an apology to JOUAM and dismissed the article as "a bit of random correspondence, passed inadvertently by the copy editor." JOUAM was not satisfied with this excuse, however, and as the Democrats and other political opponents began attacking Reid as anti-labor, the *Tribune* issued a further clarification on the twenty-eighth, explaining that Reid had not been actively involved in running the paper for more than three years because of his duties as ambassador to France and that he had been campaigning in the Midwest when the article was published. JOUAM's ire was not appeased. They continued to hold Reid responsible for the insult and denounced his candidacy in every chapter of the organization throughout the country. No one knows exactly how or when it happened, but as the pressure against Reid and the Republicans continued to mount, both Townley and his brother were sacked by the *Tribune*. In his 1931 article, Arthur Oliver recalls that it was Post Wheeler who announced the dismissals to him. "Townley Crane was fired by mail and Stevie by wire! Stevie's out now and Townley goes at the end of the season." By then, Crane had already been attacked in the local press—not by name, since the article had been unsigned, as were most articles published in the *Tribune*, but as the author of the piece. The *Asbury Park Daily Journal* described that piece as "slanderous," lacking "sense and decency, and the ability to distinguish between news matter and studied insult. . . . It is said that the *Tribune*'s regular letter-writer, J. Townley Crane, was engaged on something else last week, and delegated the task of writing up the usual Sunday gabble to another. This young man has a hankering for razzle-dazzle style, and has a great future before him if, like the good, he fails to die young."

After the firings, Arthur Oliver went to pay a condolence call on the two brothers. "Townley was as glum as a king who has lost his throne," he writes, but Crane appeared to be less rattled.

> "Stevie" greeted me with a saintly smile he always had ready for every disaster. He asked me if I had read the story, and I thought there was just a bit of pride in the look he gave me. I said I had. He asked me what I thought of it. I opined that it was clever, and good for almost any purpose except publication.
>
> "Especially publication in the *New York Tribune*," he said with a grin. Continuing he said: "You see, I seemed to have forgotten for the moment that my boss on the *Tribune* was running for Vice-President. . . . You'd hardly think a little innocent chap like me could have stirred up such a row in American politics. It shows what innocence can do if it has the opportunity!"

Hamlin Garland happened to arrive in Asbury Park a few days after Crane lost his job. When Crane stopped by his boardinghouse and told him about the firing, Garland asked if he could read the article. Crane pulled a clipping from his pocket, and once Garland had digested its contents, he handed it back to Crane and said, "What did you expect from your journal—a medal?"

Garland continues: "He smiled again in bitter reflection. 'I guess I didn't stop to consider that . . . I don't know that it would have made much difference if I had. I wanted to say those things anyway.'"

The best advice given to Crane in the middle of the JOUAM tempest probably came from Willis Fletcher Johnson, who was old enough to understand more about Crane and his future than Crane did himself.

> Stephen was much agitated . . . and came to me to know what he should do. . . . My reply was, nothing. The responsibility rested upon me, not upon him. But I "improved the occasion" with two suggestions. One was, that ordinary news reporting was not a good place for subtle rhetorical devices. The other was that a man who could write "Four Men in a Cave" ought not to waste his time reporting that "The Flunkey-Smiths of Squedunk are at the Gilded Pazaza Hotel for the season."

In November, the Republican ticket of Harrison and Reid lost the popular vote to the Democratic ticket of Grover Cleveland and Adlai Stevenson by three percentage points but was trounced in the Electoral College by nearly a two-to-one margin, 277 to 145. With or without Crane's article, it seems likely that the Democrats would have won, although in the end it is impossible to calculate how badly the Republicans were hurt by the JOUAM ruckus, which turned the labor vote against them. Years later, Whitelaw Reid wrote that Stephen Crane "was the man who beat me for vice-president. I don't know whether Grover Cleveland ever knew how much he owed him." He was probably jesting, but then again, the record tells us this: Reid retained control of the *Tribune* until his death in 1912. Although Townley was given his job back not long after he was fired, Crane had been pushed out for good, and once he began publishing novels, story collections, and poems, every one of his books was trashed by the *Tribune*, trashed loud and hard with merciless scorn, and even after Crane was dead, the paper went on attacking him—not just as an insincere literary trickster but as a loathsome human turd.

6

IN THE THICK OF THE JOUAM COMBAT, KNOWING HIS DAYS IN
Asbury Park were numbered, Crane applied to the American Press Association for a job, presenting himself as an experienced journalist who
planned to be traveling to the South and the West and hoped to write a
number of feature articles for their news service. They turned him down,
but the proposal indicates how hungry he was to explore other parts of
the country and test himself on unfamiliar ground—the first sign of his
restlessness. From then on, Crane was permanently restless, and more and
more restless as he grew older, with his itchy feet taking him to numerous
far-flung places over the years, but he couldn't travel on his own dime
back then because he had no dimes, which meant that he needed a sponsor to back his urge to hit the road. As the shortage of dimes continued
and no sponsor stepped forward to help him, he had to wait until 1895
before his wish was granted, but after he returned from that first trip to
the South, the West, and Mexico, he rarely sat still for more than a few
months at a time. Not remarkable, perhaps, for someone who never had
a fixed home as a boy.

Before that crazy summer of love and presidential politics ended, he
showed the second-to-last version of *Maggie* to both Johnson and Garland. Each man responded favorably to the manuscript, and each offered
to help him in trying to land a publisher. Garland suggested that Crane
submit the book to Richard Watson Gilder, the editor of the *Century
Magazine*, a good idea in principle but in fact no more than the longest
of long shots, since Gilder was the stuffiest and most censorious stuffed
shirt on the New York literary scene. Nevertheless, Garland wrote a letter of recommendation for Crane to pass on to him with the manuscript.
"Dear Gilder: I want you to read a *great* M.S. of Stephen Crane's making. I think him an astonishing fellow. And have advised him to bring
the M.S. to you." Johnson felt the book needed some revisions but that
it "would be worth publishing, and ought to be successful. But I warned
him that it would be difficult to find a reputable publisher who would
dare to bring it out; and that if it were published it would so shock the
Podsnaps and Mrs. Grundys as to bring upon him a storm of condem-
nation." After much thought, Johnson recommended that Crane show
the book to his "dear friend and former colleague" Ripley Hitchcock,
literary adviser to D. Appleton and Company. Crane eventually submitted the manuscript to both Gilder and Hitchcock, but not before he had

thoroughly rewritten it and produced the final version, which kept him busy throughout the fall and past his twenty-first birthday.

In the meantime, he left Asbury Park. For the next month or two he may or may not have worked as a reporter for the *Newark Daily Advertiser*, and then, in late October, the hick from New Jersey and the backwoods of Sullivan County moved to New York.

7

HIS FRIEND FREDERIC LAWRENCE, WHO HAD BEEN STUDYING MEDI-cine in the city for the past year, invited Crane to share a room with him in a boardinghouse that was mostly inhabited by other medical students at 1064 Avenue A. The Avenue A that currently begins at Houston Street and ends at Fourteenth Street on the East Side of Manhattan used to run north all the way through Harlem, but over the years different sections of it were given new names, and the site of the old building where Crane lived at number 1064 near Fifty-seventh Street now belongs to what is called Sutton Place, an address that evokes silver spoons and trust-fund indolence to contemporary New Yorkers, but back in the 1890s it was one of the least posh areas in the city. As Lawrence recounts in his memoir of Crane:

> The narrow cross-streets around us were filled with squalid habita-tions whose denizens almost filled the roadways, and here was material hitherto little used. Crane observed it all with keen and sympathetic, if detached vision. To a certain extent he could enter into an understand-ing of this submerged populace, and he made it his task to peer beneath the surface. One day he came in, his usually somber face alight, and queried abruptly: "Did you ever see a stone-fight?" When I replied in the negative, he launched into a glowing description of one that he had just seen. A little later that same day the description had been set down on paper, and the first chapter of *Maggie* was written. As the story, a sordid tale of life in the tenements and the under-world took shape in Crane's mind, he became enthusiastic, I with him, and we sallied forth into the mean streets and dangerous neighborhoods in search of the local color that would give life to the great work.

Lawrence was the privileged witness of the book's composition—and of Crane's composition methods as well. Already during their semester together at Syracuse, he had watched his friend at work, had been able to watch because unlike most writers Crane had little trouble working when other people were in the room with him, a testament to his powers of concentration, which allowed him to carve out a solitary space to hide in even when surrounded by others. As Lawrence tells it:

> For a long time he would sit wrapt in thought, devising his next sentence. Not until it had been completely formulated would he put pen to paper. Then he wrote slowly, carefully, in that legible round hand, with every punctuation mark accentuated, that always characterized his manuscripts. Rarely if ever did a word or mark require correction. That sentence completed, he would rise, relight his pipe, ramble around the room or look fixedly out of the windows. Usually he remained silent, wrapt in deep thought, but sometimes he would break into some popular song or bacchanalian ditty and sing a single bar of it over and over again while he waited for his inspiration to come. . . . Often a single page represented a day's work and rarely did the output exceed two or three pages. Sometimes he did not dip pen in ink for days at a time. Yet slowly and surely the manuscript grew, and thus *Maggie: A Girl of the Streets* came into being.

The novelette, or novella, or short novel of seventy-two pages in the Library of America edition could not have been anticipated by anything Crane had written up to that point—nor by anyone else for that matter. The setting would have been familiar to readers of the time (the New York slums) and to a certain degree the bare-bones plot would have been recognized as following the conventions of late-nineteenth-century melodrama (without the uplift of a happy ending), but stylistically the book is a declaration of war, and the effect it creates is that of a tumultuous fever dream, a mental combat zone of violent, mutating grotesques locked in perpetual combat with one another. In the most turbulent passages of the story, those characters are not characters in a novel so much as latter-day incarnations of the seething figures from the bloodiest Icelandic sagas, mythological beings decked out in 1890s costumes, archetypal forces who exist outside of time. Consequently, no addresses are given in the book, no dates are specified, and even the section of town where the protagonists live, Rum Alley, never existed on any map of New York. Scholars and critics have spent more than a century trying to squeeze *Maggie* into various boxes labeled "realism," "naturalism," "impressionism," and "determinism," but Crane's slender book eludes all fixed categories. It is a weird visionary poem, a projection of a young man's inner life thrust onto an imagined landscape that happens to coincide with a sharply observed New York City which in fact is not New York but a place that exists only in the head of the writer and the reader. That is why the book feels new and modern and why it failed to conform to what was deemed possible in 1893 America. Most people who read *Maggie* at the time were repulsed by it, including some of the more pious members of Crane's family, who stashed their copies in the attics of their houses and eventually burned them because they felt the book was offensive, immoral, and beyond the bounds of Christian decency.

To those who are unfamiliar with the contents of the novel, I would suggest a few minutes of homework before opening to the first page. First, have a look at photographs from the period, the numerous surviving images of New York from the 1890s, beginning with *How the Other Half Lives*, Jacob Riis's investigative report on the city's downtrodden population that appeared at the start of the decade, with its pictures of homeless, ragged boys sleeping in alleyways and secluded corners, young and old female sweatshop workers stitching garments together with needles and thread, the "girl of the tenements" standing alone in the rubble of a vacant lot (a plausible representation of Crane's Maggie as a child), the woman sitting at a table with six small children "making artificial flowers," the drunks sprawled out on the dirty floors of police stations, the "seven-cent lodging house" on Pell Street, the outdoor shots of Bottle Alley, Mulberry Bend, and Bandits' Roost, along with varied glimpses of Chinatown, Jewtown, and the Italian quarter, and after digesting Riis's photographs of urban poverty, move on to the work of Alice Austen from 1896, with her candid shots of a young bicycle messenger, a postman with a large leather pouch over his shoulder pulling letters out of a mailbox, a street sweeper in his white uniform holding a broom in his hands and wearing a regulation white pith helmet on his head, and a burly policeman in a long overcoat with his hands behind his back, standing alone on a cobbled street. Then turn to Alfred Stieglitz's 1892 photograph "The Terminal," which presents the cluttered, teeming vigor of a city thoroughfare with a horse-drawn streetcar in the center, the same kind of vehicle that figures in "The Broken-Down Van" and surfaced again in *Maggie*. Push on to the night spots, theaters, and dime museums of the Bowery, the Equitable Life Building, the New York Tribune Building, the Metropolitan Museum of Art, and the famous image of ice-skaters in Central Park with the immense, castle-like Dakota apartment building looming behind them. These pictures are the documentary evidence, the visual reality of the world depicted in Crane's book, and it helps to look at them in order to attain some tangible understanding of that world, but knowing the historical setting is not enough to prepare

oneself for the shock of *Maggie*. Photographs have their uses, but when
it comes to the evocative power of images, the spirit of Crane's first book
can best be found in the nightmare canvases and etchings of the deaf and
aging Goya, in particular the Black Paintings (*Fight with Cudgels, Women
Laughing, Witches' Sabbath, Two Old Men Eating Soup, Saturn Devouring
His Son*) and the human horrors and fantasies captured in *Los Caprichos* and
The Disasters of War. One can be sure that Crane himself never thought of
it, but whenever I look at the forty-third *Capricho*, I can't help seeing it as
a portrait of his state of mind while he was working on his novel. A man
sitting alone at a table has fallen asleep with his head resting in his arms as
a cohort of ghoulish specters gathers behind him. The caption says: "The
Sleep of Reason Produces Monsters."

The first monster we meet is a boy named Jimmie, who holds center
stage as the book begins:

> A very little boy stood upon a heap of gravel for the honor of Rum Alley.
> He was throwing stones at howling urchins from Devil's Row who were
> circling madly about the heap and pelting at him.
>
> His infantile countenance was livid with fury. His small body was
> writhing in the delivery of great crimson oaths.
>
> "Run, Jimmie, run! Deh'll get yehs," screamed a retreating Rum Alley
> child.
>
> "Naw," responded Jimmie with a valiant roar, "dese micks can't make
> me run."
>
> Howls of renewed wrath went up from Devil's Row throats. Tattered
> gamins on the right made a furious assault on the gravel heap. On their
> small, convulsed faces there shone the grins of true assassins. As they
> charged, they threw stones and cursed in shrill chorus.
>
> The little champion of Rum Alley stumbled precipitately down the
> other side. His coat had been torn to shreds in a scuffle, and his hat
> was gone. He had bruises on twenty parts of his body, and blood was
> dripping from a cut in his head. His wan features wore a look of a tiny,
> insane demon.

The entire project of the book is contained in these opening sentences.
The savage fight between the two camps of warring boys is simultaneously told through the rhetorical inflations used to describe their combat
(chivalric epithets such as "honor," "valiant," and "champion," coupled
with bristling, amped-up verbs, adjectives, and tropes such as "great
crimson oaths," "renewed wrath," "convulsed faces," "the grins of true

assassins," "cursed in shrill chorus," "tiny, insane demon") and the rhetorical deflations of the gutter slang used by the combatants ("Naw . . .
dese micks can't make me run"), which merge into an authorial stance
of ironic detachment, the same distancing effect to be found in the early
stories of Joyce and Hemingway, the novels of Camus, and the work of
countless other writers of the next century. Crane was the first to establish that tone. He surveys the carnage wrought by his characters with
the steady eye of a war correspondent, turning a potentially hysterical,
out-of-control scene into a starkly delineated portrait of human actions,
and because he doesn't flinch at any point in the nineteen chapters of the
narrative, his book breaks new ground, departing from both the plodding,
exhaustive naturalism of Zola and the mild-mannered realism of Howells
to establish a literature of pure telling, with no social analysis, no calls for
reform, and no psychological reflections to explain why the characters
do what they do. They simply act, and Crane tells. For the first time in
American fiction, the reader is not told what to think—only to experience
what happens in the book and then to draw his or her own conclusions.*

The Goya-like mayhem continues to the end of the first chapter and
then goes on, unrelenting, through the second and third. The stone fight
devolves into a painful rout as Jimmie's allies back off from the superior
forces of the Devil's Row children, abandoning Jimmie to battle on alone,
surrounded by his enemies at the top of the gravel heap. A stone is smashed
into his mouth, blood flows, tears fall down his face, his legs "tremble and
turn weak," and his "roaring curses" subside to "blasphemous chatter," but
just when he is about to be pummeled into submission, along comes an
older boy named Pete, "a lad of sixteen years, although the chronic sneer
of an ideal manhood already sat upon his lips." Pete apparently knows

---

* To my knowledge, there is only one other book from the period that made such a radical break with storytelling conventions of the past: Knut Hamsun's *Hunger*, published
in 1890. Often considered the first modern European novel and cited as an influence on
such divergent figures as Kafka, Gide, and I. B. Singer, its spirit is different from *Maggie*
(a solitary first-person narrator recounts his physical disintegration as he nearly starves to
death in Oslo), but its methods and approach are similarly tough and unfaltering. Written
in Norwegian, the novel was unknown to Crane at the time (it would be seven years before
someone gave him a copy of the English translation), but curious as it might sound, the life
he led in New York as an impoverished, often hungry young writer was almost identical
to the one led by Hamsun's nameless hero, even to the point of sharing certain personality
traits: the same stubbornness, the same self-punishing pride, the same walled-off resistance
to letting anyone know how hard up he was. There is no word on Crane's response to
Hunger, but by the time he read the novel he was long gone from New York and living in
England. After he finished it, he passed on his copy to Henry James.

Jimmie, and when he sees what is happening to his little friend, he says, "Ah, what deh hell" and clobbers one of the Devil's Row boys on the back of the head. The boy falls down, lets out a "hoarse, tremendous howl," and then runs off to a safe distance, followed by the other members of his gang. The Rum Alley boys step forward again, and no sooner does one of them start bragging that "we blokies kin lick deh hull damn Row" than Jimmie turns on his comrade for having left him to carry on the fight by himself. "Youse kids makes me tired," he says, and a moment later he and the other boy (Billie) begin a fresh fight of their own. Pete yells out some words of encouragement, "Smash 'im, Jimmie, kick de damn guts out of 'im," as he watches "the two little boys fighting in the modes of four thousand years ago"—a pointed remark, signaling that even if the book is set in 1890s New York, it is also set in the ancient, buried realm of eternal human conflict. As the fight between Jimmie and Billie rages on, everyone suddenly scatters because Jimmie's father has been seen walking down the street in their direction, but the young battlers are too absorbed in trying to kill each other to have noticed. The "man with sullen eyes" approaches, "carrying a dinner pail and smoking an apple-wood pipe," and when he sees the scuffle, and then sees that his son is one of the scufflers rolling around on the ground, he bellows forth a harsh reprimand, "Here, you Jim, git up now, while I belt yer life out, you damned disorderly brat," and then proceeds "to kick the chaotic mass on the ground." Billie, booted in the head, painfully disentangles himself from Jimmie and totters off, "damning." When Jimmie climbs to his feet, he doesn't apologize to his father but begins "to curse him." His father responds by delivering a fierce kick and tells the boy in a loud, belligerent voice to "stop yer jawin', or I'll lam the everlasting head off yehs." They walk home, with Jimmie trailing a dozen feet behind, swearing to himself because "he felt that it was a degradation for one who aimed to be some vague soldier, or a man of blood with some sort of sublime license, to be taken home by a father."

The second chapter begins with father and son approaching their neighborhood, which is described not in the language of nineteenth-century novels but in the allegorical tones of a medieval mystery play as "a dark region," and an instant later Crane's eye zeroes in on a single part of that region, the building where the boy and the man and the other members of the Johnson family live, which is strangely and metaphorically referred to as "a careening building," as if the bricks were alive and drunkenly on the move, and again as a quasi-animate structure in the final sentence of the chapter's first paragraph: "The building quivered and creaked from the weight of humanity stamping about in its bowels."

Between those first and last sentences, the author's roving eye stops to observe assorted particulars: "In the street infants played or fought with other infants or sat stupidly in the way of vehicles. Formidable women, with uncombed hair and disordered dress, gossiped while leaning on railings, or screamed in frantic quarrels. Withered persons, in curious postures of submission to something, sat smoking pipes in obscure corners." One can see the sentence-by-sentence method of composition that Frederic Lawrence referred to while watching Crane write. The prose doesn't rush forward in a steady flow of narrative incident but rather starts up, stops with the period, and starts up again, as if each sentence were a small work in itself, a separate photograph or drawing to be contemplated for a moment before the next one replaces it—what one might call a cinematic style before the language of movies had been invented. "Curious postures of submission to something" is memorable. "Sat stupidly in the way of vehicles" is more ambiguous, since it is hard to tell if Crane means "in the path of vehicles" or "in the manner of vehicles," but if his earlier title "The Way in Sullivan County" offers any sign of his intentions, then the altogether surprising "manner of" would be the correct reading, though even if it isn't, "path of" is still a potent image, and it contributes significantly to the world presented in this paragraph, the "dark region" that resembles nothing so much as the world of the Black Paintings.

In the next paragraph, we meet Maggie for the first time, "a small ragged girl" who happens to be Jimmie's younger sister and the daughter of the brute with the lunch pail and the apple-wood pipe. She is out on the street in front of the building dragging along her squirming, recalcitrant little brother, Tommie, and when "she jerked the baby's arm impatiently," he falls on his face and howls. She yanks him back to his feet and a moment later catches sight of her father and Jimmie approaching. Alarmed by the condition of "the blood-covered boy," she lashes out at her brother.

"Youse allus fightin', Jimmie, an' yeh knows it puts mudder out when yehs come home half dead, an' it's like we'll all get a poundin'."

She began to weep. The babe threw back his head and roared at his prospects.

"Ah, what deh hell!" cried Jimmie. "Shut up er I'll smack yer mout'. See?"

As his sister continued her lamentations, he suddenly swore and struck her. The little girl reeled and, recovering herself, burst into tears and quaveringly cursed him. As she slowly retreated her brother advanced dealing her cuffs. The father heard and turned about.

"Stop that, Jim, d'yeh hear? Leave yer sister alone on the street. It's like I can never beat any sense into yer damn wooden head."

The implication being that it's all right for Jimmie to knock around his sister indoors, but he mustn't do it in public, where other people can see him. Five pages into the book, we have already encountered the violence of the world Crane has imagined. Now, for the first time, we have seen its hypocrisy. In the next pages, we will be exposed to its self-pity as elaborated in the person of Maggie and Jimmie's mother. It is a deadly combination—violence, hypocrisy, and self-pity—and it conspires in the end to crush the soul and turn supposedly evolved human beings into savages. But such are the precepts that sustain the inhabitants of Rum Alley from one generation to the next, and the most chilling thing about it is that it is driven by its own irrefutable logic.

The father and the three children go inside, mount the dark stairway, and walk "along cold, gloomy halls" until the father "pushed open the door and they entered a lighted room in which a large woman was rampant."

Rampant, as defined in the *American Heritage Dictionary*: "1. Extending unchecked; unrestrained. 2. Characterized by uncontrolled violence, extravagance, or lack of restraint."

In the hundreds of thousands if not millions of pages I have read over the course of my life, not once outside of Crane's book have I ever come across a man, a woman, or a character in a novel referred to as "rampant." Odd as that word might be, however, it fits the person it describes.

Of all the human savages in *Maggie*, the mother is the most savage, the most unstoppable, the most fearsome. The moment she sees Jimmie's battered face and understands that he has been fighting again, she goes after him, in the process accidentally knocking down baby Tommie, who flies into a table leg and bangs his shins. She grabs hold of Jimmie, shakes him "until he rattled," and drags him to "an unholy sink," where she scrubs his wounds with such force that the boy screams in pain. The father, annoyed by Jimmie's cries, tells her to ease up. She ignores him, goes on scrubbing the boy's face with accelerated vigor and cruelty, finishes the job, and then tosses the twice-battered Jimmie into a corner. At that point: "The wife put her immense hands on her hips and with a chieftain-like stride approached her husband."

Chieftain-like stride. Not only does that phrase reaffirm that we are not, strictly speaking, confined to 1890s New York, but it also eliminates all doubt about who reigns as boss of the household.

Husband and wife quarrel. She tells him to butt out of her business, he accuses her of being drunk, and every sentence she utters during their "lurid altercation" is *screamed* or *howled* or *roared* or *thundered*. The baby hides under the table, Maggie slinks off into the corner to sit with Jimmie, and when the wife emerges as the "victor" of the quarrel, the husband grabs his hat and bolts from the apartment, "determined upon a vengeful drunk," heading down the stairs as his wife continues to shout at him from the door.

Then Crane delivers this miracle of a sentence: "She returned and stirred up the room until her children were bobbing about like bubbles." It is so good—and so unexpected—that it stands alone as the single sentence in the paragraph.

The mother prepares dinner, "puffing and snorting in a cloud of steam at the stove," and the children then scramble to the table and dig into the greasy food, Jimmie "with feverish rapidity," but "Maggie, with side glances . . . ate like a small pursued tigress."

Before long, the mother lapses into the first of many bouts of self-pity that mark her presence throughout the book.

> After a time her mood changed and she wept and carried little Tommie into another room. . . . Then she came and moaned by the stove. She rocked to and fro upon a chair, shedding tears and crooning miserably to the two children about their "poor mother" and "yer fader, damn 'is soul."

The chapter ends, however, with renewed tumult, as Maggie clears the table and carries the dishes to the sink.

> Jimmie sat nursing his various wounds. He cast furtive glances at his mother. His practiced eye perceived her gradually emerge from a muddled mist of sentiment until her brain burned in drunken heat. He sat breathless.
>
> Maggie broke a plate.
>
> The mother started to her feet as if propelled.
>
> "Good Gawd," she howled. Her eyes glittered on her child with sudden hatred. The fervent red of her face turned almost purple. The little boy ran to the halls, shrieking like a monk in an earthquake.

The intense, blow-by-blow accounts of bedlamite fury carry on through the whole of the third chapter, which concludes with Maggie and Jimmie again huddled together in a corner of the room, their eyes fixed on the "prostrate, heaving body" of their drunken mother asleep on the floor, "for they thought she need only to awake and all fiends would come from below." Crane has been pounding the reader for more than a dozen pages at this point, but in the fourth chapter he steps back and alters the pace of the narrative. The opening chapters have served as a prologue, a minutely rendered depiction of "A Day in the Life of the Johnsons," but years have passed now, and Jimmie and Maggie are no longer children. The fourth chapter and the first paragraphs of the fifth combine to form a bridge between the overture and the rest of the book, standing apart in tone, intention, and procedure, but they are essential passages, and without them the novel would not stir us or shake us as deeply as it does, for everything that happens afterward reflects back on what we learn in those pages.

Tommie has died, the father has died, both events tersely reported with no word as to how or when they died, and everything else in chapter IV is given over to a study of Jimmie's life and character as Crane marches through the catalogue of his observations with cold and merciless understanding, a doctor cutting into his patient's body with his scalpel, hands steady, eyes alert, digging to the bone.

> The inexperienced fibers of the boy's eyes were hardened at an early age. He became a young man of leather. He lived some red years without laboring. During that time his sneer became chronic. . . .
>
> Jimmie's occupation . . . was to stand on street-corners and watch the world go by, dreaming blood-red dreams at the passing of pretty women. He menaced mankind at the intersections of streets.
>
> On the corners he was in life and of life. The world was going on and he was there to perceive it. . . .
>
> After a time his sneer grew so that it turned its glare upon all things. He became so sharp that he believed in nothing.

After his father's death, he becomes a truck driver. Contemptuous of most people, in particular "obvious Christians" and the rich, afraid of "neither the devil nor the leader of society," he finds a new target for his resentment in the police, raining down curses on them as he drives his horse-drawn truck through the "turmoil and tumble of the down-town streets," but sometimes, when he goes too far, they "climb up, drag him from his perch and beat him." He also meddles in the disputes that break out among his fellow drivers in the thick of traffic, occasionally provokes them himself, and more than once has been arrested for fighting. Toward the end of the chapter, we are told that "he began to be arrested" as a little boy and by now has a substantial record, not just for fighting other truckers but for "a number of miscellaneous fights," barroom brawls, and once "for assaulting a Chinaman." Further: "Two women in different parts of the city, and entirely unknown to each other, caused him considerable annoyance by breaking forth, simultaneously, at fateful intervals, into wailings about marriage and support and infants."

There is only one thing that impresses him, that strikes fear in him, one thing in all the world that fills him with awe and demands his respect, and every time he chances upon it as he lumbers around the city with his truck and two-horse team, he submits to its power and gets out of the way.

A fire-engine was enshrined in his heart as an appalling thing that he loved with a distant dog-like devotion. They had been known to over-turn street-cars. Those leaping horses, striking sparks from the cobbles in their forward lunge, were creatures to be ineffably admired. The clang of the gong pierced his breast like a noise of remembered war.

Jimmie is a thug. Not altogether unsympathetic at times, not altogether incapable of showing an occasional flash of earnest feeling when the stars are properly aligned in the sky, but not often enough, not forcefully enough to contradict the portrait Crane gives of him in the fourth chapter, and nearly everything he does throughout the novel confirms the accuracy of that dissection. As with all the other characters in the book save one, he suffers from the triple disease of violence–hypocrisy–self-pity, and once those microbes enter your system, you can never be cured. Behold the mother. We are reintroduced to her early in the fifth chapter, and the now widowed Mrs. Johnson has turned into the neighborhood drunk, having "arisen to that degree of fame that she could bandy words with her acquaintances among the police-justices," and whenever she is hauled into court, she "besieged the bench with voluble excuses, explanations, apologies and prayers." The same woman, only worse. She still rules over her household as its most diseased member, a demented, ranting monarch who cares nothing for her children and everything for herself, but Jimmie is the head of the family now, and out in the world she has become a joke.

Only Maggie is untainted by the virus. Only Maggie is exempt from the illness that is eating away at the others, but why this should be so is never explained, is never even discussed. Crane offers her up as a sacrifice. The book would not be the book without her, and yet the victim who stands at the center of the action says little for herself, and most of the time she is mute. We are allowed into her thoughts, but Maggie is defenseless against the ones who ultimately destroy her, and because she cannot defend herself, she cannot speak—or, because she cannot speak, she cannot defend herself. Either way, one senses she is doomed from the start. The fifth chapter begins with these paragraphs:

> The girl, Maggie, blossomed in a mud puddle. She grew to be a most rare and wonderful production of a tenement district, a pretty girl.
>
> None of the dirt of Rum Alley seemed to be in her veins. The philosophers up-stairs, down-stairs and on the same floor, puzzled over it.
>
> When a child, playing and fighting with gamins in the street, dirt disguised her. Attired in tatters and grime, she went unseen.
>
> There came a time, however, when the young men of the vicinity, said: "Dat Johnson goil is a puty good looker." About this period her brother remarked to her: "Mag, I'll tell you dis! See? Yeh've edder got teh go teh hell or go teh work!" Whereupon she went to work, having the feminine aversion of going to hell.
>
> By a chance, she got a position in an establishment where they made collars and cuffs. She received a stool and a machine in a room where sat twenty girls of various shades of yellow discontent. She perched on the stool and treadled at her machine all day, turning out collars. . . . At night she returned home to her mother.

One blink later, Pete enters the apartment and the story is launched. This is the same Pete who broke up the stone fight in the first chapter, the sneering sixteen-year-old hellion now transformed into a cocky, snappily dressed bartender whose clothes look like "murder-fitted weapons." He and Jimmie have recently crossed paths again, and he has come to pick up young Johnson and take him to a boxing match in Brooklyn. Maggie watches Pete sitting on the table with his legs dangling comfortably beneath him, finds herself impressed by his loud clothes and brimming self-confidence, and concludes that "he must be a very elegant and graceful bartender." When he begins boasting to Jimmie about the pleasure he takes in tossing drunken customers out of his saloon, she is even more impressed and thinks he is "the beau ideal of a man." Crane then adds: "Her dim thoughts were always searching for far away lands . . . [and] under the trees of her dream-gardens there had always walked a lover." Pete, finally taking notice of Maggie, looks at her and remarks, "Say, Mag, I'm stuck on yer shape. It's outa sight," and then, knowing that she is listening carefully to him, he amplifies his boasting to a new level with this tender story about his good-hearted impulses toward his fellow human beings:

"I met a chump deh odder day way up in deh city," he said. "I was goin'
teh see a frien' of mine. When I was a-crossin' deh street deh chump
runned plump inteh me, an' den he turns aroun' an' says, 'Yer insolen
ruffin,' he says, like dat. 'Oh, gee,' I says, 'oh, gee, go teh hell and get off
deh eart',' I says, like dat. See? 'Go teh hell an' git off de eart',' like dat.
Den deh blokie he got wild. He says I was a contempt'ble scoun'el, or
something like dat, an' he says I was doom' teh everlastin' pe'dition, an'
like dat. 'Gee, I says, 'gee! Deh hell I am,' I says. 'Deh hell I am,' like dat.
An' den I slugged 'im. See?"

Rough stuff, one would think. Rough enough to scare off even the
boldest girl, but Pete's account of his run-in with the chump (one assumes
a wealthy chump) only increases Maggie's fascination with him. "Here was
a formidable man who disdained the strength of a world full of fists. Here
was one who had contempt for brass-clothed power; one whose knuckles
could defiantly ring against the granite of law. He was a knight."

Pete is a knight, and Maggie is a damsel in distress longing for the
knight to rescue her from the prison of her dreary factory job and carry her
off to a place where "the little hills sing together in the morning."

Madame Bovary, who fed herself on the illusions found in cheap romantic novels, was poisoned by those books in the same way Quixote was driven
mad by the books he read. It is not known if Maggie has gone to school
(nothing is said about it) or whether she is even capable of reading a book,
but her impulses are no different from those of the higher-born Emma
Bovary, and even if there are no books in her life, her imagination is fed by
stories—the wispiest of fairy tales, dreams no more solid than clouds.

So begins the courtship, which Crane presents in a series of ever more
disturbing episodes as the romance inevitably crashes to its end, following
the pretty tenement girl and the gallant bartender on their nights and afternoons out together in various music halls and theaters (all vividly drawn,
especially Maggie's identification with the heroines in the melodramas she
sees—more fairy tales to dream about), in a Bowery dime museum to gawk
at rows of "meek freaks" (their deformities fill Maggie "with awe" and she
thinks them "a sort of chosen tribe"), at the Central Park Menagerie, where
Pete tries to encourage one of the monkeys "to fight with other and larger
monkeys," and in the Museum of Arts (the Metropolitan), where Maggie looks around her and says, "Dis is outa sight." The knight is preparing
the way for his conquest of the innocent, unsuspecting lady, but even as
the romance progresses, Crane handles the physical side of it with utmost
discretion, and the only kiss ever referred to is the one Maggie does not

give Pete after their first evening out together. However obliquely told, or not told except by implication, Maggie eventually succumbs to her suitor's loutish charms. In the wake of this supposed crime, she is expelled from the family apartment by her mother and brother, quits her job at the factory, and moves in with Pete (never stated in the text, but more than strongly suggested). The romance is still in the ascendant at this point, and Maggie feels no shame in her altered circumstances, even if the word *marriage* has never come up. "Her life was Pete's and she considered him worthy of the charge. She would be disturbed by no particular apprehensions, so long as Pete adored her as he now said he did. She did not feel like a bad woman. To her knowledge she had never seen any better." Just three weeks after that, Sir Pete has already begun to tire of his lady and her "spaniel-like dependence" on him. When an old flame unexpectedly strolls into his life again, a flashy, self-assured prostitute named Nellie, described by Crane as "a woman of brilliance and audacity," he turns his back on Maggie and forgets her—as if she had never existed. He doesn't even feel guilty about it. As with everyone else who suffers from the triple disease, he is a master of self-absolution, for the dogma of those who dwell in darkness has never varied over the ages: Whatever I do is justified—because I am the one who does it.

It is a tragic turn for Maggie, but the deeper, more terrible tragedy of the book is not her seduction and abandonment by Pete but her mother's implacable heart, which burns hot with hatred even as it sits frozen in her chest, and because Mary Johnson is a woman made of both ice and fire, she does not hesitate to turn against her daughter and denounce her as a child of the devil. After all, what would the neighbors think? The smallest gesture of compassion would have spared Maggie, but neither she nor Jimmie is strong enough to stand up to the matriarch's tyrannical whims or control her sprees of drunken self-righteousness, and the one time Jimmie's disgust spills over into a direct challenge, he and his mother duke it out in the apartment and "struggle like gladiators." As Maggie observes in an earlier chapter: "It seems that the world had treated this woman very badly, and she took deep revenge upon such portions of it that came within her reach. She broke furniture as if she were at last getting her rights." The rampant woman destroys furniture and battles with her son, but she never lays a hand on Maggie. Instead, she kills her with words—and then, to finish her off, with no words. And who, she says "would tink such a bad girl could grow up in our fambly."

Turned away by her mother and brother, then turned away for the last time by Pete, whose parting words to her are "Oh, go teh hell," Maggie walks out of the saloon and wanders around the streets, so dazed by what has happened to her that the only question she can ask herself is "Who?" Not what or how or when—but who, for now that she has lost her bearings and has nowhere to go, she is beginning to disappear from herself, as if she were dissolving into a formless blot of nothingness. Eventually, she comes upon a stout man dressed in a "silk hat and a chaste black coat" whom she recognizes as a minister. "The girl had heard of the grace of God and decided to approach this man," but the beaming, benevolent-looking messenger of the Lord sidesteps her with "a convulsive movement" and walks on, thus saving his respectability instead of trying to save her soul, "for how was he to know there was a soul before him that needed saving?"

When the next chapter begins, several months have passed. Maggie, now "one of the painted cohorts of the city," is out on a wet night as the theaters are disgorging their patrons onto the "storm-swept" sidewalks. The chapter is just three pages long, but it is the best chapter in the book, a tour de force in which a brilliant formal idea coupled with an almost perfect execution of that idea manages to convey, in just a few minimal strokes, the grim, solitary life of a girl of the streets. With great moral insight, but also with great artistic acumen, the young author holds back from mentioning Maggie's name in any one of the sentences he writes about her in those three pages. Her identity has been erased by her new calling, she has been turned into an anonymous, almost nonexistent being, a no one who has ceased to merit the dignity of a name, and from beginning to end she is referred to simply as "the girl." Nor does Crane presume to tell us what she is thinking, as he has done until now whenever she appeared in earlier chapters. The images do the work for him, and because those images are so precisely rendered into words, we enter a state of heightened visual awareness, an ultra-visuality, as it were, and, as I have suggested before, the effect is eerily cinematic. An implausible, anachronistic film is suddenly playing before our eyes, and as Maggie's slow march to death begins, we follow her as if tracing the course of her life in the streets through a series of eleven harsh jump cuts, watching her pass from one potential customer to the next, each one shabbier and poorer than the one before him, each street she walks down darker and more menacing than the one before it, and whether this is all happening on that one night or over a succession of many nights is not important, for we live it in the Now of the images Crane is presenting to us, just as films are always experienced in the Now, whether they are flashing forward into the future or back into the past, and there is the first potential customer of the night, "a tall young man smoking a cigarette with a sublime air," a chrysanthemum in the buttonhole of his tuxedo jacket, looking bored, then looking interested, then abruptly losing interest when the girl comes closer and he sees that she is "neither new, Parisian, nor theatrical," and then the paragraph ends and Crane jumps immediately to the next man, "a stout gentleman, with pompous and philanthropic whiskers," whose broad back "sneers" at the girl as he walks on past her, and then jumps to the next, "a belated man in business clothes," who accidentally bangs into her shoulder, apologizes, tells her to "Brace up, old girl," and rushes off to wherever he is going, and then the next, "a young man in light overcoat and derby hat," who returns her glance with a mocking smile, saying, "Come on now, old lady, you don't mean to say that you sized me up as a farmer?," and then the next, "a laboring man . . . with bundles under his arm," who pleasantly answers her remarks (not recorded on the page), observing, "It's a pleasant evenin', ain't it?," and then the next, "a boy . . . hurrying by with his hands buried in his overcoat," who answers her smile with a smile of his own and then waves good-bye, saying perhaps another night, and then the next, "a drunken man, reeling in her pathway," who roars, "I ain't got no money, dammit," and then the next, "a man with blotched features," and then the next, "a ragged being with shifting, bloodshot eyes and grimey hands." Then, after the next jump, the girl is walking on alone as she enters "the blackness of the final block." When she is almost at the river, she sees "a great figure" standing before her in the near distance.

On going forward she perceived it to be a huge fat man in torn and greasy garments. His grey hair straggled down over his forehead. His small, bleared eyes sparkling from amidst great rolls of red fat, swept eagerly over the girl's upturned face. He laughed, his brown, disordered teeth gleaming under a grey, grizzled moustache from which beer-drops dripped. His whole body gently quivered and shook like that of a dead jelly fish. Chuckling and leering, he followed the girl of the crimson legions.

What happens next is utterly obscure. Between the end of this paragraph and the beginning of the next, Crane elides the intervening action, offering no account of what might or might not have taken place, and instead jumps forward to the final image of the chapter. There is a gap, and the reader is left to fill in the account of Maggie's death for himself. Does the hideous, gargoyle-like creature murder her? Or does she take her own life by drowning herself in the river? Impossible to say. The only thing we know for certain is that Maggie is dead and that her death has occurred off camera or, more precisely, in the space between two sentences, and it is all the more sickening because we are forced to imagine it for ourselves. It's true that Maggie and the creature are still present in the first words after the final jump—but then what?

At their feet the river appeared a deathly black hue. Some hidden factory sent up a yellow glare, that lit for a moment the waters lapping
oilily against the timbers. The varied sounds of life, made joyous by distance and seeming unapproachableness, came faintly and died away to
a silence.

Oilily is a proper word, but it sounds strange and awkward here. Say it
out loud often enough, however, and it begins to sound like a lamentation.

The final two chapters serve as a double epilogue.

In XVIII, Pete sits with half a dozen prostitutes in a saloon, grows progressively drunker and more slurred as he repeats ad nauseam, "I'm a good
f'ler, girls," professes his love of the universe as he intermittently quarrels
with the waiter, declares to Nellie, the "woman of brilliance and audacity,"
that he is stuck on her, pulls some cash from his pocket and puts it on
the table to prove his noble intentions, since he is, after all, a "goo' f'ler,"
and eventually passes out and falls to the floor. Nellie stands up, stuffs the
money into her pocket, looks down at the snoring, stupefied Pete, and says,
"What a damn fool." Then she walks out into the night.

Chapter XIX begins as if Crane were introducing a new character and
a new setting, extending his novel into a different territory. "In a room
a woman sat at a table eating like a fat monk in a picture." Who is this
woman, and why is she compared to a monk? A monk is not a woman but
a man, and why the added detail of "a monk in a picture"? What picture
is Crane referring to, and what does it have to do with the story we have
been reading? I can only speculate, but it strikes me that he is establishing
the last scene of the book by removing the action from contemporary New
York and once again evoking an earlier age, one in which, for example, fat
monks sat at tables gorging themselves on mounds of food, and since the
only monks Crane had ever seen were the ones depicted in Renaissance
paintings hanging on the walls of the Metropolitan Museum, to think of
a monk was to think of those paintings. But why a monk and not a nun?
Because there are no paintings of fat nuns gorging themselves on food. The
fat monk is a known character, a familiar type, and because this sentence
starts the chapter and stands alone in the paragraph, cutting it off from
what comes next, Crane is isolating the image and forcing us to look at it
as if it were a painting, in the same way he presented Maggie on the last
night of her life in a series of isolated, unconnected images. The power
of the image first of all—to make us see what we are looking at and look
closely at what we are seeing—and then, after we learn that the woman
is in fact Maggie's mother, we understand that Crane has desexed her,

robbed her of her femininity, and turned her into someone who cannot bear children. Therefore, she has become a man, and not just any man but a monk, a man who has sworn a vow of celibacy and is forbidden to produce children, a man who in popular lore has sublimated his sex drive into the pleasures of gluttony, and by turning Maggie's mother into a celibate, gluttonous man, Crane is silently accusing her of being an unloving, unnatural mother, a mother who has hastened the death of her daughter by refusing to shoulder the responsibilities of motherhood.

Earlier in the book, Jimmie was compared to a monk as well ("the little boy ran to the halls, shrieking like a monk in an earthquake"), and now, in the second sentence of the last chapter, Jimmie enters the room and stands before his mother, who is not named as such but is simply "the woman," just as Jimmie is simply "the man," in this instance "a soiled, unshaven man," and in the third sentence the man says to the woman, "Well, Mag's dead."

"What?" said the woman, her mouth filled with bread.
"Mag's dead," repeated the man.
"Deh hell she is," said the woman. She continued her meal. When she finished her coffee she began to weep.

This is extraordinary. A hundred things have happened in eight short sentences, and they have happened so fast that it is almost impossible to take them in on the first reading. Crane is a writer whose work demands to be read slowly and deliberately, sentence by sentence, with brief pauses between the sentences in order to digest the full import of what they contain. The prose can be choppy and disjointed, an unpredictable style that stuns and stings rather than charms, and because it does not induce the spell created by the grand, flowing novels of earlier decades, works by Dickens or Balzac or Tolstoy, you cannot curl up on a sofa and settle into a book by Crane. You have to read him sitting bolt upright in your chair.

By the next sentence, the blubbering woman has lapsed into another fugue of self-pitying sorrow. Without asking a single question about how her daughter died, she begins to act the part of grieving mother. It is a performance, and as the women from her building crowd into the apartment to witness the show, the woman raves on about the little woolen booties Maggie wore as an infant. Her acting is so persuasive that the others commiserate with her, acknowledging what an affliction it is to be the mother of a disobedient child, and soon others are weeping as well, a dozen women weeping and groaning at the same time, each one in a different key, a chaos of tears and groans filling the room as one of the weeping women, dressed in black and identified as Miss Smith, gets down on her knees beside the mourning woman's chair and begs her to forgive her wicked girl.

"Yeh'll forgive her, Mary! Yeh'll forgive yer bad, bad chil'! Her life was a curse an' her days were black an' yeh'll forgive yer bad girl? She's gone where her sins will be judged."

"She's gone where her sins will be judged," cried the other women, like a choir at a funeral.

"Deh lord gives and deh lord takes away," said the woman in black, raising her eyes to the sunbeams.

"Deh lord gives and deh lord takes away," responded the others.

"Yeh'll forgive her, Mary!" pleaded the woman in black. The mourner essayed to speak but her voice gave way. She shook her great shoulders frantically, in an agony of grief. Hot tears seemed to scald her quivering face. Finally her voice came and arose like a scream of pain.

"Oh, yes, I'll fergive her! I'll fergive her!"

The hypocrisy is so blatant and self-damning that it verges on the ludicrous, the laughable. But such is the force of Crane's bitter ending that laughter dies before it can reach the throat.

8

IN A COMIC BOW TO WILLIAM MAKEPEACE THACKERAY, CRANE called the boardinghouse on Avenue A the Pendennis Club. In Thackeray's novel, a fatherless country boy goes to London and becomes a writer, and now that the fatherless American boy had left the seashore and arrived in his own big city, carrying no earthly possessions but the pen in his pocket and a handful of pennies in his purse, he was going to become a writer as well—*and by no uncertain implication a great one.* For the rest of 1892 and into the early weeks of 1893, he worked to finish his first novella in the room he shared with Fred Lawrence, pausing between sentences to stand before the windows that looked out over the East River and Blackwell's Island, a narrow strip of land on which stood a hospital, a lunatic asylum, and a prison.* Because the world was there for him to see and he was in the world to write about it, he incorporated that prison into the first page of his book

---

* Renamed Welfare Island in 1921 and Roosevelt Island in 1973.

and used it as a backdrop to the stone fight between the children of Rum Alley and Devil's Row: "Over on the Island, a worm of yellow convicts came from the shadow of a grey ominous building and crawled slowly along the river's bank." Less than a year after Crane wrote those words, when the Panic of 1893 was beginning to demolish the American economy and millions were being thrown out of work, Emma Goldman was locked up in that same prison for telling a crowd of one thousand people in Union Square to "go into the streets where the rich dwell and ask for work, and if they do not give you work, ask for bread, and if they do not give you work or bread, then take bread." Such were the times. And such was the city Crane lived in during the rough years of little food and next to no money. His niece Helen R. Crane believed that those hardships broke his health and eventually killed him.

Nevertheless, the city was there for the taking, and he took whatever he could. According to Lawrence, he and Crane often ventured downtown to various entertainment spots on the Bowery, "then in the heyday of its multicolored existence," as well as the Atlantic Garden and Blank's, where they "could enjoy good music and passable variety at the cost of a few glasses of beer," Koster & Bial's "huge music hall" on Twenty-third Street, and dance performances by the famous Carmencita (later captured on film by Edison in one of the world's first movies) and Loie Fuller, a former headliner with the Folies Bergère who became the living emblem of Art Nouveau. Some of these places, or ones much like them, found their way into *Maggie*, but Lawrence was not the only person who accompanied Crane on his nighttime excursions, and beyond the operettas in popular music halls, there were the full-scale operas he attended, the recitals and concerts, and, to feed his ever-growing passion for it, as many jaunts to the theater as his resources would allow. Within a year of his arrival, he had dashed off "Some Hints for Play-Makers," a humor piece that could have been written only by someone who had sat through his fair share of duds ("Second Recommendation: 'A society play. Entitle this anything you please, so long as the one you hit upon does not refer . . . to anything connected with the drama'"), but when the plays were good, he was exultant. To Garland, after attending a performance of Gerhart Hauptmann's *Hannele* the following spring: "As an irresponsible artistic achievement it's great. I sat and glowed and shivered."

Once *Maggie* was finished, Crane followed the suggestions of Garland and Johnson and submitted the manuscript to both Gilder and Hitchcock. The editor of the *Century Magazine*, an advocate of tenement reform who had known Crane's father and had visited the Crane household during S.C.'s childhood, was appalled by the language and rejected the book. Hitchcock, who would later publish several of Crane's works, told Johnson that "the boy has the real stuff in him" but felt the novel had no commercial prospects and turned it down as well. Whether Crane submitted the manuscript to other publishers is not clear, but if he did, the answers he received were all negative. There were only two options left to him: either bury the manuscript in a drawer and forget about it or publish the book himself.

Whitman had done it with *Leaves of Grass*, Melville had done it with his late collections of poems, and now Crane followed their example and joined the ranks of self-published authors—a venerable if somewhat tainted American tradition. To go down that road might help repair a damaged ego, but at the same time, once you put your foot on it, you discover that the road is hexed, and whoever walks on it becomes invisible.

William, the man with many daughters, helped Crane find the money to cover the printing costs by engineering an arrangement that wound up adding to his own net worth. It is possible that he also dipped into his bank account to provide whatever extra funds were needed, but that is only speculation. I would like to think he did, if only because a man who stood up so bravely to a lynch mob deserves every benefit of the doubt, but when it came to money matters William was tough and tight, as stern as a well-oiled calculating machine, and I can also imagine him driving a hard bargain with his little brother, not through any devious intentions but simply because that was how his mind worked. What he proposed was that Crane relinquish his one-seventh share of their mother's house along with the Pennsylvania coal mine stocks he had inherited in exchange for cash at fair market value. Crane, who had no talent for thinking about or handling money (it went on slipping through his fingers to the end of his life), cared only about his book and accepted William's terms. Rather than ask around at a number of print shops to find out the going rate for producing small books such as his, he impulsively went to the only one he was familiar with, a shop on lower Sixth Avenue that he had walked past often on his rambles through the city. According to Lawrence, "they set a price and it was agreed to without demur." At $869, Crane was vastly overcharged. Nor was he put out when the printer read the book and informed him that the company's name—out of common Christian decency—would be kept off the title page, which meant that Crane's self-published book would, in effect, be published by no one. He didn't seem to care. He had

traded his inheritance for a chance to be in print, and because it was the
only chance available to him, he forked over the money without giving it
another thought.*

What he did care about was offending his family, however, and possibly being arrested for breaking the vice laws (as some friends warned
him), so he concocted a pseudonym for himself and published the book
under the name of Johnston Smith. Accounts vary on how he hit upon
that solution, but according to his friend Linson, Crane's reasoning was
simple enough: "Commonest name I could think of. I had an editor friend
named Johnson, and put in the 't,' and no one could find me in the mob of
Smiths." According to Johnson himself, Crane discovered that there were
more Smiths and Johnsons in the New York directory than any other name
and added the "t" as a flourish to throw snooping busybodies off his scent.
Post Wheeler, on the other hand, remembered that he was the one who
suggested it to Crane—as a joke. It hardly matters now who originated the
idea of Johnson-Smith, but an attentive reader will notice that among the
few last names mentioned in the novel (both Pete and Nellie are referred
to by their first names only, for example), the most prominent ones are
Johnson and Smith, as in Maggie Johnson and Miss Smith, the woman in
black who appears at the end and implores the grieving woman to forgive
her "bad, bad chil'." I wonder if Crane was even aware of this overlap. What
is clear in both instances, however—both for Crane the pseudonymous
author and for the characters in his book—is that the names are bland
and generic, not because Mr. Smith lacked the imagination to invent more
striking ones but because he was reluctant to assign names to his characters at all, feeling more comfortable with epithets such as "a woman of
brilliance and audacity," since he saw his characters as quasi-mythological
types, embodied representatives of various human attributes, each one individuated by means of his or her own distinct personality but also objectified
and continually watched from a certain distance throughout the book. This
tendency would vanish in Crane's later fiction, but in his early work it is
quite pronounced—to such an extent that he, the author of the book, chose
a name for himself that was hardly even a name, a name that turned him
into anyone, one more anyone lost in a mob of Smiths.

The finished book was ready in late February or early March. Eleven
hundred soft-bound copies with a cover of red type set against a yellow

---

* With no professional editor to review the manuscript before it was given to the printer,
numerous small errors were allowed to remain in the text—grammatical inconsistencies,
misplaced punctuation marks, and misspelled words (such as *grimey* for *grimy*). Not wanting
to tamper with the original, most subsequent editors of *Maggie* have left those errors intact.

background, three parallel red bands at both the top and bottom, and in the upper-right-hand corner a figure announcing the price at fifty cents per copy, a heftier sum than the standard ten or twenty-five cents that soft-cover books sold for at the time and not an insignificant amount when you consider that a dollar then was the equivalent of twenty-eight dollars today. Yellow: the color of the new and the radical in that era of shifting artistic perspectives, the color of the Decadent movement, the color of sexually provocative French novels, the color of Aubrey Beardsley, Oscar Wilde, and the short-lived but never forgotten *Yellow Book*. The year of *Maggie*, 1893, was also the year when Knut Hamsun's slightly younger contemporary Edvard Munch, another renegade from Norway, painted *The Scream*, and Crane's book was yellow because he felt that he too was taking part in the renegade spirit of the age. But a book has to sell some copies, or at least get talked about in the press, to make any kind of mark on the world, and *Maggie* neither sold nor got talked about. Whitman, an experienced journalist by 1855, promoted his self-published book by publishing a number of enthusiastic, self-written reviews under different pen names to spread the word of his genius—and also by sending one of the 795 first-edition copies of *Leaves of Grass* to Ralph Waldo Emerson, after which he plucked a sentence from Emerson's warmhearted response and stamped it on the spine of the second edition: "I greet you at the beginning of a great career." The much younger and less aggressive Crane lacked Whitman's talent for advertising. The one stunt he came up with, as reported by his Syracuse classmate Frank Noxon, was to hire four men "to sit all day in front of one another in New York elevated trains, reading intently and holding up the volume so that passengers would think the metropolis was *Maggie*-mad." The marketing campaign fizzled, but that pathetic, funny, juvenile effort to stir up interest in his book proves that for a short time after publication Crane still had hope that *Maggie* would succeed. The New York papers were silent. Only one early review popped up anywhere in the world—in the Crane family's provincial hometown newspaper, the *Port Jervis Union*. The reviewer predicted that the pathos of Maggie's story "will be deeply felt by all susceptible persons who read the book."

Garland was one of those susceptible persons, and Crane immediately dispatched him a copy of the novel, which in its final version bore only a scant resemblance to the manuscript Garland had read six months earlier. Crane's dedication, which includes another one of his bizarre spelling errors (*f'or* instead of *for*), is an essential document concerning how and what he thought about *Maggie*, and also, I believe, about what he didn't quite know but had expressed unwittingly in his book.

It is inevitable that you be greatly shocked by this book but continue, please, with all possible courage to the end. F'or it tries to show that environment is a tremendous thing in the world and frequently shapes lives regardless. If one proves that theory, one makes room in Heaven for all sorts of souls (notably an occasional street girl) who are not confidently expected to be there by many excellent people.

It is probable that the reader of this small thing may consider The Author to be a bad man, but, obviously, this is a matter of small consequence to

The Author

Environment, yes, which is there for all but the blind to see and has put Crane squarely in the realist-naturalist-determinist camp for generations of scholars and critics, but what about the word "Heaven" and his conviction that Maggie is with the angels now, in spite of what "excellent people" would suppose, that is, hypocrites who pretend to believe in God but believe in nothing, as personified by the falsely benevolent minister who shuns her? The word "Heaven" opens the door to further speculation about why Crane wrote the book in the first place and why he felt so drawn to the lives of the urban poor. He did not have the impulses of a reformer, took little or no active interest in politics, was not in the business of saving souls, and did not travel through those tumbledown streets in order to collect socio-anthropological data on the habits and customs of the natives. My sense is that he was horrified by what he saw—and fully caught up in it because it thrust him down deep into himself and the subterranean world of his unconscious, the dark, hidden sphere of his childhood and the religion of his parents. Life among the fallen. Not just the fallen lower classes stranded on the Darwinian battleground of capitalism, but the spiritually fallen in the kingdom of a God who might or might not exist. That was why he could tell Garland that Maggie was in heaven. Human beings had souls, and innocent souls were spared the wrath of divine punishment—assuming there was such a thing as divine punishment—and if "excellent people" were destined to land in the heaven they had imagined for themselves, then surely there was a place in it for creatures like Maggie. From early childhood, Crane had been at war with the religion of his parents. He rebelled against it, poked fun at it, dismissed it, and yet it was always there for him, pulsing faintly under his skin, as steady as the air that kept on going in and out of his damaged lungs. With *Maggie*, he took the first step toward discovering his mission as a writer. From then on, all his most important works of fiction would concern themselves with extreme situations, with matters of life and death: war, poverty, and physical danger. He wrote many other things as well, many of them good things, but the best were always written when he was afraid, trembling in his bones and scarcely aware of what he was doing—or why he was doing it.

Garland was impressed by the little novel and invited Crane to dinner at the apartment on West 105th Street that he was temporarily sharing with his brother Franklin, an actor who was performing in a play at a New York theater. Garland found Crane looking "distressingly pale and thin," but once the meal was served and the young man had downed his fill of steak and coffee, "he gave out an entirely different expression. He chortled and sang as he strolled about the room . . . and for an hour or two talked freely and well, always with precision and original tang."

It sounds as if the boy had been desperately hungry for some time.

Garland also mentions that Crane "never offered to assist with washing the dishes." Not because Garland thought he was lazy but because Crane struck him "as one remote from the practical business of living." There is probably some truth in that remark, and how eerily it meshes with Cora's scribbled note about Crane moving his soldier-buttons around the floor as a small boy: "never picked up buttons after play."

It was then or soon after that Garland suggested Crane send *Maggie* to Howells, as well as to a number of prominent reformist ministers and influential figures such as Brander Matthews (writer and theater professor at Columbia), Julius Chambers (writer and newspaper editor), and John D. Barry (novelist, playwright, and theater critic for *Harper's Weekly*). They were all solid literary men of their day, and since Garland was the only flesh-and-blood literary man Crane knew, he followed his friend's advice. The ministers said nothing. According to Linson, Crane told him, "You'd think the book came straight from hell and they smelled the smoke. Not one of them gave me a word. Icebergs, CK, flints!" The writers proved to be a bit less hostile than the clergymen. Most of them said nothing as well, but the mailed packages wound up eliciting some answers—and with those answers some consolation for the monumental, money-sucking flop he had produced.

In spite of Crane's disappointment, he dug in and continued working at his usual hectic pace. At some point before or just after the release of *Maggie*, he wrote a nimble, well-turned bit of satire and parody about a young clerk in "a little gents' furnishing store" who sits alone on a stool immersed in what he hopes will be a salacious French novel as customers straggle into the shop and interrupt his reading. The young clerk in "Why Did the Young Clerk Swear?"—yet one more fictional character with no name—skims through seventeen boring, unsexy chapters that describe "a number of intricate money transactions, the moles on the neck of a Parisian dressmaker, the process of making brandy, the milk-leg of Silvere's aunt, life in the coal-pits and scenes in the Chamber of Deputies," fixes his attention on passages such as "Silvere was murmuring, hoarsely. He leaned forward until his warm breath moved the curls on her neck," but when the clerk reaches the end of the book and discovers that it has failed to deliver on its titillating promises, he angrily tosses it aside and says, "Damn!" The sketch was published in the weekly humor magazine *Truth* and Crane received fifteen dollars for it. After subsisting on a minimal diet for the past several months, often on one meal a day and sometimes on no meal at all, he blew the entire wad on a champagne supper with a bunch of friends.

By pure coincidence, the day the piece was published was also the day when the Pendennis Club held a boisterous party to celebrate the publication of Crane's book. One of the participants elected himself "a committee for the Advancement and Preservation of *Maggie*" and managed to talk some of the guests into buying copies, which in all likelihood were the only copies out of the eleven hundred printed that anyone ever bought.* Lawrence mentions taking "a very active part in brewing the huge bowl of punch which constituted the main decoration" and how everyone was "in a highly cheerful state," producing such an uproar "that the entire neighborhood was soon hanging out of its windows in an effort to determine whether it was a riot or a political convention." Linson, who was also there, remembers Crane "thrumming chords" on a banjo, "and soon the 'Indians' were chanting to the rhythmic pound of a war dance." At around midnight, the landlady came upstairs to tell the chanters that she rented rooms to "gentlemen, not animals," and Crane "called through the door while waving a frantic hand behind, compelling quiet. 'The animals apologize and will return to their cages at once,' and to us, 'Cheese it!'" In another variant of the story collected by Schoberlin, what Crane reportedly said was: "Cheese it, for God's sake! She'll throw me out if you Indians don't die. We owe her a month's rent as it is."

Someone took a photograph that night at the party. It is an amusing picture and the only document that furnishes visual evidence of life at the boardinghouse on Avenue A. Seven young men sitting or standing around a table cluttered with drinking glasses, a bottle, and other objects

---

* Reminiscent of Thoreau's fate with his first book, *A Week on the Concord and Merrimack Rivers*, which had an original printing of one thousand. After receiving 706 unsold copies from his publisher, who no longer had room to store them, Thoreau wrote in his journal on October 28, 1853, "I now have a library of nearly nine hundred volumes, over seven hundred of which I wrote myself."

The Pendennis Club celebrates the publication of Maggie.
Crane is to the right with the banjo. (COURTESY OF SYRACUSE UNIVERSITY)

too murky to identify, as well as a pair of human skeletons with clay pipes
jutting from their mouths, no doubt procured as homework specimens by
the medical students who lived there. The skeletons are a wacky touch, a
sign of festive, college-boy shenanigans, but, somewhat curiously, at that
particular instant no one in the picture seems to be in a "highly cheerful
state." They are all looking off or down and appear to be lost in their own
thoughts, except for one of the standing men, who might or might not
be looking into the camera, and another who is kneeling or squatting on
the floor and studying (or reading) a small stub of paper. This is Lucius L.
Button, one of Crane's good friends, and immediately to Button's right is
Crane himself, sitting in a chair with a banjo stretched across his lap and
holding a pipe in his right hand. The pipe is in his mouth, we see the first
traces of a tentative, newly grown mustache, and he too is looking down at
nothing in particular with a thoughtful expression on his face. Still, there
he was, surrounded by others. For a person universally known as "taciturn"
and "introverted," Crane nevertheless thrived on fellowship and filled that
need in various ways over the years—by joining a fraternity in college, for
example, or playing on baseball teams or going on camping trips with his
friends or becoming a member of clubs—and even if he didn't talk much,
he seems to have had a magnetic quality that drew others toward him. As
Lawrence writes in his memoir:

His charm, and it was a great one, is difficult to explain. He had a great capacity for friendship, though his circle was always somewhat restricted. His sympathy was felt rather than expressed. His long silences in themselves were pervaded with this elusive factor. He was intuitive, entering into the unexpressed thoughts of his associates without effort. In short, he was a keen natural psychologist, a reader of the minds of men, and to this he owed his remarkable hold on all who got to know him well. When he spoke, it was in a pleasant rather deep drawling voice with quaint idioms of his own manufacture. It was Stephen Crane the man rather than the writings of Crane that exercised such a spell over his acquaintances.

Four days after the Pendennis Club book bash, Crane received a letter written by John D. Barry, the first true response from the list of literary men *Maggie* had been sent to. I can only imagine the mixture of happiness and despair Crane must have felt as he read through Barry's comments. The *Harper's Weekly* drama critic and assistant editor of the *Forum* (a respected magazine that covered social and intellectual matters) begins politely by thanking Crane for sending the book and adds that he has read it with "the deepest interest." A promising start, but then the other shoe suddenly drops: "It is pitilessly real and it produced its effect upon me—the effect, I presume, that you wished to produce, a kind of horror. To be frank with you, I doubt if such literature is good: it closely approaches the morbid and the morbid is always dangerous." Barry goes on for another page criticizing the book as "brutal," "black," "unhealthful," and "unpleasant," and at the end of the long first paragraph exposes his narrow, moralizing view of art by asserting that "I presume you want to make people think about the horrible things you describe. But of what avail is their thought unless it leads them to work?" That is the crux of Barry's position: art that dwells on the "horrible" and does not inspire social action is bad for the soul. After lashing into Crane with some further objections concerning style and foul language, Barry concedes that Crane has "real ability" and hopes that he "will try something else." The condescension is appalling, yet Barry closes off with a friendly overture: "I should like to talk it over further with you and should be most happy to meet you. Won't you come here some time this week?"

Linson remarks that Crane was touched by Barry's letter because it was proof of "genuine interest," but I wonder how sincerely Crane meant what he said. As Lawrence notes: "Any disappointment or rebuff that came to him . . . he kept to himself . . . [and] to even appear conscious of a slight would have seemed an unworthy concession."

As it turned out, Barry and Crane eventually met, and by the next year Barry had become a partisan and defender of Crane's poetry. It wasn't that he was a stupid man, but in spite of the fact that he was just five years older than Crane, he stood for the ideas of an older generation, and because he couldn't see his way past those ideas, he was unable to comprehend what the fledgling author had set out to accomplish in his novella. This was the start of the "beautiful war" Crane would refer to in his letter to Lily Brandon Munroe, the old versus the new, yesterday versus tomorrow, and Barry's response provides a good example of what Crane was up against as a twenty-one-year-old nobody. He didn't fit in, and after taking the punches delivered by that letter from March twenty-second, he must have felt battered and quite, quite alone—even if he refused to share his feelings with anyone.

Six days after that, Crane revealed his crumbling self-confidence in a glum note to Howells: "I sent you a small book some weeks ago. . . . Having recieved [*sic*] no reply I must decide then that you think it a wretched thing?" Howells wrote back at once, apologizing that he had been too busy to read the book, "but from the glance I was able to give it, I thought you were working in the right way. When I have read it, I will write to you again." The second letter from Howells has been lost, but without question it was a positive one, and in that letter, along with whatever comments he made about the book, there was an invitation to come to his apartment at 40 West Fifty-ninth Street for a visit. This was an essential moment in Crane's life, and without that gesture of support from Howells, it is difficult to imagine what path future events would have taken. Except for Garland, the pygmies had all turned their backs on *Maggie*, and the only one who hadn't, the sole person besides Garland who had taken the trouble to read the book, had hauled off and knocked the author flat. Now a giant had reached out his hand and pulled Crane up from the floor.

Dressed in a suit he had borrowed from his writer friend John Northern Hilliard or else from his painter friend Nelson Greene (each man had his own version of the story), Crane traveled across town and stayed with Howells well into the evening, but with typical restraint he said almost nothing about the visit to his friends on Avenue A. Johnson wrote that he would "never forget the illumination of countenance and illumination of spirit he displayed" when Crane mentioned the encounter to him, but the only report on the evening comes from Howells himself, in a letter written to Cora seven weeks after Crane's death and published in the *Academy* on August 18, 1900.

... talking about his work, and the stress there was on him to put in the profanities which I thought would shock the public from him, and about the semi-savage poor, whose types he had studied in that book. He spoke wisely and kindly about them, and especially about the Tough, who was tough because, as he said, he felt that "Everything was on him." ... Of course I was struck almost as much by his presence as by his mind, and admired his strange, melancholy beauty, in which there was already a foretaste of his early death. His voice charmed me, and the sensitive lips from which it came, with their intelligent and ironical smile, and his mystical, clouded eyes.

The gentle monarch of American writers had given Crane his blessing, and whether the visit with Howells was responsible for it or not, a torrent of work and plans for work soon followed, the *at the same time* method of attack that makes it difficult to pin down exactly what Crane did when and when he did what, since all his projects were bubbling up in him simultaneously. To begin with, if it indeed begins there, he was mapping out and perhaps writing some pages of *George's Mother*, a follow-up novella to *Maggie* which places the central characters on another floor of the Rum Alley tenement building that appears in the first book. At the same time, he was boasting to Lily about his literary success in the letter he wrote to her early that spring and also writing about his imaginary, eloping Lily in "The Pace of Youth." Linson happened to drop in on him early one morning at the Pendennis Club, just as Crane was polishing off the last paragraphs of the story. "By a far window sat Stephen, with a towel-like turban about his head. An ink bottle was on the chair beside him, sheets of foolscap on his knees, and with no further ceremony he continued his work. Presently, pages were tossed to me ... I read to the end. 'Like it?' he asked laconically. Of course I liked it." When Linson examined the headgear more closely, Crane replied: "The towel? This thing got me going and I couldn't sleep, so I got up. Been at it all night. I'm all alone in the world. It's great!"

"This thing" refers to the story. As for the towel, it is hard to know if Crane used it often or just that once. Linson is the only friend who ever referred to it, but who is to say that S.C. didn't go on writing with wet towels wrapped around his head when no one was looking?

That spring, he was also deep into his preparations for *The Red Badge of Courage*, still formless at that point but growing, beginning to take on life.

In mid-April, the building on Avenue A was sold and the Pendennis Club scattered to the winds. Crane moved with his landlady, Mrs. Jennie

Creegan, to another boardinghouse, at 136 West Fifteenth Street, but he hopped around a lot as well, retreating to Edmund's house in Lake View for long stretches and crashing here and there with friends in the city when his money was low, most often in the lofts of artists and illustrators at the old Art Students League building on East Twenty-third Street. By early fall, he had more or less moved into that large structure of "slumberous corridors rambling in puzzling turns and curves," sharing spaces with various young and impoverished fellow beginners, now-forgotten artists such as William W. Carroll, Nelson Greene, and R. G. Vosburgh, all of whom would later write vivid accounts of the time Crane spent among them, which was the time of his most important and lasting early work.*

In June, *Maggie* received its first notice in a New York publication, the *Arena*, a monthly magazine of reformist tendencies, and the reviewer was none other than Hamlin Garland. His opening comments show the same enthusiasm he had expressed to Crane in encouraging him to send the book to Howells and the others, declaring it to be "the most truthful and unhackneyed study of the slums I have yet read" and that "it has no conventional phrases," presenting "the dialect of the slums as I have never before seen it written—crisp, direct, terse. It is another locality finding voice. . . . Mr. Crane is only twenty-one years of age . . . and impresses the reader with a sense of almost unlimited resource." Those were the good things, but toward the end of the short review Garland has some harsh things to say as well: "The story fails of rounded completeness. It is only a fragment. It is typical of only the worst elements of the alley. The author should delineate the families living on the next street, who live lives of heroic purity and hopeless hardship."

So much extravagant praise, but also a profound misunderstanding of the book's structure and tone, which makes Garland only a slightly less obtuse reader than Barry, another member of the old guard who can't face the suffering presented in *Maggie* without asking for a dash of nobility to leaven the horror. By pointing to a lack of "rounded completeness," he also fails to see that the book is intentionally stripped down and fragmented because Crane did not set out to write a traditional nineteenth-century novel but was already anticipating the sensibility of the next century—no, more than anticipating it, living it. Writing in the *American Mercury* in

---

* Created in 1875, the Art Students League was originally housed in the Needham Building, on East Twenty-third Street. In 1892, it moved to its present location on West Fifty-seventh Street, but a number of artists remained at the East Twenty-third Street address for several years afterward, among them Crane's friends.

1924, the critic Carl Van Doren began his article on Crane with these words about *Maggie*: "Modern American literature may be said, accurately enough, to have begun with Stephen Crane thirty years ago." Not even Crane's supporters understood this at the time.

Crane chose to ignore Garland's negative comments and take courage from the positive ones. A natural defense for someone who had otherwise been ignored, and so his friendship with Garland carried on as if the review had been an unqualified benediction. Such was the extent of Crane's gratitude to the man who had done so much to help him ("Hamlin Garland was the first to over-whelm me with all manner of extraordinary language," as he put it to Lily Brandon Munroe), but in light of some of the less than flattering things Garland wrote about his young friend in the years after Crane's death, I suspect the harshness of that negative paragraph was motivated by more than just a difference of opinion over aesthetic principles. I don't presume to know anything about Garland's feelings toward Crane, but mingled in with all the kindness and generosity there must have been some resentment as well, perhaps a touch of envy or at least a sense of shocked bewilderment that this small, slender upstart, with his haphazard education, wobbly grammar, and penchant for splitting infinitives and misspelling words, could write circles around him.

After Garland's review, the press remained silent about *Maggie* for more than a year. As Crane put it in an 1896 letter to another inquiring journalist: "My first great disappointment was in the reception of 'Maggie, a Girl of the Streets.' I remember how I looked forward to its publication, and pictured the sensation I thought it would make. It fell flat. Nobody seemed to notice it or care for it. . . . Poor Maggie! she was one of my first loves!"

9

MAGGIE HAD BEEN PUT TO REST, THE COFFIN HAD BEEN COVERED WITH dirt, and Crane was now thinking about other things as he forged on with a preliminary draft of *The Red Badge of Courage*, but then, toward the middle or end of June, he brusquely returned to the grave site, started thinking about the Johnson family again, and resurrected the dead infant Tommie to play the central role in three short tales commonly referred to as the "Baby Stories."

Covering just eleven pages in the Library of America edition, they represent Crane's initial foray into writing about children—something he would return to in the late nineties—but this early trio stands apart from the Whilomville stories because of the narrow intensity of its focus and the unusual (if not unprecedented) nature of the enterprise: to chart as faithfully as possible the shifting moods and actions of a child so young and small that he must "go downstairs backward, one step at a time . . . holding with both hands to the step above." The boy's age is not given, but he seems to be about three or three and half, four at the most, a toddler who has not reached full boyhood or attained the capacity for reflective self-consciousness, which generally dawns in children at five or just beyond five, the moment that parents tend to call "the age of reason." The child in the stories is yet another character without a name, but we know he is Tommie because Linson reports that Crane told him who it was, and when Linson was given early manuscripts of the first two stories to illustrate, the name was in the text: "An Ominous Baby—Tommie's Home Coming."

To do what Crane does in these little works requires an unusual combination of abilities. Above all, I think, you must have a vivid memory of your own childhood, or at least a memory of how you thought as a child; next, an inborn talent for looking closely at both people and things, as well as the patience and stamina to go on looking closely for a long time; and third, an emotional attachment to your subject, that is, a deep and abiding fascination with children, even if you are not a parent yourself.

We know about Crane's love of dogs and horses, but small children should also be added to the list of his strongest affections. In one of the several memory pieces Joseph Conrad wrote about Crane, he describes his friend's intense involvement with his infant son, Borys, and the long hours Crane and the child spent together on the lawn outside his house.

> I never heard him laugh, except in connection with the baby. He loved children; but his friendship with our child was of the kind that put our mutual sentiment, by comparison, somewhere within the arctic region. The two could not be compared; at least I have never detected Crane stretched full length and sustained on his elbows on a grass plot, in order to gaze at me; on the other hand this was his usual attitude of communion with the small child—with him who was called *the Boy*. . . . In the gravity of its disposition the baby came quite up to Crane; yet those two would sometimes find something to laugh at in each other. Then there would be silence, and glancing out of the low window of my room I would see them, very still, staring at each other with a solemn understanding that needed no words or perhaps was beyond words altogether.

Somewhat older children captured his attention as well, children who could walk and talk and play games, and on his trips to Port Jervis the quiet, withheld Crane often let loose by romping around with William's daughters. In her 1926 memoir for the *Literary Digest*, Edna Crane Sidbury recalls that she and her sisters "never had a more charming playmate" than their Uncle Stephen. "Whole mornings were spent chasing us" in elaborate games of cops and robbers and "he was so entirely one of us" that when she heard about his growing fame as a writer, "I had to laugh. Uncle Stevie famous? It was a joke."

Communing with infants, cavorting with his young nieces, still close to his own childhood and never not close to it throughout his short life, still living in the afterglow of his failed book about the slums, Crane interrupted his war novel to pull the dead Tommie out of his "white, insignificant coffin," added a couple of years to the boy's age, and set him down on his feet somewhere in New York. The first story begins with this otherworldly sentence: "A baby was wandering in a strange country."

Places do not have names in the universe of the small ones, thoughts seldom crystallize into words, impulse rules. Crane does not try to put himself inside the baby's head (what would he find there beyond a few mispronounced words?), but by keeping a close watch on how the child responds to what he sees and hears, we penetrate what the child is feeling. It is a purely phenomenological approach, and as happens so often in Crane's work, the effect is both odd and arresting, for the prose manages to create a sense of intimacy even as it stands aloof from its subject, and the farther back we are made to stand, the closer we seem to be. The baby is alone. Astonishingly, there is no mother or father or brother or sister or anyone else to hold his hand and guide him through the streets. The wandering baby is an independent human monad, adrift in the great city as he drags a piece of rope behind him, the smallest of small knights-errant sallying forth in search of whatever might happen next.

The "strange country" is a street in a neighborhood far from where he lives, a wealthy area of "stolid brown houses" and "smooth asphalt," and the wanderer is from "the poor district," "a tattered child" in stained and shabby clothes that bear "the marks of many conflicts," with "an array of tiny toes" sticking out from one of his shoes. The boy toddles along slowly, "with a look of absorbed attention on his flushed face," taking in the sights and sounds of the street, the "musical rumble" of carriages as they pass by, a man with a flower going up a flight of steps, nursery maids pushing babies in their perambulators, a truck wagon roaring in the distance. The sun is shining, and the boy is in good spirits as he continues to observe the scene.

The wandering baby stopped and stared at the two children laughing and playing in their carriages among the heaps of rugs and cushions. He braced his legs apart in an attitude of earnest attention. His lower jaw fell and disclosed his small, even teeth. As they moved on, he followed the carriages with awe in his face as if contemplating a pageant. Once one of the babies, with twittering laughter, shook a gorgeous rattle at him. He smiled jovially in return.

A few seconds later, his visit to paradise is interrupted by an unfriendly nursery maid. "Go 'way, little boy," she says to him. "Go 'way. You're all dirty." Rather than take offense, Tommie looks at her with "infant tranquillity" and then trundles off with his bit of rope trailing behind him. There are other streets in paradise, after all, and he soon finds one, where he continues his explorations of the territory, studying the people and the houses with the same rapt attention he would give "to flowers and trees."

Before long, he chances upon "a pretty child in fine clothes playing with a toy," which turns out to be a small fire engine painted red and gold that a rich boy is pulling behind him at the end of a string. Is this an echo of the all-powerful fire engines that filled big brother Jimmie with such awe and devotion in *Maggie*? Perhaps. In any case, Tommie is transfixed by what he sees. "The babe with his bit of rope trailing behind him paused and regarded the child and the toy. For a long while he remained motionless, save for his eyes, which followed all the movements of the glittering thing."

The rich boy pays no attention to him. He is too busy imitating the sounds of a full-scale fire engine rushing toward a make-believe burning building to look up from his game, too engrossed in his imaginary world to notice that a boy from the real world is on the sidewalk with him and that little by little, with cautious, uncertain steps, the boy is coming closer to him, at which point Crane adds this incisive detail: "His bit of rope, now forgotten, dropped at his feet." Of course it has. The "once treasured" object has lost the glow of its importance because it is attached to nothing, whereas the rich boy's string is enchanted with the power to send the magic fire engine racing along the sidewalk. Finally, Tommie manages to get the boy's attention and asks, "Le' me play wif it?" The boy says no. When the ominous baby asks the boy if the fire engine is his, the boy says yes, drawing "his property behind him as if it were menaced." Again the baby asks if he can play with it, and again the boy says no. "It's mine! My ma-ma buyed it." Again the baby asks ("His voice was a sob. He stretched forth little, covetous hands"), and again the boy says no. The baby then asserts, rather than asks, "I want to play wif it," and when the boy refuses again, Tommie's "I want to play" turns into "I want *it*." A scuffle breaks out. The boy protects "his property with outstretched arms" as each one grabs hold of the string and tugs. In the end, the "child in tatters" wins the skirmish and runs off with the toy: "He was weeping with the air of a wronged one who has at last succeeded in achieving his rights" (which closely resembles Maggie's observation about her mother in the novel: "She broke furniture as if she were at last getting her rights"). Right or wrong, after he stops to catch his breath, the ominous baby's "little form curved with pride" and "a soft, gleeful smile loomed through the storm of tears." When he sees that the sobbing, outraged pretty child is beginning to run after him, "the little vandal turned and vanished down a dark side street as into a swallowing cavern."

The story covers just three pages. In urgent need of money, Crane was hoping to publish it as quickly as possible, but Linson had gone off to the woods on a summer camping holiday and was slow in completing the illustrations. With mounting anxiety, Crane sent off a brief note to him from his room on West Fifteenth Street: "Have you finished the 'Ominous Baby' story yet? At the present time—during these labor troubles—is the best time to dispose of it. . . . Could you send it to me shortly? I hope you are having a jolly time in the wilderness." As it happened, the story remained unpublished for close to a year, finally surfacing in the May 1894 issue of the *Arena*, the same magazine that had run Garland's review of *Maggie*. The Panic that had broken out in '93 had not diminished, and the labor troubles Crane had referred to in his note were no less destabilizing than they had been the previous summer. Almost inevitably, the story was read as a parable about the antagonisms between New York's haves and have-nots, the potential class war that was beginning to stir in that time of economic collapse and social unrest as the divide between rich and poor grew ever larger. Emma Goldman's speech got her arrested for "inciting to riot," and many felt that violent outbreaks were a distinct possibility in the near future. Crane's little story seemed to capture that feeling of imminent dread, and just to make sure the *Arena*'s subscribers got the point, the issue contained an editorial written by B. O. Flower, the director of the magazine, emphasizing the political implications of "An Ominous Baby":

The little chap who had acquired the engine and who refused the gamin the pleasure of even playing with it for a few moments, places the toy behind him the moment there is danger. The "divine right" of property, as practically held by modern plutocracy, finds a striking expression in the involuntary action of the little aristocrat, who risks a thrashing by placing himself between the toy and danger.

There is something to be said for this symbolic reading of the story, I suppose, and perhaps even Crane himself was aware of the sketch's political reverberations (e.g., *labor troubles*), but if the story is good, and I believe it is better than good, its strengths have little to do with a philosophical attack on the divine right of property and everything to do with how well Crane depicts the behavior of his tiny protagonist, how skillfully he follows the buildup of the struggle between the slum baby and the miniplutocrat, and how his deep understanding of young children enables him to deploy concrete objects such as rope and string as visible representations of the unarticulated thoughts of his little hero. B. O. Flower sees the ominous baby as a vengeful proletarian warrior. It's not that he's wrong, but based on the evidence given by the other two stories, I feel that the spirit of Crane's intentions can best be understood if we look at Tommie simply as a child—a small, hungry, love-starved child growing up in wretched, impoverished circumstances.

The second piece, "A Great Mistake," is even shorter than the first, and while it also involves a theft, the crime is of a different order, not an attack of poor against rich but of small against big, and the entire action of the story takes place in an area of about ten square feet. Day in and day out, an Italian fruit vendor sits by his stand on a corner in the baby's neighborhood. The child looks upon the vendor "with deep respect . . . as if he saw omnipotence," and the stand itself is a marvel that surpasses all other marvels, for the fruits arranged there "in dazzling rows" hold all "the sweets of the world." Day in and day out, the baby parks himself near the stand to gaze upon the "tremendous being" and his "splendid treasure," no more than "a simple worshipper at this golden shrine," until the day comes when "tumultuous desires" begin to take hold of him and he resolves to snag a piece of fruit for himself when no one is looking. The vendor appears to have nodded off in his chair. The baby approaches stealthily, trying "to maintain his conventional manner, but the whole plot was written upon his countenance," a remark that tells as much about Crane's method as it does about the baby: exposing the inner workings of the boy's mind by reading what his body does, in this case his lower lip, which starts to tremble as his panic increases because "his infant intellect had defined the Italian . . . [as] a man who would eat babes who provoked him." This is the fundamental observation of the story: he who is willing to commit a transgression in order to satisfy his craving for the sweet food in front of him imagines that he himself will be eaten by way of punishment. We are no longer in the land of parables but of fairy tales, the undernourished Hansel and Gretel devouring the candy house as a prelude to being devoured themselves and other such nightmares from the land of child-hood fears. As the baby finally extends his hand toward the fruit, "the fingers were bent, claw-like, in the manner of great heart-shaking greed," but with his eyes still turned toward the dozing vendor, he doesn't know what he has taken, only that his "rapacious fingers" have seized "a round bulb," and when the vendor suddenly wakes up and snatches the bulb from the boy's hand, it turns out to be a lemon, the one fruit from his succulent kingdom that is not sweet.

Hence the title, "A Great Mistake." Not just the mistake of stealing but—almost as bad, if not worse—of stealing the wrong thing.

The last story, "A Dark-Brown Dog," is the longest and most complex of the three, with a devastating final turn that is so unexpected and at the same time so well conceived that you cannot forget it. Read the story once, and it is bound to stay with you for the rest of your life, whether you want to remember it or not.

Some time seems to have elapsed since the botched lemon caper. Tom-mie has graduated from being called *baby* to *child*, but he is still exceed-ingly young, still prone to sudden, impetuous shifts of mood, and still "in the habit of going on many expeditions to observe strange things in the vicinity." The story opens with the child standing on a street corner, leaning against a tall wooden fence as he swings his arm back and forth and idly kicks around some gravel. It is summer, a soft wind is blowing along the dusty avenue, and the boy is in one of those dreamy trances that engulf small children when they are alone and unoccupied and outdoors in the big world with the sun bearing down on them. Moments later, a little brown dog comes trotting down the sidewalk and stops in front of the boy. A short rope is "dragging from his neck," reminiscent of the bit of rope from the first story but also a sign that the dog's owner has abandoned him or else that the dog is lost. At first, the boy is charmed by the stray puppy, but after "an interchange of friendly pattings and waggles," the dog responds with such enthusiasm that he almost knocks the child over, and just like that, without a word or hint of warning, the child strikes back by punching the dog on the head.

So begins their fraught and unequal alliance, and as Crane explores the fluid, mutating nature of their connection, he steers us through the boy's bedeviling lunges toward tyrannical dominance, sadism, devotion, and aching need as well as the dog's inborn servility, unrelenting guilt, forbearance, and adoration of his one and only master. After that first unexpected blow, the stunned dog sinks to the boy's feet, and when the first blow is followed by a second, the despairing animal rolls onto his back in a posture of prayer and supplication, and so amused is the boy at how comical the dog looks holding his paws in this "peculiar manner" that he continues to give him "little taps repeatedly, to keep him so." Then the boy suddenly loses interest and walks away. The dog trails after him, but whenever he gets within striking distance, he is beaten again, for at this point the boy holds him in "contempt" and considers him to be "an unimportant dog, with no value save for a moment." Eventually, however, the dog performs "a few gambols with such abandon" that the boy has a change of heart and decides to take him home.

Home is an apartment on one of the upper floors of a tenement building, and when the boy and the dog enter, they manage to establish a deeper rapport (another sudden shift in the boy's affections) and become "firm and abiding comrades." Then the family appears. Crane eludes any direct reference to his novella by refusing to identify them—nor does he even tell us how many they are. By the next sentence, this anonymous, unquantifiable group of family members is commenting on the dog and calling him names. "Scorn was leveled at him from all eyes, so that he became much embarrassed and drooped like a scorched plant." The boy, however, defends the dog "at the top of his voice," and in the midst of these "roaring protestations," the father of the family comes home from work and asks "what the blazes they were making the kid howl for."

> A family council was held. On this depended the dog's fate, but he in no way heeded, being busily engaged in chewing the end of the child's dress.
>
> The affair was quickly ended. The father of the family, it appears, was in a particularly savage temper that evening, and when he perceived that it would amaze and anger everybody if such a dog were allowed to remain, he decided that it should be so. The child, crying softly, took his friend off to a retired part of the room to hobnob with him, while the father quelled the fierce rebellion of his wife. So it came to pass that the dog was a member of the household.

The dog is allowed to live there, but the boy is his only ally, his only defender against the abuses of the others, various assaults in the form of kicks, whacking brooms, and missiles hurled in his direction (handfuls of coal, household objects), as well as a nasty penchant for underfeeding him, but the boy is vigilant, and by screaming bloody murder every time one of these outrages is committed against his friend, the family gradually backs off. Time passes, and the bond between boy and dog continues to strengthen, yet however much they have come to rely on each other, the boy is far from a perfect master. His is an irrational being, and therefore he has it in him to betray, even if he doesn't understand why. "Sometimes, too, the child used to beat the dog, although it is not known that he ever had what could be truly called a just cause. The dog always accepted these thrashings with an air of admitted guilt." And, needless to say, the moment the blows stop, the dog is always ready to forgive the boy. Crane is not lapsing into sentimentality here. He is simply demonstrating that the soul of a dog is different from the soul of a boy—at least this dog, who is a certain kind of dark-brown dog, and this boy, who is a certain kind of boy from a certain kind of world.

Then, on the fifth page of the six-page story, a cataclysm descends on that world and everything is blown to bits. The father comes home drunk, and while he is in the process of "[holding] carnival with the cooking utensils, the furniture and his wife," the boy and the dog return from one of their rambles through the neighborhood. Immediately understanding the severity of his father's condition, the boy dives under the table to protect himself from harm. The dog, understanding nothing, misinterprets the sudden dive to mean: "Joyous gambol." When the father sees the dog trotting toward the table, he lets out "a huge howl of joy" and "[knocks] him down with a heavy coffee pot." The astonished, writhing dog tries to run for cover, but the father kicks out at him "with a ponderous foot" and then brains him with another blow from the coffeepot. The child screams in protest, but the father ignores him and "[advances] with glee upon the dog," who by now has given up hope of escape and has rolled onto his back in a posture of submission, legs splayed as if "[offering] up a prayer." Then comes this, which is surely one of the wildest, most disturbing moments in all of Crane:

> But the father was in a mood for having fun, and it occurred to him that it would be a fine thing to throw the dog out of the window. So he reached down and grabbing the animal by the leg, lifted him, squirming, up. He swung him two or three times hilariously about his head, and then flung him with great accuracy through the window.

Most writers would stay with the dog at that point, following his downward arc through the air until he crashes to his death by landing on the roof of a shed five stories below, but in order to prolong the dog's flight, which allows the reader to imagine it as if it were happening in slow motion, Crane abruptly cuts away in another one of his clairvoyant cinematic gestures, jumping into an Eisenstein-like montage sequence that offers several points of view of the dog's descent through the air, as witnessed by various people from the neighborhood.

> The soaring dog created a surprise in the block. A woman watering plants in an opposite window gave an involuntary shout and dropped a flower-pot. A man in another window leaned perilously out to watch the flight of the dog. A woman, who had been hanging out clothes in a yard, began to caper wildly. Her mouth was filled with clothes-pins, but her arms gave vent to a sort of exclamation. In appearance she was like a gagged prisoner. Children ran whooping.

In the next paragraph, the dog crashes onto the roof of the shed, rolls off, and lands on the pavement in the alley.

In the paragraph after that, Crane returns to the apartment upstairs: "The child in the room far above burst into a long, dirgelike cry, and toddled hastily out of the room. It took him a long time to reach the alley, because his size compelled him to go downstairs backward, one step at a time . . . holding with both hands to the step above."

And then the brief final paragraph: "When they came for him later, they found him seated by the body of his dark-brown friend."

So ends the last, the longest, and the best of the three Baby Stories. According to the poet John Berryman, who published a book-length study of Crane's life and work in 1950, "A Dark-Brown Dog" "is one of the perfectly imagined American stories." It did not appear in print until after Crane was dead.

10

THE RED BADGE OF COURAGE WAS BORN OUT OF DESPERATION. CRANE was broke, and his prospects for not being broke seemed to be diminishing. He was writing constantly, but he had little to show for his efforts so far, and now that he had lost his connection to the *Tribune*, he was finding it difficult to publish in newspapers. Other than *Maggie*, which had drained all his financial resources, he managed to place just three short sketches with the humor magazine *Truth* throughout the entire twelve months of 1893, among them the already mentioned "Why Did the Young Clerk Swear?" (in March) and "Some Hints for Play-Makers" (November), as well as a mini-playlet entitled "At Clancy's Wake" (July). They are all inconsequential pieces, tossed off for some quick dollars and a few laughs, but the far superior "The Pace of Youth" languished in manuscript until early 1895, and the second Baby Story, "A Great Mistake," was still an orphan until March 1896, almost three years after it was written. For all his determination to move forward and establish himself as a legitimate professional writer, Crane was losing ground, and after nine months in New York, he was worse off than when he had moved there. That was why he temporarily abandoned *George's Mother*, which he had started writing soon after the release of *Maggie*. He simply couldn't afford to write another unpublishable book. He needed a success, and in the meantime he needed to find a job or, failing that, a steady source of income.

It wasn't that he didn't try, but just because you knock on a door doesn't mean that someone will open it and invite you into the house. In April 1893, armed with a flattering letter from Howells, he met with Edwin Lawrence Godkin (founder and editor of the *Nation*) for a job at the *New York Evening Post* and was turned down. Other attempts to find employment have not been recorded, but in late 1893 he was still at it, as his friend Frederick C. Gordon recalled in a memoir written in the early twenties, even if the newspaper in question happened to be the *New York Press* and not the *New York World*:

> On his return in October . . . he began to hunt for a job. Toward the end of a black, cold rainy day he came in to see me, soaking wet, shivering and coughing—utterly done up. He had been down to see [Edward] Marshall, who had refused to take him on the *World* staff because he believed the hectic newspaper work would ruin his genius for imaginative writing, but offered to buy special articles from him. Steve hadn't a nickel for car fare—too proud to mention it to Marshall—so he tramped in the cold downpour from the *World* building to 23rd street—no overcoat, and literally on his uppers. He was ripe for pneumonia. I got him into an extra bed I had, and in a week he was up, nearly as good as new.

It was the second time this had happened to him in the past year. First, the drenching he had received while standing outside under Lily's darkened window, followed by the long walk home in the rain, which had immobilized him with a brutal, lingering cold, and now a case of near pneumonia and a full week in bed because he wouldn't stoop to begging a nickel from Marshall, a decent, much-admired man who stuck to his word by publishing the bulk of Crane's numerous New York City sketches throughout 1894 and later shared some harrowing adventures with Crane when they were both reporting from Cuba during the Spanish-American War, but for now I want to lean in and take a closer look at the word *nickel*, which carries extra weight at this juncture in Crane's story and has everything to do with how he regarded himself and how he meant to live in regard to others, especially his family, and most of all his brother Edmund, who did whatever he could to help his impecunious little brother, mostly by housing him and feeding him at his place outside Paterson along with giving him whatever bits of cash he could spare, but however much the young one depended on his brother's generous heart, he was also ashamed of needing that help and as a point of pride did everything in his power to keep the handouts to a minimum, even if he suffered greatly because of it. A military stoicism wrapped inside his shoddy bohemian threads. A code of being, or perhaps *a test of being*, founded on honor, stubbornness, and silence. As William wrote thirty years later:

> My brother, Edmund, told the following. . . . When Stephen was gathering his impression of the Bowery, he said to my brother, who was employed on Beekman St. "Ed, if ever I come into your place and ask for a nickel, don't give me more than that." A few days later, Stephen slouched into the place, dressed shabbily and looking hungry and forlorn and asked for a nickel which Ed., without a word, handed him. There was no further conversation.

A nickel was the difference between eating and not eating, since the custom at the time in New York saloons was to throw in a free hot lunch if you could spring for the price of a five-cent beer, and as Lawrence notes in his memoir, the free lunch offered at the little saloon around the corner was often Crane's only meal of the day. Later on, when Crane was sharing a fourteen-dollar-a-month room at the old Art Students League building with three visual artists, Nelson Greene (one of the roommates) reported to Schoberlin in 1947 that "the four of us were often so hard up that we were down to $2 on Saturday morning. This was invested in a big wad of frankfurters, rye bread, coffee and condensed milk which took us through the two days." Another roommate, R. G. Vosburgh, in a 1901 *Criterion* article entitled "The Darkest Hour in the Life of Stephen Crane," recalled that their diet consisted of "two poor meals a day, a bun or two for breakfast and a dinner of potato salad and sausages warmed over the little stove that heated the room, frequently eaten cold because there was no coal for the stove." More broadly, Greene observed that "Crane's poverty and slackness kept him from eating properly. His teeth were bad . . . —very bad—and he would do nothing about them—largely from poverty. . . . His teeth, his bad hours and his disregard for his health and proper food caused us much concern—among his friends we urged better care on him but he paid no attention. I think these things helped cause his early death." Helen R. Crane took her speculations somewhat further than Greene: "There is no doubt in my mind that my uncle courted hunger and privation. This was before he realized that one may not turn the tap and cut off these unpleasant things at will. He had . . . no idea it could hurt so much."

Vosburgh: "When he returned from Lakeview [1893] he was wearing rubber boots because he had no shoes."

Crane to Hamlin Garland (April 18, 1894): "I have not been up to see you because of various strange conditions—notably, my toes are coming through one shoe and I have not been going out into society as much as I might."

Helen R. Crane: "His clothes reeked eternally of tobacco and garlic. . . . He never had a clean shirt. . . . His old gray ulster would have made quite a satisfactory stable-mop, but was scarcely good for anything else. His hands were finely textured and small, but they were always stained with cigarette yellow, and his hair—that was sailing in the general direction of the last wind."

Or as Crane once said to Linson during that period: "If I had a new suit of clothes I'd feel my grip tighten on the future—it's ridiculous but it doesn't make me laugh."*

The four young men who shared the fourteen-dollar-a-month room had one double bed and a coal box to sleep in and on, three in the bed and one on the box, tucked in fully clothed because of the chill in the room and rotating positions from night to night: the outer edge, the middle, the inner edge, the box, and then back to the outer edge, and so on. According to Vosburgh, they "pooled their resources, and the first man up was usually the best dressed for the day." When one of them had a job interview or some other plan for earning money, "the most presentable combination of clothes that could be made was gotten together for him." On the rare evenings when one or more of them happened to be momentarily flush, they would chow down together in a noisy, inexpensive restaurant on Sixth Avenue called the Boeuf-à-la-Mode—which they rechristened the Buffalo Mud. They were young and hopeful, after all, and no matter how tight their belts, they still had the energy to "discuss and argue literature, politics, art, religion—everything" (Greene) and to make fun of themselves.

---

* In *Roadside Meetings*, a book published in 1930, Garland reports that Crane said the same thing to him, almost word for word. How to account for this? Perhaps Linson read Garland's book and years later appropriated the comment without remembering its source—or perhaps Crane actually said the same thing to both of them. In the book, Garland also tells us that Crane once remarked, "I'd trade my entire future for twenty-three dollars in cash."

*Crane sleeping in the shared bed at the Art Students League building,
1893 or 1894.* (COURTESY OF THE UNIVERSITY OF VIRGINIA)

Once, while visiting Linson at his studio on West Thirtieth Street,
Crane dashed off a witty poem about his empty stomach and equally
empty purse. A moment after finishing it, he crumpled it up and tossed it
into the wastebasket, but Linson retrieved it, smoothed it out, and saved it
for posterity. With a legend at the top that reads, "I'd sell my steps to the
grave at ten cents per foot, if 'twere but honestie," it seems to have been
written by the ghost of François Villon and can be looked upon as Crane's
anthem of those hard years.

> Ah, haggard purse, why ope thy mouth
> Like a greedy urchin
> I have nought wherewith to feed thee
> Thy wan cheeks have ne'er been puffed
> Thou knowest not the fill of pride
> Why then gape at me
> In fashion of a wronged one
> Thou do smilest wanly

And reproachest me with thine empty stomach
Thou knowest I'd sell my steps to the grave
If 'twere but honestie
Ha! leer not so,
Name me no names of wrongs committed with thee
No ghost can lay hand on thee and me,
We've been too thin to do sin
What, liar? When thou wast filled with gold, dids't I riot?
And give thee no time to eat?
No, thou brown devil, thou art stuffed with lies as with
    wealth,
The one gone to let in the other.

Such was the hole Crane had fallen into by the spring of 1893. Unless he temporarily abandoned the beautiful war and wrote something that would sell, the war would be lost, for if a writer does not earn enough money to eat, a writer cannot write, and in the end he may not live. Consequently, Crane was thoroughly prepared to compromise his principles and produce something for the marketplace. Who could blame him for bowing to the pressure of his circumstances? He was too thin to do sin, his purse was haggard, and once he managed to climb out of the hole he had dug for himself, he would be back on his feet and ready to push forward again. A story about the Civil War seemed to be a good bet, a bankable project. The war had ended twenty-eight years earlier, but Americans were talking about it again all over the country, books and articles and memoirs concerning the war were becoming increasingly popular, and with Crane's interest in things military, why not crank out a heart-stopping adventure yarn for the masses, a conventional little quickie of a novel about youthful heroism on the battlefield and then watch the dollars roll in? That was the plan, in any case, but the plan to sell out soon backfired on him. As he told his good friend Louis Senger, the tall man of the Sullivan County stories: "I deliberately started out to do a potboiler, something that would take the boarding-school element—you know the kind. Well, I got interested in the thing in spite of myself, and I couldn't, I couldn't. I *had* to do it in my own way."

He did it in his own way, and the result was one of the most enduring American novels of the nineteenth century—the only one about the Civil War that still matters. If Americans know nothing else about Stephen Crane today, millions of them can tell you that he was the man who wrote *The Red Badge of Courage*, even if they don't know that the man was a kid just barely into his twenties.

II

In the twenty-five months from his first meeting with Linson in early January 1893 until his departure for Nebraska at the end of January 1895, so much happened to Crane that it is difficult to keep up with him. His material woes continued to press down on what Edward Marshall called his "thin—almost cadaverous" body, but after the rugged, fallow year of 1893, they became somewhat less terrible in 1894, and through it all he kept writing, writing slowly and steadily in his large, even hand, producing an astonishing amount of work in any number of forms: his first novel, his second novella, several short stories, the sixty-eight poems of *The Black Riders*, a dozen and a half newspaper sketches, and one long magazine article. For the sake of clarity, I will march through his various activities one at a time, but it should be remembered that they were all going on *at the same time*, often from one day to the next—and now and then more than one on the same day.

First: the composition of *The Red Badge of Courage*.

The Battle of Chancellorsville had been familiar to Crane since childhood. One of his uncles, Wilbur Fisk Peck, a rare member of the Peck clan who did not become a Methodist minister, had served as a doctor during that savage confrontation, which left nearly twenty thousand men either dead or wounded. Crane inherited his sword, which became part of the uniform he wore as a lieutenant and then captain of drilling exercises at Claverack, and one of his teachers there (in history and elocution) had been chaplain of the 34th New York Volunteers, a number that is generally assumed to have given birth to the imaginary 304th Regiment in the novel. The actual group Crane had in mind, however, was probably the 124th New York State Volunteer Regiment, often referred to as the Orange Blossoms (because its members came from Orange County, many of them from Port Jervis), which had fought at Chancellorsville during those bloody days in the spring of 1863. Most of the surviving Port Jervis veterans were still around in the early 1890s, and Crane talked to them and asked them questions, prying as much out of them as he could. As Lawrence observed, "For years he had never failed to draw out from Civil War veterans their memories, their experiences in the everyday life of an army, and he knew more of war as it appears to the private in the ranks than most of the historians."

Then there was the fortuitous meeting with Corwin Knapp Linson, which inadvertently triggered the idea of writing the book. Linson, older than Crane by seven years, was a painter and illustrator who had spent a long stretch in Paris studying at the Académie Julian as well as the École des Beaux-Arts and had crossed paths with Paul Gauguin at the Pont-Aven artists' colony in Brittany. He was also Louis Senger's cousin, and one afternoon in January 1893, with snow falling heavily on the city, Senger took Crane along to visit Linson's studio on the southwest corner of Broadway and Thirtieth Street. "Crane shed his long rain ulster," Linson writes in his book, "and was surprisingly reduced in bulk by the process, showing a comparatively slight figure, of medium height, but with the good proportions and poise of an athlete.* His face, lean but not thin, was topped by rumpled blondish hair that neither convention nor vanity had yet trained. The barely discernible shading of a mustache had just begun to fringe a mouth that smiled with engaging frankness." At first, Crane sat there in awkward silence, smoking and holding "dead cigarettes" between his "nervous fingers," but when the affable Senger induced his cousin to show them some of his work, Crane's "reserve began to crumble," and the three men went on to discuss Port Jervis, magazine editors, and assorted other topics—until (more awkwardness) Senger pulled out the newest issue of *Cosmopolitan* and showed Crane's recently published "A Tent in Agony" to Linson, who read the story with enjoyment as Crane did his best to disappear by inching to the farthest end of the sofa. When it was time to go, Crane stood up and said, "See you again soon," to which Linson replied: "Come and sleep here if you want to, the joint is open house."

So Crane returned, and before long he was immersing himself in Linson's collection of back issues of the *Century Magazine*, which had published a series entitled "Battles and Leaders of the Civil War" from November 1884 to November 1887, a massive undertaking that was later reissued as an expanded, four-volume, hard-covered set of books. Linson had acquired the magazines in order to study the work of other illustrators, and as he stood at his easel painting or drawing while snow fell and rain fell and the midtown streets clamored with traffic outside, Crane sat parked on the sofa, plowing through this material over the course of many days, drawn in particular to the accounts of enlisted men who had fought at Chancellorsville. According to Linson, the one thing he said during all that time was: "I wonder that some of these fellows don't tell how they *felt* in these scraps. They spout eternally about what they *did*, but they're as emotionless as rocks." One by one, he worked his way through the various issues, tossing the finished ones on the floor, and when at last he came to

---

* A sharp contrast to the "thin—almost cadaverous" body Edward Marshall remembered from 1894—which gives ample proof of what the hardships and penury of 1893 had done to Crane.

Crane in Corwin K. Linson's studio, 1893 or 1894.
(COURTESY OF THE UNIVERSITY OF VIRGINIA)

the end, he thanked Linson for his "charming patience" and walked out of the studio, not bothering to put the magazines back on the shelves of the bookcase.

Never picked up buttons after play.

In June, he began writing the first draft of the book, no doubt the "potboiler" version that was eventually abandoned, using *Private Fleming/ His Various Battles* as a preliminary working title, which would seem to indicate a narrower focus of attention than the book's ultimate subtitle suggests: *An Episode of the American Civil War.* By mid-June he had left the city to hole up at Edmund's place in New Jersey, and except for a couple of brief jaunts back to his boardinghouse on West Fifteenth Street, he stayed put until September. Edmund recalled that time in Lake View:

> His day began at noon when he arose and ate breakfast when my wife and the little girls ate lunch. The afternoons he spent coaching the boys of the neighborhood in football tactics. From this he gained exercise in the open air, and much amusement. The evenings were spent around the piano singing, or socially at some friend's house. When the family retired, Stephen went to the garret, where he worked and slept, and

wrote far into the night, if composition was going smoothly. As soon as the story began to take shape he read it to me as the finished parts grew. He told me he did not want my literary opinion, only to know if I liked the story. That was pretty good from a kid fourteen years my junior. I liked the story.

Nothing about wet towels wrapped around his head at night, but as it was with William's five daughters in Port Jervis, so it was with Edmund's three in Lake View. Again, his brother recounts: "He had a strenuous game he played with the girls, his nieces. Armed with newspapers rolled into clubs, the three girls would attack Stephen fiercely and he would defend himself with such determination as sometimes to rout all three. Sturdy blows were given and taken in good part."

It was a secure and comfortable life under Edmund's roof, a respite from the mental and physical stress of trying to stay afloat in New York as an unemployed freelance failure, and even when Townley married for the third time on July twentieth, neither one of his younger brothers bestirred himself from that Lake View retreat to attend the wedding in Asbury Park, although Crane understood (as he wrote to Lily) that he had lost his bet with Dottie and owed her a necklace. By and by, however, even though Crane could have stayed with Edmund for as long as he wished, his scruples got the better of him once again, and after living off his brother for the entire summer, he packed his bags and returned to New York. The exact date is not known, but on September seventh, either just before or just after he headed back to the city to look for work, a cyclone ripped through Port Jervis and destroyed the Drew Methodist Church, the congregation Crane's father had presided over during the last two years of his life. As reported by the *Port Jervis Evening Gazette*: "The greatest damage was to the Methodist Episcopal church which faces the west on Orange Square, and lay directly in the path of the storm. The wind hit squarely in the face and blew the tall steeple over the roof which was carried down with it into the interior of the church, where it lies a mass of rubbish. The church is almost a total wreck."

One more trace of his childhood was gone.

His book was also gone—or at least the potboiler version of it, the one that was going to pull him out of his hole and rescue him from misery. He had completed about one-third of the manuscript at Edmund's house, but at that point he scrapped it and started again from the beginning, by now fully engaged in giving the book everything he had in him to give, which turned out to be far more than he or anyone else suspected.

The second version of the novel was composed in New York between the fall of 1893 and April 1894, the period when Crane was sharing the one-bed-and-coal-box room with his three artist friends at the former Art Students League building, although Frederick Gordon, who put Crane up in his extra bed during the pneumonia scare, recalled that after Crane had recovered sufficiently to start working again he stayed on with him and finished writing the book in his loft. There is no reason to doubt Gordon, but neither is there any reason to doubt that Crane wrote the bulk of the manuscript in the other room. Vosburgh tells us that Crane "always worked at night, generally beginning after twelve o'clock, and working until four or five o'clock in the morning, then going to bed and sleeping the greater part of the day" and that he openly talked about the book with his roommates: "Every incident and phase of character in *The Red Badge of Courage* was discussed and argued completely before being incorporated into the story." David Ericson, who lived in yet another loft in the building and was the man who never finished the portrait of Lily, told Ames Williams in a 1942 letter that one time, when Crane was stretched out in a hammock reading over his manuscript (whether in Ericson's studio or someone else's isn't clear), he said out loud to himself, "That is great!" As Ericson remembered: "It shocked me for the moment. I thought how conceited he is. But when he read me the passage, I realized how wonderfully real it was."

Different rooms, perhaps, but all of them in the same building, and during that six- or seven-month stretch, while Crane was also busy with various kinds of newspaper and magazine work on top of writing seventy or eighty of his short early poems, he was still pining for Lily. As he declared in the letter he wrote to her that winter (1893–94): "It is beyond me to free myself from the thrall of my love for you; it comes always between me and what I would enjoy in life—always—like an ominous sentence—the words of the parrot on the death-ship: 'We are all damned.'"

When he finished the book in early April, Crane moved out of the building, finding a small apartment for himself at 111 East Thirty-third Street, and went on tinkering with the manuscript. The following week, an unexpected gift from the god of chance arrived in the form of an interview with Howells conducted by Edward Marshall for the *New York Press*. In it, Howells talked about the state of contemporary American fiction, mentioned the names of several novelists he admired, and then added: "There is another whom I have great hopes of. His name is Stephen Crane, and he is very young, but he promises splendid things. He has written one novel so far—'Maggie.' I think that as a study of East Side life in New York 'Maggie' is a remarkable book." That same day (April fifteenth), the *Press*

Crane, standing to the left, with his roommates at the Art Students League
building. R. G. Vosburgh is probably the figure at the easel,
with Nelson Greene in the foreground and William Carroll standing
next to Crane. (COURTESY OF ELIZABETH FRIEDMANN)

also ran a few extracts from the novel, along with some prefatory remarks
that were no doubt written by Marshall: "There is unquestionable truth
in it; the kind of truth that no American has ever had the courage (or is
it bravado?) to put between book covers before. It is a question if such
brutalities are wholly acceptable in literature. Perhaps, as Mr. Howells says,
they will before long."

After a year in the shadows, Crane's lost novel was beginning to come
to life again. It gave him renewed hope for the future, but at the same time
he was no less hard up than he had been the day before, and when Garland
wrote on the seventeenth to ask for news and to tell him that he was heading out west on the twenty-fifth, Crane replied with the letter about his
toes "coming through one shoe," but in a sudden burst of optimism he also
wrote: "I've moved now—live in a flat. People can come to see me now.
They come in shools and say that I am a great writer. Counting five that are
sold, four that are unsold, and six that are mapped out, I have fifteen short
stories in my head and out of it. They'll make a book." Then he sent off his

third letter to Lily. It bears no date, but given what had just happened to him, his remarks about the "beautiful war" and the "true road" must have come immediately after Howells's comments in the *Press*.

On April twenty-first or twenty-second, he traveled to West 105th Street with the rolled-up manuscript bulging in the pocket of his ulster and handed the pages to Garland, the one person he felt he could count on. As Garland sat down to have a look, Crane nervously went off to the kitchen to watch Garland's brother prepare lunch. From Garland's 1930 memoir: "Each page presented pictures like those of a great poem, and I experienced the thrill of the editor who has fallen unexpectedly upon a work of genius." But as Garland looked more closely, he realized that the manuscript stopped abruptly in the middle, and when he asked Crane where the rest of it was, S.C. flashed one of his grim, ironic smiles and told Garland that it was in hock to a typist. He owed that person fifteen dollars, and since he didn't have fifteen dollars, the second half of the manuscript was temporarily in limbo. "Much amused by his tragic tone," Garland offered to lend him the fifteen dollars if Crane promised to return with the missing pages tomorrow. Crane said he would, "and away he went in high spirits."

By the end of the month, after making some further revisions suggested by Garland, Crane submitted the book to S. S. McClure—accompanied by a letter of recommendation from his advocate on 105th Street. The hope was to place it with the McClure Newspaper Features Syndicate or the newly launched *McClure's Magazine* as a first step toward book publication. It was a sensible plan. Crane needed money, and there was extra money to be made by publishing in newspapers and magazines, but by casting his lot with the devious, sometimes underhanded McClure, Crane had stumbled into a trap, and months of frustration followed. McClure himself was low on money, nearly bankrupt, in fact, having put considerable amounts into his new magazine, which had started publication the previous June—the early Panic days of 1893—and in 1894 he was still in trouble, so desperate that he had resorted to borrowing money from his own writers and (how not to laugh?) persuading his wife's doctor to invest in the magazine. Crane would continue publishing with McClure for the rest of his life, nearly always under embattled circumstances, but the first battle they fought was the toughest one, and it nearly poisoned Crane with bitterness. McClure lacked the money to publish *The Red Badge of Courage*, but rather than tell the young author about his difficulties and return the manuscript to him on the spot, he held on to it, held on to it for six months, putting Crane off with one excuse after another, not rejecting the book but not accepting it either, locking the boy in a protracted, demoralizing stalemate of neither yes nor no.

In mid-September, after a month with friends in the woods of Pike County, Crane returned to New York, and by October he had moved back to his old digs on East Twenty-third Street. That same month, Edward Marshall rescued the novel by turning Crane in the direction of Irving Bacheller, the head of another press syndicate, and so Crane dug out the original, handwritten manuscript and resubmitted the book. From the evidence, it seems doubtful that he ever bothered to reclaim the typescript from McClure. He simply turned his back on him and moved on, hoping that Marshall, a staunch believer in his work, had given him sound advice.

From Bacheller's book *Coming Up the Road*, published in 1928:

He brought with him a bundle of manuscript. He spoke of it modestly. There was in his words no touch of the hopeful enthusiasm with which I presume he had once regarded it. No doubt it had come back to him from the "satraps" of the great magazines. They had chilled his ardor, if he ever had any, over the immortal thing he had accomplished. This is about what he said:

"Mr. Howells and Hamlin Garland have read this stuff and they think it's good. I wish you'd read it and whether you wish to use the story or not, I'd be glad to have your frank opinion of it."

The manuscript was a bit soiled from much handling. It had not been typed. It was in the clearly legible and rather handsome script of the author. I took it home with me that evening. My wife and I spent more than half the night reading it aloud to each other. We got far along in the story, thrilled by its power and vividness. In the morning I sent for Crane and made an arrangement with him to use about fifty thousand of his magic words as a serial.

Eventually, the fifty thousand words were whittled down to fifteen thousand ("much smaller and to my mind much worse than its original form," as Crane remarked after it was published in twenty-five-hundred-word installments in early December), but at least it was something, a step forward rather than backward. Crane immediately set about to have the manuscript typed up again, and once again he had to borrow the money to pay for it. This time he turned to his friend John Henry Dick, a fraternity brother from Syracuse and the person who had wrangled guests into buying copies of *Maggie* at the publication party a year and a half earlier, writing him an urgent letter that began, "Beg, borrow or steal fifteen dollars," which Dick managed to do by persuading his boss at *Godey's Magazine* to lend him the required sum. (With his habitual nonchalance regarding all matters connected to money, Crane never paid off the debt.) Once the new typescript was ready, he turned it over to Bacheller and signed a contract that awarded him ninety dollars for the serial rights, a shockingly insignificant amount by today's standards, but it was more money than Crane had held in his hands since forking over the cash to pay the chiselers who had printed his first book, and it provided him with a little breathing room, a temporary pause from his troubles.

On November fifteenth, he wrote a letter to Garland, who was still out of town:

> My dear friend: So much of my row with the world has to be silence and endurance that sometimes I wear the appearance of having forgotten my best friends, those to whom I am indebted for everything. As a matter of fact, I have just crawled out of the fifty-third ditch into which I have been cast and I now feel I can write you a letter that wont make you ill. McClure was a Beast about the war-novel and that has been the thing that put me in one of the ditches. He kept it for six months until I was near mad. Oh, yes, he was going to use it but—Finally I took it to Bacheller's. They use it in January [December] in a shortened form. I have just completed a New York book that leaves Maggie at the post [*George's Mother*]. It is my best thing. Since you are not here, I am going to see if Mr Howells will not read it. I am still working for the *Press*. Yours as ever / Stephen Crane.

The installments ran in eleven or twelve newspapers around the country from December third to the eighth, and on the ninth it finally appeared in New York, where the first of the six parts was published in the Sunday edition of the *Press*, Edward Marshall's paper. Marshall's assistant at the time was the twenty-eight-year-old Curtis Brown, the well-known figure who moved to London in the last years of the century and established the literary agency that is still a thriving concern today. Back in 1894, when Crane was writing his New York sketches and stories for the *Press*, Brown often worked as his editor, and the two young men knew each other well. In a book published in 1935, *Contacts*, Brown remembered his encounter with Crane on that long-ago Sunday. Even though it was his day off, he went to his office in the *Press* building for a few hours that morning—

and on emerging, met Stephen on that bitter, wind-swept, acute corner of Park Row and Beekman Street where the Potter Building stands, and within which *The Press* was housed. He was without an overcoat, but his face, thin and white, lit up when he saw me. He threw his arms around me and said: "Oh, *do* you think it was good?" Fortunately I could guess what he meant, and said: "It's great."

"God bless you," said he, and hurried on to anywhere in the sleet.

Brown wasn't the only person who thought it was great. As Bacheller reported in his book, "Its quality was immediately felt and recognized. Mr. Talbot Williams, the able editor of the *Philadelphia Press* [and future dean of the Columbia School of Journalism] . . . begged me to bring Crane to his office." Bacheller, described by Brown as "a jolly, blond person . . . who afterwards became famous as a novelist," and by all accounts a warm-hearted, avuncular man even then, when he was still in his mid-thirties, talked Crane into going to Philadelphia with him. "Word flew from cellar to roof that the great Stephen Crane was in the office. Editors, reporters, compositors, proof-readers crowded around him shaking his hand. It was a revelation of the commanding power of genius." Just a few days earlier, the same *Philadelphia Press* had published an article by Elisha J. Edwards (writing under the pen name "Holland") that had concluded with these words: "If Mr. Crane is careful, is true to his best impulses, follows his intuitions and pays no heed to those who write this or that about American fiction, he is quite likely to gain recognition before long as the most powerful of American tellers of tales."

He was beginning to make a splash. A little splash, to be sure, but his prospects were suddenly looking up, improving by the day, and not long after the success of the truncated newspaper version of *Red Badge*, Bacheller opened his wallet and granted Crane his long-deferred wish: the chance to travel. There would be an expense account to keep him going from one place to the next, and his only obligation would be to wire dispatches to the syndicate from his various stopping points across the South, the West, and Mexico. Crane had turned twenty-three on November first, and his departure date was set for the end of January, which gave him enough time to go about scaring up some work for himself in the interim. He paid a call on Ripley Hitchcock, the same editor at D. Appleton and Company who had turned down *Maggie*, and showed him a couple of his New York sketches as samples. When Hitchcock asked if he had a book-length manuscript that might be considered for publication, Crane followed by sending him clippings of the serialized version of *Red Badge*, and then, before taking off on his wanderings for Bacheller, he submitted the full version of the novel on the off chance that it would appeal to Hitchcock. At some point during his two-week stay in Nebraska, he received a letter from Hitchcock announcing that Appleton wanted to publish the book.

It was finally going to happen—and yet, after so many months of frustration and disappointment, how unnerving it is to discover that what seems inevitable to us today (the eventual publication of *The Red Badge of Courage*) nearly didn't happen, for as Crane later confided to Willis Brooks Hawkins, his closest New York friend throughout 1895 and 1896, he had been feeling so discouraged when he submitted the manuscript to Hitchcock that he had promised himself to burn the novel if it was rejected again.

12

NEW YORK SKETCHES.

Crane needed work, and in the early months of 1894 he began to find it. Shut out from the New York papers since the calamitous article about the JOUAM parade in the summer of '92, he had chanced upon the right person in Edward Marshall, and even if the encounter cost him a miserable week in bed, Marshall's position as Sunday editor of the *Press* gave him the power to open the door and allow Crane back into the world of journalism. Marshall was just two years older than Crane, and beyond having the wit to recognize talent when he saw it, he was a generational ally who understood what was new and original in Crane's work. Five days after Crane died at a sanatorium in the Black Forest on June 5, 1900, Marshall wrote a stunned, tight-lipped article for the *New York Herald* ("Loss of Stephen Crane—A Real Misfortune to All of Us") that focused mainly on their wartime experiences together in Cuba but also touched on Crane's first visit to the Potter Building: "One day . . . a young man came to my office with a letter of introduction. He was thin—almost cadaverous. He wanted work and got it. His article—written for a ridiculously low price—on tenement-house fire panics was one of the best things that he or any other man ever did. It was followed by other strikingly strong stories."

Marshall commissioned most of the pieces Crane wrote that year, but not all of them, and notably not the first one, which wasn't commissioned by any newspaper or magazine editor but written on spec. Composed in February and published in the October issue of *Arena*, "The Men in the Storm" gives a close, firsthand look at the ravages created by the Panic on the city's vulnerable working class. With unemployment continuing to rise and homeless men camped out on every downtown bench and street corner, New York had become the nation's capital of breadlines, soup kitchens, and shelters. Garland had already thrown out the idea of writing about these conditions to Crane, and Crane, who was young and reckless and up for any challenge, seized his chance on February 26, 1894. At three o'clock that afternoon, an immense blizzard came crashing down on Manhattan, bringing a foot and a half of snow and forty-mile-an-hour winds that "began to swirl great clouds of snow along the streets, sweeping it down from the roofs and up from the pavements until the faces of pedestrians tingled and burned as from a thousand needle-prickings. Those on the walks huddled their necks closely in the collars of their coats and went along stooping like a race of aged people." Crane rushed out into the storm and headed down to the Bowery wearing a thin jacket and no overcoat to carry out the assignment he had given himself: to keep watch on the locked door of a "charitable house" as men without work gathered in front of the door and waited for it to open. Inside, for five cents, "the homeless of the city could get a bed at night and, in the morning, coffee and bread," and as more and more men continued to show up, they huddled together in a mass of undifferentiated bodies to protect themselves from the cold, "their hands stuffed deep in their pockets, their shoulders stooped, jiggling their feet" and pressing "close to one another like sheep in a winter's gale, keeping one another warm by the heat of their bodies." Before long, Crane began to notice that the men fell into two distinct categories—the recently unemployed and the habitually unemployed ("the shifting, Bowery lodging-house element")—and that the out-of-work laborers "were men of undoubted patience, industry and temperance, who in time of ill-fortune, do not habitually turn to rail at the state of society, snarling at the arrogance of the rich and bemoaning the cowardice of the poor, but who at these times are apt to wear a sudden and singular meekness, as if they saw the world's progress marching from them and were trying to perceive where they had failed, what they had lacked, to be thus vanquished in the race."* And yet, in spite of the gruesome weather and the bleakness of the situation, Crane was impressed by the jokes that circulated among

---

* This tallies with numerous accounts about the attitudes of the unemployed during the next major depression in the 1930s and perhaps explains—or partially explains—why the American working class has never mounted a sustained ideological assault against the structures of capitalism. Crane might not have involved himself actively in politics, but he had an innate feel for the inner workings of the American psyche and, by extension, of the society he lived in.

the crowd, for "one does not expect to find the quality of humor in a heap of old clothes under a snowdrift," and even as the "winds seemed to grow fiercer as time wore on" and "some of the gusts of snow that came down on the close collection of heads cut like knives and needles . . . the men huddled and swore, not like dark assassins, but in a sort of an American fashion, grimly and desperately, it is true, but yet with a wondrous under-effect, indefinable and mystic, as if there was some kind of humor in this catastrophe." The men in the back of the line, fearful that the crowd was too big for everyone to be allowed in after the place opened, pushed forward against the ones in front of them, producing a ripple effect that closed the ranks at the head of the crowd and pinned the early arrivals against the locked door, but a policeman eventually turned up to maintain order, and no harsh words were spoken, no punches were thrown, and no one was injured. Long after darkness had fallen, the door of the shelter finally opened, and the men began to shuffle in. "The tossing crowd on the sidewalk grew smaller and smaller. The snow beat with merciless persistence upon the bowed heads of those who waited. The wind drove it up from the pavements in frantic forms of winding white, and it seethed in circles about the huddled forms, passing in, one by one, three by three, out of the storm."

Crane, who had stood out there shivering in the cold for many hours, walked back to his room on East Twenty-third Street, spent more hours writing his seven-page article, and then crawled into bed and collapsed.

The next morning, Linson came by to see him:

> At the end of February there came a driving blizzard, and after a bitter night I found Steve in bed in the old League Building looking haggard and almost ill. All the others were out. . . . Pulling a manuscript from under his pillow, he tossed it to me and settled back under cover to watch. It was that breadline classic, "The Men in the Storm." . . . I had known he was going out that night, and was anxious to know how he had come through, but I hardly expected to find him so exhausted.

Linson then asked, "Why didn't you put on two or three more undershirts, Steve?" Crane's answer, which was delivered quickly and without hesitation, can be read as a gloss on everything he believed he stood for as a writer: "How would I know what those poor devils felt if I was warm myself?"

As a piece of writing, "The Men in the Storm" is a trenchant, skillfully handled bit of work, especially when you consider the harsh conditions under which it was conceived and carried out, but even though it comes closer to what we would call "authentic journalism" than any of the other New York pieces Crane wrote that year, it does not conform to today's journalistic standards. A contemporary reporter witnessing a scene similar to the one Crane observed in 1894 would be obliged to mention the Panic and the growing unemployment rate in the city, and then, while standing among the destitute figures gathered around the door of the shelter, talk to some of them and include their statements in the article, supplying their names whenever they chose to give them, and, on top of that, the reporter would have to go into the shelter once the door was opened and describe what he or she saw there (how many rooms, how many beds, how clean or dirty), and then, finally, talk to one or more of the people who worked at the shelter to learn how the place was funded (by public charity or a private philanthropist) and how many people they served per day, per week, per month. Crane did none of that. He simply planted himself among the men and watched what they did and listened to what they said. Then he went home and sat down to record his impressions as faithfully as he could. Not once while reading the article do we suspect Crane of embellishing what he saw or intentionally making anything up, but for all that I would hesitate to classify the article as a piece of reportage. It is a piece of writing, and as such it sits squarely inside the realm of Crane's literary work and deserves the same kind of scrutiny as his novels, stories, and poems. "Sketch" is the term he and his editors used, and it is a good term precisely because it is so hard to pin down, an ambiguous term for an ambiguous form of writing that falls somewhere between fact and fiction, or facts set down by using the methods of fiction or, if you will, a story that does not tell a story but presents a picture (a sketch) of something that has happened or, in some cases, of something that happened more than once and is then told as if it were happening for the first time, as with the piece Marshall referred to in his article on Crane, "The Fire," which was not written about a single tenement fire but several fires that Crane had seen in New York and which he then distilled into the account of one fire—an imagined fire, yes, but not an imaginary one, and while the result is not journalism in the strictest sense of the word, it is nevertheless the truth, the imagined truth of something real—even if some elements in it are not based on actual events.

How would I know what those poor devils felt if I was warm myself? The comment to Linson prefigures the "little creed of art" Crane would refer to in the letter he wrote to Lily that spring, the conviction that "we are the most successful in art when we approach the nearest to nature and truth."

After tramping out into a blizzard and then standing half frozen in the ice-needle wind for several hours—for the sole purpose of writing about a crowd of abject, homeless men—Crane would seem to be arguing for the primacy of lived, personal experience over the truth-telling powers of the imagination. He might have believed it at the time—and put himself at risk because of that belief—but to carry such an argument to its logical end would eliminate novels and short stories from consideration and reduce fiction to a form of autobiography, and with Crane still hard at work on *The Red Badge of Courage* just then, a novel set in a time before he was born that tells of a war he did not participate in or even witness, his own book would have been a flagrant contradiction of what he purported to believe. Fortunately, he wasn't much of a theoretician about literature. He was a practitioner of literature, and at one time or another he followed various, often contradictory paths to accomplish his work. With "The Men in the Storm," he felt that walking out into a blizzard minus an overcoat and scarf would help him to understand his subjects more intimately and lead to a more truthful account of that frigid night than if he had bundled up to protect his body from the cold. He was probably wrong, but who are we to question the enthusiasm of a twenty-two-year-old boy burning to test his will against the elements? Crane was living the adventure of being himself, and the emotional value of such an act (courting pneumonia in order to write the best story possible) should not be discounted, for by passing the test he had imposed on himself, he had won an inner victory, and victories produce confidence, and confidence produces better and stronger work.

He did it again the following month, upping the ante to leap into another adventure with the down-and-outs of the city that didn't last hours this time but four days and three nights. Along with one of his artist roommates, William Carroll, Crane set out to explore lowlife Bowery haunts ranging from seven-cent flophouses to bottom-of-the-barrel free-lunch saloons, to mingle with the drifters, drunks, and panhandlers in order to learn something about their world, which meant standing in their shoes both figuratively and literally, and for that reason the two young men ditched their everyday clothes and dressed as bums before going underground to live as bums themselves—launching out on their mission as if they were secret agents in disguise. Carroll had a thoroughly unhappy time of it, but in a short piece written thirty years later, he recalled that while he found sleep all but impossible in the squalid lodging houses where they spent the nights, Crane "slept like a healthy baby," a sign of how quickly he had adapted to his new circumstances—

and how deeply he had immersed himself in the project. Emile Stangé, an artist friend who happened to drop in at Linson's studio just after Crane and Carroll returned from their skid row escapade, remembered the moment in a subsequent letter to Linson:

> It was a fearful day in March, raining "cats-and-dogs," wind in the northeast, cold and miserable. What I was doing out I can't imagine, but anyway, I drifted up to the studio to find Crane and another just arrived, both in rags, no overcoats, clothes all holes, toes out of their shoes, no umbrellas (of course not), and soaked to the skin, water dripping in pools about them. I noticed Crane's rather flat chest was shaking every little while with the spasms of a very hollow cough. His blond hair was matted over his eyes. A great wave of pity swept over me; I thought, "My lord! Has it come to this?" Crane, as though sensing my unspoken thought, looked at me and grinned, and you explained that they had been doing the Bowery on some assignment. I reproved Crane for taking chances with the cold he had, which he made light of. They were getting the color of tramp life.

Two versions of "An Experiment in Misery" appeared in Crane's lifetime, the newspaper version published in the *Press* (April 22, 1894) and the book version that was included in *The Open Boat and Other Tales of Adventure*, published in 1898. Crane uses a framing device to begin and end the piece in the first version but drops those passages in the second, and while losing the device makes sense (especially for a collection of short stories), it also robs the title of its meaning. The second, shorter version of the sketch is the only one that appears in books today, but in order to understand Crane's original intentions when he set out to conduct his experiment with Carroll, it helps to know what is in the missing passages.

Two men stood regarding a tramp.
"I wonder how he feels," said one, reflectively. "I suppose he is homeless, friendless, and has, at the most, only a few cents in his pocket. And if this is so, I wonder how he feels."
The other being older, spoke with an air of authoritative wisdom. "You can tell nothing of it unless you are in that condition yourself. It is idle to speculate about it from this distance."
"I suppose so," said the younger man, and then he added as from an inspiration: "I think I'll try it. Rags and tatters, you know, a couple of

dimes, and hungry, too, if possible. Perhaps I could discover his point of view or something near it."

"Well, you might," said the other, and from those words begins this veracious narrative of an experiment in misery.

The prologue continues with the young man going off to the studio of an artist friend, where he outfits himself in a hobo costume ("an aged suit and a brown derby hat that had been made long years before"), and then he disappears into the city to find an answer to his question. At that point, the first half of the framing device comes to an end, and for the next ten pages both versions of the story are identical—until the last page, when the two friends meet up again and the older one asks the younger one if he has discovered the tramp's point of view. The young one isn't sure, he says, but if nothing else, he now feels that his own point of view "has undergone a considerable alteration." In what way he doesn't tell, but that is the final sentence of Crane's experiment, and his readers are left to decide for themselves.

The frame gives a context for the title, and without it the story becomes a slightly different story—neither better nor worse, it seems to me, just different. In the newspaper version, the young man is presented as an inquiring philosopher, a seeker. In the book version, which more closely resembles a short story, the young man is presented as someone newly down on his luck, a greenhorn who has just been dealt a wretched hand by the cards of circumstance—homeless, nearly penniless, destitute. Either proposition will serve, but the essential thing to note about the story—in both versions—is that Carroll has been eliminated, which only goes to prove (again) that a sketch is not a piece of journalism as we would define it today but a separate, mongrel form of writing that is driven by journalistic impulses but at the same time adheres to the methods of fiction. Crane takes liberties with his source material because he is free to do so, and rather than write the "veracious narrative" of two young men lamming out to live among the downtrodden, he gets rid of one of them and confines himself to a single narrative perspective. It makes for a better, more concentrated story, and the overall truth of that story (minus Carroll) was confirmed by Carroll himself in his recollections from 1924 with a myriad of corroborating details, even down to the tiresome motormouth tramp who gloms onto the protagonist and clings to him throughout much of the printed sketch. "We knocked around with him and watched him panhandle several promising passersby. He steered us into some sleeping places. Finally he got so friendly he became a nuisance, and we shook him."

True to the fictional possibilities of the form he is working in, as well as to his own firmly ingrained writerly instincts, Crane tells the story in the third person, turning himself into "the youth" (yet one more character without a name), who is first shown as a solitary figure adrift in New York, walking along in the rain one night as he goes forth "to eat as the wanderer may eat, and sleep as the homeless sleep." There is no plot to the narrative, simply a succession of incidents, but the writing is acute and measured, far more under control than the hypercharged, frenetic, and sometimes overwritten sentences in *Maggie*, an advance gained from the new lessons of style he had been teaching himself while working on the still unfinished *Red Badge*, but his gift for translating the visual world into sharp, instantly seeable word-pictures continues to animate his prose: "Two rivers of people swarmed along the side-walks, spattered with black mud, which made each shoe leave a scar-like impression. Overhead elevated trains with a shrill grinding of the wheels stopped at the station, which upon its leg-like pillars seemed to resemble some monstrous kind of crab squatting over the street."

After wandering into a saloon advertising "Free hot soup to-night," the young man downs a bowl with "little floating suggestions of chicken" in it and then goes outside again, where he is approached by a rumpled, oddly dressed character who resembles "an assassin steeped in crimes performed awkwardly"—the pain-in-the-neck tramp mentioned by Carroll, henceforth referred to as "the assassin," a man given to such long-winded chatter that one of his explanations comes across as "so profound that it was unintelligible." After wheedling a few pennies out of the young man, he guides him to a seven-cent flophouse where they both spend the night, an experience that Crane plumbs fully by drawing on his own experiences of such places, but all the experience in the world won't help a writer unless he can write well, and the best writing of the piece is in the long middle section as Crane tells his story through the eyes (and nose and ears) of the young man, beginning with the "strange and unspeakable odors that assailed him like malignant diseases with wings," and four paragraphs later, "as the young man's eyes became used to the darkness he could see upon the cots that thickly littered the floor the forms of men sprawled out, lying in death-like silence or heaving and snoring with tremendous effort, like stabbed fish," and four paragraphs after that:

> And all through the room could be seen the tawny hues of naked flesh, limbs thrust into the darkness, projecting beyond the cots; up-reared knees; arms hanging, long and thin, over the cot edges. For the most part

Photograph of Crane by C. K. Linson, 1894.
(COURTESY OF SYRACUSE UNIVERSITY)

they were statuesque, carven, dead. With the curious lockers standing all about like tombstones there was a strange effect of a graveyard, where bodies were merely flung.

A couple of times, Crane comes closer to explicit social commentary than is usual for him, but the remarks are not presented as statements of fact so much as the musings of the young man, lying awake in the dark as he listens to the howls and shrieks of someone in the grip of a terrifying nightmare. "But to the youth these were not merely the shrieks of a vision pierced man. They were . . . the protest of a wretch who feels the touch of the imperturbable granite wheels and who then cries with an impersonal eloquence, with a strength not from him, giving voice to the wail of a whole section, a class, a people."

Impersonal eloquence is a profound, even transcendent idea, as is *a strength not from him*, but neither one is immediately graspable and requires some time and thought before it can be understood, yet Crane can indulge in this short lyric burst about the invisible solidarity that links the oppressed of the world to one another without disrupting his forward progress because the sketch as a whole is so thoroughly grounded in the tactile this-ness of bodily life. The next morning, for example, when the young man and the assassin sit down at the counter of a dimly lit restaurant to drink their two-cent bowls of coffee, the bowls and spoons are given the same degree of attention that Crane lavished on the men in the flophouse. "The bowls were webbed with brown seams, and the tin spoons wore an air of having emerged from the first pyramid. Upon them were black, moss-like encrustations of age, and they were bent and scarred from the attacks of long forgotten teeth." This is funny stuff, and further evidence of the dry wit that punctuates even the darkest of Crane's works, but embedded in the humor there is also something that tallies with the young man's earlier reflections about "impersonal eloquence" and "the wail of . . . a class, a people," for the bowls and spoons in restaurants are not the property of any one person, they are shared objects that temporarily belong to all the people who use them, one person after another over the years, a sort of common property passed from hand to hand and mouth to mouth and life to life, and at a moment in American history when so few had so much and so many had so little, the young man's thoughts at the close of the piece are precisely about this sense of shared life. He is back where he started at the beginning, sitting with the assassin on a bench in City Hall Park, feeling cut off from the prosperous people hustling past him on "important missions," understanding that they represent "his infinite distance from all that he valued," namely "social position, comfort, the pleasures of living," in other words, his sense of belonging to a world shared with others, and then, in the penultimate paragraph, Crane, still speaking through the thoughts of the young man, who is none other than Crane himself, delivers one of his severest indictments of money-driven America's contempt for the ones who have fallen by the wayside. "And in the background a multitude of buildings, of pitiless hues and sternly high, were to him emblematic of a nation forcing its regal head into the clouds, throwing no downward glances; in the sublimity of its aspirations ignoring the wretches who may flounder at its feet."

There were no more coatless treks into blizzards after that, no more masquerades or clandestine missions to rub shoulders with the beaten and dispossessed of the Bowery. Crane was not altogether down and out himself, perhaps, but the year and a half he had spent in New York had provided him with his own experiment in misery, and with Marshall willing to pay for any subject he chose to explore (however paltry the sums might have been), Crane pushed on with newspaper work until his departure for the West in January, publishing ten more sketches and four short stories in the Sunday edition of the *Press*, an interview with Howells for the *New York Times* ("Howells Fears the Realists Must Wait") along with a couple of other short stories that appeared in monthly magazines, and not one of those efforts is dull or pedestrian, there are a few that blaze, a few that bristle and poke fun, but all of them count, both the lesser and the greater, since they all belong to the explosion of work that came rushing out of Crane's head in that frantic, life-changing year of 1894.

By early spring, the two most important projects of that year were already behind him. Not just the war novel, which would remain hidden from the world for the next eighteen months, but the poems of *The Black Riders* as well—the two works that would establish his reputation as a prose writer and a poet. No one knew what he had accomplished yet, but the twenty-two-year-old Crane must have understood that he was no longer a beginner and that all doors had been opened. In the ten New York sketches that followed, everything was suddenly there for him, and no subject was too large or too small to capture his attention. From one piece to the next, he moves from the tragic to the boisterously comic, from high-speed action to languorous rumination, and when looked upon as a whole, these little works present a showcase of the various methods that were now at Crane's disposal to convey different moods and tones, sometimes by working in a style of short declarative sentences, sometimes spiraling forward in sinuously elongated periods, but the one thing these approaches have in common is Crane's consistent energy and the extreme internal pressure continually boiling within his prose, as if the sentences were about to burst their seams and fly out into the air as weapons. Here he is in one of his several incarnations, describing the hectic atmosphere of a large, crowded restaurant "during the noon-hour rush":

> Meanwhile the waiters dashed about the room as if a monster pursued them and they sought escape wildly though the walls. It was like the scattering and scampering of a lot of water bugs, when one splashes the surface of the brook with a pebble. Withal, they carried incredible masses of dishes and threaded their swift ways with rare skill. Perspiration stood upon their foreheads, and their breaths came strainedly. They served customers with such speed and violence that it often resembled a personal assault. The crumbs from the previous diner were swept off with one

fierce motion of a napkin. A waiter struck two blows at the table and left there a knife and a fork. And then came the viands in a volley, thumped down in haste, causing men to look sharp to see if their trousers were safe. ("In a Park Row Restaurant")

And here he is in a more reflective frame of mind, putting his words in the mouth of an imaginary, self-anointed philosopher who is wandering through the mostly empty grounds of Coney Island at the end of the season, dispensing his thoughts to the narrator:

"See those three young men enjoying themselves. With what rakish, daredevil airs they smoke those cigars. Do you know, the spectacle of three modern young men enjoying themselves is something that I find vastly interesting and instructive. I see revealed more clearly the purposes of the inexorable universe which plans to amuse us occasionally to keep us from the rebellion of suicide. And I see how simply and drolly it accomplishes its end. The insertion of a mild quantity of the egotism of sin into the minds of these young men causes them to wildly enjoy themselves. It is necessary to encourage them, you see, at this early day. After all, it is only great philosophers who have the wisdom to be utterly miserable." ("Coney Island's Failing Days")

Finally, here he is observing the imagined fire mentioned several pages earlier—yet one more modulation in tone. This passage immediately follows Crane's description of a woman who has run out of her burning building with a bamboo easel worth about thirty cents but has left her baby inside. Now that she has come to her senses and understands what she has done, she is raving hysterically in the street. A policeman has just rushed into the house to rescue the baby, but to add to the confusion of the moment, the reader is never told if he comes out or not.

Occasionally the woman screamed again. Another policeman was fending her off from the house, which she wished to enter in the frenzy of her motherhood, regardless of the flames. These people in the neighborhood, aroused from their beds, looked at the spectacle in a half-dazed fashion at times, as if they were contemplating the ravings of a red beast in a cage. The flames grew as if fanned by tempests, a sweeping, inexorable appetite of a thing, shining, with fierce, pitiless brilliancy, gleaming in the eyes of the crowd that were upturned to it in an ecstasy of awe, fear and, too, half barbaric admiration. They felt the human helplessness

that comes when nature breaks forth in passion, overturning the obstacles, emerging at a leap from the position of a slave to that of a master,
a giant. ("The Fire")

The flexibility of mood, tone, and style allows him to range freely among
his various subjects and zero in on whatever happens to grab his attention
on a particular day. The first article he wrote for the *Press*, "An Experiment in
Misery," could therefore be followed by a one-hundred-and-eighty-degree
turnaround published one week later, "An Experiment in Luxury," which
takes the young man from the previous sketch on another social investigation and plunks him down in a New York mansion for a dinner with the
family of one of his friends, Jack, the son of a millionaire. No doubt inspired
by Crane's visits to the Brandon household during his courtship of Lily, it is
a subtle, gently mocking piece that discusses the house and "its cool abun-
dance of gloom," the assorted people who inhabit the place (the snobbish
footman who answers the door, the millionaire father who plays with a
kitten throughout dinner, the rigidly correct mother—whose "features were
as lined and creased with care and worriment as those of an apple woman.
It was as if the passing of each social obligation, of each binding form of her
life had left its footprints, scarring her face"—as well as the three daughters,
described as "adorable," but "it would have been a wonder to him if he had
not found them charming, since making themselves so could but be their
principal occupation)," and the young man's conflicted feelings about the
wealth that surrounds him (surprisingly attractive but also repellent), as
when he is talking before dinner to the easygoing, warmhearted Jack and
begins to see that they are "chatting with no more responsibility than rabbits, when certainly there were men, equally fine perhaps, who were being
blackened and mashed in the churning life of the lower places," but also,
in spite of himself, how much he revels in the comfortable surroundings:
"It was delicious to feel so high and mighty, to feel that the unattainable
could be purchased like a penny bun. For a time, at any rate, there was no
impossible. He indulged in monarchical reflections." That is the strength of
this little work—its ambivalence, which is to say, its honesty. As the older
friend comments to the young man at the beginning, with droll and cutting
irony: "Nobody is to blame for anything. I wish to Heaven somebody was,
and then we could all jump on him."

Crane wandered to the New York piers one morning that spring to
watch a steamship set sail for Europe, which led to the short, unusually
touching "Sailing Day Scenes," yet another sketch written in a different key
as he observes friends and family saying good-bye to their loved ones ("It

was surprising to see how full of expression the face of a blunt, every day American business man could become"), noting the tears falling from the eyes of women and the cries of a little boy calling, "Oh, papa! Papa! Here I am!" and then, as the ship departs, the "great tumult of farewells, a song of affection that swelled into a vast incoherent roar," proving that the tough-minded, unsentimental Crane was tough enough not to squirm in the presence of deeply felt human emotion. After a break during the summer, he returned to New York and began cranking out more pieces for Marshall, on average two or three a month, including the brilliant, acerbic "Coney Island's Failing Days" and the rambunctious mayhem depicted in the Park Row restaurant sketch, traveled back in spirit if not in person to his old stomping grounds on the Jersey Shore to write two straight-faced, tongue-in-cheek accounts of the legendary revenants and specters who prowl the sands at night ("Ghosts of the New Jersey Coast" and "The Ghostly Sphinx of Metedeconk"), composed the text that Marshall called "one of the best things that he or any other man ever did," now called "The Fire" but published as "When Every One Is Panic Stricken," changed gears with a little romp about a bumbling, incoherent drunk who boards a New York streetcar ("A Lovely Jag in a Crowded Car"), and, in December, turned out one of the best of the lot, "When Man Falls, a Crowd Gathers," which recounts the story of a man and a boy, both of them Italian immigrants, who are walking along the street one day when the man suddenly falls to the ground with an epileptic seizure. In no time at all, a crowd gathers around them, and as with the anonymous neighbors in "The Fire," who stop everything to watch the blaze and the screaming woman, this crowd is drawn to the man "in a spell of fascination. They seemed scarcely to breathe. They were contemplating the depth into which a human being had sunk and this mystery of life or death held them chained. Occasionally from the rear, a man came thrusting his way impetuously, satisfied that there was a horror to be seen and apparently insane to get a view of it. Less curious persons swore at these men when they trod upon their toes."

The crowd and the individual. If there is anything that binds these disparate pieces together, it is that all the events Crane describes are witnessed by others, most of them in cluttered public spaces (a flophouse, a restaurant, a streetcar, an amusement park, a wide-open city street), and that when crowds begin to gather, the mentality of the group tends to obliterate the individual, and the larger the crowd, the more socially complex the scene becomes. Horror strikes, or sorrow, or mass confusion, but there are men who work with those situations every day, and unlike the people in the crowd, they are unaffected by them. In "Sailing Day Scenes":

"A pompous officer, obviously vain of his clothes, strode before the agitated faces upon the ship and looked complacently at the pier. It was an old story to him, and he thought it rather silly." The concluding sentences of "The Fire": "A fireman . . . wore a blasé air. They all, in fact, seemed to look at fires with the calm, unexcited vision of veterans. It was only the populace with their new nerves, it seemed, who could feel the thrill and dash of these attacks, these furious charges made in the dead of night, at high noon, at any time, upon the common enemy, the loosened flame." In "When Man Falls, a Crowd Gathers": "Then a policeman appeared. . . . He shouted: 'Come, make way there! Make way!' He was evidently a man whose life was half-pestered out of him by the inhabitants of the city who were sufficiently unreasonable and stupid as to insist on being in the streets. His was the rage of a placid cow, who wishes to lead a life of tranquility, but who is eternally besieged by flies that hover in clouds."

Crane was neither pompous nor a cow, but the attitude of those professional guardians of the peace was essentially no different from the attitude of the writer. Stay calm, keep a close eye on what is happening around you, and no matter how ugly or horrible or violent the situation you find yourself in might be, it must not prevent you from doing your duty. Crane's self-imposed duty was to write, and in order to "approach the nearest to nature and truth," he had to stand back from what he was seeing and take it in without prejudice, purging himself of all preconceived notions about human behavior, no matter if he was writing about a dinner at a millionaire's house or a crush of people gawking at a man stretched out on the pavement in the throes of an epileptic fit. In other words, for Crane to fulfill his duty as a writer, he had to disappear into the shadows and, to whatever extent he could, make himself invisible.

Then came the experiment of standing in a crowd on a night of high drama, of slipping like a phantom in among the people and listening to what they said and recording their words in his notebook, breaking down the mass into its component parts and turning the jumbled horde into a collection of individuals—no longer a chorus singing in unison but a multitude of individual voices, each one singing its own song at the same time as all the others. It was Election Night, November 1894; the city had just gone to the polls, and hundreds or thousands were milling around in front of the *Press* building as the paper used an industrial-strength magic lantern to project the steadily mounting returns on the façade of a building across the street. Not for the first time (or the last time), it was a period of corruption and scandal in New York politics, but after a ten-thousand-page report issued by the Lexow Committee had exposed the depth of that corruption as practiced by the reigning Tammany Hall Democrats, a ticket of reformist Republicans swept the election, with Levi P. Morton ousting David Bennett Hill as governor, William L. Strong defeating incumbent Hugh J. Grant for mayor, and John W. Goff winning as city recorder. Crane's piece, "Heard on the Street Election Night," carried three sub-headlines when it was first published in the *Press*, and not only do they capture the fervor of the moment, they tell us much about the tone of American journalism in that late Victorian period known as the Naughty Nineties: "Passing Remarks Gathered in Front of 'The Press' Stereopticon / HOW THEY TOOK THE GOOD NEWS / Human Nature Had Full Swing Tuesday Evening." Forty-four snippets of transcribed dialogue followed, among them these examples:

"Hully chee! Everything's dumped!"*

"Can you tell me, please, if the returns indicate that Goff has a chance?"

"Who? Goff? Well, I guess! He's running like a race-horse. He's dead in it."

"Say, that magic lantern man is a big fakir. Lookatim pushin' ads in on us. Hey, take that out, will yeh? You ain't no billposter, are yeh?"

"Well, I guess nit. If Hill wins this time, he's got to have ice-boats on his feet. He ain't got a little chance."

> "Down in Fourteenth street,
> "Hear that mournful sound;
> "All the Indians are a-weeping,
> "Davie's in the cold, cold ground."

"If Tammany wins this time, we might as well all quit the town and go to Camden. If we don't beat 'em now, we're a lot of duffers and we're only fit to stuff mattresses with."

---

* "Hully chee": slang for "Holy Jesus."

"He won't, hey? You just wait, me boy. If Hill can't carry this State at any time in any year, I'll make you a present of the Brooklyn bridge, and paint it a deep purple with gold stripes, all by myself."

Well, this is what comes from monkeyin' with the people. You think you've got 'em all under a board when, first thing you know, they come out and belt you in the neck."

"Hully chee!
"Who are we?
"The men who did up Tammanee!"

"'Eternal vigilance is the price of liberty.' That's what it is. The people lost their liberty because they went to sleep. Then all of a sudden they wake up and slug around and surprise all of the men who thought they were in a trance. They ought to have done it long ago. And now they are awake, they don't want to do a thing but sit up night and day and lay for robbers. This waking up every ten or twelve years gives me a pain."

"There was never a doubt of it. No, sir. It was playing a sure thing from start to finish. I tell you, when the avalanche starts, you want to climb a hill near by and put all your money on the avalanche."

"Tammany's in the soup."

The vox populi set loose in all its unexpurgated vigor—and no doubt one of the first "man in the street" documents ever published. Daring and entertaining as it is, however, to call this article a piece of journalism would probably be a stretch (because there are no named sources, which leaves Crane open to the charge that he invented the whole thing), and yet to call it a work of art would be something of a stretch as well. Perhaps it shares qualities of both, journalism-as-art, if you will, or art in the service of journalism, and then again, perhaps it doesn't matter how we choose to define it. What jumps out from the page is an effervescent effusion of lived life, the raw data collected one November evening in New York City and then shaped into a forty-four-part piece of splendid, cacophonous music. Stephen Crane in the crowd but not of the crowd, an invisible man watching *human nature in full swing*.

13

THE METAPHYSICS OF FEAR.

The most celebrated war novel in our literature is not a book about war so much as an examination of the effects of war on a young, undeveloped mind, a work that Crane himself would call in retrospect "a psychological portrayal of fear." A proper war novel would tell us why the war was being fought, who was fighting whom, where the fighting was taking place, and delve into such matters as politics, military strategy, and morale on the home front, but all these indispensable facts—the foundation of every other nineteenth-century war novel—are withheld in *The Red Badge of Courage*. As he did in *Maggie*, Crane strips out everything that is not pertinent to the story he means to tell. As in earlier works of his, such as "The Broken-Down Van" and "The Pace of Youth," the story is framed within a single, severely limited narrative perspective, in this case the eyes, ears, and thoughts of the protagonist. And as with the even earlier Sullivan County cycle, the work is set in a haunted landscape of vast, overarching skies, towering trees, hilly, uneven ground, perpetually shifting light, rivers, open fields, the obscuring smoke of gunfire, and dark, labyrinthine woods—demonic realms stalked by a phantom army of invisible dragons. Covering just a handful of days from beginning to end, the action unfolds in the middle of the American Civil War, and yet there is not one mention of Abraham Lincoln or the struggle to preserve the Union, not a single word about slavery, and the generals in charge of the North's humiliating defeat at Chancellorsville are not once identified by name or even so much as referred to in passing, but still, against this eerily blank canvas, the war is everywhere, the war is everything and therefore the only thing in the book, not just the background but the foreground and the entire middle ground as well, and a novel that is not strictly speaking a war novel presents us with a world in which every particle of space is suffused with war. Until Crane, no author in the English language had ever attempted such an audacious reduction of elements—to compose a novel of war with no digressions or subplots, without the sentimental trappings of a love story hovering in the wings, and confine himself solely to the combat waged by the foot soldiers in the ranks, to that and nothing else. It is a new kind of war novel, then, a novel that concerns itself not with the large matter of a country torn apart into two countries, two armies, two warring cultures, but the small matter of one man's role in the conflict, a man who is in fact a boy, a mere adolescent tossed into battle for the first time.

His age is never given, but he appears to be around sixteen, seventeen at the most. He is referred to as *the youth*. His closest young comrade is *the loud soldier*, and his most admired older comrade is *the tall soldier*. They all have names, but the unseen, third-person narrator never uses them, and we learn that they are Henry Fleming, Wilson, and Jim Conklin only when we hear them address one another during their two-way and three-way conversations. We also learn that they come from the same rural town in upstate New York and have known one another for years. Two other significant characters have no names at all and are referred to simply as *the tattered soldier* and *the man of the cheery voice*, whereas a number of minor characters in the regiment do have names (revealed in overheard conversations among other soldiers) but no substantial role to play in the story. Except for their names, they are little more than ciphers, suggestions, murky splotches dotting the canvas. Similarly, some passing remarks made by still other nameless soldiers include the words *Richmond, Washington*, and *the Rappahannock*, which obliquely situate us in the Civil War, along with comments about *rebs* and *Johnnies* (Confederate soldiers) and repeated references to the color of the soldiers' uniforms, gray and blue, which not only point to the war in question but help emphasize the primacy of color in this color-abundant work. Crane uses those random snatches of dialogue to ground the action in a precise when and where, but they are no more than hints, evanescent words that do not affect the overpowering aura of timelessness that runs through the book. Just as the New York City in *Maggie* is both a real New York and a mythological New York, the war in *The Red Badge of Courage* is both anchored in a particular historical moment (1863) and utterly outside it. The battles are real, of course, but the only one that counts is the battle Henry fights with himself.

There are just three elements in this book of vastly reduced elements, but Crane manages to juggle them and weave them together and butt them up against one another with such assurance and skill that the narrative energy of the story never flags. As I was preparing to write this chapter, I picked up the novel again and started going through it for the umpteenth time, determined to note down everything I found to be essential in each paragraph. After four chapters, I had covered twenty-six pages with my small, knotted handwriting and understood that if I carried on with the exercise through all twenty-four chapters of the book, my notes would be as long if not longer than Crane's novel. Rather than persist in burrowing down that rabbit hole, I abandoned the notebook and continued my reading with a blue pencil, underlining every sentence that struck me as important. By the time I came to the end, almost a third of the sentences were underscored in blue. Which is to say: *The Red Badge of Courage* is a book of such extreme compression that every paragraph is essential. There is no slack in it, no superfluous material, no passage that diverts one's attention from the essence of the story. That is why the book caused such a stir in 1895 and why it has never been out of print in the 125 years since then. Not so much because of the story it tells but because of how the story is told.

The three principal elements Crane draws upon to construct his book are the landscape, Henry's fellow soldiers, and the thoughts inside Henry's head. A fourth, mostly hidden element is the narrator's voice, the guiding intelligence that has elected to call Henry *the youth* and not Henry, for example, and that intervenes in the first and last paragraphs of the novel, but nearly everything else that happens is filtered through Henry's panicked, impressionable mind, creating a closed-in world of such radical subjectivity that the distinction between what is real and not real is often blurred, so blurred at times that the story begins to feel as if it is the account of a waking dream—or an out-and-out hallucination.

By *landscape*, I mean everything that surrounds Henry's body, everything he can perceive with his eyes, ears, nose, mouth, and skin, everything that is not Henry himself: the near prospect, the far prospect, the men from the two armies—both living and dead—along with the sights and sounds of battle:

> Once he saw a tiny battery go dashing along the line of the horizon. The tiny riders were beating the tiny horses.
>
> From a sloping hill came the sound of cheerings and clashes. Smoke welled slowly through the leaves.
>
> Batteries were speaking with thunderous oratorical effect. Here and there were flags, the red in the stripes dominating. They splashed bits of warm color upon the dark lines of troops. . . .
>
> As he listened to the din from the hillside, to a deep pulsing thunder that came from afar to the left, and to the lesser clamors which came from many directions, it occurred to him that they were fighting, too, over there, and over there, and over there. Heretofore he had supposed that all the battle was directly under his nose.
>
> As he gazed around him the youth felt a flash of astonishment at the blue, pure sky and the sun gleamings on the trees and fields. It was surprising that Nature had gone tranquilly on with her golden process in the midst of so much devilment.

This passage is an exemplary instance of the method Crane employs throughout the book. Henry sees the battery, the riders, and the horses as "tiny" because they are in the far distance and therefore seem exceedingly small from his point of view. The cannons and guns speak "with thunderous oratorical effect" not because weapons can talk but because Henry imagines they are talking. And now that he has been put in a position to observe a wider swath of activity than before, he understands that the fighting is everywhere, not just directly in front of him—a corrective made possible by his new vantage point—and with that greater understanding, he is awed by the fact that the sky is still blue and the sun is still shining even as slaughter reigns on the ground below.

Another instance, as Henry comes across a fallen enemy for the first time:

> Once the line encountered the body of a dead soldier. He lay upon his back staring at the sky. He was dressed in an awkward suit of yellowish brown. The youth could see that the soles of his shoes had been worn to the thinness of writing paper, and from a great rent in one the dead foot protruded piteously. And it was as if fate had betrayed the soldier. In death it exposed to his enemies that poverty which in life he had perhaps concealed from his friends.
>
> The ranks opened covertly to avoid the corpse. The invulnerable dead man forced a way for himself. The youth looked keenly at the ashen face. The wind raised the tawny beard. It moved as if a hand were stroking it. He vaguely desired to walk around and around the body and stare; the impulse of the living to try to read in dead eyes the answer to the Question.

By contrast, the second element—what I would term *Henry's fellow soldiers*—is filled with dialogue and the rough-and-tumble interactions of a regiment that is forced to march here, march there, then march back to here, all for no apparent reason until the decisive moment falls on them at last. These are the lowly men in the ranks who do what they are told without understanding why they are doing it, and at that moment in the war the 304th is composed of some veterans and a gang of fresh, young troops like Henry who have not yet been tested in battle as the book begins. Grumbling, confused, speculative, and joking, the verbal exchanges between and among the soldiers keep the story firmly rooted in the now of lived experience and prevent it from floating off into the less vivid territories of parable and fable. Their speech is rude and demotic, undercutting the more elevated language of the descriptive passages, and by shifting from one tone to another, Crane propels the narrative forward in a whirl of small, unexpected jolts. One moment, Henry is looking out at the landscape, and the next moment someone is talking, either to him or someone else. A good example of what that talk sounds like comes early in the text, when Henry asks Jim Conklin if he thinks any of the boys will run when the shooting starts. The tall soldier replies:

> "Oh, there may be a few of 'em run, but there's them kind in every regiment, 'specially when they first goes under fire.... Of course it might happen that the hull kit-and-boodle might start and run, if some big fighting came first-off, and then again they might stay and fight like fun. But you can't bet on nothing. Of course they ain't never been under fire yet, and it ain't likely they'll lick the hull rebel army all-to-oncet the first time; but I think they'll fight better than some, if worse than others. That's the way I figger."

At times, Crane clusters together long sequences of random, anonymous exchanges among the men, isolated fragments filled with rumors, gossip, and nervous chatter, all of it set down in the colloquial dialogue of Northern country speech, a mass of disembodied voices that gives human texture to the small society the youth belongs to, just as the dead and nameless Confederate soldier is granted his own humanity in the description of his worn out, paper-thin shoes. An army is a vast, multiheaded creature in which the individual is swallowed up and depersonalized by the organism as a whole, but by turning his attention to the voices produced by those heads or by fixing his eyes on the heads themselves ("the wind raised the tawny beard"), Crane is forcing us to remember that each one of those heads belongs to a man and that each man is distinct from every other man, an island unto himself, with his own history and his own separate consciousness.

The third element, *the thoughts inside Henry's head*, is the story of one such consciousness, and it is the heart of the novel, the element that distinguishes the book from other war stories and turns it into something that transcends its own setting (the battlefield) to become a drama about consciousness itself. As with Knut Hamsun's *Hunger*, *The Red Badge of Courage* is an end-of-the-century anticipation of a new aesthetic that would begin to take hold in the first decades of the next century and lead to such works as *Ulysses*, *Remembrance of Things Past*, *As I Lay Dying*, *To the Lighthouse*, and numerous other novels grounded in what I would call *a passionate interiority* that aspires to explore the *within* of its thinking, feeling subjects. I would not argue that Henry Fleming prefigures Leopold Bloom, precisely, but rather that Crane's preoccupation with the inner workings of his protagonist's mind shares many of the same impulses that drove Joyce to dig so deeply into the brain-works of his impotent, meandering hero. One book is short, the other is long. The action in the short book covers several days, the action in the long book begins and ends in just one day, but both books, remarkably, are written in the third person. Contrary to popular wisdom, intimate access does not demand an authorial *I*. *He*, as both writers prove, can do the job just as well.

Crane's *he* is a callow, self-absorbed, acutely sensitive boy endowed with a certain degree of intelligence and thoughtfulness, someone with the ability to understand when he is lying to himself but who nevertheless goes on lying whenever his actions do not measure up to the standards of conduct he perceives in others, dismissing his errors in a long chain of self-serving excuses that are twisted into supposedly rational justifications for his less than honorable behavior. His is an adolescent mind, and Crane, not far removed from his own adolescence, explores its looping trajectories, devious manipulations, and scalding anxieties with such full-bore precision as to make his study of that mind—that adolescent mind—the true subject of his book.

The first chapter presents all three elements in rapid succession and within a few short pages establishes the tone, methods, and procedures of what is to follow. Before the action begins, however, there is the mysterious opening paragraph, written in the neutral voice of the invisible narrator, a complex description of a landscape that seems to be talking about two things at the same time: the passage from night into day and then back to night as well as the passage from winter into spring:

> The cold passed reluctantly from the earth, and the retiring fogs revealed an army stretched out on the hills, resting. As the landscape changed from brown to green, the army awakened, and began to tremble with eagerness at the noise of rumors. It cast its eyes upon the roads, which were growing from long troughs of liquid mud to proper thoroughfares. A river, amber-tinted in the shadow of its banks, purled at the army's feet; and at night, when the stream had become of a sorrowful blackness, one could see across it the red, eyelike gleam of hostile camp-fires set in the low brows of distant hills.

The animism from the Sullivan County tales is back in full force: cold *reluctantly* passing from the earth; an army casts *its* eyes upon the roads, rather than the soldiers in the army casting *their* eyes, as if an army were indeed a single, multiheaded animal; *sorrowful* blackness; the red, *eyelike* gleam of fires; and the *brows* of distant hills. As for the question of time,

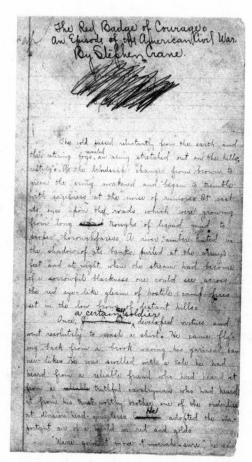

The first page of the manuscript of The Red Badge of Courage.
The original title, Private Fleming/His Various Battles, *has been crossed out.*
(COURTESY OF THE UNIVERSITY OF VIRGINIA)

Crane offers two parallel and simultaneous situations, and as the cold lifts and the fogs dissipate in the first sentence to reveal "an army stretched out on the hills, resting," one's first inclination is to assume it is morning and the men ("stretched out . . . resting"—that is, recumbent and asleep) are about to wake up. And yet the other, parallel reading would suggest that the reluctance of the cold to pass from the earth signifies the end of a long, protracted winter, that "stretched out" refers to the army as a whole camped in the hills, not the individual soldiers, and that "resting" does not refer to sleep but to an absence of activity, to an army waiting to be called into battle. The second sentence, with the landscape changing "from brown to green," is equally ambiguous, equally double, for the darkness of night eliminates color, and as the first traces of dawn begin to infuse the sky, black land turns to a dim gray-brown before turning green when the sun comes up, but at the same time this movement from brown to green can also denote the transition from winter to spring. In the same sentence, the word "awakened" can also be read both ways, literally awaking from sleep and figuratively becoming conscious of impending action, and "the noise of rumors" could be the words circulating among the men that morning or a general stir of anticipation that has been percolating for days or perhaps even weeks. Roads of liquid mud turning solid is not the work of a single night, however, but part of a longer, slower process, and yet by using the gerund "were growing" instead of "had grown," Crane is telling us that the process is still going on and that the roads are more solid today than they were yesterday. Then, in the final sentence, everything spins around and suddenly changes direction, for once Crane mentions the river that separates the encampment of this army from the encampment of the other, he heads back into an evocation of night—not just one night but every night—to reveal the menace that lurks in the hills across the water, "the red, eyelike gleam of hostile camp-fires," in other words, the many eyes of another multiheaded animal: the enemy.

The stage has been set, but no sooner have we adjusted to the tonalities of the first paragraph than Crane abruptly shifts to another tone in the second with a small bit of comic irony, which introduces us to the second element of the book.

Once a certain tall soldier developed virtues and went resolutely to wash a shirt. He came back from a brook waving his garment bannerlike. He was swelled with a tale he had heard from a reliable friend, who had heard it from a truthful cavalryman, who had heard it from his trustworthy brother, one of the orderlies at division headquarters. He adopted the important air of a herald in red and gold.

"We're goin' t' move t'morrah—sure," he said pompously to a group in the company street. "We're goin' way up the river, cut across, an' come around in behint 'em."

First, the vastly inflated, self-mocking rhetoric that attaches "virtues" to the simple act of washing a shirt, then a witty postmortem on the serpentine paths by which rumors travel, and after that a full page is given to the competing opinions of various unidentified soldiers about this fresh rumor, one of dozens that have sprung up over the past several weeks as the members of the company have languished on their hillside, restless and out of sorts. "The blue-clothed men scattered into small arguing groups. . . . A negro teamster [the only black person in the book] who had been dancing upon a cracker box with the hilarious encouragement of twoscore soldiers was deserted. He sat mournfully down. . . . 'It's a lie! That's all it is—a thunderin' lie!' said another private loudly," one who defends his position so vociferously that he nearly comes to blows with Jim Conklin as the other men continue to assault Jim with questions and "engaged in spirited debate." It is a spirited passage as well, and after just a few short paragraphs Crane has managed to thrust the reader into the thick of army life. In no time at all, the book is off and running—only to take another sharp turn an instant later. A new paragraph begins, and as Henry makes his first appearance in the opening line, the third element of the novel is put into play.

> There was a youthful private who listened with eager ears to the words of the tall soldier and to the varied comments of his comrades. After receiving a fill of discussions concerning marches and attacks, he went to his hut and crawled through an intricate hole that served as its door. He wished to be alone with some new thoughts that had lately come to him.

For the next five and a half pages, Crane casts a backward glance at the youth's history and the various circumstances that have led him to this moment. It is the only passage in the novel that is not situated in the present, but as is the case with the fourth chapter of *Maggie*, which closely examines Jimmie's character and his troubled early career as a "young man of leather," the facts offered here are essential to understanding the inner drama that unfolds throughout the rest of the novel.

"Of course," as Crane emphatically puts it, Henry "had dreamed of battles all his life—of vague and bloody conflicts that had thrilled him with their sweep and fire." He had apparently read Homer at some point, or at least had become familiar with the contents of the *Iliad*, but while he had imagined himself performing heroic deeds in battle as a young boy, he also began to suspect that the age of war had passed. "He had long despaired of witnessing a Greeklike struggle. Such would be no more, he had said. Men were better, or more timid. Secular and religious education had effaced the throat-grappling instinct, or else firm finance held in check the passions."

Still, after the outbreak of the Civil War, "he had burned several times to enlist," for even though the accounts of the battle were not "distinctly Homeric . . . there seemed to be much glory in them." The problem was his mother, who had opposed his joining up, and as the only son of a widowed woman with few resources, he had submitted to her argument with its "many hundreds of reasons why he was of vastly more importance on the farm than on the field of battle." In the end, however, inflamed by "the newspapers, the gossip of the village, [and] his own imaginings," he had rebelled against his mother and enlisted.

Continually projecting idealized outcomes onto anticipated events, the immature Henry had not prepared himself for his mother's complex, guarded reaction when he returned to the farm dressed in his uniform. She was milking one of the cows, and after pausing for a moment to say, "The Lord's will be done, Henry," she had gone back to her milking and then, unexpectedly, had shed some silent tears. Later, when he was about to leave the farm for good and begin his training, she had further disappointed him

> by saying nothing whatever about returning with his shield or on it. He had privately primed himself for a beautiful scene. He had prepared certain sentences which he thought could be used with touching effect. But her words destroyed his plans.

Those words consisted of a long, Polonius-like stream of admonitions and encouragements, heartfelt but crammed with platitudes, counseling Henry to remember that he was "jest one little feller amongst a hull lot of others," to keep quiet and do what he was told, not to worry if he had to be killed or do a mean thing because the Lord would take care of her and all the other women who had to "bear up 'ginst sech things," to remember the socks and shirts she had made for him along with the cup of blackberry jam she had put in his bundle "because I knew yeh like it above all things," and, finally, to watch out and be a good boy.

These were not the words Henry had been expecting her to say, and he listened to them "with an air of irritation," at last departing with a sense of "vague relief."

> Still, when he had looked back from the gate, he had seen his mother kneeling among the potato parings. Her brown face, upraised, was stained with tears, and her spare form was quivering. He bowed his head and went on, feeling suddenly ashamed of his purposes.

He will think about the farm from time to time in the months ahead, occasionally even long to be back there, but except for a couple of momentary flashes (once about food when he is hungry, once when he imagines himself spinning stories about his exploits to a group of women), Crane does not suggest that Henry is thinking about his mother. A devoted son would sit down and write an occasional letter, but never do we see him with a pen in his hand.

In what could be a remnant from the potboiler version of the novel—and left in as a brief, winking allusion to the sort of book Crane had become determined *not* to write—the next scene takes Henry to his school for a round of farewells with his classmates.

> They had thronged around him with wonder and admiration. He had felt the gulf now between them and swelled with calm pride. He and some of his fellows who had donned blue were quite overwhelmed with privileges for all of one afternoon, and it had been a very delicious thing. They had strutted.
>
> A certain light-haired girl had made vivacious fun at his martial spirit, but there was another and darker girl whom he had gazed at steadfastly, and he thought she grew demure and sad at the sight of his blue and brass. As he had walked down the path between the rows of oaks, he had turned his head and detected her at a window watching his departure. As he perceived her, she had immediately begun to stare up through the high tree branches at the sky. He had seen a good deal of flurry and haste in her movement as she changed her attitude. He often thought of it.

The dark-haired girl turns out to be a red herring, for even if the youth thinks of that final moment often, those thoughts never surface anywhere throughout the remainder of the book. She darts in and out of his mind just once, but that is all. So much for the love-story subplot of the traditional war novel. A fluttering instant of expectation—and then *poof.*

Certain things about Henry's character are already becoming clear in these flashbacks. Above all, his ferocious need to make a good impression on others, to stand out and be recognized as an anointed one, superior to the rest of the human horde, and once he dons his "blue and brass" he becomes so full of himself as he struts around with his fellow enlistees that he is mocked for it by the light-haired girl. Because he has not yet established a moral ground within himself, he can see himself only by imagining how others see him—not who he is, exactly (he has no idea who he is), but who he wants others to think he is. For a short time, the real had fortuitously matched up with this desire, and on the train down to Washington "the regiment was fed and caressed at station after station until the youth believed that he must be a hero . . . [and] as he basked in the smiles of the girls and was patted and complimented by the old men, he felt growing within him the strength to do mighty deeds of arms."

Then the real had turned against him, and in the disappointing "months of monotonous life in a camp," he was forced to come to grips with the everyday truth of army existence, a doleful realization that continued to weigh down on him after his training ended and he was sent into the field to face the enemy, where he and his regiment "had done little but sit still and try to keep warm." His dreams of glory had dissolved, and he had gone back to his old idea that "Greeklike struggles would be no more."

> He had grown to regard himself merely as part of a vast blue demonstration. His province was to look out, as far as he could, for his personal comfort. For recreation he could twiddle his thumbs and speculate on the thoughts which must agitate the minds of the generals. Also, he was drilled and drilled and reviewed, and drilled and drilled and reviewed.

So there he is now down in his solitary hole, trying to prepare himself for what promises to be his first combat and nervously pondering the big, unanswerable question that has come to dominate his thoughts over the last little while: whether he will run when he is thrown into action or not. He seeks to "mathematically prove to himself" that he will not, but he is soon forced to admit "that as far as war was concerned he knew nothing of himself."

> A little panic-fear grew in his mind. As his imagination went forward to a fight, he saw hideous possibilities. He contemplated the lurking menaces of the future, and failed in an effort to see himself standing stoutly in the midst of them. . . .
>
> He sprang from the bunk and began to pace nervously to and fro. "Good Lord, what's th' matter with me?" he said aloud.
>
> He felt that in this crisis his laws of life were useless. Whatever he had learned of himself was here of no avail. He was an unknown quantity. He saw that he would again be obliged to experiment as he had in early youth. He must accumulate information about himself, and meanwhile he resolved to remain close upon his guard lest those qualities of which he knew nothing should everlastingly disgrace him. "Good Lord!" he repeated in dismay.

"Disgrace" is the pivotal word in this passage. To hold his own in battle would win him the respect of his fellow soldiers. To crack under pressure and turn tail would brand him a coward, and he would carry that black mark with him for the rest of the war. Again, his overriding concern is with how others see him, not how he sees himself, but at this early point in the story, what he sees when he looks at himself is a cipher, an "unknown quantity," and when the rumor of an imminent skirmish disintegrates into yet another bogus report by the following day, the agony of the unanswered question—*Will he run or not run?*—grows ever more unbearable to him. He decides that "the only way to prove himself was to go into the blaze, and then figuratively to watch his legs to discover their merits and faults." No more mathematical calculations to posit the inevitability of one answer or the other; what he needs now is empirical evidence, a test under fire. "To gain it [the answer], he must have blaze, blood, and danger, even as the chemist requires this, that, and the other. So he fretted for an opportunity."

As he frets, he asks himself if there isn't a like-minded soul in the company, someone equally tormented by doubts who would be willing to talk to him and compare "mental notes," but when he searches around for someone who appears to be in the proper mood for such a conversation, he finds no one, and even if he did, how could he open his mouth and confess his fears when the other would probably make fun of him and insult him for being a coward? So the youth goes on suffering in silence, locked inside his head with no one to talk to but himself.

Meanwhile, his own moods lurch about in a jumble of clashing impulses and wildly inconsistent thoughts. One minute, he imagines that all the other soldiers in the regiment are heroes and reproaches himself for having committed "many shameful crimes against the gods of traditions," and the next minute he imagines that they are no different from himself, "all privately wondering and quaking." He resents the generals for their "intolerable slowness" and holds them responsible for his miseries, in effect blaming them for his fear, which continues to intensify as he waits for the decisive moment, his mind increasingly haunted by grotesque, supernatural images. "Staring once at the red eyes across the river, he conceived them to be growing larger, as the orbs of a row of dragons advancing." And even his own regiment, as it marches off into the darkness, is "now like one of those moving monsters wending with many feet." The trek comes to a halt with the "despondent and sullen" Henry still "engaged in his own eternal debate."

In the evening he wandered a few paces into the gloom. From this little distance the many fires, with the black forms of men passing to and fro before the crimson rays, made weird and satanic effects.

He lay down in the grass. The blades pressed tenderly against his cheek. The moon had been lighted and was hung in a treetop. The liquid stillness of the night enveloping him made him feel vast pity for himself. . . .

He wished, without reserve, that he was at home again making the endless rounds from the house to the barn, from the barn to the fields, from the fields to the barn, from the barn to the house. . . . He told himself that he was not formed for a soldier.

When the youth hears a rustling in the grass and spots the loud soldier walking by, he beckons Wilson over, and the two of them begin to talk. Still too afraid to bare his innermost feelings to anyone, not even to his old boyhood friend, Henry nevertheless comes close, transferring his doubts about himself into a question about Wilson and how he can be sure he won't run "when the time comes."

"'Run?' said the loud one; 'run?—of course not!' He laughed."

When Henry persists, Wilson becomes peeved at so much idle speculation, accuses Henry of talking "as if you thought you was Napoleon Bonaparte," and then stomps off in a huff. Henry calls him back, but Wilson is already gone, and from then until the youth retires for the night, "he felt alone in space . . . a mental outcast."

The next three chapters are packed with incident as the company moves from one place to another for unknown military reasons, commanded to march, commanded to run, commanded to stop, and Henry's jangled thoughts, driven by his ever-growing fear, bounce from dread to anger to despondency. The fateful hour is approaching, which is also "the stealthy approach of his death," and for a moment he imagines himself haranguing his comrades to break ranks to avoid being "killed like pigs," then stifles the impulse, knowing it will lead to a barrage of ridicule, and then, not long after, begins to imagine "it would be better to be killed directly and end his troubles," for in death "he would go to some place where he would be understood," and then, as the moment of battle nears, something unexpected happens. Wilson, the loud, cocky soldier who has shown not the smallest sign of indecision or doubt, comes to Henry with "his girlish lip . . . trembling" and hands him a packet of letters to send to his family after he is killed, for he is convinced ("Something tells me—") that he will die today, that this battle will be both the first and the last of his brief life, and when Henry stammers forth an incoherent "Why, what the devil—," "the other gave him a glance as from the depths of a tomb, and raised his limp hand in a prophetic manner and turned away."

Then come the first glimmers of chaos that prefigure the impending skirmish. Crane's short sentences follow one another as a series of swift, jabbing punches, each one aimed at a specific target, each detail clear and precise and yet adding to the overall sense of confusion.

> A shell screaming like a storm banshee went over the huddled heads of the reserves. It landed in the grove, and exploding redly flung the brown earth. There was a little shower of pine needles.
>
> Bullets began to whistle among the branches and nip at the trees. Twigs and leaves came sailing down. It was as if a thousand axes, wee and invisible, were being wielded. Many of the men were constantly dodging and ducking their heads. . . .
>
> Wild yells came from behind the walls of smoke. A sketch in gray and red dissolved into a moblike body of men who galloped like wild horses.

The company has halted at the edge of a grove of trees, and as Henry awaits his first test under fire, Crane bears down into the moment by allowing the boy's mind to wander for a few seconds just before the battle begins, fixing on a small, inconsequential memory that can be read as a sign of dissociation, homesickness, or merely as one of those stray, random thoughts that continually rush through our heads. Crane, so brilliant in his depiction of the tangible world *out there*, is equally adept at penetrating the rapid fluctuations of the *in here*, and the joining of these two talents, the visual and the psychological, is what distinguishes this book from all other American books of the period. And how subtle Crane is in pre-senting Henry's mental fugue not as a sentimental excursion into the past but as a real memory unearthed in all its tawdry, rather comical vigor—a memory of anticipation that invades the thoughts of a boy anticipating his own possible death. The memory takes on substance as one particular piles on top of another, the seconds tick by, and then a voice calls out and interrupts him, and just like that the spectacle of war begins.

> There were moments of waiting. The youth thought of the village street at home before the arrival of the circus parade on a day in the spring. He remembered how he had stood, a small, thrillful boy, prepared to follow the dingy lady upon the white horse, or the band in its faded chariot.

He saw the yellow road, the lines of expectant people, and the sober houses. He particularly remembered an old fellow who used to sit upon a cracker box in front of the store and feign to despise such exhibitions. A thousand details of color and form surged in his mind. The old fellow upon the cracker box appeared in middle prominence.

Some one cried, "Here they come!"

Contrary to his dire predictions about himself, Henry does not run— nor does he even think of running. Crane's account of this first battle covers six densely loaded pages as the regiment hunkers down to fend off a Confederate charge, and there is Henry fumbling with his rifle, not sure if he has remembered to load it or not, not sure of anything, but eventually settling down until he is methodically fighting beside his fellow soldiers and against all odds holding his own in battle.

He suddenly lost concern for himself and forgot to look at a menacing fate. . . . He was welded into a common personality dominated by a single desire. . . .

There was a consciousness always of the presence of his comrades about him. He felt the subtle battle brotherhood more potent even than the cause for which they were fighting. It was a mysterious fraternity born of the smoke and danger of death.

The sense of the group keeps him bound to the group, enables him to dissolve into the group, but for all that he is still alone in his own body, curiously poised between two physical states or else shuttling back and forth between them, at once locked in a trancelike, out-of-body experience and suffering through intense physical discomfort, as if he were both there and not there at the same time.

He was at a task. He was like a carpenter who has made many boxes, making still another box, only there was furious haste in his movements. He, in his thought, was careering off in other places, even as the carpenter who as he works whistles and thinks of his friend or his enemy, his home or a saloon. And these jolted dreams were never perfect to him afterward, but remained a mass of blurred shapes.

Presently he began to feel the effects of the war atmosphere—a blistering sweat, a sensation that his eyeballs were about to crack like hot stones. A burning roar filled his ears.

Following this came a red rage. . . .

Buried in the smoke of many rifles his anger was directed not so much against the men whom he knew were rushing toward him as against the swirling battle phantoms which were choking him, stuffing their smoke robes down his parched throat. He fought frantically for respite for his senses, for air, as a babe being smothered attacks the deadly blankets.

All three of the book's essential elements are continually at play in this chapter, zigging and zagging from one to the other with astonishing rapidity, now focusing on the soldiers and officers in the regiment, now focusing on the thoughts in Henry's head, now focusing on the scene at large, which is a scene of battle, filled with the inevitable images of the dead and wounded as each man's plight is captured in a vivid, starkly lit snapshot:

The men dropped here and there like bundles. The captain of the youth's company had been killed in an early part of the action. His body lay stretched out in the position of a tired man resting, but upon his face there was an astonished and sorrowful look, as if he thought some friend had done him an ill turn. The babbling man was grazed by a shot that made the blood stream widely down his face. He clapped both hands to his head. "Oh!" he said, and ran. Another grunted suddenly as if he had been struck by a club in the stomach. He sat down and gazed ruefully. In his eyes was mute, indefinite reproach. Farther up the line a man, standing behind a tree, had had his knee joint splintered by a ball. Immediately he had dropped his rifle and gripped the tree with both arms. And there he remained, clinging desperately and crying for assistance that he might withdraw his hold upon the tree.

The line does not bend, the attack is repulsed, and as Henry slowly comes out of his battle trance, he goes "into an ecstasy of self-satisfaction," looking back on his conduct as "magnificent" and judging himself to be "a fine fellow." Who would begrudge him these moments of relief and exaltation? He has vanquished his fears and come through the trial with his honor intact. One wonders: What can be in store for him now, and what, precisely, does it mean to talk about *a red badge of courage*? Crane quickly answers the first part of the question before the reader can pursue it any further. A soldier cries out: "Here they come ag'in! Here they come ag'in!" The entire company is shocked by this sudden turn, but even as the men pick up their rifles to defend themselves against the second attack, the addled, disbelieving Henry has trouble pulling himself together again. His strength has been depleted by the first wave, his mental command is diminished for the second, and in his eyes the enemy forces are no longer men but "machines of steel," who then turn into "redoubtable dragons," in any case and in both cases something beyond what is merely human, and he feels as if he is someone "who has lost his legs at the approach of the red and green monster," a defenseless creature waiting "to be gobbled." It doesn't help that one of the men fighting next to him suddenly stops and runs off howling, nor that one of his fellow boy soldiers, who until now has been the very picture of courage, unexpectedly turns white, throws down his gun, and flees. Others begin "to scamper away in the smoke," and before long Henry senses that the regiment is leaving him behind. If he stays where he is, he will be destroyed. A moment later, he turns and runs, and for the next forty-five pages he will continue to run—not only from the war but from the shame he has brought upon himself.

Fear is fear, an uncontrollable force that cannot be subdued by an effort of will, not so much a crime as a misfortune, a mental affliction that paralyzes its victim and leaves him powerless to resist, but in the pages that follow Henry also commits a number of moral transgressions that expose his tenuous character more dramatically than the pardonable sin of running from battle out of fear. Crane has not set out to justify the youth or turn him into a noble or sympathetic figure. Nor does he ever deign to pity him. Henry Fleming is a complex, troubled young man, flawed in the ways nearly all human beings are flawed, worse than some, better than some, an example of ordinary, run-of-the-mill life caught in the grip of extraordinary circumstances. Not a saint, not a madman, not even a hero—just a person. With the same steady gaze he applied to the characters in *Maggie*, Crane doesn't judge his flailing, panicked, self-deluding protagonist. He simply watches him and tells what he does, what he thinks, what he thinks about in the course of doing what he does, and then, once Crane has told us that, he goes on watching and tells us more. The honesty of such an approach can be excruciating, at times even unbearable, but to do it any other way would be cheating, and unlike the character in his blazing little book, Crane does not cheat.

First, the headlong sprint to the rear and into the woods, stumbling and thrashing forward, banging his shoulder into a tree, falling down, standing up again, losing his cap, losing his rifle, running, running hard, running harder and harder, driven by the thought of death gaining on him in closer and closer pursuit, running with all the other running men until he is far in front and leaving them behind, running until he is alone, until he alone has outrun death, and as shells fall and the ground explodes around him, imagining the shells with rows of cruel teeth grinning at him, then chancing upon other companies calmly going about the business of fighting and thinking them fools for not knowing they are about to be killed, and then, farther on, as he continues to run, seeing a general mounted on his horse and calling out to everyone, "They've held 'im! . . . They've held 'im, by heavens!"—and with those words the sickening knowledge that he has run away from a victory, that his regiment has pushed back the new Confederate charge and won for the second time.

A defeat would have vindicated his actions, or at least have protected him from being singled out for reprimand, but victory has turned him into a deserter and a coward, a pariah, and he feels both angry and wronged, a victim of a gross injustice whose "wisdom . . . and righteous motives" have been trampled by "hateful circumstances." Such is the world as perceived by the desperate, self-centered mind of young Henry Fleming, who rather than head back to his company to face the music goes "from the fields into a thick woods, as if resolved to bury himself."

Alone now and far from everyone, with the sounds of musket fire growing faint in the distance, he tosses a pinecone at a "jovial squirrel" and is heartened when the animal scampers off in fear. That is the law of Nature, he tells himself triumphantly. When danger comes, you don't stand and fight to the death, you turn around and run as fast as you can, and as the youth plunges on along the "bog tufts" at the edge of a swamp and travels into "deep thickets . . . going from obscurity into promises of greater obscurity," he is consoled by the fact "that Nature was of his mind," but minutes after thinking that thought he experiences a chilling epiphany that proves an altogether different proposition: Nature has no mind at all, and the minuscule travails of men are of no account to the forces that reign in heaven and on earth.

At length he reached a place where the high, arching boughs made a chapel. He softly pushed the green doors aside and entered. Pine needles were a gentle brown carpet. There was a religious half light.

Near the threshold he stopped, horror-stricken at the sight of a thing.

He was being looked at by a dead man who was seated with his back against a column-like tree. The corpse was dressed in a uniform that once had been blue, but was now faded to a melancholy shade of green. The eyes, staring at the youth, had changed to the dull hue to be seen on the side of dead fish. The mouth was open. Its red had changed to an appalling yellow. Over the gray skin of the face ran little ants. One was trundling some sort of bundle along the upper lip.

The youth backs off, terrified, and runs from the place until he is within earshot of more fighting, far louder and more intense than the two battles he was involved in: "There suddenly broke a tremendous clangor of sounds. A crimson roar came from the distance." This time, he runs *toward* the fighting, not to take part in it but to witness "a celestial battle . . . tumbling hordes a-struggle in the air," wanting to get close enough to "see it produce corpses," an impulse that is both confounding and perverse, a symptom of a mind that is flying "in all directions," and soon enough he comes upon clusters of the fallen and the dead splayed out on the ground. He then joins a procession of the wounded shuffling toward the rear, and as he plods on with "the blood-stained crowd," he finds himself walking next to a person Crane variously describes as *a tattered man, the tattered soldier*, and *the spectral soldier*, a badly wounded, sweet-tempered bumpkin who talks in a voice as "gentle as a girl's" and makes an effort to befriend the boy, but Henry is unresponsive to his overtures, not hostile so much as distracted and indifferent, and when the tattered man asks him where he was hit, that is, where and how he was wounded, Henry is so embarrassed by the question that "he turned away suddenly and slid through the crowd."

Not long after, Crane introduces the title of his book into the book itself. The question has sent the boy's mind reeling again, and "he now felt that his shame could be viewed," a sensation that leads him to wonder "if the men were contemplating the letters of guilt he felt burned into his brow." Again, it is Henry looking at himself through the eyes of the others, for when he is alone he seems perfectly capable of ignoring that guilt, or forgetting it, or pretending it doesn't exist, or even going so far as to justify his actions, but when the wounded men look at him, the shame of what he has done comes surging back into his thoughts. The next paragraph exposes his dilemma in the form of a wish:

> At times he regarded the wounded soldiers in an envious way. He conceived persons with torn bodies to be peculiarly happy. He wished that he, too, had a wound, a red badge of courage.

Suddenly, the spectral soldier is back at his side "like a stalking reproach." The wounded man is slowly but surely dying, in worse shape than he was earlier, "his eyes fixed in a stare into the unknown," and as he moves hesitantly forward, "there could be seen a certain stiffness in the movements of the body, as if he were taking infinite care not to arouse the passion of his wounds. As he went on, he seemed always looking for a place, like one who goes to choose a grave."

It is an exquisitely rendered passage, the grim, keenly observed announcement of the tattered man's deteriorating condition, a passage of dread and foreboding that is quickly followed by another narrative jolt as Henry looks up in horror and screams: "Gawd! Jim Conklin!"

And there is his friend, the tall soldier, walking down that same road with the wounded men, himself wounded and on the point of death, a figure who seems to have emerged from the great cloud of fire and fury that is war, both a fact of war and an emblem of war contained in a single dying body, and for the next four pages until the end of chapter IX Crane compels the reader to watch that death and live that death in what is justifiably considered to be one of the most remarkable passages of the book.

At first, Jim seems to be his old, good-natured self. He smiles and says, "Hello, Henry," but the youth can only stammer in response, "Oh, Jim—oh, Jim—oh, Jim—." Jim then holds out "his gory hand" and asks Henry where he's been, telling him he was worried he might have been killed, and as the boy continues to stammer, Conklin announces that he's been shot—"I got shot. Yes, b'jiminey, I got shot"—then says it again "in a bewildered way, as if he did not know how it came about." The two of them walk down the road together, with the tall soldier clutching the youth's arm, and before long, "in a shaking whisper," Jim tells Henry that his greatest fear is that he will fall down and get run over by "them damned artillery wagons." Henry promises to help, but Jim, lapsing into a sort of daze, refuses to go on leaning against him, saying, "No—no—no—leave me be—leave me be—," and it is only when the tattered soldier intervenes and urges Henry to take Jim off the road that the boy manages to guide his friend toward the fields. The tattered soldier knows that they must act quickly, for Jim is "a goner anyhow in about five minutes," and then he wonders: "Where the blazes does he git his stren'th from?"

No sooner do they turn off the road than Jim begins to run "in a staggering and stumbling way toward a little clump of bushes." Henry and the tattered soldier go after him, confused, worried that he will hurt himself, but even as Henry begs him to be careful, Jim has stopped listening, "keeping his eyes fastened on the mystic place of his intentions. 'No—no—don't tech me—leave me be—leave me be—.'" Again, Henry asks what is the matter with him, but again Jim lurches away, and both the boy and the tattered man begin to feel that there is something "rite-like in these movements of the doomed soldier," as if he were "the devotee of a mad religion, blood-sucking, muscle-wrenching, bone-crushing." When the end comes, it unfolds gradually, in a long and agonizing dance of death:

> At last they saw him stop and stand motionless. Hastening up, they perceived that his face wore an expression telling that he had at last found the place for which he had struggled. His spare figure was erect; his bloody hands were quietly at his side. He was waiting with patience for something that he had come to meet. He was at the rendezvous. They paused and stood, expectant.
>
> There was silence.
>
> Finally, the chest of the doomed soldier began to heave with a strained motion. It increased in violence until it was if an animal was within and was kicking and tumbling furiously to be free.
>
> This spectacle of gradual strangulation made the youth writhe, and once as his friend rolled his eyes, he saw something in them that made him sink wailing to the ground. He raised his voice in a last supreme call.
>
> "Jim—Jim—Jim—"
>
> The tall soldier opened his lips and spoke. He made a gesture. "Leave me be—don't tech me—leave me be—"
>
> There was another silence while he waited.
>
> Suddenly, his form stiffened and straightened. Then it was shaken by a prolonged ague. He stared into space. To the two watchers there was a curious and profound dignity in the firm lines of his awful face.
>
> He was invaded by a creeping strangeness that slowly enveloped him. For a moment the tremor of his legs caused him to dance a sort of hideous hornpipe. His arms beat wildly about his head in expression of implike enthusiasm.
>
> His tall figure stretched itself to its full height. There was a slight rending sound. Then it began to swing forward, slow and straight, in the manner of a falling tree. A swift muscular contortion made the left shoulder strike the ground first.
>
> The body seemed to bounce a little way from the earth. "God!" said the tattered soldier.
>
> The youth had watched, spellbound, this ceremony at the place of meeting. His face had been twisted into an expression of every agony he had imagined for his friend.
>
> He now sprang to his feet and, going closer, gazed upon the pastelike face. The mouth was open and the teeth showed in a laugh.
>
> As the flap of the blue jacket fell away from the body, he could see that the side looked as if it had been chewed by wolves.

The youth turned, with sudden, livid rage, toward the battlefield. He shook his fist. He seemed about to deliver a philippic.

"Hell——"

The red sun was pasted in the sky like a wafer.*

Not long after that, Henry commits his first sin. There will be two more in the chapters that follow, but in spite of revealing the youth's heartlessness, his willingness to lie in order to save face, and a lack of scruples that leads him to indulge in the equivalent of moral blackmail to protect his secret from exposure, the boy will gradually emerge from the nightmare of his fear to perform ably on the battlefield the next day and win some form of redemption for himself. Depending, of course, on how one defines the word *redemption*—and also depending on how one interprets the novel's murky, ambiguous conclusion.

After Jim's death, Henry throws himself on the ground "and [begins] to brood" as the tattered man rambles on about the horrendous thing they have just witnessed and then proposes that they shove off and continue their trek down the road. His condition is getting worse ("I'm commencin' t' feel pretty bad . . . pretty damn bad"), and he's not sure how much farther he can walk, but he continues to worry about the boy as well, afraid that Henry has some kind of internal injury (which he does, of course, although not a physical one), and when he asks him where this wound is located, then asks the same question again, Henry becomes unhinged. With a "furious motion of his hand," he shouts, "Oh don't bother me!," so

---

* This last line, the most thoroughly examined, lauded, and debated sentence in all of Crane's work, was used by some scholars back in the fifties and sixties to promote a now-debunked reading of *Red Badge* as a novel rife with religious symbolism that turned Jim Conklin (J.C.) into a stand-in for Jesus Christ and interpreted the sky-borne wafer as a reference to the sacrament of the Eucharist, but there are other meanings of the word *wafer* as well, one of which comes from the domain of law: a small disk of adhesive material used as a seal for legal documents. That is probably what Crane had in mind and would account for the word "pasted" in the sentence. What makes the passage so stunning in my opinion, however, has nothing to do with either religion or the law but with the music of Crane's lightning-quick jumps and juxtapositions, the harsh cut from earth to sky at the end but first of all the cut from the impulse to deliver a long blast of denunciation (philippic) that suddenly collapses into a single word, *hell*, which is both an exclamation and a description of the scene, and then, following the long triple dash after the world *hell*, which has kept us suspended on the earth, Crane suddenly points to the sun in the sky, and for a moment we can feel it burning up there in all its bloody redness, utterly indifferent to Jim Conklin and every other soldier on the battlefield. The language becomes a physical force felt in the body, and consequently it is an emotional force as well, in the same way a choral blast of fifty or a hundred voices erupting from a quiet passage in Bach can shake us to our toes and fill our eyes with tears.

angry by now that he feels he could strangle the tattered man, who has been nothing but good to him, nothing but kind and solicitous and helpful in spite of his own mortal wounds. In a disgusting act of self-pity, fueled by an utter lack of regard for the suffering of a fellow creature, Henry abruptly decides to leave. "Good-by," he says—with curt, sucker-punching effect— and as the tattered man looks at him "in gaping amazement," shocked by the boy's cruelty but also fretting about what will happen to him, Henry decamps.

> The youth went on. Turning at a distance he saw the tattered man wandering about helplessly in the field.
> He now thought that he wished he was dead.

A twinge of conscience, perhaps, but not enough to stop him from leaving, and off he goes, consumed by his own torments as he abandons the spectral soldier to his lonely, painful death.

The second transgression, which occurs later that day, turns the entire book around and points it in another direction. It is Crane's masterstroke, the event that makes the novel what it is, and the irony embedded in this narrative happenstance is so rich with meanings and counter-meanings that my head starts to spin whenever I try to parse them. An unlucky thing is turned into a lucky thing, the answer to a prayer as fervent as any wish in a fairy tale, and yet only by lying about what happened to him can Henry cover up the shame of his former misdeeds and go on with his life, even if that life is essentially a fraud. Under the circumstances, it is understandable that he should lie—most people would—but once he tells his lie, Henry acts as if he believes his false version of the story, so much so that he seems to forget that he lied in the first place, and rather than thank the fates for giving him false absolution, he carries on as if he had been blameless from the outset. That is the real fraud. Not that he has allowed himself to perpetuate the fraud but that he no longer considers it to be a fraud, that he is dishonest with himself even about his own dishonesty.

After leaving the tattered man, he blunders around in a swirl of confusion as "the furnace roar of battle" grows louder and a retreating mass of soldiers files past him in the woods "like soft, ungainly animals." The youth is momentarily comforted by this sight, interpreting it as proof of his own wisdom in having run from battle, but then he sees other soldiers advancing toward a new confrontation, and "the black weight of his woe" presses down on him again. His mind begins to shuttle back and forth between opposing impulses: to join up with those men and return to the front, imagining himself "a blue desperate figure leading lurid charges with one knee forward and a broken blade high," then longing for a rout of his own army with thousands running as he has run and with this projected defeat finding a measure of solace for "his unprecedented suffering," but an instant later he recoils from such vile hopes and denounces himself "as a villain . . . the most utterly selfish man in existence." Crane plows on in this mode for six pages, spending a full chapter on his fierce journey through the labyrinth of Henry's consciousness and arriving at the dead center of his book with this plunge into the interior of a soul trapped in self-devouring speculations that take him round and round and then back to his starting point and then round and round again. Kierkegaard called this state of mind *the sickness unto death*. A century later, Sartre called it simply: *No Exit*. However you choose to define the condition, the fact is that Henry has come to a wall, and because the wall is too high for him to climb over it, he is stuck—not just temporarily but forever.

Then, as if by a miracle, he is granted his red badge of courage and a possible way out. He comes upon another retreating company, "dark waves of men . . . sweeping out of the woods and down through the fields," charging toward him "like frightened buffaloes." Henry understands that a major battle has been lost and that "war, the red animal, war, the blood-swollen god, would have bloated fill." Desperate to find out what is happening, he pushes himself into the crowd, and when he grabs hold of a soldier's arm and tries to question him, the enraged, frightened man yells, "Let me go! Let me go!" and because Henry doesn't let go, the man drags the boy along with him for several paces, and then, "adroitly and fiercely," smashes his rifle into Henry's skull.

> He saw the flaming wings of lightning flash before his vision. There was a deafening rumble of thunder within his head.
> Suddenly his legs seemed to die. He sank writhing to the ground. . . .
> In his efforts against the numbing pain he was like a man wrestling with a creature of the air.
> There was a sinister struggle.

There is also blood—trickling out of the spot where his scalp was gashed—and as evening comes on and he continues to stagger around in pain, that blood will become his false salvation. The pain eventually subsides, but it still isn't clear to him how badly he is wounded. Early evening turns into dusk, and before long it is near-night, dark enough for him to wonder if he shouldn't begin to look for a place to bed down until morning. He is alone now and lost in the woods, dazed and deeply exhausted, hungry, thirsty, and undone, but then a second miracle occurs in this hour of two miracles, arriving in the form of a cheery voice, which becomes a man with a cheery voice, another soldier who can see (*see in the dark*) that the boy is in "a pretty bad way" and offers to guide him back to his regiment, a task he accomplishes as if he possesses a magic wand, threading "the mazes of the tangled forest with a strange fortune," and once they reach their destination and the man "who had so befriended him was thus passing out of his life, it suddenly occurred to the youth that he had not once seen his face."

As Henry rejoins the men of the 304th, he has not yet prepared his lie and is fully expecting to "feel in his sore heart the barbed missiles of ridicule," but when the first man he encounters turns out to be his friend Wilson standing guard in the blackness, the loud soldier is so glad to see him that Henry immediately begins to concoct a false story about his adventures, and because the blood trickling from his head is a protective shield against suspicion, he manages to get away with it.

> "Yes, yes, I've—I've had an awful time. I've been all over. Way over on the right. Ter'ble fightin' over there. I had an awful time. I got separated from th' reg'ment. Over on th' right. I got shot. In th' head. I never see sech fightin'. Awful time. I don't see how I could a' got separated from th' reg'ment. I got shot, too."

A day of battle has produced enormous changes in Wilson. The swagger and bombast of his "tinsel courage" are gone, and he has now "climbed a peak of wisdom from which he could perceive himself as a very wee thing," a fundamental shift in perspective that astonishes Henry and convinces him "that ever after it would be easier to live in his friend's neighborhood." As Wilson bustles around like "an amateur nurse" tending to Henry's needs— clumsily bandaging the wound with a large handkerchief, giving him his bedroll for the night, plying him with ample doses of food and coffee in the morning, even as he breaks up a scuffle between two quarreling soldiers in the encampment—one feels that Wilson's miraculous transformation into a person with "new eyes" can mostly be understood by how *connected* he has become to others, whereas Henry, in spite of what he has been through in the past twenty-four hours, is still locked in isolation, a being apart who has gone on judging himself as big—the biggest man in all creation—and therefore a man who has neither the power nor the will to think of anyone but himself.

And so he commits the third transgression, which is not an overt act as the first two were but a potential act that he keeps to himself as an insurance policy to guard against exposure of his guilt, a small-scale version of the panic that courses through Raskolnikov in *Crime and Punishment* and leads him to commit a second murder in order to cover up the first, for Henry is equally desperate to remove all traces of his original crime, and the person most likely to unmask him is none other than Wilson, formerly known as *the loud soldier*, now referred to merely as *the friend*, who he fears will begin asking too many questions about what happened to him yesterday. On the morning after Henry's return, as the regiment stands at arms awaiting the order to march, the youth remembers the packet of letters Wilson entrusted him with in a moment of weakness prior to their first combat, sobbing with the conviction that he was about to be killed, and although Henry is tempted to say something about it, he stifles the impulse, resolving "not to deal the little blow," but for all that he is glad.

> He now rejoiced in the possession of a small weapon with which he could prostrate his comrade at the first signs of cross-examination. He was master. It would now be he who could laugh and shoot the shafts of derision.

This is an ugly bit of business, a scathing look into the soul of a bloodless manipulator, and when Wilson finally plucks up his courage and asks Henry to return the letters to him, the youth exults in his triumph. He now has the goods on his friend and is home free, safe from the potential humiliation of having to give an honest account of his flight from battle.

> His self-pride was now entirely restored. In the shade of its flourishing growth he stood with braced and self-confident legs, and since nothing could now be discovered he did not shrink from an encounter with the eyes of judges, and allowed no thoughts of his own to keep him from an attitude of manfulness. He had performed his mistakes in the dark, so he was still a man.

A man—or a hypocrite? In Henry's mind, it would seem there is no difference between the two, and therefore all bets are off when it comes to preserving one's reputation. Still trapped in the adolescent delusion of always looking at himself through the eyes of others, he conceives of manhood not as a state of inner groundedness but as a form of respect granted by other men. If you can hold your head high among those other men, you are a man. No matter that you have committed shameful acts and would be ostracized if anyone knew about them. As long as the others don't know, you are a man.

Three paragraphs down, the word crops up again as the emboldened youth takes stock of his situation:

> There was a little flower of confidence growing within him. He was now a man of experience. He had been out among the dragons, he said, and he assured himself that they were not so hideous as he had imagined them. Also, they were inaccurate; they did not sting with precision. A stout heart often defied, and defying, escaped.
>
> And, furthermore, how could they kill him who was the chosen of gods and doomed to greatness?

There is a breathtaking complexity to these remarks, suggesting both signs of potential change in Henry and a congenital persistence of his egotism and immaturity. Crane comes down hard on the boy, but that doesn't mean he considers him to be a lost cause. Muddled and groping, perhaps, hemmed in by his conflicts and weaknesses, but nevertheless someone capable of learning from his missteps, even if he has lied in order to wash the slate of his conscience clean, even if the grandiosity of his self-regard is so inflated as to be absurd, for "doomed to greatness" or not, one senses that Henry is evolving by small degrees. It is unlikely that he has it in him to undergo a monumental transformation on the scale of Wilson's, but he is still young enough to start again, and the conditions for a new beginning are all in place. The lie about the red badge of courage has set him on his feet, the nasty hold he has gained over Wilson will protect the lie and keep him standing, and the question now becomes: Where will he go from here?

The question is answered in the final third of the book as Henry is thrown into the fire again and the story moves from anxiety to action, from fear to rage. Crane's battle passages are electrifying in their vividness, a sustained onslaught of thirty-six pages that demonstrates his command of large scenes filled with masses of men engaged in a multitude of different activities at the same time. Whether you want to call him a painter or a cinematographer, his ever-watchful eye is in constant motion, swooping in for a close look at a small detail in one paragraph, then pulling back in the next to take in the full panorama, and as he charts the advance, the retreat, and then the second advance of the 304th, his highly controlled language creates a breathless effect: "It was a blind and despairing rush by a collection of men in dusty and tattered blue, over a green sward and under a sapphire sky, toward a fence, dimly outlined in smoke, from behind which spluttered the fierce rifles of enemies." Or: "On the slope to the left there was a long row of guns, gruff and maddened, denouncing the enemy, who, down through the woods, were forming for another attack in the pitiless monotony of conflicts." Or: "With his soiled and disordered dress, his red and inflamed features surmounted by the dingy rag with its spot of blood, his wildly swinging rifle and banging accouterments, he looked to be an insane soldier."

Henry is that insane soldier, and as the events of the day unfold in all their teeming chaos, his earlier conception of war is overturned when he loses himself in the frenzy of battle. The dragons have disappeared, along with the supernatural imagery of the first half of the book. He is a young soldier in an army of men and boys fighting another army of men and boys, and there is no Greeklike glory in such a struggle, since war in the mid-nineteenth century is not an arena where men try to prove their moral worth through bravery on the battlefield but a simple matter of life and possible death, a physical confrontation replete with muskets, cannons, and swords to amplify the savagery of direct hand-to-hand combat. Just as fear is an uncontrollable force that overwhelms the intelligence, so too is the fury of battle, which Crane describes as a form of delirium or madness, and how can a man feel responsible for turning himself into a crazed savage when he scarcely knows who he is anymore? Courage is no more an act of will than the cowardice that prompts a man to run from battle, and they both derive from the same irrational source. Yesterday, Henry ran. Today, he finds himself swept up in the madness of battle, consumed by a hatred of the enemy that leads him to perform bravely, at times even recklessly, and yet for all his heroism in combat, his most important victory is the bond he forms with Wilson, the once-loud soldier who stands side by side with him in the battles they fight that day, the two of them equal partners in a common struggle. Still, much of the old Henry remains intact, and he is far from having acquired his friend's wisdom of perceiving himself as "a very wee thing." In a crucial episode, Henry overhears one of the officers tell a general that the men of the 304th "fight like a lot 'a mule drivers," meaning that they are both expendable and insignificant, which throws Henry into a tantrum of indignation, and in the ensuing battle he fights as much from a hatred against his own commanding officers as from a hatred of the enemy. He refuses to think of himself as small. He will not be diminished by anyone—and he must, at all costs, shine.

How much has Henry changed by the end of the novel?

A bit—quite a bit, perhaps—but not as much as he seems to think.

As the last chapter begins, he is marching with his regiment away from the scene of battle, and as his head slowly clears and he can "comprehend himself and his circumstance," he is able to reflect on what has happened to him over the past two days and "study his deeds, his failures, and his achievements." The writing in these closing paragraphs is so eloquent and flat-out moving at times that it is hard not to fall under Crane's spell and accept Henry's ruminations at face value. But there is much going on beneath the surface, and in order to make sense of the book's conclusion, careful attention must be paid.

First of all, he is glad to have come through the battle in one piece, to be alive, to know that after having been to "where there was red of blood and black of passion," he has escaped. This is fundamental, and the unspoken thought underlying his happiness is the fact that he held his ground and did not run, that his fear of battle is behind him. A well-earned victory— and a legitimate cause for celebration.

Then he thinks back on "his public deeds" and the "performances which had been witnessed by his fellows," actions that seem to go "gayly with music" and give him much "pleasure" as he calls them to mind. Music suggests a military parade down a grand boulevard flanked by a cheering, adoring crowd of onlookers, a fantasy that allows him to indulge in a preening sort of self-congratulation and fulfill his need to shine under the gaze of others. This is Henry in all his adolescent Henryness, but given what he has been through on the battlefield, let us grant him his moment of inner glorification. No sooner does the parade pass by, however, than the text leaps into a startling new register with these blunt remarks: "He saw that he was good. He recalled with a thrill of joy the respectful comments of his fellows upon his conduct."

If I understand the word *good* correctly, Henry is not calling himself a good soldier or a good comrade but a good person, a categorical judgment of his moral worth, but the ironic, puzzling thing about those who are truly good is that they rarely if ever think of themselves as good. They tend to doubt their own goodness, which is what makes them good in the first place, whereas the less than good or only partially good, the ones who blunder about and always find an excuse to forgive themselves for their mistakes, call themselves good without understanding that they are not, in fact, who they think they are. A means of self-preservation, perhaps, or else a form of delusion. Henry is still an unformed, deluded character, and he still needs "the respectful comments of his fellows" to validate himself in his own eyes.

Immediately after that, however, his thoughts turn inward, and for the first time in the book Henry launches into an honest grappling with his flaws, his errors, and his less than shining moments. The memory of his flight from battle surges up in him, he blushes, "his soul flickered with shame," and once that bad memory departs, it is quickly followed by an even worse memory.

A specter of reproach came to him. There loomed the dogging memory of the tattered soldier—he who, gored by bullets and faint for blood, had fretted concerning an imagined wound in another; he who had loaned his last of strength and intellect for the tall soldier; he who, blind with weariness and pain, had been deserted in the field. . . .

. . . Whichever way his thoughts turned they were followed by the somber phantom of the desertion in the fields. He looked stealthily at his companions, feeling sure that they must discern in his face evidence of this pursuit . . .

For a time this pursuing recollection of the tattered man took all elation from the youth's veins. He saw his vivid error and he was afraid that it would stand before him all his life. He took no share in the chatter of his comrades, nor did he look at them or know them, save when he felt a sudden suspicion that they were seeing his thoughts and scrutinizing each detail of the scene with the tattered soldier.

This is progress. To feel the sting of such wretchedness, to wallow in such blistering self-contempt for his callous behavior is an encouraging sign of dawning maturity, but pure as Henry's anguish might be (*he was afraid that it would stand before him all his life*), there is another element to his distress, another source of panic that has become all too familiar by now: the fear of being found out, the dreadful possibility that others will learn what he has done and expose his secret, which is the same sort of panic that has been chasing him since the start of the book.

His desertion of the tattered soldier is far and away the worst of his crimes, but it should be noted that he never stops to think about the two others: the nonexistent gunshot wound to his head and the scheme to checkmate his friend into silence and submission by bringing up the embarrassing letters. Those transgressions have vanished from his mind—not so much erased as expunged.

Then, in one of those mental contortions that necessity seems to demand in the face of unbearable guilt, Henry solves his problem by simply jumping over it.

"Yet gradually he mustered force to put the sin at a distance."

Rather than go on tormenting himself for the rest of his life, he chooses to bury the thing he has done and never return to the grave.

Has he repented enough to justify this act? Perhaps he has, perhaps he hasn't, but it is certain that Henry believes he has, and once he manages *to put the sin at a distance*, the tenor of his thinking undergoes a profound shift, and the book ends in a beautiful if strange gush of soaring contradictions and puzzlements.

> Yet gradually he mustered force to put the sin at a distance. And at last his eyes seemed to open to some new ways. He found that he could look back upon the brass and bombast of his earlier gospels and see them truly. He was gleeful when he discovered that he now despised them.
>
> With this conviction came a store of assurance. He felt a quiet manhood, nonassertive but of sturdy and strong blood. He knew that he would no more quail before his guides wherever they should point. He had been to touch the great death, and found that, after all, it was but the great death. He was a man.

There is no doubt that his ideas of war have changed and that he is no longer terrorized by the thought of dying in battle, but do these illuminations now qualify him to join the ranks of manhood? Not yet. He has taken some small steps in the right direction, but he still has a long way to go, for declaring himself to be *a man* is of the same order as declaring himself to be *good*, a hopeful assertion, perhaps, but by no means proven yet.

In the penultimate paragraph, Henry's thinking goes into a weird flight of hyperbolic imagery, wonderfully seductive and convincing as it moves from sentence to sentence but at the same time increasingly unmoored as it wobbles farther and farther from his actual circumstances at that moment.

> It rained. The procession of weary soldiers became a bedraggled train, despondent and muttering, marching with churning effort in a trough of liquid brown mud under a low, wretched sky. Yet the youth smiled, for he saw that the world was a world for him, though many discovered it to be made of oaths and walking sticks. He had rid himself of the red sickness of battle. The sultry nightmare was in the past. He had been an animal blistered and sweating in the heat and pain of war. He turned now with a lover's thirst to images of tranquil skies, fresh meadows, cool brooks—an existence of soft and eternal peace.

These are the dreams of a boy, and they make it sound as if the war is over when in fact it is just beginning for Henry and the other boys in his company. There are more battles to be fought ahead, and in order to acquit himself well—as he has done in today's fighting—he will have to turn himself into a savage again and plunge back into the red sickness of war. Henry is still a boy, but that doesn't mean he lacks the potential to become a man. Almost certainly, he will become a man—as long as he isn't killed in another battle the next day, or the next month, or the next year.

In the final sentence of the book, the invisible narrator returns to report on the conditions brewing in the sky.

"Over the river a golden ray of sun came through the hosts of leaden rain clouds."

Light mixed with dark. Dark mixed with light. The doubleness of the real.

14

IN THE DEPTHS OF A COAL MINE.

In May 1894, not long after Crane had submitted *The Red Badge of Courage* to McClure and was still counting on a prompt decision about the book, he and Linson were hired by McClure to travel to Scranton, Pennsylvania, to report on conditions in the coal mines. Payment would come only after the article was published, and with Crane's purse in its usual hungry state, he borrowed fifty dollars from Linson to cover the costs of the trip. Once again, it was a loan he never paid back.

The assignment came to him through a recommendation from Garland, who had just written a piece for *McClure's Magazine* on Homestead in the aftermath of the vicious strike that had taken place at Carnegie's steelworks, and so off Crane and Linson went, armed with pens and pencils to write the report and draw the pictures that would accompany it. They stayed at a hotel in Scranton called the Valley House, visited the Oxford mine on the first afternoon, and that evening, through a local artist friend of Linson's, John Raught, were put in contact with James Young, foreman of the Dunmore mines, who arranged a trip to Number Five for them the next morning. On one of their evenings in town, they also managed to pay a call on Crane's maternal uncle Reverend Luther W. Peck, D.D., a genial old man who talked to them at length about his passion for butterflies.

One asks: Was Crane thinking about the coal mine stocks owned by his family or the shares he had inherited and then sold to his brother in order to publish his first book? Probably. Much had happened to him since then, but *Maggie* had come into the world just fourteen months earlier, and now, having washed his hands of coal mines, here he was traveling deep under the earth to write about them.

It is one of Crane's strongest and most vivid reports, a closely observed first-person account of what it feels like to approach, enter, and go down to the bottom of a pit more than one thousand feet under the ground where an army of men, boys, and mules is toiling to extract ton after ton of anthracite from the bowels of a torch-lit hell. Crane moves through the experience in a methodical, step-by-step manner, beginning with the land-scape surrounding the mine, the breakers that "squatted upon the hillsides and in the valley like enormous preying monsters eating of the sunlight, the grass, the green leaves," takes note of the other structures grouped around the central building, the "sheds, engine-houses, machine-shops, offices, [and] railroad tracks," and then pauses to take in the spectacle of the "little slate-pickers," the young boys in ragged shirts with "shoulders black as stoves" who are responsible for plucking chewed-up fragments of coal from the troughs that carry the chunks up from the bottom, and as Crane watches the boys go about their work he comments:

> The slate-pickers, all through this region, are yet at the spanking period. One continually wonders about their mothers and if there are any school-houses. But as for them, they are not concerned. When they get time off, they go out on the culm-heap and play base-ball, or fight with boys from other breakers, or among themselves, according to the opportunities. And before them always is the hope of one day getting to be door-boys down in the mines and, later, mule boys. And yet later laborers and helpers. Finally when they have grown to be great big men they may become miners, real miners, and go down and get "squeezed," or perhaps escape to a shattered old man's estate with a mere "miner's asthma." They are very ambitious.
>
> Meanwhile, they live in a place of infernal dins. The crash and thun-der of the machinery is like the roar of an immense cataract. The room shrieks and blares and bellows.... All the structure is a-tremble from the heavy sweep and circle of the ponderous mechanism. Down in the midst of it, sit these tiny urchins, where they earn fifty-five cents each day.... They have this clamor in their ears until it is wonderful that they have any hoodlum valor remaining. But they are uncowed; they continue to swagger.

A few minutes later, Crane and Linson are hurtling downward in an elevator to the bottom, clinging to the iron bars to steady themselves "as the dead black walls slid swiftly by.... When the faculty of the balance is lost, the mind becomes confusion. The will fought a great battle to comprehend something during this fall, but one might as well have been tumbling among the stars." As their guide leads them through the tunnels, Crane is struck by how the men they encounter, with their blackened faces and equally blackened clothes, are discernible only by their eyes and teeth, which shine "white as bleached bones," and how, in the first mine, they "speedily lost all ideas of time, direction, and distance." As noted earlier, there is a long passage about the mules in their stable, which he compares to a dungeon and the mules themselves to "enormous rats" (page 31), but also some remarks on the dangers of gas leaks and another long passage on the detonations set off in the nether zones of the colliery, which he correctly judges to be the soul of the enterprise—and also its most perilous aspect.

Crane at the Scranton coal mine with Linson, spring 1894.
(COURTESY OF SYRACUSE UNIVERSITY)

There is booming and banging and crashing until one wonders why the tremendous walls are not wrenched by the force of this uproar. And up and down the tunnel, there is a riot of lights, little orange points flickering and flashing. Miners stride in swift and sombre procession. But the meaning of it all is in the deep bass rattle of a blast in some hidden part of the mine. It is war. It is the most savage part of all in the endless battle between man and nature. These miners are grimly in the van. They have carried the war into places where nature has the strength of a million giants. Sometimes their enemy becomes exasperated and snuffs out ten, twenty, thirty lives. Usually she remains calm, and takes one at a time with method and precision. She need not hurry. She possesses eternity. After a blast, the smoke, faintly luminous, silvery, floats silently through the adjacent tunnels.

Crane was appalled, not only by the conditions under which these men worked and the low wages they were given (three dollars a day for the miners, a dollar and twenty-five cents for their laborer assistants), but also by the greed of the profit-driven mine owners who perpetuated this system of exploitation, and for once he lost his composure and took sides, blasting forth with an angry, sarcastic rant toward the end of the article. First:

One cannot go down in the mines often before he finds himself wondering why it is that the coal-barons get so much and these miners, swallowed by the grim black mouths of the earth day after day get proportionately so little.

Second:

While I was in Wilksbarre, there was an accident at a mine near there that threatened the lives of about twenty coal-brokers and other men who make neat livings by fiddling with the market. The elevator and the fan became paralyzed so that the visitors were menaced with death from gas in a mine ten hundred feet deep. The miners helped them up ladders to the surface. Upon their arrival, they promptly fainted or agitatedly drank whiskey, according to their dispositions. They were weak with the horror of it.

Third:

I hasten to express my regards for these altogether estimable coal-brokers and there is of course no doubt that there was the usual pro-

portion of good and generous men among them but I must confess to
a delight at for once finding the coal-broker associated in hardship and
danger with the coal-miner. I confess to a dark and sinful glee at the
description of their pangs and agonies. It seemed to me a partial and
obscure vengeance.

Fourth:

If all men who stand uselessly and for their own extraordinary profit
between the miner and the consumer were annually doomed to a certain
period of danger and darkness in the mines, they might at last comprehend the misery and bitterness of the men who toil for existence at these
hopelessly grim tasks. They would begin to understand then the value of
the miner, perhaps. Then maybe they would allow him a wage according
to his part. They will tell you all through this country that the miner is a
well-paid man. If you ask the miner about his condition he will tell you,
if he can confide in you, that the impersonal and hence conscienceless
thing, the company

The rest of the passage is missing because the next two pages of the
original manuscript have been lost, and not one word from any of these
four paragraphs was ever published. Even McClure, with his muckraker's
heart and insatiable love of controversy, felt that Crane had gone too far,
and so, without telling his twenty-two-year-old author what he was planning to do, he pulled out his editor's knife and cut that material from the
piece. When the pared-down version of "In the Depths of a Coal Mine"
was published in July, Linson reports that after Crane looked it over, he
grunted, tossed it aside, and said, "The birds didn't want the truth after all.
Why the hell did they send me up there then? Do they want the public to
think the coal mines gilded ball-rooms with the miners eating ice-cream
in boiled shirt-fronts?"

15

POEMS.

Early on in that year of years, roughly from January to the middle of
March, while still working on his novel but not yet contributing regularly
to the *Press*, Crane took a sudden, unexpected swerve in another direction,
and just like that, without rhyme or reason—literally without rhyme, though
perhaps not without reason—he found himself writing poems, one poem

after another until there were more than enough of them to make a book. They were mostly short, some consisting of just three or four lines, and all of them were oddly worded, enigmatic, and infinitely strange. They didn't look like poems or sound like poems, and even Crane himself rarely called them poems, preferring to use the more humble term he invented for them, "lines," although "lines" was occasionally transformed into "pills," no doubt as in *bitter pills*, and yet, for all that, his lines and pills were most definitely poems.

> Many red devils ran from my heart
> And out upon the page.
> They were so tiny
> The pen could mash them.
> And many struggled in the ink.
> It was strange
> To write in this red muck
> Of things from my heart.

Where did they come from? When Linson asked him that question, Crane pointed to his forehead and answered: "They came, and I wrote them, that's all." A few weeks later, when he showed some samples to Garland, his friend, "astounded by their power," asked if he had written any others, and again Crane pointed to his head, this time his temple, and replied: "I have four or five up here, all in a little row. That's the way they come—in little rows, all ready to be put down on paper. I wrote nine yesterday." A year after that, when the poems had been assembled and published as a book by the Boston firm of Copeland and Day, Hawkins "asked him how he came to hit upon that peculiar form of verse," and Crane answered: "I don't know. It just seemed to be the perfectly honest way of expressing what I felt at the moment. . . . I have a sneaking idea that those feelings which cannot be expressed satisfactorily in prose should be put into verse. I couldn't have written those things in prose form . . . any more than I could have chewed up green paper and spit out ten dollar bills."

> If I should cast off this tattered coat,
> And go free into the mighty sky;
> If I should find nothing there
> But a vast blue,
> Echoless, ignorant,—
> What then?

Except for some lost poetry written in college and the comic lament about his haggard purse that was tossed off and then crumpled up in Linson's studio, Crane's energies of the past few years had been concentrated on prose, and the several forms his prose had taken—novels, stories, satires, sketches—had all been marked by the same abundant, image-laden, muscular style. The poems that came spilling out of him in early 1894, however, were all skin and bone, stripped down to the barest, most elemental articulations, so aggressively anti-lyrical and primitive that the poetry in them is finally less apparent than it is in the prose.

> A man feared that he might find an assassin;
> Another that he might find a victim.
> One was more wise than the other.

Crane's tiny pills stood in such radical opposition to the florid, ultra-literary poems that passed as good poetry in America at the time that he often recoiled at the mere mention of the word "poet," which he said "continually reminds me of long-hair and seems to be the most detestable form of insult." Crane's aversion to the "poet," however, should not be construed as an aversion to poetry itself. In fact, he had read more than his fair share by then, not just the already mentioned Keats but Burns, Shelley, Browning, Dryden, et al., along with ample doses of Shakespeare, and he had no trouble manufacturing conventional rhyming verses when the spirit moved him, as in this jeering quatrain composed at school after he had been compelled to read (and perhaps memorize) Longfellow's dreadful "A Psalm of Life," and how prophetic that it should attack the very thing his later poems would also attack—and sometimes be attacked for: "Tell me not in joyous numbers / We can make our lives sublime / By— well, at least, not by / Dabbling much in rhyme." To a substantial share of the poetry-reading public, this hostility to convention turned him into a barbarian outlier, a self-taught bumpkin who had failed to grasp the first thing about verse techniques, but the passage of time tells a different story, and in 1950 John Berryman would calmly assert that "Crane is the most important American poet between Walt Whitman and Emily Dickinson on the one side, and his tardy-developing contemporaries Edwin Arlington Robinson and Robert Frost with Ezra Pound on the other."*

---

* The impact of *The Black Riders* extends beyond the world of poetry. No fewer than three postwar American novels use lines from Crane's poems as their titles: *In a Lonely Place*, by Dorothy B. Hughes, 1947 (turned into a film directed by Nicholas Ray and starring

> "Think as I think," said a man,
> "Or you are abominably wicked;
> "You are a toad."
> And after I had thought of it,
> I said, "I will, then, be a toad."

His first critics were his roommates, the rowdy, wisecracking artists who lived with him on East Twenty-third Street, and much as they stood by Crane as a friend and fellow artist, they found his weird, gnomic concoctions ripe for abuse. Uncharacteristically upset, he complained about it to Garland: "I wanted to write some more last night but those 'Indians' wouldn't let me do it. They howled so loud over the other lines that they nearly cracked my ears. . . . They think my verses are funny. They make a circus of me."

> If there is a witness to my little life,
> To my tiny throes and struggles,
> He sees a fool;
> And it is not fine for gods to menace fools.

Once, when Linson was visiting him, Crane "pointed to a pinned-up squib on the wall with a graphic profile of himself above it. . . . 'See what they do to me,' he said with a grin. 'They think I'm a joke, the Indians! They pin up these slams about me when I'm out. They make me ill!'" Writing from what he confessed was "slipping memory," Linson recalls that Crane also said (more or less): "The mutts yowl like bobcats when I try to write, but I'll get my innings. I'll put 'em in a book, the lobsters. They're a husky lot." A year and a half later, Crane did put them in a book, each one renamed and disguised but nevertheless drawn directly from those impoverished days at the old Art Students League building, and there they all are in *The Third Violet*, the last of Crane's novels set in New York and by far the most autobiographical work of fiction he ever published.

> "Truth," said a traveller,
> "Is a rock, a mighty fortress;
> "Often have I been to it,
> "Even to its highest tower,

"From whence the world looks black."
"Truth," said a traveller,
"Is a breath, a wind,
"A shadow, a phantom;
"Long have I pursued it,
"But never have I touched
"The hem of its garment."
And I believed the second traveller;
For truth was to me
A breath, a wind,
A shadow, a phantom,
And never had I touched
The hem of its garment.

Even Howells was perplexed, and in a brief letter sent to Crane early that fall he admitted that "these things are too orphic for me. It is a pity for you to do them, for you can do things solid and real, so superbly. . . . I do not think that a merciful Providence meant for the 'prose-poem' to last."

Once, I knew a fine song,
—It is true, believe me,—
It was all of birds,
And I held them in a basket;
When I opened the wicket,
Heavens! They all flew away.
I cried, "Come back, little thoughts!"
But they only laughed.
They flew on
Until they were as sand
Thrown between me and the sky.

But the poems had their early supporters as well, Linson and Garland to begin with and soon after John D. Barry, the same man who had written the supercilious letter debunking *Maggie* the year before. The poems excited him, however, and more than anyone else he was responsible for bringing them into the world—first by standing up and reading portions of Crane's manuscript to the assembled guests at an important New York literary gathering in April, and then by putting Crane in contact with the Boston firm that eventually published his poems in a lavishly designed book the following year. Barry's help was indispensable, although he was probably wrong to suppose that Crane had been influenced by Emily Dickinson.* He based that theory on an event that might or might not have happened, but if it did happen, he was the only person who seemed to know about it. According to Barry, when Crane first visited Howells in 1893, "Mr. Howells took from his shelves a volume of Emily Dickinson's verses and read some of them aloud. Mr. Crane was deeply impressed ... afterward he showed me thirty poems in manuscript [which] furnished the bulk of the volume entitled *The Black Riders*. It was plain enough to me that they had been directly inspired by Miss Dickinson." Although Howells might have read Dickinson out loud to Crane, he never mentioned it to anyone, and neither did Crane, who is not known ever to have spoken or written a single word about Dickinson. That isn't to say that Barry deliberately lied. Perhaps Howells did talk to him about it—to him and no one else—or perhaps he heard the story secondhand, but the more important thing to consider is this: in spite of certain superficial resemblances—their brevity and concision, their disdain of traditional forms, their emphasis on asking big questions rather than small questions—Dickinson and Crane have almost nothing in common as poets.

> There was a man who lived a life of fire.
> Even upon the fabric of time,
> Where purple becomes orange
> And orange purple,
> This life glowed,
> A dire red stain, indelible;
> Yet when he was dead,
> He saw that he had not lived.

Other supporters looked for other influences to account for the birth of Crane's bizarre little lines. One camp pointed to the French Symbolists (he had never read them), another saw his poems as a condensed form of Whitman (free verse, no rhymes), and yet another, considering him to be "the Aubrey Beardsley of poetry," imagined Crane to be a follower of the Decadents. They were all wrong. For better or worse, Crane's

---

* Dickinson had died unknown and unread in 1886, but following the initial publication of her poems in 1890, she had come to be regarded as the most brilliant and powerful poet in America. Even dead, she was still a *new poet* in 1894, and with Whitman now buried in Camden, New Jersey, she had no living rival. Howells was one of her many enthusiasts.

poems have no literary antecedents, and whether they are good poems or bad poems or merely eccentric poems, they plant themselves in the mind and are not soon forgotten. What Crane called a "poetic spout" had been opened, and out came the poems, or lines, or pills, which were in fact rhythmic eruptions from the jungle of his unconscious, blasts of psychic energy that could be sustained only for brief, ecstatic intervals, and when the first one passed, the second one came, and then the third and the fourth and the fifth until, after a couple of months, the spout ran dry.

> Black riders came from the sea.
> There was clang and clang of spear and shield,
> And clash and clash of hoof and heel,
> Wild shouts and the wave of hair
> In the rush upon the wind:
> Thus the ride of sin.

That is the first poem in the collection, and of the sixty-seven others that follow, a few can be classified as love poems (for the most part bleak and despairing), a few as war poems (parables of human idiocy), a few as philosophical quest poems (a man seeks counsel from a sage, who invariably turns out to be no wiser than the man), and a good number as attacks against organized religion and the God of wrath and vengeance who dominated Crane's childhood, poems often steeped in the language of the Bible and, as with the phrase "mighty fortress," the lyrics of Protestant hymns. Puny, pitiable man, set down on an Earth that is either hostile or indifferent to him, is a creature born out of sin and doomed to a life of sin with no recourse but to seek consolation in the arms of a compassionate, forgiving God, but if the All-Powerful One shows Himself to be a cruel and violent God, then man must resist Him at every turn, even if he is ultimately crushed for standing up in revolt.

> "And the sins of the fathers shall be visited upon the heads of the children, even unto the third and fourth generation of them that hate me."

> Well, then, I hate Thee, unrighteous picture;
> Wicked image, I hate Thee;
> So, strike with Thy vengeance
> The heads of those little men
> Who come blindly.
> It will be a brave thing.

And when this God isn't smashing His fist on the heads of little men, He can be distracted and irresponsible, even when it comes to creating the world.

> God fashioned the ship of the world carefully.
> With the infinite skill of an all-master
> Made He the hull and the sails,
> Held He the rudder
> Ready for adjustment.
> Erect stood He, scanning His work proudly.
> Then—at fateful time—a wrong called,
> And God turned, heeding.
> Lo, the ship, at this opportunity, slipped slyly,
> Making cunning noiseless travel down the ways.
> So that, forever rudderless, it went upon the seas
> Going ridiculous voyages,
> Making quaint progress,
> Turning as with serious purpose
> Before stupid winds.
> And there were many in the sky
> Who laughed at this thing.

All in all, the poems of *The Black Riders* can be looked upon as a sort of delirium that overwhelmed Crane and sent him plunging into the depths of a rage that had been smoldering inside him for years. Or if not a delirium, an exorcism, a personal battle to silence the voices that were still clamoring in his head, the haranguing, supremely confident voices of his harsh, dogmatic ancestors—who had felt they owned the truth when in fact they had owned nothing but their dogma. During that two-month-long fit of near-incessant composition, Crane learned that his rightful place was among the sinners, the lost ones, the tormented ones who squat in the desert eating of their own hearts. That poem, which begins with the lines "In the desert / I saw a creature, naked, bestial" and is reproduced on page 5, hinges on a single word, and that word, beyond its importance to this poem, is the animating force that lies at the center of Crane's book as a whole. The man who comes upon the naked creature neither judges him nor is repulsed by him but merely observes what he is doing. Then, without the slightest touch of irony, he addresses him as "friend." He could just as well have called him "brother."

When Barry invited Crane to read his poems to an audience of fellow writers and assorted guests at a meeting of the Uncut Leaves Society in mid-April, a full-dress literary affair to be held at the posh Sherry's restaurant, Crane turned him down, declaring that he would "rather die than do it." Linson was planning to go, Senger and Lawrence had come down from Port Jervis to go as well, and Button had traveled all the way from Rochester to join them, but when Crane's friends tried to talk him into changing his mind, S.C. held his ground and refused to budge. He had a horror of speaking in public, detested black-tie gatherings, and had no interest in sitting through a reading by the guest of honor, children's author Frances Hodgson Burnett (who had published *Little Lord Fauntleroy* by then but not *A Little Princess* or *The Secret Garden*). Most of all, he was probably terrified by the reception his poems would be given by such an upstanding, stodgy crowd—described in an article about the event as "cultured litterateurs"—and after the scorching of *Maggie* one year earlier, he couldn't risk another public humiliation. Barry had already offered to read the poems for him, but Crane still refused to attend, and now that the moment had come, he waved off Linson and the others, instructing them to tell him about it after they returned, and then he stayed behind and sweated it out alone.

Against all his expectations, the reading was a success. According to the same syndicated article written by Elisha J. Edwards, "Mr. Barry read the poems with delightful elocution, suggesting their perfect rhythmical quality, although they were not arranged in metrical form. If the opinion of those who heard the poems is a just one, they are likely to suggest high talent when they are published." When Crane's four friends burst in on him to deliver the good news, he thought they were pulling his leg, and it took some time before they managed to convince him that the crowd had indeed been favorably impressed. After which, in Linson's words, "the glowing report sent him to bed happy."

The next day, the *Press* published Marshall's interview of Howells with its generous words about Crane along with Marshall's introduction to a number of extracts from *Maggie*.

More signs of life.

16

MR. BINKS AND OTHERS.

He wrote some short stories that year as well, seven published and two unpublished by my reckoning, but in spite of the earlier Sullivan County stories, "The Pace of Youth," the Baby trio, and some microscopic bonbons such as "Why Did the Young Clerk Swear?," he was still a novice at the form. That would change in due course, change to such an extent that within the next two years the short story would become his preferred method of operation, but for now he was still feeling his way and testing out the possibilities.

Most of them fall flat for one reason or another—too melodramatic or too trivial, too long-winded or not developed enough—but among those failed efforts there are four exceptions, and each one is good enough to deserve mentioning. "A Night at the Millionaire's Club," which appeared in the humor magazine *Truth* just one day before the publication of "An Experiment in Misery," is a fine little bit of juvenile silliness, a blunt satire that mocks the pompous ignorance of the filthy rich with all the subtlety of a sledgehammer, but nevertheless it does its job and manages to be quite funny. A dozen aging plutocrats are sitting around in the library of their club, where the ceiling decorations "cost seventy-four dollars per square inch" and each chair occupies "two thousand dollars worth of floor," when a "seventeen-cent lackey upholstered in a three hundred dollar suit of clothes" enters the silent chamber and announces that there are four gentlemen outside who wish to enter the club. Their names are Ralph Waldo Emerson, Nathaniel Hawthorne, George Washington, and Alexander Hamilton. The club members, who are not familiar with those names, ask the lackey where the men are from, and when the servant replies that "they said they were from America," several members call for immediate and drastic action ("Don't let 'em in here!" "Throw 'em out!" "Kill 'em!"), but the calmer head of Erroll van Dyke Strathmore prevails. He instructs the lackey:

> "You will tell them that as we know no one in America . . . if they will repair quietly to any convenient place, wash their hands and procure rubber bibs, they may return and look at the remains of a cigarette which I carelessly threw upon the door-step. . . . Afterward, you will sponge off the front steps and give the door-mat to one of those downtown clubs."

So much for the masters of the Gilded Age, who get a nice poke in the eye over the course of that nine-hundred-word bagatelle, but then comes the longer, more carefully constructed "Mr. Binks' Day Off" (the *Press*, July 8). Putting aside the Baby trio, it is the first story Crane ever wrote that is not a fairy tale, a spoof, or a burlesque, something less close in spirit to Kipling or Twain than to Chekhov or (to invoke his name again) the young James Joyce, who was born just ten years after Crane.

Binks is a humble, diligent New York office worker who lives in a small Harlem flat with his wife and three young children. One afternoon, while riding uptown on a Broadway cable car, he looks out the window at the stone city and glimpses a patch of "radiant green" in Madison Square Park, a sight that unaccountably stirs him and fills his head with "subtle memories" and "the melody of his past." After a rocky dinner at home that evening, during which the downcast Binks offends his irritated wife and snaps at his children, he resolves to organize a family outing to the country on Sunday. Because they are too strapped for money to consider a full-scale excursion, they settle on a visit to Mrs. Binks's Aunt Sarah, who lives at the foot of the Ramapo Hills in New Jersey.

The beauty of this simple story is all in the details, the minutely described interactions between husband and wife, the activities of the children, the presentation of the rural setting, and how these tense city people gradually adjust and fall into the drowsy rhythms of this other world, at first horrified by the quiet and stillness around them ("I should go crazy if I had to live here," says Mrs. Binks) but little by little slowing down, until the "warm, sleepy air, pulsating with the sounds of insects, had enchained them in a great indolence." And then, as the sun begins to set, Mr. and Mrs. Binks climb a hill to take in the view below. After an intentionally banal opening on a Broadway cable car, the story ends with a somber, epiphanic vision of ultimate things:

> This song of the trees arose in low, sighing melody into the still air. It was filled with an infinite sorrow—a sorrow for birth, slavery, death. . . . Each man finds in this sound the expression of his own grief. It is the universal voice raised in lamentations. . . .
>
> The Binkses had been silent. These songs of the trees awe. They had remained motionless during this ceremony, their eyes fixed upon the mighty and indefinable changes which spoke to them of the final thing—the inevitable end. Their eyes had an impersonal expression. They were purified, chastened by this sermon, this voice calling to them from the sky. . . . Binks finally stretched forth his arm in a wondering gesture.
>
> "I wonder why," he said; "I wonder why the dickens it—why it— why——"
>
> Tangled in his tongue was the unformulated question of the centuries, but Mrs. Binks had stolen forth her arm and linked it with his. Her head leaned softly against his shoulder.

One could argue that the final passage is overwritten, which it probably is, but it also shows Crane pushing toward a new register, the same register that the young Joyce was also pushing toward in the short stories of *Dubliners*, which were also written when he was in his early twenties, a desire to build on the realism of Flaubert and inject a spiritual quality into the mundane, earth-bound struggles of ordinary human beings—which evolved into one of the central ambitions of twentieth-century modernism. There is no other story in Crane's work that resembles "Mr. Binks' Day Off." He was not someone who wrote about marriage or parenthood or the pressures of middle-class life, but in this promising if somewhat unfulfilled story he does all three, and the result is both poignant and unexpected—a brief glimpse of the path not taken.

"Stories Told by an Artist" (the *Press*, October 28) is an early stab at taking on the "husky lot" from the old Art Students League building and is written with the same down-to-the-ground realism as "Mr. Binks." Just seven and a half pages long, it is divided into three separate stories: "How 'Great Grief' Got His Holiday Dinner," "As to Payment of the Rent," and "How Pennoyer Disposed of His Sunday Dinner." Linson appears momentarily as an artist named Corinson, but the central characters are Crane (Little Pennoyer, or Penny) and his roommates Nelson Greene (Purple Sanderson), R. G. Vosburgh (Warwickson, a.k.a. Great Grief), and William Carroll (Wrinkles). The caustic humor that occasionally surges up in the three episodes comes from the characters themselves and not from an act of willful intention on the part of the author—an advance—and Crane is particularly adept here at capturing what I would call *an air of good-natured nastiness* in the dialogue, the taunting, teasing exchanges of young men forced to live together in cramped quarters, and the episodes glide along smoothly and convincingly with no wrong turns.

Then there is Crane's first story about the American West, an inconsequential but amusing lark that was written before he ever crossed the Mississippi and saw the West with his own eyes—which can only mean that the place-names alone (Denver and Omaha) provided enough inspiration to get him started. "An Excursion Ticket" (the *Press*, May 20) is a picaresque shaggy-dog story told by a veteran tramp named Billie Atkins to a group of men in a lodging house "just off the Bowery." Last winter, when Billie found himself in Denver, he was seized by a powerful urge to go to Omaha—not for any special purpose but simply because "it suddenly occurred to him that he wished to be in Omaha." So Billie hops one train after another, is beaten by one brakeman after another, and finally makes it to Omaha in such a ragged, disheveled condition that he asks to be arrested so he will have shelter for the night, and then, as he is falling asleep in his jail cell, another powerful urge comes over him, and he decides that he must go back to Denver in the morning. Charming fluff. Still, there is one sentence in the story that stands out from the others. Crane had finished *The Red Badge of Courage* in April. Now it was May, and with what I imagine must have been an unbridled sense of inner hilarity, he wrote these words to begin the most buoyant, entertaining paragraph of "An Excursion Ticket": "The rest of the trip is incoherent, like the detailed accounts of great battles." How good it must have felt to mock himself in this way, to ridicule his own book with such supremely detached irony. No doubt he paused for a moment to savor the private joke, and then, gathering his forces again, plunged on and completed the paragraph:

> Billie boarded trains and got thrown off on his head, on his left shoulder, on his right shoulder, on his hands and knees. He struck the ground slanting, straight from above and full sideways. His clothes were shredded and torn like the sails of a gale blown brig. His skin was tattooed with bloody lines, crosses, triangles, and all the devices known to geometry. But he wouldn't walk, and he was bound to reach Omaha. So he let the trainmen use him as a projectile to bombard the picturesque Western landscape.

If the short stories from that year are largely warm-ups, with a few verging on excellence and others deservedly forgotten, some of their flaws can probably be attributed to the haste with which they were written. Crane was simultaneously working on books that were far more important to him, and he had already made his bargain with the devil to churn out sellable material in order to sustain himself while he forged on with those other projects. Dollars damned him no less than they did Melville, Poe, and countless other nineteenth-century American writers, and to prove how desperately Crane needed dollars during those tough times, I should point to another one of his less than good stories from the period, "A Christmas Dinner Won in Battle," which found its way into print on January 1, 1895. The hero of the tale, a young man named Tom, happens to be a plumber in the prairie town of Levelville. Willing to publish in any newspaper or periodical that would pay him, Crane wound up selling the story to the *Plumbers' Trade Journal, Gas, Steam, and Hot Water Fitters' Review.**

---

* Melville to Hawthorne (June 1, 1851): "Dollars damn me; and the malicious Devil is forever grinning in upon me, holding the door ajar. . . . What I feel most moved to write, that is

17

MAGGIE'S NEIGHBOR.

If *Maggie* is a book set in hell, *George's Mother* is set in purgatory. If *Maggie* is a full-blown flash of blinding crimson, the color of *George's Mother* is a deep, solid gray. *Maggie* pierces the heart; *George's Mother* descends as an all-enveloping cloud of sadness. *Maggie* roars and stuns you into submission; the quieter, more subtle *George's Mother* leaves you bereft. *Maggie* can stand on its own, but *George's Mother* gains strength when it is seen as the second half of a two-part hymn to a world in which even God is on the rolls of the unemployed.

Just sixty-three pages long, Crane's little book begins with one of the most confounding first sentences in all of American literature: "In the swirling rain that came at dusk the broad avenue glistened with that deep bluish tint which is so widely condemned when it is put into pictures." Before the reader has had a chance to take a breath and plunge into the story, the story and the manner of its telling have been called into question. What deep bluish tint is he talking about—and why is it condemned when it is found in paintings? On the one hand, Crane is asserting that this bluish tint exists as a real color in the real world (why else would he put it in his book?), but others who live in that same world (critics of paintings) oppose the use of that color because . . . because of what? Not, I assume, because the color per se offends them (how can anyone be offended by a color?) but because they have convinced themselves that this color does not exist in the natural world and therefore is an offense to the truth—or to their ideas about art—when it shows up in a painting. But Crane (or the omniscient third-person narrator of his book) has just told us that he has seen it, that the rain falling on the broad avenue has a deep bluish tint, the precise shade of bluish tint that so offends critics of paintings, but because he is compelled to tell the truth as he perceives it, he says to them: Here is your cursed bluish tint, whether you like it or not.

In other words: Here is my little book, whether you like it or not.

The first sentence of that book is a manifesto, an encoded declaration of Crane's principles as an artist, and everything that follows in the book will be based on the certainty that the deep bluish tint is real, is the very sign, in fact, of *the real* itself, for unlike *Maggie*, which was mistakenly understood to be a novel in the realist tradition (even by Crane himself),

---

banned—it will not pay. Yet, altogether, write the *other* way I cannot. So the product is a final hash, and all my books are botches."

George's Mother is not a book of apparitions and monsters but of closely observed human misery and profound spiritual pain.

The difference is stark, and the reasons for the shift in tone from one book to the other are various. To begin with, close to a year and a half had gone by since Crane had abandoned his first attempt to write *George's Mother*, and when he picked it up again in May of '94 he had produced a hefty pile of work in the interim: no fewer than seventy-five poems, *The Red Badge of Courage*, and three of his most scintillating New York sketches ("The Men in the Storm" and the two "Experiments"). He was a more seasoned and accomplished writer now, but because he was still unknown and not yet standing on firm ground, he had allowed the criticisms leveled against *Maggie* in Garland's review and Barry's letter to get under his skin. If the book had been a success, he might have been better able to defend himself against their misgivings, but having gained no readers and just the scantest critical attention, and with *Red Badge* still locked in the purgatory of McClure's stalling tactics, he deferred to what he imagined was their superior knowledge of how to write fiction. A serious mistake, given that *Maggie* far surpasses anything either of those two men ever wrote, but at the same time it was an opportunity as well, an invitation to test himself in another arena. Garland had recommended that "the author . . . delineate the families living on the next street, who live lives of heroic purity and hopeless hardship," and Linson reports that when Crane told him about his meeting with Barry, one of the suggestions he had been given was to use more dialogue in his future work because "talk reveals, it lightens narrative." In *George's Mother*, Crane followed the advice of both men, for there is indeed more dialogue in it than there is in *Maggie*, and although Crane didn't travel to the next street to look for his central characters (George Kelcey and his mother live in the same tenement building as the Johnsons), they are subdued working-class folk and in no way resemble the violent grotesques who dominate the first novella. At the same time, it should also be remembered that *George's Mother* was conceived *before* Crane read Garland's review or talked with Barry. He had been intending to write an altogether different kind of book from the start (another reason, perhaps, why he welcomed their advice), a story that would concentrate on intimate psychological warfare as opposed to the wild physical battles presented in the Johnson family saga—a study in gray rather than crimson.

There was surely an autobiographical component in this as well, although how big or small cannot be precisely measured. A man named Bill Sickle from the country town of Handyville is mentioned on the second page, undoubtedly inspired by the Van Sycles, the relatives who had housed eight-year-old Stephen and his brother Edmund at their farm in Sussex County following the death of Reverend Crane, that difficult moment when the family had to leave the parsonage and temporarily dispersed to several spots in New Jersey and New York State. Then there is George's last name, Kelcey, which derives from a saloon in Asbury Park owned by a certain William B. Kelsey, one of Townley's drinking haunts, and in this story about a lost and embattled son who veers into self-destructive alcoholism, it seems certain that Crane's often inebriated brother served as one of the models for George. Harvey Wickham, Crane's boarding school classmate at Claverack, writes in his 1926 piece for the *American Mercury* that the mother and son in the book were partly based on relatives of his and that Crane had met them, a pair of middle-class people whom he later "transposed . . . to the slums, preserving only the characters—a plausible and worthless young man with an indulgent and credulous parent." Wickham could well be right, but that doesn't remove Townley from the picture, and then, to throw one more possible source into the mix, there is Crane himself. In the book, George is the last of five sons. The four others are dead, as is the father, and after spending their lives in rural Handyville, George and his mother are now in the city, inhabiting an apartment on the Lower East Side. The reason for the move is never discussed, but Crane was the youngest in a family of many children as well, and a number of his siblings were dead. A possible underground connection, but when you add in the fact that the mother is a pious Christian temperance advocate who is continually urging the impious, indifferent George to attend prayer meetings with her, the connection seems more than just possible. And yet, in spite of those similarities, the mother in the book is not a portrait of Crane's mother. She is uneducated, for one thing, which Crane's mother was not, and she is also portrayed as a weak and ineffective person, which Crane's mother most definitely was not. Nor is George modeled directly on Crane or his brother Townley or Wickham's relative. And yet, casting aside all references to the living and the dead, there is something in the interactions between George and his mother that strikes home.

The story is simple enough, almost skeletal in its construction. George Kelcey, "a brown young man" of perhaps twenty or twenty-two is trudging homeward in the glistening rain with the deep bluish tint, carrying a lunch pail under his arm and puffing on a corncob pipe, evidently "a man who worked with his muscles." He runs into Charley Jones, a former acquaintance from Handyville. An effusive fellow bubbling over with excessive goodwill, Jones invites George to have a drink with him, and off they go to a saloon, where Jones orders a whiskey and George a beer, which eventually becomes two beers, then hesitantly a third, and as they chew the fat about the old days and Jones rattles on about the five dead Kelcey men and George's mother ("The last time I remember she was as spry as a little ol' cricket, and was helpeltin' aroun' th' country lecturin' before the W.C.T.U.'s an' one thing an' another"), he tells George about the "great crowd" he hangs out with at the saloon and suggests that George come around and join them one evening, any evening, perhaps even tonight, and George says, "I will if I can."

The next chapter jumps to the tenements. No longer the dark satanic realm of careening buildings and gruesome doorways found in *Maggie*, the buildings are just buildings now, and sticking his head out a window in one of those buildings is "a man with a red, mottled face" shouting violent curses.

> He flung a bottle high across two backyards at a window of the opposite tenement. It broke against the bricks of the house and the fragments fell crackling upon the stones below. The man shook his fist.
>
> A bare-armed woman, making an array of clothes on a line in one of the yards, glanced casually up at the man and listened to his words. Her eyes followed his to the other tenement. From a distant window, a youth with a pipe, yelled some comments upon the poor aim. Two children, being in the proper yard, picked up the bits of broken glass and began to fondle them as new toys.

The target of the errantly thrown bottle is a flat across the way in which "a little old woman" is cleaning house. As she goes about her work, she is singing a Methodist hymn in a voice that "quavered and trembled out into the air as if a sound-spirit had a broken wing" until it becomes "a strange war-chant, a shout of battle and defiance, that rose and fell in harsh screams." It is this voice—and this song—that have driven the man half out of his mind with rage.

The little old woman is George's mother, and in contrast to the characters in *Maggie*, who have first names but no last names, she has a last name but no first name and is identified throughout as "the little old woman," which makes her sound like a figure from a nursery rhyme or a fairy tale. Her principal occupation besides singing hymns and attending prayer meetings is cleaning house. Maggie's mother revels in smashing furniture; with like-minded fury and conviction, George's mother cleans it to within an inch of its life.

Those occupations are central to her, but even more dominant is her preoccupation with her son, the last living link to her former days as a wife and mother in Handyville and the embodiment of all her hopes for the future. Young George has a job and supports her financially, but with Crane's by now rigorously developed practice of stripping out all but the most essential elements from his stories, we are told almost nothing about the job—except that it is in a "shop" of some kind and that George is one of several (if not many) employees who work under the supervision of a foreman. George usually returns home a little past five, but on this particular day he is sitting in a saloon drinking beer with Charley Jones, and as the little old woman goes about her household chores, she stops for a few moments at five o'clock to look out the window at the "enormous brewery" that towers over the other buildings, already anticipating George's homecoming, but forty-five minutes later he still hasn't arrived, and as the third chapter begins, she has given up her frantic dusting and scrubbing and is sitting in a chair looking at the clock. It is seven by now, and she is nervously playing out in her mind all the "mishaps and obstacles" that might have interrupted her son's journey between work and home. Up to this moment in the story, nothing unusual has happened. A mother is fretting over her precious son's whereabouts, a standard response to a standard situation—but then, suddenly, it starts to get interesting. She hears George coming up the steps in the hallway, and rather than show the smallest sign of relief or happiness, she bounds from the chair and begins to "bustle about the room. The little fearful emotions passed at once from her face. She seemed now to be ready to scold." Why scold? If George is normally on time, which all her previous actions have suggested, wouldn't she give him the benefit of the doubt and let him explain why he was delayed before feeling an urge to scold? With one deftly positioned word, Crane has just informed us that there is long-standing trouble between them. If she won't give him the benefit of the doubt, that means she already doubts him, and if she is at that point in the early pages of the book, then the trouble has been building for some time. *Scold.* Until now, nothing in Crane's work has prepared us for such a nuanced understanding of the intricate psychological machinery whirring inside his characters. It marks something new for him, an inward turn that goes beyond the exploration of just one mind (the cut-off, solitary Henry Fleming) to bring in a second mind, and because there are two now, the space between them becomes part of the drama as well, for that invisible zone of the between is not empty space—it is a fraught and highly combustible no-man's-land, the shifting, unstable locus of all human interactions.

It is instructive to chart those inner movements in the third chapter to see how Crane draws us into the complex, highly ambiguous push-pull dance of feelings between mother and son. George enters the apartment and drops his lunch pail in a corner, "evidently" (from the mother's point of view) "greatly wearied by a hard day of toil" (and by the consumption of three post-work beers). Before he can say a word, "the little old woman hobbled over to him and raised her wrinkled lips. She seemed on the verge of tears and an outburst of reproaches." Choosing to ignore those hostile signs, George says hello to her in a cheerful voice and then asks if she has "been gettin' anxious," indicating that he already knows she has been worried because he knows his mother as well as she knows him and is just as irritated by their frequent bouts of discord as she is. Rather than cut him some slack by brushing off the question, she begins to complain. "Yes," she says. "Where yeh been, George? What made yeh so late? I've been waitin' th' longest while." Without pausing to let him answer, she then blurts out: "Don't throw your coat down there. Hang it up behind th' door." Crane doesn't mention it in the text, but the implication is that George was about to drop his coat on the floor, something he is wont to do and which continues to be a major bone of contention between them throughout the book. In this instance, however, George silently does as she asks, then goes over to the sink and washes up. It is only now that he finally has a chance to tell her why he was delayed. "Well, yeh see, I met Jones—you remember Jones? Ol' Handyville fellah. An' we had t'stop an' talk over ol' times. Jones is quite a boy." By way of response, "the little old woman's mouth set in a sudden straight line. 'Oh, that Jones,' she said. 'I don't like him.'"

For the first time since coming home, George gives his mother a less than friendly look, interrupting "a flurry of white towel" to ask why she would say such a thing about a man she probably hasn't talked to once in her life, but his mother stands firm and says that Jones isn't the sort of person he should be going around with. "He ain't a good man," she says. "I'm sure he ain't. He drinks." George bursts out laughing, but at the same time he isn't "shocked at this information." His mother nods her head for emphasis and then goes on to explain that she once saw Jones coming out of a hotel in Handyville "an' he could hardly walk. He drinks! I'm sure he drinks!" Still refusing to pick a fight with her, George lets out an exasperated "Holy smoke!" and that is that—for now.

When the next paragraph begins, some time has passed. They are sitting at the table, well into their dinner, and the mood is one of relative peace. "The youth leaned back in his chair, in the manner of a man who is paying for things. His mother bended alertly forward, apparently watching each mouthful. She perched on the edge of her chair, ready to spring to her feet and run to the closet or the stove for anything he might need. She was as anxious as a young mother with a babe."

This is the other side of their elaborate two-step dance, the pull side as opposed to the push side, the maternal-filial bond that never fully comes undone because it can't, but the balance between attachment and repulsion is so delicately poised in both of them that no sooner does one pull than the other begins to push, which is precisely what happens next, for now that mother and son are temporarily in harmony, she cannot leave well enough alone and does the one thing that is sure to annoy him and upset the balance again. Mustering all her courage, as if "she had arrived at a supreme moment," she asks George to go to the prayer meeting with her that night. The young man drops his fork and tells her she must be crazy. Undaunted, the mother begins to plead, throwing out one argument after another to induce him to change his mind (he never goes out with her anymore, it's such a long and lonely walk, "and don't yeh suppose that when I have such a big, fine strappin' boy, I want 'im t' beau me aroun' some?") but never anything about how beneficial it will be to his soul if he attends the meeting, whereas the meeting is uppermost in George's thoughts: "A vision came to him of dreary blackness arranged in solemn rows. A mere dream of it was depressing." It's not that George wants to disappoint his mother, but after doing his best to humor her and fend her off, he finally has to give a straight answer, and so the third chapter ends:

> "Well, now, y'see," he said, quite gently, "I don't wanta go, an' it wouldn't do me no good t' go if I didn't want to go."
>
> His mother's face swiftly changed. She breathed a huge sigh, the counterpart of ones he had heard upon like occasions. She put a tiny black bonnet on her head, and wrapped her figure in an old shawl. She cast a martyr-like glance upon her son and went mournfully away. She resembled a limited funeral procession.
>
> The young man writhed under it to an extent. He kicked moodily at a table-leg. When the sound of her footfalls died away he felt distinctly relieved.

The rest of the book unfurls from that scene, spinning forward in a compact spiral of small, ever more alarming events as George slowly loses his grip on himself and sinks to the bottom of the world—which ends up destroying his mother, who dies in the last sentence of the book. Crane's original title was *A Woman Without Weapons*. It is unclear why he abandoned it for the published version, but it gives a sharper idea of what he was thinking when he began the project than the anodyne choice he eventually made. Mrs. Kelcey sees herself as a soldier in God's Christian army, but the only weapon she carries is her faith, and while there are no doubt countless souls out there who long to be redeemed by that faith, George is not one of them. With her own boy, she is powerless.

George goes to pieces, but there is no simple explanation to account for what happens to him. Multiple forces are at work, and each blow comes at the precise moment when it seems calculated to cause the most harm to his fragile, unformed self. He has been in New York for three years when the book begins, but he is still isolated and apparently without friends. He has his job and his fellow workers (none of whom he sees outside work) and beyond that nothing but his doting, fretful, scolding mother and the suffocating confines of a small tenement flat. Starved for companionship, he downs three beers to prolong his chance encounter with Charley Jones, and then, the moment his dejected mother sets off for her prayer meeting, he slips out of the flat to join the ex-Handyville man and his cronies at the saloon. They are an older, more experienced, hard-drinking lot who welcome George into their circle, and before long he begins to feel that he is "passing the happiest evening of his life," unable to see that his companions are no more than a bunch of pathetic blowhard buffoons.

He drinks heavily that night, swept up in the camaraderie of "those fine fellows," and as he goes on drinking one beer after another, "he felt his breast expand with manly feeling" and imagines himself performing great and noble sacrifices on behalf of his new friends. When someone announces that it is one o'clock, however, he is startled by the lateness of the hour and rushes home, since he must be off to work by seven.

A fierce hangover exacts its revenge on him in the morning, and for the next week or so he drinks nothing and returns home directly from the shop every evening. His mother is encouraged. George seems to have settled back into his "sunny-tempered," amiable self, and for a time she becomes convinced that she is "a perfect mother, rearing a perfect son," but another blow is about to descend on George, and when it comes—in a flash of brutal disappointment—it strikes so hard that it staggers him and ultimately knocks him off his feet. When he tries to stand up again, he discovers that his legs are broken.

George is pining for Maggie. He caught his first glimpse of her one afternoon on the stairway of their building, coming up with "a pail of beer in one hand and a brown-paper parcel under her arm," and although the look she gave him was both "indifferent" and "unresponsive," the encounter turns him upside down: "As she came to the landing, the light from a window passed in a silver gleam over the girlish roundness of her cheek. It was a thing that he remembered." More than remembered, it is a thing that begins to haunt him until "the shade of this girl was with him continually," and every time he hears Mrs. Johnson go off on one of her loud, drunken binges upstairs, he is almost happy because it allows him "to sit in the dark and make scenes in which he rescued the girl from her hideous environment." George is a dreamer, one of those stifled, maladroit young men who burn with passion but are unable to express themselves, and as was the case with Maggie in the other book, his head is crammed with hackneyed visions of idealized romantic love, an impossible realm in which he, as the principal actor, is no longer himself "but himself as he expected to be," a gallant figure lifted from the pages of the novels he has read, brainless, high-flown books that have taught George to believe "there was a goddess in the world whose business it was to wait until he should exchange a glance with her." Now that the glance has been exchanged, he deludes himself into thinking that she must know how he feels about her because—after all—those feelings are blazing so brightly in him that they must be visible even to the blind.

> He laid clever plans by which he encountered her in the halls, at the door, on the street. When he succeeded in meeting her he was always overcome by the thought that the whole thing was obvious to her. He could feel the shame of it burn his face and neck. To prove to her that she was mistaken he would turn away his head or regard her with a granite stare. . . .
>
> He saw that he need only break down the slight conventional barriers and she would discover his noble character. Sometimes he would see it all in his mind. It was very skillful. But then his courage flew away at the supreme moment. Perhaps the whole affair was humorous to her. Perhaps she was watching his mental contortions. She might laugh. He felt that he would then die or kill her. He could not approach the dread moment.

He never does. Before he can find the gumption to look her in the eye or address a single word to her, George is approached by a stranger in the halls of the building who asks him where "the Johnson birds live." Two flights up, George says, and then he notices the man's impressive, fashionable clothes, "the fine worldly air, the experience, the self-reliance, the courage that shone in his countenance" and understands that his dream of winning Maggie for himself is dead. The man is doubtless Pete the bartender, "that pig of the world in his embroidered cloak" who has come to escort the pretty Johnson bird out into the city on their first date, and the defeated George slinks off "flushing and ashamed." He enters the Kelcey flat, and an instant later, "in a high key of monotonous irritability," his mother is after him again about not hanging up his coat. For the first time, George erupts in anger, turning toward her with a look "hard with hate and rage." The two of them stare at each other in silence, and after a long moment the distraught mother stumbles off to her room, inadvertently banging her hip into the corner of the table as she heads for the door and finally goes in. George sits down in a chair, thrusts out his legs, sticks his hands in his pockets, and lowers his head onto his chest, looking blankly at nothing. "There swept over him all the self-pity that comes when the soul is turned back from a road."

This is the defining moment of the story, and from then on there is nothing to stop George's inevitable collapse into hard, steady drinking, the loss of his job, and his new life among a band of shiftless thugs. "Self-pity" is the crucial word in the last sentence of the seventh chapter, and as the eighth chapter begins Crane pushes forward and unravels the psychological consequences of that perilous state of mind. For George, the loss of Maggie is not simply a personal setback or an unlucky turn on the path to love, it is a metaphysical catastrophe, the destruction not only of the little world of his immediate surroundings but of his entire view of the world at large.

> During the next few days Kelcey suffered from his first gloomy conviction that the earth was not grateful to him for his presence upon it. When sharp words were said to him, he interpreted them with what seemed to be a lately acquired insight. He could now perceive that the universe hated him.

One evening, George runs into Charley Jones again and is asked to come to "a blow-out t'morrah night." More in need of companionship than ever, George jumps at the chance, and then Crane turns the last screw of his startling disquisition on the inner workings of George Kelcey's mind: "As he walked home he thought that he was a very grim figure. He was about to taste the delicious revenge of a partial self-destruction. The universe would regret its position when it saw him drunk."

In an early chapter of *Maggie*, Mr. Johnson storms out of the apartment "determined upon a vengeful drunk." The object of that revenge is his wife, but here the stakes are much higher, so high that it is now a question of partly destroying yourself in order to punish the universe. It is the attitude of a small, petulant child—a self-pitying child—but that is what George has become now: a child in the body of a man, a puny being with no more weight than a feather, liable to be blown in any direction by the first gust of wind that comes his way.

He drinks too fast and too much at the party, embarrassing himself with slurred, barely coherent declarations about Maggie ("I lovsh girl live down my shtreet. Thash reason 'm drunk, 'tis!") until he passes out, dead to the world as he sleeps it off in a tangle of overcoats piled on the floor. Once again, he resolves to mend his ways, going so far as to allow his mother to talk him into attending a prayer meeting, but listening to the minister's sermon does nothing for George except to prove, once again, that he is "damned." The effort to reform ebbs away into sullen indifference, he slips back, discovers that he can down "from ten to twenty glasses of beer" over the course of an evening, and when his mother tries to lure him to the church one more time, he puts his foot down and says no. Increasingly resentful and bitter, he begins to treat her more and more harshly, and every question she asks him is answered with a lie. He gravitates toward a gang of witless toughs, young know-it-alls who spend their time boozing, fighting, and hanging out on street corners, an admirable fraternity in George's eyes, every one of them bored and contemptuous and "too clever to work." The pot is boiling now, and when George finally explodes in an ugly confrontation with his mother, life in the apartment devolves into a tense, unbearable standoff.

> For three days they lived in silence. He brooded upon his mother's agony and felt a singular joy in it. As opportunity offered, he did little despicable things. He was going to make her abject. He was now uncontrolled, ungoverned; he wished to be an emperor. Her suffering was all a sort of compensation for his own dire pains.
>
> She went about with a gray, impassive face. It was as if she had survived a massacre in which all that she loved had been torn from her by the brutality of savages.
>
> One evening at six he entered and stood looking at his mother as she peeled potatoes. She had hearkened to his coming listlessly, without emotion, and at his entrance she did not raise her eyes.
>
> "Well, I'm fired," he said, suddenly.
>
> It seemed to be the final blow.

And yet, the very next day, as a new calamity arrives and sets everything spinning around again in a sudden half turn, we discover that the bond between mother and son—which seems to have been broken for good—is still intact. It is one of the masterstrokes of this painful little book, and it underscores how deeply its young author has penetrated the minds of his two principal characters.

George is standing on the corner with his pals when three boys run up to him and announce that he is wanted at home because his "ol' woman" is sick. "A swift dread struck Kelcey," the air around him turns "ominous and dark," and a pall of disaster descends upon "the street, the buildings, the sky, the people." When George looks over at his friends, he sees that they are watching him, and rather than try to explain himself, he turns his back on them and starts for home, "glad that they could not see his face, his trembling lips, his eyes wavering in fear." One day earlier, he had been rejoicing in his mother's agony. Now that she could be dying, he is panicked.

It turns out to be a false alarm. When he enters the apartment and finds his mother sitting calmly in a chair, he feels "an unspeakable thrill of thanksgiving." She explains that she had a dizzy spell, nothing more than that, and after she fell down behind the stove, Mrs. Callahan (their neighbor) helped her back to her feet and called in a doctor, who said she would probably be all right within a couple of hours. Speaking in a voice that has "the ring of vitality in it," she assures him that "I don't feel nothin'," to which George responds: "Lord, I was scared."

Relieved but still not fully recovered from his panic, George is suddenly at a loss about what to do next. He asks if there is anything he can get for her. No, nothing, she says, and yet there George sits, eagerly looking at her, his eyes filled with love, and if not "for the shame of it he would have called her endearing names." They talk a little about hunting for a new job (the sorest of sore subjects), but George insists that he is going to try, try as hard as he can to land one. Empty talk, perhaps, but he has convinced himself that he believes what he is saying, and from his tone the little old woman understands that "he was making peace with her." George winds up cooking dinner for them. As they sit at the table eating together, they share some laughs over George's feigned ineptitude as a chef. The chapter ends with the two of them sitting side by side in chairs looking out the window. The mother's hand is resting on her son's head.

Do not be deceived, however. This tender moment does not signify a permanent reconciliation so much as another truce, one more pause in a long succession of flare-ups and pauses, and if time were not running out on them, there would be more flare-ups ahead. The false alarm has served as a jolt to reactivate George's sympathies for his mother, but George himself is still plunging downward. The next chapter begins with young Kelcey asking his middle-aged drinking companions for a loan, but they all turn him down with one feeble excuse or another, and he understands that they regard him as someone "below them in social position." They have lost interest in him now that he is desperate and unemployed, and after such a promising start with affable Charley Jones and company, he has been expelled from the group.

In the next paragraph, he is back with the toughs, the other small society he is struggling to find a place in, still a newcomer and not yet completely trusted or accepted, which puts him in the position of having to do reckless, foolish things in order to gain full status among them. On this particular day, Fidsey, Corcoran, and their several accomplices have procured a "big can" (a large tin pail of beer) by swiping it from the new bartender at the corner saloon, and they goad George into accompanying them to a nearby vacant lot to drink down their spoils by challenging his loyalty and accusing him of "gittin' t'be a reg'lar willie." In the lot, a dispute breaks out between Fidsey and another tough known as Blue Billie, and George, who is looking away and "apparently deep in other matters," is suddenly appointed to settle accounts with Blue Billie. Just as they are squaring off, however, a little wild-eyed boy comes charging down the slope toward them, bursting out "in a rapid treble" that Kelcey is wanted at home, his mother is sick again, and "yehs better run." George backs off from Blue Billie and says he thinks he should go. By way of support, his would-be friends howl at him. He tries to explain: "'Well,' he continued, 'I can't——I don't wanta——I don't wanta leave me mother be——she——,'" but "his words [are] drowned in the chorus of their derision."

Exiled again. First by the older ones, and now by the younger ones. There is nowhere for him to go now except back to his mother and what is described in the first sentence of the final chapter as "the chamber of death."

Throughout the book, Crane has handled the scenes in the apartment as if they were small bits of theater, with ample dialogue and vividly mapped-out stage directions, along with emotional cues to suggest why someone sits down or stands up or thrusts his hands into his pockets, as well as remarks about lighting, sound, props, and scenic design. *Maggie* has a cinematic feel to it, but the interior action in *George's Mother* evokes the atmosphere of a play, and until now the cast of that play has been limited to just two characters. In the final act, the two become five, and then, in the final half page, seven, as a pair of offstage voices is heard (to great effect) coming from the hallway outside the apartment. There is a young doctor attending to Mrs. Kelcey when George enters his mother's bedroom. There is a young minister who comes at the end to replace the young doctor, and there is Mrs. Callahan throughout, "feverishly dusting" and polishing and cleaning, arranging "everything in decorous rows" and "preparing for the coming of death."

When George walks in, the little old woman is stretched out on her bed, "sickeningly motionless, save for her eyes, which rolled and swayed in maniacal glances." She is unable to recognize her son when he talks to her. Her mind has withdrawn to a distant place, and specters from her past have crowded into the room. She calls out to her dead husband, Bill, who is plowing in a field: "Bill——o-o-oh, Bill——have yeh seen Georgie? Is he out there with you? Georgie! Georgie! Come right here this minnet! Right——this——minnet!" A moment later, she is telling the invisible people in the room to get out, she doesn't want them there anymore, and they should go away, go away, go away.

Seven lines down, the novella heads toward its conclusion:

> The little old woman lay still with her eyes closed. On the table at the head of the bed was a glass containing a water-like medicine. The reflected lights made a silver star on its side. The two men sat side by side, waiting. Out in the kitchen Mrs. Callahan had taken a chair by the stove and was waiting.
>
> Kelcey began to stare at the wall-paper. The pattern was clusters of brown roses. He felt them like hideous crabs crawling upon his brain.
>
> Through the door-way he saw the oil-cloth covering of the table catch a glimmer from the warm afternoon sun. The window disclosed a fair, soft sky, like blue enamel, and a fringe of chimneys and roofs, resplendent here and there. An endless roar, the eternal trample of the marching city, came mingled with vague cries. At intervals the woman out by the stove moved restlessly and coughed.
>
> Over the transom from the hall-way came two voices.
>
> "Johnnie!'
>
> "Wot!"
>
> "You come right here t'me! I want yehs t' go t' d' store fer me!"
>
> "Ah, ma, send Sally!"
>
> "No, I will not! You come right here!"
>
> "All right, in a minnet!"
>
> "Johnnie!"
>
> "In a minnet, I tell yeh!"
>
> "Johnnie——" There was a sound of a heavy tread, and later a boy squealed. Suddenly the clergyman started to his feet. He rushed forward and peered. The little old woman was dead.

Another mother and another son, and who can say what the future holds for little Johnnie from across the hall?

By the time Crane finished *George's Mother*, in November 1894, *The Red Badge of Courage* had been accepted for serial publication by Bacheller. After one possible rejection (no one knows for sure), he decided to hold on to his new manuscript until the verdict on *Red Badge* had come in, since the success or failure of that book would determine what happened to the other. The results of the serial version were inconclusive, and so he went on waiting until *Red Badge* was released as a book in September 1895. It was only then that he sent out *George's Mother*, which was finally published in 1896. After the sterling notices and vigorous sales of *Red Badge*, expectations must have been high, but Crane's second little book about the New York tenements arrived with a barely audible thud—just as the first one had. A grim and hopeless book, the reviewers said. They were probably right. It is a grim and hopeless book, but it is also an exceptional one—just as *Maggie* is. For the first time since coming to New York, the normally impetuous Crane had played his hand cautiously, but it hadn't done him any good. Slum stuff turned people off.

18

PIKE COUNTY PUZZLE AND BATTLES WITH BOSTON.

What intrigues me most about Crane is his many-ness. Not just the several selves he carried around with him in his small body (every one of us is a spectrum of multiple, contradictory selves) but his talent for being able to think one thought while also thinking another thought and perhaps a third and even a fourth without losing track of the first, or, to put it another way, the ability to inhabit different states of mind in rapid, vertiginous succession. Without that talent, the efflorescence of 1894 would be inexplicable. While working on his novel, he was also working on his poems, and while working on his novel and poems he was also working on his newspaper sketches and various stories, and while working on his newspaper sketches and various stories after he had finished the novel and the poems, he was working on his novella, and while working on his novella—that grimmest of grim, hopeless books—he took a month-long summer break, went off into the wilds with a gang of friends, and wrapped up his holiday by co-producing the nuttiest, most outlandish comic absurdities that had tumbled from his head since the Great Bug Hoax of 1891.

To celebrate her son's appointment to the staff of Hahnemann Medical College in Philadelphia, Fred Lawrence's mother sponsored a group outing to the woods near Twin Lakes in Pike County, Pennsylvania. More than two dozen young men and women were invited, and they set off in the company of Mrs. Lawrence and two other women, who served as chaperones and cooks during those days and nights of tent-living, sports and games, musical soirées, and ceaseless joking that lasted throughout the entire month of August. Linson joined the party sometime during the first week and later recorded that "Steve was happy there as a colt in pasture. The freedom of the woods and the youthful horseplay on land and water sports were good medicine. Three times daily we fed at a long table, standing like the animals we were. In the orange light of a great campfire we gathered of evenings and perched on low branches and logs, Stephen with his back to a tree picking at a guitar." Linson also gives the only surviving account of Crane playing baseball after he had dropped out of college:

> One afternoon it was demonstrated to me that, in spite of his slight appearance, Stephen was no weakling. We were playing baseball. He was behind the bat. I was legging out a home run past third base and somewhat in a hurry. By some inadvertence I had not seen the ball go in ahead of me by a bare second or two, but I found it at the end of Steve's arm. The impact was like hitting the end of a wagon tongue. "Sorry, CK, you're out." Very casual, but effective. I *was* out, for the rest of the game.

The tradition among Twin Lakes campers was to produce a commemorative keepsake to mark the time they had spent there—a photograph, a funny poem, whatever struck their fancy. In 1894, with the help of his friend Louis Senger, Crane took on the ambitious task of creating a four-page newspaper, the *Pike County Puzzle,* which was run off on the presses of the *Port Jervis Union* after the camping party had left Twin Lakes. It isn't clear if they worked on it over the course of the month or whipped it up in a frenzied burst of nonstop composition immediately after returning to Port Jervis, as Linson's remarks would suggest: "Steve and Lou spent one hilarious night in Senger's home editing this unique literature. In an adjoining room I might have slept two hours."

However it was composed, the results are indeed hilarious. As a participant in the enterprise, the *Union* proudly took note of the one-off paper and commended Crane on his good work:

The "Puzzle" from beginning to end is the product of the prolific genius Mr. Crane and all that it contains, including editorials, advertisements, telegraphic dispatches, reading notices and puffs, were written by him. . . . The editor has clearly aimed to be clever, amusing, funny, satirical, ironical and witty at the expense of his associates (not even sparing himself) and has succeeded in producing a clever burlesque.

Printed in four columns across four maximum-width broadsheet pages and set in type small enough to be read most comfortably with a magnifying glass, the contents of the *Puzzle*, when reconfigured into book form for volume VIII of the collected works, stretch out over twenty-seven and a half pages. Dated August 28, 1894, the *Pike County Puzzle* masthead includes the paper's inspirational motto (attributed to Senger), "HSTR WITH XZOASCVAR," and in the numerous articles and squibs that follow nearly everyone is mocked, nearly everyone is given a nickname (Wicked Wickham, Stormy Tubbs, Ravenous Pierce), and the pancake-loving Crane, known as Pan-Cake Pete, is later transformed into Signor Pancako Peti in a report entitled "GRAND CONCERT":

Signor Peti broke his voice across his knees, spliced it simply with a silk handkerchief and sang: "Give Me Back My Whiskey Slings," with intense emotion and feeling. Next he held it between his thumb and finger in plain sight of the audience, when, presto, it was gone. The wondering multitude gaped when the Signor, passing down the centre aisle, laughed playfully and drew his voice from the left vest pocket of Ontario Bradfield's sweater. The Signor passed from one feat to another in his dazzling Italian manner, and as the curtain fell for the last time, all united in declaring that they had spent one of the most pleasant, enjoyable, and disastrous evenings of their lives.

That gives a fair idea of the tone, which at its funniest achieves the kind of spirited nonsense found in Lewis Carroll and S. J. Perelman, at its wildest resembles the mashed-up yoking of incongruous elements found in Dada and the pages of *Mad*, and at its least inventive smacks of the winking sarcasm found in college humor magazines. In the aggregate, the *Puzzle* is a telling reminder of just how young Crane still was in the summer of 1894, for in spite of all he had accomplished in the past few years, if he had stuck with college and earned his degree at Syracuse, he would have graduated with the senior class just weeks before the summer holiday in Pike County.

What is most appealing about this flood of wacky exuberance are the moments when Crane pokes fun at himself—especially at his own serious-ness. In a one-sentence morsel under the headline ACCIDENT, we learn that "As Stephen Crane was traversing the little rope ladder that ascends the right hand side of the cloud-capped pinnacle of his thoughts, he fell and was grievously injured." Later on, in an advice column filled with ques-tions such as "Do you recommend mixed drinks?," "Have you ever seen anything of my table manners?," and "Would you advise me to smile so freely?," Stephen Crane writes in and asks, "What can I do with my voice?" The answer: "In the spring, Stephen, you can plough with it, but after corn ripens you will have to seek employment in the blue-stone works. We have seen voices like yours used very effectively as cider presses."

As a rule, the more insane the writing becomes, the more pleasurable it is to read: "As Mr. S. Energetic Brinson was running a lawn mower lightly over his beard, a blade caught and interfered with his features so seri-ously that . . . his sister, Miss Charlotte Montague Brinson, the marvelous impersonator of activity, swooned and became paralysed in both arms. It is said that she will not be able to wash dishes for four years."

And yet, at the same time (to use those words again), in the midst of such widespread merriment, Crane was also brooding about his poems. The manuscript of *The Black Riders* was sitting in the Boston offices of Copeland and Day, and whether it had been sent to them by Barry or by Crane at Barry's suggestion, some time had passed, and Crane had received no word about whether they were intending to publish it or not. On or about August 23, while still at Twin Lakes, he sent off a worried note to Boston.

> Dear sirs:——
> I would like to hear from you concerning my poetry. I wish to have my out-bring all under way by early fall and I have not heard from you in some time.* I am in the dark in regard to your intentions.
> Yours very truly
> Stephen Crane

---

* "Out-bring" is a bizarre locution, archaic enough to sound as if Crane were writing in Anglo-Saxon, but there it stands on page 1270 of *Webster's New Universal Unabridged Dic-tionary* (second edition, 1983) defined as "to bring or carry forth," which seems to sug-gest something akin to "output." In general, Crane's 1890s vocabulary does not sound dated in the early twenty-first century, but every now and then there is a word that jars to some degree—the past tense of "bend," for example, which Crane nearly always writes as "bended" rather than the more contemporary "bent."

There must have been a quick reply, since Crane sent off another letter to them from Hartwood on September ninth, not the least bit pleased by what they had written. We must remember that McClure was now in his fifth month of torturing Crane with his refusal to commit himself on the war novel, and Crane's frustration had been steadily mounting. The letter from Copeland and Day had demanded a number of changes and cuts, and Mr. Funny-Bones of the *Pike County Puzzle*, who was equally the author of *The Black Riders*, wrote back to them in a monumental snit.

> Dear sirs:——We disagree on a multitude of points. In the first place I should absolutely refuse to have my poems printed without many of those which you just as absolutely mark "No." It seems to me that you cut all the ethical sense out of the book. All the anarchy, perhaps. It is the anarchy which I particularly insist upon. From the poems which you keep you could produce what might be termed a "nice little volume of verse by Stephen Crane" but for me there would be no satisfaction. The ones which refer to God, I believe you condemn altogether. I am obliged to have them in when my book is printed. There are some which I believe unworthy of print. These I herewith enclose. As for the others, I cannot give them up—in the book.
>
> In the second matter, you wish I would write a few score more. It is utterly impossible to me. We would be obliged to come to an agreement upon those that are written.
>
> If my position is impossible to you, I would not be offended at the sending of all the retained lines to the enclosed address. I beg to express my indebtedness to you and remain
>
> Yours sincerely
>
> Stephen Crane

He was still a no one at that point, but this magnificently vituperative letter in defense of his ethical and aesthetic position—the *anarchy*, the energy, the savage contempt for what is considered "nice"—demonstrates that however keen he was on having his work published, he was willing to forgo publication if the publisher dared to compromise his work. Good for him, but also good for Copeland and Day that they stuck with him and saw the project through to the end. Seven poems were eventually cut (with Crane's approval), but their absence in no way diminishes the anarchy that courses through *The Black Riders* from the moment the riders emerge from the sea and begin their wild rush upon the world.

Crack twenty-seven and a half pages of jokes one day, and then, twelve days after that, when you feel yourself backed into a corner, put on your boxing gloves and start punching. For a person who rarely punched, the little man's right was exceptionally strong.

19

WE ALREADY KNOW WHAT HAPPENS NEXT. CRANE COMES BACK TO New York in mid-September and continues his freelance work for the *Press*. In October, Marshall puts him in contact with Irving Bacheller, and a truncated version of the war novel is accepted for serial publication. In November, he finishes *George's Mother*. After the truncated version appears in eleven or twelve newspapers around the country in early December, he gives *The Red Badge of Courage* to Ripley Hitchcock, and eventually the book will be accepted for publication by D. Appleton and Company. Meanwhile, Bacheller has commissioned him to travel west, south, and down to Mexico on a lengthy tour as a newspaper-syndicate reporter, and as Crane packs his bags and prepares to leave for Nebraska by way of Philadelphia and St. Louis in late January 1895, I want to stop for a moment and begin to address some of the issues I raised earlier (page 63). To do that will require probing more deeply into who Crane was and, to whatever degree possible, discovering what he saw when he stepped back and looked at himself when no one else was in the room.

LOOKING AT OTHERS. The starting point is Crane's 1892 letter to his friend Tommie Borland and the words "I—I think black is quite good— if—if its yellow and young." An astonishing number of things are going on here at the same time. Not only does Crane sound guilty ("read these word in a whisper"), and not only is he giving his younger, worshipful friend the lowdown on the secrets of "the ways of a man with the maid," he is exposing a racist attitude toward black people (black is fine as long as it isn't too black) and in the same breath denigrating women by reducing them to nothing more than objects of male sexual desire. Crane was twenty when he wrote those words, and for all the adolescent bravura lurking behind them, they raise important questions about who he was and how he regarded those he perceived as different from himself, which encompasses not only black people but American Indians, Asian Indians, the Chinese, Mexicans, and all white European immigrants who were not English-speaking Protestants, in particular the ones who were most visible in 1890s New York: Irish people, Italians, and Jews. As an artist, Crane was a man ahead of his time, but as a man he was of his time as much as any other white Anglo-Saxon Protestant, and in that era of Jim Crow and *Plessy v. Ferguson*, of the double-barreled Chinese Exclusion

Act, of massive resistance to southern and eastern European immigration (as represented by the members of JOUAM), of universal anti-Semitism, and of the American cavalry's final war against the Indians, Crane stands out as a mostly tolerant and egalitarian member of his class, but not even he was altogether immune to its prejudices and deep-in-the-bone tribal assumptions, and here and there those ethnic antagonisms crop up in his work, most blatantly in an early, unpublished piece that was probably written during his semester at Syracuse in 1891, "Greed Rampant," which came as a shock to me the first time I read it.

A dramatic skit set in Paradise, N.J., and taking place at a time indicated as "the end of it," the little work sports a cast that includes Mr. John P. St. Peter, a "Crowd of Gentiles," and a "Mob of Jews." Mr. St. Peter is dozing comfortably on a small box next to the turnstile at the central gate of his kingdom in Paradise, N.J. A roar of "loud voices raised in wrath, discussions, dissensions, quarrels, bickerings, and the noise of wildly scrambling feet" is heard from without, and in rushes the mob of Jews, comprised of "thirteen clothes dealers" and "two-score pawnbrokers" among various anonymous others. After much pushing, shoving, and fighting, they eventually sit down in the front seats. Next come the Gentiles, who "march in an orderly and modest manner," and when they discover that all the good seats are occupied by Jews, that "the entire front is a wriggling mass of big noses and diamonds," they are "grieved." One of them, described as "thoughtful," eventually comes up with a plan. Pulling a fountain pen from his pocket, he prints out a sign on a stray piece of cloth, mounts it on a walking stick, and then parades up and down the room with his banner: "JOB LOTS. JOB LOTS. DOWN IN SHEOL, CAPE MAY COUNTY, NEW JERSEY. Selling out at 2 per cent of cost." The Jews jump at the deal, and as "an avalanche of bargain-hunters" goes pouring out of the room, the Gentiles move up and take over the good seats.

It is impossible to know what prompted Crane to write this three-page farce or what audience he was intending to amuse with it, but I am hard-pressed to imagine that anyone but the most locked-in anti-Semite would feel inclined to laugh. Crane was young, but not so young as to be unaware of what he was doing, yet he sat down and wrote this dismal nonsense, sufficiently pleased with the result to have the manuscript typed up by someone, perhaps with the thought of trying to publish it somewhere. The only positive thing I can say about "Greed Rampant" is how lucky it was for him that it never saw the light of day again until it landed in an archive at the University of Virginia seventy years later.

That was 1891. On July 26, 1896, an article by Howells appeared in the *World* comparing Crane's *Maggie* to the recently published *Yekl: A Tale of the New York Ghetto*, by Jewish author Abraham Cahan, contending that "both of these writers persuade us that they have told the truth" and adding that "I cannot help thinking that we have in him [Cahan] a writer of foreign birth who will do honors to American letters."* On August 15, Crane wrote to Howells. After thanking him for the kind remarks about his work, he begins the next paragraph by saying, "I would like to know Mr. Cahan. I am reading his book and I am wondering how in the name of Heaven he learned how to do it." Hardly the words of a man who had an axe to grind against the Jews, and when Crane and Cahan met ten days later at Howells's summer retreat in Far Rockaway, the encounter so impressed Cahan that he was moved to write about it in his memoirs thirty-two years later. Noting Crane's thinness and "intelligent appearance," he went on to observe that "rarely does the talent of a gifted person mirror itself in his face. With Crane, his talent was infused throughout his entire being."

If nothing else, this tells us that Crane was not someone who shunned Jews as a matter of principle. He admired Cahan's work, and not only did he welcome the chance to meet the author of *Yekl*, he initiated the meeting himself by contacting Howells and asking for Cahan's address. Should we therefore look upon "Greed Rampant" as a youthful aberration and let the matter drop? Mostly yes, I think, but not entirely. Cahan stood out for Crane as a fellow writer of talent, a man worthy of respect, but on the rare occasions when Jewish characters flit through Crane's work, not one of them stands out from the ethnic stereotypes of the era. Jews are either pawnbrokers or earn their living in the needle trade, just as Italians are either fruit vendors or musicians (e.g., Signor Pancako Peti). In Asbury Park, there are the "brown-skinned sons of India" and the "self-possessed Chinaman," but in his New York writings the Chinese tend to be remote human blurs, and when they come into the foreground it is only briefly, as when Maggie's brother is arrested "for assaulting a Chinaman." The Irish of the tenements are consistently portrayed as drunks (Maggie's parents), but when Crane traveled to Ireland in 1897, he started paying closer attention and his thinking changed,

---

* Abraham Cahan (1860–1951) was born in Lithuania and made his way to New York in 1882. A socialist and bilingual writer, he was editor of the Yiddish-language *Jewish Daily Forward* for forty-six years and also contributed articles to numerous English-language dailies, among them the *New York Press* and the *New York Sun*. His best-known novel is *The Rise of David Levinsky* (1917).

which led to a series of short, deeply sympathetic articles about life in small Irish villages along the southern coast. Which is to say, he mostly wasn't paying attention, and unless he did start paying attention—for one reason or another—his reflex was to fall back on the standard biases that dominated the white Protestant view of the world. On the other hand, a thorough reading of his published writings and letters shows that he largely kept himself within the perimeters of that world, and the instances of what I would call *lazy thinking* about the ones who lived outside the perimeter are so infrequent as to be negligible, statistically irrelevant. Beyond his work, in the jostle and flow of his day-to-day life, he was not given to ranting about Jews, Italians, or anyone else. From all I can gather, he seldom even thought about them.

Ancestors of Crane's had fought against the Indian allies of the British during the Revolutionary War, and given Crane's attachment to his family's history, Indians were of far greater concern to him than the immigrants he crossed paths with in New York. Three sketches from the Sullivan County cycle (1891–92) and three stories written during the last year of his life ("Tales of the Wyoming Valley," 1899) take on the subject of Indians directly, but those works are all set in the past, most of them in the late eighteenth century, and they tell us little about Crane's attitude toward Indians in his own lifetime.* At that late date in American history—following the massacre at Wounded Knee in December 1890—it is instructive to recall that the supposedly wise and open-hearted William Dean Howells, who first came to national prominence as the author of Abraham Lincoln's 1860 campaign biography, could state in print just one month after Wounded Knee that the Sioux were "butchers," the Cheyennes "idiotic murderers," and that he longed for the day that the

---

* "The Battle of Forty Fort," "The Surrender of Forty Fort," and "'Ol' Bennet' and the Indians" were all derived from Crane's reading of a book written by his maternal grandfather, the Reverend George Peck, that was published in 1858: *Wyoming: Its History, Stirring Incidents, and Romantic Adventures.* One of the illustrations was made by Crane's mother, and Crane himself owned two copies of the book, which he held on to for his entire life. When the six-year-old Crane and his mother traveled to the Wyoming Valley to attend the WCTU conference in July 1878 (those heady days of cigarettes and beer), the one-hundredth-anniversary reenactments they witnessed of Revolutionary War battles—and massacres—were the same ones recounted in his 1899 stories. To further enhance the family connection, the primary source for Crane's source (his grandfather's book) was an unpublished memoir written by Martha (Bennet) Myers, Crane's grandfather's mother-in-law, who was the daughter of Thomas Bennet, the crusty, opinionated Ol' Bennet of the stories and—to cinch the knot of family connections even more tightly—Crane's great-great-grandfather.

"Indians should have ever been treated otherwise than in severalty"—that is, kept apart from the rest of the American population. Such opinions were still common among whites throughout the country, embraced not only by the common folk but by intellectuals as well. Crane's thinking was more nuanced and informed, perhaps, but it was also highly ambiguous.

In the fall of 1896, less than a month before Crane headed to Florida on his way to Cuba and abandoned his life in New York for good, he escaped the controversy of the Dora Clark Affair by traveling up to Cambridge, Massachusetts, on two successive weekends to cover Harvard football games for the *New York Journal*. The first one was played on October thirty-first and pitted Harvard against the team from the Carlisle Indian Industrial School in Pennsylvania, founded seventeen years earlier by Captain Richard Pratt of the United States Army and the first of several all-Indian schools that were established around the country, which put into practice Pratt's theory of "Kill the Indian: Save the Man." As Pratt wrote: "A great general has said that the only good Indian is a dead one. In a sense, I agree with the senti-ment, but only in this: that all the Indian there is in the race should be dead." In this benighted attempt to turn Native Americans into true-blue citizens of the Republic by cutting all ties to their ancestral past, the students were encouraged to participate in contemporary sports, and before long they were excelling at football.* The team Crane covered in 1896 was a national pow-erhouse and trotted onto the field that Saturday afternoon in Cambridge as heavy favorites against Harvard. Crane acknowledges this in the first para-graph of his article: "It was understood beforehand that the Indians were sure winners. Everybody declared that the Harvard team was composed mainly of cripples, and everybody recited the glory of the aborigines."

Aborigines. It is unclear to what extent Crane is being ironical by using that word, which carries a whiff of racial insult, but whether he is writing from his own point of view or merely aping the language of the anti-Indian majority (Howells and all the others) cannot be known at this early point in the article. Crane's talent for mockery ran deep, and at one time or another he had already turned his sarcasm on white millionaires, middle-class vacationers in Asbury Park, shambling marchers of the nativist work-ing class, profit-hungry coal brokers, and various others, often mimicking their own language and patterns of thought in order to expose them as

---

* Carlisle's best-known graduate, Jim Thorpe—Olympic gold medalist in the decathlon, pro-fessional baseball player, college and professional football star—is widely considered to be the greatest all-around athlete in American history.

hypocrites without calling them that by name. In the second paragraph of "Harvard University Against the Carlisle Indians," his intentions become even more opaque and confusing:

> Fifteen thousand people expected a surprise. They were there to observe how the red man could come from his prairies with a memory of four centuries of oppression and humiliation as his inheritance, with dark years, perhaps utter extinction before him, and yet make a show of the white warriors at their favorite sport.

Crane is reporting not just on a football game but on a clash of civilizations. The inflated rhetoric suggests more mockery, more irony, and more double-edged or even triple-edged thinking, but where in fact does Crane himself stand on the matter? Again, it is difficult to know. One reading establishes that he is well aware of the indignities and abuses Indians suffered from the moment white men started invading their lands. Another reading turns the first reading on its head and seems to be making fun of that sorrowful history, and with the war now lost and possible extinction on the horizon, the only possible revenge is a symbolic one—to defeat the white man at his favorite sport—which trivializes the whole matter of the Indians' painful past. Is *red man* a negative term, a positive term, or a neutral term? Depending on how you read the paragraph, it can be any one of them—or all of them.

By the fourth paragraph, the mocking tone swells into pseudo-Romantic bombast, and one senses that Crane doesn't really care what his position is. He had come to Massachusetts to escape his troubles, and with the gigantic mess still swirling around him in New York, which must have been on his mind, distracting him from his usual focus on the task at hand, he begins to lose his grip on what he is trying to say, assuming he ever knew what it was to begin with.

> How old Geronimo would have enjoyed it! The point of view of the warriors was terse but plain: "They have stolen a continent from us, a wide, wide continent, which was ours, and lately they have stolen various touchdowns that were also ours. . . . If sacrifice of bone and sinew can square the thing, let us sacrifice, and perhaps the smoke of our wigwam camp fire will blow softly against the dangling scalps of our enemies."

The rest of the piece darts this way and that. In the fifth paragraph, Crane goes back to a pre-game encounter with the Carlisle team at their hotel, emphasizing how quiet they were, barely talking to one another as they sat around in their blue-and-red uniforms: "They were remarkably modest in their ways. They were like children, mightily well-behaved and docile children. It required long observation to find in these serene countenances the nerve which the men have displayed to such a tremendous degree." Crane then gives the lineups of the two squads and launches into a thorough account of the game, which turned out to be a tense affair that resulted in a narrow victory for Harvard by a score of 4 to 0.* Mostly referring to the teams by their school names (Harvard, Carlisle) or their nicknames (the Crimson, the Indians), Crane varies his language in a few spots: "the aboriginal fifteen-yard line," "the noble red men," and "simple savages." Again, it is hard to know if Crane is mocking or mimicking with those epithets, but his use of the word "simple" probably meant something quite different to him than it would mean to us today. Earlier that year, in his autobiographical letter to John Northern Hilliard, he had referred to his father as "a great, fine, simple mind." He was not calling his father stupid. On the contrary, he meant to suggest something akin to "purity" or "unwavering inner strength." He seems to have felt a similar kind of admiration for the Carlisle team, but rather than stick to football and the performance of the team on the field, he couldn't stop himself from branching off into those bizarre, quasi-humorous asides about Indian history and revenge. They are rhetorical lead balloons, undoubtedly in bad taste, but not malicious—just wrongheaded and ill-conceived. Crane did not hate people who were not like himself. He simply didn't understand them, and rather than make an effort to penetrate their thinking or attempt to see the world through their eyes, he stood back and watched, either with indifference (immigrants) or fascination (Indians) but nearly always with a sense that the person he was looking at was alien to him, an inscrutable Other. So ends his first and second-to-last attempt to write about football: "After the game the Indians moved off through the dusk with all their old impassiveness." But never does Crane ask why.

His parents had run two schools devoted to educating black men, women, and children in Port Jervis when Crane was a boy, and of all the Others who haunted the periphery of his life, black people were the least alien to him, the ones he felt most comfortable with, to such a point that he welcomed having sex with black women ("I—I think

---

* The allotment of points at the time was: touchdown 4, successful kick after touchdown 2, safety 2, field goal 5.

black is quite good") and put a number of significant, full-fledged black characters into the fiction he wrote during the last three years of his life (*The Monster* and *Whilomville Stories*). And yet, for all his democratic impulses and goodwill, black people were still the Other to Crane, and he could never entirely free himself from the racial stereotyping that was rampant in white American culture back then and is still very much with us today.

One work will suffice to expose these blind spots in Crane. Just seven pages long, it happens to be the last newspaper sketch he wrote about New York, and when it was published by the Bacheller Syndicate on December 20, 1896, Crane had already been in Florida for more than three weeks. "STEPHEN CRANE IN MINETTA LANE" is the headline (attesting to the enormous clout he had achieved since publishing *The Red Badge of Courage*), followed by a different set of sub-headlines in each paper that ran above the article. The one from the *Galveston Daily News* is probably the most vivid: "Stephen Crane Describes One of New York City's Most / Notorious Thoroughfares // ITS WORST DAYS HAVE PASSED // But Its Inhabitants Include Many Whose Deeds Are Evil—The / Celebrated Resort of Mammy Ross."

After the Dutch allowed "partially freed" slaves to farm there in the mid-seventeenth century, Minetta Lane, a narrow, twisting alleyway that connects with Sixth Avenue at one end and MacDougal Street at the other, became a center of black life in New York. "Mannetta" was the name of the brook that ran through there until it was covered up in the early nineteenth century, an Algonquin word alternately translated as "spirit water" and "demon water," and by 1827, when slavery was abolished in New York, the area became known as Little Africa, with a population of roughly fourteen thousand. As the years passed, it acquired a reputation as one of the most menacing, crime-ridden enclaves in Manhattan. Crane knew all that, and with his startling talent for absorbing new things quickly, he prowled the lane and collected stories about the criminals who had been active there before the police clamped down on them and cleaned up the neighborhood, recounting the exploits of such figures as Bloodthirsty, No-Toe Charley, Black-Cat, and Guinea Johnson, as well as tracking down three aged survivors of the bad old days—Mammy Ross, Pop Babcock, Hank Anderson—and getting them to share their memories with him. It is a lively, expertly written piece, but in spite of Crane's sympathy for the subjects of his report, it is also riddled with a number of condescending, racist remarks. From the second paragraph:

To gain a reputation in Minetta Lane, in those days, a man was obliged to commit a number of furious crimes, and no celebrity was more important than the man who had a good honest killing to his credit. The inhabitants for the most part were negroes and they represented the very worst elements of their race. The razor habit clung to them with the tenacity of an epidemic, and every night the uneven cobbles felt blood.

If Crane had been investigating a band of white criminals, he would not have commented on their race. If anything, he might have said that "they represented the very worst elements of humanity," but black people cannot be seen as representative of humanity. They represent only themselves—and they are a race apart, eternally banished from the domain of the universal, which belongs only to whites. As for the man known as Bloodthirsty, who is still at large and wanted for murder, Crane describes him as "a large negro and very hideous," with "a rolling eye that shows white at the wrong time." During his drunken sprees before he vanished from the lane, Bloodthirsty "would rave so graphically about gore that even the habituated wool of old timers would stand straight." A few pages after that, the dapper Hank Anderson is called "the guiding beacon" of "the dusky aristocracy of the neighborhood." "Wool," "dusky," and "rolling eye" were in current use well into the twentieth century and persist even today. They are small, offensive markers that signify a deeper, often unconscious prejudice of white against black, and I doubt that it ever even occurred to Crane that clichés of that sort can wound. One wants to forgive him for these lapses, since the rest of the article is mercifully devoid of such ingrained bias, but then, in the final paragraph, he resorts to the biggest, most offensive cliché of them all, and there he leaves us, standing on the stage of a two-bit minstrel show.

But they are happy in this condition, are these people. The most extraordinary quality of the negro is his enormous capacity for happiness under most adverse circumstances. Minetta Lane is a place of poverty and sin, but these influences cannot destroy the broad smile of the negro, a vain and simple child but happy. They all smile here, the most evil as well as the poorest. Knowing the negro, one always expects laughter from him, be he ever so poor, but it was a new experience to see a broad grin on the face of the devil.

The vast majority of his white readers would have swallowed this without a second thought. As for Crane himself, it is almost certain that he thought he was being kind.

LOOKING AT WOMEN. The thwarted, failed romance with Lily Brandon Munroe. A brief infatuation with Nellie Crouse, a stunningly attractive but shallow upper-class girl from Akron, Ohio, whom he met once—only once—at a New York tea party he was taken to by his friend Lucius Button (also from Akron) and to whom he wrote seven long, rambling letters between December 31, 1895, and March 1, 1896, in a frantic, short-lived effort to win her affections. His head had been turned by a pretty girl, he lunged, the girl eluded him, and that was that. And then, finally, during his last months in New York before absconding to Florida, he fell for a twenty-one-year-old prostitute named Amy Leslie, lived with her for a time, seemed to be genuinely in love, but ultimately slipped away from her under obscure circumstances.

Those were Crane's most serious entanglements between the ages of twenty and twenty-five, the ones that are known, in any case, although there could have been others, perhaps several others that have never come to light. A perplexing, unexplained letter written to his friend Willis Brooks Hawkins on March 15, 1896, full of apologies for an apparent wrong he had committed against him, begins with the words "It was a woman! Don't you see? Nothing could so interfere but a woman" and ends with "I am sure, of course that you have been very much offended but it is a woman, I tell you, and I want you to forgive me," but who that woman was remains a puzzle.* Then there is an intriguing bit of conjecture that revolves around a young woman named Grace Hall. A wealthy midwesterner who came to New York to study voice and prepare for a career in opera, she traveled in the same Art Students League social circle as Crane, but the extent of their involvement with each other is one more blank in Crane's story. And yet, how to ignore this curious link: the love object of the central character in *The Third Violet* (written in 1895) is named Grace Fanhall, which seems to point directly to Grace Hall herself. Evidence of another entanglement?—a crush?—or merely a name that suited his purposes? In what must have been a disappointing turn for her, the real Grace Hall had to abandon her career as an opera singer because of a childhood illness that had damaged her eyes and made them inordinately sensitive to theater lights. So she returned to Oak Park, Illinois, and married her fiancé, Dr. Clarence Hem-

---

* The editors of *The Correspondence*, Stanley Wertheim and Paul Sorrentino, speculate that it could have been Amy Leslie, but they are by no means certain of it.

ingway. Her second child, born in 1899, was named Ernest, who held Crane in the highest regard after he became a writer himself.*

Three respectable, well-bred women born into comfortable surroundings, but also a woman with no resources or background who rented out her body to cash-paying customers in order to keep herself clothed and fed, and, as we already know, Amy Leslie was not the first prostitute to have put her arms around Crane. The question, however, is how many had there been before her and how often had his nights ended (or begun) with a trip to a brothel. Five times a week? Five times a month? Five times a year? No one can answer that question because there isn't enough information to answer it, which leaves us with yet one more blank. Journalist John Northern Hilliard (1872–1935), an intense admirer of both Crane and his work, wrote in 1922 that his friend

> had a hankering after the women. He took up with many a drab and was not overly particular as to her age, race or color. Many a time I have heard him say that he would have to go out and get a nigger wench "to change his luck." Time and again he would bring a lady from the streets to his room. He had no eye for women of his own class or station. He preferred the other kind. I can understand this. Women of his own class would have given him nothing. In the slums he got life. He got the real thing, and that was what he was always looking for—the real, naked facts of life.

Hilliard is both right and wrong. He clearly knew nothing about Lily Brandon Munroe (which proves that he was less intimate with Crane than he thought he was), and as for the ugly term "nigger wench," we have only his word (written long after the fact) that Crane actually used it, and even if Crane did, he might have said it to impress the impressionable Hilliard, who seems to have been a young bohemian hell-raiser with a fondness for that kind of loose, masculine talk—although, in light of Crane's remarks about "happy grinning negroes," anything is possible.† On the other side

---

* "The good writers are Henry James, Stephen Crane, and Mark Twain. That's not the order they're good in. There is no order for good writers." (From *The Green Hills of Africa*, 1935.) And in *Men at War*, an anthology he edited in 1942, Hemingway called *The Red Badge of Courage* "a great boy's dream of war . . . one of the finest books in our literature."

† The N-word, so repulsive to our ears today, was common coin in the late nineteenth and early twentieth centuries. Not just in private but in public as well—often on the covers of books. As recently as 1939, Agatha Christie published a mystery novel with the title *Ten Little Niggers* (based on the lyrics of a popular British blackface song), but the title was

of the ledger, there is a second, independent account that confirms what Hilliard says about Crane's habit of inviting streetwalkers to come in out of the cold and accompany him back to his room. Harry B. Smith (1860–1936), a composer and music-critic friend of Willis Brooks Hawkins's, was asked to join Hawkins and some other men for an evening of poker at Crane's apartment in late 1895 or 1896. He later wrote,

> My impression is that the building ... was somewhere in the West Twenties. We went to the top floor, an extensive loft. In one corner was a bedroom partitioned off. . . . There was no literary pose about Crane. He seemed to be what Hawkins had said—"just a kid"; but thin, pallid, looking like a consumptive. We played cards till two or three o'clock in the morning and, as we started for home we passed the window of the partitioned bedroom. A girl was asleep in the bed.
> "Gosh!" said Crane. "I didn't hear her come in."
> There were facetious comments. "Is it *Maggie?*" asked one of the ribald, referring to Crane's story.
> "Some of her," said Crane.

A different side of Crane is revealed by a story told in the mid-twenties by journalist Robert H. Davis (1869–1942), who met Crane for the first time one chilly night as Davis was standing under the Sixth Avenue El at Broadway and West Thirty-third Street with another reporter, who happened to know Crane. Just then, as if he had materialized out of thin air, there was Crane himself, walking down the street with his eyes "bent upon the pavement," and because Davis was familiar with Crane's work and considered himself a fan, he asked his friend to introduce him. "I pressed his thin veal-like hand with unfeigned warmth," Davis writes, and before the three of them had a chance to say much of anything to one another, the reporter dashed off to another appointment, leaving Davis alone with Crane. They chatted for a minute or two, and after learning that Davis was also a minister's son, Crane remarked dryly on how much the world exulted whenever a minister's son was "overtaken by misfortune." "This is the point of view," he continued. "The bartender's boy falls from the Waldorf roof. The minister's

---

changed for the American publication in 1940 to *And Then There Were None*. Apparently, the word had been deemed too offensive by 1940 to be used in American public discourse, but what people said in private was another matter, and the word lives on even today among bigots from all classes of society. The point being, however, that back in Crane's time and well beyond it, the word was used in polite society as well.

son falls from a park bench. They both hit the earth with the same velocity, mutilated beyond recognition."

A moment after talking about ministers and their sons, Crane saw a prostitute coming down the street. He turned his attention from Davis to look at her, and suddenly she stopped and began looking at him.

Straightaway he detached himself from my side, tossed his cigarette into Greeley Square, placed his left hand upon his heart, removed his hat and made a most gallant bow. I have never seen a more exquisite gesture of chivalry than this youth sweeping the pavement with his black felt. . . .

"A stranger here?" inquired Crane with the utmost delicacy in his speech as though addressing one lost in a great city.

The girl stood there with her lips parted and a queer expression of indecision on her face. . . . She caught her breath.

"Well, suppose I am a stranger. Can you show me anything?"

"Yes," replied the author of *Maggie*, "I can show you the way out. But if you prefer to remain—" Crane made another gesture with his felt and bowed with an air of magnificent finality.

The girl suddenly found an extra button at the throat of her coat and fastened herself in. The light seemed to go out of Stephen Crane's eyes as though some one had turned down a lamp from within.

"You shouldn't hang out here, kid," said Maggie in a throaty voice. "You look cold. You can't stand it. This fat guy can."

At last I was recognized.

The girl sauntered off utterly indifferent in the direction of Shanley's, Burns's, Delmonico's—

"This is a long cañon," said Crane. "I wonder if there *is* a way out . . ."

This was hardly the conduct of a whore-mongering, philandering rake, and in spite of Hilliard's comments, whatever lustful urges Crane harbored throughout his late teens and early twenties were tempered by a profound reserve in the presence of women, no matter what class or station they happened to belong to. Shy, hesitant, awkward, polite, decorous, and often ill at ease in female company, he was a young man of multiple contradictions, at once a *gentleman* in the old sense of the word (according to his friend Gordon) and also what I would call a *puritanical hedonist*, ever and always a minister's son even as he went on fighting his war with God. Part of the problem in understanding Crane is that he developed far more rapidly as an artist than he did as a man, and it wasn't until he left New York and met the twice-married Cora Taylor at the Hotel de Dreme in Jacksonville, Florida, that he managed to form a sustained connection with a woman. Whatever ups and downs they might have gone through together, he stuck with her from his twenty-fifth birthday until the end of his life three and a half years later, inching ever closer to full maturity during those last years but still a boy when he died.

OTHERS LOOKING AT HIM. Opinions vary on Crane's appearance, so much so that it is difficult to pin down precisely what others saw when they looked at him. His New York painter friend Nelson Greene, who would have been in the habit of looking at faces more closely than most people, observes the following: "light hair, almost blond, light bluish gray eyes—very direct glance. He had very good features, excellent pointed nose—face slightly narrower than medium—eyes fairly wide apart. He had a . . . kindly, tired tolerance in his eyes, face and attitude." Linson, who had lived in France and eventually painted Crane's portrait, saw something unusual in his friend's nose the first time they met: "Against the window his profile silhouetted in a cleancut reminiscence of the young Napoleon." Bacheller's initial impression was even more admiring: "One day a slim youth with gray-blue eyes, a rather dark skin and a cast of countenance 'comely and good to look upon,' as the ancients were wont to say, came to my office. His head was picturesque and beautiful in its shape and poise." Cahan and Howells have already been heard from—two more men struck by Crane's aura—but then there are these comments from Garland, which undercut the remarks of Bacheller, Howells, and the others. After reading Crane's poems for the first time: "I was astounded by their power. I could not believe that they were the work of the pale, laconic youth before me." And then, a month or two later, following his first look at *The Red Badge of Courage*: "I brooded over his case, and looking across at him, sallow, yellow-fingered, small and ugly, I was unable to relate him in the slightest degree to the marvelous manuscript which he had placed in my hands."

We all know how different our faces can look from one photograph to another, from one random moment to another—at times presentable and even attractive and at times hideous. The angle, the light, the tilt of the head, a sudden change of mood while being photographed, not to speak of illness or lack of sleep, can all play a part in how we come across to others. Beyond the written accounts of friends and acquaintances on how they perceived Crane's physical self, there are a number of photographs from those years as well, not many of them but enough to give a rather muddled, contradictory idea of what Crane looked like. As with all of us, he appears to be somewhat different from image to image, at times presentable and even attractive, at times homely and frail. About the only thing he and everyone

Oil portrait of Crane by C. K. Linson, 1894.
The words at the top of the canvas read: "Stephen Crane Aged 22 1894
Author The Red Badge of Courage."
(COURTESY OF THE UNIVERSITY OF VIRGINIA)

else seemed to agree on was that his complexion tended to be *sallow*, a fact that can probably be attributed to unstable health, inadequate diet, punishing hours, and whatever microbes were brewing inside him that led to his death at such a young age. Without his tough athlete's body to defend him against the earliest assaults, it seems unlikely that he would have lasted as long as he did. As Cora succinctly put it in the notes she compiled for the biography she never wrote: "Fate sets its stamp upon the faces of those who are doomed to an early death."

By all accounts, he was a pungent conversationalist, quick-witted, incisive, with an exceptional gift for inventing new and salty idioms on the spot, more dazzling as a talker than as a writer, according to many of his friends, but the words came out of his mouth slowly, in a languid, idiosyncratic drawl that embarrassed him and made him feel self-conscious in front of strangers, and until the final year of his life he dreaded the thought of speaking in public. Hence his refusal to accept Barry's invitation to read his poems to the Uncut Leaves Society in 1894—so anguished at the prospect of disgracing himself that he declared he would rather die than do it.

Another quirk that impressed nearly everyone who knew him was how seldom he laughed. As Conrad noted, he never heard Crane emit a single sound that resembled a laugh except when parked on the lawn with infant Borys, while niece Helen R. Crane is even more emphatic on this point, insisting that "We never heard him laugh," *period*, adding that "former friends of his I have met say the same thing." This is altogether bizarre—a man who never laughed—and yet, as if to compensate for any apparent shortfall in the mirth department, Crane was also known for the frequency of his smiles, not just one form of smile continually repeated but many of them, a different smile for each different circumstance, variously seen by those who knew him as charming, ironic, humorous, bitter, compassionate, tender, distant, happy, saintly, and thoughtful. He might not have laughed much himself—or not at all—but his niece tells us that he "always kept his hearers laughing and urging him on to say more."

The many-ness I referred to earlier is confined to a rather narrow spectrum with Crane. He was not a violent person, for example. He did not pick quarrels or shout when he disagreed with someone or try to dominate those around him. He had no criminal impulses, manifested no signs of mental illness, and beyond the transitory bouts of sadness all human beings are prey to, he was not prone to depression. Any psychiatrist examining him would have concluded that he was a normal person—that is, someone who did not think he was the Second Coming of Jesus Christ, someone who understood that he belonged to a world of others and was not the center of that world, someone who was capable of love, generosity, and kindness, and yet someone who was also capable of standing up for himself when pushed. In other words, not a madman, not a debilitated neurotic, and not a potential suicide. No doubt all this has become obvious by now, but before looking into Crane's personality, character, and the effect he had on others, it is necessary to exclude everything he was not in order to clear the ground and find the correct place to start digging. There are some fairly demented artists out there, after all, but Crane was not one of them.

The personal testimonies that have come down to us about him were all written by friends, people who cared about him when he was alive and went on caring about him after he was dead, but even his closest allies were far from unanimous in who they thought he was.

Post Wheeler: "Shy, sensitive, quick-tempered, restive, reckless, and generous to a fault, that is the Stephen Crane I knew. I never knew him to do a mean thing.... The aloof manner he showed to strangers was the protective coloration which one sees so often in the British."

John Northern Hilliard: "Crane was a big man as well as a big writer—the biggest writer, to my mind, this country has produced. He lived his own life, a free, untrammeled life; he had great courage (he was the most utterly fearless man I have ever known); he faced poverty blithely, and he wrote absolutely to please himself.... And then when the gods were kind, and a newspaper editor gave us a check, it was ho! for the fleshpots and an all-night session at poker. It was those days, those play times that remain freshest in my memory, for Crane was always playing. He played all his life."

Corwin K. Linson: "It was impossible at any time for any who knew him to regard him with any degree of indifference. He was loved or disliked with an almost equal warmth. The most human of companions, in our early relation he attracted, intrigued, delighted, and irritated me, and I jarred him more than once, but he held my admiration to the last. Incapable of malice of any sort, he pronounced his dislikes openly, but with the unoffending candor of a boy."

Three different views from three different men. Wheeler, the childhood smoking pal, Asbury Park colleague, and New York apartment-mate, who had known him longer and perhaps better than any of the others. Hilliard, a year younger than Crane, the worshipful enthusiast and late-night chum, who felt his own life had been enhanced if not validated by having known the dead genius. And Linson, seven years older than Crane, looking back from a distance of many years, honest enough to admit to a certain irritation with his young friend (the unpaid fifty-dollar loan?) but still flooded with affection for him. Each man remembers a different Crane, and if there is any common thread that links all three of their accounts, it would be the nervous energy they all felt coursing through him, the keyed-up, playful, opinionated, quickness of a body and mind in constant motion. There seems to have been nothing soft or lethargic about Crane. He sits ramrod straight on the saddle of his horse, and in no photograph do we see him looking bored or lolling around in one of those indolent poses cultivated by the Decadents in England and France. His country was America, "a nation forcing its regal head into the clouds," and Crane, the self-imposed outsider, was nevertheless in and of America from the tip of his Napoleonic nose to the roots of his crumbling teeth: restless, tightly sprung, sprinting.

He moved in and out of several different worlds during the years he spent in New York, the world of his friends first of all, some of whom he had known previously, such as Lawrence and Senger, and others (the medical students, the young artists, Linson) with whom he formed new friendships, writing his work in their midst, eating with them, bunking down with them, at times frank and outspoken, at times funny, at times remote, at times an object of jesting ridicule, a part of the gang but also an independent, somewhat mysterious figure who would disappear for a time or else pop up without warning, knocking on the doors of acquaintances around town to crash at this one's or that one's place whenever his pockets were empty. The next world consisted of newspaper editors, publishers, and fellow journalists (Marshall, McClure, Bacheller, Hilliard), where he struggled at first and was often kept waiting for long hours in the reception areas of various offices, but things gradually improved for him, and as it was in the world of his friends, he held his own and managed to make a place for himself among them. With the working-class and unemployed people from the Bowery and other impoverished neighborhoods, he mostly watched and listened, trying to blend in with his surroundings in order to soak up as much as he could and further his education. With big brothers and fathers such as Garland, Howells, and Hawkins (who was nineteen years older than Crane), the young one was deferential, earnest, and yet not too intimidated to speak his mind and defend his positions. To the degree that he felt comfortable anywhere, he traveled through those first four worlds in relative comfort, but the fifth world, the world of the New York rich ("My daughter does not speak French, Mr. Crane") and the provincial, churchgoing bourgeoisie (reencountered every time he went to William's house in Port Jervis), aggravated him to the point of discombobulation and rudeness. It is worth quoting Helen R. Crane at length about his rebellion against the smugness of that milieu:

> He wilfully and painstakingly went about to shock them. . . . The bourgeois complacency of everyone, even of his brothers and their families, goaded him to act in a manner which at times was a bit disconcerting.
>
> His sisters-in-law never knew what he was going to do. There were instances when he behaved very nicely, but there were more when he did not. Sometimes, on being introduced to a socialite, he would assume an East Side accent (which he could do perfectly) and blare forth yarns he had picked up in the night-courts.
>
> My mother and my aunts never quite got used to the idea that he

might suddenly interrupt a dinner conversation which was running along smoothly on croup or hats to inquire earnestly if any of the guests had ever seen a Chinaman murdered in Mott street. Nor did they feel any happier when he called attention to his black eye and explained how he had got it in a grand fight on the Bowery.

It was impossible for him to be a social lion, because he could not understand small talk. He could spend hours with Mike Flanagan who drove a beer-truck on the East Side . . . and talk all night with Theodore Roosevelt, Hamlin Garland, or William Dean Howells about the virtues of the Single Tax or the genius of Flaubert, but when it came to the inanities of ordinary gossip, he was sunk. And he did not get along with young people, the boys and girls of his own age. They thought he was cracked and he thought they were stupid.

Lest that be the final word about Crane's conduct in Port Jervis, there are also the comments offered by the other niece who wrote about him, Edna, one of William's daughters, who played cops and robbers with her uncle when she was a child and took special pleasure in preparing him silver mugs filled with fresh lemonade in the summer, which he would drink down with an equal show of pleasure and then inevitably declare it to be "Out of sight." Yes, Crane had a soft spot for children and was always kind to his nieces, but in her article from 1926 Edna Crane Sidbury also tells us that "my mother and Mrs. Edmund Crane were very fond of him . . . and always glad to see him" and that "my uncle was very popular with the young people in our town . . . and young ladies came frequently to play croquet upon our front lawn."

Another story, or perhaps another side of the same story—just for the record. Proving, yet again, that no man is one thing to all people. The two pictures seem to cancel each other out, but in fact they don't. They stand side by side, each one as true as the other.

There is much to admire about Crane both as an artist and as a man—his ferocious commitment to his work, his taciturn but warm companionability as a friend, the gentlemanly code of honor he tried to follow in his interactions with others—but, needless to say, he had his flaws and blundering moments as well, his less than admirable qualities, which with Crane seemed to spring mostly from his tortured, incoherent relationship with money, a persistent problem that dogged him to the end of his life and often led to devious, irresponsible behavior. I am not just talking about his habit of seldom if ever paying back loans, since he lent others money as freely as he borrowed from them,* nor even his occasional lapses of attention,† but his slipshod and sometimes unscrupulous dealings with the editors and publishers who paid him for his work. When he returned from his travels for Bacheller in the spring of 1895—to cite one early example—he fudged his expense account by passing off a revolver he had borrowed from a friend as one he had bought to protect himself on the trip. Hardly a serious crime, no doubt the sort of small-scale chicanery practiced by most struggling journalists, but given the high ethical standards Crane normally adhered to, one would have expected better from him. In this case, however, he didn't feel the least bit guilty about scamming his employer. His artist friend Nelson Greene happened to accompany him to Bacheller's office that afternoon, and when he saw Crane produce the gun, he blurted out that it looked "just like Doc. Biggs' gun." Afterward, when they were out on the street, Crane said to him: "Greene, damn you, what was the matter with you about that gun. You nearly queered my expense account."

This was small potatoes, amounting to no more than a few dollars, but as time went on and Crane's reputation began to grow, he would commit a number of naïve and thoughtless errors in his transactions with publishers and agents, slithering around the agreements written into contracts by submitting the same work to two different publications, for example, or not understanding the unwritten rules of the publishing world, as when he turned over *George's Mother* to the Anglo-American firm of Edward Arnold instead of giving it to Hitchcock at Appleton, who had no legal claim on the manuscript but who assumed, as the publisher of four of Crane's other books, that he would have first crack at seeing all of Crane's new material. When Hitchcock called him out on it, Crane was apologetic—but not excessively so—and tried to defend his behavior in a letter written on March 26, 1896:

Dear Mr. Hitchcock: I have not told you that I am beset—quite—with publishers of various degrees who wish—or seem to wish—to get my

---

* One telling exchange with Post Wheeler in 1894 offers written proof: "Dear Stevie—Are you in a hurry for that twenty? Post W," to which Crane scrawled a reply at the bottom of Wheeler's letter and promptly sent it back to him: "Good heavens! Forget all about it! Don't ever mention it! S."

† His artist friend David Ericson reported that Crane invited him to lunch one afternoon, but once they sat down at their table in the restaurant, Crane "immediately pulled out his pad and pencil and began to write," and when they finished the meal, Crane—forgetting that he had offered to pay for the lunch—simply stood up and walked out, leaving Ericson to cover the check.

books and who make me various offers. . . . I have not considered at all
the plan of playing one house against another but have held that the
house of Appleton would allow me all the benefits I deserved. Without
vanity I may say that I don't care a snap for money until I put my hand in
my pocket and find none there. If I make ill terms now there may come
a period of reflection and so I expect you to deal with me precisely as if
I was going to write a *great* book ten years from now and might wreak
a terrible vengeance on you by giving it to the other fellow. And so we
understand each other. . . .

    You know of course that my mind is just and most open but perhaps
in this case I violated certain business courtesies. But, before God, when
these people get their fingers in my hair, it is a wonder that I escape with
all my clothes. My only chance is to keep away from them.

The letter is uncommonly nasty in tone, perhaps the nastiest of any
of Crane's letters, with its unveiled threat of "wreak[ing] a terrible vengeance on you," but even though the potential breach with Hitchcock was
quickly mended, it is interesting to see how nimbly S.C. shifts the blame
from himself, apparently excusing his actions because he is inexperienced,
vulnerable to the predatory stratagems of others, and the only way he can
protect himself is to steer clear of them entirely. Just one sentence in the
letter rings true from start to finish, a sentence that inadvertently reflects
his ungrounded, immature approach to what Garland called "the practical
business of living": *I don't care a snap for money until I put my hand in my
pocket and find none there.* This was Crane in a nutshell, and what agonizing
troubles that approach would cause him in the last two years of his life.

    No talent for the practical side of things, then, and a rather sloppy, even
shoddy manner of handling the dull obligations of day-to-day existence,
summed up by his inability to understand "small talk," as his niece put it,
which can be translated into an inability to understand "small anything,"
but beyond the claustrophobic interiors of New York publishers' offices and
1890s Victorian drawing rooms, whenever the stakes were truly high Crane
could be magnificent. Standing up for a falsely accused prostitute in court,
for one thing—which seriously damaged his reputation—and then, after
he left New York, the steadfast calm he showed as his ship foundered and
sank off the coast of Florida, followed by the thirty hours he spent adrift
at sea in a small boat with two members of the crew and the captain, who
called him "the spunkiest fellow out . . . a thoroughbred, and a brave man,
too, with plenty of grit," and, most remarkably, while covering the fighting
in Cuba, taking a dispatch written by his friend Edward Marshall, who had

been badly shot and could not move, and running several miles through the jungle to deliver it to Marshall's newspaper, which led his own paper to sack him for helping a rival journalist. This was what Hilliard meant when he called Crane "a big man." Sometimes small, yes, but never not big when the circumstances demanded it.

LOOKING AT HIMSELF. The friends and relatives who wrote about him offered their varied impressions of who he was and told of what he did or how he acted when they were with him (Linson on Crane's disgust at seeing the final version of the coal mine piece, for example), but not one of them ever recorded an instance when Crane let down his guard and talked about himself: no accounts of a secret confession or a long heart-to-heart chat, no glimpses into what he thought of his own character or what he saw when he looked at himself with his own eyes. In his letters, many of them to journalists, he gives details about his family and early life, often discusses his approach to writing or makes more general remarks about the purpose of literature and where he stands on the aesthetic debates of the moment, but only in a handful of letters from that early period (before he left New York) does he open up and examine who and what he was. One of them, to Viola Allen on March 15, 1896, has already been quoted, but it is worth recalling the self-deprecation that runs through the letter and his closing words to his former classmate: "I was such an ass, such a pure complete ass—it does me good to recollect it." That letter is about the past, a retroactive opinion on the idiocies of his youth, but he was just as capable of looking at himself in the present and coming to similarly harsh judgments. On the same day he answered Viola Allen, he also wrote to Hitchcock, a prelude to the more combative letter that followed eleven days later, but in this one Crane seems to understand what a difficult person he could be, and rather than attempt to defend himself, he honestly presents himself as someone close to incorrigible.

> Dear Mr. Hitchcock: Of course eccentric people are admirably pictur-esque at a distance but I suppose after your recent close range experi-ences with me, you have the usual sense of annoyance. After all, I cannot help vanishing and disappearing and dissolving. It is my foremost trait. But I hope you will forgive me and treat me as if you could still think me a pretty decent sort of chap.

Then there is the letter he wrote two weeks earlier to a certain Daisy D. Hill, which is probably the most revealing and self-damning letter in all of Crane's correspondence, but it is also a fascinating human document in its own right, for not only does it show Crane sticking daggers into himself but also how delicately he tries to spare Miss Hill's feelings in responding to the conundrum posed by her letter—which appears to have been a fan letter, no doubt a gushing one, so excessive in its praise that the recipient was nothing short of embarrassed.

> My dear Miss Hill: I have been wondering if you are not making game of me. And yet I suppose the egotism of the average man is large enough to make it all appear perfectly sincere. Assuming then that you mean what you say, your letter makes me mournful. In the first place, I am such a small pale-yellow person with a weak air and no ability of pose that your admiration, or whatever it may be—if admiration is too strong a term—causes me to feel that I am an imposter and am robbing you of something. Of course your letter appeals to me. It is the expression of a vibratory sensitive young mind reaching out for an ideal. But then I cannot for a moment allow you to assume that I am properly an ideal. Ye Gods! I am clay—very common uninteresting clay. I am a good deal of a rascal, sometimes a bore, and often dishonest. When I look at myself I know that only by dint of knowing nothing of me are you enabled to formulate me in your mind as something of a heroic figure. If you could once scan me you would be forever dumb.
>
> Your mind must be of a finer mold than the minds around you or the fingers of your soul would never reach into the distance. That is why I am glad to write to you and tell you the truth as I know it. Of course, I wish for the sake of the episode that I could tell you that I *am* a remarkable person but, alas, poor romance, I am most hideously ordinary.

Beyond the interpersonal realm of morals, ethics, or just plain manners, there is also the question of how this "small pale-yellow person" lived within himself, not what others saw when they looked at him but the more primal fact of who he was as a physical being and how his strong but less than healthy body affected both his work and his behavior. None of this can be fully known—for the simple reason that it is impossible to stand inside another person's skin—but it strikes me as incontestable that there was something singular about Crane's neurological makeup, that he was more tightly wired than most people, which allowed him to perceive visual phenomena more rapidly and precisely than most of us, that something in him was constantly *buzzing*. An extreme example of such a person can be found in Crane's contemporary Nikola Tesla, the inventor who gave the world alternating current, neon light, remote control, and the principles of the radio before Marconi, and who, it is said, was so highly sensitive to sound that he could hear a fly land on a wall in the next room. Crane did not dwell at that far edge of semi-delirium, but he too was an excessively vibrant, vibrating creature—a human tuning fork—and the strangeness and originality of his work is as much a product of the body he was born into as the mind he cultivated and developed: the visual immediacy of it, the primitive force of its animism, and above all the steady bombardment of color. The dog has "yellow famine" in his eyes, Jimmie Johnson lives "some red years," and George Kelcey is "a brown young man." These are not mere literary effects but a spontaneous manifestation of Crane's synesthesia, a condition shared by such well-known people as the physicist Richard Feynman, the writer Vladimir Nabokov, the musician Duke Ellington, the painter Vincent van Gogh, and possibly Arthur Rimbaud, who if nothing else articulates the essential characteristics of synesthesia in his poem "Vowels," which famously begins: "A black, E white, I red, U green, O blue." One day, while Crane was out walking around the Brooklyn waterfront with his friend Hawkins, a boat almost rammed into the pier, and when a sailor let out a cry of warning, Crane suddenly said, "Great heavens! What a green voice!" As Hawkins later reported in an article published in the *Brooklyn Daily Eagle* (April 18, 1907), he was struck by Crane's comment and asked if he was trying to be "poetic." "Certainly not," Crane answered. Every sound triggered off a color in his mind, he said, and rather than seem odd or unusual to him, he found it hard to understand that the same thing didn't happen to everyone. Sounds as colors, but also emotions as colors and various shades of thought. These responses were felt deep within and absorbed into Crane's body, which was the site of a constant inrush of raw sensation, and not only can the traces of these collisions between the outside and the inside be found all over his work, it seems perfectly plausible that a man with such a finely tuned nervous system should have been known for his darting, restless, inconstant personality.

A Dark-Brown Dog. The Black Riders. The Red Badge of Courage. The Bride Comes to Yellow Sky. The Blue Hotel. An Illusion in Red and White.

Any assessment of Crane must also take into account the matter of his health, beginning with the rash of illnesses he suffered throughout his childhood, which might have included an early case of tuberculosis—a disease prevalent in his family—that could have gone dormant for some years only to be rekindled by his immersion in the New York slums after moving to the city, not to mention frequent colds and brushes with pneumonia, and in spite of his passion for baseball and tennis and the vigorous outdoor activities he took part in whenever possible, it seems that he understood he was not destined to have a long life, and already at twenty he was dropping hints about the limited future that lay in front of him, not just to Lily Brandon Munroe but to Nellie Crouse and even to Willa Cather, whom he met in Lincoln, Nebraska, on his trip out west, responding to her comment that he would be a significant someone within ten years by telling her, "I can't wait ten years. I haven't time."

Nearly all young people think they will live forever. Crane knew otherwise, and unlike most of us when we are ten and twenty and twenty-five, he was never granted the luxury of living under that delusion.

20

DURING A BRIEF STOPOVER IN ST. LOUIS ON JANUARY 31, 1895, HE dashed off a note to his friend Button—"Dear Budge, I'm en route to kill Indians"—and the next day he was in Lincoln, Nebraska, where the most daunting part of his assignment was about to begin: a news story of national interest, as opposed to the travel pieces he would be filing with Bacheller as he pushed on through Hot Springs, New Orleans, Galveston, San Antonio, and Mexico City in the months ahead. A harsh summer of drought and violent windstorms had ravaged large swaths of western and central Nebraska, and now that an unusually cold winter had settled on those same lands, with frequent blizzards and astonishing accumulations of snow, thousands of families in the afflicted areas were suffering, some of them ruined and heading out of the state and others, also ruined, living on the point of starvation. The *Omaha World Record* had run a fifteen-part series of articles on the crisis in December, and now that Crane had traveled halfway across the country to cover the story, the *Nebraska State Journal* treated his arrival as a newsworthy event:

> Stephen Crane, representing a large syndicate of newspapers of national reputation and influence, arrived in Lincoln last evening, drawn to the state by the distressing special dispatches sent out of Omaha to advertise the drouth. . . . Mr. Crane's papers have asked him to get the truth, whether his articles are sensational or not, and for that reason his investigation will be welcomed by the business interests of Nebraska.

This was a different sort of job from Crane's previous work for newspapers, not just the semifictionalized New York sketches but the Pennsylvania coal mine report as well, which had been an overview of general conditions, whereas Nebraska was an urgent calamity that needed to be investigated, analyzed, and presented to the public as quickly as possible. He spent close to two weeks on the story, interviewing the governor and various state officials in Lincoln, then traveling west into the drought-damaged areas on the fourth and fifth of February, followed by another trip to the north-central part of the state from the sixth to the eighth, where he holed up in the small town of Eddyville ("as inanimate as a corpse") and conducted additional interviews with farmers as an immense, twenty-four-hour bliz-zard rushed through Dawson County with sixty-mile-an-hour winds and temperatures of fourteen to eighteen degrees below zero for the entire three days. The thermometer in his unheated hotel room registered "pre-cisely one and a half degrees below zero," Crane wrote, and one wonders how he managed to keep his fingers warm enough to hold a pen in his hand. The experience of that mighty tempest stayed with him, and two years later it would return in one of his finest stories, "The Blue Hotel," which is set on the ferocious, godforsaken plains of Nebraska.

Running over four thousand words and examining the situation from several different vantage points, Crane's article is the most thorough piece of journalism he had written so far. "Nebraska's Bitter Fight for Life" offers numbers and statistics, demarcates the exact areas hit by the drought, and delves into the relief efforts mounted by other states around the country, which led to some corrupt distribution practices that wound up putting donated food, clothing, and coal into the hands of undeserving people while those who needed it most got nothing. The strongest and most eloquent passages, however, are found in Crane's conversations with the struggling farmers and in his descriptions of the blighted landscape:

> The leaves of the corn and of the trees turned yellow and sapless like leather. For a time they stood the blasts in the agony of a futile resis-tance. The farmers helpless, with no weapon against this terrible and inscrutable wrath of nature, were spectators at the strangling of their hopes, their ambitions, all that they could look to from their labor. It was as if upon the massive altar of the earth, their homes and their families were being offered in sacrifice to the wrath of some blind and pitiless deity.
>
> The country died. In the rage of the wind, the trees struggled, gasped through each curled and scorched leaf, then, at last, ceased to exist, and

*Drawing of Crane by C. K. Linson, early 1895, just prior to Crane's departure
for the West and Mexico as roving correspondent for the
Bacheller Syndicate.* (COURTESY OF THE UNIVERSITY OF VIRGINIA)

there remained only the bowed and bare skeletons of trees. The corn shivering as from fever, bent and swayed abjectly for a time, then one by one the yellow and tinder-like stalks, twisted and pulled by the rage of the hot breath, died in the fields and the vast and sometimes beautiful green prairies were brown and naked.

Offered in sacrifice to the wrath of some blind and pitiless deity echoes the Crane of *The Black Riders*, and *the inscrutable wrath of nature* had been a presence in his work as far back as the Sullivan County tales, but beyond these familiar marking stones of the Crane universe, there are a couple of other points about this article that demand a closer look—one of them a thing that could easily escape notice and the other what might be called a further step in the evolution of Crane's thinking, a deepening of his understanding of the world.

"Nebraska's Bitter Fight for Life" is a wholly factual piece, eleven pages of professionally responsible journalism, and yet the vivid, lushly written passage just quoted describes changes to the landscape that occurred in the summer of 1894, and Crane did not set foot in Nebraska until February 1, 1895. No doubt he was told many stories about the drought from numerous local sources, but he did not witness—could not have witnessed—those events himself, and yet how precise he is in detailing the havoc of the summer windstorms and the damage they caused to the crops and surrounding vegetation—"leaves . . . sapless like leather," "corn shivering as from fever," "the yellow and tinder-like stalks"—pinpoint observations that in fact were not directly observed but *imagined*, and so well imagined that no one ever questioned the accuracy of Crane's reportage. This is one more instance of the dilemma that occurs when fact goes to bed with fiction, for even as a writer of facts, Crane was above all a writer of fiction, and in the best of his fiction (this is where it begins to get strange), his observations of imagined scenes carry all the force of lived experience, to such an extent that countless readers of *The Red Badge of Courage* came away from the book astonished that its author was not a Union veteran himself. Similarly, with the report on the Nebraska drought, it is hard to believe that Crane wasn't there in the summer. His words seem to put him there, but in truth he was twelve hundred miles to the east, concocting the proto-Dada inanities of the *Pike County Puzzle*.

After the relative calm of Lincoln, his journey to the scorched and frozen hinterlands had a profound effect on him, and the normally dubious if not skeptical Crane could not help marveling at the fortitude of the people he encountered there. He was well acquainted with hardship and misery by then—the New York slums and flophouses, the Pennsylvania coal pits—but the battle for survival on the western tundra was even more extreme, and what struck him about those destitute farmers was their toughness, stoicism, and lack of self-pity. In one memorable conversation with a farmer from Lincoln County, Crane learns that the man has received no aid and asks, "How did you get along?" The man replies, "Don't git along, stranger. Who the hell told you I did get along?" Self-pity, the disease that poisons so many of the characters in *Maggie* and *George's Mother* and turns life into an unrelenting war of all against all, is absent in the devastated heartland, and as with the coal miners in Scranton, the only war they are fighting is against the capricious, implacable forces of nature. With one another, however, the men and women of the plains stick together, and the spirit of pioneer solidarity Crane discovered among those wastelands of hunger and want jolted him into a new awareness of the human potential for grace—even under the harshest, most life-threatening circumstances. He writes: "They are fearless folk, completely American," and as he comes to the end of the article, he pauses for a moment to reflect on the precarious months ahead that will either restore the region to health or bring about a "catastrophe that would surely depopulate the country," then finishes off with these admiring words, which until then would have been all but unthinkable for him: "In the meantime, they depend on their endurance, their capacity to help each other, and their unyielding courage."

Besides the article, Crane also wrote from Nebraska to his Syracuse college friend Clarence Loomis Peaslee, an aspiring writer who published one of the first feature stories about Crane ("Stephen Crane's College Days," August 1896), and it was in Peaslee's article that a portion of the letter Crane sent to him on February 12, 1895, from Lincoln is quoted—which is the only surviving fragment from what seems to have been a long discussion about literature that culminated in these sentences:

> As far as myself and my own meagre success are concerned, I began the war with no talent, but an ardent admiration and desire. I had to build up. I always want to be unmistakable. That to my mind is good writing. There is a great deal of labor connected with literature. I think that is the hardest thing about it. There is nothing to respect in art, save one's own opinion of it.

This is one of Crane's essential early statements about his work as a writer, and so accurately did it express his true feelings that he recycled some of the same sentences in a letter he sent to Hilliard just days after writing to Peaslee, which bears noting because it clarifies the intended meaning of the word *unmistakable*. To Hilliard: "I had to build up, so to speak. And my chiefest desire was to write plainly and unmistakably, so that all men (and some women) might read and understand. That to my mind is good writing." In other words, *unmistakable* as that which is immediately comprehensible, or not obscure, not fussy, not "literary": literature as meaning and not mere show. It sounds perfectly sensible today, but back then, in that mostly blank period between the end of the American Renaissance and the beginning of modernism, when literature had been reduced to little more than an exercise in genteel entertainment, Crane's position was a bold one, especially in his implied dismissal of critics and the marketplace. The writer is the judge of his own work, and if he believes in what he is doing, then he can respect that work and stand by it, regardless of anyone else's opinion. Crane might have added: And be prepared to duck when they start throwing eggs at you—for in spite of the respect he would eventually gain from others, there were still others who couldn't resist attacking him, and the more he was respected, the more he was attacked as the years went on.

During the four months he spent on the road, Crane must have met and talked to dozens of people, perhaps hundreds of people, but only one of them ever took the trouble to record her impressions of the East Coast man's visit to the West. Willa Cather, just two years younger than Crane, was a senior at the University of Nebraska and the drama critic for the *Nebraska State Journal*. Two months earlier, she had copyedited the serialized version of *The Red Badge of Courage*, and when Crane arrived in Lincoln on February first, he and Cather met in the offices of the paper.* On the thirteenth, they met there again and had what seems to have been a rather long conversation, which provided the bulk of the material for Cather's article, "When I Knew Stephen Crane." Written in June 1900 (just days after Crane's death) and originally published under one of Cather's journalistic pseudonyms, Henry Nicklemann, the piece bears a striking resemblance to its author's name in that a good part of the text is pure invention.

Cather gives the time of their meeting as the spring of 1894, not the winter of 1895. The weather is "oppressively warm," not frigid. She is a junior in college, not a senior. Crane's hair is black, not blond. His eyes are dark, not blue-gray. His serialized book was given to Bacheller through a connection with Howells, not Marshall. He is twenty-four, not twenty-three. He is carrying "a little volume of Poe ... in his pocket," no doubt because she has made Crane dark and wants him to look like Poe or, even more fancifully, to present him as a reincarnation of Poe.

Can anything in her article be trusted? Perhaps some things, but it is difficult to know which ones. "He stated that he was going to Mexico to do some work for the Bacheller Syndicate and get rid of his cough." Perhaps Crane said those words, perhaps he didn't. "He was thin to emaciation, his

---

* If legend is to be believed, he walked in at around midnight, and there he came upon Cather, standing on her feet with her eyes closed, fast asleep and motionless as a statue. The astonished Crane is reported to have said that he had never seen anything like it.

face was gaunt and unshaven . . . [his hair] shaggy and unkempt. His gray clothes were much the worse for wear. . . . He wore a flannel shirt and a slovenly excuse for a necktie . . . his shoes were dusty . . . and badly run over at the heel." It is possible that the often poorly dressed Crane looked like this, but Cather's depiction is so extreme that it is hard not to suspect her of exaggerating for poetic effect (or Poe-etic effect).

Still, Cather is a beautiful writer, and whether she is exaggerating or not, her portrait of a dejected, distracted Crane might have some validity. He was, after all, still waiting to hear from Hitchcock about *The Red Badge of Courage*, which must have been a cause of anxiety—his future as a writer hanging in the balance—and yet when Cather asserts that he was "entirely idle" during his days in Lincoln, the facts are against her, since we know that Crane was hard at work on his article while still in town, interviewing, among others, Governor Holcomb and L. P. Ludden, the man in charge of coordinating the relief efforts, and then writing the article itself in Lincoln after he returned from his trip to Eddyville and other ravaged zones of the state. Nevertheless, Cather writes impressively—and with apparent conviction:

Crane was moody most of the time; his health was bad and he seemed profoundly discouraged. Even his jokes were exceedingly drastic. He went about with the tense, preoccupied, self-centered air of a man who is brooding over some impending disaster, and I conjectured vainly as to what it might be. . . . His eyes I remember as the finest I have ever seen, large and dark [*sic*] and full of lustre and changing lights, but with a profound melancholy always lurking deep in them. They were eyes that seemed to be burning themselves out.

As he sat at the desk with his shoulders drooping forward, his head low, and his long, white fingers drumming on the sheets of copy paper, he was as nervous as a race horse fretting to be on the track. Always, as he came and went about the halls, he seemed like a man preparing for a sudden departure. Now that he is dead it occurs to me that all his life was a preparation for sudden departure. I remember once when he was writing a letter he stopped and asked me about the spelling of a word, saying carelessly, "I haven't time to learn to spell." Then, glancing down at his attire, he added with an absentminded smile, "I haven't time to dress either; it takes an awful slice out of a fellow's life."

On the night of the thirteenth, Cather reports, Crane opened up to her and began to talk about the difficulty of sustaining "a double literary life;

writing in the first place the matter that pleased himself, and doing it very slowly; in the second place, any sort of stuff that would sell," with Cather remarking that "in all his long tirade, Crane never raised his voice; he spoke slowly and monotonously and even calmly, but I have never known so bitter a heart in any man as he revealed to me that night." No one else who wrote about him ever detected such bitterness in Crane, but granting Cather the right to her own opinion, let us assume that Crane was feeling especially bitter just then, frazzled and exhausted from his days in the countryside, in the dumps. A moment or two after that, however, she quotes him as saying something he could not have said because it is a paraphrase of something that was said about him by someone else—the British critic Edward Garnett, who was the husband of the Russian translator Constance Garnett and a friend of Crane's during S.C.'s last years in England. Crane, as quoted by Cather: "What I can't do, I can't do at all, and I can't acquire it." Garnett on Crane (from an article published in December 1898): "What he has not got he has no power of acquiring." We know that Cather was familiar with Garnett's article (she quotes from it later in her own article), which makes it all the more mysterious why she should have put Garnett's words into Crane's mouth. A small, niggling point, perhaps, but further proof that Cather's memorial piece on Crane was in large measure a work of fiction.

For all that, how interesting it is to learn that the two best American writers of their generation happened to have met at twenty-one and twenty-three in a small newspaper office in Lincoln, Nebraska. Cather would review some of Crane's lesser works in the years ahead, often harshly, but when she sat down to write about him after his death, she generously gave him his due, describing "The Open Boat" as "unsurpassed in its vividness and constructed perfection" and calling Crane "the first writer of his time in the picturing of episodic, fragmentary life." As for the other quotation she uses from Garnett in her article, there is no reason to doubt that the Englishman's words express her feelings about the dead burning boy as well: "I cannot remember a parallel in the . . . history of fiction. Maupassant, Meredith, Henry James, Mr. Howells and Tolstoy were all learning their expression at an age when Crane had achieved his and achieved it triumphantly."

It is unclear exactly when Crane heard from Hitchcock about *The Red Badge of Courage*, but the letter must have come sometime after his gloomy conversation with Cather (if in fact it was as gloomy as she said it was), for when he pulled into Hot Springs, Arkansas, on February fifteenth, he seems to have been in excellent spirits. He was just passing through, on his way to New Orleans in the morning, but he saw enough of the little resort town to zip out a charming, bubbly, five-page nothing of a story that was published on March third and, for all we know, could have been written on the train as he barreled ahead to his next stop.

The charm of "Seen at Hot Springs" is predominantly a matter of phrasing, tone, and a whimsical understanding of how deeply unimportant the piece is. After the life-and-death issues confronted on the Nebraska prairie, one feels Crane exhaling in the balmy Arkansas weather and joyously winging it from one sentence to the next. A stream of water "looks like a million glasses of lemon phosphate," the stage men and baggagemen at the railway station badger, roar, and gesticulate, "as unintelligible . . . as a row of Homeric experts," and when Crane visits the renowned bathhouses, he concludes that once inside those vaporous enclosures "a man becomes a creature of three conditions. He is about to take a bath—he is taking a bath—he has taken a bath." By the fourth page, he seems to have run out of things to say about the town, which strikes him as unique in the United States for mixing up so many contrasting elements that it resembles "the North and the South, the East and the West," and starts spinning a little story about a commercial traveler for a hat firm in Ogallala, Nebraska, and a "youthful stranger with . . . blonde and innocent hair," and whether it is based on a real event or spun from whole cloth is of little importance. The two men repair to a saloon for some liquid refreshments. Another man, standing at the bar and "ruffling his whiskers," offers to "shake" for the drinks. The traveler agrees and they start to gamble, first for a dollar, then for "two bones," then for "four bones," until the traveler has won "fifty dollars in 'bout four minutes." The man with the whiskers vanishes, and the delighted traveler, still standing at the bar next to the youthful stranger with the blond and innocent hair, proposes that they split the money and "blow it," but the Crane stand-in demurs, perhaps suspecting an intricate con in the making, and ditches the bewildered, irritated traveler with these parting words: "I guess I'll stroll back up-town. I want to write a letter to my mother." What a fine, dumbfounding non sequitur that is, but even better is the last sentence of the article—"In the back room of the saloon, the man with the ruffled beard was silently picking hieroglyphics out of his whiskers"—which is surely one of the most beguiling, crackpot sentences Crane ever wrote.

He rode that wave of exultant good humor on into New Orleans, and three days after his arrival he sent off a zinging nonsense letter to Linson in a mashup of Creole, German, and clunky beginner's English:

Mon ami Linson: Friedweller die schonënberger je suis dans New Orleans. Cracked ice dans Nebraska, terra del fuega dans New Orleans. Table d'hotes sur les balconies just like spring. A la mode whiskers on the citizens en masse, merci, of the vintage de 1792.

Frequented I all the time here again l'etoile de Virginitie sur St. Louis Street. Sic semper tyrannis! Mardi gras tres grande but it does not until Tuesday begin. Spiel!

He had never been so far from home. Untethered, unpressed, liberated from all responsibilities to anyone but Bacheller and himself, it was the first time in three and a half years that he could stop worrying about where his next dollar and his next meal were coming from. More than that, he was *on the move*, living out his old dream of escaping the narrow, cobbled streets of New York for the unearthly expanses of the American West, and with his poems on the brink of publication and his war novel finally accepted, why wouldn't he have been feeling giddy over this sudden turn in his fortunes? The Hot Springs article and the letter to Linson are signs of a young man punch-drunk with happiness, and while the articles he produced for Bacheller were mostly undistinguished, the value of the trip for Crane was immeasurable: four months of new impressions and new thoughts that would generate a remarkable effusion of stories after he returned to New York, first the terrifically good, tightly wrought Western and Mexican tales from 1895–96 ("One Dash—Horses," "The Five White Mice," "A Man and Some Others") and then the two narrative astonishments from 1897–98 ("The Bride Comes to Yellow Sky," which is set in Texas, and "The Blue Hotel," which takes place during a Nebraska blizzard identical to the one he experienced in Eddyville). If not for the trip, none of these works would have been written, meaning that if not for the trip that inspired those works (among the best he wrote), Crane never would have become Crane.

He knew that the Wild West of his boyhood was dead. The frontier had been pronounced officially closed after the 1890 census, and with no more virgin territory to be explored and conquered, no more Indians to be rounded up and killed, no more gunslingers to square off against one another in saloons and dusty corrals, progress was coming in the form of Civilization. Crane arrived in the region on the cusp of these changes, changes he would later exploit to great effect in his two Western masterpieces, but even as the towns grew into cities and commerce spread, the landscape stood there in all its cosmic grandeur, and whatever encroachments the East was making on the West, the West was still a place apart, another America from the one Crane had known in New Jersey and New

York. Six months after his return, he wrote to his friend Hawkins from Port Jervis:

> I have always believed the western people to be much truer than the eastern people. We in the east are overcome a good deal by a detestable superficial culture which I think is the real barbarism. . . . Damn the east! I fell in love with the straight out-and-out, sometimes-hideous, often braggart westerners because I thought them to be truer men and, by the living piper, we will see in the next fifty years what the west will do. They are serious, those fellows. When they are born they take one big gulp of wind and they live.

It wasn't that he slacked off on his work for Bacheller—fourteen articles in four months hardly qualifies as a dereliction of duty*—but he was distracted by his own excitement, I think, and it turned out that the job of travel writer was not well suited to his talents. Crane was best when he was telling stories, even the smallest of stories, such as an account of a traffic jam on a New York street, but now that his assignment was to travel from place to place and collect bits of local color, he seems to have been at loose ends, or at least uninspired, which gives the sketches a rather dogged, workmanlike feel. The articles are uniformly well written and often entertaining, more than good enough to have pleased Bacheller, but except for two or three of them, they lack Crane's customary spark.

Not much is known about what he was up to during those four months. He dawdled in New Orleans for fifteen or sixteen days, notably working on a freshly typed version of *The Red Badge of Courage* that Hitchcock express-mailed to his hotel, and before Crane sent it back to D. Appleton and Company he revisited the novel with enough detachment and clarity of mind to cut out one of the chapters, discard the final paragraphs of several others, trim roughly two thousand words from the text as a whole, and make—as he put it to Hitchcock—"a great number of small corrections." When he wasn't tinkering with his manuscript, he was attending two opera performances, suffering through a case of dyspepsia (according to Linson's memoir), and looking over a copy of Copeland and Day's publishing prospectus for *The Black Riders* (complete with flattering excerpts from Garland's review of *Maggie*), but other than the two dispatches he sent off

---

* Or seventeen, if one counts the three fables he also wrote in Mexico or immediately after his return, all of them published by Bacheller: "The Voice of the Mountains," "How the Donkey Lifted the Hills," and "The Victory of the Moon."

from New Orleans, the rest of his stay at the Hotel Royal is a blank. The first article is a laudatory piece about the historical importance and current state of opera in the city, and the second is a detailed, blow-by-blow report of the Mardi Gras celebration on February twenty-sixth, which must have been wired in a bit behind schedule, since Bacheller didn't publish it until the next Mardi Gras rolled around the following year. Then he was off to Texas, arriving on March fifth in Galveston, where he spent most of the day in two long drinking sessions with local big shots, first the mayor and then the managing editor of the *Galveston Daily News*. Afterward, he described the experience in a letter to his artist friend James Moser:

> To my honor be it said that I didn't mention the managing editor to the mayor nor the mayor to the managing editor, but withstood both assaults with good manners and tranquility. If any man hereafter says I can't hold my liquor, he lies. I am a liquor holder from Holdersville. . . . Galveston is a great town I think, and all heavy wit aside I am deeply indebted to you for introducing me to such a royal good fellow as Sam Penland.

It is the same jaunty good humor found in the Hot Springs article and the letter to Linson from New Orleans, and something of that spirit must have communicated itself to the people he met, among them Penland, who later that month sent off a letter of thanks to Moser for connecting him with Crane—which is the first of only two short written accounts besides the longer piece from Cather of anyone running into Crane during his western travels:

> The quiet demeanor and unobtrusive manner of Mr. Stephen Crane together with his impressive countenance made him a special mark of interest to several of my friends to whom I had the pleasure of introducing him. His stay with us was altogether agreeable from our point of view and we anticipate with great interest his return from the City of Mexico.

This proves that Crane did not shut himself up in his hotel room during his weeklong stay in Galveston, that he spent time among the local citizenry and made a good impression on them, but there is nothing else on record to tell us what he said or did or thought while he was there. Apparently, he took extensive notes for the article he was planning to write about the town, but he didn't manage to finish it until much later, so much later that it didn't appear in print until five months after his death. For the most part, it is a travel essay that attacks the fundamental principle of a travel essay, which is to seek out what is new and different in whatever place the travel writer happens to land, whereas most American towns tend to be more alike than different, Crane feels, as is the case with the ever more modernized Galveston, with its "square brick business blocks . . . mazes of telegraph wires . . . [and] trolly-cars clamoring up and down the streets," so that "an illustration of Galveston streets can easily be obtained in Maine." On the other hand, there are the people to consider as well, and the article ends with praise for the Galvestonians' "Southern frankness, the honesty which enables them to meet a stranger without deep suspicion, and they are masters of a hospitality which is instructive to cynics." By cynics, of course, Crane is referring to himself.

The story was much the same in San Antonio. An unfinished article that wasn't published until years later (January 8, 1899) and a crackingly funny letter to a friend. This time it was Button, and after prematurely announcing his imminent departure for Mexico (he left the following week), Crane takes a quick swipe at himself and the drudgery of travel reporting ("I would tell you of many strange things I have seen if I was not so bored with writing of them in various articles") and then turns to the matter at hand, which is to describe his encounter in New Orleans with a man from Button's hometown—

a most intolerable duffer . . . who let it be known that he was from Akron, O., although I don't see why he should. He told me that he knew your friends there or your friends who have escaped or are about to escape, or are about to plan to escape from there.

He had fingers like lightning rods and on the street he continually pointed at various citizens with the exclamation: "Look at that fellow!" People in New Orleans don't like that kind of thing, you know. No doubt his ingenuous Akron spirit was amazed at many things but for my own part I felt that he should have controlled his emotion. . . .

He enthusiastically requested me to stop off on my way home in the spring and visit him. I modestly replied that while I appreciated his generosity and his courage, I had to die early in the spring and I feared that I would have to hurry home for the funeral but I had an open date in 1997 and would be happy to see him in hell on that occasion.

Well, at any rate, I lie, for I was considerate to him, treated him well at times, and was careful of his childish innocence. But there should be a tariff on that kind of export from Akron, O.

The last glimpse of Crane in the American West is provided by Frank Bushick, the editor of the *San Antonio Express,* who puts himself and the visiting correspondent on Alamo Plaza one evening in front of a Mexican food stand as a relaxed and bantering Crane chats with one of San Antonio's legendary Chili Queens—attractive waitresses who flirted with potential customers in order to lure them into buying the tamales, enchiladas, and frijoles offered by the stands they worked for (food that Crane subsequently characterized as tasting "exactly like pounded fire-brick from hades"). Her name was Martha, a woman renowned for her luscious, dark-haired beauty, and as she stood there dressed in an above-the-ankle "flaming red skirt" and a blue blouse that exposed her bare arms and "full bosoms," she seemed to take a sudden shine to Crane and complimented him on his good looks. Shedding his customary reserve, he offered his own compliment by saying she was "prettier than ever tonight," a gallant but absurd remark that would suggest they had been friends for years, and as the witty Martha looked him over again and finally understood how young he was, she asked Crane if his mother knew he was out. Quickly affirming that she did, he prolonged the game by telling Martha he had heard a lot about her and that was why he had come around to see her, at which point Martha laughed and said, "Oh, my! You're a big kidder, too. Here, you must have a flower for that," and then she pinned a red rose on the lapel of Crane's jacket.

Bushick recorded this anecdote thirty-nine years after the fact in a book entitled *Glamorous Days: In Old San Antonio.* Such a long passage of time doesn't discount the possibility that it was true, however, and if it does happen to be true, it would verify that Crane's good humor was still intact after a month and a half on the road, regardless of how bored he had become with the job of cranking out travel articles to pay for the trip.

The belated report about San Antonio renews his grievances against the modernization of Texas cities as he condemns the "uproar [of] the terrible and almighty trolley car" and speculates that "if the trolley car had trolleyed around Jericho, the city would not have fallen; it would have exploded." Even the remnants of old Spanish mission architecture still standing in the Mexican quarter are under threat and "must get trampled into shapeless dust which lies always behind the march of this terrible century." For all that, he seems to have preferred San Antonio to Galveston and was particularly drawn to the Alamo and the suicidal, last-stand battle waged there in 1836 by a small group of Texans led by Travis, Crockett, and Bowie against Santa Anna's four-thousand-man army. In a rare burst of maudlin rhetoric, Crane calls the Alamo "the greatest memorial to courage which civilization has allowed to stand," but by the next page, as he tells the story of Colonel Travis preparing his men for certain death—after he had given them the choice to stay and die or depart and live—Crane reverses course and zeroes in on the one man who chose to depart, the only so-called coward in the bunch, who announced, "I'm not prepared to die, and shall not do so if I can avoid it," but rather than condemn this man, whose name was Rose, Crane calls him "a kind of dogged philosopher" and is impressed by his "strange inverted courage," for much as he admired heroism in battle, he also admired the man with enough conviction to stand alone against the will of the crowd.

On March seventeenth, he left San Antonio for Laredo. There he boarded another train, and sixty hours and one thousand miles later, he arrived in Mexico City, where for the next nine weeks he managed to make himself all but invisible.

Judging by the stories he wrote later that year and the next, it would seem that Crane spent a fair amount of time with other Americans in Mexico City, the expats, the drifters, the barmen of a transplanted, south-of-the-border Yankee world, leading Berryman to conclude that "the lazy, alcoholic, gambling life of Americans in a foreign city had never been so well observed before," but that was not the only world he traveled in during those nine undocumented weeks, for there was the shock of Mexico to be absorbed as well, both its land and its people, and he pushed on dutifully with his investigations and reports, at times disoriented by the newness of it all, at all times burdened by the sense of himself as an ignorant stranger, but even as he struggled to penetrate Mexico and its culture, he persisted in his writer's obligation to keep his eyes open and communicate what he saw.

On the train heading south: "In Mexico the atmosphere seldom softens anything. It devotes its energy to making high lights, bringing everything forward, making colors fairly volcanic."

By the side of a creek, as women bathed in the water: "In the stream that flowed near there was a multitude of heads with long black hair. A vast variety of feminine garments decorated the bushes that skirted the creek. A baby, brown as a water-jar and of the shape of an alderman, paraded the bank in utter indifference or ignorance or defiance."

In Mexico City: "The bull-fighters ... move confidently, proudly, with a magnificent self-possession. People turn to stare after them. There is in their faces something cold, sinister, merciless. There is history there too, a history of fiery action, of peril, of escape. You would know, you would know without being told that you are gazing at an executioner, a kind of moral assassin."

At the Viga Canal: "Out from behind the corner of the garden-wall suddenly appeared Popocatepetl, towering toward the sky, a great cone of creamy hue in the glamor of the sunshine. Then later came Iztaccihuatl, the white woman, of curious shape more camel than woman, its peak confused with clouds. A plain of fervent green stretched toward them."

In Mexico City: "The burro, born in slavery, dying in slavery, generation upon generation, he with his wobbly legs, sore back, and ridiculous little face, reasons not at all. He carries as much as he can, and when he can carry it no further, he falls down."

On money and prices: "If a young Mexican clerk, who is, for instance, on a salary of $60 per month, but who, nevertheless, thinks considerable of himself, as young clerks are apt to do—if this young clerk wishes to purchase a suit of clothes commensurate with his opinions, he will have to spend more than a month's pay to get it. . . . Young clerks do not become great dudes in Mexico."

On pulque, the national drink: "It resembles green milk. The average man has never seen green milk, but if he can imagine a handful of paris green interpolated into a glass of cream, he will have a fair idea of the appearance of pulque. And it tastes like—it tastes like—some terrible concoction of yeast perhaps. Or maybe some calamity of eggs—One understands then that education is everything, even as the philosophers say, and that we would all be eating sandwiches made from doormats if only circumstances had been different."

These extracts from the nine articles he sent to Bacheller convey something of their gist, something of the guidebook tone he chose to settle for. They are exercises in style rather than substance, marked by occasional surges of wit and Crane's irrepressible talent for the surprising image (*sandwiches made from doormats*), but they all approach Mexico from the outside and rarely even attempt to crack the surface of the visual spectacle unfolding around him. Travel notes of a befuddled tourist—to help prepare other Americans for their own befuddled adventures in the "mystic south." All nine articles were duly published in multiple venues by the syndicate, but the most important piece Crane wrote in Mexico, the only one of any importance, was a small essay that remained unpublished for more than half a century and did not find its way into print until 1967, smack in the middle of the Vietnam War. Bearing no title and unused by Bacheller for reasons that have never been explained (perhaps Crane didn't bother to send it in, perhaps it was rejected for being too provocative), it is now known by two different titles, "Above All Things" (from the first words of the essay) and "The Mexican Lower Classes" (as published in the Library of America edition, which was released in 1984). Just three and a quarter pages long, it is one of Crane's most incisive works of nonfiction, an intimate, questing, wholly honest effort to grapple with the mysteries of culture, society, and the fate of individuals born into one set of circumstances or another—a crucial step forward in Crane's evolving search for his own philosophical position.

> Above all things, the stranger finds the occupations of foreign peoples to be trivial and inconsequent. The average mind utterly fails to comprehend the new point of view and that such and such a man should be satisfied to carry bundles or mayhap sit and ponder in the sun all his life in this faraway country seems an abnormally stupid thing. The visitor feels scorn. He swells with a knowledge of his geographical experience. "How futile are the lives of these people," he remarks, "and what incredible ignorance that they should not be aware of their futility." This is the arrogance of the man who has not yet solved himself and discovered his own actual futility.
>
> Yet, indeed, it requires wisdom to see a brown woman in one garment crouched listlessly in the door of a low adobe hut while a naked brown baby sprawls on his stomach in the dust of the roadway—it requires wisdom to see this thing and to see it a million times and yet to say: "Yes, this is important to the scheme of nature. This is part of her economy. It would not be well if it had never been."
>
> It might perhaps be said—if any one dared—that the most worthless literature of the world has been that which has been written by the men of one nation concerning the men of another.

In one fell swoop, Crane demolishes everything he has thought and written about Mexico so far, understands that in fact he understands nothing about the place, and in spite of the vast material differences between himself and the impoverished Indians he has studied, he cannot presume to look down on them from a position of moral or cultural superiority. To call someone else's life futile is a failure to grasp one's own insignificance in the big scheme of things, a failure to grasp oneself. Abandon your preconceptions, he is telling us, do not judge the stranger by the norms and measures of your own society, and above all do not rely on your first impressions as an accurate gauge of the truth, for even Crane himself admits, "At first it seemed to me the most extraordinary thing that the lower classes of Indians in this country should insist upon existence at all. Their squalor, their ignorance seemed so absolute that death—no matter what it has in store—would appear as freedom, as joy."

This is an extreme if not outlandish statement, so coldhearted and unsettling that it verges on indecency, but it soon becomes apparent that the joyful embrace of death he imagines for these downtrodden peasants is no more than a rhetorical point. Crane is building an argument, and in the next paragraph he turns his attention to another, more familiar form of poverty, that of the New York slums:

> The people of the slums of our own cities fill a man with awe. That vast army with its countless faces immovably cynical, that vast army that silently confronts eternal defeat, it makes one afraid. One listens for the first thunder of the rebellion, the moment when this silence shall be broken by a roar of war. . . .
>
> They are becoming more and more capable of defining their condition and this increase of knowledge evinces itself in the deepening of those savage and scornful lines which extend from near the nostrils to the corners of the mouth. It is very distressing to observe this growing appreciation of the situation.

Crane is referring to the widespread fear in the mid-nineties that America was heading toward an outbreak of class warfare. The Panic had entered its third year of economic hardship and social disintegration, and unemployed slum dwellers were becoming ever more conscious of the forces that were aligned against them, ever more aware of the causes of their suffering, and while Crane does not discount the possibility that the Mexican lower classes have attained a similar awareness, he "cannot perceive any evidence of it" and concludes that they do not feel "the modern desperate rage at the accident of birth," for even if "the Indian can imagine himself a king . . . he does not apparently feel that there is an injustice in the fact that he was not born a king any more than there is in his not being born a giraffe." Then, as Crane comes to the end of the first part of his argument, he suggests that the difference between the two forms of poverty is largely a matter of knowledge versus ignorance: "He [the impoverished Mexican] has not enough information to be unhappy about his state. Nobody seeks to provide him with it. He is born, he works, he worships, he dies, all on less money than would buy a thoroughbred Newfoundland dog and who dares to enlighten him?"

The second part of the essay abandons the angry, increasingly militant American masses and introduces another sort of comparison:

A man is at liberty to be virtuous in almost any position of life. The virtue of the rich is not so superior to the virtue of the poor that we can say that the rich have a great advantage. These Indians are by far the most poverty-stricken class with which I have met but they are not morally the lowest by any means. Indeed, as far as the mere form of religion goes, they are one of the highest. They are exceedingly devout, worshipping with a blind faith that counts a great deal among the theorists.

But according to my view this is not the measure of them. I measure their morality by what evidences of peace and contentment I can detect in the average countenance.

The tranquil faces of the Mexican poor, in contrast to the "savage and scornful lines" on the faces of the American poor, as well as the classless imprint of virtue, which transcends both the rich and poor alike and places them on equal footing. Even here, in what is probably Crane's most abstract, speculative piece of writing, writing so important to him that he took the unusual step of casting it in the first person, even in this quasi-theoretical work he continues to ground his thoughts in the observable, the tactile, the immediacy of a world pouring into his mind through the electric hum of his senses, and therefore he presents us with faces, the expressions he has observed in human faces as evidence to support his conclusions about virtue, morality, and the depth of religious belief. Hardly a scientific approach, but Crane was not a scientist, after all, he was a writer, and this piece of writing stands out not so much for the airtight logic of its propositions as for what it tells us about Crane's thinking at that moment in his journey— not just through Mexico, but his journey through life.

In the next paragraph, he comes to the central point of the essay:

If a man is not given a fair opportunity to be virtuous, if his environment chokes his moral aspirations, I say that he has got the one important cause of complaint and rebellion against society. Of course it is always possible to be a martyr but then we do not wish to be martyrs. We prefer to be treated with justice and then martyrdom is not required.

There is much to explore in these sentences. On the one hand, Crane is presenting what amounts to a declaration of his political beliefs—the conditions under which a person has the right to rebel against society—and yet, by invoking the terms *justice* and *fair opportunity* (what we now call *equal opportunity*), he is not primarily concerned with economic or social advancement but with an individual's *moral aspirations*, in other words, the

quality of a person's soul and his chance or lack of chance to lead a virtuous life. Morality is not just a question of a person's individual conduct,
however, it is a question of how we interact with one another, a product
of the spiritual ground upon which a society stands, and if the potential
within us to pursue a virtuous, moral life is thwarted by our environment,
we are justified in challenging the status quo and attempting to change
the world around us. The logical next step in this line of reasoning would
then be to examine the ways in which an unjust society could be made
just without producing a mountain of dead martyrs, but Crane doesn't go
there. He stops at the threshold of what could be called the realm of the
political—the more than one—to remain with the one, the individual, in
this case himself, a young American far from home looking at the world
from a new perspective.

"I am of the opinion that poverty of itself is no cause," he writes in
the next paragraph, comparing his own situation to that of the rich,
because in spite of his own impoverished circumstances of the past
few years, he understands that he has had his own fair opportunities
and has not been choked by the environment, which makes him no
worse off than the rich. "Their opportunities are no greater," he continues. "They can give more, deny themselves more in quantity but not
relatively. We can each give all that we possess and there I am at once
their equal."

The essay concludes:

> I do not think however that they would be capable of sacrifices that would
> be possible to me. So then I envy them nothing. Far from having a griev-
> ance against them, I feel that they will confront an ultimate crisis that
> I, through my opportunities, may altogether avoid. There is in fact no
> advantage of importance which I can perceive them possessing over me.
>
> It is for these reasons that I refuse to commit judgement upon these
> lower classes of Mexico. I even refuse to pity them. It is true that at night
> many of them sleep in heaps in door-ways, and spend their days squat-
> ting upon the pavements. It is true that their clothing is scant and thin.
> All manner of things of this kind is true but yet their faces have almost
> always a certain smoothness, a certain lack of pain, a serene faith. I can
> feel the superiority of their contentment.

One can hardly fault Crane for failing to predict the Mexican Revolution of 1910, along with the massive peasant revolt led by Emiliano Zapata
in Morelos. If we went down that road, we could also blame him for not

predicting the San Francisco earthquake of 1906 or the stock market crash of 1929. What counts is that Crane was continuing to make progress, and the two good things he managed to compose on his trip, "Nebraska's Bitter Fight for Life" at the beginning and "The Mexican Lower Classes" at the end, are significant milestones in his development, two more steps on the way toward the thinking that would inform what are probably his greatest, most indelible stories, "The Open Boat," *The Monster*, and "The Blue Hotel."

Then there is this. Although it cannot be verified with absolute certainty, the evidence seems persuasive enough to back the story that at some point during his weeks in Mexico Crane had a frightening, near-death encounter with a gang of bandits somewhere in the countryside—a heart-in-the-throat adventure of menace, escape, and pursuit on horseback worthy of the most thrilling cowboy film, all of it depicted in the story "One Dash—Horses," *one dash* being a gambler's term for an all-or-nothing roll of the dice.

From a letter written to Hawkins in September 1895: "I am engaged at last on my troubles in Mexico." From a 1948 letter written by one of Crane's nieces to Schoberlin: "I did hear about the Mexican trip and heard him describe the toughness of the bandits." And then, most compelling of all, these sentences from Linson's memoir about Crane's return to New York:

Just as abruptly as he had departed . . . just so abruptly he returned. One evening I was alone. A knock on the door brought me face to face with Steve. That evening was a riot of talk. For once his tongue found freedom. But it has all gone from me but one tale of a wild midnight of alarming uncertainties, a pursuit by bandits, and a ride filled with foreboding until it ended in an almost comic surprise in the arms of a company of Rurales scouting the hills at dawn.

The plot of "One Dash—Horses" closely follows Crane's verbal account of the incident. An American traveler named Richardson, accompanied by his Mexican guide, José, journeys out onto the plains. At night, they take shelter in the back room of an adobe tavern, in separate quarters divided from the main room by a thin blanket. They fall asleep, but before long they are awakened by a loud party of men (the bandits) whom they overhear plotting to kill Richardson before they steal his money, pistol, saddle, and spurs. Someone pushes aside the blanket, and in walks "a fat, round-faced Mexican" followed by five or six other men. Richardson, clutching his revolver under his own blanket, is terrified, too afraid to move as "his knee-joints turned to bread." The irrationality of his response is the most convincing aspect of the scene and suggests that Crane could well have been remembering his own response at that moment: "The American did not move. He was staring at the fat Mexican with a strange fixedness of gaze, not fearful, not dauntless, not anything that could be interpreted. He simply stared." Because he does not "cry out and turn pale, or run, or pray them mercy," the Mexicans conclude that he is either a great fighter or an idiot, and therefore they hesitate to act, but when they shine their torch into another part of the room, they discover José and immediately pounce on him and give him a good, thorough pounding. Still, Richardson does not move, clutching his gun under the blanket as he continues to stare at them with blank eyes. In the middle of this standoff, a bunch of laughing women enter the main room of the tavern, and with the business of Richardson's murder still pending, the fat man and the others go off to cavort with "the girls." Richardson and José take advantage of the interruption to slip outside, mount their horses (as cited on pages 30–31), and gallop off into the breaking dawn, eventually pursued by "a wild mob of almost fifty drunken horsemen," but before the mob can catch up with them, Richardson and José run into "a detachment of Rurales, that crack corps of the Mexican army that polices the plains so zealously," and are saved.

Could this have happened to Crane? There is a good chance that it did, and if it did, there is every reason to believe that it was one more turning point in his life: proof that he had the courage not to panic or whimper or beg for mercy when he found himself looking into the eyes of death.

He headed back to New York on May fifteenth, carrying the things he had acquired during his four months on the road: a pistol, a serape, an assortment of riding gear, and a small bag filled with a dozen colorful stones he had bought from a street vendor in Mexico City, thinking they were opals when in fact they were nothing more than gleaming bits of worthlessness. He gave away the stones to his friends and held on to everything else, even going to the trouble of lugging his collection across the ocean in 1897 when he moved to England, where for the rest of his life he kept those objects on display as treasured souvenirs. Talismans.

21

THE BLACK RIDERS WAS PUBLISHED ON MAY FIRST, AND BY THE TIME Crane returned to New York in the middle of the month, the book was beginning to make a small noise in literary circles around the country, as shown by these comments from a Chicago newspaper on the eleventh: "There is not a line of poetry from the opening to the closing page. Whitman's 'Leaves of Grass' were luminous in comparison. Poetic lunacy would be a better name for the book." There would be a number of more positive reactions as well, along with other, equally scathing assessments, but for a work as unorthodox as *The Black Riders*, the fact that the reviews were mixed and not universally hostile ranks as something of a triumph. In any case, done in by his long journey home and not in the best physical shape, Crane crashed briefly at Nelson Greene's loft at the old Art Students League building (where he met Greene's model Gertrude Selene, who would become the inspiration for the character Florinda in *The Third Violet*), stopped by the offices of the Bacheller Syndicate to hand in his expense account (which included the cost of the phantom gun), and then went north to Port Jervis to rest up and recover.

On June eighth, he wrote to the publishers of *The Black Riders*, Copeland and Day, to inform them that he had recently returned from Mexico and was taking some time off in the country "because I am not in very good health." Then, turning to more important business, he asked for news of his book: "I would be glad to learn of *The Black Riders*. I hear they are making some stir. My address will be c/o Lantern Club, 126 William St, N.Y.C."

Once he was on his feet again, Crane moved back into Greene's loft on East Twenty-third Street, but the bulk of his social life revolved around the newly formed Lantern Club—sometimes spelled "Lanthorn" or "Lanthorne"—which he had helped set up with Irving Bacheller, Edward Marshall, Willis Brooks Hawkins, Post Wheeler, and other young and not-so-young writers and journalists. Bacheller was named permanent president, and the club convened in a shack that was perched on the roof of a building in lower Manhattan near the Brooklyn Bridge, a building so old that it was reported to be the oldest building in the city, a place that had once been the home of Captain Kidd and had later served as a hideout for Washington and other generals during the Revolutionary War. As Bacheller recalled in 1901:

The shanty on the roof was occupied by an old Dutchman, who gladly gave up possession for the sum of $50. Then the organizers, among whom was Stephen Crane, employed a cook and fitted up the shanty so that it looked like a ship's cabin. There, far above the madding crowd, the "Lanthornes" held high intellectual revels. A luncheon was served every day, and the members let their hair grow long and their minds grow high. Every Saturday night they held a literary banquet. Each week some member of the club was assigned to write a story, and it was read at the dinner. Encomium and favorable criticism were prohibited. After the reading of the story the members jumped upon it as hard as they could, pointed out the flaws in it and pooh-poohed it generally, if possible. The highest tribute that a story could receive was complete silence. That was the best any writer ever got.

After the fraternity in college, the Pendennis Club on Avenue A, and the long stint of impoverished group living on East Twenty-third Street (which would come to an end by early fall), Crane was now traveling with his fellow writers and satisfying his need for human interaction in their company. Guests came as well, some of them prominent national figures, and the informal ship's-cabin atmosphere must have helped the reticent Crane let down his guard a bit and talk to them with a certain degree of comfort. Howells showed up, but other visitors included the young Ethel Barrymore in the early days of her acting career, the architect Stanford White, Nathaniel Hawthorne's prolific writer son, Julian, Theodore Roosevelt (current friend, future antagonist), and, more than once, Samuel Clemens, who was friendly to Crane and whom Crane liked personally, even if he preferred Clemens the man to the work of Mark Twain the writer (excluding *Life on the Mississippi*). Most afternoons, Crane ate lunch at the club, slept there every now and then, and however little he contributed to the group discussions, he did muster the courage one Saturday night to stand up and read a story of his to the assembled gathering—which qualifies as a minor miracle and suggests that he felt more at home there than anywhere else.

Meanwhile, the public response to *The Black Riders* was gaining momentum—in both directions. The poems themselves were challenging enough, but readers also had to contend with the book's unusual design. In her introduction to the first reprint of the collection in 1926, the Imagist poet Amy Lowell began by recalling the box that contained the new poet's little pills:

> I remember perfectly when *The Black Riders* came out. . . . The book was published in fanciful guise by two enthusiastic and aesthetic young men whose firm name, Copeland and Day, stood for quality in literature, quality of a somewhat esoteric variety, as a rule. . . . The virility and harsh passion of Stephen Crane's fistful of verses accorded ill with the form in which they were presented to the public—fifty special copies on vellum, and . . . the regular edition [of five hundred] bound in grey boards with a conventionalized orchid in black trailing across both covers. For

some unfathomable reason, the printing throughout was in capitals, and pursuing an unhappy custom just coming into vogue the poems spurted from the tip-top of the pages. . . . No method more certain to obscure the sincerity of the work could well have been devised.

Influenced by the Arts and Crafts movement and a recent wave of small presses in England devoted to publishing innovative books in fine, limited editions, Copeland and Day had been founded in Boston in 1893 and ceased operations just six years later, but in its short life the company launched the careers of several young Americans, brought out works by English, Irish, and Scottish authors such as Stevenson, Yeats, Wilde, and Elizabeth Barrett Browning, and served as the American publisher of *The Yellow Book*. Crane had next to nothing to do with the design preparations for his own entry onto the Copland and Day list. He asked his artist friend Fred Gordon to furnish a drawing of the black orchid for the front and back covers, but Gordon's proposal was turned down and then reconfigured by someone else in Boston. Still, Crane was pleased with the final result and had no objections to THE CAPITAL LETTER FORMAT OF HIS POEMS. When the book's design was attacked in the press, he concluded a letter to Copeland and Day with an enthusiastic show of support: "I see they have been pounding the wide margins, the capitals and all that but I think it's great."

As for the contents of the book, the mixed verdict of reviewers tended to oscillate between the extremes of disgust and admiration. The *New York Tribune*, in the first of its foul-tempered rants against Crane, closed off by driving a wooden stake into the heart of the poems: "In their futility and affectation they strike the impartial reader as so much trash." Another unsigned review, in *Munsey's Magazine*, contended that Crane "has the skepticism and cynicism of a man who imagines instead of knows, and none of the exquisite sense of sound that belongs to the poet as to the musician," and then asked, as if in bewildered supplication: "Is this poetry?" The estimable Thomas Wentworth Higginson, however, commander of the first black regiment in the Civil War and co-editor of the first publication of Emily Dickinson's poems in 1890, defended Crane in his review for the *Nation* and felt that the power behind the poems lay in a "vigorous earnestness and a fresh pair of eyes." Harry Thurston Peck, writing in the magazine he edited, the *Bookman*, went a good deal further than that and called Crane "a true poet . . . who stimulates thought because he himself thinks. It's no exaggeration to say that the small volume that bears his name is the most notable contribution to literature to which the present year has given birth."

It was more or less a wash, with the two sides canceling each other out, but the fascination (and contempt) inspired by Crane's poems did not stop with the reviews, and for months after the release of the book, parodies of his lines kept popping up in newspapers and magazines. It was the same sort of mocking abuse his friends had dished out to him while he was writing the poems, but now the taunts had evolved into a sport to be played in full view of the public. Post Wheeler dubbed the wisecracking verses "stephencranelets," and close to a hundred of them found their way into print—a record number of parodies for any American poet of the nineteenth century. One example will suffice. The text of Crane's now often anthologized original reads as follows:

> I saw a man pursuing the horizon;
> Round and round they sped.
> I was disturbed at this;
> I accosted the man.
> "It is futile," I said,
> "You can never—"
> "You lie," he cried,
> And ran on.*

On August eleventh, the *Buffalo Press* published this:

> I saw a meter measuring gas.
> On and on it ran.
> I was disturbed at this,
> Because no gas was being used.
> "It is futile," I said,
> "You can't register"—
> "You lie!" it cried.
> I did.
> It ran on.

Crane being Crane, he managed to shrug off these whimsical attacks, or at least keep them at bay by pretending to ignore them, but that doesn't mean he was unaware of the parodies or that they didn't hurt, as this letter written to Hilliard the following January would seem to suggest:

---

* A recent example would be the current *Oxford Book of American Poetry* (edited by David Lehman, 2006), in which this poem is one of seven chosen to represent Crane's work.

The one thing that deeply pleases me in my literary life—brief and inglorious as it is—is the fact that men of sense believe me to be sincere. "Maggie," published in paper covers, made me the friendship of Hamlin Garland and W. D. Howells, and the one thing that makes my life worth living in the midst of all this abuse and ridicule is the consciousness that never for an instant have those friendships at all diminished. Personally I am aware that my work does not amount to a string of dried beans—I always calmly admit it. But I also know that I do the best that is in me, without regard to cheers or damnation. When I was the mark for every humorist in the country I went ahead, and now, when I am the mark for only 50 per cent of the humorists in the country, I go ahead, for I understand that a man is born into the world with his own pair of eyes and he is not at all responsible for his quality of personal honesty. To keep close to my honesty is my supreme ambition. There is a sublime egotism in talking of honesty. I, however, do not say that I am honest. I merely say that I am as nearly honest as a weak mental machinery will allow. This aim in life struck me as being the only thing worth while. A man is sure to fail at it, but there is something in the failure.

Not responsible. At first glance, a puzzling statement—implying that a person is not accountable for his own behavior—but ultimately (I think) a defense of an inborn moral imperative to conduct one's life as honestly as he can, which is not a trait granted to all men but only to some, himself included. We know that Crane wobbled from time to time, but we also know that in the face of "cheers or damnation," he held his ground with steadfast equanimity, not allowing the cheers of praise to swell his ego with the poison of self-aggrandizement nor the howls of damnation to crush his spirit. He simply went ahead, and he continued going ahead with his eyes fixed on the road until death stopped him five years later.

22

As he reacclimated himself to New York City, Crane entered a fallow period in which his output dropped off for a while, at least in comparison to the frenetic pace he had kept up throughout 1894. No doubt he was exhausted, both mentally and physically, but in terms of his work, this period was less a slump or a falling off than a time for regrouping—the case of a young writer who has come to a crossroads and isn't quite sure which path to follow next. After his return, the articles he had written about Mexico began appearing in various newspapers around the country, but Crane took on no more journalistic assignments, which must have meant that his purse was momentarily less empty than usual. That spring was important, however, for even if he left little behind to show for it, those months mark the beginning of a gradual turn toward the short story as the medium best suited to his inclinations and disposition as a writer. Until then, he had merely dabbled in stories, but bit by bit they became a serious enterprise for him, and before long they were the heart and substance of his work.

Still living under the spell of *The Red Badge of Courage*, he wrote two stories that spring, both of them set in the Civil War, in much the same way that the spell of *Maggie* had induced him to write the Baby Stories in the afterglow of that book's publication. The first one, "A Grey Sleeve," is something of a botch. Well written, yes, but given what the story is about—a Northern soldier and a young woman from the South begin to fall for each other, hinting at further romantic developments after the war is over—it is probably the most sentimental and conventional piece of fiction Crane ever wrote, which could have meant, after all, that the contents of his purse were dwindling. We do know that Crane struggled mightily to finish it, perhaps from physical and mental exhaustion, perhaps because he had trouble believing in the story itself, perhaps both. After coming to the end of the first part, he said to his roommate Greene, "Ned, I'm all written out, my mind's a blank. I can't write anymore. I don't believe I'll ever write again. I'm through." Early the next year, after the story had been syndicated by Bacheller, Crane sent the printed newspaper version to Nellie Crouse but forewarned her: "It is not in any sense a good story." When she wrote back telling him that she had liked it, he answered, "It is good that you like 'A Grey Sleeve.' Of course, they are a pair of idiots. But yet there is something charming in their childish faith in each other. That is all I intended to say."

The second story, on the other hand, "A Mystery of Heroism," represents a startling breakthrough. It was as if Crane had chanced upon a key, and when he discovered that the key slipped into the lock he had unconsciously designed for it, a door sprang open, and once he stepped inside, he found a new way of thinking about narrative, which in effect was no different from finding a new way to breathe. His lungs were compromised, after all, and the rigors of long-distance running put an undue strain on his body. The short burst was more in step with his impulses as a writer (lapidary, episodic, swift), creating a breath-rhythm that allowed him to release the full force of his spiritual and somatic energies, and from then on all of his best work would be accomplished in one of several lengths of sprint: the sixty-yard dash (under ten pages), the hundred-yard dash (ten to twenty pages), the two-hundred-yard dash (twenty to forty pages), and the longer quarter-mile run (forty to sixty pages), which he managed to pull off just twice—with the forty-two-page "War Memories" and the fifty-seven pages of *The Monster.*

In some respects, "A Mystery of Heroism" can be looked upon as a nine-page version of *The Red Badge of Courage.* There is a subtitle similar to the one Crane used for the novel, *A Detail of an American Battle* (just a hairs-breadth off from *An Episode of the American Civil War*), and a number of the tropes he employed earlier are used again with equal effect, as when the company is described as a "long animal-like thing" that turns its "four hundred eyes" on the protagonist, Fred Collins, or when the "gentle little meadow" where the skirmish is being fought is transformed into "the object of the red hate of the shells." Most important—following the example of the novel—the action is set exclusively on the battlefield, in the midst of heavy combat.

Yet in many other ways, the story is markedly different from the novel. For one thing, the language is flatter and more concise, more propulsive and at the same time more restrained, and because the number of elements is even further reduced, each one stands out in sharp relief against the mayhem in the background, rotating from one to the other in the manner of a tautly composed fugue. What becomes abundantly clear in retrospect—but only in retrospect—is how slyly Crane introduces the main character of the story, who first appears in such a fleeting, offhanded manner that one assumes he is of little significance, but bit by bit, after being mentioned and then dropped a couple times as the battle rages on through the first three and a half pages, he begins to command center stage, and an actor with little more than a walk-on part emerges as the star of the show by the second act. In *Red Badge*, Henry Fleming makes his first appearance early in the first chapter and from then on dominates all the subsequent action, but in the shorter work Crane takes his time before letting us in on his secret, and by means of this unexpected delaying tactic he manages to convince us that his main character is a no one, the quint-essential anyone, which is the ultimate point of the story, never announced as such but there for all to see—in retrospect.

Fred Collins is thirsty. In the second paragraph, even as shells are exploding around him, we hear him say, "Thunder, I wisht I had a drink. Ain't there any water round here?" and then, after delivering those two sentences, Collins evaporates out of the scene as the noise and chaos roar on. A house in the meadow directly in front of A Company is "blown . . .

to fragments," there is loud scuffling in the woods with "the crashing of infantry volleys," soldiers are shot, wounded, laid flat, killed, and an injured lieutenant on horseback holds "his right arm carefully in his left hand . . . as if this arm were not at all a part of him, but belonged to another man." After two pages of hellish combat, Collins suddenly reappears: "Some comrades joked Collins about his thirst. 'Well, if yeh want a drink so bad, why don't yeh go get it?'" Collins replies, "Well, I will in a minnet if you don't shut up," and then he promptly vanishes from the text again. Another page goes by, during which the wounded lieutenant on horseback is hit again after riding into the meadow and can now be seen "lying face downward with a stirruped foot stretched across the body of his dead horse." At that point, the movement of the story finally shifts over to Collins—first, engaged in an argument with his fellow soldiers, who are continuing to taunt him for not having the guts to risk his life by going off to look for water; second, approaching his commanding officers (a captain and a colonel) and requesting permission "to go git some water from that there well over yonder." The officers try to discourage him, knowing how dangerous it would be to attempt such a thing, but Collins is adamant, and when they finally give in to his request, it still isn't clear to them if he wants to go or not, which is also true of Collins himself by now, who has come to understand that he has no idea why he has chosen to embark on this absurd mission. As he is about to leave, the colonel calls after him and says: "Take some of the other boys' canteens with you an' hurry back now."

So Collins begins his fraught and ridiculous journey toward the well that stands beside the destroyed house in the meadow, heading straight into the thick of ferocious artillery fire with half a dozen canteens dangling from his shoulders and clanking against his body. One of his comrades observes, "Well, sir, if that ain't th' dardnest thing. I never thought Fred Collins had the blood in him for that kind of business."

The focus of the narrative turns inward at that point, and as the befuddled Collins advances toward his goal, he begins thinking about the subject announced in the title of the story, the same subject that had bedeviled the youth in *The Red Badge of Courage*, but here it is treated from an entirely different emotional perspective, for other than the fact that they are both soldiers, Fred Collins and Henry Fleming have nothing in common.

> It seemed to him supernaturally strange that he had allowed his mind to maneuver his body into such a situation. He understood that it might be called dramatically great.
>
> However, he had no full appreciation of anything excepting that he

was actually conscious of being dazed. He could feel his dulled mind groping after the form and color of this incident.

Too, he wondered why he did not feel some keen agony of fear cutting his sense like a knife. He wondered at this because human expression had said loudly for centuries that men should feel afraid of certain things and that all men who did not feel this fear were phenomena, heroes.

He was then a hero. He suffered that disappointment which we would all have if we discovered that we were ourselves capable of those deeds which we most admire in history and legend. This, then, was a hero. After all, heroes were not much.

No, it could not be true. He was not a hero. Heroes had no shame in their lives and, as for him, he remembered borrowing fifteen dollars from a friend and promising to pay it back the next day, and then avoiding that friend for ten months. When at home his mother had aroused him for the early labor of his life on the farm, it had often been his fashion to be irritable, childish, diabolical, and his mother had died since he had come to war.

He saw that in this matter of the well, the canteens, the shells, he was an intruder in the land of fine deeds.

From then on, the story devolves into a grim comedy of mishaps, frustrations, and grotesque bungles, a tragic farce that strikes a new note in Crane's work and by the last sentence leaves the reader suspended between an urge to laugh and a state of horrified wonder at the inanities of war—or perhaps just the inanities of life, for in Crane war is always a continuation of life (not politics) by other means.

With the noise of combat resounding in his head—as if "two demon fingers were pressed into his ears"—and the ground shaking underfoot from the impact of falling shells, Collins eventually reaches the house. When he lowers one of the canteens into the well, however, the water comes in "slowly . . . with an indolent gurgle," and because that "maddening slowness" is putting him at ever greater risk, he abandons his efforts with the canteens and instead decides to fill up the bucket, which is attached to "a length of rusty chain," but even then there are difficulties, and with the bucket knocking against the inner walls of the well as he hoists it up, some of the water spills out. Deeply terrified by now, Collins begins to make his way back to the A Company line, "anticipating a blow that would whirl him around and down. He would fall as he had seen other men fall, the life knocked out of them so suddenly that their knees were no more quick to touch the ground than their heads." He runs for dear life, lugging the heavy bucket as he crosses the "terrible field . . . in the manner of a farmer chased out of a dairy by a bull," but before he can get to the "impossible star" of the A Company line looming before him, he comes upon the fallen artillery officer lying in the meadow, whose groans are drowned out in "the tempest of sound" created by the bullets and exploding shells. Summoning all his strength, the officer asks Collins for a drink of water, and from that moment until the end of the story, Crane packs an entire universe of misadventures into a single page:

> "I can't," he screamed, and in this reply was a full description of his quaking apprehension. His cap was gone and his hair was riotous. His clothes made it appear that he had been dragged over the ground by his heels. He ran on.
>
> The officer's head sank down and one elbow crooked. His foot in its brass-bound stirrup still stretched over the body of his horse and the other leg was under the steed.
>
> But Collins turned. He came dashing back. His face had now turned grey and in his eyes was all terror. "Here it is! Here it is!"
>
> The officer was as a man gone in drink. His arm bended like a twig. His head drooped as if his neck was of willow. He was sinking to the ground, to lie face downward.
>
> Collins grabbed him by the shoulder. "Here it is. Here's your drink. Turn over! Turn over, man, for God's sake!"
>
> With Collins hauling at his shoulder, the officer twisted his body and fell with his face turned toward that region where lived the unspeakable noises of the swirling missiles. There was the faintest shadow of a smile on his lips as he looked at Collins. He gave a sigh, a little primitive breath like that from a child.
>
> Collins tried to hold the bucket steadily, but his shaking hands caused the water to splash all over the face of the dying man. Then he jerked it away and ran on.
>
> The regiment gave him a welcoming roar. The grimed faces were wrinkled in laughter.
>
> His captain waved the bucket away. "Give it to the men!"
>
> The two genial, sky-larking young lieutenants were the first to gain possession of it. They played over it in their fashion.
>
> When one tried to drink the other teasingly knocked his elbow. "Don't, Billie! You'll make me spill it," said the one. The other laughed.
>
> Suddenly there was an oath, the thud of wood on the ground, and a swift murmur of astonishment from the ranks. The two lieutenants glared at each other. The bucket lay on the ground empty.

Crane says not a word about it, but the added irony that emerges with the final sentence harks back to the beginning of the story. Fred Collins is half mad with thirst. He risks life and limb to fetch some water to appease that thirst, but even after he has found the water, events conspire against him, and not once does he manage to take a drink himself.

In mid-June, not long after he resettled in New York, Crane was finally offered a contract for *The Red Badge of Courage* from Appleton. It was a notably unfair agreement, but he was still a newcomer to the world of commercial publishing and did not raise any objections. A ten percent royalty to be paid once a year—as opposed to the standard twice a year—but not one penny would be turned over to him until the full production costs of the book had been covered. Beyond that, there was nothing about foreign rights, which meant that Appleton could make an arrangement with a British publisher, for example, and not have to give Crane anything. It is likely that Crane didn't know enough to push any harder, but my guess would be that he had also lost interest in the book, which seems to have burned him out, and once he'd put the finishing touches on the manuscript in New Orleans, he was more than ready to leave it behind him. When Hitchcock wrote in August to announce that the proofs had arrived from the printer, Crane answered with a brief, two-sentence note, in the first one giving the address where they should be sent, and then, remarkably, in the second one reversing himself and telling Hitchcock, "As a matter of fact I don't care much to see the page proof." Chances are he did go over the proofs, but never before have I heard of a writer, whether young or old, so reluctant to read the galleys of his own book. Short as it was, the novel had been a long, painful slog for him, with multiple revisions, corrections, deletions, and changes of heart about the final version, and after the wrenching standoff with McClure and the further contortions that had gone into making the abridged, serialized version for Bacheller, he was probably sick and tired of the whole business and no longer wanted to think about it.

Also in June, tentative plans to bring out two more books with Copeland and Day rapidly fizzled into no books because Crane didn't know where to find them. His Boston publishers had offered to reprint *Maggie* in a proper edition, but with roughly a thousand copies floating around New York and various points to the north, west, and south, Crane couldn't track down a single one, a telling example of how indifferently he treated his own past work (no sooner written than forgotten), and then, when he proposed that they publish eight of the Sullivan County stories instead ("grotesque tales of the woods which I wrote when I was clever"), Lily, the one person he had ever given copies to, failed to send them, no doubt because they had been destroyed by her husband in one of his jealous rampages.

Not long after signing the *Red Badge* contract, Crane left New York again and went on another one of his summer camping trips in Pike County. On August ninth, he wrote to Hawkins:

> I am cruising around the woods in corduroys and feeling great. I have lots of fun getting healthy. Feel great . . .
>
> There are six girls in the camp and it is with the greatest difficulty that I think coherently about any other subject.

After his return from the woods, Crane was led to assume that he had been hired as a drama critic for the *Philadelphia Press*—full employment, with a regular salary for the first time in his life—and on September sixth he wrote again to Hawkins, this time from Philadelphia: "Dear Willis: It's dramatic criticism and nuttin else. I've taken it and am going to go to work at once." Four days later, he wrote back to give Hawkins the disappointing news that the job had not panned out.

> Dear old man: Things fell ker-plunk. Stranded here in Phila. . . . Nice town. Got lots of friends, though, and 23,842 invitations to dinner of which I have accepted 2.
>
> The Press wanted me bad enough but the business manager suddenly said "Nit."

He stayed in Philadelphia for another week or two (most likely with his friend Lawrence), where he turned his "personal troubles in Mexico" into the splendid "One Dash—Horses," the first of the stories inspired by his experiences on the road while working for Bacheller.

He returned to New York sometime after the twentieth. On September twenty-seventh, Appleton applied for American copyright of *The Red Badge of Courage*, meaning that the book had been printed and was ready to be released.

In early October, Crane abandoned his current living arrangements and moved into a loft apartment with Post Wheeler at 165 West Twenty-third Street. A number of all-night poker sessions took place in that apartment, along with an untold number of nighttime visits from girls who wound up sleeping in Crane's bed, even on the nights when he was busy playing poker in the other room.

By then, his book was beginning to circulate around the country, and before the month was out, the life he had been leading for the past four years came to an abrupt and permanent end. Without warning, and with scarcely a breath in between them, Crane's next life began.

23

THE PRAISE WAS FAR FROM UNANIMOUS, BUT IT WAS MORE THAN enough to drown out the book's detractors and turn *The Red Badge of Courage* into both a critical and a commercial success, with two more printings in 1895 and another fourteen the following year in the United States. In England, the response was just as strong, perhaps even stronger, and it was there that the most intelligent and thorough review published by anyone on either side of the Atlantic appeared (written by ex–career soldier and literary critic George Wyndham for the *New Review*), which argued that the novel surpassed both Tolstoy and Zola in the truth of its depiction of war and that "Mr. Stephen Crane, the author of *The Red Badge of Courage*, is a great artist, with something new to say, and consequently, with a new way of saying it. His theme, indeed, is an old one, but old themes re-handled in the light of novel experience, are the stuff out of which masterpieces are made, and in *The Red Badge of Courage*, Mr. Crane has surely contrived a masterpiece."

In what must have been a severe disappointment to Crane, however, his most ardent and influential American supporter weighed in with a mixed review for *Harper's Weekly* on October twenty-sixth: "[Stephen Crane] has now attempted to give a close-at-hand impression of battle as seen by a young volunteer in the civil war, and I cannot say that to my inexperience of battle he has given such a vivid sense of it as one gets from other authors." As with his response to Crane's poems, Howells simply couldn't grasp what the novel was about, and in his bafflement—or resistance—closed himself off to the spirit of the book, even as he continued to express confidence in Crane's future and "the greater things that we may hope from a new talent working upon a high level, not quite clearly as yet, but strenuously." In spite of the mixed review, Crane wrote an earnest, appreciative letter to Howells from Hartwood on January first to acknowledge the "interest which you have shown in my work" and to seize "the New Year's Day as an opportunity to thank you and tell you how often I think of your kind benevolent life." A display of undiminished gratitude from the young man, to which the older man replied toward the end of the month:

Your New Year's greeting was very pleasant to me, and I have been enjoying for your sake your English triumphs. I am glad you are getting your glory young. For once, the English who habitually know nothing of art, seem to know something. . . . For me, I remain true to my first love, "Maggie." That is better than all the Black Riders and Red Badges.

You have got a lot of work in you, and the whole of a long life to get it out.

I wish you could come sometime to see me.

Extremely gracious, but not without another dig at the poems and *Red Badge*, and while it is uncertain what Crane felt about Howells's generous but ultimately condescending words, we do know that after delaying for several months he sat down and inscribed a copy of *Red Badge* with an effusive dedication to the man he looked upon as his literary father—and then, afterward, could never summon the nerve to send it.

Other dissenting voices were heard from as well, with the most hostile one blasting from the pages of the eternally hostile *New York Tribune*, which followed its slam of *The Black Riders* with another kick to the groin, calling the novel "a chromatic nightmare . . . as tedious as a funeral march." And then, by the spring of 1896, after the success of the book had been assured, there was the inevitable backlash from an older generation of disgruntled American readers. One of them, General Alexander C. McClurg (1832–1901), who happened to own the company that published the *Dial*, expressed his outrage in his own magazine by calling the novel "a vicious satire upon American soldiers and armies. The hero of the book . . . without a spark of patriotic feeling, or even of soldierly ambition, has enlisted in the army from no definite reason that the reader can discover." Not content to leave it there, the general further complains that there is "an entire lack of any literary quality" in the book and concludes that "respect for our own people should have prevented its issue in this country."

Attacks of this kind were rare, however, and most of the reviews were either good or very good, with many of them exceedingly warm in their enthusiasm for the book and others written in what appears to have been a state of unbridled exaltation. Edward Marshall, in an unsigned piece for the *New York Press* (October 13): "One should be forever slow in charging an author with genius, but . . . *The Red Badge of Courage* is open to the suspicion of having greater power and originality than can be girdled by the name of talent." The *New York Times* (October 19): "[Private Henry Fleming's] emotions, his mental vagaries, his experience with the dead and dying, and the terrible nervous ordeal he undergoes are depicted by

Mr. Crane with a degree of vividness and original power almost unique in our fiction." Sydney Brooks, in an unsigned piece for the British *Saturday Review* (January 11, 1896): "Mr. Crane, in the supreme moments of the fight, is possessed by the fiery breath of battle, as a Pythian priestess by the breath of God, and finds an inspired utterance that will reach the universal heart of man."

As with *The Black Riders*, however, the reviews alone did not tell the full story. There was also the public agitation that followed the release of the book, pushing it beyond the confines of the literary world until large numbers of people had an opinion about it, whether they had read the book or not. With Crane's poems, the agitation had expressed itself through a barrage of insults and feeble-witted spoofs. With the novel, there was an outbreak of stunned adulation, a gasp of awe that spread through American and British society as more and more people came to understand that an author so young and so unknown had produced a book of such radical innovation and brilliance. *The Red Badge of Courage* was more than just a novel, it was a sensation, one of those rare works of art that transcend art to become a cultural marker, a thing that divides time in half and puts everything else either before it or after it. In the history of American literature, I can think of only one other case of a young novelist taking the country by storm as Crane did in 1895–96: F. Scott Fitzgerald in 1920, with the publication of *This Side of Paradise*. Like Crane, Fitzgerald was a notoriously bad speller, and, like Crane, he achieved the uncommon distinction of becoming *a household name* for the rest of his life.

The American writer Harold Frederic, who lived in England and reported on British cultural events for the *New York Times*, published a long article on January 26, 1896, that tracked the growing acclaim for *Red Badge* in London, beginning with the assertion that "this mysteriously unknown youth has really written an extraordinary book" and then describing how people began to talk about it, first one person and then another person until it became "more talked about than anything else in current literature." After calling it "one of the deathless books" that everyone who cared about literature would eventually read, Frederic attempted to explain why:

> If there were in existence any books of a similar character, one could start confidently by saying that it was the best of its kind. But it has no fellows. It is a book outside of all classification. So unlike anything else is it that the temptation rises to deny that it is a book at all. When one searches for comparisons, they can only be found by culling out

selected portions from the trunks of masterpieces, and considering these detached fragments, one by one, with reference to the *Red Badge*, which is itself a fragment, and yet it is complete. Thus one lifts the best battle pictures from Tolstoi's great *War and Peace*, from Balzac's *Chouans*, from Hugo's *Les Miserables* . . . and studies them side by side with this tremendously effective battle painting by the unknown youngster. Positively they are cold and ineffectual beside it. The praise may sound exaggerated, but really it is inadequate. These renowned battle descriptions of the big men are made to seem all wrong. The *Red Badge* impels the feeling that the actual truth about a battle has never been guessed before.

This comes close to sanctification, perhaps even deification, and while a part of Crane must have been glad to discover that he now ranked above Tolstoy, Balzac, and Hugo, another part of him must have been frightened to death, for no sooner had he been placed on his throne of glory than he took off the crown, bolted from his seat, and ran for the hills.

In mid-October, just as the clamor was beginning, he left New York for Hartwood, where he hid out at his brother Edmund's place for several months, working on his next novel, riding his horse through the woods, and staying in touch with his friends by letter. He had attained a new and exalted status in the eyes of the world, but the fact was that he was still broke, and because of the bad contract he had signed with Appleton, it would be a long time before his success earned him any money. Everything was different now except for one thing, and that thing was still remarkably the same.

It wasn't that he didn't read the reviews of *Red Badge* or was uninterested in what people were saying about him, but he preferred to do it from a distance, keeping up on the news about himself by subscribing to a clipping service, which sent him fresh reviews and articles as they came in. There was no question that he was pleased, but this sudden rise to prominence also had unexpected consequences, and throughout his months at Hartwood he lived in a scramble of ups and downs and morbid rumination. To Howells on January twenty-seventh:

I had just become well habituated to abuse when this bit of a flurry about the red badge came upon me. I am slightly rattled and think it best to cling to Hartwood where if I choose to shout triumphant sounds none can hear me. However I have not yet elected to shout any shouts. I am, mostly, afraid. Afraid that some small degree of talk will turn me ever so slightly from what I believe to be the pursuit of truth, and that my block-head will lose something of the resolution which carried me very comfortably through the ridicule. If they would only continue the abuse. I feel ably to cope with that, but beyond I am in great doubt.

That same day, he also wrote separately to Hawkins and Hitchcock about a recent excursion down to the city and how badly it had unnerved him.

My dear Willis: There are none of my friends whom I could treat so shamefully and none who can make me feel so utterly dejected over it afterward. But oh you don't know how that damned city tore my heart out by the roots and flung it under the heels of it's noise. Indeed it did. I couldn't breathe in that accursed tumult. On Friday it had me keyed to a point where I was no more than a wild beast and I had to make a dash willy-nilly . . .

Dear Mr. Hitchcock: I fear that when I meet you again I shall feel abashed. As a matter of truth, New York has so completely muddled me on this last visit that I shant venture again very soon. I had grown used to be called a damned ass but this sudden new admiration of my friends has made a gibbering idiot of me. I shall stick to my hills.

One set of facts had replaced another set of facts. The reality of a life had been turned into the reality of a different life, and as Crane struggled to regain his footing and adjust to his new circumstances, Hartwood served as a refuge from the tumult churning around him. What he failed to understand, however, was that the tumult was as much inside him as it was in the streets of cities and the book-review pages of magazines, and during this period of self-imposed rustication, which lasted well into February, his mind swung back and forth through a myriad of inner conflicts and unanswered questions about himself. Isolated from everyone but his family, he wrote more letters than was usual for him, reaching out to his friends and associates (mostly Hawkins) to maintain contact with the world, and in those letters we can see him bouncing from one contradictory mood to the next, at times charming and self-confident, at times downright chatty by his standards, and at other times wallowing in doubt, self-reproach, and, just once (but how unusual it was for him), erupting in a burst of irrational anger against . . . nothing at all. To Hawkins, dated November nineteenth:

Edmund Crane's house on the Mill Pond in Hartwood, New York.
(COURTESY OF THE MINISINK VALLEY HISTORICAL SOCIETY)

I lost my temper to-day—fully—absolutely—for the first time in a good many years. I sailed the cat-boat up the lake today in the stiffest breeze we've had in moons. When I got near the head of the lake, the boat was scudding before the wind in a manner to make your heart leap. Then we got striking snags—hidden stumps, floating logs, sunken brush, more stumps,—you might have thought ex-Senator Hollman of Indiana was there.* Anything that could obstruct promptly and gracefully obstructed. Up to the 5th stump I had not lost my philosophy but at the 22nd I was swearing like cracked ice. And at the appearance of the 164th, I perched on the rail, a wild and gibbering maniac. It is all true. I cant remember when I was so furiously and ferociously angry. Never before, I think.

A rage had been building up in him, a storm of inchoate feelings that eluded comprehension but had everything to do with the conflicts that were roiling inside him, and as in a bad dream, the stumps and logs and various other impediments thwarting the progress of his boat were reflected embodiments of his own inner frustrations, which prompted the habitually even-tempered Crane to lose his composure and snap. He recounts the episode to Hawkins with humorous astonishment (his anger had passed by then), but he must have been disturbed by the intensity of this rare tantrum, which would explain why he bothered to mention it in the first place. Otherwise, why talk about it? Without

---

* William Steele Holman (1822–1897). Not a senator but a longtime congressman, famous for his stubborn opposition to government spending.

understanding what had happened to him, Crane had lived through a parable of his current situation.

But that situation had its emboldening effects as well, and for every doubt and confused thought that assailed him during those months, there was an equal and opposite surge of pride in his success, as captured by the ebullient tone of his letter to Hawkins on October twenty-fourth, not long after he arrived at Hartwood:

> My dear Willis: The brown October woods are simply great. There is a kitten in the stables who walks like Ada Rehan* and there is a dog who trims his whiskers like the late President Carnot's whiskers.† Gypsey, cousin to Greylight and blood relative of the noble Lynne bel, who lost the Transylvania so capably at Lexington this season—well, Gypsey ran away with me. What can be finer than a fine frosty morning, a runaway horse, and only the still hills to watch. Lord I do love a crazy horse with just a little pig-skin between him and me. You can push your lifeless old bicycles around the country but a slim-limbed thoroughbred's dauntless spirit is better. Some people take much trouble to break a horse of this or that. I dont. Let him fling himself to the other side of the road because a sumac tassle waves. If your knees are not self-acting enough for that sort of thing, get off and walk. Hartwood scenery is good when viewed swiftly.
>
> I missed my first partridge yesterday. Keh-plunk. Bad ground,'though. Too many white birches. I haven't written a line yet. Dont intend to for some time. Clip anything you see in the paper and send it. Remember me to everybody at Greene Ave. I have heard indirectly from Brentano's that the damned "Red Badge" is having a very nice sale.

There it is: the first reference to *Red Badge*—with the adjective "damned" before it, which can be read as a curse if one takes the dark view or as a backslapping term of endearment if one doesn't. Hard to tell at this point, but as time went on Crane's ambivalent feelings about his own book become more and more pronounced. Not because he didn't stand behind what he had written but, more subtly, more insidiously, because he had come to fear that the success of the book might become a burden to him, an object as heavy as a piano that he would be forced to carry around on his back as he made his way into the future.

The ambivalence began once he started writing his new novel in late

---

* American actress and comedian (1857–1916) known for her "personality style" of acting.
† President of France from 1887 until his assassination in 1894.

October. At first, the book seemed to be advancing smoothly, and on the twenty-ninth he reported to Hitchcock that "the story is working out fine. I have made seven chapters in the rough, and they have given me the proper enormous interest in the theme. I have adopted such a 'quick' style for the story that I don't believe it can work out much beyond twenty-five thousand words—perhaps thirty—possibly thirty-five." Just one week later (November fifth), he wrote to his friend Wheeler: "I am working out-of-sight. Novel third done." Three days later, however, he suddenly voiced some misgivings to Hawkins: "The novel is one-third completed. I am not sure that it is any good. It is easy work. I can finish a chapter each day. I want you to see it before it goes to Appleton's." Again to Hawkins on the eleventh or twelfth: "The novel is exactly half finished. It seems clever sometimes and sometimes it seems nonsensical. I hope to show it to you in less than two months." And again on the nineteenth (from the same letter in which he talks about losing his temper at the lake): "The new novel is two-thirds done. I gave the first eighteen chapters to my brother Teddie [Edmund] to read. He finished them without a halt. He is an awful stuff in literature. I am a little dubious about his performance. Seems to me it throws rather a grimly humorous light on the situation. Understand, he thinks my style wouldn't be used by the devil to patch his trousers." Then, briefly changing the subject in his next letter to Hawkins, on the twenty-fifth, he addresses the matter of his now-empty purse: "I have been frantically hustling of late to make some money but I haven't achieved a cent, mainly because I want it so badly." On December twenty-seventh, he mailed the completed manuscript to Hitchcock in New York. As Crane had predicted, it turned out to be a short book: just 107 pages in the Library of America edition, roughly halfway between the length of *Maggie* and the length of *Red Badge*. Four days after that, in the last hours of 1895, he wrote to Curtis Brown and finally made the connection between the new novel and the one that had driven him into hiding: "Thank you for your kind words and for your *Sketch* clipping. I hear the damned book 'The Red Badge of Courage' is doing very well in England. In the meantime I am plodding away. I have finished my new novel—'The Third Violet'—and sent it to Appleton and Co., as per request, but I've an idea it won't be accepted. It's pretty rotten work. I used myself up in the accursed 'Red Badge.'" Modulating his tone somewhat after Hitchcock accepted the manuscript after all, Crane dropped the epithet *rotten work* to describe what he had done but nevertheless continued to measure the two books against each other and to denigrate what he had accomplished in his war novel.

I think it is well to go ahead with The Third Violet. People may just as well discover now that the high dramatic key of The Red Badge cannot be sustained. You know what I mean. I dont think The Red Badge to be any great shakes but then the very theme of it gives it an intensity that the writer cant reach every day. The Third Violet is a quiet little story but then it is serious work and I should say let it go. If my health and my balance remains to me, I think I will be capable of doing work that will dwarf both books.

Crane was right on both counts. He did manage to produce stronger work in the years ahead, but he was also correct to assume that any book he published from then on would inevitably be judged by the standard he had set for himself when he was just twenty-three years old. Now he was twenty-four, and as he plunged on with new stories and sketches and various other projects, he understood that the sensation he had caused with his first full-length novel was both a blessing and a curse. A blessing because it had thrust him into public view and turned him into a writer whose work would continue to attract a substantial audience—and a curse because no matter how much he accomplished in the future, he would never match the success he had already achieved. As the months passed, his position eventually hardened into a tough-minded wariness against the perils of fame—as shown by these anguished reflections, which were printed in a popular magazine in May 1896:

Before "The Red Badge of Courage" was published I often found it difficult to make both ends meet. The book was written during this period. It was an effort born of pain, and I believe that this was beneficial to it as a piece of literature. It seems a pity that this should be so,—that art should be a child of suffering; and yet such seems to be the case. . . .

Personally, I like my little book of poems, "The Black Riders," better than I do "The Red Badge of Courage." The reason is, I suppose, that the former is the more ambitious effort. In it I aim to give my ideas of life as a whole, so far as I know it, and the latter is a mere episode,—an amplification. Now that I have reached the goal for which I have been working ever since I began to write, I suppose that I ought to be contented; but I am not. I was happier in the old days when I was always dreaming of the thing I have now attained. I am disappointed with success. Like many things we strive for, it proves when obtained to be an empty and fleeting joy.

24

> Finally Hawker said that he thought "Hearts at War" was a very good play.
>
> "Did you?" she said in surprise. "I thought it was very much like the others."
>
> "Well, so did I," he cried hastily. "The same figures moving around in the mud of modern confusion."
>
> *The Third Violet* (Chapter XXVI)

THE THIRD VIOLET IS SUCH A RADICAL DEPARTURE FROM CRANE'S previous work that it could easily be mistaken for the work of another writer. Not just because it abandons the life-and-death issues of his first three books (urban poverty and war) to take on the thoroughly conventional subjects of courtship and marriage, but also because Crane adopts an altogether different narrative method from the one he had been developing and refining over the past four years—the "'quick' style" that he referred to in his letter to Hitchcock, as opposed to the "thick style" of his other novels. In the case of *The Third Violet*, "quick" turned out to mean a story written almost exclusively in dialogue, making the book read less like the novel of manners it purports to be than a screenplay for a film of manners—another one of Crane's bewildering anticipations of cinematic language—and how curious it is to learn that just as he was finishing his book at the end of 1895, the Lumière brothers were projecting the first moving pictures on a large screen before a paying audience of seven hundred people in Paris (December 28) by means of their newly invented device, the cinematograph. A quirk of historical timing, yes, but something was definitely in the air, and it seems both fitting and uncanny that movies as we know them today were born at the very moment Crane was delivering his most movie-like novel to his publisher. Even if he knew nothing about the Lumière brothers, and even if he could have known nothing about the still-to-be-invented form of writing we now call the screenplay, Crane's book-in-dialogue draws heavily on his love and knowledge of the theater, and because much of that book is set outdoors in a natural world far too large to be encompassed by a standard proscenium stage, the effect it has on us is now cinematic—necessarily cinematic—and no matter how bizarre it might sound, there is some justification in calling *The Third Violet* the world's first screenplay.

The origins of the novel can probably be traced back to the Sunday editions of the *New York Press* and the *New York Times* on October 28,

1894, both of which carried pieces written by Crane. Some of the material from the first one, "Stories Told by an Artist," would be lifted out and used again in the novel, not just the characters based on the "husky lot" of young artists Crane had lived with at the old Art Students League building (Wrinkles, Great Grief, Pennoyer, and Purple Sanderson), but whole sentences and passages as well. In this one, describing the room they all share, only a couple of words have been changed on the journey from newsprint to book:

> The flood of orange light showed clearly the dull walls lined with sketches, the tousled bed in one corner, the masses of boxes and trunks in another, a little dead stove and a wonderful table. Moreover, there were wine-colored draperies flung in some places and on a shelf high up, there were plaster casts with dust in the creases. A long stove-pipe wandered off in the wrong direction and then turned impulsively toward a hole in the wall. There were some elaborate cobwebs in the ceiling.

The artists are in the book because the principal male character—the suitor in the love drama that occupies much of the story—is a painter named Hawker (William to his family, Billie to everyone else), and Wrinkles and Company live across the hall from his studio and are among his closest friends. Hawker seems to have been modeled partly on Linson (a country boy from Sullivan County who has studied art in Paris), but the name itself is undoubtedly a nod to another friend of Crane's, Hawkins, with the added twist of transforming it into the verb *to hawk* (peddling goods by calling out in the street to promote your wares), which neatly sums up the pressure on artists to earn enough money to survive. In Billie Hawker's case, that meant returning to New York from his studies in Paris and being obliged to crank out "the beautiful red and green designs that surround the common tomato can" until his own paintings began to be noticed.

The article that appeared in the *Times* that day was Crane's interview with Howells ("Howells Fears the Realists Must Wait"), which was conducted about eighteen months after their first meeting and serves up Howells's views on the state of contemporary American fiction as Crane (who identifies himself simply as "the other man") sits there listening to the Great One talk and chimes in with an occasional comment of his own. "Ah," says Howells, "this writing merely to amuse other people—why, it seems to me altogether vulgar. A man may as well blacken his face and go out and dance on the street for pennies. The author is a sort of trained bear, if you accept certain standards. If literary men are to be the public fools, let us at any rate have it clearly understood, so that those of us who feel differently can take measures. But on the other hand a novel should never preach and berate and storm. It does no good. As a matter of fact a book of that kind is ineffably tiresome."

By contrast, Howells believes "it is the business of the novel to picture the daily life in the most exact terms possible with an absolute and clear sense of proportion. That is the important matter—the proportion." It sounds good, but because he has yet to define what he means by proportion, it is still rather vague at this point, and after he has rambled on for a little while, the other man interjects: "I suppose that when a man tries to write 'what the people want'—when he tries to reflect the popular desire, it is a bad quarter of an hour for the laws of proportion." Rather than give his young friend a straight answer, Howells launches into a gentle harangue on one of his pet peeves—the love story, or, as he puts it, "the hosts of stories" that begin when the hero sees "a certain girl" and end abruptly when he marries her. "Love and courtship was not an incident, a part of life—it was the whole of it. All else was of no value. Men of that religion must have felt very stupid when they were engaged in anything but courtship. Do you see the false proportion?"

At last, Howells is beginning to make sense. To talk about one thing to the exclusion of all others is to lose a sense of proportion—which leads to the writing of bad books that do not reflect the reality of lived experience. He goes on: "Here and there an author raised his voice, but not loudly. I like to see novelists treating some of the other important things in life— the relation of mother and son, of husband and wife, in fact all these things that we live in continually."

The other man then remarks that there must be "two or three new literary people" who have taken that approach, but then he adds: "Books along these lines that you speak of are what might be called unpopular. Do you think them to be a profitable investment?"

Howells insists that they are and that it is all "a question of perseverance—courage. A writer of skill cannot be defeated because he remains true to his conscience. It is a long serious conflict sometimes, but he must win, if he does not falter."

It sounds as if Howells is talking directly to Crane here, encouraging him to take heart in his own future, but Crane refuses to share the master's optimism.

"Mr. Howells," said the other man suddenly, "have you observed a change in the literary pulse of the country within the last four months. Last winter, for instance, it seems that realism was almost about to capture things, but recently I have thought that I saw coming a sort of counter-wave, a flood of the other—a reaction, in fact. Trivial, temporary, perhaps, but a reaction, certainly."

Surprisingly, Howells does not disagree with him, and as the interview comes to a close, he says, dropping "his hand in a gesture of emphatic assent, 'What you say is true. I have seen it coming. . . . I suppose we shall have to wait.'"

One year after the article was published, Crane began working on a novel that sought to reexamine the issues he and Howells had touched on in their conversation: the dilemma of pursuing art in a culture dominated by the pursuit of money (the conundrum of art versus commerce or art *as* commerce) and the conflict between artistic integrity and popular taste (the perils of becoming a trained bear). These were deeply personal issues to Crane—the beautiful war he had been engaged in ever since his move to New York—but, then, as if in defiance of Howells, or at least disregarding Howells's open contempt for the courtship novel, Crane chose to wrap those issues inside a story about a young artist's quest for love, as if to prove that he could pull off such a book without turning into a trained bear. A difficult challenge, but Crane was still just twenty-three when he started writing his little romance, and after toiling on a book drenched in the violence of war, followed by another book set in the New York slums, he must have been hungry to try something new, *to write against himself* and see where the experiment took him. Banal as the subject might have been, it too was a deeply personal one for Crane, and now that his courtship of Lily Brandon Munroe had ended in failure, he took it upon himself to fictionalize his own experience and tell the story of a struggling painter from a family of no wealth who falls for a beautiful and spirited young woman born into great wealth, a boy raised on a farm in love with a New York heiress. Lily was the primary source (their initial meeting at a resort hotel, Crane's visits to her father's house in the city, both of which are echoed in the novel), but Ernest Hemingway's future mother, Grace Hall, also must have played a part in the creation of Grace Fanhall, and then there was Nellie Crouse, the rich, attractive girl from Akron, Ohio, whom Crane had met just once at a New York tea party but who was surely in his thoughts as well, since he began courting her by letter immediately after the book was finished.

As for the bare-bones plot, it seems to owe something to Verdi's *La Travi-ata*. The heroine, whose name is Violetta, gives Alfredo a camellia in the first act as a sign of her growing affection and asks him to come back as soon as the flower has begun to wilt, that is, to come back the next day, and Crane's manipulations of the three violets in his story serve a similar erotic purpose.

The book is divided into two distinct halves, the first one set in the countryside of Sullivan County and the second one in New York City, the two places in the world Crane was most familiar with, his two homes. The Hawker farm is modeled on Edmund's house at Hartwood (where Crane wrote most of the novel), and Hawker's New York studio is located in what seems to be an exact duplicate of the old Art Students League building, where Crane had lived and starved and written several of his early books.

What was not familiar to him, however, was the narrative territory he had chosen to enter with his new project, but just as he had turned the conventions of the war novel inside out with *The Red Badge of Courage*, he was now proposing to do the same with the novel of manners—by dramatically different means. In the earlier instance, he had taken a subject that normally lends itself to objective accounts of physical action and transformed it into a story about consciousness and the inner life, and now, almost perversely, but with a similar kind of daring, he set out to dismantle the love story, which is normally about feelings, perhaps only about feelings, and transform it into a novel of pure action. As he had done in his previous books, Crane began by stripping out everything that was not relevant to his purpose. We know that every character in the book thinks Grace is beautiful, for example, but we have no idea what she looks like, whether tall or short, blond or brunette, with straight teeth or crooked teeth, nor are we ever told what any of the other characters look like, nor what clothes they wear from scene to scene, nor what happens to their faces when they smile, nor much of anything about the houses and rooms they live in—the plentitude of details that provide the meat and bone of the classic novel of manners. Here, in an abrupt reversal of norms, the most vivid physical presence in the book belongs to the one character who cannot speak: Hawker's dog, Stanley, described as "a large orange and white setter" who expresses emotion "by twisting his body into a fantastic curve and then dancing over the ground with his head and his tail very near to each other." More than that, Stanley can think, and from time to time Crane even lets us in on his thoughts, as when the dog is "wagging his tail in placid contentment and ruminating upon his experiences." By contrast, the two-legged characters are opaque, and Crane never ventures inside them as he did with Henry Fleming, George Kelcey, and Maggie Johnson in his other novels. They think, of course, but their thoughts are revealed to us only through what they say to one another in the conversations that inform the action of the book, that *form* the action of the book, and the one time Crane is about to go inside's someone head and tell us what the expression on his face could mean, he pulls back at the last second—"in his eyes was a singular expression which perhaps denoted the woe of the optimist pushed suddenly from his height." The *perhaps* undercuts any certainty about what the man is actually thinking. As with the characters in a screenplay, the men and women in *The Third Violet* are all surface, and because Crane gives us almost nothing to see of that surface, we must imagine them for ourselves. The curious power of this bare, enigmatic book is that the reader, in the act of reading it, is also writing it along with Crane, and one by one all the blanks get filled in.

Few descriptions, then, scarcely a look at the physical world, and not a single moment of introspection, which until now had been Crane's two most formidable strengths as a writer. As if he had chosen to blindfold himself and then tie his right hand behind his back and compose with his left hand, he had reduced his storytelling options to one method and one method only: the utterances of the human voice. Seventy-five to ninety percent of the novel consists of talk (depending on the chapter), meaning that the book stands or falls on the quality of that talk, and against all odds, how the dialogue reads on the page turns out to be the most captivating element of Crane's experiment. Again and again, characters repeat themselves, again and again they say "What?" when someone says something to them, and again and again—especially at moments of emotional confusion or distress—they lapse into inarticulate stammering, breaking off their sentences before they can finish them, too flustered to translate their feelings into words. By and large, the dialogue in conventional nineteenth-century novels is coherent, but here as elsewhere Crane ignores convention and uses incoherence to convey uncertainty and psychological turmoil in his characters—to such an extent, at times, that the dialogue begins to resemble the speech patterns found in the plays of Harold Pinter, who didn't start writing until fifty years after Crane's death.

"Yes—no. I don't know."

"You would rather sit still and moon, wouldn't you?"
"Moon—blast you. I couldn't moon to save my life."
"Oh, well. I didn't mean moon exactly."

"Yes, but not—"

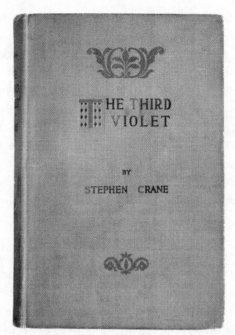

Front cover of The Third Violet, *published in 1897.*
(PHOTOGRAPH BY SPENCER OSTRANDER)

"Hold on. You were going to say that she was not like any other woman, weren't you?"

"Not exactly that, but—"

"What did she say?" whispered the younger Worcester girl.

"Why, she said—oh nothing."

"Look! Honest now, there's the stage. See it! See it!"

"It isn't there at all," she said.

Gradually, he seemed to recover his courage. "What made you so tremendously angry? I don't see why."

After consideration, she said decisively. "Well, because."

"That's why I teased you," he rejoined.

"Well, because—because—"

"Go on," he told her finally. "You're doing well." He waited patiently.

"Well," she said, "it is dreadful to defend somebody so—so excitedly and then have it turn out just a tease. I don't know what he would think."

"Who would think?"

"Why—he."

"Well, of course I like him, but—but—"

"What?" said Pennoyer.

"I don't know," said Florinda.

"Well, I still care for you and so I can only go away somewhere—some place 'way off—where—where—See?"

There are thirty-three chapters in the novel, which averages out to roughly three pages per chapter, and each one is presented as a self-contained scene, a dramatic moment in which two or more characters are caught in the middle of a conversation that advances the story in one direction or another, and once the scene ends, the next chapter begins with a destabilizing jump to another place and another set of characters caught in the middle of another conversation that could be happening an hour later or a day later or the following week. As with a film, the story is told through an accumulation of small bits and pieces, and what the story boils down to is the manner in which it is told, that is, the telling of the story itself, for all the characters in it seem to be aware that they are characters in a story, which demolishes the illusion that the story is an imitation of life, and therefore Crane's love story is in fact a parody of a love story, a critique of the popular fiction of the day, a book so densely constructed in its word-by-word progress and yet ultimately so thin in substance that it resembles a spider's web: an intricate, many-faceted marvel that can be swept away with a single thrust of a broom.

Hawker, the bungling, tormented, ill-at-ease suitor, stops for a moment on a walk through the countryside with Grace, points to a waterfall, and then proceeds to tell her the legend of the rocks on the other side of the river—a story within a story, their story at one remove, of course (the *of course* is essential), which is none other than the same old love story everyone has heard a thousand times before.

"Once upon a time there was a beautiful Indian maiden, of course. And she was, of course, beloved by a youth from another tribe who was very handsome and stalwart and a mighty hunter, of course. But the maiden's father was, of course, a stern old chief, and when the question of his daughter's marriage came up, he, of course, declared that the maiden should be wedded only to a warrior of her tribe. And, of course, when the young man heard this he said that in such case he would, of course, fling himself headlong from the crag. The old chief was, of course, obdurate, and, of course, the youth did, of course, as he had said. And, of course, the maiden wept." After Hawker had waited for some time, he said with severity: "You seem to have no great appreciation of folklore."

The principal storytelling character in the novel, however, is the man who serves as the link between Hawker and Grace, a foppish, cynical writer named Hollanden, who has left New York to spend the summer at the Hemlock Inn in Sullivan County, as has Grace, along with her sister-in-law and her sister-in-law's two young children, and with Hawker back on his family's farm for an extended break from city life, during which he plans to do as much painting as possible, there they all are, in close proximity to one another as the story begins, with Hollanden serving as go-between, prompter, and mischievous creator of the courtship drama that unfolds in the bucolic, Arcadian setting of Crane's rural nowhere—the classic spot for love stories over the centuries, from Shakespeare's *A Midsummer Night's Dream* to Ingmar Bergman's *Smiles of a Summer Night*.

Hawker has already seen Miss Fanhall in the opening pages of the book, but he has no idea who she is. By the time he runs into Hollanden on the morning of his first full day in the country, all he knows is that he crossed paths with a young woman and felt an immense and immediate attraction to her. It happened at sundown the day before, just after he arrived in Nowheresville. As he was disembarking from the train, he accidentally clunked a little boy on the head with his easel (foreshadowing the emotional clumsiness he will display throughout the book—while also telling us what kind of work he does), and then, as Hawker stood on the platform looking for a driver to take him to his parents' farm, Miss Fanhall (the boy's aunt) approached him from behind, asking if he knew which stage was the one for the Hemlock Inn.

> Hawker turned and found a young woman regarding him. A wave of astonishment whirled into his hair and he turned his eyes quickly for fear that she would think that he had looked at her. He said: "Yes—certainly—I think that I can find it." At the same time he was crying to himself: "Wouldn't I like to paint her, though. What a glance—oh, murder. The—the—the distance in her eyes."

To be attracted to that distance suggests a long struggle ahead, as if Hawker is one of those men doomed to want what they can't have, manically twisting himself into knots in his quest for the unattainable, but such is the way the artist's mind works, and how can such a man resist a woman who causes a wave of astonishment to whirl into his hair the instant he sees her for the first time?

Because the farm was in the same direction as the inn, Hawker wound up sharing the stage with Miss Fanhall and the others in her party, but chance saw to it that he was seated across from the two children rather than the astonishing woman. Reminiscent of the obstacles and contortions imposed on the lovers in "The Pace of Youth," Hawker's frustration vented itself with an absurd exercise in the art of twist and turn, for even though he wanted to go on looking at Miss Fanhall, he didn't want to offend her by appearing to be too forward.

Fate had arranged it so that Hawker could not observe the girl with the—the—the distance in her eyes without leaning forward and discovering to her his interest. Secretly and impiously he wriggled in his seat and as the bumping stage swung its passengers this way and that, he obtained fleeting glances of a cheek, an arm or a shoulder.

That was all he managed to see—a few fragments of her—and then he had to get off at the crossroads and finish his journey on foot as the stage rumbled off toward the inn. For all his interest in her, Hawker had not even learned her name—and that, apparently, was the end of that.

After uniting with Stanley the dog and spending the night with his parents and two sisters at the farmhouse, Hawker goes out early the next morning to paint. He knows that his "writing friend" is staying at the inn, but "he could not hope to see Hollanden before eleven, as it was only through rumor that Hollanden was aware that there was a sunrise and an early morning." So Hawker settles down to business, choosing to plant himself "in front of some fields of vivid yellow stubble on which trees made olive shadows," for he is a landscape painter, no doubt working in the mode of the French Impressionists, and while he is still struggling to sell his canvases, his reputation has been growing, raising his status to that of a promising new figure who seems poised to take the next step into broader recognition—much as Crane was in the months before the release of his war novel. Unexpectedly however, "a white-flannel young man walked into the landscape." This is one of the few times anyone's clothing is mentioned, but how evocative that white flannel is to us today, stirring up a host of images from that turn-of-the-century world when the young men and women who were to become our grandparents and great-grandparents and great-great-grandparents walked around in their summer whites—a symbol of leisure, indolence, and prosperity, even if one was only a middle-class office clerk or a manual laborer. The young man in white is of course Hollanden, and as Hawker waves "Hi, Hollie" at him with his brush and tells him to "get out of the color scheme," Hollanden grins and saunters over to his friend, saying how glad he is to see him. After taking a quick look at the canvas portraying "the vivid yellow stubble with the olive shadows" (Crane repeats the words), he suddenly turns his eyes on the painter and asks, "Say, Hawker, why don't you marry Miss Fanhall?" And with those words the novel bolts out of the starting gate and begins its hectic run around the track.

> Hawker had a brush in his mouth, but he took it quickly out and said: "Marry Miss Fanhall? Who the devil is Miss Fanhall?"
>
> Hollanden clasped both hands about his knees and looked thoughtfully away. "Oh, she's a girl."
>
> "She is?" said Hawker.
>
> "Yes. She came to the inn last night with her sister-in-law and a small tribe of young Fanhalls. There's six of them, I think."
>
> "Two," said Hawker. "A boy and a girl."
>
> "How do you—oh, you must have come up with them. Of course. Why, then you saw her."
>
> "Was that her?" asked Hawker, listlessly.
>
> "Was that her?" cried Hollanden, with indignation. "Was that her?"
>
> "Oh," said Hawker.
>
> Hollanden mused again. "She's got lots of money, he said. "Loads of it. And I think she would be fool enough to have sympathy for you in your work. They are a tremendously wealthy crowd, although they treat it simply. It would be a good thing for you. I believe—yes, I'm sure she could be fool enough to have sympathy for you in your work. And now if you weren't such a hopeless chump—"
>
> "Oh, shut up, Hollie," said the painter.

Hollanden should not be confused with a matchmaker. He is an inventor, an instigator, a plot builder improvising his story as he goes along, and rather than urge his two characters to fall in love quickly, dash to the altar, and live happily ever after, he wants to make the story as interesting and dramatic as possible, so impediments are just as valuable to him as encouragements, and whenever the story seems in danger of becoming too dull, he throws in another element to spice up the action—by overstating the qualities of a potential rival suitor (Oglethorpe) to discourage Hawker, for example, or by dragging Grace into teasing, circular, nonsensical conversations during which he pretends to bad-mouth Hawker in order to confuse her about the artist's intentions. Hollanden is the most entertaining figure in the book, a court jester–Cupid armed with a quiver full of pungent, self-deprecating wit-darts, and he is amusing himself on his summer holiday by cooking up a diversion that will distract him from the boredom of tennis, picnics, and more tennis with the tale of a man who woos without knowing how to woo and the woe that follows from his ineptitude, even if his case is far from hopeless, since the object of his desire seems more than willing to be conquered. Hollanden is creating a spectacle, and because every spectacle needs an audience, Crane provides him with one by putting fifteen older women at the Hemlock Inn (fifteen out of a total of forty-two guests), a band of curious onlookers whom Hollanden describes to Hawker as "middle-aged ladies of the most aggressive respectability. They have come here for no discernible purpose save to get where they can see people and be displeased at them. They sit in a large group on that porch and take measurements of character as importantly as if they constituted the jury of heaven." The women serve as a kind of modern-day Greek chorus, shadowy presences without faces who have been positioned in a back corner of the stage to offer their comments as the story of the protagonists unfolds, involving themselves in the Hawker-Fanhall romance in the same way readers become involved in courtship novels or viewers get hooked on the roller coaster plots, subplots, and sub-subplots of five-day-a-week soap operas. In the second half of the book, when the action shifts to the city, the women on the porch disappear, but their part in the story is handed over to Hawker's artist friends, who follow the romance with the same avidity as the original onlookers and can scarcely talk about anything else. Aside from the leading man and woman, every other character's role in the story is to follow the story and speculate on where it is going and how it will come out in the end. Trapped in a self-enclosed mirror-world, the book is ultimately about the expectations one brings to the reading of stories, and—to say it again—what it tells is the story of the story itself.

The novel advances by misdirection, foiled anticipations, and unexpected lurches to one side or the other of the main action. In the early scene when Hollanden walks into the landscape and Hawker sees him for the first time, the suggestion that Hawker marry Miss Fanhall is followed by the jousting conversation between the two men, which concludes at the end of the chapter with Hawker accusing Hollanden of being *ridiculous*, to which Hollanden replies:

"I'm not ridiculous."

"Yes, you are, you know, Hollie."

The writer waved his hand despairingly. "And you rode in the train with her and in the stage."

"I didn't see her in the train," said Hawker.

"Oh, then you saw her in the stage. Ha-ha, you thief. I sat up here and you sat down there and lied." He jumped from his perch and belabored Hawker's shoulders.

"Stop that," said the painter.

"Oh, you old thief, you lied to me. You lied—Hold on—bless my life, here she comes now."

But she doesn't come, at least not in the text. We turn the page, fully expecting to see Miss Fanhall approaching them, but Crane gives us something else instead. "One day," the fourth chapter begins, and there is Hollanden telling Hawker about the fifteen middle-aged women who spend their days sitting on the porch of the inn. This is typical of how Crane proceeds throughout the book—promising something, then rescinding the promise and pushing forward with another line of thought, threatening to trip us with the numerous holes he leaves in the narrative ground, and because of that unstable ground, we are kept continually off-balance and on our guard, unsure of our footing and therefore unable to predict what will happen next, even though the story we are reading is an utterly conventional one at heart, a string of a hundred *of course*s that thread sinuously through all thirty-three chapters of talk and more talk and still more talk until the book comes to its unexpectedly ambiguous conclusion.

By the second page of the fourth chapter, apropos of nothing, Hollanden suddenly blurts out something.

"By the way," he added, "you haven't got any obviously loose screws in your character, have you?"

"No," said Hawker, after consideration. "Only general poverty—that's all."

"Of course, of course," said Hollanden. "But that's bad. They'll get on to you—sure. Particularly since you come up here to see Miss Fanhall so much."

This is how we find out that Hawker has already begun his courtship of the astonishing woman—indirectly, at one remove, with the entire business having been conducted offstage, in other words, beyond the perimeter of the book, which digs yet one more hole in the narrative ground we are walking on. What follows from that revelation is a dialogue between the two young men that carries on until the end of the chapter and demonstrates the sharp difference in their personalities— Hollanden's buoyant playfulness as opposed to Hawker's stuffy rectitude and quickness to anger—as well as showing Hollanden's mind at work as he puts together his "dramatic situation" and counsels Hawker on how to fit into the "play" that is in fact his own life (as conceived and directed by Hollanden), and when Hawker is reduced to stuttering incoherence as the scene draws to a close, the meaning of the book's title is unveiled in the final sentence.

"What's the matter with you? Haven't you ever been in love before?"

"None of your business," replied Hawker.

Hollanden thought upon this point for a time. "Well," he admitted finally, "that's true in a general way, but I hate to see you managing your affairs so stupidly."

Rage flamed into Hawker's face and he cried passionately, "I tell you it is none of your business." He suddenly confronted the other man.

Hollanden surveyed this outburst with a critical eye and then slapped his knee with emphasis. "You certainly have got it. A million times worse than I thought. Why, you—you—you're heels over head."

"What if I am?" said Hawker, with a gesture of defiance and despair.

Hollanden saw a dramatic situation in the distance and with a bright smile he studied it. "Say," he exclaimed, "suppose she should not go to the picnic to-morrow. She said this morning she did not know if she could go. Somebody was expected from New York, I think. Wouldn't it break you up, though! Eh?"

"You're so dev'lish clever," said Hawker with sullen irony.

Hollanden was still regarding the distant dramatic situation. "And rivals, too. The woods must be crowded with them. A girl like that, you know. And then, all that money. Say, your rivals must number enough to make a brigade of militia. Imagine them, swarming around. But then it doesn't matter so much," he went on cheerfully. "You've got a good play there. You must appreciate them to her—you understand—appreciate them kindly like a man in a watch-tower. You must laugh at them only about once a week and then very tolerantly, you understand—and kindly—and appreciatively."

"You're a colossal ass, Hollie," said Hawker. "You—"

"Yes—yes—I know," replied the other peacefully. "A colossal ass. Of course." After looking into the distance again he murmured: "I'm worried about that picnic. I wish I knew she was going. By heavens, as a matter of fact, she must be made to go."

"What have you got to do with it?" cried the painter in another sudden outburst.

"There—there," said Hollanden, waving his hand. "You fool. Only a spectator, I assure you."

Hawker seemed overcome then with a deep dislike of himself. "Oh, well, you know, Hollie, this sort of thing—" He broke off and gazed at the trees. "This sort of thing—It—"

"How?" asked Hollanden.

"Confound you for a meddling, gabbling idiot," cried Hawker suddenly.

Hollanden replied: "What did you do with that violet she dropped at the side of the tennis court yesterday?"

The mysterious first violet. Dropped by accident or design by Miss Fanhall, and if by design as a gesture of—what? It is too early to tell. Perhaps as a token of affection—but to whom? Hollanden seems to imply that Hawker picked it up or might have picked it up—but not even that is certain at this point. Much later, we will learn that the artist has indeed pocketed the violet, and by the time Miss Fanhall offers him a second one on the day she leaves the inn to return to the city, Crane has delineated the first stage of their bumpy, hot-and-cold, yet ever more serious romance—as orchestrated by the chortling, whimsical Hollanden.

Who is this devilish young man in the white flannel? Or, as one of the young female guests at the inn asks him at the beginning of chapter IV, "What makes literary men so peculiar?" After telling her that "I've inquired of innumerable literary men and none of 'em know," he switches direction and offers to give them his "personal history," which is met by the young Worcester girl's older sister with an enthusiastic "Oh, do!" (In the speech that follows, note how Crane uses the term invented by Howells in their interview from the previous October: *trained bear*.)

"Well—you must understand—I started my career—my career, you understand—with a determination to be a prophet, and although I have ended in being an acrobat, a trained bear of the magazines, and a juggler of comic paragraphs, there was once carven upon my lips a smile which made many people detest me, for it hung before them like a banshee whenever they tried to be satisfied with themselves. I was informed from time to time that I was making no great holes in the universal plan, and I came to know that one person in every two thousand of the people I saw had heard of me, and that four out of five of these had forgotten it. . . . Meanwhile I created a gigantic dignity, and when men saw this dignity and heard that I was a literary man they respected me. I concluded that the simple campaign of existence for me was to delude the populace or as much of it as would look at me. I did. I do. And now I can make myself quite happy concocting sneers about it. . . ."

"I don't believe a word of it is true," said Miss Worcester.

"What do you expect of autobiography?" demanded Hollanden.

He is Crane's nightmare double—the sellout writer who has given in to the demands of the marketplace, an extreme example of the sort of person he does *not* want to become, and consequently the embodiment of his worst fears about himself. And yet, how jovial Hollanden is, how comfortable in his derision of himself and others, so resigned to his mediocrity that he seems almost happy about it, as if, in having given up the struggle to turn himself into a prophet, an immense burden has been lifted from his shoulders, freeing him to cavort as irresponsibly as the nincompoops of fashion who appreciate his comic paragraphs. Or so it would appear from listening to him talk, but the Worcester girl sees right through him, understanding that he doesn't mean a thing he is saying. Then comes his witty rejoinder, "What do you expect of autobiography?," meaning that when one tells (or writes) about one's "personal history," the result will be no less a literary artifact than the words found in any piece of fiction, which happens to be true and which can also be read as a comment from Crane about his own book, for even if *The Third Violet* draws liberally on elements from his own life, it is not, strictly speaking, an autobiographical novel, even though the two principal male characters are both artists, each of whom represents something about his own conflicts in trying to establish a place for himself in the literary world. As for Hollanden, his true feelings are perhaps best expressed in a subsequent conversation with Oglethorpe when Hawker's supposed rival, the all-but-perfect candidate to win Miss Fanhall's hand in marriage (for he is widely considered to be the richest, handsomest, most likable fellow on the face of the earth), oafishly contends

that the men who made the most money from books were the best authors. Hollanden contended that they were the worst. Oglethorpe said that such a question should be left to the people. Hollanden said that the people habitually made the wrong decisions on questions that were left to them. "That is the most odiously aristocratic belief," said Oglethorpe.

"No," said Hollanden. "I like the people. But, considered generally, they are a collection of ingenuous blockheads."

"But they read your books," said Oglethorpe, grinning.

"That is through a mistake," replied Hollanden.

For once, Hollanden seems to be telling the truth. And then again, perhaps he isn't, and it is precisely the doubt embedded in this *perhaps* that makes him such an intriguing character. The self-negating force of his ironies spins round and round in an ever-deepening whirlpool of more ironies and contradictions, and the reader must be cautious in taking anything he says at face value. What he has just told Oglethorpe is that he knows the difference between good writing and bad writing and that any reader who thinks he is a good writer is wrong. Does he mean this? Probably. But if he does, that would also imply that Hollanden is bitter about his failure to live up to his earlier ambitions, and not once in the book does Crane show that bitterness. Hollanden never removes his mask, and because of that we can never fully trust what he says.

Hawker is another sort of artistic animal—dedicated, focused, driven by a burning compulsion to turn his canvases into weapons of the truth. His artist friends have a deep admiration for what he does, which is a convincing sign of how uncommonly gifted he is, but as with most people who push toward higher and higher levels of excellence, Hawker is uncommonly hard on himself, and no matter how good or admired his paintings might be, he is rarely satisfied with them. That is the paradox every genuine artist is forced to grapple with: to live in a state of perpetual doubt and yet to forge on from painting to painting or book to book in the hope of doing better the next time, and then, even when it is better, to feel another surge of disappointment at not having made it better enough. In that respect, Hawker's inner trajectory as an artist closely resembles Crane's, but there are a number of external resemblances as well, especially in Hawker's early struggles with poverty and neglect, which he talks about several times in his conversations with Miss Fanhall. One instance, from chapter VIII:

"But, still, the life of the studios—"

Hawker scoffed. "There were six of us. Mainly we smoked. Sometimes we played hearts and at other times poker—on credit, you know—credit. And when we had the materials and got something to do, we worked."

After he tells her about painting the red-and-green designs on the common tomato can and then graduating to corn and asparagus, Miss Fanhall repeats her opening remark, as does Hawker:

"But, still, the life of the studios—"
"There were six of us. Fate ordained that only one in the crowd could have money at one time. The other five lived off him and despised themselves. We despised ourselves five times as long as we had admiration."
"And was this just because you had no money?"
"It was because we had no money in New York," said Hawker.
"Well, after a while, something happened—"
"Oh, no, it didn't. Something impended always, but it never happened."

Another instance, from chapter XXIX, after Miss Fanhall has asked him to tell her about his beginnings as a painter:

"Well, I started to study when I was very poor, you understand. Look here, I'm telling you these things because I want you to know, somehow. It isn't that I'm not ashamed of it. Well, I began very poor, and I—as a matter of fact—I—well, I earned myself over half the money for my studying and the other half I bullied and badgered and beat out my poor old dad. I worked pretty hard in Paris and I returned here expecting to become a great painter at once. I didn't, though. In fact, I had my worst moments then. It lasted for some years.... However, things got a little better and a little better, until I found that by working quite hard I could make what was to me a fair income...."
"Why are you so ashamed of this story?"
"The poverty."
"Poverty isn't anything to be ashamed of."
"Great heavens, have you the temerity to get off that old nonsensical remark. Poverty is everything to be ashamed of. Did you ever see a person not ashamed of his poverty? Certainly not. Of course when a man gets very rich he will brag so loudly of the poverty of his youth that one would never suppose that he was once ashamed of it. But he was."
"Well, anyhow, you shouldn't be ashamed of the story you have just told me."

"Why not? Do you refuse to allow me the great right of being like other men?"

"I think it was—brave, you know."

"Brave—nonsense. Those things are not brave. Impression to that effect created by the men who have been through the mill for the greater glory of the men who have been through the mill."

"I don't like to hear you talk that way. It sounds wicked, you know."

"Well, it certainly wasn't heroic. I can remember distinctly that there was not one heroic moment."

"No, but it was—it was—"

"It was what?"

"Well, somehow I like it, you know."

In Hawker, Crane is not presenting a portrait of himself so much as conjuring up a kindred spirit, a fellow artist who approaches his art with an intensity similar to his own and has lived through humiliations similar to the ones he has experienced himself, but even though they share some personality traits as well (shy, bottled up, awkward around women), there is an essential difference between them that in the end makes all the difference: Crane had a sense of humor and Hawker does not. Even in his darkest moments of penury and hunger, Crane had it in him to step back from himself and mock his destitution with the zany, puffed-up verses of "Ah, haggard purse, why ope thy mouth," whereas Hawker would be utterly incapable of such a gesture. He is grim, whereas Crane often smiled through his troubles. He is quick-tempered and embattled, whereas Crane was mostly calm and collected, with an ability to make people laugh at his jokes, but Hawker doesn't smile, and he never tells a joke. So much for the autobiographical element of the novel, for what, after all, can we expect of autobiography? Crane has used parts of himself to fashion two characters named Hollanden and Billie Hawker, but they are both inventions, and *The Third Violet* is a novel, a work of the imagination that follows the ins and outs of a love story that never happened anywhere but inside the author's head.

Hollanden's interference complicates that love, as does the arrival of Oglethorpe, but the biggest obstacle standing between the two lovers comes from Hawker himself, for in spite of having moved up the social ladder (earning "a fair income"), he is intimidated by Miss Fanhall's wealth or, rather, to be more precise about it, by the class she was born into and seems to represent (the distance in her eyes is also the distance that separates them socially), and no matter how glorious his position might become in the future, Hawker can never escape the story of his humble background and the shame of his early struggles. Rich girl that she is, however, Miss Fanhall is not a snob, and she has no impulse to look down on that humble background or condemn those early struggles and is, quite frankly, baffled by Hawker's attitude. Why *shame*? If you have done nothing wrong, how can you possibly feel shame? Nevertheless, that is the word Hawker uses, but what he actually means by it is *self-hatred*, which twice earlier in the text has been called "a deep dislike of himself." In other words, Hawker is at odds with himself, and in his pursuit of Miss Fanhall that condition exposes him as a man equally torn between love and anger, so that the more enamored he becomes of the girl with the distance in her eyes, the more contentiously he behaves with her—to such a degree that when she tells him that "poverty isn't anything to be ashamed of," he dismisses her remark and interprets it as a sign of condescension. In a fascinating reversal of roles, the tortured, self-tormenting painter is the one who turns out to be the snob.

The most pertinent episode in the first half of the novel occurs in chapter XIV, when Hawker and Grace are walking through the woods not long after he has finally found the courage to announce that he "cares" for her, which for him carries all the weight of a declaration of love. Lagging behind the others in the group, they run into Hawker's father and (at Grace's request) hitch a ride with him back to the inn in his oxcart. Hawker the snob is embarrassed by this chance encounter between aristocrat and peasant, but the egalitarian, open-hearted Grace is charmed by it, and as the "tall and tattered" farmer drives them to their destination, talking easily and amiably with the society girl sitting next to him on the plank in front, his wincing, unhappy son stands silently in the back. By the next morning, the Oxcart Incident has become the talk of the front porch at the inn, and one of the gossiping women insults Grace by complimenting her on her "prank." "Prank?" Grace asks, and the woman replies: "Yes, your riding on the ox cart with that old farmer and that young Mr. What's-his-name, you know. We all thought it delicious." Agitated by the woman's rudeness, Grace marches off in a snit, and later that morning Hawker, unable to understand the true reason for her indignation (her attraction to him, her sympathy for his good father), tries to appease her by shouldering the blame for the woman's insult.

"I know what Mrs. Truscot talked to you about."
She turned upon him belligerently. "You do?"

"Yes," he answered with meekness. "It was undoubtedly some reference to your ride upon the ox wagon."

She hesitated for a moment and then said: "Well?"

With still greater meekness he said: "I am very sorry."

"Are you—indeed?" she inquired loftily. "Sorry for what? Sorry that I rode upon your father's ox wagon, or sorry that Mrs. Truscot was rude to me about it?"

"Well—in some ways it was my fault."

"Was it? I suppose you intend to apologize for your father's owning an ox wagon, don't you?"

"No, but—"

"Well, I am going to ride in the ox wagon whenever I choose. Your father, I know, will always be glad to have me. And if it so shocks you there is not the slightest necessity of your coming with us."

A moment later, she tells him that she and her family will be leaving the inn next week. The blindsided Hawker can scarcely believe what he has heard, and then, to emphasize the depth of her irritation with him, Grace casually says that she meant to tell him earlier but it kept slipping her mind. Following that hurtful disclosure, she augments the hurt by pretending to have forgotten what he told her yesterday ("I care for you, of course"), and when he accuses her of not remembering on purpose, she calls him "a ridiculous person . . . more ridiculous now than I have yet seen you." Then she stomps off to the tennis courts with Hollenden, who has promised to teach her a new stroke called "the slam."

Her slam of the obtuse Hawker is fully justified at this point, but all is not lost, and the rattled suitor is far from ready to give up. On the last evening before Miss Fanhall's departure, Hawker returns to the inn, chastened but still determined, and in spite of the presence of several other people around her, among them Oglethorpe (who has come and gone and come back again), he does his best to convey his feelings to her under those constrained circumstances. "I shall miss you," he says; "This has been quite the most delightful summer of my experience," he says; "I shall miss you," he says again; "It will be very lonely here," he says; "I dare say I shall return to New York myself in a few weeks," he says, and Miss Fanhall stiffly replies, "I hope you will call," which he answers with an equally stiff "I shall be delighted," and for once the reader can sympathize with him and feel the agony of his predicament. Some moments later, as she is about to go in and retire for the night:

Hawker said to the girl: "I—I—I shall miss you dreadfully."

She turned to look at him and smiled. "Shall you?" she said in a low voice.

"Yes," he said. Thereafter he stood before her awkwardly and in silence. She scrutinized the boards of the floor. Suddenly she drew a violet from a cluster of them upon her gown and thrust it out at him as she turned toward the approaching Oglethorpe.

"Good-night, Mr. Hawker," said the latter. "I am very glad to have met you, I'm sure. Hope to see you in town. Good-night."

He stood near when the girl said to Hawker: "Good-by. You have given us such a charming summer. We shall be delighted to see you in town. You must come some time when the children can see you, too. Good-by."

"Good-by," replied Hawker, eagerly and feverishly trying to interpret the inscrutable feminine face before him. "I shall come at my first opportunity."

The action then travels south to New York, where we meet Hawker's impecunious artist friends and the courtship staggers along in a succession of three one-on-one conversations between Hawker and Grace at her family's uptown mansion, described as an "endless building of brown stone about which there was the poetry of a prison." Absorbing as the country passages have been, the story takes on added life in the city, for it is there that Crane gives us the book's finest creation, the artists' model Florinda O'Conner, known to her friends as Splutter, who is far and away the most touching, fully realized female character in all of Crane's work.* Significantly, Oglethorpe has disappeared from sight, and instead of wondering which man the heiress will choose, we now wonder which woman the painter will choose—because we know, from the instant she turns up in chapter XIX, that Splutter is heels over head for him.

Hollanden is still there, but he no longer occupies center stage as he did in the first half of the book, appearing at several crucial moments to keep his plot spinning forward, as Wrinkles and Company take over the bulk of

---

* Nelson Greene, in a 1947 letter to Schoberlin, wrote that Crane "met my model, Gertrude Selene, who was probably the 'Florinda.' She was reputed at 18 to have the best figure of any model in New York City. She had beautiful blond hair, gray eyes and she was not beautiful. Nevertheless she was attractive and distinctly a man's girl. Kindly do not use her name. She later married a doctor and became highly respectable. She and Crane got on very well. She admired his keen mind and often talked with him and discussed him with me. He never tumbled with her however."

the scenes. They are an amusing, high-spirited gang of innocents, vivacious mopers battling through various forms of adversity (rejections, hunger, delayed payments for published work, monthly rent panics) in the dogged hope of establishing themselves as magazine illustrators and cartoonists. Their living conditions are directly drawn from Crane's yearslong sojourn in the land of male cohabitation, and the room they share (referred to as *the den*) is identical to the one he shared with Greene, Carroll, and the others— even down to the coal bin masquerading as a piece of furniture. Every once in a while, a member of the gang will deliver an unforgettable remark, as Pennoyer does when he understands that they are all facing a weekend of empty stomachs ("Singular thing. . . . You get so frightfully hungry as soon as you learn that there are no more meals coming") or as Grief does when he prances around the room delivering a comic monologue about the preference of successful American painters for foreign subjects over American ones, aping their scornful attitude by declaring, "How the devil can I paint America when nobody has done it before me?"—but mostly they banter among themselves, play cards, prepare their skimpy meals if and when they have food, and take an inordinate interest in Hawker's affairs. Once Hawker returns to New York and Pennoyer accidentally catches him looking at the violets in "the palm of his hand," that interest evolves into an obsessive preoccupation with his *affair*: the mystery of the two flowers and the name of the unknown woman those flowers represent. It matters to them because Hawker is their shining star, the friend who has made good, the brilliant painter who springs for their rent whenever they are squeezed, and because the god from across the hall no longer seems to be himself, they suspect that whatever is wrong with him can be answered by solving the riddle of the two violets. On top of that, they are just plain curious, dying to know simply for the sake of knowing, so they enter the story by becoming observers of the story, and once again, with a few additions and subtractions to and from the cast of characters, the story in the second half of the book continues to be the story of the story itself.

Splutter is one of the boys and not one of the boys, the sole female presence ever admitted into their squalid, one-room fraternity house. "A lithe and rather slight girl," she comes around to the den often and shares meals with them, smokes with them, drinks with them, and once even cooks a spaghetti dinner for them (exposing her "wonderful arms" when she rolls up her sleeves), and those two shorthand comments about her appearance make her the only central character in the novel whose looks are referred to at all. In that enclosed male world of teases and insults, she holds her own with the young men by calling them "idiots" and "dubs" (losers), and they tease her back by calling her "a poor outspoken kid": "Don't you know that when you are so frank you defy every law of your sex, and wild eyes will take your trail?"—which in fact is a compliment and proof of how much they care for her. They have helped her out of "scrapes" several times in the past, and now that they are down on their luck and she is on her feet again because of her modeling work, she wants to return the favor by helping them through this rough patch, but they are too embarrassed to accept her help and turn it down by "acting like a set of dudes," that is, by posing as chivalric gentlemen who would rather starve than accept help from a girl. What holds them together is their universal admiration of the god from across the hall. All of them agree that Billie Hawker is an extraordinary person, and because the boys know that Splutter is in love with him and Billie is not in love with her, their affection for her is also tinged with pity. The sad truth is that she knows it herself, which is what makes her such a poignant, shimmering character: not the star of the show but the one all eyes turn to whenever she appears, the one who steals the audience's heart. Early on she says, "Billie Hawker doesn't give a rap for me and never tried to make out that he did." That seems to be a definitive pronouncement, but this is a romance, after all, and obstacles are the stuff that drives readers of love stories to go on turning the pages, and perhaps Crane is setting us up for the moment when the girl with the wonderful arms will manage to overcome the obstacles that stand between her and Billie.

She never does, but the ride to that impasse travels through the most engaging parts of the book, for the dense, chuckleheaded Hawker has no clue about her feelings for him and thoughtlessly degrades her again and again, too preoccupied with his own love drama to understand what he is doing. On his first day back in the city, when he walks into the den and doesn't bother to say hello to her, she turns around and remarks, "Well, Billie Hawker. . . . You don't seem very glad to see a fellow." (*Fellow*: a sign of her wit, but also of her despair.) Hawker brusquely replies, "Heavens, did you think I was going to turn somersaults . . . ?" Later that same day, with Hawker decked out in his best clothes and sporting an elegant pair of gray gloves (about to go uptown to call on the lady of the violets), he runs into Splutter charging up the darkened staircase carrying food and drink for a dinner with the boys. When they move toward the light seeping through a small window, she looks him over and says, "Oh, cracky. . . . How fine you are, Billie. Going to a coronation?" He mumbles something about having to visit "a friend," and when she asks him to join them for dinner after he returns ("It's fun when we all dine together. Won't you, Billie?"), he hems and haws with a noncommittal "I'll see . . . I can't tell." When he arrives uptown and comes to the door of "a certain austere house," it turns out that Grace isn't there. More than disappointed, he acts as if he has been betrayed, and "when he rounded the corner his lips were set strangely as if he were a man seeking revenge."

Cut to the dinner preparations at the den. Splutter is chilling the wine on a window ledge as she cooks the spaghetti in her rolled-up sleeves, and Grief and Wrinkles are arguing about which one of them should go out to buy the potato salad. They hear someone approach, "whistling an air from 'Traviata,' which rang loud and clear and low and muffled as the whistler wound around the intricate hallways. This air was as much a part of Hawker as his coat." Eventually, Hawker and Florinda volunteer to fetch more provisions (claret, cognac, cigarettes, among other things), and as they are going down the stairs, she bluntly asks him, "What— what makes you so ugly, Billie?" Is he really ugly? he asks. "Yes, you are ugly as anything." Thrown back by her comments and the "grievance in her eyes," he says that he doesn't want to be ugly, speaking in a tone that is suddenly and unexpectedly "tender," or at least "seems" to be tender, which prompts Florinda to place her hand on his arm as they continue down the "intensely dark" staircase, suggesting that they have arrived at a truce and the matter has been settled. When they stop in at the "illustrious purveyors of potato salad on Second Avenue," however, Florinda offers to carry the package so Hawker's gloves won't get "soiled," and without warning he explodes at her about "this blasted glove business," accusing her of

> "intimating that I've got the only pair of grey gloves in the universe, but you are wrong. There are several pairs, and these need not be preserved as unique in history."
>
> "They're not grey. They're—"
>
> "They are grey. I suppose your distinguished ancestors in Ireland did not educate their families in the matter of gloves, and so you are not expected to—"
>
> "Billie!"
>
> "You are not expected to believe that people wear gloves excepting in cold weather, and then you expect to see mittens."

He has stomped on her with his words, assaulted her family and her background, humiliated her. When they return to the building, he makes a small, wordless show of contrition by offering to guide her up the dark stairs, but when he reaches for her arm, she pulls it away. Understandably. After his cruel outburst, why would she want him to touch her?

We see them alone together for the last time in the next chapter. There has been another group dinner at the den, and as it is getting late (past eleven), and as the neighborhood is too dangerous for an unaccompanied woman to walk through it at night, the boys play a hand of poker to decide which one of them, as Grief puts it, "will have the distinguished honor of conveying Miss Splutter to her home and mother." Hawker wins the hand with three sevens, and as the two of them go off into the night, heading toward her apartment building on Third Avenue ("a flat with fire escapes written all over the face of it"), Crane momentarily departs from his "'quick' style" to offer up a one-paragraph digression about the constant repair work inflicted on New York's streets and the mountains of fresh paving stones that block the sidewalks, which have created the "tangled midnight" through which Hawker is conducting Florinda home and the air of "grim loneliness" that hangs over "the uncouth shapes in the street." As they approach her apartment house, Florinda asks him a question similar to the one she asked in the previous chapter, and at last something begins to stir inside Hawker's thick skull.

> "Billie," said the girl suddenly, "what makes you so mean to me?"
>
> A peaceful citizen emerged from behind a pile of debris, but he might not have been a peaceful citizen, so the girl clung to Hawker.
>
> "Why, I'm not mean to you, am I?"
>
> "Yes," she answered. As they stood on the steps of the flat of innumerable fire escapes, she slowly turned and looked up at him. . . .
>
> He returned her glance. "Florinda," he cried, as if enlightened, and gulping suddenly at something in his throat. The girl studied the steps and moved from side to side, as do the guilty ones in country schoolhouses. Then she went slowly into the flat. There was a little red lamp hanging on a pile of stones to warn people that the street was being repaired.

That's it. Hawker has finally understood that she is in love with him, but other than call out her name, he says nothing, and other than swallow hard, as if choked up with a sudden rush of feeling, he does nothing. Then, as Florinda sways back and forth and looks down at the steps, no doubt waiting for Hawker to say something or do something, Crane follows with a curious, unexpected comparison—likening her to a guilty schoolgirl—which all at once infantilizes Florinda and seems to bar her from consideration as a sexual being, and because Crane's imaginary schoolhouse is not in the city but the country, she has also been turned into an unsophisticated hick—hardly the sort of woman the social-climbing Hawker would be attracted to. And yet, in the last sentence, there is the mysterious red lamp, the universal sign of prostitution, in this case dangling from a pile of stones to warn pedestrians that there is a risk in walking down this street, and perhaps there is a risk, perhaps even a sexual risk, for at this point in the New York half of the novel Hawker has yet to see Grace again, and those rooting for the noble Splutter to turn his snob head toward her, and in the process reclaim his own inherent nobility, still have reason to hope. So ends chapter XXIV, with Crane managing to perform the impossible trick of having his cake and eating it, too, twisting his parody of love story conventions into such a merry, tangled knot that we can enjoy watching him poke fun at them even as we wait to see what will happen next. Two violets! "Gulping suddenly at something in his throat"! These are the ingredients of soaring Italian operas and steamy, pseudo-pornographic French novels—not unlike the one by Zola that Crane ridiculed in "Why Did the Young Clerk Swear?" back in the spring of '93. But Splutter breaks through those hackneyed tropes to become something real, and however contrived the plot might be, we want to know how things will turn out for her.

Three chapters go by before she is mentioned again, but the outcome is still far from certain at that point, and it helps Florinda's case that the person who speaks up for her is a disinterested party, a walk-on character who has been referred to just once, ten chapters earlier. He is a successful painter with the delicious name of Lucian Pontiac (no more Smiths and Johnsons in this book) who has employed Florinda as a model and thinks the world of her. Hawker is out one evening with Hollanden at a crowded restaurant-café when Pontiac comes over to their table and is asked to sit down, and thus the two painters meet for the first time. After a few complimentary words to Hawker about his "abilities," Pontiac tells him that he occasionally uses one of his models. "Must say she has the best arm and wrist in the universe. Stunning figure—stunning." When Hawker asks if he is talking about Florinda, Pontiac replies, "Yes. That's the name. Very fine girl. . . . And honest, too. Honest as the devil. . . . I've been much attracted to your girl, Florinda." "My girl?" Hawker says. Pontiac goes on to explain that last week, when he wanted to use her on Friday, she turned him down because Billie Hawker was back in the city and might need her then, and he was impressed by what he calls her "obedience and allegiance and devotion." When he asks if Hawker did in fact use her on Friday,

Hawker says no, and a moment after that, as if expressing the thoughts of the reader, Hollanden says, "Poor little beggar."

"Who?" said Pontiac.

"Florinda," answered Hollanden. "I suppose—"

Pontiac interrupted. "Oh, of course, it is too bad. Everything is too bad. My dear sir, nothing is so much to be regretted as the universe. But this Florinda is such a sturdy young soul. The world is against her, but, bless her heart, she is equal to the battle. She is strong in the manner of a little child. Why, you don't know her. She—"

"I know her very well."

"Well, perhaps you do, but for my part I think you don't appreciate her formidable character. And stunning figure—stunning."

"Damn it," said Hawker to his coffee cup, which he had accidentally overturned.

"Well," resumed Pontiac, "she is a stunning model and I think, Mr. Hawker, you are to be envied."

Is that enough to turn Hawker in Florinda's direction? Perhaps Crane wants us to think it is, at least for a little while, but no, it is not enough, and just days after that conversation in the restaurant, when Florinda gets her first look at Miss Fanhall through an upstairs window, she understands she hasn't a prayer of competing against such beauty. That leads to the heartbreaking thirty-first chapter, the one passage in the book that attains a genuine emotional power, a short, quiet scene as Pennoyer walks Florinda back home following her devastating glimpse of Hawker's beloved, and the exquisite thing about this chapter is that we know by now that Pennoyer is secretly in love with her, that he has been pining for Florinda from the moment the two of them entered the book, which turns their walk through the streets into a back-and-forth exchange of two equals, two battered souls talking at cross-purposes in a conversation that evolves into a small piece of music through repetition, rhythm, and the "one string" that goes on playing throughout: Crane's modern, down-to-the-ground version of a classic opera duet—*La Traviata* without the orchestra, *The Third Violet* without the violets. Crane never would have been capable of writing such a passage earlier, and he never tried to do anything like it again. Just two pages long, the chapter demands to be quoted in full.

In the evening Pennoyer conducted Florinda to the flat of many fire escapes. After a period of silent tramping through the great golden avenue and the street that was being repaired, she said: "Penny, you are very good to me."

"Why?" said Pennoyer.

"Oh, because you are. You—you are very good to me, Penny."

"Well, I guess I'm not killing myself."

"There isn't many fellows like you."

"No?"

"No. There isn't many fellows like you, Penny. I tell you most everything and you just listen and don't argue with me and tell me I'm a fool because you know that it—because you know that it can't be helped anyhow."

"Oh, nonsense, you kid. Almost anybody would be glad to—"

"Penny, do you think she is very beautiful?" Florinda's voice had a singular quality of awe in it.

"Well," replied Pennoyer, "I don't know."

"Yes, you do, Penny. Go ahead and tell me."

"Well—"

"Go ahead."

"Well, she is rather handsome, you know."

"Yes," said Florinda, dejectedly. "I suppose she is." After a time she cleared her throat and remarked indifferently: "I suppose Billie cares a lot for her?"

"Oh, I imagine that he does. In a way."

"Why, of course he does," insisted Florinda. "What do you mean by 'in a way'? You know very well that Billie thinks his eyes of her."

"No, I don't."

"Yes, you do. You know you do. You are talking in that way just to brace me up. You know you are."

"No, I'm not."

"Penny," said Florinda, thankfully, "what makes you so good to me?"

"Oh, I guess I'm not so astonishingly good to you. Don't be silly."

"But you are good to me, Penny. You don't make fun of me the way— the way the other boys would. You are just as good as you can be. But you do think she is beautiful, don't you?"

"They wouldn't make fun of you," said Pennoyer.

"But you do think she is beautiful, don't you?"

"Look here, Splutter, let up on that, will you? You keep harping on that one string all the time. Don't bother me."

"But, honest now, Penny, you do think she's beautiful?"

"Well, then, confound it—no. No. No."

"Oh, yes you do, Penny. Go ahead now. Don't deny it just because you are talking to me. Own up now, Penny. You do think she is beautiful!"

"Well," said Pennoyer, in a dull roar of irritation, "do you?"

Florinda walked in silence, her eyes upon the yellow flashes which lights sent to the pavement. In the end she said: "Yes."

"Yes, what?" asked Pennoyer sharply.

"Yes, she—yes, she is—beautiful."

"Well, then?" cried Pennoyer, abruptly closing the discussion.

Florinda announced something as a fact. "Billie thinks his eyes of her."

"How do you know he does?"

"Don't scold at me, Penny. You—you—"

"I'm not scolding at you. There! What a goose you are, Splutter. Don't for heaven's sake go to whimpering on the street. I didn't say anything to make you feel that way. Come, pull yourself together."

"I'm not whimpering."

"No, of course not; but then you look as if you were on the edge of it. What a little idiot!"

In spite of certain hints and in spite of certain expectations founded on those hints, it seems clear now that Florinda never had a chance with Billie. But what of Billie's chances with Grace? We will not know the answer until the final sentence of the book, and even then the resolution will be murky, with multiple, contradictory interpretations radiating out from that fiendishly complex last moment.

They have talked to each other twice so far, both times at the Fanhall mansion, which has been presented as a prison-like fortress, a barren environment devoid of people and objects, a vacuum of pure mental space that has been set apart from the physical world for the sole purpose of allowing the lovers to talk—as if on an empty stage. Other than noting a chandelier that gleams "like a Siamese headdress" and lace curtains that sweep down "in orderly cascades, as water trained to fall mathematically," Crane tells us nothing about where we are, and during those first two visits to the house, we have no idea whether Hawker and Grace are standing or sitting while they talk.

On the first visit, Hawker's anxiety makes him so tense that he can't get his "tongue to wag to his purpose." He begins by reversing himself on his opinion of the play, conceding that, yes, it is no more than the same old characters wallowing "in the mud of modern confusion," then continues to sabotage the visit with a word storm of clumsy, inappropriate comments, and Grace, still miffed over the oxcart dispute, is no more than coldly polite to him during their testy, unsatisfactory encounter. The second visit goes more smoothly, building up to Hawker's confession about his early struggles and Grace's sympathetic remarks about his bravery, which in turn induces her to visit Hawker's studio with Hollanden and one or two others, but that scene takes place off camera, as it were, with the lens pointed at the den dwellers across the hall as they listen closely at their closed door and manage to hear nothing but "a dulled melodious babble" coming from the other room. The chapter ends with Florinda standing at the window and looking down at Grace as she leaves the building—a crushing moment for poor Splutter—but Crane has left us in the dark about any further developments in the Hawker-Fanhall romance.

Toward the end of the book, Hollanden reemerges as a principal player in the action. Before Pontiac turns up in the restaurant scene—a brilliantly orchestrated bit of business, with Hollanden talking to Hawker in one part of the room as a violent quarrel breaks out in another—we learn how disappointed the writer has become with his friend's behavior: "You will become correct. I know you will. I have been watching. What's the matter with you? You act as if falling in love with a girl was a most extraordinary circumstance." After pausing to comment on the fight, which is taking place behind Hawker's back, Hollanden continues: "You have got an eye suddenly for all kinds of gilt" (guilt about gilt in the Gilded Age?) and then delivers this harsh judgment: "You are in the way of becoming a most unbearable person." When Hawker tries to defend himself, insisting that he hasn't changed at all, his companion cuts him off. "'You are gone,' interrupted Hollanden in a sad voice. 'It is very plain. You are gone.'"

Gone or not, Hawker is in a bad way, and when we see him standing before a newly finished canvas in the penultimate chapter, several months have gone by and snow is falling on the great stone city. In an earlier chapter, we have already witnessed him hard at work on another canvas, going at it "fiercely, mercilessly, formidably"—as if "thrusting with a sword"—but now, as he looks over his most recent painting, he is revolted by what he has done. Hollanden walks into the studio, and when he sees the scowl on Hawker's face, he asks, "What's wrong, now?" Everything is wrong, and with words similar to the ones Crane spoke to his friend Ned Greene about not being able to write anymore, Hawker tears into his own work, calling the picture "vile" and then declaring, "I can't paint. I can't paint for a damn. I'm not good. What in thunder was I invented for, anyhow, Hollie?" Hollanden calls him a fool, an idiot, but suspecting that Hawker's meltdown has something to do with Grace, he says, "Just because she—" Before

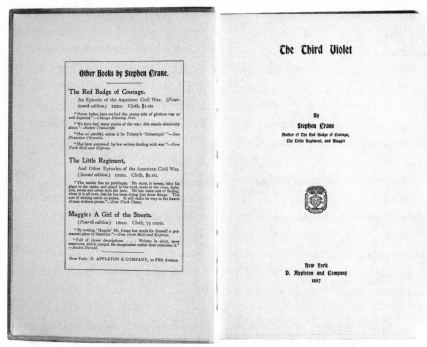

Title page of The Third Violet *and list of Crane's previous books published by D. Appleton and Company, along with extracts of reviews, on facing page.*
(PHOTOGRAPH BY SPENCER OSTRANDER)

he can finish, Hawker interrupts and says that *she* has nothing to do with it, although *she*, now that they are on the subject, doesn't "care a hang" for him, in fact doesn't even care "an old tomato can" for him, and why should she? By way of response, Hollanden begins lecturing Hawker on the irrationality of women, reprising that stale, ever-popular argument men have been broadcasting for centuries to assert their superiority over women, but Hollanden is a true believer and stands by the argument, concluding that "the safety of the world's balance lies in woman's illogical mind" and "thank heaven for it"—to which Hawker replies: "Go to blazes."

Again the house. Again the chandelier, which Hawker studies with "defiance and hatred" as he enters the blank room, sits in a chair (the first mention of a chair), and waits for the encounter to begin. Then it begins. Grace has not entered the room, she is simply in the room as Hawker starts the conversation by telling her that "perhaps" he is going away. Astonishment, followed by a decorously worded "We shall be sorry to lose you." The *we* spares her from any obligation to express her own feelings about his impending trip as she dissolves into a generalized Fanhalldom that includes her sister-in-law and the children (we have already learned that her older brother, presumably the husband of the sister-in-law, is dead, and Crane says nothing at all about her parents, who could be dead themselves or lurking in another room). Hawker reminds her that he once told her that he cared for her and that even now he still cares for her and will carry the two violets with him as a way to remember her on his travels, which will take him far from New York and could go on for a long time, possibly forever. After that cornball moment of operatic excess, she tugs at her gown, removes a third violet, and "thrusts it at him," which he interprets as a gesture of "supreme insolence." Suddenly annoyed, suddenly on the verge of anger, he sounds a further operatic note by insisting that he doesn't want to be "melodramatic" or "to act like a tenor" and that the last thing he wants is for her to pity him. The conversation quickly collapses into a series of mutual misunderstandings, and the violet that was thrust at him is turned into the violet that was flung at his head. No, not flung at his head, she protests, but "freely-given."

> "Do you know," said Hawker, "it is very hard to go away and leave an impression in your mind that I am a fool. That is very hard. Now, you do think I am a fool, don't you?"
> She remained silent. Once she lifted her eyes and gave him a swift look with much indignation in it.
> "Now you are enraged. Well, what have I done?"
> It seemed that some tumult was in her mind, for she cried out to him at last in sudden tearfulness: "Oh, do go. Go. Please. I want you to go."
> Under this swift change, Hawker appeared as a man struck from the sky. He sprang to his feet, took two steps forward and spoke a word which was an explosion of delight and amazement. He said: "What?"
> With heroic effort, she slowly raised her eyes until, a-light with anger, defiance, unhappiness, they met his eyes.
> Later, she told him that he was perfectly ridiculous.

The screen goes black, the curtain comes down, the book is over. And what, we ask ourselves, has just happened?

One possible reading: If we fix our attention on Grace's sudden loss of control, then her tearful outburst commanding Hawker to leave the house can be interpreted as a sign of passion—passion as an indication of love—for Grace is a woman, and as master of ceremonies Hollanden has just told us, women are irrational creatures, meaning that Hawker's "explosion of delight and amazement" comes from his recognition that

Grace has finally let down her guard and expressed her true feelings toward him, which mirror his own feelings toward her, and even if her eyes are "a-light with anger, defiance, unhappiness," those things count for little when a woman is in the heat of passion, for in the intensity of that upside-down moment anger means love and defiance means capitulation and unhappiness means joy, and therefore all ends well for the mismatched couple, and as they climb into bed on their wedding night, she gently teases him about how ridiculously he acted with her until that breakthrough moment.

Another possible reading: If we fix our attention on the word *Later*, then the happy-ending outcome most readers will take for granted is suddenly cast into doubt, for *later* is a relative length of time, an unspecified length of time, and what if Crane was not thinking of an immediate later but a more distant one, two or three years later, for example, and after Hawker's solitary travels to unknown parts of the universe have ended, he comes back to New York, goes to a gathering where he runs into Grace (who is now married to Oglethorpe or some other prince from the leisure class), and when they slip off to the terrace for a word in private, she tells him that the reason she broke it off two years ago was because she was in fact angry, defiant, and unhappy that afternoon and felt he had behaved with her in a manner that was (to repeat the words of the book) *perfectly ridiculous.*

The reader is left to decide which ending is the proper one—or else not decide and hold on to both of them at once, which is what I suspect Crane had in mind by closing his love-opera with such a cryptic, ambivalent scene. By divulging so little, he has allowed himself to offer two opposite and equal endings, a strategy that is fully in tune with the parodic, self-reflexive spirit of the book as a whole. It is not an either-or proposition, then, but rather one of either *and* or. Both at the same time.

This is intricate, maddeningly nuanced stuff, and it will hardly come as a surprise to learn that the novel died a quick death after it was published in May 1897. Crane was in the Mediterranean by then, covering the Greco-Turkish War as a correspondent for Hearst, and was spared from having to face the firing squad of American reviews, which attacked *The Third Violet* as "a weak sister" (*Buffalo Enquirer*), "not realistic . . . in any plausible sense" (*New York Tribune*), "leaves a distinct impression of dissatisfaction" (*Brooklyn Daily Eagle*), "as inane a story of summer resort flirtation as was ever written" (*Springfield Republican*), and "a book with badness written large all over it" (*Providence Journal*). *Godey's Magazine* was the only New York publication that seemed to have any inkling of what Crane had accomplished, and the anonymous reviewer, while calling the book "devoid of flesh and blood" (not without reason), praised it for being "a remarkable display of purely literary craft; as a study in handling and technical originality it is something unprecedented." After further praising the "jerky, fragmentary" dialogue and the vividness of Crane's language, the reviewer observed that "there is a constant display of a strong ability to suggest underlying subtleties of meaning and mood by careless-looking speech"—which was dead on target. What surprises me now, however, more than a century after the novel's release, is how little attention has been given to the book in the years since then, even by Crane scholars and devoted advocates of his work. *The Third Violet* has mysteriously slipped through the cracks, which explains why I have devoted so much time to it in this chapter—because it continues to be neglected, and because it deserves a fresh look from a new generation of readers. Compared to Crane's most powerful stories and novels, it surely falls into the category of "minor," but minor does not mean insignificant, and by trying his hand at a novel of manners at the same moment his war novel was turning him into an international figure shows something about his willingness to take risks, to experiment, to thrash out into new territory. That he largely managed to succeed with his experiment by undermining the conventions of the form he had chosen to tackle proves, I think, how far in advance of his time he was. Not only is *The Third Violet* the world's first screenplay, it is probably the world's first postmodern novel as well.

Crane never attempted such a project again. After his two-month holiday on the Island of Love, he returned to the mainland, unfastened the blindfold he had wrapped around his head, picked up his pen with his right hand, and plunged back into darkness.

25

THERE WERE NO LITERARY PRIZES IN AMERICA BEFORE THE TURN OF the century. No foundations had been created to disburse grants and fellowships to writers, and no colleges or universities employed writers to teach other writers how to write. The market ruled all literary business in that era of raw, unfettered capitalism, and when it came to the business of honoring writers who had distinguished themselves with an exceptional work or a lifetime of work, the honors were bestowed by private literary clubs and informal associations of fellow writers at banquets marked by the consumption of much food and wine along with speeches—many speeches—in praise of the honoree. Crane had already been invited to one of those gatherings a year and a half earlier—the celebration of Frances Hodgson Burnett hosted by the Uncut Leaves Society in New York—but he had refused to go out of dread, terrorized by the thought of watching John Barry stand up and read his poems to what he assumed would be a hostile audience. Now the tables had been turned, and as the freshly anointed celebrity author of *The Red Badge of Courage*, Crane was thrust into the uncomfortable position of being asked to attend more and more of these dinners as the guest of honor himself. In spite of his misgivings, he usually accepted—for all the standard reasons to begin with (gratitude, common courtesy, a chance to shine in public for a few hours)—but once he understood how much those dinners meant to certain folks in and around Port Jervis, he also accepted from a deeper, more urgently felt desire to impress his older brothers with his new standing in the world. Most of all William, the biggest of the brothers and therefore a kind of substitute father to him for the past sixteen years, and what son doesn't want to show his father that he isn't the no-account wastrel he once appeared to be? On January 7, 1896, after Crane learned that Hitchcock was organizing a dinner for him at the Authors Club to be held in early March, he wrote to Hawkins:

> The dinner scheme mingles my emotions. In one sense, it portends an Ordeal but in the larger sense it overwhelms me in pride and arrogance to think that I have such friends.
>
> By the way, you ought to see the effect of such things upon my family. Ain't they swelled up, though! Gee! I simply can't go around and see 'em enough. It's great. I am no longer a black sheep but a star.

But how frazzled that black sheep–star could become when plans were afoot to honor him, and never more frazzled than the first time, which happened to occur during his months at Hartwood, with the invitation arriving in early November from East Aurora, New York, just days after Crane had announced to Hawkins that the first third of *The Third Violet* was finished, which means that all through the final two-thirds of the book he lived in a state of ever-mounting panic, cursing himself for having accepted and yet too timid to withdraw with some fabricated excuse—a broken leg, perhaps, or a virulent eruption of hives—appealing to Hawkins again and again for moral support, logistical support, sartorial support, and making such a big to-do about such a nothing-at-all that it could be seen as a purely comic episode if not for how things turned out in the end. Crane had been duped by a con man, and through his own naïveté and readiness to believe in the good intentions of others, he never held that man responsible for the fiasco that took place at the Genesee Hotel on the evening of December 19, 1895. Even more astonishing, he remained a friend of that man for the rest of his life.

A former soap manufacturer turned writer, publisher, and self-appointed "ex-officio General Inspector of the Universe," the man was saddled with one of the more pungent, comical names of the era: Elbert Hubbard. W. C. Fields would later make a good living by inventing characters with names like that one, but Hubbard managed to elude the unfortunate *Elbert* in boyhood by masquerading under the nickname of Bertie and as an adult took to calling himself Fra Elbertus, which provided the name of one of the magazines he published, *Fra*. A hustling blowhard with a penchant for visionary pronouncements and a flair for self-promotion, he became a disciple of the Arts and Crafts movement and in 1895 was inspired by the example of William Morris's Kelmscott Press in England to found his own American version outside Buffalo, the Roycroft Press, along with establishing a small community of artisans known as the Roycrofters, who worked variously at printing, binding, handmade paper production, and the building of Arts and Crafts furniture. In June of that year, he launched the first of his magazines, *The Philistine: A Periodical of Protest*, which jabbed at the stodges from the New York literary establishment, mocked the complacent banalities of middle-class American life, and was bound in brown butcher paper to alert the world that there was "meat" to be found inside its covers. Most of the contributions were written by Hubbard himself (the other contributors were unpaid as a matter of principle), and at the peak of its popularity *The Philistine* attained a circulation of more than one hundred thousand—a remarkable number for a magazine of that kind. In the inaugural issue, Hubbard joined the chorus of glib archers shooting arrows at Crane's book of poems, wondering why the black riders were black when they "might as easily have been green or yellow or baby-blue for all the book tells about them," and then later that same month, he had the effrontery to send a letter to Crane, "trusting you will not take to heart the little stunt on The Black Riders," and ask him to furnish them with "a bit of ms. You can help us and we will try awfully hard to help you." It was the first time a magazine had solicited a poem from him, and Crane must have been flattered, flattered enough not to bear any hard feelings about the insult, and so rather than ignore the request, he sent off a poem to Hubbard for the next issue, and then another poem for the issue after that, and so the story began, with Crane falling for Hubbard's line about the two of them helping each other when in fact Hubbard only wanted to use Crane to help himself. Still, the man had offered to publish his poems, which made them allies, Crane felt, fellow renegades in the beautiful war against the status quo, and even if they didn't see eye to eye on all things, the man wanted to use his work, and what harm could come from tossing an occasional bone to a hungry dog?

The harm, as Amy Lowell pointed out in her introduction to the reissue of *The Black Riders*, had to do with Hubbard's reputation and the negative effect it had on Crane's reputation as a poet. "It was difficult for the world to believe that a man championed by the arch-poser, Elbert Hubbard, could have merit. . . . It was a thousand pities that poems such as these should appear under the aegis of the Roycrofters." Crane, however, still so young, and still so inexperienced, failed to notice the problem, and without giving the matter much thought, he kept on going to the cupboard and feeding Hubbard his bones.

Then the invitation showed up in the mail, blasting into the stillness and seclusion of Hartwood in the form of a letter dated November tenth *From the Committee For the Philistine Society* (a one-off, otherwise nonexistent organization) that began: "Recognizing in yourself and in your genius as a poet, a man whom we would like to know better, the Society of the Philistines desire to give a dinner in your honor early in the future." The signatories included Hubbard, his partner Henry P. Taber, and nine other men representing newspapers from Buffalo, Syracuse, Boston, New Orleans, Denver, and Washington. Overwhelmed, Crane reacted by immediately writing to Hawkins to ask his friend what he should do. Two years older than S.C.'s brother William and editor of the magazine *Brains* (one of the first publications devoted to advertising), Hawkins would surely have a better grasp of the situation than he did.

The reply was swift and decisive: "You may answer the Buffalo fellows without delay, for you must—you just *must*—accept their invitation. There is a business side to life that must not be wholly ignored. It hasn't a leg to stand on, and there's no honest reason for it's being, but here it is and— there you are. . . . You go ahead and accept. Tell me of the day you fix on, and I'll agree that you'll be togged properly for the occasion." Leaving nothing to chance, Hawkins continued by asking Crane for his chest measurement, what size shoe he wore, and the length of his leg from crotch to heel, since he knew that Crane's wardrobe was deficient on all fronts and that he lacked the funds to do anything about it. With the zeal of a true friend, the less than wealthy Hawkins was willing to do anything he could to help.

Buoyed by that enthusiastic support, Crane wrote back to Hubbard and accepted, humbly adding, "I am a very simple person and I am dejected when I think of the disappointment of my friends, the Philistines, if they have been good enough to form any opinion at all favorable of my ability or my personality." That day or the next, Crane wrote to Hawkins with thanks for the advice and to tell him how embarrassed he felt "when I think I was low enough to grab at your generosity." Then he provided the information Hawkins had asked for: "My chest, bad luck to it, measures 35 inches—scant—and my leg is a 33—worse luck. And foot—rot it—is a seven. There! It is over. I feel I have told you I am a damned thief"—for he knew that Hawkins would have to dig into his own pocket to rescue him. "Heaven send you rest, Willis, and in your old age may you remember how you befriended the greatest literary blockhead in America."

Early on, Crane sent Hubbard a list of the people he wanted to invite, and before long the regrets began trickling into the *Philistine* office, not as snubs to the guest of honor but from wariness of the host, who had already established the reputation Amy Lowell would write about thirty years later and who was clearly capitalizing on Crane's recent success to promote himself and his magazine. Irving Bacheller, Hamlin Garland, Ripley Hitchcock, and William Dean Howells were all otherwise engaged and sent their best wishes. Ambrose Bierce was in California, Richard Harding Davis was somewhere else, and S. S. McClure wrote that much as he appreciated Crane's talent, he preferred to "admire the valiant Philistines— from a safe distance." Undaunted, Hubbard pushed on with his plans as the large dinner shrank to a smallish dinner of approximately twenty-five confirmed guests, printing a thick souvenir menu that included a previously unpublished poem by Crane and the responses of the more than three dozen people who found it impossible to attend. Meanwhile, back at Hartwood as the nineteenth of December approached, Crane had slowly worked himself into a glorious, unrelenting nervous fit. To Hawkins on December fifteenth:

> I have mapped out my two or three shekels so that I will return home smiling but broke and in the smoking-car. I bought today one full dress shirt and what goes with it. I have a damn fine hat. I have no overcoat save that little gauze one which you may remember. Nor no dress-suit. My brother has—(had)—a pair of patent leathers and I am sleeping with them under my pillow. . . .
>
> And now, Willis, old man, when I get in all this flumy-doodle business and see you behind there moving the scenes and knowing

all the time what a damned fool I am and what a ridiculous hole I'm in, I get fair feeble-minded with dwelling upon it. I leave it all to you. For my part I wish the whole thing was in Ballywhoo because while I look forward to it as probably the greatest pleasure of my life, I feel as if I were astride your shoulders. And if I could stop the thing now I would.

Still optimistic, Hawkins wrote back on the seventeenth:

If you reach the Genesee before I do either wait for me or leave a note for me. I shall express an overcoat to you this afternoon. In Buffalo we will fix up the dress suit question. You bring along your shirt, hat & shoes. I will attend to coat, vest and trousers.

I like this sorto' thing. Don't let it bother you a bit. . . . We'll have a bully time.

That was the fun part, the comic tangle of frets and jitters and anxious second thoughts, but the dinner that Hawkins and no doubt Hubbard himself imagined would be a cozy, dignified affair turned into an embarrassment, an unruly verbal brawl provoked by a number of razzing, drunken newsmen sitting at one end of the long table. Several eyewitness accounts of the scene have come down to us, and while they differ somewhat in the details, there are no discrepancies in the overall impression of what happened. Crane's Syracuse fraternity brother Frank Noxon, then working as a drama critic for the *Boston Record*, was one of the self-described "freaks and near-freaks" in attendance. He had been placed next to Claude Bragdon, a set designer and architect, who was seated across from Crane and Hawkins. Hubbard's partner, Henry Taber, sat at the head. "After dinner," Noxon wrote in 1928,

Taber rose and began his speech. "Probably," he said, "the most unique—" That was as far as he got. A voice somewhere down toward Hubbard [at the other end of the table] called out "Can 'unique' be compared?" This was the signal. It determined the tone of the festivities. In the best clown and gridiron manner Taber and all the other speakers were guyed and ragged from start to finish. Crane . . . was called up, and they had as much fun with him as the others.

Bragdon, writing in 1905, offers his own description of the mayhem:

That dinner, held in a private room of a Buffalo hotel, is still a distressing memory—like the site of a young ox led to a slaughter. At first the dinner was dominated by a lot of drunken pseudo-reporters, who had come there with the evident intention of turning the whole affair to ridicule by their ribald and irrelevant interruptions, much to the distress, naturally, of Hubbard and us others.

Hawkins, sitting immediately to Crane's left, had a more intimate understanding of what the guest of honor had to endure. In one of his "All in a Lifetime" pieces from the 1920s, he wrote:

Thursday evening, December 19, 1895, Stephen and I sat next to each other at that dinner. He was in immaculate evening clothes, but he was ill at ease. The many speeches lauding his literary work had double effect on him. Nothing in his outward behavior indicated whether they pleased him or displeased him, but every now and then he would nudge me and utter a nearly suppressed groan or half-whispered word of disapproval of what I knew he regarded as kindly-intended bosh; for he had repeatedly assured me that he had done nothing to warrant any of this praise.

When Hubbard, who presided, had, in glowing terms, extolled the honored guest as man and genius, he called on Crane for a few words. Stephen, with manifest reluctance, rose. Evidently, he was panic-stricken. Wetting his pale, parched lips, he seemed for a moment unable to utter a word. At last his innate courage came to his relief, but he could say only that he had done nothing in a literary way but to tell in his own poor words what he saw and as he saw it. . . .

The fact is, Stephen was in a blue funk.

Both Bragdon and Hawkins were too modest to discuss the roles they played in the proceedings that night, however, and it is only in Noxon's account that we learn what they did and how Hawkins was the one who prevented the dinner from degenerating into an out-and-out calamity.

When Crane sat down up rose Claude Bragdon. After 31 years I can still hear the sound of his voice and see the look on his face. "I come here," he said, "to do honor to Stephen Crane, not to ridicule him. I regret to take this step, but I cannot longer remain in the room." The door was on the far side of the table. To get out, Bragdon had to walk around Taber and Crane. Hawkins stood and blocked him. "One moment," he said. "I am the oldest man in this room. I know Stephen Crane better than any one else here. I have slept with him, eaten with him, starved with him, swum with him. I know him through and through, every mood. I have taken part in all that has occurred, and he knows I love him and admire him. He knows that you all do. I have come here, like our friend, to do honor to Stephen Crane. I assure you that he feels more complimented by the spirit of this meeting than he would have been by all the solemn eulogies that could be pronounced." Crane was nodding his head off. Everybody applauded.

"I am sorry," said Bragdon, "if I have made a mistake. I ask your pardon."

"Pardon is granted you," Hawkins answered, "on one condition."

Bragdon looked up inquiringly.

"That condition," said Hawkins, "is that you turn around and take your seat."

And Bragdon did it. *

Somehow or other, the dinner plodded on to its conclusion without further incident. The next day, a journalist from the *Buffalo Evening News* who had attended the affair reported that thirty-one guests had been present "and every seat was filled." Ignoring the ruckus that had taken place at the "interesting gathering," he summarized the speeches given by Taber and Hubbard and then turned his attention to the author of *The Red Badge of Courage*, "which is exciting widespread interest just now":

Mr. Crane responded modestly and gracefully, saying he was a working newspaperman who was trying to do what he could "since he had recovered from college" with the machinery which had come into his hands—doing it sincerely, if clumsily, and simply setting forth in his own way his own impressions. The poet made a very good impression. He is a young fellow, 24, with a smooth face and a keen eye and doesn't take himself over-seriously.

---

* Years later, in a book published in 1938 (*More Lives Than One*), Bragdon revisited that night and confessed that he was the culprit who had "cowed them," although he never would have spoken out as he did if he hadn't been "a little drunk." He also understood that the dinner "was really a bit of shrewd advertising of Hubbard himself" and then, with great feeling and insight, wrote these words about the guest of honor: "Crane made a deep impression on me, though I never saw him except that once: a youth sincere and ardent, with an inward fire greater than that of other men—so great, indeed, that it was even then burning him up." The author gives thanks to the ghost of Claude Bragdon (1866–1946), whose last remark inspired the title of this book.

Always quick to pounce on its favorite target, the *New York Tribune* countered with an article of its own on the twenty-ninth in which the Philistines were denounced for supporting "the irrepressible mediocrity which insists upon affronting public intelligence though the heavens cry out for shame. We had thought the 'Philistines' would help to quench the Minor Poet. Instead they give him a dinner and sing his praises to the moon!"

However he might have suffered at that dinner, Crane never felt any resentment toward the man who had lured him up to the Genesee Hotel, and he went on publishing his work in Hubbard's magazines until the end—poems mostly, but also a number of short prose pieces—unable to turn his back on the person who declared in print, just three months after the dinner, that Stephen Crane had rescued "the fag-end of the century from literary disgrace." As for Hubbard, he continued to flourish for the next twenty years, maintaining his Roycroft empire as he churned out novels, articles, newspaper columns, and close to two hundred pamphlets, none more popular than *A Message to Garcia*, a tract on courage, devotion to duty, and honor at all costs that sold several million copies in the decades following its 1899 publication and was twice adapted into films, a silent from 1916 and a feature from 1936 starring Barbara Stanwyck and Wallace Beery, a work that sent its long tentacles so far into the future that in 1960 it was assigned to me and the other thirteen-year-olds in my eighth-grade English class by our teacher Mrs. Brown, a woman on the brink of retirement whose life surely overlapped with Crane's.

Following a visit to Europe, Hubbard died in the wreck of the *Lusitania* off the coast of Ireland in May 1915 when he, his wife, and 1,196 other people went down with the ship after it was torpedoed by a German U-boat in the second year of the First World War.

26

BACK AT HARTWOOD AFTER SPENDING CHRISTMAS IN NEW YORK, Crane sent off the manuscript of *The Third Violet* to Hitchcock on December twenty-seventh, declined an invitation to do a series of articles on Civil War battlefields for the McClure syndicate on the thirtieth, and wrote three letters on the thirty-first, one of them the "rotten work" critique of his new novel to Curtis Brown and another to Hawkins, in which he reports that he has taken to wearing corduroys again and will be shipping the overcoat back to him that night. After going on to tell him that "Hubbard and Taber think you are just the smoothest guy in the world," he asks Hawkins if he was "satisfied with the dinner," confessing that "I didn't drink much but the excitement soon turned everything into a grey haze for me and I am not sure that I came off decently," and then, having finished the letters to his two friends, he closed off the year by writing a third letter to Nellie Crouse in Akron, Ohio.

It made no sense at the time, and it continues to make no sense now. Crane had met her only once—all the way back at the beginning of the year—and he had not written a word to her in the many months that had gone by since then. She had been the most attractive woman at the tea party his friend Button had dragged him to that afternoon in early January ("Stunning figure—stunning," to repeat the words of Lucian Pontiac), and Crane had monopolized her attention the whole time he was there—in fact had talked to no one else. The flirtations of a bored young man at a boring party or the first signs of a genuine crush? By all accounts, Nellie Crouse was a "prim, thoroughly conventional young woman," a far cry from the ideal Crane had expressed to Linson on another afternoon in New York ("I don't know anything finer than the natural talk of a nice girl with brains in her head"), but if Nellie Crouse lacked brains, she most definitely had looks and possessed all the qualifications to rank as a nice girl. Young men fall fast and hard for attractive young women. That is a law of the universe, but if Crane had fallen for the good-looking girl he encountered on one of the first days of the year, why did he wait until the last day of the year before making his next move?

Several answers come to mind, but none of them is wholly convincing. It could be that the seclusion at Hartwood had begun to drive him stir-crazy. Shut off from his friends for the better part of the past two and a half months, starved for female company in his little monk's room on the second floor of Edmund's house, young Crane must have been thinking about women to the point of distraction, not only about the imaginary Grace and Splutter in his novel but about real women as well, and as he considered his chances among the various prospects parading through his head, he fixed his eyes on the face of the tea-party girl from Akron—the fairest of them all—and wondered if she might not be worth pursuing. Or, having just spent two months dwelling on the dramas of courtship in his now-completed novel, he was ready to take a stab at courtship himself, to follow the example of Billie Hawker and set his sights on a well-heeled, unattainable beauty—even at the cost of appearing to be *perfectly ridiculous*. Or (less likely), he had been thinking about Nellie Crouse every day for the past year but had held back from approaching

Nellie Crouse, 1896. (COURTESY OF SYRACUSE UNIVERSITY)

her again because he had felt he needed to enhance his credentials as a suitor before going on the attack, and now that he had earned those credentials with his recent success, he was finally in a position to make his next move. Or, still rattled by that success, still struggling to come to terms with it, and further agitated by the several commotions produced by the Philistine dinner in Buffalo, he had gone slightly bonkers and didn't know what he was doing. Whatever the reason, the seven letters he wrote to Nellie Crouse between December thirty-first and March eighteenth are both sublimely ridiculous and deeply amusing—Crane's *Guide for the Perplexed* transformed into the chronicle of a bungled romance. Round and round he goes, twisting himself into ever-tightening knots of self-conscious bluster, second guesses, apologies, apologies for the apologies, more second guesses of the apologies for the apologies, proceeding in a manner so inept and tortured that you feel sorry for him even as he makes you laugh with his mocking asides and rhetorical somersaults, writing his head off in a storm of chatterboxing brilliance until the sham, one-way courtship runs aground against the shoals of inanity. He had conjured a figment, an invented girl who could have been better used as a secondary character in *The Third Violet*, and once he understood that she was too dense to understand a fraction of what he was saying to her, it was as if he were writing to himself, chewing off his own ear as he yelled into the void, and then, after charming her and flattering her and making every effort to crack through her doltish impenetrability, she turned him away and he gave up, no doubt disgusted with himself, but also in a dark place, a hole of pure despond—at least for a time—and then he crawled out of it and moved on.

But how brightly it all began, with a nutty, jocular letter that set the tone for what was to follow as the nervous suitor launched his campaign by presenting her with a batch of press clippings about the Philistine dinner on the nineteenth (his new credentials—which would have bulked up the envelope, signifying Important Material Contained Within) and commenting on them in the two opening paragraphs with self-deprecating nonchalance, which in turn would prove that he was such a big man now that he could make fun of his own bigness. Not a bad strategy, perhaps, but nevertheless a strategy, for at this point he didn't know where he stood with her and was obliged to mask his true intentions. Then comes the weird third paragraph, which tentatively begins to allude to his purpose with this arch and stilted disavowal: "I do not suppose you will be overwhelmed with distinction when I tell you that your name is surrounded with much sentiment for me." In other words: I like you, but why should you care that I like you, and how on earth would it do you any good to know that I like you? Immediately after that, he begins to tell a story:

> I was in southern Mexico last winter for a sufficient time to have my face turn the color of a brick side-walk. There was nothing American about me save a large Smith and Wesson revolver and I saw only Indians whom I suspected of loading their tamales with dog. In this state of mind and this physical condition, I arrived in the city of Puebla and there, I saw an American girl . . .

We should remember that he was trying to impress the daughter of rich society people from a small city in the provinces, a virgin princess who dressed in fine clothes and lived within the protective cocoon of her family's wealth, and here was Crane strutting around in his first letter with a sunburned face and a six-shooter on his hip looking positively un-American as he prepares to chow down with his Indian friends on dogmeat tamales. Would Miss Crouse know enough to detect the humor in his portrait of southern Mexico or would she be repelled by his tough-guy swagger and the barbarous eating habits of the natives? Crane would find out if and when she bothered to answer him, but for now he calmly went on with his tale of the American girl in Puebla, whom he saw just four times in all—once in the hotel corridor and three times in the street—and with whom he never exchanged a word, but the sight of that American girl "in a new spring gown" nearly caused him "to drop dead," and so he ran to the railroad office and promptly bought a ticket for the next train to New York. Or so he says. But why is he saying it? Because the girl "resembled you," he writes, and because of that she wasn't an individual to him but a symbol, "and I have always thought of you with gratitude for the peculiar thrill you gave me in the town of Puebla, Mexico," never explaining why he didn't think to write her about it on the trip home or immediately after his return, nor, for that matter, ever explaining what he meant by the word *thrill*. The thrill of seeing an American girl who resembled her—which propelled him to rush back to America—or the thrill, quite simply, of seeing a girl who resembled her, whether he remained in Mexico or not? The jury is still deadlocked.

Having said nearly all he has to say, Crane closes off with two more startling leaps in the final paragraph, abruptly changing the subject to write three of the best-known sentences from his correspondence—"The lives of some people are one long apology. Mine was, once, but not now. I go through the world unexplained, I suppose"—and then, fearing that his letter will be taken as "an incomparable insolence," he hopes that she will not be angry and asks—out of the blue, apropos of precisely nothing—if she knows where their mutual friend Button can be found, pretending that this was his reason for writing to her all along. "I lost him almost a year ago and have never been able to discover him. I suppose it is his size [Button was an extremely small person]. He could so easily be overlooked in a crowd." Then he signs off: "Yours sincerely/Stephen Crane."

It was a strange, almost nonsensical performance, but he got what he wanted from it—a reply—and so their correspondence began, with Crane the unexplained promising to explain himself only to her, to share his work only with her and sending along a copy of "A Grey Sleeve" ("not in any sense a good story") to prove it, confessing that he used Button's whereabouts merely as a pretext to write to her, and then (all this just in his second letter) springing into an absurd, convoluted song and dance about wanting to go to Arizona to study the Apaches because "a man in Boston was unwise enough to ask me to write a play for his theatre and

I wish to have some Apaches in it," which is no more than a preamble to inform her that if he does go to Arizona he intends to travel west "on the Erie," which he distinctly remembers makes a stop at Akron, and even if he doesn't go to Arizona, he will surely go to Buffalo, "and if you will please tell me that Akron is not far from Buffalo, I will make an afternoon—or possibly evening—call on you. Sure." Not sure, of course, but he had finally owned up to his intentions, and a face-to-face meeting was uppermost in his thoughts—as a first step to whatever might or might not happen between them, which at that point, of course, was not at all sure.

Crouse's letters have been lost, but it isn't hard to guess what she wrote from Crane's answers to her, since he tends to use her remarks to jump off into his long, meandering responses, which inevitably have as much to do with himself as they do with her. When he isn't yattering on with high-flown, disingenuous homilies about the meaning of life, he is doing everything he can to accommodate her, bending over backward to present himself as a soul mate so perfectly in harmony with her that he can feel her smallest fluctuation of mood as if it were his own, as when he opens a letter by saying, "How dreadfully weary of everything you are" and then proceeds to tell her that, for his own part, "I am minded to die in my thirty-fifth year" because life "doesn't strike me as particularly worth the trouble" or to ingratiate himself with her by dispelling her potential misgivings about him, as when he replies to her teasing complaint "of being aghast at being left alone with such a clever person" by saying, "I am often marvelously a blockhead and incomparably an idiot. I reach depths of stupidity of which most people cannot dream." Anything to show what a good-hearted, sympathetic fellow he is, and again and again through the bulk of the correspondence we see him trying on different masks, feverishly looking for the one that would allow him to embody the form of manhood that would make the most favorable impression on her, nowhere more ludicrously than when he decides to portray himself as "an intensely practical and experienced person, in fear you might confuse the word 'poet' with various kinds of crazy sentiment." He must have imagined her father to be that sort of practical person, and why not try to emulate a man who had served as a foot soldier in the Civil War and had worked his way through the ranks of American business to become one of the principal backers of the Goodyear Rubber Company and the Diamond Match Company and who knows how many other companies, but it turned out that Crouse wasn't interested in a man who resembled her father, she was more disposed to prefer "the man of fashion," and so

Crane, the self-described "shaggy barbarian," would convert himself into a man of fashion for her sake—and watch him squirm as he struggles to reconcile himself to the thing he most despises in the world, again and again putting his foot in his mouth until he finally takes it out and then shoots himself in the other foot.

> Your recent confession that in your heart you like the man of fashion more than you do some other kinds of men came nearer to my own view than perhaps you expected. . . . For my part, I like the man who dresses correctly and does the right thing invariably but, oh, he must be more than that, a great deal more. But so seldom is he anything more than correctly-dressed and correctly-speeched, that when I see a man of that kind I usually put him down as a kind of idiot. Still, as I have said, there are exceptions. There are men of very social habits who nevertheless know how to stand steady when they see cocked revolvers and death comes down and sits on the back of a chair and waits. There are men of very social habits who know good music from bad, good poetry from bad—(a few of 'em)—good drama from bad—(a very few of 'em)—good painting from bad. There are very many of them who know good claret and good poker-playing. There are a few who can treat a woman tenderly not only when they feel amiable but when she most needs tender-treatment. There are many who can ride, swim, shoot, sail a boat, a great many. There are an infinitesimal number who can keep from yapping in a personal way about women. There are a large number who refuse to haggle over a question of money. There are one or two who invariably mind their own business. There are some who know how to be frank without butchering the feelings of their friends. . . .
>
> I swear by the real aristocrat . . . one who will stand the strain whatever it may be. He is like a thorough-bred horse. His nerves may be high and he will do a lot of jumping often but in the crises he settles down and becomes the most reliable and enduring of created things.
>
> For the hordes who hang upon the out-skirts of good society and chant 143 masses per day to the social gods and think because they have money they are well-bred—for such people I have a scorn which is very deep and very intense. . . . In Hartwood I have a great chance to study the new-rich. The Hartwood Club-house is only three miles away and there are some of the new rich in it. May the Lord deliver me from having social aspirations.

That was the sixth letter, written on February eleventh, the sixth letter he had sent to her in about as many weeks, but eighteen days went by before he sat down to write the seventh and shortest one, which he didn't quite manage to finish, and then he let another seventeen days go by before he picked up his pen and wrote the last paragraph of his last letter to the invisible Nellie Crouse. It is difficult to know why he went to the trouble of buying a stamp and mailing it to her, since she had already dropped him for someone else by then, but perhaps he wanted to have the last word, and after so much playacting and buffoonery in the run-up to the end, the last word was surprisingly bitter.

The final two paragraphs from that final letter, separated by a distance of two and a half weeks—

March 1: Dear me, how much am I getting to admire graveyards—the calm unfretting unhopeing end of things—serene absence of passion— oblivious to sin—ignorant of the accursed golden hopes that flame at night and make a man run his legs off and then in the daylight of experience turn out to be ingenious traps for the imagination. If there is a joy in living I cant find it. The future? The future is blue with obligations— new trials—conflicts. It was a rare old wine the gods brewed for mortals. Flagons of despair—

March 18: Really, by this time I should have recovered enough to be able to write you a sane letter, but I cannot—my pen is dead. I am simply a man struggling with a life that is no more than a mouthful of dust to him.

He had made a fool of himself, but no more than most of us do when we are young, especially when we are chasing after love and have no idea how to go about it. If nothing else, Crane seems to have learned his lesson, and after that disappointment in the early months of 1896, he abandoned his pursuit of nice girls and girls with money and girls he had met only once at tea parties and all the other apparitions who were no more than reveries of girls who lived only in his head. He would commit a number of other mistakes with women in the future, but not that mistake, not that one ever again.

The following year (June 1897), Nellie Crouse married a Harvard graduate named Samuel E. Carpenter and moved with him to Ridgefield, Connecticut. They had six children (two of whom did not survive infancy) and were divorced in 1914. She relinquished custody of the children to her ex-husband's family in Philadelphia, lived in Paris for an unspecified length of time, and then moved to Philadelphia herself, where she died in 1943.

27

THE FAILED EPISTOLARY ROMANCE WITH CROUSE WAS ONLY ONE OF Crane's problems as the new year began. Still at loose ends, and more broke than ever after earning no money throughout the writing of his novel, he allowed himself to be talked into pursuing several ill-advised projects that ultimately came to nothing—and also to make one serious error of artistic judgment. That was in January, when he met with Hitchcock at the Appleton offices and agreed to the plan of issuing a new edition of *Maggie*—in a toned-down, expurgated, and more "acceptable" version. A dangerous proposition on several fronts, it seems to me, and even if one chooses to ignore my entrenched conviction that writers should never, *never under any circumstances*, tamper with their old work, at least four other objections remain. One: S.C. was three years removed from the original publication of the book, and in those three years he had come so far as a writer that he was no longer in a position to judge what his younger self had produced. Two: To pacify the rebellion of the original would negate the reason for having written the book, and Crane, who had fought so hard to preserve the anarchy and "ethical sense" of his poems—even if it meant withdrawing the manuscript from Copeland and Day and never publishing *The Black Riders*—had now capitulated to Appleton's demands and was willing to go along with "a nice little volume by Stephen Crane"—and in so doing betray himself and his work. It was entirely within his power to say no to them or even to insist on republishing the novel with no changes except for correcting misspelled words and typographical errors, and if Appleton refused, he could have taken it elsewhere. What had happened to the bold and uncompromising young hellcat? My suspicion is that he was afraid—even more afraid than he let on to Howells after returning from his trip to New York, where the plan for the new *Maggie* had been put in motion—and I would contend that this fear was one more by-product of his sudden, unexpected rise in the world, his so-called success, which was still so new to him, and therefore still so unsettling, that he had temporarily lost track of himself and didn't quite know who he was anymore. And so, instead of standing up for himself, he flinched. Three: It was a waste of his time. He had better things to do than revisit an old book he no longer seemed to believe in, and why go back to it when the only plausible step for him was to keep moving forward? Four: The project was doomed to fail, and in the end it did fail. Whose delicate sensibilities would be protected by going through the pointless exercise of changing every *hell* and *damn* to *h—l* and *d—n*? And what aesthetic purpose would be achieved by butchering the magnificent seventeenth chapter and eliminating the last two men Maggie encounters on the night of her death? The remake was a disaster, and the proof of how bad it was lies in the judgment of history: The 1896 edition was discarded long ago, and for many decades now the only version available in print has been the original *Maggie* as it was published in 1893.

The job of defanging the wild beast he had created as a twenty- and twenty-one-year-old beginner took about two months. At first, Crane seemed optimistic about the enterprise and wrote to Hitchcock on February second that "I am very glad to hear you speak as you do about *Maggie*. I will set to work this month rewriting it." Two or three days later he reported that "I have dispensed with a goodly number of damns," and on the tenth that "I have carefully plugged at the words that hurt," leaving no doubt that he was a willing accomplice in the "nicification" of his book. One week later, however, he sent a copy of *The Black Riders* to his English publisher, William Heinemann, and in the letter that accompanied it he mentioned the coming reprint: "*Maggie* was born into a world of enemies three years ago but I have toned it down somewhat at the request of the Appletons. . . . For my own part, I hate the book." After what must have been a lull in his progress (from apathy? from disgust?), he assured Hitchcock on March twenty-third that "I will begin to drive Maggie forward," but on April second, with the job now finished and the galleys lying in front of him, he wrote to his editor that "the proofs make me ill. Let somebody go over them—if you think best—and watch for bad grammatical form & bad spelling. I am too jaded with Maggie to be able to see it." He also told Hitchcock that he was "engaged in the preface," but chances are that he crumpled it up and threw it away, for when the altered version of *Maggie* was published by Appleton in early June—two days before Edward Arnold's publication of *George's Mother*—there was no preface in the book, and all traces of whatever Crane might or might not have started to write about his first novella have disappeared. The reader is left to draw his or her own conclusions.

Even more dangerous was the decision to allow S. S. McClure back into his life. After two miserable episodes with him in the past—the six-month ordeal of waiting for a response to *Red Badge* and the harsh amputations administered to the coal mine report—one would think that he had had

enough of the man to keep him at a safe distance, but as Crane continued his lurching advance toward adulthood, he was proving himself to be
one of those rare people who find it impossible to hold a grudge. He had
forgiven the rascal Hubbard for mocking his poems and taking advantage
of him with the Philistine dinner, and now, when the bigger and more
cunning rascal McClure approached him with various proposals for work,
Crane was willing to forget the past and listen. Needless to say, McClure
was hoping to cash in on the boy's new celebrity, and needless to say the
boy was aware of that, but the boy also needed money, and if the rascal
could deliver, why not bury the hatchet and give him another chance?
Crane was a much-solicited figure now, but mostly he was being asked to
join clubs and societies and to give interviews to newspapers and magazines, and McClure was the only one who came to him with dollars on his
mind—and an opportunity for Crane to replenish his empty purse.

The first documented overture came from McClure's partner, John
Phillips, with the proposal to visit Civil War battlefields for a series of
syndicated articles—which Crane turned down in his letter from December thirtieth, begging off because he was too busy with other work—but it
seems that he had already been approached by McClure sometime before
that with a proposal to publish new stories about the Civil War, and with
"A Grey Sleeve" and "A Mystery of Heroism" already behind him, Crane
plunged in and started another. As early as January seventh, he told Hawkins that "I am writing a story—'The Little Regiment'—for McClure. It
is awfully hard. I have invented the sum of my invention in regard to war
and this story keeps me in eternal despair. However I am coming on with
it very comfortably after all." So comfortably that he traveled down to
northern Virginia about a week later for a long look at the site of the Battle of Fredericksburg to research the setting of his story in progress, and
after he finished "The Little Regiment," he wrote three other war stories
in fairly rapid succession, making for a total of six, which turned out to
be long enough to gather into a volume of stories that Appleton hustled
to press and released in November under the title *The Little Regiment and
Other Episodes of the American Civil War*. Crane's distinguished publisher
was no less eager than McClure to cash in on the spoils of *Red Badge*, so
war trumped love and the stories appeared in book form six months in
advance of *The Third Violet*, which was syndicated in serialized fragments
that same fall by none other than . . . McClure.

Another one of McClure's proposals turned into a time-wasting dud. The
offer to publish new war stories from Crane had worked out well because,
without quite knowing it himself, Crane had wanted to return to the sub-

ject of war. To write a novel about national politics, on the other hand, was
something that had never occurred to him, yet when McClure presented
him with the tantalizing offer of financing a trip to Washington in order to
research a prospective novel about politicians and politics, Crane thought
there might be something to the idea and journeyed down to the capital to
see what he could see and learn what he could learn before committing himself to the project. His willingness to go was one more sign of how confused
and destabilized he was during those months, for Crane was a writer who
wrote from the inside out—not the other way around—and no amount of
research was ever going to ignite the inner spark he needed to hurl himself
into a new novel. He had already come up with the idea of *Maggie* before
he started prowling the slums for more details to work into his story, and
he had already conceived the plan for *The Red Badge of Courage* before he
settled down to his historical investigations of the Civil War. In the case
of *The Third Violet*, nearly everything had come directly from his own life.
Now he was proposing to work from the outside in, and the only thing that
came of it was a long visit to Washington that lasted from early March to
April second in the pleasant surroundings of the Cosmos Club, where he
worked on his war stories and wrote a number of striking letters, among
them the "mouthful of dust" conclusion to his romance with Crouse, the
nasty threat to Hitchcock during their contretemps over *George's Mother*,
and the spirited, self-teasing remarks to Viola Allen about being "such an
ass—such a pure complete ass" while they were at school together. The novel
about Washington, however, the thing that had brought him to Washington
in the first place, crashed into a brick wall. Fortunately, he was intelligent
enough to recognize when he was defeated, and after writing to Hitchcock
as late as March twenty-third that he was "gradually learning things" and
had already visited "a number of senatorial interiors," he wrote again just a
week later to tell Hitchcock that he was giving up: "You may see me back in
New York for good by the end of this week. These men pose so hard that it
would take a double-barreled shotgun to disclose their inner feelings and I
despair of knowing them." One day after that (March thirty-first), he wrote
to Hawkins and simply said: "Washington pains me."

Underneath these misfires and errors of judgment was the question of
money, the fundamental problem of how to earn a steady enough income
to sustain himself without running into blank periods that would threaten
him with belt-tightening shortfalls and, even worse, lapses into the poverty
that had marked his early years in New York. There was no question that
Crane's work was in demand now, that he could count on publishing nearly

everything he wrote, but the fees paid by newspapers and magazines were small, thirty dollars here, twenty-five dollars there, occasionally as much as fifty or seventy-five, but even the serialization of a full-length novel such as *The Third Violet* brought in only one hundred and fifty. As Crane struggled to find a new equilibrium in this disorienting moment of transition, he was not only battling to adjust to his new inner circumstances but looking for a way to organize his economic future, and with no one to give him advice, and with his own less than cautious impulses often clouding his decisions, he found himself being suckered into arrangements that looked good on the surface but ultimately worked to his disadvantage, diminishing his income rather than increasing it, which threw him into the conundrum of having to do more and more in order to earn less and less. One such arrangement was the bargain he struck with McClure, who capitalized on Crane's anxieties about not having enough ready cash on hand by offering to put him on a sort of retainer, in other words, paying him in advance for work not yet written, so that when Crane turned in a piece to him, McClure did not give him cash for the work but merely credited it to his account—while taking a commission for the service he had provided. Early on, Crane seemed to sense the potential difficulties that lay ahead of him when he wrote to McClure on January twenty-seventh: "I think the agreement with you is a good thing. I am perfectly satisfied with my end of it but your end somewhat worries me for I am often inexpressibly dull and uncreative and those periods often last for days." Only *days*. But what if one of those periods lasted for two weeks or a month—or even longer? By August, Crane understood that he was effectively in servitude to his purported benefactor, and in his frustration he turned elsewhere, entering into an agreement with Paul Revere Reynolds, America's first literary agent, to sell one of his recent stories (which happened to be one of his best, "A Man and Some Others") for what he hoped would be as much as $350, concluding a letter he wrote to him on September ninth with these words of caution: "Don't go to Bacheller or McClure."*

But placing his work in newspapers and magazines was only part of the story, and if Crane intended to earn his living exclusively from his writing, he needed to have conscientious, dedicated book publishers as well, and not

---

* Reynolds (1864–1944) opened his agency in 1893, and over the years his clients included H. G. Wells, Edith Wharton, Jack London, George Bernard Shaw, Willa Cather, Paul Lawrence Dunbar, Joseph Conrad, Émile Zola, and Leo Tolstoy. Although Crane mentions Bacheller and McClure in the same sentence, his relationships with the two men were quite different. Bacheller, who had always treated Crane kindly and fairly, was not in a position to pay such an exalted sum as $350, whereas Crane felt trapped with McClure and needed help in circumventing the bad agreement he had made with him.

only did he have to be paid fairly by those publishers, it was essential that he maintain good relations with them. Since he had self-published *Maggie* and then published the five-hundred-copy edition of *The Black Riders* with the small Boston firm of Copeland and Day, the move to D. Appleton & Company in New York was his first experience with a large, commercial house. Founded in 1831, Appleton was a venerable name in American publishing, with a list of authors that included Lewis Carroll, Charles Darwin, Rudyard Kipling, Thomas Huxley, and Henry James—to mention just a few—and the man who served as his editor there, Ripley Hitchcock, was both highly intelligent and tough, a Harvard-educated art historian on the one hand and, on the other, a diligent literary adviser who understood that publishing was a business and that his job was to ensure that Appleton remained a profitable concern. He and Crane mostly got along, but there were tensions between them from time to time as well, none worse than when Crane succumbed to the pressure of a former Claverack classmate who worked as the American representative of the Anglo-American firm Edward Arnold and handed him the manuscript of *George's Mother* without bothering to inform Hitchcock. That led to Crane's hostile, uncharacteristically threatening letter of March twenty-sixth, a conflict that in all likelihood was defused when Hitchcock made the mollifying gesture of increasing Crane's royalties from ten to fifteen percent, but the problem flared up again that summer, as Crane scholar J. C. Levenson reports:

> Evidently the change from 10 to 15 percent was made about this time [early spring], for Crane's next letters to Hitchcock were tranquil businesslike communications. But when Arnold, having lost out on *Maggie*, tried to get the English rights to later works and thus undo Appleton's arrangement with Heinemann, the old problem came to a head. The matter was cleared up when Crane wrote, not to Hitchcock, but to Mr. Appleton himself [July 6]: "I have written to Arnold that your arrangement with Heinemann concerning The Little Regiment and The Third Violet must stand—that it was a prior and just contract and that I intend to see that Heinemann's rights in the books shall be guarded." This letter, written on Appleton stationery and bearing a date filled in by someone other than Crane, bears the marks of having been done in the Appleton office with Hitchcock standing over Crane's shoulder and breathing some strong words on the meaning of legal obligation.

The dressing-down must have been hard on him, but the truth was that he deserved it, and once the letter was put in Appleton's hands, the matter seems to have been settled. At least for now, and at least with Hitchcock, but after publishing three more books with him in the space of a year (the new *Maggie*, *The Little Regiment*, and *The Third Violet*), Crane wandered off to other publishers—and to more bumps in the road ahead.

How innocent it looks in retrospect to invoke the letter he wrote to Hitchcock in early February, asking for a one-hundred-dollar advance against royalties to buy a "saddle horse" he had set his heart on, and when Hitchcock came through with the money, Crane thanked him for his "prompt sympathy" and added, "It is a luxury to feel that some of my pleasures are due to my little pen." The horse's owner was Elbert Hubbard, and Crane had seen the young gelding on his trip to Buffalo and East Aurora in December, but rather than stand firm on a price of one hundred dollars, Hubbard was flexible enough to let the horse go for sixty. One wonders how Crane spent the extra forty he had pocketed from Hitchcock—how many cigarettes smoked, how many meals consumed, how many nighttime excursions to the back of beyond?

Renamed Peanuts by his new owner, the animal was transported to Hartwood in the spring of 1896 and spent the rest of his life there, outlasting the man who had bought him by many years.

28

AFTER CRANE RETURNED FROM WASHINGTON, HE MOVED BACK INTO the apartment he shared with Post Wheeler on West Twenty-third Street, and before long he was writing about New York City again, picking up where he had left off prior to his travels through the West and Mexico. He had thought he would be working on his now-defunct political novel, and with no plans to embark on any other major project in the foreseeable future, he split his time over the next several months between short story writing and journalism. Not a lot of journalism, but enough to bring in some money, and the articles he produced were good ones, five in all between mid-May and mid-August, each one syndicated by McClure (under Crane's copyright) and covering such varied topics as roof-garden restaurants, a day in the life of a Broadway cable car, and the fad for high-speed bicycle sprints that had caught on among athletic young men and bloomer-clad young women who made a sport of wheeling their way past pursuing cops down "the Western Boulevard" (Fifty-ninth Street) between Columbus Circle and the river. All sharply written, all little jewels of close observation and humor, but the one that stands out and goes deepest, that explores an aspect of New

York life that was all but invisible to the rest of the world, is the first one, a six-page article that appeared on May seventeenth under the headline "Opium's Varied Dreams."

It could be that McClure had assigned him to work on the story, but it seems more likely that Crane suggested it himself. He was back in New York after an absence of several months, and for all his growing disenchantment with the city, it was still a source of fascination to him. Especially the poor and the marginalized, the fallen ones, the ones who had been cast out and driven underground, and as a veteran nighthawk and chronicler of flophouses and slum saloons, he now turned his eyes on the subterranean fraternity of opium addicts, some twenty-five thousand strong by his reckoning, concentrated in two separate areas of Manhattan—Chinatown, where it all began, and the Tenderloin, with its population of "cheap actors, race track touts, gamblers and the different kinds of confidence men."

In that era of yellow-press sensationalism, Crane handles his sensational subject with solemn detachment, as if presenting a scientific report to a room filled with doctors and sociologists. His language is dry and circumspect, devoid of personal commentary or rhetorical flourish, and he provides no specific cases (no stories) to advance his argument, preferring instead to give a general overview of the phenomenon as he understands it. No, he says in the first paragraph, the opium habit is not confined exclusively to the Chinese and the majority of smokers are in fact white men and white women. Until the police crackdowns of recent years, there were splendid "joints" scattered throughout the city, opulent enough to be considered "palatial if not for the bad taste of the decorations," but now "opium [has] retired to private flats." The first trial is often unpleasant, he says, with the room and everything in it whirling "like the insides of an electric light plant," followed by "a thirst, a great thirst," but if the beginner chooses to try again, "Gradually, the power of the drug sinks into his heart. It absorbs his thought. He begins to lie with more and more grace to cover the shortcomings and little failures of his life. And then finally he may become a full-fledged 'pipe fiend,' a man with a 'yen-yen.'" At that point, he explains, the newly addicted person will learn how to prepare the opium himself—how to "cook it"—which is a delicate operation that involves rolling "the pill" and heating it over a small lamp, and "when a man can cook for himself and buys his own 'layout,' he is gone, probably. He has placed upon his shoulders an elephant which he may carry to the edge of forever." Crane then goes on to give a long, meticulous account of the cooking procedure, beginning with the pipe itself and its clay bowl, bamboo stem, and ivory mouthpiece (which bears no resemblance to the popular conception of the opium pipe as portrayed in newspaper drawings) and then moving on to the role of the "yen-hock," which he describes as "a sort of sharpened darning needle," a multipurpose instrument used to spear the opium from its box and then hold it over the flame until it achieves the consistency of "boiling molasses" as the thumb and forefinger of the other hand work it into the proper shape, at which point the pill is transferred to the bowl of the pipe and then further manipulated by the yen-hock "until it is a little button-like thing with a hole in the centre fitting squarely over the hole in the bowl."

After that exacting inventory of the mechanics of opium consumption, Crane turns his attention to the smokers themselves, who always gather in small groups, passing around a single pipe from one to the other as the cook prepares a new bowl for each smoker, and because of the quiet intimacy of the closely huddled participants, Crane is led to offer an unlikely but apt comparison between "a group of men about a midnight camp-fire in a forest and a group of smokers about a layout tray with its tiny light . . . [for] just as the lazy eyes about a camp-fire fasten themselves dreamfully upon the blaze of logs so do the lazy eyes about an opium layout fasten themselves upon the little yellow flame." In both cases, there is the camaraderie of the group, but at the same time the isolation of each member of the group from all the others. Alone together, as it were, or together and yet alone as each man sinks into his own thoughts and drifts away from his comrades, transfixed by the light in front of him.

It is only in the last two paragraphs that Crane returns to the individual smoker and finally addresses the problem of addiction, but those paragraphs are so strong that they overwhelm the nineteen others that come before them, ambushing the reader with their frankness and unbiased understanding of the lure drugs represent. Dispassionate, wholly free of moral judgments, Crane's words transmit a deep sensitivity to the psychological vortex that traps the user in an endless, spinning dance of desperation and transcendent release from the pain of being alive: the mind and body engaged in a constant war with each other until the body finally wins.

If a beginner expects to have dreams of an earth dotted with white porcelain towers and a sky of green silk, he will, from all accounts, be much mistaken. "The Opium Smoker's Dream" seems to be mostly a mistake. The influence of "dope" is evidently a fine languor, a complete mental rest. The problems of life no longer appear. Existence is peace. The virtues of a man's friends, for instance, loom beautifully against his own sudden perfection. The universe is re-adjusted. Wrong departs, injustice vanishes; there is nothing but a quiet, a soothing harmony of all things—until the next morning.

And who should invade this momentary land of rest, this dream country, if not the people of the Tenderloin, they who are at once supersensitive and hopeless, the people who think more upon death and the mysteries of life, the chances of the hereafter, than any other class, educated or uneducated. Opium holds out to them its lie, and they embrace it eagerly, expecting to find a definition of peace, but they awake to find the formidable labors of life more formidable. And if the pipe should happen to ruin their lives they cling more closely to it because then it stands between them and thought.

It is useless to ask whether Crane tried opium himself or not. Given how he had prepared himself to write some of his other New York pieces—living as a bum in order to write about the bums in "An Experiment in Misery," for example—I would say probably yes, but there is nothing on record to confirm my suspicion, and no one knows how he came to write the article, nor why he wrote it, nor what kind of research he did beforehand. It would matter to us now only if Crane had become an opium addict himself, which he didn't, and therefore it shouldn't, but nevertheless it does for this simple, gruesome reason: Sometime during his work on the article, he procured an opium layout (again, no one knows how or why), and after the article was finished, he mounted the layout on a wall in his apartment as a souvenir, something he was wont to do with objects that appealed to him (the plaques of Mozart and Beethoven, the spurs from Mexico), but some months later, when Theodore Roosevelt and the New York Police Department turned against him for testifying against one of their own in the Dora Clark trial, they ransacked the apartment, found the layout, and used it to charge him with running an opium den—one more piece of damning evidence that helped drive him from the city and then kept him moving until he was clear across the ocean. In the mind of the New York police, he had become a man with an X on his back.

With all that looming in the near but still-distant future, Crane blithely went about his business, working on his stories and articles, frequenting the Lantern Club, attending literary dinners where he was often the object of warm, laudatory toasts from his fellow writers, accepting membership in the Authors Club after being recommended by Howells, and bit by bit coming back to his senses after the shock of *Red Badge*, although by no means fully restored and with no particular plans in front of him.

The new *Maggie* and *George's Mother* were published almost simultaneously in early June. However badly he had compromised his book, it was still
more or less the same book as the original, enough the same in any event
to provoke the same response an exact reprint of the original would have
caused, and many of the reviews were predictably negative. Ever reliable in
its disdain for him, the *New York Tribune* lashed into the novella with an
assault of such vituperation and disgust that it achieved the ridiculousness
of high (or low) comedy: "He puts on paper the grossness and brutality which are commonly encountered only through contact with the most
besotted classes. . . . He has no charm of style, no touch of humor, no hint of
imagination. . . . The book shocks by the mere fact of its monotony and stupid
roughness. To read its pages is like standing before a loafer to be sworn at
and have one's face slapped twice a minute for half an hour."

Other reviewers, not understanding that *Maggie* was an early work, saw
it as a sign of disintegrating talent and regression, and still others were
bored, hostile, or indifferent to the book's language and lowlife setting, but
then there were those who found it good, even exceptional, with the *New
York Times* calling *Maggie* a book written by "the hand of an artist" and
praising the author as "a master of slum slang." More strong responses came
in after that from other quarters, and before long the equally maligned
George's Mother was drawing its fair share of positive notices as well, so that
in the end the overall response to Crane's two-pronged book launch can be
qualified as a resounding *perhaps*. Then, just as the noise was beginning to
die down, out came Howells's three-thousand-word essay on both novellas
in the *World* on July twenty-sixth, and all the short reviews that had been
published so far, the good as well as the bad, suddenly disappeared from
memory—as if they had never been written.

"He's a good boy," Howells said about Crane in a letter to Hamlin
Garland written just a few days before the article came out, a good boy
"with lots of outcome," he added, meaning that Crane's work was not
only good but limitless in its potential, and in spite of Howells's disgruntled response to *Red Badge* and what he called S.C.'s *prose poems*, his new
essay was unreserved in its admiration for the two short novels and, alone
among critics of the time, he was able to situate them in their proper—and
broader—historical context.

> There is a curious unity in the spirit of the arts; and I think that what
> strikes me most in the story of *Maggie* is that quality of fatal necessity
> which dominates Greek tragedy. From the conditions it all had to be,
> and there were the conditions. . . . Another effect is that of an ideal of

artistic beauty which is present in the working out of this poor girl's squalid romance as in any classic fable. This will be foolishness, I know, to the foolish people who cannot discriminate between the material and the treatment in art [the subject and the style], and who think that beauty is inseparable from daintiness and prettiness, but I do not speak to them. I appeal rather to such as feel themselves akin with every kind of human creature, and find neither high nor low when it is a question of inevitable suffering, or of a soul struggling vainly with an inexorable fate.

About *George's Mother*, which Howells told Garland was his wife's favorite among Crane's books, "the best of all," he remarked that "The wonder of it is the courage which deals with persons so absolutely average, and the art that graces them with the beauty of the author's compassion for everything that errs and suffers."

Crane was off on another one of his summer jaunts with Senger and company in the Pennsylvania woods, which prevented him from reading the article until after he returned. From his letter to Howells on August fifteenth: "It is of course the best word that has been said of me and I am grateful in a way that is hard for me to say. In truth you have always been so generous with me that grace departs from my pen when I attempt to tell you of my appreciation."

In the same letter he also talks about his admiration for Abraham Cahan, whose recently published *Yekl* was given several paragraphs in Howells's article for the *World*, which led to the meeting between Crane and Cahan at Howells's cottage in Far Rockaway, a subsequent one-on-one dinner not long after, and finally to an event at the Lantern Club on September twenty-second honoring Garland, Crane, and Cahan "as three young exponents of so-called realism in fiction" (*New York Press*), where Cahan talked about his dreams of becoming a writer as a young man in Russia and Crane read the manuscript of a new story, which, needless to say, "was duly criticized" by the audience, as per the regulations of the club.

A week before Howells's article was published, a two-column profile of Crane appeared on the "Literary Den" page of the *Illustrated American*, written by a young man named Herbert P. Williams, who had been promoted to the job of literary editor at the *Boston Herald* just one year earlier. The piece is unusual because Crane allowed Williams into his apartment (a rare if not unprecedented invitation to a journalist), which gives us a chance to see his private world and understand something about how he lived in that enormous room at the top of a house near the heart of the city, in the shopping district. The furniture of the room is curiously typical of the man: a tinted wall is relieved at intervals by war trophies and by impressionistic landscapes.... The small bookshelf contains batches of gray manuscript and potential literature in the form of stationery. One of the two chairs stands between the windows and the writing table at which a club might dine. An ink-bottle, a pen and a pad of paper occupy dots in the vast green expanse. A sofa stretches itself near the window and tries to fill the space. No crowded comfort is here—no luxury of ornament—no literature, classical or periodical; nothing but the man and his mind.

Describing Crane as "frank, open, natural, and completely devoid of affectation," Williams then manages to extract from him a sentence that strikes me as the most eloquent description he ever gave of the inner work that was necessary before he could move on to the actual work of writing. "His method, he told me, is to get away by himself and think over things. 'Then comes a longing for you don't know what; sorrow, too, and heart-hunger.' He mixes it all up. Then he begins to write."

Heart-hunger.

A blind plunge into the self, a search for something that cannot be named—that must not be named—and then the slow work of pulling the words up and out and onto the page, where the words that once belonged to you now belong to others. Crane was still just twenty-four when he spoke to Williams, but he had been living in words for many years by then, and he understood that the solution to the mystery of how art gets made is itself the ultimate mystery.

29

TREADING WATER FOR A TIME, THEN BEGINNING TO MAKE PROGRESS, and as the year ticked on his production continued to grow until he was working at a pace that rivaled the frenzied output of 1894. On top of the articles for McClure, he wrote some new poems and published close to a dozen short fictions of two, three, and four pages in a wide spectrum of tones and styles (chiefly with Bacheller's syndicate), but his most important works from 1896 are two Civil War stories ("The Veteran," which was included in *The Little Regiment* volume, and a four-and-a-half-page masterpiece, "An Episode of War," which was not) along with two adventure stories written at Hartwood during the summer, "The Five White Mice" (set in Mexico City) and "A Man and Some Others" (set in southwestern

Texas). He wrote some other Western and Mexican stories that year as well, all of them good or at least interesting, but those two are the best ones, and each deserves a bronze plaque in the Crane pantheon of most memorable works. The same holds true of "A Mystery of Heroism" and the two other war stories from 1896, but the remaining four in *The Little Regiment*—"A Grey Sleeve," "Three Miraculous Soldiers," "An Indiana Campaign," and the title story—do not measure up to the greatness of the best ones. They are eminently readable and skillfully done, but with so many dozens of small and large pieces cramming the ten volumes of Crane's collected works, I have to be selective in what I write about, or else we'll all be here until the cows come home.*

"The Veteran" stands apart from Crane's other works as both a curiosity and an exorcism—a story written in response to another story that is at once a sequel and an act of destruction. Henry Fleming is brought back, is given a chance to live again for a few pages, and then Crane kills him off in a brutal, symbolic murder that seems to have been committed in the hope of putting an end to the drama of the "accursed *Red Badge*."

Fleming is old now, old enough to be the grandfather of at least one grandchild, and on the first page of "The Veteran" he is referred to as "old" no fewer than five times, but if Crane has set his story in the year it was written (1896), the math tells us that Fleming can't be more than around fifty. That is too young for Crane's purposes, however, so he fudges the calendar a bit to comply with the emotional demands of the story he wants to tell and turns Fleming into a venerable old geezer, a man whose life consists of all past and no future, which makes his death in the concluding paragraph somewhat more bearable—not a grotesque accident that cuts down a life in mid-course but the fulfillment of that life as it comes to its noble, logical end.

The story begins with Fleming chewing the fat with a small group of men in a country grocery store one spring afternoon as his friends ask him questions about his days as a young soldier in the Civil War. One by one, Crane revisits the crucial events from *The Red Badge of Courage*, but now we get to hear about them from the protagonist himself. When one of the men asks if he was ever frightened in battle, Fleming looks down, grins, and surprises them by saying he was. "Pretty well scared, sometimes. Why,

---

* On the subject of cows, see Crane's humor piece from 1895 or '96, "Art in Kansas City" (*Works*, volume VIII), in which the narrator recounts a story told to him by his Uncle Clarence about a cow with a genius for painting watercolors, but because her milk is becoming thin and she refuses to work in oils, her owner has forbidden her to paint anymore, thus depriving Kansas City of its most brilliant artist.

in my first battle I thought the sky was falling down. I thought the world was coming to an end. You bet I was scared." The men laugh, charmed by Fleming's candor and admiring him all the more for it because they know of his outstanding record and his rise through the ranks to become an orderly sergeant, "so in their opinion his heroism was fixed." Now that Fleming has opened up to them, however, the memories continue to pour in on him, and he goes on with his recitation for some time, as if unable to stop himself.

"The trouble was," said the old man, "I thought they were all shoot- ing at me. Yes, sir. I thought every man in the other army was aiming at me in particular and only me. And it seemed so darned unreasonable, you know. I wanted to explain to 'em what an almighty good fellow I was, because I thought then they might quit all trying to hit me. But I couldn't explain, and they kept on being unreasonable—blim!— blim!—bang! So I run!"

Two little triangles of wrinkles appeared at the corners of his eyes. Evidently he appreciated some comedy in this recital. Down near his feet, however, little Jim, his grandson, was visibly horror-stricken. His hands were clasped nervously, and his eyes were wide with astonishment at this terrible scandal, his most magnificent grandfather telling such a thing.

"That was at Chancellorsville. Of course, afterward I got kind of used to it. A man does. Lots of men, though, seem to feel all right from the start. I did, as soon as I 'got on to it,' as they say now, but at first I was pretty flustered. Now there was young Jim Conklin, old Si Conklin's son—that used to keep the tannery—you none of you recollect him— well, he went into it from the start just as if he was born to it. But with me it was different. I had to get used to it."

From one paragraph to the next, the scene suddenly shifts, and we are no longer in the grocery store but out on the street with Fleming and his grandson, the two of them walking past the shops in the little town as the agitated boy grips two of his grandfather's fingers, ignores the old man's remarks about the handsome colt "over in the medder," and finally asks him if what he said in the store was true. Yes, Fleming says, it's true that he ran. "It was my first fight, and there was an awful lot of noise, you know." This confirmation has a powerful effect on the boy, who can be seen as a kind of latter-day incarnation of Fleming's own delusions about the glory of combat when he was a raw, untested volunteer: "Jimmie seemed dazed that this idol, of his own will, should so totter. His stout boyish idealism

was injured." When the old man continues to talk about the colt, asking
Jimmie if he wouldn't want to own such a fine animal himself, the boy
shrugs him off by saying it isn't as nice as their colts and then lapses into
"another moody silence." The colts seem to be an incidental distraction
at this point, but they aren't, and by the end of the story they prove to be
essential. Crane has planted a seed, and when the plant springs forth in
the final paragraphs, the colts turn out to be the cause of Fleming's death.

A one-line space follows, and then the second part of the story begins.
Out on Fleming's farm, one of the hired hands—identified simply as "a
Swede" and thereafter as "the Swede" or "this Swede"—goes off to town
one day and returns to the farm that night drunk, so drunk that he tips
over a lantern and accidentally sets the barn on fire. Fleming, roused from
sleep by the commotion, rushes out of the house as several hired hands
rush out as well, but the old man is the only one daring enough to open
the doors of the burning barn and go in to rescue the animals.

> He flung a blanket over an old mare's head, cut the halter close to the
> manger, led the mare to the door, and fairly kicked her out to safety. He
> returned with the same blanket and rescued one of the work-horses.
> He took five horses out, and then came out himself with his clothes
> bravely on fire. He had no whiskers, and very little hair on his head.
> They soused five pailfuls of water on him. His eldest son made a clean
> miss with the sixth pailful because the old man had turned and was
> running down the decline and around to the basement of the barn
> where were the stanchions of the cows. Some one noticed at the time
> that he ran lamely, as if one of the frenzied horses had smashed his hip.

Scorched and hobbled, Fleming acts as if he were reliving a battle
scene from his youth (the youth that was invented for him by Crane),
and he throws himself into the chaos of the fire with the same reckless-
ness and lack of thought that sustained him in combat during the war—
irrational, beside himself, blind to every risk that stands in his way. So far,
his courage has spared a number of horses from certain death, and now
that he has gone back and rescued all the cows but one, Fleming and the
hired men return to the front of the barn and stand there "sadly, breathing
like men who had reached the final point of human effort."

That should be the end of it, but after a few moments the drunken
Swede cries out, "as one who is the weapon of the sinister fates. 'De colts!
De colts! You have forgot de colts!'"

It is true. Fleming has forgotten a pair of colts at the back of the barn, and when he tells the others that he must go back and try to get them out, all the men protest, saying that "it's sure death," "it's suicide for a man to go in there," but their frantic warnings have no effect on him.

"Old Fleming stared absent-mindedly at the open doors. 'The poor little things,' he said. He rushed into the barn."

And that is the end of him. Crane spares us the horrific details of Fleming's death by fire, choosing instead to jump to the final paragraph, which is an odd and unusually bombastic paragraph for such a hard-nosed, disciplined writer, but in his struggle to give Fleming a proper send-off, an elegy fit for a hero, Crane can't help overstating his case, for he knows that Fleming's last act was not heroic so much as stupid, an impulsive, sentimental gesture performed by a man no longer in his right mind.

> When the roof fell in, a great funnel of smoke swarmed toward the sky, as if the old man's mighty spirit, released from its body—a little bottle— had swelled like the genie of fable. The smoke was tinted rose-hue from the flames, and perhaps the unutterable midnights of the universe will have no power to daunt the color of this soul.

Taken as a story in its own right, "The Veteran" is nearly incomprehensible. When considered as an addendum to *The Red Badge of Courage*, however, it takes on a certain poignancy, not as a work of art, perhaps, but at least as a marking stone in the trajectory of Crane's inner life. Not many novelists go to the trouble of killing off the characters who have brought them their greatest success, but success for Crane had been both the best thing and the worst thing that had happened to him, at once a source of fulfillment and trauma, and perhaps Crane had felt he needed to get rid of the thing that most fully represented the trauma to him, and so Henry Fleming, who had been born as a figure of Crane's imagination, could be put to death in Crane's imagination as well.

The corpse remained quiet for years, but toward the end of Crane's life, as he was working on his last book of short fiction, *Whilomville Stories*, which are mostly about the adventures of a little boy named Jimmie Trescott, the old Henry Fleming comes back to life and makes a last walk-on appearance—along with the maniac Swede who burned down the barn in "The Veteran." The story is called "Lynx-Hunting," and after Jimmie picks up a rifle for the first time and accidentally wounds one of Fleming's cows with an errant bullet, the angry Fleming comes after him brandishing a whip. "Well, what did you shoot'er fer?" he asks.

Jimmie thought, hesitated, decided, faltered, and then formulated this: "I thought she was a lynx."

Old Fleming and his Swede at once lay down on the grass and laughed themselves helpless.

No longer a spirit-cloud hovering over the unutterable midnights of the universe—but an old man rolling around on the grass, laughing himself silly.

On the last day of October 1895, a letter was sent to Crane by the corresponding editor of *The Youth's Companion* inviting him to submit work to the magazine: "In common with the rest of mankind we have been reading The Red Badge of Courage and other war stories by you . . . and feel a strong desire to have some of your tales." Advertising itself as "an illustrated Family Paper," the *Companion* was a national institution with an immense readership that began its life in 1827 and remained on the American scene for more than a hundred years. Never more popular than in the 1890s, it published work by every important writer from Mark Twain to Booker T. Washington, and, as the corresponding editor pointed out in his letter to Crane, "the substantial recognition which the Companion gives to authors is not surpassed in any American periodical." On top of that, it paid well.*

Crane was hard at work on *The Third Violet* just then, but he wrote back on November fifth to say that he "would be very glad to write for the Companion" and promised to send them something "in the future." The future arrived in March, when he mailed off the manuscript of "An Episode of War" to the offices in Boston, mentioning in the last line of his cover letter that "this lieutenant is an actual person"—possibly someone he had heard about from his uncle Wilbur Peck, who had served as an army doctor during the war.

The shortest of Crane's Civil War stories from 1895–96, "An Episode" is also the strongest, the boldest, and the most moving—a thoroughly modern work that takes on the issue of war trauma with pinpoint clarity and perceptiveness. The condition has been a part of human life ever since the first war was fought between battling clans thousands of years ago, and even though it has gone by several different names in America over the course of our history—*soldier's heart* during the Civil War, *shell shock* during

---

* Erle Stanley Gardner, a great fan of the magazine when he was a boy, used the name of its founder for the lawyer hero of his best-known stories and novels: Perry Mason.

World War I, *war neurosis* during World War II, and *post-traumatic stress syndrome* (PTSD) during the Vietnam War and on through subsequent wars in Iraq, Afghanistan, and elsewhere—its symptoms have never varied, and the affliction is the same one in all wars, repeated again and again in an eternal pattern of inner brokenness and wordless suffering.

The story begins in mid-action as the lieutenant (never named) is conscientiously dividing up and distributing coffee rations to each squad in the regiment. "Lips pursed," "frowning and serious," he is using his sword to separate the mass of coffee beans spread across his rubber blanket into squares that are "astoundingly equal in size," and just as he is about to finish this "great triumph in mathematics," with various corporals still thronging around him to claim their allotted shares, the lieutenant cries out in pain, looks at the man next to him "as if he suspected it was a case of personal assault," and an instant after that, when the others notice blood on the lieutenant's sleeve, they cry out as well. No, the lieutenant has not been punched by a fellow soldier; he has been struck by an enemy bullet.

Crane has managed to tell all this in a mere six sentences, and now, with dozens of narrative options before him, he hunkers down over the next two paragraphs and minutely examines the immediate responses of both the lieutenant and the men to this abrupt, wholly random event, "this catastrophe which had happened when catastrophes were not expected." No one says a thing. The lieutenant, clearly beginning to go into shock, looks out over the breastwork and stares at the green woods in front of him, which are now dotted with "many little puffs of white smoke." After a moment, the still-silent men look there as well and contemplate "the distant forest as if their minds were fixed upon the mystery of the bullet's journey." The silence is crucial, and Crane prolongs it for an almost unbearable length of time, stretching it out because he is writing about a world in which soldiers are supposed to be shot in battle, not when they are distributing coffee beans to other soldiers, and the mystery of that silent, invisible bullet is powerful enough to stun the witnesses into a state of speechless awe. As for the man who was hit, he has entered a zone in which words are utterly beyond him.

Then comes the intricate business of what to do with the sword. The lieutenant's right arm is immobilized, and therefore he has transferred it to his left hand, grasping it not by the hilt but somewhere along the middle of the blade, "awkwardly," and all at once that familiar object, which is the very emblem of his soldierhood, has become strange to him. This is one of the purest examples of Crane's ability to explore emotions through inanimate things, and by focusing his attention on the sword, he leads us through the lieutenant's gradual dissociation from the reality he belonged to just minutes earlier, his growing detachment from what is now and will forever after be his former self as he withdraws into the isolating grip of what was then called *soldier's heart*. The process continues when the lieutenant tries to put the sword back in its sheath, an all but impossible task when the sword is in your left hand and the scabbard is on your left side, especially when you are holding the sword in the middle of the blade, and most especially when the sword has become strange and meaningless to you, and as the wounded man engages in a "desperate struggle with the sword and the wobbling scabbard . . . he breathed like a wrestler."

> But at this instant the men, the spectators, awoke from their stone-like poses and crowded forward sympathetically. The orderly-sergeant took the sword and tenderly placed it in the scabbard. At the time, he leaned nervously backward, and did not allow even his finger to brush the body of the lieutenant. A wound gives strange dignity to him who bears it. Well men shy from this new and terrible majesty. It is as if the wounded man's hand is upon the curtain which hangs before the revelations of all existence, the meaning of ants, potentates, wars, cities, sunshine, snow, a feather dropped from a bird's wing, and the power of it sheds radiance upon a bloody form, and makes the other men understand sometimes that they are little. . . .
>
> There were others who proffered assistance. One timidly presented his shoulder and asked the lieutenant if he cared to lean upon it, but the latter waved them off mournfully. He wore the look of one who knows he is the victim of a terrible disease and understands his helplessness. He again stared over the breastwork at the forest, and then turning went slowly rearward. He held his right wrist tenderly in his left hand, as if the wounded arm was made of very brittle glass.
>
> And the men in silence stared at the wood, then at the departing lieutenant—then at the wood, then at the lieutenant.

With these piercing formulations and precisely chosen narrative details, Crane delineates the lieutenant's expulsion from the regiment that has been under his command. The alienating force of the wound has driven him into himself and out of the group, severing his ties with his comrades, and from now on he is a man alone, still in the war but no longer a combatant, invalidated out of the army even as he remains in uniform, and for the next two pages he wanders around in a kind of stupor as he searches for the field hospital, looking at the world as if he were a stranger from another universe, curious but indifferent, cut off from the meanings of things that until now have meant everything to him. When he sees a general mounted on a black horse, for example, and then watches an aide gallop up to him "furiously" and present him with a piece of paper, it was, "for a wonder, precisely like an historical painting." Later on, when he sees the swirling, thunderous charge of a battery off to his right, with shouting men on horseback and "the roar of wheels" and "the slant of the glistening guns," he simply watches—emotionless, walled off, elsewhere. Some stragglers tell him how to find the field hospital, and a few minutes later he is approached by an officer who begins to scold him for not taking proper care of his arm. The officer then "appropriated the lieutenant and the lieutenant's wound," cutting the sleeve and bandaging the exposed tissue and mangled flesh with a handkerchief, rattling on in a tone that "allowed one to think he was in the habit of being wounded every day. The lieutenant hung his head, feeling, in this presence, that he did not know how to be correctly wounded."

At last he makes it to the low white tents surrounding an old schoolhouse that serves as the makeshift hospital, a muddy, clamorous place where two ambulance drivers have interlocked wheels and are shouting at each other, while inside the ambulances, "both crammed with the wounded, there came an occasional groan," and outside "an interminable crowd of bandaged men" shuffles past as another dispute breaks out on the schoolhouse steps and the lieutenant looks at a man sitting with his back against a tree smoking a corncob pipe—his "face as grey as a new army blanket," a silent, wounded soldier easing himself into the arms of death. No more than that—a single, haunted image—and then Crane pushes on to the end of the story, with its enormous, startling leap between the last two paragraphs:

> A busy surgeon was passing near the lieutenant. "Good morning," he said with a friendly smile. Then he caught sight of the lieutenant's arm and his face at once changed. "Well, let's have a look at it." He seemed possessed suddenly of a great contempt for the lieutenant. This wound evidently placed the latter on a very low social plane. The doctor cried out impatiently. What mutton-head had tied it up that way anyhow. The lieutenant answered: "Oh, a man."
>
> When the wound was disclosed the doctor fingered it disdainfully. "Humph," he said. "You come along with me and I'll 'tend to you." His voice contained the same scorn as if he were saying: "You will have to go to jail."

The lieutenant had been very meek but now his face flushed, and he looked into the doctor's eyes. "I guess I won't have it amputated," he said.

"Nonsense, man! nonsense! nonsense!" cried the doctor. "Come along, now. I won't amputate it. Come along. Don't be a baby."

"Let go of me," said the lieutenant, holding back wrathfully. His glance fixed upon the door of the old school-house, as sinister to him as the portals of death.

And this is the story of how the lieutenant lost his arm. When he reached home his sisters, his mother, his wife, sobbed for a long time at the sight of the flat sleeve. "Oh, well," he said, standing shamefaced amid these tears, "I don't suppose it matters as much as all that."

So ends this astonishing piece of work, which to my mind is one of Crane's most brilliant little stories, a four-page sixty-yard dash run at full tilt from start to finish without a single misstep or stumble along the way, so perfect in its execution that it justifiably ranks as one of the finest war stories in American literature. The jump between the last two paragraphs lands with the force of an explosion, and there we find the one-armed lieutenant among his weeping relatives, a hollowed-out man devastated by the trauma of war who has become so diminished in his own eyes that he can't even bring himself to regret the loss of his arm. To use Crane's term, he has discovered that he is "little," and why should the universe care about the subtraction of one little arm from the body of yet one more little man?

The Youth's Companion read the story and paid Crane for the right to publish it, which effectively turned the magazine into the owner of "An Episode of War" and explains why it was not included as the seventh story in *The Little Regiment*, but after paying for the rights, the magazine began to have second thoughts and ultimately decided not to use it. The publication represented the American public, after all, and the editors felt that patriotic Americans would not look kindly upon such a dark representation of the realities of war. Sometime later, in an effort to recoup the money they had forked out for the story they had killed, they sold the British rights to a magazine called *The Gentlewoman* (!), where it was published in December 1899, six months before Crane's death, which means that "An Episode" was never circulated among American readers in Crane's lifetime. Years passed, and in 1916 *The Youth's Companion* dug into its dead-matter file, pulled out the story it had bought from the now long-dead Crane back in 1896, and published it in America for the first time. That was in the middle of the Great War, of course, and with articles from the trenches and hospitals about a new phenomenon known as *shell shock* everywhere in the world press, perhaps the current editors felt that Crane's old story had at last become timely—and acceptable to the readers of their magazine. Lest we have forgotten, however, another year would go by before America entered the war, meaning that the story was published when American troops had not yet begun to suffer from the disease that had been ravaging their French and British allies since 1914. By the time the war ended, in November 1918, more than thirty thousand of them had.

During an extended visit to Hartwood in June and July 1896, Crane took a further step forward with two philosophical tales wrapped in the clothing of adventure stories, or, to be more precise, life-and-death dramas of *thought in action*. Earlier in the year, he had published a pair of stories inspired by his experiences in the West and Mexico—"One Dash—Horses" (January) and "A Freight-Car Incident" (April)—and now he returned to those places in three additional stories that got progressively better the more deeply he dug. The first was a so-so warm-up effort called "The Wise Men," but in it Crane found the setting and the characters for the second, "The Five White Mice," which begins slowly and then builds—and builds—to a jaw-dropping conclusion.

The setting is a gringo dive in Mexico City, and the characters are a couple of disaffected young Americans known as the New York Kid and the 'Frisco Kid, each one the alter ego of the other and both together perhaps a split-in-two projection of Crane himself, his twin doppelgängers. The five white "mice" are the dice used in a version of seven-up poker, and the story is centered on the clash between chance and destiny—and whether a human being has any control over his own fate. It is the first of what I have come to think of as Crane's *existential puzzles*.

> Freddie was mixing a cocktail. His hand with the long spoon was whirling swiftly and the ice in the glass hummed and rattled like a cheap watch. Over by the window, a gambler, a millionaire, a railway conductor and the agent of a vast American syndicate were playing seven-up. Freddie surveyed them with the ironical glance of a man who is mixing a cocktail.

Right away, we can hear something new in the sound of the prose, a new sound for the new environment he has chosen to write about, what Berryman called "the lazy, alcoholic, gambling life of Americans in a foreign city," which no American before Crane had ever portrayed in a work of fiction. There was Henry James, of course, with his wealthy Americans struggling to keep their balance among the European upper classes, but not this lowlife world of Americans abroad, which seems to anticipate the expat subculture in Paris depicted by Hemingway and Fitzgerald in the 1920s and '30s, and beyond the question of milieu there is the language of that opening paragraph as well, with its blunt, deadpan, hard-boiled tone, which anticipates the style perfected by Raymond Chandler in the thirties and forties, so much so, it seems to me, that if one did not know Crane was the author of those sentences, they could easily be mistaken for an early passage written by Chandler himself.

The first half of the fourteen-page story zeroes in on the subject of chance as the New York Kid and several other men throw themselves into an intense round of seven-up on the counter of Freddie's bar at the Casa Verde, and once "they had passed beyond shaking for drinks for the crowd, for Mexican dollars, for dinner, for the wine at dinner" and then "separating the cigars and cigarettes from the dinner's bill and causing a distinct man to be responsible for them," they have run out of ideas about what to gamble for until one of them suggests playing "for a box at the circus" that night, which they all agree is an excellent plan. The Kid has been down on his luck of late, but he is still in the game as the last hand comes to its conclusion, needing one more ace to trump the other man's five queens, and as he begins to shake the dice for his final roll, "he addressed a gambler's slogan to the interior of the cup":

> Oh, five white mice of chance,
> Shirts of wool and corduroy pants,
> Gold and wine, women and sin,
> All for you if you let me come in—
> Into the house of chance.

After the Kid loses, the others jeer at him by chanting, "Five white mice! Five white mice!" and even as they go off to the circus together, they continue to mock him by suggesting that he look to other animals besides mice for help—"rabbits, dogs, hedge-hogs, snakes, opossums"—but he stands his ground and argues "that if one is going to believe in anything at all, one might as well choose the five white mice." Along the way, he runs into the 'Frisco Kid and a man named Benson, who have "a little scheme" of dragging him along with them on an all-night binge, but the New York Kid says he can't, he has to take the others to the circus, and when they insist that he forget about the others and the circus, he insists back at them that he can't, that he's stuck because of the lost bet, and as he begins to walk away, "they yelled with rage, 'Well, meet us, now, do you hear? In the Casa Verde as soon as the circus quits! Hear?' They threw maledictions after him."

A small pause in the action follows as Crane extols the virtues of the Circo Teatro Ornin, which he calls one of the best in the world and far superior to any of the big-top entertainments up north. "At this circus the Kid was not debased by the sight of mournful prisoner elephants and caged animals forlorn and sickly. He sat in his box until late and laughed and swore when past laughing at the comic, foolish, wise clown."

After laughing and swearing at the foolishness of the clown's wise performance, the Kid returns to the Casa Verde looking for his friends, but Freddie tells him they left a few minutes ago, which sends him back outside to look for them. "At midnight a little Mexican street burrowing among the walls of the city is as dark as a whale's throat at deep sea"—but eventually they are found, both snockered and leaning together against a wall, Benson fully blitzed and the 'Frisco Kid about halfway there. For the next two pages, we watch the irritated, cold-sober New York Kid try to get his drunken friends home, a hilarious scene in its way, with some sterling examples of slurred speech, such as "comonangetadrink" and "gome" as a contraction of "go home," but after a while we begin to wonder what Crane is up to and where this pointless, meandering story can possibly be headed when, from one moment to the next, *it happens*, and suddenly the story becomes another story as the hammer of chance descends on the three ne'er-do-wells. Without the inconsequential non-sense that preceded it, the last part would not have the chilling impact it does, for this is how the world works, and when the do-or-die moment of danger thrusts itself into our stupid lives, it always comes when we are least expecting it.

This is one of Crane's principal obsessions: the unforeseen encounter with death. It was so much a part of his thinking that he even let it slip out—absurdly, inappropriately—in his letter to Nellie Crouse about the man of fashion: "There are men of very social habits who nevertheless know how to stand steady when they see cocked revolvers and death comes down and sits on the back of a chair and waits." A year earlier, he had already written about such a confrontation in "One Dash—Horses," the first of his Mexican stories: the sudden, terrorizing moment when a stranger pulls a gun on you and everything falls away and there you are, alone in the universe, unexpectedly looking at your own death, and how you handle this moment—for which there is no preparation, no experience from any other moment of your life to instruct you on what to do—will determine whether you wind up dead on the floor or not. The showdown. One person facing another person, each looking into the other's eyes. This has nothing to do with the random, depersonalized death of a soldier in war—except in the case of hand-to-hand combat. In all other instances, the bullet or shell that kills you is fired by someone you can't see, an anonymous stranger standing in the far distance. With the one-on-one showdown, you are standing face-to-face with the person who will kill you. Dread as opposed to out-and-out fear. And hence the paradox: What to do when you have no idea what to do?

As the two drunken boys are led through the streets by the sober Kid, "it chanced that three other pedestrians were passing in shadowy rank" and Benson's shoulder accidentally jostles one of them. A simple apology would undo the offense, but Benson is too drunk to apologize. The jostled Mexican stranger wheels around, shoots his hand toward his hip (as if going for a knife), and says, "Does señor want fight?" The dazed Benson says nothing. Just as the New York Kid is about to pull Benson away, the 'Frisco Kid steps forward, pushes Benson aside, and answers the question for him: "Yes!"

Immediately after that word is spoken, Crane gives us this:

> There was no sound nor light in the world. The wall at the left happened to be of the common prison-like construction—no door, no window, no opening at all. Humanity was enclosed and asleep. Into the mouth of the sober Kid came a wretched bitter taste as if it had filled with blood. He was transfixed as if he was already seeing the lightning ripples on the knife-blade.

For the next five pages, everything slows down as Crane plants himself inside the New York Kid and tracks every racing thought that darts through his head, even as he continues to look at the developing showdown through the Kid's eyes. Inner and outer are eerily and magnificently in balance, and as the slow-motion waltz of anticipated violence unfurls in the Kid's mind, Crane builds the scene into one of the most gripping passages in all his work. The Mexican, who has yet to draw his knife, leans toward the Kid and whispers, "So?" His face is "lit with a sinister decision," and suddenly the Kid is reminded of the face "of a man who had shaved him three times in Boston in 1888," and, both "fascinated" and "stupefied," he imagines he can follow "the progress of the man's thought toward the point where a knife would be wrenched from its sheath."

But the Kid is armed as well, and he too has his hand on his hip, clutching his large revolver, and no sooner does he touch the gun than another irrelevant thought surges up in him: "He recalled that upon its black handle was stamped a hunting scene in which a sportsman in fine leggings and a peaked cap was taking aim at a stag less than one eighth of an inch away."

The big and the small blur together, miniature men in peaked caps are hunting miniature animals while three pairs of full-sized men are squaring off against one another in a dark city street, all of them armed except the inebriated, semiconscious Benson, and once he has looked over at his friends, the New York Kid understands that he is

> going to be killed. His mind leaped forward and studied the aftermath. The story would be a marvel of brevity when first it reached the far New York home, written in a careful hand on a bit of cheap paper topped and footed and backed by the printed fortifications of the cable company. But they were often as stones flung into mirrors, these bits of paper upon which are laconically written all the most terrible chronicles of the times. He witnessed the uprising of his mother and sister and the invincible calm of his hard-mouthed father who would probably shut himself in the library and smoke alone. Then his father would come and they would bring him here and say: "This is the place." Then, very likely, each would remove his hat. They would stand quietly with their hats in their hands for a decent minute. He pitied his old financing father, unyielding and millioned, a man who commonly spoke twenty-two words a year to his beloved son. The Kid understood it at this time. If his fate was not impregnable, he might have turned out to be a man and have been liked by his father.

After that intricate mental flight about cablegrams and taciturn millionaire fathers, the Kid imagines how the other Kid would mourn his death—"preternaturally correct," "without swearing"—and then, shifting course, Crane turns his attention to the images flooding the Kid's mind, calling them "perfectly stereopticon, flashing in and away from his thought with an inconceivable rapidity," and one sentence after that he jumps again and formulates another startling idea: "And here is the unreal real: into the Kid's nostrils, at the expectant moment of slaughter, had come the scent of new-mown hay." More smells quickly follow, all of them bucolic, all of them evoking peace and soothing tranquility, not imagined smells but real smells invading his nostrils from the "unreal real" as he waits "for pain and a sight of the unknown," which immediately turns into another thought about the other Kid, who, he realizes, is about to be killed as well, which provokes yet another round of disconnected associations, a dizzying zigzag that mirrors the motions of a panicked mind at work. It's a wild onslaught, but one that is thoroughly under control, and because I have not read every story that was written in the world before Crane wrote this story, I can't say for certain that no one in the years leading up to 1896 had ever done anything quite like this, but I am hard-pressed to think of any writer before the twentieth century who attempted to follow the inner workings of a mind in crisis as Crane does in these paragraphs.

The Kid then understands that his only hope is to draw his revolver and "face down all three Mexicans." If he can do it quickly enough, he will probably win. If he can't, then he and his friends will be dead. As the showdown moves into its next and final act, the words of the poem about "the five white mice of chance" are repeated, not spoken by the Kid this time but simply there, suspended in the middle of the page to signal the beginning of the end of the story.

The next three paragraphs are all about the revolver and the Kid's anxieties about pulling it from the holster without fumbling, an operation that must be accomplished at a moment when "the eels of despair lay wet and cold upon his back." To his surprise, "the revolver . . . arose like a feather," no doubt because "the Kid had unconsciously used nervous force sufficient to raise a bale of hay," and there he is, suddenly in control as the Mexican emits "a low cry" and takes a quick step backward. In control now, yes, but also angry at himself for having been so afraid, for having overestimated the courage of the Mexicans, and this upsets him greatly, for now "the Kid was able to understand . . . that they were all human beings" and that all along his opponents' fear has been equal to his. "Upon the instant he pounced forward and began to swear, unreeling great English oaths as thick as ropes and lashing the faces of the Mexicans with them. He was bursting with rage because these men had not previously confided to him that they were vulnerable. The whole thing had been an absurd imposition."

The showdown ends in a standoff, and as the Mexicans disappear into the night, Crane concludes his existential puzzle with a short conversation between the New York Kid and Benson that recapitulates the philosophical underpinnings of the story, with the sloshed Benson taking the logical, Enlightenment view of a mechanistic universe ruled by the forces of cause and effect and the sober Kid suggesting that in the end—perhaps—life is ruled by chance, which is as much as to say that life is inexplicable. Why things happen as they do is surely life's greatest mystery, but *how* they happen, which would seem to be a matter of close observation and study, can also be problematical.

Then, to top things off, there is the story's last sentence, three short words that arrive with the suddenness of a match struck in the darkness—igniting the pages we have read so far and forcing us to think our way through them again.

> "Well," said the sober Kid crossly, "are you ready to go home now?"
>
> The 'Frisco Kid said: "Where they gone?" His voice was undisturbed but inquisitive.
>
> Benson suddenly propelled himself from his dreamful position against the wall. "Frishco Kid's all right. He's drunk fool and he's all right. But you New York Kid, you're shober." He passed into a state of profound investigation. "Kid shober 'cause didn't go with us. Didn't go with us 'cause went to damn circus. Went to damn circus 'cause lose shakin' dice. Lose shakin' dice 'cause—what make lose shakin' dice, Kid?"
>
> The New York Kid eyed the senile youth. "I don't know. The five white mice, maybe."
>
> Benson puzzled so over this reply that he had to be held erect by his friends. Finally the 'Frisco Kid said: "Let's go home."
>
> Nothing had happened.

After reading "A Man and Some Others" for the first time in the fall of 1897, Joseph Conrad wrote Crane to tell him that Garnett considered it to be "immense" and that he himself admired it "without reserve."

> I am envious of you—horribly. . . . Your temperament makes old things new and new things amazing. I want to swear at you, to bless you—perhaps to shoot you—but I prefer to be your friend.
>
> You are an everlasting surprise to me. You shock—and the next moment you give perfect artistic satisfaction. Your method is fascinating. You are a complete impressionist. The illusions of life come out of your hand without flaw. It is not life—which nobody wants—it is art—art for which everyone—the abject and the great hanker—mostly without knowing it.

A solitary man in the middle of nowhere. Dark mesquite stretching from horizon to horizon, a desert world without people, as silent and bleak as the landscape of a Beckett play, but far bigger, an American vastness of pure sky, pure earth, and nothing else, so huge that it resembles a dreamland, a site of cosmic struggle. It is the same world as the one depicted in the poems of *The Black Riders*—the same limitless desert in which men squat upon the ground and eat of their own hearts.

The man's name is Bill. He is alone in that Texas wilderness because he is a sheepherder, "the only white man in half a day's ride," and as the six-part fifteen-page story begins, we find him bent over a campfire preparing his dinner. A Mexican sheepherder approaches the camp and warns Bill that he and his friends want him off the range. If Bill doesn't "geet out," they will "keel" him. Unperturbed, Bill replies with some harsh words of his own, telling José that he has just as much right to be there as they do, and if they come after him with their guns, he will "plug about fifty per-cent of the gentlemen present, sure." So ends the brief powwow. Neither man has budged, and consequently it is only a matter of time before the showdown begins.

In spite of Bill's tough talk, Crane leaves no doubt in the reader's mind that his hero is doomed. Outnumbered by eight to one, he has no chance of getting out of the confrontation alive. The story, then, will not be about how a lone Odysseus manages to outwit his enemies and overcome the odds against him, but how a stubborn, violent, cantankerous roughneck drifter chooses to make his last stand. All the tropes of the classic Wild West tale are present, but Crane subverts them, turns them inside out, and uses them to fashion another one of his existential puzzles. The question here is not one of chance and destiny, however, but of *why*. Why stay when reason tells you to run, when staying is all but certain to lead to your death? An all but unanswerable question until we remember the Alamo. And remember how deeply Crane admired those doomed men who held their ground and fought until every last one of them had been killed. And remember, too, how much sympathy he had for the one man who chose to leave, Rose, whom he called "a kind of dogged philosopher" possessed of a "strange, inverted courage." The essential word is *choose*, which in Rose's case, Bill's case, and the case of Bowie, Crockett, and the others at the Alamo is a *philosophical choice*, and if you choose to die (for whatever reason—personal honor, faith in a cause, a hunger for martyrdom), the question then becomes *how*. How will you handle yourself when the moment of reckoning comes?

In the second part, Crane takes the unusual step of backtracking into Bill's past. In most of his short stories, he tells us little or nothing about the lives of his characters before we discover them in the middle of whatever situation he has thrown them into. We know nothing about Fred Collins in "A Mystery of Heroism," nothing about the lieutenant in "An Episode of War," and nothing about the New York Kid in "The Five White Mice" except that he comes from a rich family, but here Crane takes the trouble to fill us in on Bill's background—an indirect method of explaining why he has chosen not to run, for Bill himself never says a word about it and, as far as we can tell, never even stops to examine the implications of his choice—which is a choice that equals death.

In just over three pages, Crane tells the story in a swiftly charging narrative rush as sentence jams into sentence and occasionally explodes into acerbic psychological commentary, a whirl of incident that follows Bill's long fall from wealthy mine owner in Wyoming to lowly sheepherder in Texas. The process begins with an unlucky night at poker

> when three kings came to him with criminal regularity against a man who always filled a straight. Later he became a cowboy, more weirdly abandoned than if he had never been an aristocrat. By this time all that remained of his former splendor was his pride, or his vanity, which was the one thing which need not have remained. He killed the foreman of the ranch over an inconsequent matter as to which of them was a liar, and the midnight train carried him eastward. He became a brakeman on the Union Pacific, and really gained high honors in the hobo war that for many years had devastated the beautiful railroads of our country. A creature of ill fortune himself, he practised all the ordinary cruelties upon these other creatures of ill fortune. . . . He had already worsted four tramps with his own coupling-stick, when a stone thrown by the ex–third baseman of F Troop's nine laid him flat on the prairie, and later enforced a stay in the hospital in Omaha. After his recovery he engaged with other railroads, and shuffled cars in countless yards. An order to strike came upon him in Michigan, and afterward the vengeance of the railroad pursued him until he assumed a name. This mask is like the darkness in which the burglar chooses to move. It destroys many of the healthy fears. It is a small thing, but it eats that which we call our conscience. The conductor of No. 419 stood in the caboose within two feet of Bill's nose, and called him a liar. Bill requested him to use a milder term. He had not bored the foreman of Tin Can Ranch with any such request, but had killed him with expedition. The conductor seemed to insist, and so Bill let the matter drop.
>
> He became a bouncer of a saloon on the Bowery in New York. . . . He nearly killed Bad Hennessy, who, as a matter of fact, had more reputation than ability, and his fame moved up the Bowery and down the Bowery.
>
> But let a man adopt fighting as his business, and the thought grows

constantly within him that it is his business to fight. These phrases became mixed in Bill's mind precisely as they are here mixed; and let a man get this idea in his mind, and defeat begins to move toward him over the unknown ways of circumstances. One summer night three sailors from the U.S.S. *Seattle* sat in the saloon . . .

As it happened, Bill chose to pick a quarrel with the sailors, and after he tossed them out of the bar, they regathered their forces on the sidewalk, chanced upon a stray beam of wood ("a scantling"), and used it as a battering ram "to punch him in the bulwarks of his stomach" as he stood triumphantly in the doorway, causing a wound to open up in him that the ambulance surgeon compared to "an excavation." Thus Bill landed in southwestern Texas, where he began his new life as a sheepherder. As Crane puts it earlier in the passage: "Strange and still strange are the laws of fate."

The third part begins with Bill examining his revolver immediately after the conversation with José. He killed the ranch foreman with this gun, has used it in "free fights" during which he may or may not have killed others, and by now it is his "dearest possession," an object he loves "because its allegiance was more than that of man, horse, or dog. It questioned neither social nor moral position; it obeyed alike the saint and the assassin. It was the claw of the eagle, the tooth of the lion, the poison of the snake; and when he swept it from its holster, this minion smote where he listed, even to the battering of a small penny."

This is Crane writing at full stretch and in full command of what he is doing, exploring the mythology of the gun in a language both biblical and deadly ironic, never more sure of the gifts at his disposal, at once able to plunge deep and range wide, traveling in a single sentence from claws to teeth to minuscule pennies, but no sooner do we settle in and begin to contemplate the lone, desperate battle this burned-out man is about to fight than another character suddenly and unexpectedly appears, invading "the desolation" and "stillness" of the desert as Bill looks up and sees "a motionless horseman in black outline against the pallid sky." Another oddly cinematic moment; another solitary figure plunked down in the denuded, primal landscape; another surprise. Not once in the story do we see or hear any of the sheepherder's sheep (because they are irrelevant), but this stranger, who turns out to be a young American greenhorn from "a far, black Northern city," is essential. Never named, he will become the witness to the story, and everything that happens from now on will be seen through his eyes. He is Nick Carraway to Bill's Gatsby, the innocent, rational, "eddycated man" poised midway between author and reader to function as the interpreter of the irrational forces that will lead to the violent death of the violent, gun-loving Bill.

The two men size each other up. Although Bill is fully prepared to shoot the stranger if necessary, what he sees upon closer examination is a harmless fellow decked out "in some Mexican trappings of an expensive kind," a fairly ridiculous Yankee tourist of "a type which did not belong in the mesquit." What the stranger sees is a "tattered individual with a tangle of hair and beard, with a complexion turned brick-color from the sun and whiskey." When he asks the bearded one if he can spend the night in his camp, Bill puts him off by explaining that "some of these here greasers are goin' to chase me off the range tonight; and while I might like a man's company all right, I wouldn't let him in for no such game when he ain't got nothin' to do with the trouble."

Because he is an outsider, the stranger can ask all the questions an insider would not or could not ask. He can be shocked, outraged, and confused (just as the reader is), but the actors in the drama, Bill and José, are too absorbed in the action to step back and consider the consequences of what they are doing. Therefore, the stranger can bluntly ask: "And—great heavens! will they kill you, do you think?" To which Bill replies: "Don't know. Can't tell till afterwards." And then, as he goes into the various ways in which the scene could play out, Bill concludes, "It's awful hard on a man's mind—to git a gang after him." Appalled by what he is hearing, not only that Bill is determined to fight but that he will be outnumbered eight to one in that fight, the stranger cries out, "Well, why in the name of wonder don't you go get the sheriff?" It is, of course, a dumb question, perhaps the dumbest question he could have asked—further proof of his naïveté and ignorance, his failure to grasp the full meaning of the situation he has stumbled into. Bill is so disgusted by the question that he doesn't even bother to answer it. Instead, he barks out a single one-syllable, four-letter word—not so much a curse as a sign of exasperation.

The stranger has been told to "hit the trail," and in the fourth part he is nowhere to be seen. Night falls, and before Crane begins to show us the battle that will soon take place in the darkness, he pauses to set the scene of the confrontation while at the same time announcing the philosophical intentions of his story. This is not just another shoot-out in another Wild West adventure yarn, he is telling us; it is an examination of the futility of human endeavor on an earth that has no time to trouble itself with the lives and deaths of mere men.

Long, smoldering clouds spread in the western sky, and to the east silver mists lay on the purple gloom of the wilderness.

Finally, when the great moon climbed the heavens and cast its ghastly radiance upon the bushes, it made a new and more brilliant crimson of the camp-fire, where the flames capered merrily through its mesquit branches, filling the silence with the fire chorus, an ancient melody which surely bears a message of the inconsequence of human tragedy—a message that is in the boom of the sea, the sliver of the wind through the grass-blades, the silken clash of hemlock boughs.

This is the do-or-die moment, but if Bill can do rather than die, the only thing in front of him will be another round of fighting, for the odds are against him, and how can he expect to kill all eight of the men who are out to kill him in the first round? But how clever he is that night, and how like Odysseus he is with his cunning strategy to outwit his opponents by stuffing his bedroll by the fire with various objects to give the impression that he is sleeping when in fact he is hiding somewhere in the bushes, and as José and his crew empty their sawed-off shotguns into the bedroll, how hard he laughs at them, such "a fearsome laugh of ridicule, hatred, ferocity" that it scares them into silence, and as they begin to run from the invisible revolver in Bill's invisible hand, he manages to kill one of them as the rest scamper off into the darkness. A moment later, all goes quiet in the wilderness again, and the fire chorus goes on singing "the ancient melody which bears the message of the inconsequence of human tragedy." By repeating this phrase, Crane transforms it into a kind of dirge.

The fifth part begins with a comment from the stranger.

"'Now you're worse off than ever,' said the young man, dry-voiced and awed.

"'No, I ain't,' said Bill rebelliously. 'I'm one ahead.'"

Not gone, then, as Bill had asked, but still there, having lurked about in the vicinity all during the exchange of gunfire, and now that dawn has begun to break, he and Bill approach the campfire to assess the damage. Bit by bit, the young man has insinuated himself into the story and by now he is no longer strictly an observer but something close to a participant as well. A reluctant, horrified participant who has no business being there, of course, one so out of his element that he promptly becomes unhinged when he chances upon a clear view of the dead man's face through an opening in the thicket. "That man there takes the heart out of me," he says, "and makes me feel like a murderer," and when Bill reminds him that "you didn't shoot him, mister, I did," the young man answers, "I know;

but I feel that way somehow. I can't get rid of it." He is so rattled by the bloodshed that he wants to leave, to put the whole gruesome affair behind him, but before he can mount his horse and ride away from the impending slaughter, José and his men are suddenly back for round two, arriving with "a roar of guns" and filling the air with "such hooting and whistling as would come from a swift flock of steam-boilers." The commotion spooks the young man's horse, and when the animal bolts from the scene, the stranger is stuck there, forced to witness the last battle and, in the end, take part in it himself.

He and Bill throw themselves onto the ground, and for the rest of Part V Bill, José, and the others exchange insults, insults that grow increasingly ugly and bitter as Bill's anger mounts.

> His hidden enemies called him nine kinds of coward, a man who could fight only in the dark, a baby who would run from the shadows of such noble Mexican gentlemen, a dog that sneaked. They described the affair of the previous night, and informed him of the base advantage he had taken of their friend. In fact, they in all sincerity endowed him with every quality which he no less earnestly believed them to possess. One could have seen the phrases bite him as he lay there on the ground fingering his revolver.

The sixth and final part, all seen from the stranger's point of view, quickly devolves into a blur of fragmented chaos, an episode from a dream that resembles a picture that is only "half drawn." The enraged Bill wants to go after them, but the young man yells out, "Don't you budge an inch! Don't you budge!" Ignoring the stranger's command, Bill casts his eyes on the bushes in front of him, no doubt beginning to lift his head, for the young man then cries out, "Put your head down!"—but by then it is too late.

> As the guns roared, Bill uttered a loud grunt, and for a moment leaned panting upon his elbow, while his arm shook like a twig. Then he upreared like a great and bloody spirit of vengeance, his face lighted with the blaze of his last passion. The Mexicans came swiftly and in silence.

From then on, the images begin to break apart into "the rush of feet, the spatter of shots, the cries, the swollen faces seen like masks on the smoke," and two short paragraphs down, in an obliquely told, after-the-fact account, we learn this stunning bit of news about the stranger's role in the skirmish: "He killed a man, and the thought went swiftly by him, like the feather on the gale, that it was easy to kill a man."

This is the final step in an ineluctable process that was set in motion by pure chance. An unsuspecting innocent wandered into a world of violence, and from neutral observer he became a reluctant participant, then an active participant, and by the end of the story he has become a part of the violence himself. With this terrible knowledge now buried in him for the rest of his life, "he suddenly felt for Bill, this grimy sheep-herder, some form of idolatry. Bill was dying, and the dignity of last defeat, the superiority of him who stands in his grave, was in the pose of the lost sheep-herder."

After a one-space blank, the story unwinds in the last four paragraphs as the stranger sits on the ground wiping sweat and gunpowder from his face. "He wore the gently idiot smile of an aged beggar as he watched three Mexicans limping and staggering into the distance." Three left out of seven, and counting the other one killed the night before, five of the eight Mexicans who came after Bill are dead. The now-dead Bill is the sixth corpse. The stage is cluttered with corpses, as bloody as in any final scene of a Shakespeare tragedy, but no Fortinbras will be coming to restore order to the world, and as the stranger finally stands up, he walks over to Bill, whose hands are wrapped around the throat of another dead man. He loosens the hands, and then, "swaying as if slightly drunk, he stood looking down into the still face." Eventually, an idea comes to him, and he walks off to retrieve his multicolored Mexican blanket "from where it lay dirty from trampling feet." Carefully dusting it off, he returns to Bill and lays it over the sheepherder's body. This is not a moment for solemn introspection, however, and as the story comes to its end, there is one last jolt of fear.

> There he again stood motionless, his mouth just agape and the same stupid glance in his eyes, when all at once he made a gesture of fright and looked wildly about him.
>
> He had almost reached the thicket when he stopped, smitten with alarm. A body contorted, with one arm stiff in the air, lay in his path. Slowly and warily he moved around it, and in a moment the bushes, nodding and whispering, their leaf-faces turned toward the scene behind him, swung and swung again into the stillness and the peace of the wilderness.

A month or two went by before Crane got around to handing the story over to Paul Revere Reynolds, his new agent. Understanding the power of the work he had been given, Reynolds sold it to Richard Watson Gilder of the *Century* for five hundred dollars, the largest sum Crane had ever received for one of his stories. With Gilder's strict policy of banning all coarse language and swearing in the pages of his magazine, however, there was some wrangling over the use of certain words, "B'Gawd" and "hell" in particular. When the story was published in the February 1897 issue (with a full-page illustration by Frederic Remington), those shocking epithets were modified to read "B'G——" and "h——." Just two months earlier in Paris (December 10, 1896), Alfred Jarry's revolutionary, modernist play *Ubu Roi*, which begins with a variant of the word *Shit*, provoked a riot in the theater on opening night and was closed after just one performance. W. B. Yeats, who happened to be present, famously commented, "After us the Savage God."

Following his immensely productive stay at Hartwood, Crane returned to New York to begin work on a series of articles about the Tenderloin district, also known as "Satan's Circus." By mid-September, the ground he had been walking on unexpectedly began to crumble, and because the laws of fate are strange and still strange, both New York and Hartwood would soon vanish as the centers of his world.

30

ENTER THEODORE ROOSEVELT. ENTER WILLIAM RANDOLPH HEARST. One shoe dropped, then the other shoe dropped, and within a matter of weeks Crane was up to his neck in trouble.

T.R. Roosevelt—one of the great stone faces now carved into the south-eastern wall of Mount Rushmore—was another precocious American phenomenon who not only devoured books (one before breakfast every day, often two or three more in the evening) but wrote them as well (close to forty), along with hundreds of essays and articles and no fewer than 150,000 letters. After serving three terms as an assemblyman in the New York State legislature, he left politics in 1884 when, within the space of eleven hours, both his wife and his mother died on different floors of the same house. He went out to North Dakota and lived as a rancher for the next two years, wrote three more books, and then returned to politics and New York, where he ran for mayor in 1886 and lost, after which he published a bestselling history, *The Winning of the West*, and married for the second time. Appointed to the United States Civil Service Commission by the Harrison administration, he lived in Washington for the next several years, but following the 1894 Republican sweep in the New York elections (reported by Crane in "Heard on the Street Election Night"), he left the capital and returned to his hometown, where the new reform mayor, William Lafayette Strong, had chosen him to be president of the board of New York City Police Commissioners, making Roosevelt the chief law enforcement official of the largest city in the country at age thirty-six.

W.R.H. Hearst was young as well—just thirty-three when he signed up Crane to furnish articles and sketches about the Tenderloin—but by 1896 he was already an experienced newspaperman. After being expelled from Harvard nine years earlier, he had become the editor of the *San Francisco Examiner* (owned by his father, a wealthy U.S. senator), and when Hearst moved to New York in 1895 and took over the failing *Journal*, the yellow-journalism war between his paper and Joseph Pulitzer's *World* was launched. One year into it, Hearst had acquired a reputation for paying his writers well, and when he sent a telegram to Crane on August eleventh asking, "How much money do you require?," one more writer was added to the *Journal* payroll.*

T.R. It is likely that Crane met Roosevelt at the Lantern Club in late 1895 or early 1896, but their friendship did not begin in earnest until the summer, when McClure was toying with the notion of asking Crane to write an article about the police department. That led to a request for an interview, and on July twentieth Roosevelt sent a brief note to Crane about where and when they could talk: "Court opens at ten, but eleven o'clock would be the time for you to come around. I have much to discuss with you about 'Madge.'" He was referring to the new edition of *Maggie* that had been published in June, and although the piece for McClure was never written, Crane and Roosevelt dined out together a number of times that summer, at least twice in the company of Jacob Riis, Roosevelt's fellow reformer and ally. After a long absence, Hamlin Garland had come back to New York for a summer visit, and in an undated message from July that Crane left at his hotel (along with an inscribed copy of *George's Mother*), he wrote: "Just heard you were in town. I want you to dine with me tonight at the Lantern Club. Sure!! Roosevelt expects to be there. Don't fail. I

---

* The term *yellow journalism* derives from a character named the Yellow Kid in Richard F. Outcault's Sunday comic strip *Hogan's Alley*, which was originally published in Pulitzer's *World*. When Hearst lured Outcault into working for the *Journal* (along with other members of the *World* staff), Pulitzer countered by hiring another artist to continue the strip in his paper. "Yellow Kid Journalism" soon became "yellow journalism," a catchword for the sensationalized reportage practiced by both papers. Each sold roughly one million copies per day.

will call here at six—again."* The next month, Crane wrote another letter to Roosevelt about police matters and included with it a copy of *George's Mother* and a typescript of the recently finished "A Man and Some Others." The first paragraph of Roosevelt's response from August eighteenth shows how carefully he kept up with Crane's work, and, in spite of his denigrating, prejudiced remarks about the Mexican characters in the story, how diligent a reader he was. Closing off with an amiable "I hope soon to see you again," it is the letter of a man who considered himself to be Crane's friend:

> I am much obliged to you for "George's Mother" with your own auto-graph on the front. I shall keep it with your other books. Some day I shall try to get you to write your autograph in my "Red Badge of Cour-age", for much though I like your other books, I think I like that book the best. Some day I want you to write another story of the frontiersman and the Mexican Greaser in which the frontiersman shall come out on top; it is more natural that way!

W.R.H. One day after receiving Hearst's telegram, Crane went to Madison Square Garden to watch (and perhaps write about) William Jennings Bryan's first major address as the Democratic candidate for president. Bryan had been nominated a few weeks earlier at the party convention in Chicago, where he had delivered his famous "Cross of Gold" speech (which denounced the gold standard as a tool of the rich in suppressing the interests of the laboring class) and the incumbent president, Grover Cleveland, had been dumped by his own party—the same Grover Cleveland who had been elected (according to Crane's former boss at the *Tribune*, Whitelaw Reid) because of Crane's 1892 JOUAM article. A spell of hot, dog-day weather was pounding New York (temperatures in the nineties), and with a large crowd expected at the Garden that night, it was Roosevelt's job to ensure that adequate police protection was on hand. The one thousand cops he provided should have been enough to maintain order in a twelve-thousand-seat arena, but forty thousand people turned up, and mayhem ensued as the undermanned security force allowed in people who had no tickets and barred others from entering who did, causing a great commotion on the street outside the Garden, where two different waves of incensed Bryan supporters crashed through the police lines.

T.R. There was much criticism in the press the next day, and Crane,

---

* The inscription read: "To Hamlin Garland / of the great honest West / From Stephen Crane / of the false East. / New York City / July 1896."

uncommonly irked by what he had seen, wrote to Roosevelt about it soon after—not to complain so much as to inquire about how and why things had gotten out of control. On August eighteenth, in the second paragraph of the letter that began with Roosevelt thanking Crane for the gift of the book and the story, he addressed the problem directly:

> This evening I shall be around at the Madison Square Garden to see exactly what the Police do. They have a very difficult task with a crowd like that, because they have to be exceedingly good humored with the crowd, and they also have to please the Managers of the meeting who know nothing about crowds, and yet they have to control twenty thousand people. I will say one thing for them at the Bryan meeting; we have not had a single complaint of clubbing or brutality from any man claiming to have suffered; the Managers of the meeting and the Manager of the Garden have both written us in the warmest terms.

Earlier in the same letter, Roosevelt announced that he was "leaving in a few days for a three weeks trip to the West," and Crane took advantage of that absence to hammer home his irritation in print. Why he should have been so angry at the police department is unclear. He had witnessed numerous injustices in New York and elsewhere in the past without taking the trouble to write about them, and only once earlier, in the coal mine piece from 1894, had he ever let himself go in a full, splenetic outburst over a political or economic issue—paragraphs that were later cut from the text by McClure. Now, for whatever reason (a long-smoldering resentment that had ignited into fury after what he witnessed at the Garden? a personal grievance against the patrolmen of the Tenderloin?), he was riled up again, agitated enough to sit down and vent his feelings on paper, and yet, not wanting to attack his friend Roosevelt in the New York press, he cautiously hedged his bets and published his complaints in a series of articles for the remote *Port Jervis Evening Gazette* over three successive weeks in late August and early September, burying his remarks about the police in a column entitled "From the Metropolis" (tidbits from New York, not unlike the tidbits he had once written about Asbury Park) and then protecting himself still further by using his initials in the byline rather than his full name. The first piece is far and away the most vituperative. Before moving on to such topics as the fatalities from the current heat wave in New York (record numbers of people, fifteen hundred horses), the growing fad for bicycles, and the opening of a new department store, Crane kicks off the piece with a one-paragraph rant:

The wretched mismanagement which marked the police arrangements at the recent Bryan and Sewall notification at Madison Square Garden has occasioned a great deal of unfavorable comment, finding an echo in the columns of the daily press. The brutality and unnecessary harshness with which the large crowd was handled would have been inexcusable at any time, and on the evening in question it was simply shameful. Such blundering as was painfully in evidence on the night of the 12 inst. would not have been possible under the Byrnes regime [the former police superintendent, who had been dismissed by Roosevelt], and that fact is another reminder that what we have gained in official honesty through administrative reforms is more than counter-balanced by the effects of official incapacity and inexperience.

The article from the following week contains eight items, two of which take on other examples of police misconduct. After describing the spread of delicatessens in Manhattan to serve the growing need for "the hasty lunch," Crane adds:

For some unexplained reason the reformed police administration, early in its career, singled out the harmless and petty traders as subjects whom they could annoy with impunity. An obnoxious sanction of blue laws regulating the time of opening and closing the shops was made the basis of a systematic police persecution, and violators were promptly hauled before a city magistrate, to be promptly discharged. The dealers are now strongly organized for protection, public opinion is with them, and they will probably have something to say on Election day.*

In the sixth item, he is at it again:

It is to be hoped that an example will be made of the policeman who arrested an unoffending and innocent woman on 6th avenue the other night. This is a form of outrage that has become very frequent of late, and the disgrace and exemplary punishment of some of the official brutes would have a beneficial effect in serving as a warning to over zealous policemen.

---

* The Republicans were swept out of office in November, and the Tammany Democrats regained control of the city. The following April, Roosevelt left his job with the police department to become assistant secretary of the navy in the newly installed McKinley administration.

The innocent party in question was a prostitute named Ruby Young (a.k.a. Dora Wilkins and Dora Clark), and how odd, or prescient, or downright spooky that Crane should mention her in his column. He still hadn't met her at that point, but this was the woman who would cross paths with him in the early morning hours of September sixteenth, triggering the controversy that led to the longest police trial in the city's history, public humiliation for Crane, and his eventual departure from New York.

Finally, in the article from September ninth, he alludes to one of the most contested policies of Roosevelt's administration: strict enforcement of the recently enacted Raines Law, which banned saloons from operating on Sunday. Almost all men with jobs worked six days a week, and by denying them the small pleasure of gathering with their friends for a casual drink on their one day off, the law was seen as an unwarranted punishment of the working class and generally despised throughout the city. Only hotels with ten or more rooms were allowed to sell liquor on Sunday now, but only to guests, and only if accompanied by sandwiches. To circumvent these restrictions, saloon keepers expanded their establishments by renting out back rooms and upstairs rooms in order to qualify as hotels. Because most of the "guests" were prostitutes, one of the unintended results of the Raines Law was to increase the number of brothels across the city.*

After returning to New York on September eleventh, Roosevelt organized a lunch with four of his male friends, and whether planned or not, each happened to represent one of his abiding interests: Crane (literature), Jacob Riis (tenement reform), Hamlin Garland (the West), and big-game hunter William Chanler (killing large animals). In his memoir from 1930, *Roadside Meetings*, Garland recalled that Roosevelt chatted comfortably with everyone but Crane, who scarcely said a word throughout the meal and sat there looking "like a man in trouble." Could Roosevelt have known about the Port Jervis articles? Unlikely. But it could be that Crane thought he did, or at least suspected he did, which was enough to put him on edge. Several times in the war novel, Henry Fleming is so overcome by guilt that he fears his fellow soldiers can see that guilt written across his face. Was Crane in a similar kind of quandary with Roosevelt? Perhaps. If nothing else, he must have felt embarrassed to be sitting at the table with a man

---

* The law had its comical aspects as well. In *The Battle with the Slum* (Macmillan, 1902), Jacob Riis reports on the invention of "brick sandwiches"—a single brick clamped between two slices of bread—which were placed on bars in mocking compliance with the statute. Real sandwiches were sometimes placed there for show, but once, when an unsuspecting customer picked one up and was about to start eating it, "the police restored the sandwich to the bartender and made no arrests" (p. 224).

he had just attacked in print, the same man, as it happened, who was no doubt paying for his lunch.

W.R.H. The Tenderloin was given its name in 1876 by police captain Alexander "Clubber" Williams. Following his transfer to the Twenty-ninth Precinct, one of the most corrupt areas of the city, he is reported to have said: "I've been having chuck steak ever since I've been on the force, but now I'm going to have a bit of tenderloin." Williams seized the opportunity he had been given, and over the next nineteen years he built a fortune that included a house and other properties in New York, a second house in Connecticut, real estate in Japan, and enough money collected from graft to invest the loot and turn several hundred thousand dollars into millions.

A midtown neighborhood with fluctuating borders over the years, the Tenderloin originally encompassed the east-west blocks between Fifth and Eighth Avenues and the north-south blocks between Twenty-third and Fifty-seventh Streets. By the time Crane began writing his pieces for Hearst, it had shrunk somewhat and now extended between Fourth and Seventh Avenues on one axis and between Twenty-third and Forty-second Streets on the other. But as Crane put it in one of his *Journal* sketches: "The Tenderloin is more than a place. It is an emotion." Along the avenues of that emotion were the majority of theaters and hotels in the city, and down its darkened side streets nearly all the gambling houses, opium dens, and brothels—yet one more double world in which light rubbed shoulders with darkness and virtue pretended to ignore its fraternal bond with sin.*

Crane started his investigations for Hearst in the middle of September (around the same time as the awkward lunch with Roosevelt), but for some weeks before that he had been dropping in at the Jefferson Market Police Court to observe the arraignments, hearings, and trials of various Tenderloin figures brought before the bench, one of whom was probably Dora Clark, which would account for her mention in the Port Jervis article from August twenty-eighth. On the night of September fifteenth, he conducted a prearranged interview with two chorus girls who worked in the neighborhood. Whether they were legitimate theatrical performers or

---

* For all the new administration's efforts to abandon the Clubber Williams philosophy of law enforcement, sin remained a profitable business because the police were still on the take, collecting their weekly protection-money envelopes from the hundreds of enterprises that filled the darkened blocks—from peep shows to dope houses to bordellos (both straight and gay) to raunchy bars with private rooms for indulging in this, that, and the other. As long as these underground establishments stayed clear of the boulevards and brightly lit thoroughfares, the law continued to play an active role in keeping them open.

something else is not known, since in local jargon the term "chorus girl" also meant prostitute, and the names (and identities) of the two young women were never made public. The three-way conversation began at one of the area's "Turkish smoking parlors," a euphemism for low-end drug establishments where hashish (inexpensive, widely available, and not illegal) was regularly sampled by the customers, but sometime before midnight Crane and the two women left the smoking parlor on West Twenty-ninth Street, wandered over to the Broadway Garden, "a notorious hangout for prostitutes," and went on talking for another two hours. Toward the end of those hours, Dora Clark, an acquaintance of one of the chorus girls, walked over to the table to say hello and was invited to sit down with them. Not long after, they all decided to go home. They left the Broadway Garden together, and while Crane accompanied one of the chorus girls to an uptown cable car, Dora Clark and her acquaintance waited for him on the corner of Broadway and Thirty-first Street. As Crane strolled back to them after putting the first chorus girl on the car, he saw that they were deep in conversation. Two men walked quickly past them, no doubt headed for home after a long night out, and when Crane was within a few feet of the corner, another man unexpectedly sprang from the shadows and grabbed hold of the women. They both began to scream. An instant later, Crane understood that the man, evidently a plainclothes cop, was in the act of arresting his companions for soliciting the two men who had just walked by.

That was the beginning of the sordid tangle known as the Dora Clark Affair, the prelude to the first act of a play in several acts that dragged on through the end of October and continued to hover around Crane for the rest of his life and even beyond. In his written account of that night and the following morning (published in the *Journal* as "Adventures of a Novelist" just four days later), it was "a plain tale of two chorus girls, a woman of the streets, and a reluctant laggard witness." Crane fudges some of the preliminary details by reducing the smoking parlor and Broadway Garden to a single "resort on Broadway where the two chorus girls and the reluctant witness sat the entire evening" and disclaiming any prior knowledge of Clark, when in fact he had already written about one of her previous arrests, but those are small matters, even insignificant matters compared to Crane's decision to stick out his neck and involve himself in Clark's defense. He knew that standing up for her could cause serious damage to his reputation, and yet he went ahead and did it, in spite of how important that reputation was to him—as shown by his reluctance to speak out boldly against the police actions that had so infuriated him,

Ink portrait of Crane accompanying "Adventures of a Novelist,"
New York Journal, *September 20, 1896.*

planting his remarks in a busybody news column of metropolitan trivia
published in a paper so far from the metropolis that his voice was bound
to go unheard. This time was different, however, and therein lies the nub
of the affair.

In Crane's telling, after the policeman announced why he was arresting
the two women, he, the reluctant witness, cried out: "What two men?" The
men who had just passed by, said the cop, at which point the girls began
to sob "hysterically" and try

to pull their arms away from the grip of the policeman. The chorus girl
seemed nearly insane with fright and fury. Finally she screamed:

"Well, he's my husband." And with her finger she indicated the reluctant witness. The witness at once replied to the swift, questioning glance
of the officer, "Yes, I am."

If it was necessary to avow a marriage to save a girl who is not a prostitute from being arrested as a prostitute, it must be done, though the
man suffer eternally. And then the officer forgot immediately—without
a second's hesitation, he forgot that a moment previously he had arrested
this girl for soliciting, and so, dropping her arm, released her.

But he still had the other one, declared the cop ("as picturesque as a wolf"), and then the nonsensical conversation started up again in much the same spirit as before, with the reluctant witness asking why bother to arrest either one of them and the officer answering it was because of the two men she had solicited, but no, the reluctant witness replied, "she didn't solicit those two men." Rather than trouble himself by responding to that assertion, the cop changed the subject and asked Crane and the chorus girl if they knew "this woman." Yes, the chorus girl answered, she'd seen her two or three times, but "the reluctant witness said at once that he knew nothing whatever of the girl."

"Well," said the officer, "she's a common prostitute."

There was a short silence then, but the reluctant witness presently said: "Are you arresting her as a common prostitute? She has been perfectly respectable since she has been with us. She hasn't done anything wrong since she has been in our company."

"I am arresting her for soliciting those two men," answered the officer, "and if you people don't want to get pinched, too, you had better not be seen with her."

Then began a parade to the station house—the officer and his prisoner ahead and two simpletons following.

The officer, whose name was Charles Becker, told the desk sergeant at the station house that he had seen the arrested woman "come from the resort on Broadway alone" (not true) and that as she was approaching Broadway and Thirty-first Street, she solicited the two men (also not true), at which point (that is, only afterward) she ran into a man and a woman at the corner (Crane and the chorus girl) and started talking to them as they stood on the curb (again not true), all the while neglecting to say anything about his temporary arrest of the chorus girl. On the strength of this account, the desk sergeant had the prisoner removed to one of the cells at the rear of the building. As she was being led away, she "screamed out a request to appear in her behalf before the Magistrate."

Meanwhile, as Becker told his untrue story, the chorus girl went on sobbing in "a paroxysm of terror," and Crane was fully occupied in trying to calm her down and prevent her from "making an uproar." After Dora Clark was locked up, the two of them left the station house, but once they were outside, the still-weeping girl shouted at him: "If you don't go to court and speak for that girl you are no man!" Thrown back by her words,

Crane stammered out in protest: "By George! I cannot . . . I can't afford to do that sort of thing. I—I—-"

After seeing the girl home, however, he began to have second thoughts. The arrest was wrong, he said to himself, and even if the girl was a prostitute, she had not been arrested for prostitution but for solicitation. As Crane reflects:

> "If I ever had a conviction in my life, I am convinced that she did not solicit those two men. Now, if these affairs occur from time to time, they must be witnessed occasionally by men of character. Do these reputable citizens interfere? No, they go home and thank God that they can still attend piously to their affairs. . . .
>
> "But this girl, be she prostitute or whatever, was at the time manifestly in my escort, and—Heaven save the blasphemous philosophy—a wrong done to a prostitute must be as purely a wrong as a wrong done to a queen," said the reluctant witness—this blockhead.
>
> "Moreover, I believe that this officer has dishonored his obligation as a public servant. Have I a duty as a citizen, or do citizens have duty, as a citizen, or do citizens have no duties? Is it a mere myth that there was at one time a man who possessed a consciousness of civic responsibility, or has it become a distinction of our municipal civilization that men of this character shall be licensed to depredate in such a manner upon those who are completely at their mercy?"

So Crane returned to the station house and talked to the desk sergeant, asking if there was anything he could send the girl to make her more comfortable and then giving a full account of the arrest as he had seen it. The sergeant had no opinion on the matter. Perhaps Crane was telling the truth and the officer had lied, he said, but the fact was that the girl was a known prostitute and that was why he had ordered her to be put in a cell. Again, Crane said what he had already said to Becker at the time of the arrest and later to himself:

> "But she was not arrested as a common prostitute. She was arrested for soliciting two men, and I know that she didn't solicit the two men."
>
> "Well," said the sergeant, "that, too, may all be true, but I give you the plain advice of a man who has been behind this desk for years, and knows how these things go, and I advise you simply to stay home. If you monkey with this case, you are pretty sure to come out with mud all over you."

"I suppose so," said the reluctant witness. "I haven't a doubt of it. But I don't see how I can, in honesty, stay away from court in the morning."

"Well, do it anyhow," said the sergeant.

"But I don't see how I can do it."

The sergeant was bored. "Oh, I tell you, the girl is nothing but a common prostitute," he said, wearily.

The reluctant witness on reaching his room set the alarm clock for the proper hour.

At eight-thirty in the morning, Crane walked into the building that housed the Jefferson Market Police Court, hair combed, dressed in a dark blue suit, ready to do his part as a witness to the unlawful apprehension of an innocent girl, but just as the desk sergeant had advised him some hours earlier, his fellow reporters all urged him to go home and forget about it because, as one of them remarked, involving himself in the case wouldn't look "very respectable," while another tried to soothe his conscience by telling him that "it [was] only a temporary wrong." Hard-pressed to understand the meaning of a "temporary wrong," Crane wrote:

> Thus—if the girl was wronged—it is to be seen that all circumstances, all forces, all opinions, all men were combined to militate against her. Apparently the united wisdom of the world declared that no man should do anything but throw his sense of justice to the winds in an affair of this description. "Let a man have a conscience for the daytime," said wisdom. "Let him have a conscience for the daytime, but it is idiocy for a man to have a conscience at 2:30 in the morning in the case of an arrested prostitute."

Rapidly coming to the conclusion of his five-page article, Crane reported that after Clark gave her testimony—which the reluctant witness understood to be perfectly true and yet was bound to be believed by no one present but himself—he stepped forward to confirm the accuracy of what she had said, "and the Magistrate discharged the prisoner."

That is precisely what happened, and there are no errors in Crane's account of the trial. At that point, the affair seemed to be over and done with, and since Crane's piece was primarily focused on his own actions and why and how he came to feel it was necessary for him to speak up in Clark's defense, he didn't bother to include Clark's lengthy testimony, which he must have assumed was irrelevant by then. If there had been no second act to the story, his assumption would have been correct, but after the story started up again a few weeks later, knowledge of Clark's testimony becomes fundamental to understanding the complicated nature of the affair.

Several papers reported on the brief trial. If anyone other than Crane had been involved, the articles might never have been written, but he was a known figure by then, and his presence in court that morning was deemed interesting enough to warrant news coverage—especially when it concerned a steamy bit of business about a young, highly attractive woman of the night. According to one of the articles, after Becker gave his version of the arrest,

the young woman denied this story and wept as she told the Magistrate that she was being persecuted.

This is the story she told: "The police have been persecuting me ever since I was arrested about three weeks ago by Policeman Rosenberg of the same station as Detective Becker. On that occasion, I was walking on Broadway, where it was rather dark, and Rosenberg approached me and spoke. I told him to go about his business, calling him a negro. Then he arrested me, and when I told the Magistrate when I was arraigned the following morning of the mistake I had made in supposing that Rosenberg was a negro the policeman became angry.

"He threatened to arrest me for spite. Two nights later I was talking with a friend at Twenty-third street, and I was warned by two hackmen that Rosenberg and Policeman Conway were looking for me. I waited until after I thought they had gone and then I started home through a side street. Conway was following me and he arrested me when there was no one about.

"The next morning I was fined. Since that time I have been arrested on sight by all of the precinct police in citizen clothes.

"I was in the Broadway Garden last night with a man and woman and we left the place together. Becker came across the street and, while the man was placing the other woman on the car, he took hold of my arm and placed me under arrest. I had spoken to no one."

Novelist Crane then told Magistrate Cornell that he wished to testify. He said that he was searching for material for sketches, and that last night he was introduced to the prisoner in the Broadway Garden. He said that he, the prisoner and two other women left the Broadway Garden together and walked to Thirty-first street, where he left the Clark woman for a minute, and he knew that she did not speak to any men.

"The testimony of this gentleman, whom I know," said Magistrate Cornell, "causes me to discharge you this time."

"But, your Honor," said the prisoner, "I will be arrested on sight the next time I show my face in the precinct."

"I will look out for that," said Magistrate Cornell.

Nothing is known about Policeman Rosenberg, and therefore what kind of Rosenberg he happened to be is anyone's guess (Danish or Jewish or something else), but Clark's testimony seems to imply—*maybe*—that he had stopped her on the street with some sort of sexual proposition. However, incorrectly assuming he was a black man, that is, a person she would never consent to sleep with (not surprising in racist New York during those openly racist times), she had brushed him off, and not only was he frustrated by her refusal but deeply insulted by her error, infuriated by it. After that night, the pretty streetwalker had become the target of every cop in the precinct, Rosenberg and his partner Martin Conway to begin with, then Becker, and then all the way up to the captain, a powerful figure named Chapman. That was the background to the mess Crane had unknowingly walked into on Broadway and Thirty-first Street, and, as he would later find out, in speaking up for Clark he had done more than challenge the testimony of one bad cop—he had impugned the reputation of the entire precinct and, by extension, the entire New York City police force, including headman Roosevelt himself.

For the time being, however, the matter seemed to be closed, and when Crane walked out of the courtroom on the morning of September sixteenth, the general feeling among the press was that he had handled the situation admirably. As the headlines of the next day's *Journal* announced:

**STEPHEN CRANE AS
BRAVE AS HIS HERO
SHOWED THE "BADGE OF COUR-
AGE" IN A NEW YORK
POLICE COURT.
BOLDLY AVOWED HE HAD BEEN
THE ESCORT OF A TENDER-
LOIN WOMAN.**

It made sense that the *Journal* would vigorously defend its own reporter, but even the neutral papers were respectful in their headlines and singled out Crane as the central attraction of their reports, with many of them also running excerpts from the interviews he gave to various journalists on the afternoon of the sixteenth. The fullest exchange appeared in the *Journal* on the seventeenth, and it bears quoting for a number of reasons: the insight it gives into Crane's state of mind immediately after the trial, the fact that he went on record with a comment about his willingness to support Clark if and when she decided to bring perjury charges against Becker, and especially for what the concluding paragraphs tell us about the attitude of the police toward Crane's testimony—a small sign of what was to come.

"I was strongly advised by Sergeant McDermott not to try to help her, for I seemed a respectable sort of man, he said, and it would injure me. I well knew I was risking a reputation that I had worked hard to build. But," he added, "she was a woman and unjustly accused, and I did what was my duty as a man. I realized that if a man should stand tamely by, in such a case, our wives and sisters would be at the mercy of any ruffian who disgraces the uniform. The policeman flatly lied, and if the girl will have him prosecuted for perjury I will gladly support her."

[*Journal*]: "While waiting to speak in the court room, and to thus openly dare the censure of the public, did you not feel like your own hero in 'The Red Badge of Courage' before his first battle?"

He smiled. "Yes, I did. I was badly frightened, I admit, and would gladly have run away, could I have done so with honor."

[*Journal*]: "And now that it is over, I presume you are also like your hero, in being ready to face a sword ordeal without a tremor?"

"No, no!" Mr. Crane exclaimed. "I differ from my own hero, for I would be just as frightened the next time!"

"Just how would you describe the girl, Mr. Crane?"

"Why," he said, "she was really handsome, you know, and she had hair—red hair—dark red"—

"Yes"—

"And she was dressed, I'm pretty sure, in some kind of shirt waist," he concluded, desperately.

At the Nineteenth Precinct Police Station it was learned last evening that the girl's fears of re-arrest were well founded.

"I only hope she'll be out to-night and be run in here," said Sergeant Daly, chuckling gleefully at the thought.

Captain Chapman said he fully believed Becker's story.

[*Journal*]: "Does it make no difference that a man of world-wide reputation states that she committed no offense?" he was asked.

"Who is this Crane? An actor?"

"No. An author."

"Never heard of him before. Becker is a good man, and has been on the force four years. I know him well, and so do the police generally. And I believe him."

He admitted, however, that very recently Becker had made a similar arrest, and that a number of reporters had alleged that the girl in that case was innocent.

Articles were published in New York, Boston, Philadelphia, and beyond, and not one of them could resist bringing *The Red Badge of Courage* into the discussion or treating the affair in the most melodramatic terms (young knight-errant rescues damsel in distress), which Crane must have found to be both ridiculous and annoying, but at least the early coverage was favorable. As soon as the next day, however, he was being gently mocked by the *Boston Herald* ("Stephen Crane, novelist, has been distinguishing himself in the New York police courts in a manner that does credit to his heart, if not to his head"), and with more snide comments and distortions surely on the way (they were), Crane decided to clear the air by offering his own account of what had happened in "Adventures of a Novelist" (an illustrated, front-page story published by the *Journal* on Sunday the twentieth), hoping to quiet the chatter and refocus the public's attention on the most important aspect of the case: not himself, and not even Clark, but the problem of police abuse.

He put an unusual amount of effort into writing the article, going through several drafts before he handed it in, paring it down and revising until he had achieved what he felt was the proper balance. One of the discarded passages is significant, however, a five-sentence screed that crystallizes the thoughts Crane had been developing ever since the Madison Square Garden fiasco in mid-August—which had driven him to write the Port Jervis articles—but by now he had gained a better understanding of the fundamental issues involved and was able to express himself with a new clarity and forcefulness:

> Everyone who thinks is likely to know that the right of arrest is one of the most dangerous powers which organized society can give to the individual. It is a power so formidable in its reaches that there is rarely a situation confronting the people which calls for more caution. A blackguard as a private citizen is lamentable; a blackguard as a police officer is an abomination. Theoretically the first result of government is to put control into the hands of honest men and nullify as far as may

Additional drawings of scenes described in "Adventures of a Novelist,"
New York Journal, *September 20, 1896.*

be the ambitions of criminals. When government places power in the hands of a criminal it of course violates this principle and becomes absurd.

Perhaps he thought he was beginning to sound like a soapbox orator, so he cut the passage and replaced it with a single sentence: "I believe that this officer has dishonored his obligation as a public servant." True enough, but in the longer version he explains why he believes that—which also explains why he declared himself willing to stand up for Clark again if she decided to pursue a case against Becker. Becker was the one Crane cared about, for Becker and other cops of his ilk were not guardians of the peace, they were destroyers, and they deserved to be brought down.

31

MEANWHILE, HE PUSHED ON WITH HIS WORK, AND THE WHEELS OF the world cranked forward. Just two days after the publication of "Adventures of a Novelist," he took part in the joint reading with Cahan and Garland at the Lantern Club. A new poem of his appeared in the *Bookman* ("I explain the silvered passing of a ship at night"), Reynolds came on board as his agent, the new version of *Maggie* appeared in England, and his most recent books, *The Little Regiment* and *The Third Violet*, were about to appear in print as well. As for the work he produced that fall, most of it consisted of stories, sketches, and articles about the Tenderloin, some of them perfunctory while others are impressively good, even stellar. It is hard to pin down exactly when they were written (a Mexican piece composed in the spring of 1895, for example, did not surface until October 1896), but the notable thing about these new efforts is that there is no difference in quality between the ones he wrote before his encounter with Clark and the ones he wrote after. A rare case of armored defensiveness, perhaps, or else a singular tenacity, but Crane was a person who wrote, who wrote and wrote and wrote, and once he applied himself to the particular writing task he had chosen to take on (whether for love or money), he vanished into the page in front of him.

Two microscopic gems of two pages each were written before the storm. One was a combination sketch-article inspired by Crane's visit to the Jefferson Market Police Court on September fourteenth (one day before his rendezvous with the chorus girls at the Turkish smoking parlor), and the other was a story syndicated by Bacheller on August thirtieth, about two weeks before Crane started working for Hearst.

"A Detail" begins with a tiny old woman in a black dress and a "curious little black bonnet" slowly making her way through the midafternoon tumult of the Sixth Avenue shopping district. Overwhelmed by the crowds and the noise around her, she wants to ask someone a question, but each time she is about to open her mouth and talk, her courage fails her. Then she sees two elegantly dressed young women looking into a shop window, scanning the goods on display as if they had all the time in the world. The reader understands at once that they are prostitutes ("they wore gowns with enormous sleeves that made them look like full-rigged ships with all sails set"), but the old woman has no inkling of what they do and takes them for a pair of fine, sophisticated young ladies. She sidles up to them, looks into the window herself, and then asks the question she was too timid to ask anyone else: "Excuse me but can you tell me where I can get any work?" The girls look her over, are about to "exchange a smile" but suppress the impulse and marvel at her wrinkles, which show "no trace of experience, knowledge," and the expression in her eyes, which has "the trustfulness of ignorance and the candor of babyhood." She explains that she is looking for work because she needs the money, and even though she isn't strong, she can sew well, and if she could land in a place "where there was a good many men folks," she could do the mending for the household. At that point, the girls at last exchange a smile, but it is a "subtly tender smile, the verge of personal grief." No, madame, one of them says, she doesn't think she knows anyone, but an instant after that, seeing the disappointment in the old woman's face, she asks for her address and promises to contact her if she manages to find a potential employer.

> The tiny old lady dictated her address, bending over to watch the girl write on a visiting card with a little silver pencil. Then she said: "I thank you very much." She bowed to them, smiling, and went on down the avenue.
>
> As for the two girls they went to the curb and watched this aged figure, small and frail, in its black gown and curious black bonnet. At last, the crowd, the innumerable wagons, intermingling and changing with uproar and riot, suddenly engulfed it.

A slight but moving episode, which if handled differently could have degenerated into farce or a swell of sobbing violin music, but those traps are avoided through linguistic restraint and emotional reserve to achieve an unsentimental pathos, that is, a genuine pathos and not some maudlin facsimile of it, and how fitting that the last paragraph is not told by an omniscient observer but seen through the eyes of the two young prostitutes as they watch the tiny figure in black disappear into the great maw of the city streets. Another cinematic moment, and, if I am not mistaken, this short, lightning-fast vignette is the only work of Crane's in which all the principal characters are women.

"An Eloquence of Grief" also concerns a woman in trouble, a young woman this time, a servant girl who has been accused of stealing by her employers and is about to be crushed in the grindworks of the criminal justice system—one case among the many Crane observed during his visits to the court. He opens with an ironic description of the setting, comparing the courtroom to a church with its "high and saintly" windows and the policeman posted at the door—who tells all who enter, "Take off your hat"—to "a priest when the sanctity of a chapel is defied or forgotten." He moves on to the various clusters of people in the courtroom, those involved in cases and those who have come to watch "for curiosity's sake," hoping to inject some thrill into their "jaded, world-weary nerves—wires that refused to vibrate for ordinary affairs." Then, and only then, does he present the servant girl, who is standing in a corner under the guard of a plainclothes detective, weeping her heart out as the tears fall from her eyes and leave "fierce pink marks on her face." From time to time, she looks across the room "where two well-dressed young women and a man stood waiting with the serenity of people who are not concerned as to the interior fittings of a jail." These are her employers, and when the case is brought before the bench, the two women testify "calmly and moderately" that the girl stole fifty dollars' worth of silk underwear from one of their rooms. By contrast, when the girl is given a chance to tell her story, she is so nervous and afraid that her lips have turned white. The lawyer for the plaintiffs questions her—"with the air," Crane tells us, "of a man throwing flower-pots at a stone house"—and then the short hearing concludes with the judge declaring that the evidence is strong enough "to commit the girl for trial."

> Instantly the quick-eyed court officer began to clear the way for the next case. The well-dressed women and their escort turned one way and the girl turned another, toward a door with an austere arch leading into a stone-paved passage. Then it was that a great cry rang through the court-room, the cry of this girl who believed that she was lost.

The cry is so loud, so piercing, that it cuts through the crowd like a blade. The girl falls back into the arms of a court officer, and as "her wild heels clicked twice on the floor," she bellows out in horror: "I am innocent! Oh, I am innocent!"

It is an extraordinary, wholly unexpected outburst, so outside the norms of conventional public behavior that Crane cuts away in the next paragraph to examine the scream itself and its effect on the people in the room—which is to say, finally, the effect it had on him.

> People pity those who need none, and the guilty sob alone; but innocent or guilty, this girl's scream described such a profound depth of woe—it was so graphic of grief, that it slit with a dagger's sweep the curtain of common-place, and disclosed the gloom-shrouded spectre that sat in the young girl's heart so plainly, in so universal a tone of the mind, that a man heard expressed some far-off midnight terror of his own thought.

It is a curiously bumpy passage for Crane at this point in the evolution of his prose, one that begins powerfully with its epigrammatic assertions, builds its argument with the sudden, compassionate turn into "a profound depth of woe" (not just the girl's but the woe of everyone who has ever suffered greatly), and then loses its footing with the clumsy "graphic of grief" and the overblown "gloom-shrouded spectre," only to right itself in the last phrases and end as powerfully as it began. Who knows how quickly these two pages were written and under what circumstances, but the small stylistic stumbles carry their own emotional weight, for they show the generally sure-handed, ever-articulate Crane beginning to stammer as he gropes for the words to convey the enormity of the girl's scream—the transcendent force of a human soul laid bare in full view of others and, as a consequence, its deeply personal impact on those others, Crane himself above all.

Nevertheless, the true subject of the piece is not the girl or her agony or the decision rendered in her case but the court itself and how blind justice plods on in its execution of the law—rapidly, mechanically, with supreme indifference to the lives of the people it judges. No sooner does the girl's case end than the next one begins, and Crane concludes his brief report by jumping into an entirely different register:

> The cries died away down the stone-paved passage. A patrolman leaned one arm composedly on the railing, and down below him stood an aged, almost toothless wanderer, tottering and grinning.
>
> "Please, yer honer," said the old man as the time arrived for him to speak, "if ye'll lave me go this time, I've nivver been dhrunk befoor, sir."
>
> A court officer lifted his hand to hide a smile.

Yes, it is funny, but more important than funny, it seethes with ironic disdain, even contempt. Just moments before, a servant girl had ripped apart the heavens with her howl of grief, but those cries have been forgotten now, and because the tragic and the comic are always indistinguishable from one another in a court of law, it is always business as usual there, and now that we've moved on to the next case, let's see if we can stop ourselves from laughing at that funny Irish drunk.

In what must have been the fastest journey between conception and publication of any of his stories, the magazine *Town Topics* sent Crane's newest little fiction out into the world on October first. Written just days after he had testified in court, "In the Tenderloin: A Duel Between an Alarm Clock and a Suicidal Purpose" followed fast on the heels of the already finished "Adventures of a Novelist," and it is interesting to note that alarm clocks figure in both works. I doubt that Crane himself was aware of the repetition, but there they are, as bright as one-hundred-watt bulbs, and when we put the two of them together for a closer look, they turn out to be remarkably similar and yet wholly different, for the real alarm clock in Crane's room allowed him to get up in time to go to court and save a Tenderloin prostitute from wrongful arrest, whereas the second one, the imaginary one, is used by a pimp to clunk a Tenderloin prostitute on the head. Was Crane voicing his exasperation with Clark for having dragged him into the compromising swirl of controversy and public attention that had put his name in dozens of headlines across the country? Such exasperation that a part of him wanted to bash in her skull with the clock that had summoned him to her defense? Possibly. And if so, a telling indicator of how torn he felt about having put his reputation on the line, but we should also remember that every work of fiction has an autobiographical component in it somewhere, however obscure or submerged or unknowable it might be, and with or without the shadowy presence of Dora Clark, this work happens to be a good one—rich, deeply complex, and strange, by far the best of the Tenderloin stories Crane wrote during those rough weeks prior to his twenty-fifth birthday.

He opens with a facetious, first-person prologue in which he complains that everyone already seems to know everything there is to know about the Tenderloin, from clergymen to police forces to his distant "friends from the stars," but now that he is about to tell of the battle fought in the Tenderloin between an alarm clock and a suicidal purpose—"a matter of no consequence"—he feels that it could be the one Tenderloin incident not previously reported to every person in the world.

A tone has been quickly established—arch, playful, distant, and self-conscious—and Crane hews to it until the end of the story, which recounts a harrowing night-to-dawn episode that nearly undoes a pimp named Swift Doyer and his unnamed prostitute girlfriend but is also a commentary on storytelling itself and the contrast between life lived by real people and the lives of imaginary characters presented in stories.

Swift and his girl are quarreling in their small Tenderloin flat. He has caught her out in a lie, and now he is letting her have it because he is "jealous in the strange and devious way of his kind," thundering forth accusations in a repetitive, unhinged tirade that gives the sobbing girl no chance to defend herself. Eventually, after calling her a liar a dozen times in twelve slightly different ways, he pauses, stands up from the table to light a cigarette, and orders her to stand up as well "and let me see you lie!"

There was a flurry of white in the darkness, which was no more definite to a man than the ice floes which your reeling ship passes in the night. Then, when the gas glared out suddenly, the girl stood before him. She was a wondrous white figure in a vestal-like robe. She resembled the priestess in paintings of long-gone Mediterranean religions. Her hair fell wildly on her shoulder. She threw out her arms and cried to Swift in a woe that seemed almost as real as the woe of good people.

"Oh, oh, my heart is broken! My heart is broken!"

But Swift knew as well as the rest of mankind that these girls have no hearts to be broken, and this act filled him with a new rage. He grabbed an alarm clock from the dresser and banged her heroically on the head with it.

That terminates the first sequence of events. After the clunking, the girl staggers off to the mirror. Swift assumes that she wants to inspect the damage to her head, but when he starts in with another verbal attack, she gazes at her own image and says, "I've taken morphine, Swift!"

The yelling stops, the anger stops, everything stops. Swift jumps over to "a little red pill box" and sees that it is empty. Eight quarter-gram doses are gone. It is enough to kill someone, and as Crane wryly notes in the next sentence, "The Suicidal Purpose was distinctly ahead of the Alarm Clock." Then, "with great presence of mind," that is, with no presence of mind, Swift throws the empty pill box out the window, as if that could do either one of them the least bit of good, since the pills that had previously been in the box are now in the girl's stomach.

A furious struggle against time suddenly begins as Swift marshals his forces to save her, for in spite of his raging temper tantrum of just a moment ago, he loves the girl and cannot imagine his life without her. He pours whiskey down her throat in order to keep her awake, then starts punching her in order to keep her awake, and if punching seems an odd way to revive someone in danger of passing out, Crane defends the tactic by observing that "our decorous philosophy knows little of the love and despair that was in those caresses," and as Swift goes on punching her and plying her with whiskey, he talks to her as well, calling "the light into her eyes" and "her soul back from the verge," but for all his efforts, she slides "limply in her chair like a cloth figure." Not knowing what else to do, he props her up in the chair and runs off to the kitchen to make coffee. A difficult task, in that his fingers seem reluctant to obey him, but eventually he manages to will them into completing the job. "When he lifted the girlish figure and carried her into the kitchen, he was as wild, haggard, gibbering, as a man of midnight murders." A bit excessive, perhaps, but well in keeping with the hyperbolic tone maintained throughout ("Oh, oh, my heart is broken!"), and then Crane polishes off the sentence with this somewhat bizarre notion (made more bizarre by the fact that "juke" is probably a misprint of "duke"): "and it was only because he was not engaged in the respectable and literary assassination of a royal juke that almost any sensible writer would be ashamed of this story."*

Why ashamed? Because respectable assassinations are literary ones committed against high-born jukes or dukes, and Doyer is a "man of midnight murders" (or looks like one, in any case) and therefore is not respectable, which means that any writer who chooses to tell his story ought to be ashamed of himself for scorning literary assassinations in favor of real ones. It is all a joke, of course. Again, Crane is making fun of the genteel pieties of standard contemporary fiction, but at the same time he is also defending himself (by reverse logic) for his interest in characters such as Swift Doyer, a preoccupation that was not always looked upon kindly by the arbiters of good taste. Later that month, for example, another one of his lowlife reports printed in the *Journal*, "The Tenderloin as It Really Is," was attacked by a San Francisco newspaper as "the veriest filth," so revolting that "we have yet to see even the 'Police Gazette' descend to such depths."

After that sentence about respectable and unrespectable assassinations, the story leaps several hours ahead, and "when the steel-blue dawn came and distant chimneys were black against a rose sky, the girl sat at the dining-room table chattering insanely and gesturing." She is still under the influence of the morphine, but she is still breathing as well, and as Swift watches her from the other side of the table, "he had to repeat to himself that he, worn-out, stupefied from his struggle, was sitting there

---

* It is also possible that in a clever double twist Crane was toying with the common slang meaning of "juke" in the late nineteenth century as a derogatory reference to the rural poor. A book published by sociologist Richard L. Dugdale in 1877, *The Jukes: A Study in Crime, Pauperism, Disease, and Heredity*, charts the history of several generations of an ever-expanding family of criminals. The name Jukes (a pseudonym) and the word "juke" were in the air during Crane's lifetime, and perhaps "royal juke" is meant to signify the top man in a gang of bumpkin outlaws, in other words, the lowest of the low, which would add another layer of meaning to this jesting passage. Then again, "juke" might well be a misprint of "duke," which would make the humor simpler and more straightforward—but still cutting. It is almost certain, however, that the name Swift Doyer is meant to evoke the crime-ridden alley in Manhattan's Chinatown that gave birth to the expression "As crooked as Doyers Street."

awaiting the moment when the unseen hand should whirl this soul into the abyss, and that then he should be alone."

At that point, something happens that turns the story around again, a most beautiful and unexpected something that makes this story the exceptional little work it is. In a stroke of pure inventive brilliance, Crane introduces a fly into the air around the table, a humble, ordinary housefly, the smallest of small insignificant creatures, and when the fly lands on a picture hanging from the wall, the girl's attention is suddenly drawn to it. "Oh," she says, "there's a little fly." She stands up, sticks out her finger, and leans forward to touch it. "Hello, little fly," she says, but no sooner does her finger come into contact with it than the fly ("perhaps too cold to be alert") drops to the floor. The girl cries out, sinks to her knees, and searches for her little friend, all the while "uttering tender apologies," and once it is found, she picks up the fly and carries it over to the gas jet in order to revive it—a rescue operation similar to the one Doyer has just performed on her. Like a drugged Ophelia floating through a mental ward, she babbles to herself in a semidelirious monologue filled with both pity and remorse.

> "Poor little fly," she said, "I didn't mean to hurt you. I wouldn't hurt you for anything. There now—p'r'aps when you get warm you can fly away again. Did I crush the poor little bit of fly? I'm sorry—honest, I am. Poor little thing! Why I wouldn't hurt you for the world, poor little fly—"

Swift is no longer a participant in the drama but merely an observer now, a stunned witness parked in his chair at the table watching what he imagines to be the death throes of his beloved. But something is off, he realizes, for death as he has seen it depicted in plays and stories is not supposed to happen as it appears to be happening now. Like Maggie Johnson with her fairy-tale dreams of love and Henry Fleming with his Homeric delusions about war, tough guy Swift Doyer has fallen prey to the snares of conventional storytelling about death. Humorous as the following passage might be, it is another sneak attack launched by Crane in the long and beautiful war he had been fighting for years.

> Strange things invariably come into a man's head at the wrong time, and Swift was aware that this scene was defying his preconceptions. His instruction had been that people when dying behaved in a certain manner. Why did this girl occupy herself with an accursed fly? Why

in the name of the gods of drama did she not refer to her past? Why, by the shelves of the saints of literature, did she not clutch her brow and say: "Ah, once I was an innocent girl"? What was wrong with this death scene? At one time he thought that his sense of propriety was so scandalized that he was upon the point of interrupting the girl's babble.

But here a new thought struck him. The girl was not going to die. How could she under these circumstances? The form was not correct.

Crane concludes this deft little piece of work with a morning tableau of his two exhausted characters and, at the very end, a final twist of his storyteller's corkscrew:

> For an hour the girl talked to the fly, the gas-jet, the walls, the distant chimneys. Finally she sat opposite the slumbering Swift and talked softly to herself.
>
> When broad day came they were both asleep, and the girl's fingers had gone across the table until they had found the locks on the man's forehead. They were asleep, and this after all is a human action, which may safely be done by characters in the fiction of our time.

Swift Doyer reappears as a secondary character in another Tenderloin story published the following month, "Yen-Hock Bill and His Sweetheart," a vigorously told black comedy about an opium-addict con man stricken with pneumonia, which also mentions another character from yet another story of the period, Jimmy the Mole in "Diamonds and Diamonds," a concert tenor with "a Tenderloin voice" who doubles as a con man himself and whose game is swindling pompous, well-heeled marks into buying diamond rings that have no diamonds in them. "Yen-Hock Bill" came out in the *Journal* on November twenty-ninth, but "Diamonds and Diamonds" seems to have been lost in a muddle of Crane manuscripts and slept on unnoticed through two world wars until it was found and finally published in the *Bulletin of the New York Public Library* in 1956. Both stories can be considered minor works, but minor for Crane is nevertheless good or even very good, and either one of these brisk, hard-boiled miniatures would more than hold its own in an anthology of classic New York stories.

He also published two reports on the Tenderloin for Hearst, unremarkable but entertaining strings of real or imagined anecdotes about the night spots of the district. The better one, "The Tenderloin as It Really Is," was provocative enough to inspire the "veriest filth" comment from the *Wave* in San Francisco, probably because it includes a blow-by-blow account of a fierce barroom brawl, but there is also this droll, deadpan vignette that strikes me as something that would fit comfortably into a mid-twentieth-century absurdist play:

> Five men flung open the wicket doors of a brilliant café on Broadway and, entering, took seats at a table. They were in evening dress, and each man held his chin as if it did not belong to him.
>
> "Well, fellows, what'll you drink?" said one. He found out, and after the ceremony there was a period of silence. Ultimately another man cried: "Let's have another drink." Following this outburst and its attendant ceremony there was another period of silence.
>
> At last a man murmured: "Well, let's have another drink." Two members of the party discussed the state of the leather market. There was an exciting moment when a little newsboy slid into the place, crying a late extra, and was ejected by the waiter. The five men gave the incident their complete attention.
>
> "Let's have a drink," said one afterward.
>
> At an early hour of the morning one man yawned and said: "I'm going home. I've got to catch an early train, and—"
>
> The four others awoke. "Oh, hold on, Tom. Hold on. Have another drink before you go. Don't go without a last drink."
>
> He had it. Then there was a silence. Then he yawned again and said: "Let's have another drink."

Crane's most compelling newspaper work during the Clark Affair had nothing to do with the Tenderloin or New York City, however, and when one stops to imagine the turmoil he must have been living through that fall, it seems fitting that he should have accepted an assignment from Pulitzer's *World* to travel north to a small Hudson River town in the company of a staff illustrator to write a report about the electric chair at the local prison, Sing Sing. A doleful job, to be sure, but given Crane's circumstances at the time, perhaps he was in the proper mood to contemplate death in its most modern, mechanically efficient form. Death had been the subject of three of his best new stories, both the near deaths of the New York Kid and Swift Doyer's girlfriend and the consummated death of Bill the sheepherder, but those had been imagined deaths in works of fiction, not real deaths of living men and women, and even if the report from Sing Sing did not require him to witness an execution, looking at the empty wooden chair in the execution chamber would be hard enough.

All the whimsy and bounce and sprightly turns of phrase in the Tenderloin sketches and stories are absent in "The Devil's Acre." No doubt Crane had been keeping his spirits up with those rhetorical high jinks, but now that he had arrived at Sing Sing, the fun stopped.

He begins by going directly into the chamber. The walls and ceiling are lined with polished wood, and the only object in the room is the chair, also made of polished wood. It is a large chair, the kind of thing a prosperous banker might sit in, and the place reeks of varnish, a smell so strong that it produces an atmosphere similar to the one inside a carriage factory. A long pipe sticks out from behind a partition, and hanging from the end of it is an electric wire, "as thick as a cigar." Some broad, thick straps are draped haphazardly over the arms of the chair. The courteous, helpful man who has guided Crane and his companion into the room tells them that "the whole business takes about a minute from the time we go after them," but when he asks if they would like to be strapped into the chair "to imagine how it feels," they politely turn down the offer. They know his time is valuable, they explain, and they wouldn't want to put him to such trouble.

Crane begins to muse on the contrast between the tranquility of the setting and its morbid purpose, "for the room is a place for the coronation of crime and the chair is the throne of death," and all these "ordinary things"—"an odor of oiled woods, a keeper's ... unemotional voice ... a broom ... in a corner near the door, a blue sky and a bit of moving green tree at a window so small that it might have been made by a canister shot"—only augment the horror "of this comfortable chair, this commonplace bit of furniture that waits in silence and loneliness, and waits and waits and waits."

> It is patient—patient as time. Even should its next stained and sallow prince be now a baby, playing with alphabet blocks near his mother's feet, this chair will wait. It is as unknown to his eyes as are the shadows of trees at night, and yet it towers over him, monstrous, implacable, infernal, his fate—this patient, comfortable chair.

Crane leaves the building and wanders off to a hillside overlooking the Hudson, where little ships pass slowly along the "silver sheet" of water and all is still on the beautiful ground above, which happens to be the site of the convicts' graveyard.

> Simple white boards crop out from the soil in rows. The inscriptions are abrupt. "Here lies Wong Kee. Died June 1, 1890." The boards front the

wide veranda of a cottage. . . . If people on this veranda ever lower their eyes from the wide river and gaze at these tombstones they probably find that they can just make out the inscriptions at the distance and just can't make them out at the distance. They encounter the dividing line between coherence and a blur.

The last two sentences seem to capture the essence of the Crane project in all its multiple forms, fiction and nonfiction alike, for at the heart of his writing the keenest attention is given to the vagaries of the perceived world, the eye looking out and trying to make sense of what it sees and the mind looking inward at the jumble of contradictory impulses and emotions that continually bombard consciousness, and nowhere in his work does he manage to express it more precisely than he does in this passage. Looking out at something from a distance that shuttles back and forth across the boundary between what is legible and illegible, *the dividing line between coherence and a blur*, and that line, that place of indeterminacy, where the subjective and the objective merge, is the narrow ground on which most of Crane's work is played out, and because this ground had never been so fully explored by anyone in the past, he stands as the discoverer of a new territory. That accounts for his importance to American literature, I believe, and explains why he was the one who opened the door on what would happen next.

The passage continues:

It is a most comfortable house, and yet a person properly superstitious would possibly not care to offer more than $3 for it. For, after all, it is impossible for the eye to avoid these boards, these austere tributes to the memory of men who died black souled, whose glances in life fled sideways with a kind of ferocity, a cowardice and a hatred that could perhaps embrace the entire world.

These dark thoughts take an even darker turn as he tries to imagine the graveyard at night, conjuring up "gruesome figures," "the laugh of the devil," and "clutching, demoniac fingers," a catalogue of terrors that is summed up in the title of the piece and underscored by a blunt, eight-word sentence in the middle of the paragraph: "It is the fiend's own acre, this hillside." Just when he is about to be carried away by this flood of gothic imagery, however, he returns to dry land and starts talking about the cows grazing on the hillside.

It takes more than this to arouse the awe of a cow. A cow cares little for superstition. A cow cares for grass. Good grass grows here. Kind, motherly old cows wander placidly among these new and old graves. Ordinarily it would be very annoying to have tombstones constantly in one's way. A solemn inscription at every turn is enough to vex the most gentle spirit. But these matters cannot move the deep philosophy of a cow. It is not a question of sentiment; it is a question of pasturage.

Nightmares followed by levity, the same doubleness that infuses so much of Crane's work, but before long he settles down into a careful description of the place and, doing what he does best, tells us exactly what he sees as he roams through that field of dead and forgotten criminals, ending his excursion to the devil's acre in near silence as he looks at a sundered cross jutting through the weeds.

Time deals strokes of rain, wind and sun to all things, and a board is not strong against them.

Soon it falls. There is none here to plant it upright again. The men that lie here are of the kind that the world wishes to forget, and there is no objection raised to the assault of nature. And so it comes to pass that the dates on the boards are recent. These white boards have marched like soldiers from the southward end of the field to the northward. As they at the south became dim, rotted and fell, others sprang up at their right hand. As these in turn succumbed, still others appeared at their right. It is a steady travel towards the north. In the other end there are now no boards; only a sinister undulation of the earth under the weeds. It is a fine short road to oblivion.

In the middle of the graveyard there is a dim but still defiant board upon which there is rudely carved a cross. Some singular chance has caused this board to be split through the middle, cleaving the cross in two parts ... but the aged board is still upright and the cross still expresses its form as if it had merely expanded and become transparent. It is a place for the chanting of monks.

Years would go by before it happened, and Crane himself would never know about it, but on July 30, 1915, Charles Becker, the policeman who had falsely arrested Dora Clark, was put to death in the same electric chair Crane had written about after his visit to Sing Sing in 1896. Becker was the first police officer in American history to be executed for the crime of murder.

To add to the strangeness, Becker was just one year older than Crane and had spent the first twenty years of his life in Sullivan County.

He moved to New York in 1890, worked at a number of odd jobs, and wound up as a bouncer in a German beer hall just off the Bowery. When he joined the police department in November 1893, he was assigned to the Twenty-ninth Precinct and put under the command of Clubber Williams, who served as his teacher in the Clubber Williams School of Law Enforcement Ethics. With the return of Tammany Hall to power after the Republican defeat in 1896, Becker's career prospered, and as the years went by he rose through the ranks to become a sergeant, then a lieutenant, and managed to accumulate more than one hundred thousand dollars in extortion money from owners of Manhattan brothels and illegal gambling houses.

After he was promoted to lieutenant, his good fortune continued when the department blinked (or closed its eyes) and made him head of the Gambling Squad. In that capacity, he formed a close business association with Herman Rosenthal, a bookie and small-time gambling operator with a joint on West Forty-fifth Street, but in 1912, when Rosenthal refused to kick in five hundred dollars to the defense fund of Becker's press agent (who had been charged with killing a man during a raid on a gambling den), Becker turned on Rosenthal by ordering a raid on his establishment. Rosenthal retaliated by going to the press, and two days after the *World* published his affidavit accusing Becker and his partner of skimming twenty percent off his weekly profits, he was gunned down and killed by four Jewish mobsters from the Lower East Side as he was walking out of the Hotel Metropole on West Forty-third Street near Times Square. Two weeks later, Becker was arrested for instigating the murder, and at his trial that fall the jury found him guilty as charged. The verdict was overturned in a court of appeals, but at the retrial in 1914, he was found guilty again and sent to Sing Sing, where he was strapped into the electric chair the following year. According to the keeper of the death chamber who had spoken to Crane in 1896, the executions took no longer than a minute, but Becker's dragged on for more than nine minutes, and according to one writer on the subject, "it was long considered to be the clumsiest execution in the history of Sing Sing."

The Becker-Rosenthal case was national news for years, and its repercussions spread so far and so wide that there is a reference to the murder in a novel written by the heir to Crane's wonder-boy crown, F. Scott Fitzgerald. In chapter 4 of *The Great Gatsby* (1925), the gambler Meyer Wolfsheim sits with Gatsby and Nick Carraway in a Times Square hangout reminiscing about the old days at the Metropole:

> "Filled with faces dead and gone. Filled with friends gone now forever. I can't forget so long as I live the night they shot Rosy Rosenthal there. It was six of us at the table, and Rosy had eat and drunk a lot all evening. When it was almost morning the waiter came up to him with a funny look and says somebody wants to speak to him outside. 'All right,' says Rosy, and begins to get up, and I pulled him down in his chair.
>
> "'Let the bastards come in here if they want you, Rosy, but don't you, so help me, move outside this room.'
>
> "It was four o'clock in the morning then, and if we'd of raised the blinds we'd of seen daylight."
>
> "Did he go?" I asked innocently.
>
> "Sure he went." Mr. Wolfsheim's nose flashed at me indignantly. "He turned around in the door and says: 'Don't let that waiter take away my coffee!' Then he went out on the sidewalk, and they shot him three times in his full belly and drove away."
>
> "Four of them were electrocuted," I said, remembering.
>
> "Five, with Becker."

32

ON SEPTEMBER 20, 1896, THE SAME DAY "ADVENTURES OF A NOVEL-ist" appeared in the *Journal*, Becker and his partner, Michael J. Carey, shot and killed John Fay, alias John O'Brien, at Thirty-fifth Street and Seventh Avenue. The event was reported on the front page of the *New York Times* the following morning in an article that criticized the police as "brutal and reckless in the use of bludgeons and firearms." Although Carey was the one who fired the pistol that cut down Fay/O'Brien, both he and Becker were temporarily reassigned to desk duty at the precinct house pending an investigation, which turned up nothing and led to no further disciplinary action.

On October second, Dora Clark, with the aid of a lawyer who had been provided to her with funds from two charitable organizations and the assurance that Crane would back her testimony, preferred charges of false arrest with Police Chief Conlin against Conway and Becker.

That same day, the *Boston Traveler* harked back to Crane's September appearance in court with an editorial note that questioned the truthfulness of his testimony: "Stevie Crane seems to have gotten into warm water by his valiant defence of a young woman in police court at New York. The chances are that the youthful literary prodigy was on a genuine 'lark,' and, when his companion was apprehended, invented the tale about searching for book material. That is simply the way it looks to a cold and unprejudiced world." Much of that unprejudiced world still found it hard to accept Crane's involvement in the affair without casting suspicion on his motives for standing up in Clark's defense. Another example of the always pertinent if well-worn adage: No good deed goes unpunished.

On October fourth, at three o'clock in the morning, Becker hunted down Clark and gave her a brutal thrashing in front of several witnesses to let her know what he thought of the charges she had filed against him. As reported in the *Journal* on October eighth, after Clark brought new charges against Becker for the beating, she said in her complaint:

"I was standing on the corner of Sixth avenue and Twenty-eighth street early last Sunday morning talking to a group of cabmen, when Becker came along dressed in citizen's clothes. He walked straight up to me and said: 'So you made charges against me did you?' at the same time using profane language.

"'You're a loafer to talk that way,' I replied, whereupon he seized me by the throat, kicked me and knocked me down. I got up and he threw me down again. The bystanders then interfered and Becker went."

In spite of the overpowering evidence against him, Becker swatted away the charge by contending that he had been at the station house during the time of the beating, and the cabmen who had promised to serve as Clark's corroborating witnesses mysteriously went silent and refused to support her. Without question, they had been bribed or intimidated by the police into changing their stories, a tactic that was also used against several witnesses in the false-arrest trial that took place the following week. As a result, Clark had no choice but to follow the recommendation of her lawyer, David Neuberger, and withdraw the assault charge against Becker.

On October tenth, *Harper's Weekly* declared that "Roosevelt and other high authorities of the police force are sceptical of Mr. Stephen Crane's observation in the case of that young woman who he thought had been wrongfully arrested." Hamlin Garland later reported in his 1930 memoir that he saw Crane several times during "his troubles with the New York police, and while I sympathized with him in his loyalty to a woman whom he considered had been unjustly accused of soliciting, his stubborn resolve to go on the stand in her defense was quixotic. Roosevelt discussed the case with me and said, 'I tried to save Crane from press comment, but as he insisted on testifying, I could only let the law take its course.'"

The next day, October eleventh, an article in the *Journal* began with a marathon headline that read:

NOVELIST CRANE A
HARD MAN TO SCARE.
RUMORS OF POLICE MUDSLING-
ING CAN'T FRIGHTEN HIM
FROM HIS DUTY. SAYS HE WILL
STICK BY UNFOR-
TUNATE DORA CLARK TO
THE END.
NEVER HAD ANY IDEA OF ABANDONING
HIS SHARE IN THE PROSECUTION OF
DETECTIVE BECKER.
DENIES HAVING BEEN COERCED.
CURRENT TENDERLOIN GOSSIP WAS THAT THE
POLICE HAD THREATENED TO SHOW HIM UP
AS A FAST LIVER AND KEEPER OF
AN OPIUM JOINT.

The first half of the article repeats all the information in the headline; the second half consists of the remarks attributed to Crane in an interview about the impending trial:

"There is not an atom of truth in any report that I shall fail to appear against Becker. I have not tried to avoid subpoena servers, and I have not left town. My address is with a lawyer, who will notify me when the time arrives to appear. I have not received any intimations from the police that I would be 'shown up' if I appeared against Becker, either. It wouldn't have made the slightest difference to me if I had. I have never, since I testified in the police court, had any idea of refusing to proceed further in the case."

When asked about his opium joint, Crane laughed. "I have an opium lay-out in my room," he said, "but it is tacked to a plaque hung on the wall.

"I consider it my duty," he said, "having witnessed an outrage such as Becker's arrest of this girl, to do my utmost to have him punished. The fact that I was in her company, and had just left what the detective called a resort for thieves, prostitutes, and crooks, does not bear on the matter in the least. I had a perfect right to be there, or any other public resort anywhere else in the city where I choose to go."

As it happened, he did leave town not long after giving his answers to the *Journal* reporter, perhaps that same day, perhaps the next, hoping to avoid further interactions with the New York press by traveling to Philadelphia and camping out at Fred Lawrence's place for a brief, unspecified length of time. During that visit, he sent a telegram to Roosevelt informing him that he fully intended to appear in court, which was confirmed by Roosevelt's comment to Garland that Crane "insisted on testifying," but Lawrence, who knew Crane well and had been one of his closest friends for the past five years, was justifiably worried. "If Crane had been wisely counseled," he wrote, "he would have seen the folly of such an attempt against the system. . . . He would have realized . . . that the whole force of the police power would be turned against him. But no, he explained; young Theodore Roosevelt had just been made Police Commissioner of New York, and he would see that he had a square deal." So the wire was dispatched to Roosevelt from a telegraph office in downtown Philadelphia, and immediately after that, as Lawrence puts it, "Mr. Galahad caught the next train."

The trial that began on the night of October fifteenth and lasted well into the morning of the sixteenth took place in a special court whose sole purpose was to rule on matters of alleged police misconduct. Clark was the plaintiff in the case, Conway and Becker were the defendants, and Crane's role was no more than that of a witness who had agreed to testify on the plaintiff's behalf. Neither Clark nor Crane was on trial, but due to the aggressive, hammer-and-tongs lawyering of Becker's counsel, Louis D. Grant, and the lax control exercised by the police-commissioner judge, whose name was also Grant—Frederick D., son of the late president and Civil War general—the questions were allowed to stray into territory far outside the purview of the court, and before long the accusers had been turned into the accused. Clark's charity-sponsored lawyer raised numerous objections to his opponent's line of inquiry, but in nearly every instance he was overruled by judge Grant, which enabled lawyer Grant to forge on with his attacks against the credibility of the plaintiff and her key witness. In a courtroom jammed with Becker's fellow cops and commanding officers—man after man in full-dress department blue—the trial unfolded as if it were a lopsided sporting event in which one team owns the ball, the field, and the loyalty of every spectator in the crowd.

Not knowing that the police had raided his apartment while he was out of town—nor that they had been conducting an undercover operation to probe into every hidden corner of his private life—Crane turned up at police headquarters a little in advance of the appointed time of three in the afternoon. The docket was full that day, however, and hours passed before the Conway-Becker case was called before the judge. For the first hour, as the *Journal* reported, Crane "leaned against a window in the corridor smoking a cigar, apparently oblivious of the scowls of the policemen who were awaiting trial for various offences. . . . At 4 o'clock Mr. Crane was told that he would probably be called to the stand at 5:30; at 5:30 Clerk Kip thought the case would come up at 7; at 7 o'clock there was a prospect that it might be reached in another hour, and the young novelist who had a dinner engagement at 8 sent a telegram and dined on a ham sandwich and a glass of beer in a Mulberry Street saloon." The case finally began at nine, but with a horde of witnesses scheduled to testify before him, Crane went on walking up and down the corridor, smoking cigarette after cigarette until 1:55 in the morning as "the women with artificial manners and complexions sneered at him" and "the hack drivers winked at each other and pointed." As the last of the witnesses, he was barred from entering the courtroom for the first five hours of the trial, and therefore he knew nothing about the nature of the defense lawyer Grant had prepared.*

Conway came first, and the matter was quickly resolved when he and Rosenberg falsely claimed that Clark had been soliciting three men at the time of her arrest. To back their testimony, according to the *Journal*, "another woman of the streets who had come to headquarters to testify in Dora Clark's favor, but who had some conversation with officers of the Nineteenth Precinct before the case was called, swore in corroboration of the evidence of Conway and Rosenberg when she was put on the stand."

The Becker case started at ten. After the two sides presented their competing versions of the facts, an army of Tenderloin characters marched to the stand to support the police version in order to save their skins or their livelihoods or, depending on their line of work, both. One of them, "a legendary prostitute of the nineties," Big Chicago May, "was famous for her

---

* The transcript of the trial no longer exists. The only accounts I have read are in the reports published by the *World* (October 18, 1896), the *New York Journal* (October 16 and 17), and the *Sun* (October 16), which were reprinted in *The New York City Sketches of Stephen Crane and Related Pieces*, edited by R. W. Stallman and E. R. Hagemann (New York University Press, 1966).

method of biting the stones out of men's scarf-pins while she amorously pretended to bury her face against their chests." The article in the *Journal* on October seventeenth underscored the extent to which those witnesses lied:

> All the women with diamonds and all the hackmen were absolutely certain that Dora Clark left the Broadway Garden alone. They positively swore so. One woman, known in the Tenderloin as "Big Chicago May," went further. She is a huge blonde, whose diamond earrings are as big as hickory nuts. Miss "Big Chicago May" is as familiar on Sixth Avenue and on Twenty-third street after dark as is the Masonic Temple. Calmly she swore that Dora Clark offered her $25 if she would swear falsely against Becker.
>
> "Dora Clark went to other women," swore Miss "Big Chicago May." "She said, 'We must protect ourselves. Becker is persecuting us. We must break him. Then I'm going to Europe.'"
>
> "What's your occupation?" Mr. Newburger [*sic*] asked this woman, whose blushes are not visible.
>
> "I'm a typewriter," she retorted.
>
> "On what machine do you typewrite?"
>
> She did not know.
>
> "Name one typewriting machine."
>
> She could not.
>
> "Did you earn those diamonds with your wages as a typewriter?"

Lawyer Grant's interrogation of Clark was relentless. Described in the same *Journal* article as "good looking" and with "good manners," she had prepared herself for her appearance in court by putting on a black dress "trimmed with purple velvet" and "a large black hat adorned with black feathers." Both "veiled and gloved," she wore no jewelry except for "a diamond star at her throat." An impressive figure of just twenty-one who seemed to be "above the level of her class," and yet, to lawyer Grant and the assembled policemen, she was nothing but a shabby, run-of-the-mill Manhattan whore. When Grant asked her where she lived, she refused to divulge the address, telling him that she would be run out of the place if she did, just as she had been run out of all the other places where she had lived since the police began their persecution campaign against her. Grant pressed on, however, and eventually extracted the information from her. Even more damning (and no doubt based on diligent detective work), he bullied her into admitting that she was a "kept woman" and "had received money lately from a wealthy man who lives at the Waldorf" (the *World*, October 16). Which raises a question: If she was supported by someone with the financial resources to live in the city's finest hotel, why would she bother to solicit unknown men in the streets of the Tenderloin? Lawyer Grant, of course, failed to ask that question.

When Crane's turn finally came at two in the morning, he had been waiting outside the courtroom for eleven hours. The instant Neuberger opened the door to announce that they were ready for him, a man who had been watching Crane all through those eleven hours slipped into the courtroom, whispered something into lawyer Grant's ear, and a moment later Grant jumped up and shouted: "This is an outrage, unjust to all concerned. This witness, Crane, has heard everything that has been said in this room, has been waiting outside within earshot."

Again, not true, but one more example of Grant's pugnacious strategy to stay on the attack and do everything in his power to discredit the ones who were about to discredit his client. If nothing else, his outburst should have warned Crane about what he would be up against when he took the stand. The atmosphere was already hostile enough, and in a courtroom packed with "policemen, policemen, policemen" a well as "women with yellow hair and white diamonds" and a contingent of Tenderloin hack drivers (all of them pro-police), it must have been fairly intimidating. On top of that, Crane was exhausted and emotionally spent, so exhausted and so spent that the *Journal*'s description of his appearance that night is perhaps the most unflattering portrait of him on record:

> a thin, pale, young man, with straight hair plastered down on a curiously shaped head, with a poorly nourished mustache, a large nose, prominent teeth; a young man who does not look brainy, but who has proved he has brains.

In all fairness, he made a weak showing of himself that night. He handled the questions from Neuberger with "self-control ... cold as ice," repeating the story he had already given numerous times in the past month about the events of the night in question, but when lawyer Grant's turn came and the grilling began, Crane froze into the defensive posture of a man under assault as he struggled to ward off the blows that kept coming at him. Grant's objective was to prove that Crane was a liar, but in order to achieve his goal he first had to prove that Crane was a worthless human being, beginning with the accusation that he was an opium smoker and had been under the influence on the night in question ("dopey," as several earlier witnesses had testified, and therefore unable to remember what had happened), which advanced to the further accusation that he owned and operated an opium den, and then shifted to the accusation (as the *World* reported in its account of the trial) that he earned his living as a pimp:

> Lawyer Grant wanted to know if it was not a fact that Mr. Crane lived by money given to him by women of the Tenderloin.
> Mr. Crane denied that such was the case, but said that he made money by writing for newspapers and magazines.
> So thick and fast did Lawyer Grant fire the red-hot questions at the witness that he finally put his hands up to his face as if to prevent them from burning into his brain.

Another exchange reported by the *Journal* shows how Grant's barrage of random, scattershot questions kept Crane continually off-balance and forced him to refuse to answer many of them.

> Mr. Grant questioned this young unmarried man . . . as to where he lived in New York. The cross-examination proceeded like this:
> Mr. Crane (freezingly)—Yes, I lived in a flat house on West Twenty-second Street.
> Mr. Grant (sneeringly)—With what woman did you live there?
> Mr. Neuberger—As your adviser, Mr. Crane, I tell you not to answer that question. It has absolutely nothing to do with the case in hand here.
> Mr. Crane (wearily)—I refuse to answer.
> Mr. Grant (triumphantly)—On what ground?
> Mr. Crane—Because it would tend to degrade me.
> Mr. Grant—Perhaps you think to answer this will tend to disgrace you. With whom did you live at such and such a place?
> So it went . . .

According to the *World*,

> Lawyer Grant then took another tack. He asked the witness whether he knew a woman named Sadie or Amy Huntington. It was presumed that Lawyer Grant had reference to Sadie Traphagen, who was the friend of Annie Goodwin, the cigarette girl, who was a victim of Dr. McConigal. It will be remembered, as the Goodwin case was widely published at the time, that the girl was the victim of malpractice.*

---

* A botched abortion that resulted in Annie Goodwin's death.

Whether Amy Huntington was really Sadie Traphagen was not developed.

"Did you ever smoke opium with this Sadie or Amy in a house at 121 West Twenty-seventh street?" asked Lawyer Grant.

"I deny that," said Mr. Crane.

"On the ground it would tend to degrade or incriminate you?"

"Well—yes," hesitatingly.

The report in the *Sun* provides some added details: "In the summer he visited a certain house in West Twenty-seventh Street. He refused to say how many times he had visited the house, and also refused to say whether or not he was acquainted with Sadie or Amy Huntington."

West Twenty-seventh was a street long known for its houses of prostitution and the hookers who lined its sidewalks after dark, but what possible connection could that have to the rest of the case? Although Grant's question seemed to be just another random assault at the time, it turned out to be a crucial element in his effort to destroy Crane's credibility, but that would become clear only when a surprise witness was called after Crane had stepped down from the stand. Meanwhile, the beating continued, and whenever Grant wanted to return to the fundamental issue of Crane's habitual lying, he would trot out the one lie of Crane's he was aware of, which happened to be the supremely innocent lie he had told Becker on the night in question, pretending to agree with the chorus girl who was about to be arrested that he was her husband. From the *Journal*, in its concluding remarks about Crane's testimony:

Mr. Grant turned over and over the fact that Mr. Crane told Becker that one of the women he arrested was his wife.

"She is not your wife?"

"No."

"Why did you say she was?"

"Because I know she was guiltless. It was impossible that she solicited, because she was under my protection; because I felt bound to protect her."

The policemen smiled at each other. The women were puzzled. Being of the Tenderloin, it was utterly impossible for them to understand the motive Mr. Crane expressed. So, having finished the course he laid out for himself, Stephen Crane arose, bowed to Commissioner Grant, turned on his heel and left Headquarters.

It was over—and then it wasn't over. Judge Grant adjourned the trial, but before anyone could move, Becker's commanding officer, Captain Chapman, leapt to his feet and asked that one more witness be called to the stand. The judge allowed it, and in walked James O'Conner, the janitor of the building at 121 West Twenty-seventh Street, the same address that lawyer Grant had accused Crane of visiting in order to smoke opium with Sadie or Amy Huntington or Traphagen. According to O'Conner, Crane had lived there with a woman "as man and wife" for six weeks during the summer, whereupon he mentioned the name of the woman, which did not appear in any of the press reports of the trial. Neuberger angrily objected, calling the statement "outrageous" and utterly irrelevant to the case. Judge Grant concurred and excluded it from the record, but the words had been spoken, they had been heard by the press, and because the press had sharp ears and a loud voice, they would soon be heard by everyone in the city.

O'Conner went on to say that some of the women who lived in the house made a practice of luring men into their apartments and then robbing them once they were there. He named a certain Effie Ward as the worst of the offenders, and because Miss Ward happened to be present in the courtroom, the moment the trial ended she joined the dispersing crowd, followed O'Conner out of the building, and "planted her fist in his face with such force as to send him on the run down the steps to the sidewalk." The *Journal* report continues:

> Before the infuriated woman could reach him again she was pulled to one side by a number of policemen. She was released again, and in an instant she was at a young woman who appeared in behalf of the policeman, tooth and nail. She had grabbed a handful of the young woman's hair and was twisting it out by the roots when she was again seized and hauled off.
>
> She was taken away by a reporter and disappeared around the corner into Bleecker street.

It goes without saying that Becker and Conway were found innocent of all charges.

Crane had been ambushed by the combined forces of an indignant police department, a zealous, cunning defense attorney, and the incompetence of a police-commissioner judge who had once been described as a man who liked "nothing so much as to sit and stare into space." Crane's double life had been exposed, and no matter how vigorously he was defended in the editorials and articles that were published over the next few days, his name was now forever attached to scandal. The front-page headlines alone would have been enough to make him want to crawl under a rock and hide there until hell froze over or the city went up in flames.

The *World*, accompanied by a large portrait of the new poster-boy scoundrel:

CRANE HAD
A GAY NIGHT
RACY STORY BROUGHT OUT IN
THE TRIAL OF BECKER
AND CONWAY
A JANITOR CONFESSED THAT THE
NOVELIST LIVED WITH A
TENDERLOIN GIRL
AN OPIUM SMOKING EPISODE

Even the *Journal*, Crane's staunchest advocate among the papers that covered the trial, could not resist joining in on the fun:

CRANE RISKED ALL
TO SAVE A WOMAN
HIS BOHEMIAN LIFE IN NEW
YORK LAID BARE FOR THE
SAKE OF DORA CLARK

In the days that followed, the *Brooklyn Daily Eagle*, the *New York Press*, and the *Journal* itself all rallied to Crane's defense and excoriated the proceedings as a perversion of justice, correctly insisting that a police court had no legal authority to try citizens and that Crane, "a gallant gentleman," "a man who had not violated any laws," had been forced to answer questions that had no bearing on the case against Becker and Conway. The argument was sound, the writing was impassioned and even eloquent, but however consoling those articles might have been to Crane, they made no difference in the end, for the harm had already been done, and it was beyond repair.

At nine o'clock in the evening on Saturday, October thirty-first, Dora Clark was walking down Sixth Avenue near Thirty-first Street when Big Chicago May attacked her with a blow to the head. Clark struck back, Big May pounced, Clark punched again, and both women were arrested for disorderly conduct and fined by the magistrate at the Jefferson Market Police Court the next morning.

The last word about the mysterious, embattled Dora Clark comes from an article published in the *Sun* on January 2, 1897, that is summarized in Paul Sorrentino's biography of Crane:

> In early December, she rented a room in a boardinghouse; but when other boarders complained about her late-night activities, she was evicted. Seeking revenge, Clark broke into the landlady's room, woke everyone up by banging out "Coming through the Rye" on a piano, shredded the curtains, and scattered ink all over the carpet and rugs. Despite a warrant for her arrest, she was last seen cavorting nightly with affluent boys in Broadway's roof-garden dance halls.

As for Crane's thoughts about his own predicament, there are two bits of writing that offer some clues. One is impossible to date and comes from a manuscript fragment currently housed in the University of Virginia Library, but it seems to have been written in the immediate aftermath of the trial.

> A man who possessed a sense of justice was a dolt, a simpleton, and a double-dyed idiot for finally his sense of justice would get him into a corner and, if he obeyed it, make him infamous. There is such a thing as a moral obligation arriving inopportunely. The inopportune arrival of a moral obligation can bring just as much personal humiliation as can a sudden impulse to steal or any of the other mental suggestions which we account calamitous.

These are bitter sentences, and they show how deeply Crane understood what had happened to him, but at the same time they do not carry any sense of regret over his doltish, idiotic behavior—merely an awareness of its possible consequences, which in this case unfortunately came to pass. But his conscience was clear, and that fact outweighs all the others when we ask ourselves how he managed to find the strength to pick himself up from the floor and recover from his public humiliation—for he did ultimately recover, even if he lost some friends along the way. A clear conscience meant no regrets, and no regrets meant that he would have done the same thing again if he ever found himself in the position of having to decide between doing the right thing and doing nothing.

The second, more calmly stated remark comes from the final paragraph of a long letter sent to his brother William from Florida on November twenty-ninth:

> I forgot to mention the Dora Clark case. If I should happen to be detained upon my journey, you must always remember that your brother acted like a man of honor and a gentleman and you need not fear to hold your head up to anybody and defend his name. All that I said in my own article in the Journal is absolutely true, and for my part I see no reason why, if I should live a thousand years, I should ever be ashamed or humiliated by my course in the matter.

His closest friends stood by him and never wavered in their loyalty, even after he was dead. Lawrence, Marshall, Linson, and Hawkins all understood that the drug charges against him were absurd, that the pimping accusation was a contemptible slander, and that how he chose to conduct his sexual life was strictly his own business. Yes, he enjoyed drinking beer from time to time, but not one of them had ever seen him drunk, and even the cigarettes he was constantly smoking often burned out before he had finished them and would remain in his mouth because he rarely remembered to relight the extinguished butts.

Howells was apparently "distressed" by the newspaper reports until the true facts of the case were put before him by someone in a position to know the facts. After that, he and Crane carried on with their friendship, seeing each other whenever Crane returned to New York in the years ahead, and the warm letter Howells wrote to Cora in 1900 proves that his memory of Crane was not spoiled by any doubts about his young friend's character or conduct.

Roosevelt, on the other hand, turned his back on Crane and never took the trouble to ask him to give his side of the story. Because the soon-to-be ex–police commissioner accepted the department's version of the affair, S.C. was cast out from his circle of acquaintances and shunned as a debauched, dishonest, delinquent soul. Roosevelt, a squeamish prig when it came to sexual matters, who once boasted that his "small hand" had "caressed only two women" (his two wives), must have been shocked to learn that Crane had been sharing his bed with a prostitute that summer, which to Roosevelt's mind would have been an unforgivable trespass against the laws of decency.

In September 1902, one year into his first term as president, Roosevelt was traveling somewhere on a train with his secretary, George B. Cortelyou, and Jimmy Hare, a celebrated photojournalist who had been a good friend of Crane's in Cuba. Cortelyou was reading Crane's story collection about American soldiers during the Spanish-American War, *Wounds in the Rain*, and the conversation naturally came around to the dead author. Roosevelt said to Hare, "You knew this fellow Crane rather well, didn't you, Jimmy?" Hare replied, "Yes, sir, very well indeed." "I remember him distinctly myself," Roosevelt said. "When I was Police Commissioner of New York I once got him out of serious trouble." Scrambling the facts somewhat, Hare recalled that it had happened while Crane was "collecting data" for his first book, *Maggie*. "Nonsense!" Roosevelt thundered back at him. "He wasn't collecting any data! He was a man of bad character and he was simply consorting with loose women." Hare, a little man who scarcely weighed one hundred pounds, stood up angrily and said: "That is absolutely not so! Nothing could be farther from the truth!" Realizing that he had overstepped the bounds of decorum by talking to an American president in that way, Hare sat down and apologized. "I'm sorry," he said, struggling to keep himself under control. "You see, I happen to know the story behind that incident. My friend, Crane, was merely taking the part of a woman who was being hounded by the police; that was the whole reason for his getting into a scrape with the law." Roosevelt, who had calmed down by then, answered with a slight, condescending nod. "All right, Jimmy," he said. "Have it your own way."

More disturbing—because closer to home and therefore more important to Crane—was the chill that descended on his friendship with Garland. No one had done more to advance Crane's career, no one had been more enthusiastic or given more encouragement to his early efforts as a writer, and without the older man's help Crane might still have been knocking on doors that refused to open. All that is certain, and Crane himself was perfectly aware of it, but as I have suggested earlier, what Crane didn't know is that deep within Garland, perhaps so deep that Garland himself didn't know about it either, there was a festering sore of envy and resentment and anger against the young man for his superior gifts, and beyond those gifts, the fact that they had been granted to a "hungry, seedy boy," "a strange, willful, irresponsible boy" who managed his life so carelessly and sloppily when Garland, who was anything but careless and sloppy, had toed the line and played by the rules established for him by others, and even though he managed to establish himself as a certain someone in the land of those rules, in the land of art, where there are no rules, he couldn't hold a candle to the sloppy boy. The Clark Affair seemed to be the opening Garland needed to reassert himself over Crane, and now that "the shady side of his bohemian life was turned to the light,"

Garland could slip back into his former patronizing, avuncular role and pretend to have Crane's best interests at heart. After the trial, he tells us in his memoir, he ran into Crane at McClure's office and recommended that he cut his ties to the city, return to his brother's farm in Sullivan County, and "get back his tone" by writing "a big book up there." It's not that this was bad advice (which Crane said he would follow and of course didn't), but for all of Garland's supposed caring about what happened to Crane, at bottom I don't think he cared much at all. Not unlike his friend Roosevelt, Garland was shocked by what had been brought out at the trial and found it morally reprehensible, and from then on he began to distance himself from Crane, little by little withdrawing until they lost contact, and so estranged did they become over time that when Garland traveled to England after Crane had moved there, he invented an excuse not to see him. Then Crane died, and no sooner was he buried than the man who had discovered him wrote, "He was too brilliant, too fickle, too erratic to last. He could not go on doing stories like 'The Red Badge of Courage.' The weakness of such highly individual work lies in its success by surprise. The words which astonish, the phrases which excite wonder and admiration, come eventually to seem tricky. They lose force with repetition and come at last to be distasteful."

In 1930, when copies of *Maggie* had become so scarce that they were fetching high prices in the first-editions market of the rare book trade, Garland sold his inscribed copy for twenty-one hundred dollars and then turned around the money to finance the new house he had bought in Hollywood, where he palled around with Will Rogers and Robert Benchley and spent the last ten years of his life exploring psychic phenomena.

33

IT GETS MORE COMPLICATED. HOWEVER UNFAIR THE TRIAL, AND however irrelevant the last witness's testimony was to the case, the janitor had told the truth about Crane and the woman who had lived together in his building that summer. Nor was her name in doubt, although in that demi-world of pseudonyms and aliases, where murder victim Fay called himself O'Brien and prostitute Ruby Young called herself both Dora Wilkins and Dora Clark, the woman who lived at 121 West Twenty-seventh Street variously went by three different names rather than one. Like her twenty-four-year-old sister, Sadie, a veteran prostitute who shared the flat with her, twenty-year-old Amy was born with the last name Traphagen, which she eventually abandoned for Huntington, and when that no longer suited her, she began calling herself Amy Leslie instead.*

Other than the janitor's testimony in court, there is nothing on record about her affair with Crane, and if not for a bewildering money transaction that occurred two weeks after the trial, the Amy Leslie chapter probably would have been reduced to a single footnote in the story of Crane's life. Her name and address appear in a list of names and addresses that were jotted down in a bank book from the American Security and Trust Company in Washington, where Crane had opened an account in early March, not long after he began his monthlong stay at the Cosmos Club. Another piece of evidence is a photograph of himself that he sent to Amy's sister, Sadie, on April twenty-ninth, with these words written on the back: *To Kid / From Stephen Crane.* Neither one adds up to much—except to prove that Amy was known to him well before the summer—but then there are the five letters Crane wrote to her after he left New York in the final week of November, along with the worried letter and three short notes he wrote to Hawkins *about* her. The letters to Amy are passionate declarations of love, more ardent and more direct than any of the letters he wrote to Lily Brandon Munroe or Nellie Crouse, but the letter and notes to Hawkins are all about the money and never would have been written if the transaction hadn't taken place. Without those messages to Hawkins, the letters to Amy would have stood as mysterious remnants of a brief, inexplicable affair, establishing that Crane had been in love with someone and left her—but who? Even with the public mess that followed from the money transaction, it took more than a hundred years to come up with the answer. Without the mess, it would still be a mystery today.

---

* To complicate matters even further, there was a second Amy Leslie in Crane's life, a long-distance friend who worked as the drama critic for the *Chicago Tribune*. She was sixteen years older than Crane, but because she was a well-known figure, and because she was known to be on good terms with Crane, for more than a hundred years every Crane scholar in America believed that she was the Amy Leslie who had lived with him in the summer of 1896. The fact that there were two Amy Leslies was not uncovered until 2000, when Kathryn Hilt and Stanley Wertheim published a masterful piece of literary detective work, "Stephen Crane and Amy Leslie: A Rereading of the Evidence" (*American Literary Realism* 32, no. 3 [Spring 2000]), which establishes the existence of Amy Traphagen-Huntington-Leslie from New York and proves that she was Crane's lover—not the forty-one-year-old Amy Leslie from Chicago. The final twist is that neither woman was born with that name. The Chicago journalist had been Lillie West, a prominent singer who had performed in opera houses throughout the country, but after she retired from the stage and began her new career, she wrote for the *Tribune* under the pen name Amy Leslie, which became her legal name as well. She lived until 1939, and to her dying day she angrily insisted she was *not* the woman who had been romantically involved with Crane, but no one believed her.

On Saturday, October thirty-first, Crane was in Cambridge, Massachusetts, reporting on the football game between Harvard and Carlisle, but he returned to New York that night or early the next morning and was back in Manhattan to celebrate his twenty-fifth birthday on November first. That afternoon or evening, Amy supposedly gave him eight hundred dollars in cash to deposit in a bank for her. At the time—and in fact well into the heart of the twentieth century—single, widowed, or divorced American women were prevented by law from opening a bank account without the presence of a man to cosign the application, so Crane was compelled to deposit the money into his own account, but when he finally got around to doing it on Thursday, November fifth, he put in six hundred dollars rather than the full eight hundred. This raises a number of difficult, if not unanswerable questions. One: If Amy indeed gave him the money, why did she do it? The answer is clear: We will never know. Two: Given the laws in force at the time, why didn't she accompany him to the bank and open an account of her own? Three: Why did Crane hold on to the money for so long, dawdling around for three business days with eight hundred dollars in his pocket before he put it in the bank? Several explanations jump to mind: (a) he was distracted and/ or occupied by other matters and didn't have the time; (b) he forgot; (c) he was lazy and kept putting it off; (d) he never received money from her in the first place. Four: What happened to the missing two hundred dollars? If they in fact had been given to him, the obvious answer would be that Crane stole them or, if outright theft seems unlikely, that he appropriated them with the intention of paying them back whenever he could, which might have been never. And yet, having just been accused in court of living off money "given to him by women of the Tenderloin," would he have had the gall to turn around and do the very thing lawyer Grant had charged him with doing? In light of what we know about Crane's inveterate laxness with money, it has to be considered a possibility, but in light of everything else we know about him, it can't. What, then, happened to the missing two hundred dollars? No one seems to know, nor has anyone ever explained how or why the dollars went missing—if in fact they were missing.

Meanwhile, circumstances were closing in on the young couple. Following the trial, Crane understood that it was imperative for him to leave the city, that staying in New York would subject him to continual harassment from the police and that a sustained career in journalism would no longer be possible for him there. He had already left Manhattan twice since the middle of October (up the river to Sing Sing and then farther north to Cambridge), and the following Saturday (November seventh) he was in Cambridge again to report on the Harvard-Princeton football game, but those were only temporary measures, not the long-term solution he required. Then help came from an old friend. Hoping to rescue his failing syndicate, which was too small to compete against the large operations of McClure, Hearst, and Pulitzer, Irving Bacheller offered Crane an assignment to travel to Cuba to report on the growing insurrection of the Cubans against the Spanish, which had started in early 1895. Crane jumped at the chance, telling Bacheller he was ready to leave at a moment's notice, but his departure hinged on the availability of a boat to carry him from Florida to Cuba, and for the next several weeks he sat around and waited, filling the dead time with other work for Bacheller's syndicate, which included the strong but problematical piece about the vanished black underworld of Minetta Lane.

Nevertheless, a solution had been found, and yet as Crane quickly discovered in the days that followed, by solving one problem for himself he had only created another. Amy had come unglued. Anguished by the thought that she was about to be deserted, she did everything she could to prevent him from leaving, and in the whirl of pressures she began to put on him, one seems to have been the false claim that she was pregnant, which Crane apparently believed (causing untold further confusions), but in the end not even the prospect of a child could deter him from following through with his plan.

All that was hard enough, but then there was the question of the eight hundred dollars, and what happened next was so murky, so deeply at odds with the laws of common sense that little sense can be made of it. Sometime after the middle of November, Crane was told by Bacheller that he should prepare to leave for Jacksonville on November twenty-sixth or twenty-seventh, and on the twenty-fifth, with his bank account now totaling $776.50, he wrote a check for five hundred dollars to Hawkins, who had agreed to look after Amy while Crane was gone and to dole out portions of the money to her when and as she needed them. Eight hundred dollars had become five hundred dollars, all of which rightfully belonged to her (or so she would later contend), and if Crane no longer had the eight hundred, why not give her, *himself*, the full five hundred or, for that matter, the full seven hundred and seventy-six? And why take the trouble of asking Hawkins to serve as an intermediary when the whole matter could have been dispensed with before Crane's departure? Something doesn't smell right here, and with Hawkins surely in the dark about the original eight hundred (which might or might not have belonged to Amy), he undoubtedly thought that Crane was using his own money to help her. If one accepts Amy's position in the matter, then everything points to Crane as the culprit in the affair. Not only did he seem to be pulling a fast one by withholding her own money from her (*why would he do that when he professed to love her?*) but the missing two hundred had suddenly grown into the missing three hundred, and now that he had set up the byzantine arrangement with Hawkins for the remaining five hundred, it begins to look as if Crane spent the missing money and had no intention of paying it back. Again one asks: Why would he do such a thing? For the first time in his life, he was reasonably flush just then, with more food in his stomach and better clothes on his back than in all the years he had been in New York, which would eliminate desperate need as a possible cause for taking the money, but if he hadn't taken it, where was it? The mind spins round and round looking for an answer, for the fact is that the letters he wrote to Amy after he arrived in Jacksonville are so filled with love and worry and heartbreak that it borders on the inconceivable that he could have stolen money from her. And yet, looking squarely at the evidence—from Amy's point of view—what else are we to think?

Then again, perhaps we should consider this. Crane never mentioned to anyone that he had received eight hundred dollars from Amy, and the assumption that he had comes exclusively from her. It could be that he talked about giving her eight hundred dollars one day, perhaps even promised to give it to her, and that the two deposits of six hundred and one hundred and seventy-six dollars were royalty earnings from his books (*Red Badge* went through fourteen printings that year) as well as money earned from newspapers and magazines. That would explain why Hawkins knew nothing about the eight hundred dollars—because they didn't exist—and therefore, when he was given the five-hundred-dollar check from Crane, he took it for granted that it was Crane's money to give. As early as December first, just days after Crane arrived in Florida, Amy began pressing Hawkins for money and kept on pressing until the last week of September 1897 ("I am broke and need the money very much"; "I must have it"; "I do not know how I am going to live if I do not get those cheaks" [*sic*]), and while Hawkins did what he could to help (sending money by messenger and arranging a modeling job for her with one of his artist friends), he eventually gave up in disgust and withdrew from his role as Crane's proxy banker. Amy then turned to a lawyer, George D. Mabon, and began a legal action to recuperate the five hundred and fifty dollars she insisted she was still owed. Why that amount? If Hawkins had already given her five hundred, shouldn't she have been asking for the remaining three hundred? Again, the mind spins round, and again there are no answers. The *New York Times*, the *Chicago Tribune*, and other newspapers ran articles about the suit, which turned the private quarrel into a public mess and established eight hundred dollars as the sum in question. The press seemed disposed to believe her—mistakenly assuming she was the other Amy Leslie from Chicago—but if the young A.L. had lied about the pregnancy to hold Crane in New York, there was every reason to suspect she was lying now in order to punish him for having abandoned her. Mabon pushed hard and had an attachment order issued against Crane's royalties from Appleton, but in the end the case was settled out of court with legal help from Crane's brother William. It is worth noting that the matter was never referred to anywhere in the correspondence between the two brothers, nor did Crane ever mention the sum of eight hundred dollars in any of the letters he wrote to Amy, nor did he ever suggest that he had done anything wrong in his financial dealings with her—not to Amy herself, not to Hawkins, not to William, not to anyone. Most important, not once in any of her letters did Amy badger Hawkins by insisting that the money belonged to her. From start to finish, her attitude was that of a woman living off the generous support of her absent lover—which would suggest that Crane was probably innocent, after all.

She rode with him on the train as far as Washington, and then she got off and returned to New York while he pushed on to Jacksonville. He had been told that the boat for Cuba would be leaving the morning after he arrived, which explained why she had accompanied him for only part of the trip, but things did not go according to plan, and several weeks went by before the boat finally left. From Jacksonville, dated "Sunday" (November 29, 1896), his first full day in town (written in the simple, baby-talk language he used in all his letters to her):

> My Blessed Girl: I have dictated a long letter to you today but as it was dictated to a stenographer I could not very well tell you how much I loved you and how sorrowful I am now over our temporary separation. The few moments on the train at Washington were the most painful of my life and if I live a hundred years I know I can never forget them. I want you to be always sure that I love you. We start tomorrow night probably but if you have written today I will get it before the boat sails. Be good, my darling, my sweet. Don't forget your old hubber. I think of you at all times and love you alone.
>
> Your Lover.

And then another from the twenty-ninth, dated "Sunday night":

> My dearest: Two letters will reach you soon after this one. Just happened to get time to send this to you on the northern mail which leaves in ten

minutes. God bless you and keep you safe for me. Yours with all the love in the world.

S.

Prepared to depart the next morning, and not knowing what would happen to him in the days and weeks ahead, he sent off two more letters that afternoon, one written to his brother William in Port Jervis (outlining the contents of his will) and the other (by dictation) to Hawkins in New York, which was largely about Amy.

In case you see Amy from time to time encourage her in every possible way. . . . I was positively frightened for the girl at the moment of parting and I am afraid and worried now. I feel that no one . . . could need a friendly word more than this poor child, and I know that you are just the man to do it in a right way if the chance presents itself. . . . It broke my heart to leave the girl but I could feel comparatively easy now if I could feel that she had good friends. There is not a man in three thousand who can be a real counsellor and guide for a girl so pretty as Amy. . . . Her sister is a good hearted sort of creature, but she is liable to devote most of her attention to herself and besides that Amy is mentally superior to her in every way. The sister is weak, very weak, and so I am sure that she would be of no help to Amy in what is now really a great trouble.

After the two letters he had sent to her on November twenty-ninth, he waited twelve days before writing to her again. He had met someone else in the meantime, which no doubt had cast him down still further into *the mud of modern confusion*, but he was not about to share this new entanglement with Amy, which in all likelihood would end as quickly as it began, and so he continued to shower her with his customary endearments. December eleventh:

My own Sweetheart: I have not written until now because every moment we have expected to get off and I have wished to save my last word here for you. We have had a great deal of trouble to get a boat ready and I think within 24 hours we will be on our way to Cuba. It breaks my heart to think of the delays and to think that I might have had you with me here if I had only known. . . . Remember me sweetheart even in your dreams. From now on I will have time to write oftener and you may expect to hear now every day . . . from your poor forlorn boy. I know you

wont forget me. I know you love me and I want you always to remember
that I love you.

　　Your lover

Not every day, as it turned out, but only the next day, which was the last
time he wrote to her from Florida. Dated Saturday, December twelfth, it
begins and ends with the following:

My Beloved: It has been altogether a remarkable series of circumstances
which has delayed us here so long and it breaks my heart to think that I
might have had you with me a few days longer—as I wrote you yesterday. . . .

　　Sunday—Today we are spending in misery at the hotel with a strict
rule about drinking and no one to play with. I can do nothing but think
of you. I love you, my sweetheart, my sweetheart.

　　Monday: Seems sure that we leave tomorrow. I love you, mine own
girl. Be good and wait for me. I love you.

But he didn't leave tomorrow, nor the tomorrow after that, nor the
tomorrow after that, and when he finally set sail for Cuba on the last day
of the year, the boat sank.

EXILE

✿

I

A MONTH IN JACKSONVILLE, FLORIDA, WITH NOTHING TO DO BUT
wait. Nine hundred miles to the north, New York City had turned into a
mirage, and Dora Clark, Charles Becker, Theodore Roosevelt, and lawyer
Grant could no longer touch him. He had left the weeping Amy on a train
platform in Washington, and while he continued to send her occasional
bits of money and wrote to her one last time in the fall, he never saw her
again. Something new was on the verge of happening, an abrupt turn into
a new way of living and thinking and breathing that would carry him
through the last three and a half years of his life, and as Crane languished
in Florida during that monthlong interval before the steamship *Commodore* set out for Cuba, one wonders if he had any idea how thoroughly the
past had closed behind him.

Bacheller had given him a money belt filled with seven hundred dollars
in gold, and following the practice of other journalists who had come to
Jacksonville on their way to Cuba, Crane registered at his hotel under
a pseudonym, Samuel Carlton.* The false names were a ruse to deflect

---

* No doubt a winking nod to the American poet Will Carlton, who supported the cause of
Cuban independence and had written a widely read poem urging the United States to inter-
vene on the rebels' behalf. Spurred on by anti-Spanish reports in the yellow press (Hearst
and Pulitzer), American opinion was largely sympathetic to the Cubans, but the government
was still neutral at that point, and a blockade had been put in force by the American navy to
prevent clandestine boats carrying arms, rebel soldiers, and journalists from entering Cuba.

attention from the Spanish spies in Jacksonville who were keeping watch on suspicious Americans. In his December twelfth letter to Amy, Crane shrugged off the potential difficulties. "We are troubled occasionally by Spanish spies. They follow us a good deal but they seem very harmless." In fact, they were not harmless. The Spanish government had declared that any American journalist who managed to enter Cuba would be treated as a spy and dealt with accordingly. A few months earlier, a young reporter from the *Key West Equator-Democrat*, Charles Govin, had reached Cuba on a boat similar to the one that had been lined up for Crane. Immediately after he landed, Govin was captured, tied to a tree, and executed by firing squad. Then, to discourage others who might have been tempted to follow his example, the Spanish soldiers took out their machetes and hacked his body to pieces.

The crossings to the island, which had been under Spanish control since 1511, were organized by Cuban rebels in Jacksonville (the Junta), who had two tugs and one small steamship at their disposal for carrying out these "filibuster" operations between Florida and off-limits Cuba. Not "filibuster" as it applies to debating tactics in the United States Senate but as its first meaning is defined in *Webster's New Universal Unabridged Dictionary*: "A freebooter or soldier of fortune who engages in unauthorized warfare against a foreign country with which his own country is at peace in order to enrich himself: first applied to buccaneers in the West Indies who preyed on Spanish commerce to South America." Crane and the other Americans who had gathered in Jacksonville were not looking to enrich themselves so much as to participate in an adventure, the kind of derring-do that many of them had dreamed about as children, and as Crane put it in one of his articles, "The Filibustering Industry," "The romance of it catches the heart of the lad. The same lad who longs to fight Indians and to be a pirate . . . longs to embark secretly at midnight on one of these dangerous trips to the Cuban coast." Crane, too, was looking forward to the adventure, and also to what promised to be his first glimpse of actual combat between living men in a real war, but there were delays, many delays over the weeks that followed, and there was nothing for him to do but sit tight until the *Commodore* was ready.

On arriving in Jacksonville, however, he had been fully expecting to leave for Cuba the next morning, and so he had sat down and written what he assumed was his farewell letter to Amy—quickly followed by a postscript the same day—and another letter to Hawkins filled with anxieties about Amy and her "great trouble," imploring his friend to look after her in his absence, as well as a last letter to his brother William about the terms of his will. Knowing the perils of the "dangerous trips to the Cuban coast," and surely aware of what had happened to Charles Govin in July, Crane understood that he might never return, or, as he obliquely expressed it to Hawkins, "in case my journey is protracted by causes which you can readily imagine." Hence the will—and the urgent need to put his affairs in order, just in case.

He had made out a will at some point in the recent past, but the document had been lost or left behind in New York, and with no time to wait for William to send a fresh copy from Port Jervis, he did his best to recall what he had previously judged to be "perfectly satisfactory." On top of that, there were a number of new bequests that had occurred to him since then, and although he wasn't sure that mentioning them in an unnotarized letter would "stand for anything in court," he had been planning to bring them up the next time he saw William.

The old terms were simple enough. William would be the sole executor. William and Edmund would each receive one-third of his estate, and one-sixth each would go to his brothers George and Townley. (Neither Wilbur nor his sister Nellie was mentioned.) Then came the new items. "For instance my saddle horse [Peanuts] I would not like to have sold. I would prefer that he be kept in easy service at Hartwood and have him cared for as much as possible by Ed himself, or by somebody whom it is absolutely certain would not maltreat him. As for the furniture of mine at Hartwood I would like that all to go to Ed except small things which the other members of the family might care to keep as mementoes of me."

His horse, his furniture, his small things, and then he moved on to his literary estate, appointing Howells, Garland, Hawkins, and Hitchcock as his executors, men who would "no doubt be good enough to trouble themselves with my affairs." Howells "of course" would be in charge of deciding on the contents of posthumous books drawn from work previously published in newspapers and magazines. In his desk at Hartwood, he added, there was a list he had compiled of his published stories, and although tracking them down would entail considerable effort, "there are some of them which I would hate to see lost." Countering the misconception that journalism was of no importance to Crane and that he had cranked out his newspaper sketches simply for the money, he went on:

> Some of my best work is contained in short things which I have written
> for various publications, principally the New York Press in 1893 or there-
> about [1894]. There are some fifteen or twenty short sketches of New
> York street life and so on which I intended to have published in book

form under the title of "Midnight Sketches." That should be your first care and after that sketches of outdoor life such as "One Dash Horses", "The Wise Men", "The Snake" and other stories of that kind could also be published in book form if the literary executors thought that they were up to my standard. There will be a story in the January or February Century which also could go very well with this collection ["A Man and Some Others"].

The will ends there, and as it is with all wills made by all people, the finality of its pronouncements gives an X-ray view into the mind of the person who has written it. Young Crane's last will and testament tells us what he thought of his work as a writer and identifies the people who counted most for him: four of his brothers, two of them in particular, with the mass of his other siblings and their many children left to duke it out among themselves over his "small things." Although they are not named as beneficiaries, the letter also shows his absolute trust in Howells and the others to watch over his literary work after he is gone. There is something odd or even comical about describing "One Dash—Horses" and "A Man and Some Others" as *sketches of outdoor life*, I suppose, but even odder and far less comical is the omission of Amy Leslie's name from the will. He had written to her just before he wrote to William, or was about to write to her just after he finished the letter to William—*twice* within the space of a few hours—calling himself her "hubber," a conflation of "husband" and "lover" that seems to suggest both the pleasures of good sex and the promise of long-term devotion, and in his own words she was his "blessed girl," his "darling," his "sweet," his "dearest," and yet in spite of those fervent declarations, he did not mention her to William. It would have been difficult to do that, of course, both difficult and embarrassing, but a will is not an ordinary letter, and when a young man is facing the prospect of his own end, the obliteration of his life for all eternity, one would expect that man to tell the truth, to come clean and own up about the woman he loves, but Crane couldn't bring himself to do that, which proves that for all his gushing adoration and sweet-talking pronouncements, he didn't love her as much as he thought he did.

Nor should we overlook the question of Amy's "great trouble." It seems clear that Crane was referring to her pregnancy when he wrote those words to Hawkins, the fictitious pregnancy that Amy had invented in order to trap him into marrying her, and even if her "great trouble" was founded on a lie, it appears that Crane had fallen for it, which means that when he left New York for Florida in late November, he assumed he was facing the prospect of becoming the father of an illegitimate child. That turned out to be a false assumption, but he didn't know it at the time, nor did he know that Amy had further deceived him by simultaneously carrying on an affair with another man, a traveling salesman named Isidor Siesfeld, who suggested hiring lawyer Mabon to launch the suit against Crane and eventually seems to have married Amy (the 1920 census report lists her as his widow), but what was true and what was false is not what counts in the matter of Crane's will—only what he believed to be true when he dictated the letter to William on November twenty-ninth. He believed he was about to become a father, and that unborn child, whether legitimate or not, would one day have a legitimate right to a share of his estate, but as it was with Amy, so it was with his potential offspring: not one word.

By not saying what he could have said, this is what Crane's will tells us about his blessed girl and her imaginary baby: If he happened to die in Cuba, he did not want them to be part of his legacy or to have anything to do with his brothers, and, because of that, if he happened to make it back alive, they had already been written out of his plans for the future.

Alternately described in the press as the "southern Newport" and the "American Nice," Jacksonville was a pleasant resort town of twenty-eight thousand inhabitants with a lively winter tourist trade and the largest, most splendid hotel south of the Mason-Dixon Line, the St. James, which could accommodate more than five hundred guests. Along with many of his fellow American journalists, Crane had booked a room there, but in order to protect his secret identity, he shied away from the rich crowd that milled around in the lobby and made himself as scarce as possible. Another well-known journalist, Sylvester Scovel, who would become a good friend of Crane's when they both covered the Greco-Turkish War that spring, had registered under the name of George H. Brown, and within a week of their arrival, the *Daily Florida Citizen* wrote that Samuel Carlton and two other men, George H. Brown and H. K. Sheridan, were "being closely watched by Spanish spies." Brown was reported to be an "expert dynamiter" and Carlton "an ex-lieutenant in the army" who was "fully up to war tactics and maneuvers."

According to another journalist friend, Charles Michelson, who first met Crane in Jacksonville and later worked side by side with him during the Spanish-American War, S.C.'s vanishing act in Florida was typical of his behavior in all the spots where he landed:

Crane on horseback with Sylvester Scovel, Jacksonville,
late 1896 or early 1897. (COURTESY OF THE MISSOURI HISTORICAL SOCIETY)

Crane always disappeared on his arrival in a new town. He dived into
the deep waters of society and stayed under. His associates knew where
to find him and haled him forth when the time came, but he never was
to be looked for about his hotel or in the bright cafés where the rest of
us sunned ourselves during the waiting-time. . . . Night after night Stephen loitered in the back room of a grimy water-front saloon, partially,
doubtless, because it was so close to the dock, but largely because there
people did not talk to him about his books—book, rather, for *The Red
Badge of Courage* was the only one people knew about then.

This was the period when he was supposed to be sunk in debauch-
ery. Actually he was consuming innumerable bottles of beer—I never
knew him to take anything stronger—and listening to the talk of oilers,
deck hands, sponge fishermen, wharf-rats and dock thieves, and all the
rest of the human flotsam that is washed into a port that has the West
Indies for a front yard. This was his way of soaking in knowledge . . .
of the kind of men he loved to write about, and while he was at it he
was one of them—a sombre, silent member, contributing no adventure
of his own, never flushing his quarry with a word that was not in their
vocabulary.

Of all the war correspondents who worked with Crane and later wrote about him, Michelson is the most acute and observant witness, the one who captures his elusive subject more fully than any of the others, but reliable as Michelson is, he overstates one small thing in this passage. While *The Red Badge of Courage* was unquestionably the only book of Crane's most people were aware of, that did not hold true for all people, as Michelson seems to imply, and among those who happened to have read other books by Crane as well, there was a person in Jacksonville who owned and operated a business on the corner of Ashley and Hawk in the La Villa district, and that woman, who had entered the world in Boston as infant Cora Ethel Eaton Howorth and later became Cora Murphy and then Cora Stewart and now called herself Cora Taylor, would become the most important person in Crane's life—his companion for the next three and a half years, the woman he called his wife when they set up house together in England, and the person who was in the room with him on the day he died.

2

HER GREAT-GRANDFATHER GEORGE HOWORTH WAS AN ART DEALER and gallery owner who had invented a special process for restoring oil paintings that had produced enough money for him to invest it in Boston real estate and become a wealthy man. Her maternal grandfather, Charles Holder, had been the first manufacturer of pianos in New York. Cora's father, John, was a painter, and among her uncles and cousins were decorated Civil War veterans (from both the army and the navy), naturalists, musicians, and the biographer of Darwin and Agassiz. Another relative on her mother's side was John Greenleaf Whittier, the poet. Which is to say that Cora Howorth, an only child, was surrounded by a world in which art and literature were part of daily life and certain comforts were taken for granted. But Cora was a rebellious, high-spirited prankster, a blonde bombshell in pinafores who found her greatest pleasure in rousing her friends to insurrectionist acts of defiance and mischief. Years later, when she told Crane about one of her childhood stunts, he turned it into the catalyzing event of "The Angel Child" (in *Whilomville Stories*), which features a character named "little Cora," a cunning provocateur who induces her playmates to follow her into a barbershop to have their long children's hair cut down and drastically reduced without their parents' permission. As for little Cora's parents in Crane's story, the mother is "quick, beautiful, imperious," and the father is "quiet, slow, and misty." Whether this is an accurate portrayal of the real Cora's parents is uncertain, but what we do know is that her gentle, much-adored artist father died painfully and young, still in his mid-thirties when he was struck down by the same disease that would kill the other man of her life in 1900—tuberculosis. Cora was six years old.

The record becomes somewhat obscure after that. Her mother remarried, the family settled in New York, and some years later, after her mother died during a difficult pregnancy, Cora moved in with her widowed aunt, Mary Holder, at 125 West 128th Street. The rest of her early life is a blank, but on or around her sixteenth birthday she came into what her biographer, Lillian Gilkes, has called a "substantial inheritance" from her great-grandfather's estate, the bulk of which had been passed on to the old man's widow, then to Cora's father, John, and after her father's death, to her mother, Elizabeth, and now some of that money had found its way to Cora, and whatever the amount was, it was enough for her to strike out on her own. There had been no quarrel with her aunt, and they remained on good terms for years afterward, but for the willful, supremely confident Cora, the move was a declaration of independence—the beginning of her life as an emancipated being, for as time went on she would become one of the rare American women of the late nineteenth century who felt herself as free as any man to follow her impulses and do exactly as she wished.

Through it all, she read voluminously, insatiably, and by the time she reached her late teens or early twenties, she had begun copying out significant passages in a series of commonplace books. Mixed in among her quotations from Shakespeare, Dante, Ibsen, Byron, Dickens, Emerson, Thoreau, and scores of others, there are many from forgotten novels of the period, but some of them are highly pertinent and offer a clear passage into understanding who Cora Howorth was and, just as important, who she thought she was—an image of herself as expressed through the words of others. One example: "Sometimes I like to sit at home and read good books, at others I must drink absinthe and hang the night with scarlet embroideries. . . . I never know how I shall spend the evening until the evening has come—I wait for my mood." Another: "If more allowance were made for the innocent impulses common to men, as gregarious animals, there might be less of the dangerous sense of the pleasure of forbidden fruit in their enjoyment." And still another: "I am a strange woman to whom fear of many kinds is unknown. I could dare, or do some strange things without flinching if I were driven."

At seventeen, she became the mistress of Jerome Stivers, the thirty-two-year-old heir to a carriage-manufacturing fortune known as "an all around man about town" and "a friend of the Duke of Manchester."

During one prolonged stretch in the four years they were together, Stivers owned or managed the London Club on West Twenty-ninth Street just off Fifth Avenue, a chic gambling house at the eastern edge of the Tenderloin where Cora worked as the hostess. Prostitutes undoubtedly worked there as well, but that was not Cora's trade and never would be, although the lessons she learned at the London Club must have been helpful to her when she opened her own night spot in Jacksonville a decade later.

During that early period, she also tried her hand at the theater and proved herself a capable enough singer and dancer to secure a role in the chorus of a comic opera, *Pepita, or The Girl with the Glass Eyes*, which starred the celebrated Lillian Russell and opened at the Union Square Theatre in March 1886. The production had a successful nine-week run, and while Cora did not pursue other roles after that, the mere fact that she had auditioned for this one on a blind whim and had been offered the part confirms that she was a young woman of spirit, a person who was both unafraid and willing to try anything.

At twenty-one, not long after the affair with Stivers ended, Cora married Thomas Vinton Murphy, the twenty-five-year-old son of the wealthy, well-connected Thomas Murphy, a former state senator and collector of the Port of New York during the Grant administration who was now in charge of the racetrack at Monmouth Park, just outside Long Branch, New Jersey, which had been one of Stivers's favorite haunts. The marriage crashed, ending in divorce two years later, in large part (most likely) because Murphy's devout Catholic father was opposed to it and pressured his son into extricating himself from the clutches of a scarlet woman who had lived openly in sin with another man in the years before her marriage. Daddy got his way, and Cora was dumped.

Not long after, she formed a new liaison with still another feckless, gadabout son who lived off his father's money (in this case a father who had helped found the First National Bank of the City of New York in the 1860s and Chase National Bank in the 1870s), but Ferris S. Thompson was a cut above the others, a young man not only of immense wealth but of infinite charm who had excelled on the Princeton track team and was now planning to devote the remainder of his youth to traveling around the world and living the good life. He was everything Cora wanted. She fell in love with him, ferociously in love, and as soon as her divorce with Murphy was finalized, she was fully expecting to take the plunge again and change her name to Thompson. Meanwhile, the two vagabonds, armed with a line of credit as long as the Mississippi, set off on an extended round of travels through the major capitals and neglected backroads of Europe, at one

Cora Crane, 1889.
(COURTESY OF SYRACUSE UNIVERSITY)

point journeying all the way to Constantinople on the Orient Express, but the handsome, magnetic Thompson, the most generous donor to Princeton in the history of the college, was prey to self-destructive impulses as well. He drank too much and could not control it; beautiful women kept throwing themselves at him, and he could not control it; he had no interest in books, music, or art (matters of vital importance to Cora) and could not control it. There were disputes and breakups, reconciliations and more breakups, and once, after they had reconciled yet again, Cora met up with him in Paris, only to discover that he was in the midst of an affair with a

French actress. Enraged and distraught, Cora picked up the object closest to hand—a penknife—and stabbed Thompson in the arm. They reconciled again, and then he betrayed her again, and Cora took off for London.

As if to punish him for what he had done to her, she took up with some-one else, a man she might have met as far back as her early days with Stivers or as recently as during one of her protracted visits to London with Thompson, but however long she had known ex-captain Donald William Stewart of the 92nd Gordon Highlanders, she now decided to marry him. The military son of a military man who had been made a baronet after his retirement as commander in chief of Her Majesty's forces in India, young Stewart had served under his father's command in Afghanistan, where he was gravely wounded in battle. After a short stint in the Transvaal, he was transferred to India, where he worked as his father's aide-de-camp for two years and was again nearly killed in battle—the noble record of a tall, strapping man who seemed to embody all the self-proclaimed virtues of the British Empire—but Stewart was also a spendthrift, a womanizer, a gambler, and an angry drunk, and in 1888 he was forced to resign his commission because mounting debts had pushed him into the embarrassing spot of having to declare bankruptcy. When Cora understood that he had married her for her money, she backed off. Thompson reentered the picture, the affair resumed, and as the cuckolded victim of his wife's treachery, Stewart sought to cash in by suing Thompson for "alienation of affection" in the amount of fifty thousand dollars, the equivalent of more than a million dollars today. The case dragged on until it was ultimately dismissed, no doubt because Thompson had settled the matter quietly out of court. Still going by the name Lady Stewart, Cora imagined that divorce would be the next step, but Stewart exacted further revenge by refusing to grant her one. She was stuck. The romance with Thompson puttered along for a while, but whatever chance she had had of marrying him was now gone. Bit by bit, she would have to train herself how to stand on her own two feet, and when Thompson finally vanished from her life, she began to take her first steps forward.

For reasons unknown, she landed in Jacksonville, Florida, in early 1895. Also for reasons unknown, she was now calling herself Cora Taylor, and under that name she bought the property at the corner of Ashley and Hawk Streets from Carrie B. Mudge on March twenty-first. For some time, Mrs. Mudge had been leasing the two-story structure to a woman named Ethel Dreme, who ran a boardinghouse there that in all probability was more than just a boardinghouse, and when Cora agreed to pay off Ethel Dreme's debts in addition to the purchase price of the property, she took sole possession of what would soon become the pearl of Jacksonville nightlife, for if anyone understood the meaning and the power of the night, it was Cora Howorth, the woman of many names. "Whatever is too precious, too tender, too good, too evil, too bashful for the day happens in the night," she wrote in her commonplace book. "Night is the bath of life, the anodyne of heartaches, the silencer of passions, the breeder of them too, the teacher of those who would learn, the cloak that sets a man in with his soul."

In a town where the local population shared space with countless transients—tourists, Spanish spies, American reporters, Cuban rebels, and Michelson's "human flotsam"—there was little else for a displaced man to do after dark beyond drinking away the hours in a saloon or "going down the line" on Ward Street to visit one of Jacksonville's many brothels. Cora's new place in La Villa was far from that seedy row of fornication houses, and once she had revamped Mrs. Mudge's old property into the elegant sporting club she had mapped out in her imagination, she hung a sign over the door that read HOTEL DE DREME and opened for business.

From kept woman and wayward wife, Cora had advanced to a new level of self-knowledge, and by sheer strength of will she had finally taken control of her destiny. Through long and often painful experience, she had come to understand what men wanted, but now she would give it to them without paying a personal price, as she had in the past. Instead, the men would pay the price in the form of dollars, and by reversing the old formula, she would transform her wisdom into a lucrative operation that would grant her a life of total independence.

Cora's establishment was both a whorehouse and not a whorehouse, and if sex was one of the services offered to clients of the Hotel de Dreme, it was no more than an accompaniment to the roulette wheel, the good dinners, and the inexhaustible bottles of champagne. No girls lived on the premises, and no girls were employed by Cora as prostitutes, but if one of her male visitors chose to use the hotel for a private assignation, he was free to conduct his private business in one of the upstairs rooms after Cora herself had retired for the night. The downstairs parlor was where she entertained her guests, and with a man called the Professor playing tunes on the piano, the atmosphere was discreet, civilized, and even decorous. From the Gilkes biography:

> Cora remained in the parlor rooms during the first part of the evening to greet the guests and start things off. For she knew they came to see her. Her personality and wit drew them back and kept their dollars rolling in.

With her luminous smile and a bright word for each, she passed among the tables, joining in conversation when some youth or balding cavalier pleaded to buy her a drink—beer or champagne: no spirits or hard liquor was served to the public. Cora disliked drunkenness. Beer was one dollar a bottle, the standard price "down the line."

Later, as couples began to leave or drift upstairs, Cora said good night and . . . withdrew to her own apartments, to which none but the inner circle gained entrée. To these favored few she was "Miss Cora," or sometimes "Ma."

Attractive but far from beautiful, an impressive bearing but small in stature and decidedly plump, no one special, it would have seemed, and yet Cora had whatever it is that endows certain women with the self-assurance to make men want to look at them, to know them, to stand near them and breathe within their orbit. Her best features were her abundant blond hair—shimmering, spectacular—and her vivid blue eyes. Arresting, to be sure, though not enough to make a real difference in the long run. That she read books, could draw well, and wrote a decent sentence were all points in her favor, as was her gift for subtle, intelligent conversation, but what counted most was her inordinate vitality and, just as important, her utter lack of cynicism. She had entered a profession that makes women hard, but in the two years she ran her little pleasure resort in Jacksonville, Cora never became hard. She was an optimist, and in spite of the knocks that were dealt to her over the years, she never lost faith in herself or the promise of her own future. When she met Crane in early December, she was thirty-one. She told him she was twenty-eight, and because of who she was and how she must have said it, he believed her.

By one account, the affair began when Crane saw her reading a book of his that was not *The Red Badge of Courage*. She had bought an early printing of the war novel back in 1895, but this was something more recent, most likely *George's Mother*, although it could have been his newly published story collection, *The Little Regiment*. She didn't know that the author of the book, who happened to be one of her favorite contemporary writers, was the person watching her read the book, however, since he had come to her place under the guise of shadow-man Samuel Carlton, but when one of his friends blurted out his real name, our source tells us, "the news pierced the lady's very liver" and caused "an instantaneous mutual attraction."

So says Ernest W. McCready,* in any case, who purports to have heard about the incident from Ralph D. Paine,† who was supposed to have witnessed the scene on a night when McCready wasn't there, although the latter visited often enough to have retained a sharp memory of Cora, whom he calls "handsome, of some real refinement, aloof to most" (Crane was the exception). "Fact is," he goes on, "she was a cut above us in several ways, notably poise and surety of command of herself and others. If she had any false notes I was then all too unskilled in recognizing authentic 'class,' or lack of it, to detect any."

An instantaneous attraction, yes, but not quite as mutual as McCready would have it. Cora fell fast and hard, and almost from the instant she saw him she was prepared to jump into a lifetime of shared intimacy with a man she would playfully call her "mouse" and, in dead earnest, her "guiding star." Crane, however, tiptoed into the romance with extreme caution. He had been rejected in love by Lily Brandon Munroe, had failed in his antic pursuit of Nellie Crouse, and now he was struggling to sort out the disaster he had brought upon himself with Amy Leslie. With the New York scandal just behind him and the uncertainties of Cuba just ahead, it was hardly the moment to be making decisions about love or anything else.

Nevertheless, Crane had finally met his match, his spiritual double, the living embodiment of a female version of himself. Cora was a woman who spurned the conventions and moral hypocrisies of their world just as thoroughly as he did, a woman who had no fear of sex and understood that erotic desire was an essential fact of the human condition, a woman who loved books—among them *his books*—and, as her history showed, a woman who could be just as reckless as he was.

She was frank with him about that history, even when they were just getting to know each other, and barely a day or two after they met, Crane presented her with three books. One was a collection of poems by Kipling in which Cora later noted: "The first thing my mouse ever gave me was this book." The second contained an inscription that began "To C.E.S." (Cora Ethel Stewart), an irrefutable sign that she had opened up to him

---

* Another journalist friend who was with Crane in Florida and later in Cuba during the Spanish-American War. He served as the model for the character known as "Shackles" in three of Crane's stories from 1899 ("God Rest Ye, Merry Gentlemen," "Virtue in War," "The Revenge of the *Adolphus*") and appears as McCurdy in the autobiographical "War Memories."

† The third member of the Asbury Park trio of cub-reporter friends in the early nineties. The other two were Post Wheeler and Crane.

about her second marriage, and if she had done that, she had probably talked about her first marriage and many other details about her life as well. Under the initials Crane wrote: "Brevity is an element / that enters importantly / into all pleasures of / life and this is / what makes pleasure sad / and so there is no / pleasure but only sad- / ness." Not the words of a man who had much hope in their future together—or even in the idea that there could have been a future for them.

The third book was *George's Mother*, and in that one he simply wrote: "To an unnamed sweetheart." Eventually, he would give her a name—his own name—but only after he had gone off on his journey into the waters between Florida and Cuba and come back from the dead.

3

THESE ARE THE FACTS. SEVENTY-ONE FILIBUSTER BOATS SET OUT from Florida to Cuba between 1895 and 1898, and more than half of them were stopped by the American or Spanish navies. Although the policies of the two countries were identical, America's actions stemmed from legal obligation (to enforce the neutrality laws), whereas Spain's were political (to thwart the rebellion). By the end of 1896, the steamship *Commodore* had attempted to reach Cuba four times but had managed to get there only twice. Still, there were loopholes that sometimes came into play, and they could be exploited to gain clearance from the authorities, which seems to have happened with the *Commodore's* fifth expedition on New Year's Eve when the U.S. secretary of the treasury signed off on the venture. A pro-rebel Cuban lawyer had argued that where a ship was going and what it happened to be carrying were two distinct issues. In other words, once approval had been granted by the American government, it should not matter if the ship was carrying "arms or sausages." Approval was required from the Spanish government as well, and in this case greed turned out to be the motivating factor that led Pedro Solis, the Spanish consul in Florida, to put his name on the document, even after it was pointed out to him that the *Commodore* would be carrying more than two hundred thousand cartridges, one thousand pounds of giant powder, forty bundles of rifles, two electric batteries, and three hundred machetes. When asked if he would clear the ship for departure, Solis replied, "Certainly I will . . . just the same as if the cargo were potatoes for the Spanish army." Then he reminded them that among the benefits of his job as consul, he was paid a fee for all transports to Cuba. The heavier the load, the greater the sum that went into his pocket.

It was an open secret, then. The *Commodore* was engaged in a filibuster operation to provide arms to the Cuban rebels, and when it set sail at eight o'clock in the evening on December thirty-first, a large crowd of rebel supporters gathered on the dock to cheer the ship as it left the port. One hundred and twenty-two feet long, twenty-one feet wide, and weighing one hundred and seventy-eight tons, it carried a human cargo of Cuban nationalists, American officers and deckhands, and one journalist—twenty-seven men in all. Crane had signed on as a working member of the crew, but no one from the local press was taken in by the decoy. The *Florida Times-Union* announced that S.C. was aboard the vessel "as the representative of a syndicate of Northern newspapers. He will not be employed in the capacity of a newsgatherer, but will write Sunday letters to the newspapers of New York, Philadelphia, Chicago, Pittsburgh, and Boston. He was asked how long he expected to stay in the island, and replied that he could not tell. He shipped as a seaman at a salary of $20 a month."

The trouble began almost at once. Two miles from Jacksonville, as the pilot steered the *Commodore* through heavy fog down the St. Johns River toward the open sea, the ship jammed into a sandbar and was stuck there until dawn. Help was sought from the revenue cutter *George S. Boutwell*, which normally was in the business of trying to impede filibuster craft from slipping through the blockade, but this time the captain chose to ignore official policy and towed the *Commodore* back into the water, then continued to pull her in the direction of the sea. He, too, was clearly in on the open secret of the *Commodore*'s mission, and because he was less neutral in his sympathies than the American government, he kept the *Boutwell* close to the *Commodore* after the towline was detached. Not long after, the *Commodore* struck land again at Mayport, but this time the ship managed to free herself when the engines were thrown into reverse. As Captain Kilgore of the *Boutwell* looked on, he called to the other ship, "Are you fellows going out to sea today?" Captain Murphy of the *Commodore* called back, "Yes, sir." The *Commodore* whistled a friendly salute, and as Kilgore took off his cap and waved it at Murphy, he shouted, "Well, gentlemen, I hope you have a pleasant cruise."

Captain Edward Murphy had been on other filibuster missions in the past and was an experienced commander, with sailing master's licenses from both England and America, but this was his first voyage with the *Commodore*, as it was for the two engineers on board, and because they were unfamiliar with the ship, or simply because it didn't occur to them, not one of them thought to inspect the hull for damage after the first grounding in the St. Johns River, and so, damaged or not, the *Commodore* headed for the open sea.

The water was rough that day, a stiff wind was blowing, and as Crane described it in his four-thousand-word account of the catastrophe, the *Commodore* pitched and rolled over the waves "and on deck amidships lay five or six Cubans, limp, forlorn, and infinitely depressed . . . and presently even some American seamen were made ill by the long wallowing motion." Captain Murphy told the *New York Press* (January 4) that "even old sailors got seasick when we struck the open sea after leaving the bar, but Crane behaved like a born sailor. He and I were about the only ones not affected by the big seas which tossed us about. As we went south he sat in the pilot-house with me, smoking and telling yarns. When the leak was discovered, he was the first man to volunteer aid."

The pumps had stopped working, water was rushing in through a rent in the hull, and at ten o'clock that night the chief engineer entered the pilot-house to inform the captain that there was trouble in the engine room. Minutes later, Crane was down there in the bowels of the ship with a line of other men, bailing water as they passed the buckets back and forth between them, working in the insufferable heat while "soapish sea water swirl[ed] and swish[ed] among machinery that roared and banged and clattered and steamed." Captain Murphy ordered the men to feed the furnace with wood, oil, and alcohol—anything that would burn—in the hope of keeping the engines alive long enough to carry them to Mosquito Inlet, which was about eighteen miles to the west, but, as he told the *New York Herald* (January 5), "the water gained upon us slowly and surely, and we had not proceeded three miles when the fires were quenched. There was no hope of saving the ship."

Meanwhile, up on deck, men were beginning to panic. A coal heaver emerged from the hold carrying a package of dynamite and asked the captain to get it over with and blow them up before they drowned. "The dynamite was carefully taken from him, and then Captain Murphy's fist did the rest. 'Lie there, you cowardly dog!' shouted Captain Murphy. 'Obey orders, and we'll all get off'" (the *World*, January 4). The same article reports that one of the sailors lost his mind, scrambled up the rigging all the way to the yard, and then tried to stand on his head. A Cuban about to jump into the water was pulled back by the second mate, and "another was so thoroughly demoralized that he knelt down at the Captain's feet and prayed to be thrown overboard."

In his own article, Crane avoids dwelling on his conduct during the crisis, but the men around him were all struck by how calmly he acted under pressure and the clear-headed, unflagging bravery he showed in trying to maintain order on the ship. The steward, Charles Montgomery, told the *New York Press* (January 4) that "one of the Cubans got rattled and tried to run out one of the boats before time, and Crane let him have it right from the shoulder, and the man rolled down the leeway, stunned for the moment." Captain Murphy commented in the same article: "That man Crane is the spunkiest man out. . . . His shoes, new ones, were slippery on the deck, and he took them off and tossed them overboard, saying with a laugh: 'Well, Captain, I guess I won't need them if we have to swim.' He stood on the deck by me all the while, smoking his cigarette, and aiding me greatly while the boats were getting off. . . . He's a thorough-bred, and a brave man, too, with plenty of grit." Montgomery shared the captain's opinion:

> "That newspaper feller was a nervy man. He didn't seem to know what fear was. . . . He insisted upon doing a seaman's work, and he did it well, too. When aroused Saturday morning he never quailed when he came on deck and saw the foaming and raging billows and knew that the vessel was sinking. . . . He stood on the bridge with glasses in hand, sweeping the horizon in an effort to get a glimpse of land. . . . I thought sure that he would be swept off as the vessel rolled from side to side, her yards almost touching the water as she rolled."

The *Commodore*'s rescue equipment included three lifeboats, a ten-foot dinghy, and however many life jackets the ship was carrying. In his piece, Crane remarks that when a stoker was seen "prowling around, done up in life preservers until he looked like a featherbed," the captain cursed him out, which would suggest that the supply of jackets was limited, and indeed, when Crane wound up in the dinghy with the captain, steward Montgomery, and an oiler named Billy Higgins, there were only two life jackets in the boat, not four. To make matters worse for the captain (and finally for all of them), a wave had smashed into the deckhouse and broken his arm, which was now in a sling, immobilized and useless.

As the first lifeboat was being lowered into the water, Crane happened to observe another instance of raw, terror-driven panic: "A certain man was the first person in the first boat, and they were handing him in a valise about as large as a hotel. I had not entirely recovered from my astonishment and pleasure in witnessing this noble deed, when I saw another valise go to him." The *noble deed* was in fact the escape of a coward, and the *certain man* was Paul Rojo, the person in charge of the Cubans on board and the representative of the ship's owners. Eleven more Cubans followed him into the boat, and when they reached shore at ten o'clock in the morning (January 2), Rojo hired a sailboat, but instead of using it to return to the *Commodore*, he sailed on to the town of New Smyrna, where at last he wired Jacksonville about the trouble at sea. He asked them to send help, but no help ever came. As S.C. later told Horatio S. Rubens, general counsel of the Cuban Junta: "He reminded me of George Washington. First in war, first in peace—and first in the lifeboat."

The second lifeboat could not be yanked from its moorings, at least not without a mighty effort from Crane, Higgins, two stokers, and the first mate:

> We wrestled with that boat, which I am willing to swear weighed as much as a Broadway cable car. She might have been spiked to the deck. We could have pushed a little brick schoolhouse along a corduroy road as easily as we could have moved this boat. But the first mate got a tackle to her from a leeward davit, and on the deck below the captain corralled enough men to make an impression upon the boat.

It finally went down into the water, and the remaining Cubans were sent off. Traveling through the predawn darkness, they reached shore by the time the sun was directly above them.

The American crew was next, eleven men including Crane, and now that four of them had decided to chance it with the dinghy, the other seven would take the sturdier lifeboat. Everything was going according to plan, and if the third lifeboat had been the solid, seaworthy craft they all assumed it was, the plan would have worked. The seven would have been saved, but because the third boat was defective, they were not saved, and what should have been the story of a brilliant, last-minute rescue was turned into a tragedy of horror and meaningless death.

After the third boat set off toward the coast, the captain instructed Crane to prepare the dinghy for boarding. One by one, the four men climbed into the little rowboat and steered it several hundred yards from the sinking ship, where they intended to stay until the *Commodore* went under. By the time they settled into position, however, they saw that the seven men from the lifeboat had returned to the ship. "The men on board were a mystery to us," Crane writes, "as we had seen all the boats leave the ship. We rowed back to the ship, but did not approach too near, because we were four men in a ten-foot boat, and we knew that the touch of a hand on our gunwale would assuredly swamp us.

"The first mate cried out from the ship that the third boat had foundered."

In the meantime, the men had hastily constructed three makeshift rafts, which had been thrown into the water and were floating beside the ship. When they called out to the captain and asked if he would be willing to tow the rafts behind the dinghy, he agreed to give it a try and then told them to "jump in." As Crane recounts: "Four men, I remember, clambered over the railing and stood there watching the cold, steely sheen of the sweeping waves." Four men, but the three others inexplicably held back. The old chief engineer jumped in first, followed by a stoker, and after that a seaman named Tom Smith, who earlier had told Crane that this would be his last filibustering job, that he had had enough and was planning to enter a new line of work. They all managed to catch hold of the rafts, but the last of the four, the first mate, whom Crane had already described as "losing his grip" during a temper tantrum over the stuck second boat, suddenly "threw his hands over his head and plunged into the sea. He had no life belt, and for my part, even when he did this horrible thing, I somehow felt that I could see in the expression of his hands, and in the very toss of his head, as he leaped thus to his death, that it was rage, rage, rage unspeakable that was in his heart at the time."

Rage against the circumstances that had trapped him in this hopeless situation, but rage against the captain for having abandoned the ship as well, and the sight of Murphy sitting securely in his little boat must have been too much for the first mate, and rather than try to save himself, he ended his life in an act of savage protest.

Crane continues:

On board the *Commodore* three men strode, still in silence and with their faces turned toward us. One man had his arms folded and was leaning against the deckhouse. His feet were crossed, so that the toe of his left foot pointed downward. There they stood gazing at us. . . .

The colored stoker on the first raft threw a line and we began to tow. Of course, we perfectly understood the absolute impossibility of any such thing; our dingy was within six inches of the water's edge, there was an enormous sea running, and I knew that under the circumstances a tugboat would have no light task in moving these rafts. But we tried it, and would have continued to try it indefinitely, but that something critical came to pass. I was at an oar and so faced the rafts. The cook controlled the line. Suddenly the boat began to go backward, and then we saw this negro on the first raft pulling on the line hand over hand and drawing us to him.

He had turned into a demon. He was wild, wild as a tiger. He was crouched on this raft and ready to spring. Every muscle of him seemed to be turned into an elastic spring. His eyes were almost white. His face was the face of a lost man reaching upward, and we knew that the weight of his hand on our gunwale doomed us. The cook let go of the line.

We rowed around to see if we could not get a line from the chief engineer, and all this time, mind you, there were no shrieks, no groans, but silence, silence, and silence, and then the *Commodore* sank. She lurched to windward, then swung afar back, righted and dove into the sea, and the rafts were suddenly swallowed by this frightful maw of the ocean. And then by the men on the ten-foot dingy were words said that were still not words, something far beyond words.

For the next thirty hours, the men in the dinghy struggled to reach the shore, but the frail boat was not equipped to handle such rough waters, and threatened by the drift and the undertow and the presence of sharks, they had to row and bail with all their strength just to prevent themselves from being pushed farther out to sea. The captain had only one usable arm, the cook could not swim, and with Crane and Higgins doing most of the work, they fought for an entire day and all through a long winter night before hazarding a last run at the beach the following morning. Before they could land, however, the boat capsized, throwing them into the water, and they had to swim the rest of the way.* In his article, Crane skips over all that. "The history of life in an open boat for thirty hours would no doubt be very instructive for the young," he writes, "but none of that is to be told here." He told it some weeks later, in what is probably the greatest and most perfect of his short stories, but for now—just two days after his rescue—the exhausted, emotionally ravaged Crane concluded his article by underscoring "the splendid manhood of Captain Edward Murphy and of William Higgins, the oiler" and praising the man on the beach ("John Kitchell of Daytona") who shed his clothes and ran into the surf when he saw them floundering among the waves after they had been tossed from the boat. He was the one who hauled them onto dry land, but even then, the tragedy of the *Commodore* had not yet drawn to a close:

---

* The captain had given the life jackets to Montgomery and Crane. The instant S.C. found himself in the water, he unbuckled the money belt to rid himself of the encumbrance. Seven hundred dollars in gold (the equivalent of around twenty thousand dollars today) sank to the bottom of the ocean. A short time later, Bacheller left the newspaper syndicate business to become the Sunday editor of the *World*, then turned his attention to writing short stories, poems, essays, and novels—more than thirty of them—one of which (*Eben Holden*, 1900) sold nearly a million copies.

"He dashed into the water and grabbed the cook. Then he went after the captain, but the captain sent him to me, and then it was that we saw Billy Higgins lying with his forehead on sand that was clear of the water, and he was dead."

Higgins, the stoutest member of the group, the best swimmer among them and the man who had worked most tirelessly during their thirty hours at sea, had been struck on the head by the overturned dinghy as he swam ashore, and the blow had killed him.

It was Sunday morning, January third. In no time at all, local residents began rushing toward the beach with clothes, coffee, and blankets for the three survivors. Lodging was arranged for them, and they all wound up spending the night in Daytona, ninety miles down the coast from Jacksonville.

When the first reports of the *Commodore* disaster had been published in the press the day before, it had been generally assumed that Crane was dead, and officials in Jacksonville had told Cora to "fear the worst." Now, on learning that he was alive, she answered his telegram with one of her own: "Telegram received. Thank God your safe have been almost crazy."

Another telegram, from Edward Marshall in New York, was forwarded to him by a clerk at the St. James Hotel: "Congratulations on plucky and successful fight for life. Dont wire. But write fully from Jax. will wire money today."

Then, still on the third, Cora sent him another telegram: "Come by special today never mind overcharges answer and come surely." There were no trains on Sunday, however, and so he stayed where he was, intent on going to Billy Higgins's funeral and then (no one is quite sure) perhaps traveling south to look for another way to get to Cuba. Whatever he was planning, Cora promptly took charge of the situation by catching the early train from Jacksonville the next morning and turning up in Daytona at around noon. In spite of his apparent reluctance to see her again (if in fact he was reluctant), their reunion was not an unhappy one. Before they began the return trip to Jacksonville, an indiscreet, overly curious telegraph operator at the Daytona station kept a close watch on them. "They sat in a corner of the waiting room with their arms around one another," he said, "kissing and hugging like love birds, until time for the afternoon northbound train. That's the last I saw of them."

A crowd of more than a hundred Cubans cheered when Crane disembarked in Jacksonville, but he slipped out as quickly and quietly as he could, shunning the applause and nonsensical clamor (what had he done, after all, but not die?), and then he returned to the St. James Hotel, still dressed in his ragged seaman's clothes, which had shrunk to half their original size. In the lobby, he ran into a nine-year-old girl named Lillian Barrett, a future writer who was staying at the hotel with her parents and who had gotten it into her head that Crane was "the divinely appointed savior" of Cuba. Before his departure on New Year's Eve, she had asked him to sign her autograph book, but he hadn't had the time to do it. Now he did. "Where's that album?" he asked. Turning to a fresh page, he wrote: "Stephen Crane, Able Seaman, S.S. Commodore, January 4, 1897."

On the fifth, the *World* published an article with the headline STEPHEN CRANE SAFE. In it, they quoted a telegram he had sent to their office— probably on the fourth: "I am unable to write anything yet but will later." Later came soon, perhaps the same day the article was published, for Crane's account of his experience on the *Commodore* was in print by the seventh. In the meantime, according to a newspaper from Asbury Park, "a New York paper wired him an offer of $1000 for 1000 words about the affair . . . but he kept faith with the syndicate."

A telegram he sent to the *Atlanta Journal* on the sixth confirms that finding another way to reach Cuba was uppermost in his thoughts: "Seven of the Commodore's men are now unaccounted for. The ship was probably not scuttled.* I will stay in Jacksonville until another expedition starts for Cuba."

On the seventh, he wired Hawkins to thank him for sending money and to salute the members of the Lantern Club, who were planning to honor him for his "manly bearing in the presence of great danger": "Thanks awfully old man greeting to club send mail here." That same day, his article ran in several papers across the country and in two London papers as well. Featured on the front page of the *New York Press* under the headline STEPHEN CRANE'S OWN STORY, it was accompanied by a large picture of the author surrounded by a bright yellow halo. Not three months earlier, he had been portrayed as an archvillain of loose morals and scandalous habits for the newspaper readers of New York, and now he was being heralded as a shining figure of dauntless courage and exemplary inner strength. As a newspaperman himself, he undoubtedly understood the irony of his shifting status in the public mind. Nor was

---

* In the days following the disaster, numerous articles contended that sabotage had destroyed the *Commodore*—most likely caused by someone tampering with the pumps. There was an official investigation, but no evidence was found either to prove or disprove that idea.

he ever deluded about the innate contradictions of the organism that both fed him and devoured him throughout his working life: the modern press. "A newspaper is a collection of half-injustices," he wrote in one of his later poems. "A newspaper is a court / Where everyone is kindly and unfairly tried / By a squalor of honest men. . . . / A newspaper is a market / Where wisdom sells its freedom . . . / A newspaper is a game / Where error scores the player victory / While another's skill wins death. / A newspaper is . . . / A collection of loud tales / Concentrating eternal stupidities, / That in remote ages lived unhaltered, / Roaming through a fenceless world."*

He was done in by the time he washed ashore, utterly drained after three days of strenuous exertion on little or no sleep, and, as Montgomery described it to a reporter, Crane had become "so worn out that he could scarcely hold his oar straight." Had he suffered permanent damage to his health? Quite possibly, although it would be hard to measure exactly how much. For now, his most urgent need was rest and a chance to recover his strength. He let Cora take care of him in Jacksonville, and she did everything she could as far as he would allow it, indulging him with games of cards and sumptuous dinners of quail on toast and champagne in her private apartment at the Hotel de Dreme, but Crane was morose and withdrawn, disheveled and "rather slouchy," according to a Jacksonville doctor who stopped in to spend some time with them, even though "you could see she was simply crazy about him." Not long after his return, he inscribed another book to her, paraphrasing his recently published poem, "I explain the silvered passing of a ship at night" in a way that transforms it into a gloss on the wreck of the *Commodore* and his struggle to come to terms with what had just happened to him.

> To C.E.S.
> Love comes like the tall
> swift shadow of a ship at
> night. There is for a mom-
> ent, the music of the water's
> turmoil, a bell, perhaps, a

---

* From Crane's second collection of poems, *War Is Kind* (1899). The composition date of the newspaper poem has not been established, but in all likelihood it was written during the period when Crane was attracting so much negative and positive attention in the press.

man's shout, a row of gleaming yellow lights. Then the
slow sinking of this mystic
shape. Then silence and a
bitter silence—the silence
of the sea at night.
Stephen Crane*

The period of rest and recuperation lasted only seven days, during which
Crane was working on his article as much if not more than he was attending to his health, and with immediate passage to Cuba still uppermost in
his mind, he left Jacksonville on the eleventh, apparently bound for Tampa
(as reported by the *Florida Times-Union* on the twelfth), from which he was
planning "to go to Cuba via the Plant steamer Olivette if he cannot make
the trip in any other way," but at the last minute he scrapped the plan to
go south and took a train to New York, where he arrived on the thirteenth.

Of all places, why New York?

Only one person could tell us, and he is no longer available for comment.

The first thing he did there was apply for a passport to travel to Cuba,
Mexico, and the West Indies. It was issued on the fifteenth, the same day
the *Port Jervis Union* published an article about the hometown hero in
which he said, "I am feeling stronger, and after a short rest I shall make
new plans for my visit to Cuba."

Among the things he did during his short rest was attend a dinner in
his honor at the Lantern Club and accept an invitation to go to a party
for seven thousand people at Madison Square Garden on the night of the
eighteenth, but there is nothing to suggest that he tried to contact Amy
Leslie at any point during his visit to Manhattan.

Crane seems to have acquired a new sense of himself as a public figure
by then, and accepting the invitation to the annual French Ball thrown
by the Cercle Français de l'Harmonie would give him a chance to see
where he stood with his friends from the New York Police Department
and whether they still had it in for him after his resurrection in the pages

---

* The published poem reads: I explain the silvered passing of a ship at night / The sweep of
each sad lost wave / The dwindling boom of the steel thing's striving / The little cry of a
man to a man / A shadow falling across the greyer night / And the sinking of the small star.
// Then the waste, the far waste of waters / And the soft lashing of black waves / For long
and in loneliness. // Remember, thou, oh ship of love / Thou leavest a far waste of waters /
And the soft lashing of black waves / For long and in loneliness.

of the popular press. The yearly ball was one of the most lavish, epicurean indulgences of the Gilded Age, an event that began in a stately, dignified manner but often devolved into a free-for-all of drunken men in tuxedos sliding down banisters or trying to dance on champagne bottles, prostitutes floating among the crowd, and impromptu slugfests among the inebriated. If Crane did not go to see all that, he went to be seen, for none other than Captain Chapman, Officer Becker's friend and precinct commander, was in charge of security that night, so Crane donned the dreaded black-tie accoutrements and allowed himself to be seen, and what happened to him when he left the ball gave a definitive answer to his question. The police tried to arrest him for drunkenness, but because he wasn't drunk and had never been seen drunk by anyone in his life, they had to let him go. When they tried to arrest him again a day or two later as he was walking down Madison Avenue with a fellow journalist, the message was clear: Nothing had changed.

He went north after that to his brothers and his friend Louis Senger, who remarked that he "looked like a man from a grave. He jerked and thrashed in his sleep, and sometimes he cried out in anguish." Shuttling between the houses of William and Edmund, Crane spent the next three weeks with a pen in his hand, scratching out his brief instruction manual for the young. It was his last extended visit to Port Jervis and Hartwood, and in the cold of that New York State winter, the burning boy traveled down to Florida and jumped back into the waves that had nearly killed him.

4

In the presence of extraordinary actuality, consciousness takes the place of imagination.

—Wallace Stevens

"THE OPEN BOAT" STANDS APART FROM ALL OF CRANE'S OTHER work, not only because it is the most personal of his stories, the one based on a purely autobiographical experience, but also because it is the only thing he ever wrote that was driven by a double impulse: to present the facts of an actual event and at the same time to interpret those facts in order to understand their meaning. Until now, he had been splitting his energies between two forms of prose, fiction and journalism, but in "The Open Boat" he draws on both forms to create something new, a third something that is outside both categories and yet firmly anchored in each, something that could be called, perhaps, a *documentary fable*. Crane announces his intentions in the subtitle of the story: *A tale intended to be after the fact. Being the experience of four men from the sunk steamer Commodore.* "Tale" implies a work of the imagination, a fiction. "After the fact" implies the opposite: a piece of journalism, which is always written "after the fact." And by mentioning the "sunk steamer 'Commodore,'" Crane leaves no doubt about which fact he is referring to, a fact so well known to his readers that the single word "Commodore" is enough to identify it. Up to this point, all his short stories and novels had dealt with situations "during the fact," but now he will be telling a story that has already happened, a remembered story of an experience that involved him and three other men, and because that experience is so vital to him and therefore so powerfully remembered, the power of the story asserts itself from the first sentence and then sustains that power through the thirty pages that follow. It no longer matters what form Crane is working in, whether fiction or nonfiction or something else. He has us in the palm of his hand. He tells, and we listen, then he tells some more, and we listen some more, and before long we realize that the hand has tightened around us, locking us in the story in the same way the men are locked in the boat.

"None of them knew the color of the sky." So the account begins, and in one short sentence we understand that we are already in the middle of the account promised by the title and its explanatory subtitle: four men who have escaped a shipwreck are in an open boat somewhere in the Atlantic Ocean, and because their situation is perilous, their eyes are fixed on the water that surrounds them, which prevents them from turning their heads upward to look at the sky. The sentence propels us into the immediate, perceptual world of the men in the boat, and by using "them" rather than "us" Crane has informed the reader that this will not be an introspective, first-person retelling of what happened to him but an objective report of what happened to all four of them together. *A tale intended to be after the fact.* We are not in the now but in the then, and that allows the narrator to maintain a certain distance from the action even as he immerses himself in the memory of it and lives through the action *again*. Wordsworth: Poetry "takes its origin from emotion recollected in tranquillity." Crane recollects, and if his story is not a poem, it is nevertheless a prose poem that articulates the confrontation between the outer and inner worlds of nature and man, shot through with biting, ironic observations, several dashes of sly, deadpan humor, and, from start to finish, an all-pervasive feeling of dread.

The first paragraph continues with a precise description of what the men who do not know the color of the sky are seeing:

> Their eyes glanced level, and were fastened upon the waves that swept toward them. These waves were of the hue of slate, save for the tops, which were of foaming white, and all of the men knew the colors of the sea. The horizon narrowed and widened, and dipped and rose, and at all times its edge was jagged with waves that seemed to thrust up in points like rocks.

The tone then changes abruptly into a kind of jocular derision as boats are compared to bathtubs, then changes again into the mock-fussy exactitude of "small boat navigation," proving that our narrator is a flexible sort of person, open to various modes of discourse and emotional registers—someone capable of surprising us:

> Many a man ought to have a bath-tub larger than the boat which here rode upon the sea. These waves were most wrongfully and barbarously abrupt and tall, and each froth-top was a problem in small boat navigation.

The four principal characters are then introduced, one by one, over the next four paragraphs: the cook (Montgomery), the oiler (Higgins), the correspondent (Crane), and "the injured captain" (Murphy). The cook is bailing water from the bottom of the boat; the oiler is steering with one of the oars ("a thin little oar" that "often seemed ready to snap"); the correspondent is pulling at the other oar, wondering why he is there; and the captain is lying in the bow, brooding over the loss of his ship and remembering "the stern impression of a scene in the grays of dawn of seven turned faces, and later a stump of a top-mast with a white ball on it that slashed to and fro at the waves, went low and lower, and down." That is all that is ever said about the sinking of the *Commodore*, and although the captain is in a "profound dejection" and "there is something strange in his voice," he is fully up to the challenge of commanding the men in the boat. The first words of dialogue in the story are his:
"'Keep'er a little more south, Billie,' said he.
"'A little more south, sir,' said the oiler in the stern."
Higgins, the one who dies at the end, is the only character addressed by name. The correspondent, who represents the author, is not the one who is telling the story. That role belongs to an invisible, third-person narrator, but the narrator never presumes to enter the thoughts of any

character except the correspondent. For the simple reason that Crane knew what he was thinking during those thirty hours at sea but was not privy to the thoughts of the others. A subtle point, perhaps, but a crucial one, for *after the fact* means fact, not speculation, and the narrator's one brief excursion into the captain's state of mind is drawn from observation and Crane's own memory of the sinking of the ship. The "seven turned faces" from that early passage become "the seven mad gods who rule the sea" when the correspondent tries to imagine what could be in store for them nine pages later. The seven crewmen are always present, and because they have been swallowed by the sea, they have become the embodiment of the sea and the destructive powers within it—phantoms haunting the depths.

As he did with nearly all of his longer short stories, Crane divides "The Open Boat" into chapters, or a succession of numbered scenes, and the rest of the first part continues to introduce the reader to the basic conditions of life in the boat, that is, life in the middle of a churning, unstable expanse of ocean while trapped in a dinghy no larger than a bathtub. "The craft pranced and reared, and plunged like an animal. As each wave came, and she rose for it, she seemed like a horse making at a fence outrageously high." Not just a leap upward, as he goes on to explain, but a leap downward as well: "Then, after scornfully bumping a crest, she would slide, and race, and splash down a long incline and arrive bobbing and nodding in front of the next menace."

In the midst of this remembered turmoil, the narrator steps back from time to time to look at the scene from a broader, more tranquil perspective, pausing to note, for example, that "there was a terrible grace in the move of the waves, and they came in silence, save for the snarling of the crests." If the lives of the men were not at risk, there would be beauty in the motion of those waves, a natural beauty wholly at odds with the menace it brings when men entangle themselves within it, and three sentences after that, as Crane steps back still farther, he imagines looking down on the scene from above: "Viewed from a balcony, the whole thing would doubtlessly have been weirdly picturesque." And yet, as he quickly adds, "the men in the boat had no time to see it," *it* being not "the whole thing" but the supposition that they could be regarded as picturesque, for they are too busy looking at the water and trying to row themselves ashore to imagine themselves from the outside or even to notice the sun inching "steadily up the sky," and for that reason "they knew it was broad day because the color of the sea changed from slate to emerald green, streaked with amber lights, and the foam was like tumbling snow." That is what the men see, and therefore "the process of the breaking day was unknown to them." Perception is all, and constrained by the limitations of their predicament, they can see only what they need to see in order to survive. For now, the rest of the world is invisible, and if it is there, it can be conjured into view only *after the fact*—in the calm of recollection.

The chapter ends with the first sustained dialogue in the story as the cook and the correspondent begin to argue about "the differences between a life-saving station and a house of refuge," with the cook saying there is a house of refuge just north of the Mosquito Inlet lighthouse, which means that once their boat is spotted off the shore, rescue boats will be mobilized to bring them in, and the correspondent answering that "houses of refuge don't have crews."

> "Oh, yes, they do," said the cook.
> "No, they don't," said the correspondent.
> "Well, we're not there yet, anyhow," said the oiler, in the stern.
> "Well," said the cook, "perhaps it's not a house of refuge that I'm thinking of as being near Mosquito Inlet Light. Perhaps it's a life-saving station."
> "We're not there yet," said the oiler, in the stern.

An example of how the men in the boat interact with one another, and also a brief look at their contrasting personalities: the not too bright cook, the stickler correspondent—who will correct anyone who does not have his facts straight—and the stolid oiler, who prefers to do his job rather than get dragged into useless talk about hypothetical situations that have no bearing on the present. In just a few lines, Crane has given us a clearer notion of who these men are. We are two and a half pages into the story at this point, and already we are in deep.

Details accumulate as the narrative pushes forward, a barrage of precisely rendered descriptions that chart the shifting behavior of the ocean, the ominous arrival of pestering gulls (one of them lands on the captain's head), the "brown mats of seaweed" that appear on the surface whenever the boat comes within range of the shore (only to be pushed back again and again), and the dogged, muscle-draining work of endless rowing ("In the meantime the oiler and the correspondent rowed. And also they rowed"). Interspersed among the onrush of sensory particulars, there are passages that address the mood among the four men, which seems to fluctuate as rapidly as the wind and water around them. Early on, they scarcely know what to think. They feel it would be "childish and stupid" to express any optimism about their chances, and yet, as the narrator explains, the alternative would be no better, for "the ethics of their condition was decidedly against any open suggestions of hopelessness." The quandary therefore ends in a standoff: "So they were silent."

The ethics of their condition means the responsibility each man has assumed for the welfare of the three others, for they are all in the boat together, literally *in the same boat*, and it would be an ethical violation to say anything that would threaten the morale of the group. In this case, silence is the only solution, and what each man is thinking is known only to himself. In a world that has been reduced to a population of four, each man carries the burden of one-fourth of humanity, and whatever he does or doesn't do will affect the entire world. "The Open Boat" will turn on this condensation of the real into "a wee thing . . . at the mercy of five oceans" filled with four little men on their way to an uncertain future, and until that future comes, *the oiler and the correspondent rowed. And also they rowed.*

The mood lifts toward the end of the second chapter when they sight land for the first time—a tiny pinpoint in the distance, identified by the captain as the lighthouse at Mosquito Inlet—and if the wind holds and the boat doesn't swamp, the captain assures them, they are bound to make it all the way in. "'Bail her, cook,' said the captain, serenely." And the cook, now described as "cheerful," happily does as he is told. Which leads to the quasi-ecstatic first paragraph of the third part, in which Crane sets forth his new understanding of the world:

> It would be difficult to describe the subtle brotherhood of men that was here established on the seas. No one said that it was so. No one mentioned it. But it dwelt in the boat, and each man felt it warm him. They were a captain, an oiler, a cook, and a correspondent, and they were friends, friends in a more curiously iron-bound degree than may be common. The hurt captain, lying against the water-jar in the bow, spoke always in a low voice and calmly, but he could never command a more ready and swiftly obedient crew than the motley three in the dingey. It was more than a mere recognition of what was best for the common safety. There was surely in it a quality that was personal and heartfelt. And after this devotion to the commander of the boat there was this comradeship that the correspondent, for instance, who had been taught to be cynical of men, knew even at the time was the best

experience of his life. But no one said that it was so. No one mentioned it.

Twice before in his work, Crane had commented on a similar revelation, but in both instances he had been talking about others, first in Nebraska, where he had been awed by the solidarity he had witnessed among the suffering farmers, and then in Galveston, where the graciousness and honesty of the people had been "instructive to cynics," but now the cynic is directly involved in the experience himself, a terrible experience by any objective standard, but because of the "subtle brotherhood of men ... established on the seas," he declares it to be the best experience of his life. He was changed by what happened to him in that little boat, and from then on he found himself living in a different world from the one he had known before, a potentially different world, in any case, depending on whether one lived strictly for oneself or for and with and because of others as well. When *The Open Boat and Other Stories* was published as a book in 1898, Crane added a formal dedication for the first time in his writing life—a salute to the men who had trained him in the mysteries of the subtle, unarticulated brotherhood, which in a universe without meaning is man's only defense against unmitigated despair:

TO

THE LATE WILLIAM HIGGINS

AND TO

CAPTAIN EDWARD MURPHY AND STEWARD C. B. MONTGOMERY

OF THE SUNK STEAMER COMMODORE

The men fashion a makeshift sail by attaching an overcoat to an oar, and when they reach the top of the waves now, they can see the land growing larger in front of them, but then, unexpectedly, the wind dies down. The progress of the boat stalls, and the oiler and the correspondent take hold of the oars and start rowing again. Crane remarks:

Shipwrecks are *apropos* of nothing. . . . Of the four in the dingey none had slept any time worth mentioning for two days and two nights previous to embarking in the dingey, and in the excitement of clambering about the deck of a foundering ship they had also forgotten to eat heartily.

Hunger and exhaustion coupled with the slog of continual rowing, and the correspondent begins to wonder how anyone could possibly think that rowing is "amusing" when in reality it is a "diabolical punishment," "a horror to the muscles and a crime against the back." Still, they are all reasonably optimistic at that point. The land is looming closer, the distant lighthouse is well within view, and even if the surf is too strong for them to risk heading into it, they are working on the mistaken assumption that someone is in the lighthouse and they will be seen, and once they are seen, help will come to save them. They expect to be ashore within an hour, and when the correspondent discovers eight cigars in the top pocket of his coat, four of them soaked through with seawater and the four others miraculously dry, they all light up, "and with the assurance of impending rescue in their eyes, [they] puffed at the big cigars and judged well and ill of all men. Everybody took a drink of water."

But nothing happens. "Funny they don't see us," the cook says as the fourth chapter begins, and before long those words are repeated and then repeated again as the men puzzle over the lack of response from the shore: "Funny they don't see us."

> The light-heartedness of a former time had completely faded. To their sharpened minds it was easy to conjure pictures of all kinds of incompetency and blindness and, indeed, cowardice. There was the shore of the populous land, and it was bitter and bitter to them that from it came no sign.

The captain concludes that they should make a try for it themselves, reasoning that "if we stay out here too long, we'll none of us have the strength to swim after the boat swamps." As the oiler turns the dinghy toward the shore, the captain, understanding how perilous this charge on the breakers will be, asks the men if they know where to send the news of his "finish" if he doesn't make it, and for the first time in the story the subject of death is confronted head-on.

> They then briefly exchanged some addresses and admonitions. As for the reflections of the men, there was a great deal of rage in them. Perchance they might be formulated thus: "If I am going to be drowned—if I am going to be drowned—if I am going to be drowned, why, in the name of the seven mad gods who rule the sea, was I allowed to come thus far and contemplate sand and trees? Was I brought here

merely to have my nose dragged away as I was about to nibble the sacred cheese of life? It is preposterous. If this old ninny-woman, Fate, cannot do better than this, she should be deprived of the management of men's fortunes. She is an old hen who knows not her intention. If she has decided to drown me, why did she not do it in the beginning and save me all this trouble. The whole affair is absurd. . . . But no, she cannot mean to drown me. She dare not drown me. She cannot drown me. Not after all this work." Afterward the man might have had an impulse to shake his fist at the clouds. "Just you drown me, now, and then hear what I call you!"

It is a complex passage, at once serious and mocking, and as Crane presents his argument, he seems to know how ridiculous he must sound, for shaking your fist at the clouds and cursing Fate after she has killed you are surely empty, meaningless gestures. Man has no say in what nature decides to do with him, and it is a telling point, I think, that Crane should compare man to a mouse, the lowly, insignificant mouse who *nibbles the sacred cheese of life*, a phrase at once so humorous and dark that it would be difficult not to see it as another one of Crane's ironic jabs at the platitudes of conventional thinking: the *Woe is me* response to impending death. But this passage is only a first step on the road toward a deeper understanding of the experience he has lived through. There is more to come, and the rage and petulance of this imagined inner monologue will disappear as the story advances. Bit by bit, the walls of imprisoning selfhood will crumble, and the world will shine through—not just the water, but the sky as well—for what seems at first to be nothing more than a real-life adventure tale is in fact a philosophical journey through the various stages of dawning consciousness toward a somber, stoical, painfully earned wisdom.

The oiler points the boat toward the shore, but the billows are intense, growing "more formidable," and "they seemed always just about to break and roll over the little boat in a turmoil of foam." There is still a long way to the shore, but even from that distance the water is too rough to advance in safety. The oiler announces that "she won't live three minutes more and we're too far out to swim." He asks the captain if he should "take her to the sea again," and the captain answers yes, go ahead. The assault on the beach has failed.

They remove themselves to a safer distance, studying the beach for signs of life, anything that would offer some hope that they will, in the end, be rescued. Several pages go by in which the men do nothing but watch, wait, and row. Then one of them spots a man on the beach. The four men in the boat turn their full attention on him, studying his gestures, commenting on what he is doing, and in the long skein of dialogue that follows Crane holds back from attributing a speaker to what is said: the words hang in the air, and we have no idea who is saying them—whether it is the captain, the correspondent, the oiler, or the cook, for by now they are of one mind, one purpose, and it no longer matters who is saying what. This is the subtle brotherhood in action, and no further gloss is required. The action speaks for itself, which in this case is the act of speaking, and who speaks is in fact all of them together, each one in his turn, for what happens to one of them will be something that happens to all of them. Their fates have become indistinguishable.

The man seems to be waving at them. Then he is no longer waving, he is running. Then he has stopped running. Suddenly another man appears, running, it seems, but no, he is on a bicycle, and he has joined the other man. They both wave. Then something comes rolling along the beach. It could be a boat on wheels, they think, but no, it is an omnibus—one of the omnibuses from the large hotels nearby. A man on the bus is waving a black flag, but no, it isn't a flag, it's an overcoat, and why would a man wave an overcoat around his head? The men in the boat speculate. The people from the hotel have come to the shore to watch them drown. Or the people think the four men in the boat are fishing. Or what? It goes on, it goes on and on until the men in the boat are trapped on the uncertain *dividing line between coherence and a blur*, and then, little by little, the light steadily dims, and the day has been lost.

> The shore grew dusky. The man waving a coat blended gradually into this gloom, and it swallowed in the same manner the omnibus and the group of people. The spray, when it dashed uproariously over the side, made the voyagers shrink and swear like men who were being branded.
>
> "I'd like to catch the chump who waved the coat. I feel like soaking him one, just for luck."
>
> "Why? What did he do?"
>
> "Oh, nothing, but then he seemed so damned cheerful."
>
> In the meantime the oiler rowed, and then the correspondent rowed, and then the oiler rowed. Gray-faced and bowed forward, they mechanically, turn by turn, plied the leaden oars. The form of the lighthouse had vanished from the southern horizon, but finally a pale star appeared, just lifting from the sea. The streaked saffron in the west passed before the all-merging darkness, and the sea to the east was black. The land

had vanished, and was expressed only by the low and drear thunder of the surf.

As the fifth chapter begins, Crane pushes further into the darkness that surrounds the boat:

> A night on the sea in an open boat is a long night. As darkness settled finally, the shine of the light, lifting from the sea in the south, changed to full gold. On the northern horizon a new light appeared, a small bluish gleam on the edge of the waters. These two lights were the furniture of the world. Otherwise there was nothing but waves.

"Furniture of the world" is both stunning and unexpected—stunning in the sense of *beautiful*, unexpected in the primary sense of *stunning*—especially because the furniture is no more substantial than two distant sources of light, and coming just after the unexpected conclusion to the fourth chapter, when the cook suddenly turns to the oiler and asks, apropos of nothing (in the same way shipwrecks are apropos of nothing), "Billie, what kind of pie do you like best?," the weave of textures and tones in the story has attained a new thickness, a new complexity of meaning. With the continual return to several key phrases throughout ("the oiler rowed, and then the correspondent rowed, and then the oiler rowed" along with the refrain of "If I am going to be drowned—if I am going to be drowned—if I am going to be drowned," which has been repeated toward the end of the fourth chapter and will be repeated again at the beginning of the sixth, each time somewhat shorter, with fewer sentences from the original version left in), it is becoming clear that "The Open Boat" has been structured as a piece of music, a fugue in which the separate voices or strands increasingly overlap until they begin to merge, and with the coming of night the fugue has entered the early stages of its stretto, the finale that will gather up the disparate voices and turn them into one, a resolution that will create a different sound from the ones heard in the earlier portions of the text, a sound as deep as the thunder of the surf.

The oiler and the correspondent take turns rowing in the darkness. While one sleeps in the cold water sloshing around the bottom of the boat, the other mans the oars until he is too exhausted to go on. When that happens, he gently rouses the sleeper from the "dead sleep" and asks if he will spell him for a little while, and if it is the correspondent who happens to be sleeping, he will answer, "Sure, Billie," and then the two of them will trade places until the time comes for them to trade places again.

Their politeness with each other is both serene and courtly, and not once does either of them complain.

The correspondent rows on alone in the night, looking down at the sleeping cook and oiler, one with his arm thrown around the other's shoulder, and thinks of them as "the babes of the sea, a grotesque rendering of the old babes in the wood." Even the ever-wakeful captain seems to have dozed off, "and the correspondent thought that he was the one man afloat on all the oceans. The wind had a voice as it came over the waves, and it was sadder than the end." A shark appears alongside the boat, no more than an oar's length away—"a long flash of bluish light . . . an enormous fin speed[ing] like a shadow through the water"—but the threat leaves the correspondent strangely unmoved. He wishes that one of the others was awake to share the experience with him, but all three are dead to the world, fast asleep in the sloshing water at the bottom of the boat, and the solitary correspondent rows on.

Chapter V gives way to chapter VI, and the correspondent is still alone, meditating on the seven mad gods of the sea as he mutters his familiar refrain, "If I am going to be drowned—if I am going to be drowned—if I am going to be drowned," but now he begins to push his thinking beyond mere petulance into a broader view of his situation, no longer treating it as a personal insult but as a philosophical problem that can afflict any man who finds himself confronting the irrational forces of the elements.

> When it occurs to a man that nature does not regard him as important, and that she feels she would not maim the universe by disposing of him, he at first wishes to throw bricks at the temple, and he hates deeply that there are no bricks and no temples. Any visible expression of nature would surely be pelleted with his jeers.
>
> Then, if there be no tangible thing to hoot he feels, perhaps, the desire to confront a personification and indulge in pleas, bowed to one knee, and with hands supplicant, saying: "Yes, but I love myself."
>
> A high cold star on a winter's night is the word he feels that she says to him. Thereafter he knows the pathos of his situation.

The correspondent's mind wanders, inexplicably going back to a poem he read in childhood, so long ago that he has "forgotten that he had forgotten the verse," a dreadful bit of hokum about a *soldier of the Legion* who *lay dying in Algiers* and would *never more* see his *native land*, a work that made no impression on him as a boy, for while he knew he was supposed to be filled with sorrow for the dying soldier, "it was less to him than the breaking of a pencil's point."

> Now, however, it quaintly came to him as a human, living thing. It was no longer merely a picture of a few throes in the breast of a poet, meanwhile drinking tea and warming his feet at the grate; it was an actuality—stern, mournful, and fine.
> ... In the far Algerian distance, a city of low square forms was set against a sky that was faint with the last sunset hues. The correspondent, plying the oars and dreaming of the slow and slower movements of the lips of the soldier, was moved by a profound and perfectly impersonal comprehension. He was sorry for the soldier of the Legion who lay dying in Algiers.

Another one of Crane's stream-of-consciousness divagations, similar to the barrage of thoughts tumbling through the head of the New York Kid in "The Five White Mice," but also a parable of how Crane chose to write his story, a fable within the true-life fable that is "The Open Boat," a work set in Florida but written in the cold of an upstate New York winter, no doubt in a room warmed by a comfortable fire, not unlike the room the correspondent imagines the poet to be sitting in when he writes about the soldier in hot, distant Algiers. The poem is still a bad poem, and because of its dead language the soldier is already dead before he dies, but the boy who failed to respond to it is now a man, a correspondent rowing for his life in the darkness who has at last understood the *pathos of his situation*, which has allowed him to attain a "perfectly impersonal comprehension" that cuts through the dead language of the poem and gives him the dying soldier again in all the pathos of *his* situation. He can be moved by the poem now, not because it is a good poem but because the poem no longer matters. It is the *human, living thing* that counts, the human situation, which is no less human than his own, and therefore he can feel "sorry for the soldier of the Legion who lay dying in Algiers."

All to the point, certainly, but somewhat cracked as well, for this mental detour is also the product of duress, the extreme discombobulation brought on by a full day and half a night spent in an open boat: a psychological fact engendered by a mind that has started to buckle under the physical demands of the ordeal.

The captain stirs back to consciousness, the correspondent and the oiler trade places again, and as the correspondent lies down next to the sleeping cook, his teeth are chattering from the cold and "playing all the popular airs." He sleeps so soundly that no more than an instant seems to go by before he hears a voice "in the last stages of exhaustion": "Will you spell me?" And the correspondent replies: "Sure, Billie."

A bit later, the captain instructs the cook "to take one oar at the stern and keep the boat facing the sea." That will enable the correspondent and the oiler "to get respite together" and give them "a chance," as the captain says, "to get into shape again." So they sleep the dead sleep one more time, "and the ominous slash of the wind and the water affected them as it would have affected mummies." At this point in the struggle, their principal task is to keep the dinghy poised in a delicate balance between sea and shore, and whatever skills they possess in the art of small-boat navigation must be used to prevent the dinghy from coming too close to the treacherous surf and at the same time prevent it from drifting too far out and losing contact with the land. Another shark, or perhaps the same one, appears alongside the boat as the cook mans the oar. Then it is the correspondent's turn to row again. The captain gives him whiskey and water to steady "the chills out of him," and when the correspondent reaches the point of exhaustion for the umpteenth time, he turns to the oiler and asks, "Billie. . . . Billie, will you spell me?" and for the umpteenth time the oiler says, "Sure."

The last chapter begins as the correspondent opens his eyes and sees dawn breaking around him. The sky is gray at first, but as the minutes pass, "carmine and gold was painted upon the waters. The morning appeared finally, in its splendor, with a sky of pure blue, and the sunlight flamed on the tips of the waves." He knows the color of the sky now, and because he has achieved an "impersonal comprehension" of things, he is capable of looking at the world with an objective eye, an unclouded eye. He studies the distant shore, and what he sees is this: sand dunes, a number of small black cottages, and a tall white windmill towering above them. Signs of life, it would seem, but everything is deserted. No people, no dogs, no bicycles—nothing.

A conference was held in the boat. "Well," said the captain, "if no help is coming, we might better try a run through the surf right away. If we stay out here much longer we will be too weak to do anything for ourselves at all." The others silently acquiesced in this reasoning. The boat was headed for the beach. The correspondent wondered if none ever ascended the tall wind-tower, and if then they never looked seaward. This tower was a giant standing with its back to the plight of the ants. It represented in a degree to the correspondent, the serenity of nature amid the struggles of the individual—nature in the wind, and nature in the vision of men. She did not seem cruel to him then, nor beneficent, nor treacherous, nor wise. But she was indifferent, flatly indifferent.

Crane had visited this place in his mind many times before, but now he was experiencing it in the flesh, relearning the lessons he had already learned in a way that would imprint them in his bones forever, and from now on he would feel his way toward a new understanding of his mission as a writer. If nature is indifferent to the struggles of mankind, that does not mean it is cruel or even hostile, simply that it has no intrinsic meaning, or a meaning so far beyond the grasp of human intelligence that it has, in the end, no meaning. A design, perhaps, but no purpose or reason for existing except to perpetuate itself as a blind force, and mankind is left to cope for itself, to find meanings for itself in the subtle, unarticulated human bond, as in the case of four men stranded together in a boat that cannot reach the shore. Crane the gambler knew that when the dice rolled out of the cup, the result was a matter of pure chance. Forget God, forget destiny, forget fate—and understand that we are ruled by arbitrary forces beyond our control. Four men are stranded in a boat. They suffer through the same ordeal, but three of them will live and one of them will not. Why? Not only does the question have no answer, it has no meaning. Billie Hawkins dies. Mourn him by remembering him, remember him by mourning him, and then, if you happen to be a person who writes, put him in your story, and if your story from 1897 is good enough, it will go on being read for a long time to come, as it is being read today by a man sitting alone in a room in Brooklyn, New York, one hundred and twenty-two years after the fact.

They are heading toward the beach. It is certain that the boat will be swamped long before they get there, and as the oiler steers the dinghy in backward, the biggest question is when they will be swamped and how far they will have to swim. "The monstrous inshore rollers heaved the boat high," the narrator tells us, and then the last element of the story is brought into play, the final voice of the fugue, which suddenly changes the odds of surviving the battle ahead: fatigue, an immense and overpowering physical fatigue. The correspondent's "mind was dominated at this time by the muscles, and the muscles said they did not care. It merely occurred to him that if he should drown it would be a shame." He must fight for his life at the very moment when his will to live is draining out of him, and no sooner does he think this thought than the battle begins. A gigantic white wave "came roaring down upon the boat. . . . The boat slid up the incline, leaped at the furious top, bounced over it, and swung down the long back of the wave." Then the next wave comes: "The tumbling boiling flood of white water caught the boat and whirled it almost perpendicular. Water swarmed in from all sides." The captain warns them that "the next one will do for us, sure"—and it does. "The third wave moved forward, huge, furious, implacable. It fairly swallowed the dingey, and almost simultaneously the men tumbled into the sea. A piece of life-belt had lain in the bottom of the boat, and as the correspondent went overboard he held this to his chest with his left hand."

What follows is a blow-by-blow account of his struggle in the icy water, his mind flailing between confusion and clarity as he pushes on through his mounting exhaustion. The oiler is swimming "strongly and rapidly." The cook, girdled in a life jacket, has followed the captain's instructions and is lying on his back with an oar in his hands, moving along "as if he were a canoe." The captain is clinging to the overturned boat with his one good hand and riding the waves inward. Meanwhile, the correspondent is dog-paddling slowly and "leisurely" in order to preserve his strength, conscious of little but the "noisy water" and the shifting currents below him as his thoughts become more and more dissociated, so detached that when he looks ahead to the shore, it "was spread like a picture before him. It was very near to him then, but he was impressed as one who in a gallery looks at a scene from Brittany or Holland." For the last time, he repeats the refrain that has been running through his head from the beginning, but it is muted now, simpler and more direct, with all the rhetorical flourishes stripped out as his weary body paddles on toward land.

He thought: "I am going to drown? Can it be possible? Can it be possible? Can it be possible?" Perhaps an individual must consider his own death to be the final phenomenon of nature.

The captain, sensing that the correspondent is in trouble, calls out to him to come to the boat, but that will not be easy, for the magnitude of the effort required is mostly beyond him now.

In his struggle to reach the captain and the boat, he reflected that when one gets properly wearied, drowning must really be a comfortable arrangement, a cessation of hostilities accompanied by a large degree of relief, and he was glad of it, for the main thing in his mind for some moments had been horror of the temporary agony. He did not wish to be hurt.

He seems to be giving up, resigning himself to death in the waves even as he is within shouting distance of the land, but then he gets lucky, so lucky that what rescues him is one of the killer waves that have been threatening to drown him, a wave so large and so powerful that it vaults him clear over the boat and deposits him in water that is only waist-deep. He stands up, but the correspondent is too exhausted to stand, and a moment later he falls down. The waves lash into him again, again the undertow pulls at him, and once again he gets lucky. A man on the shore "who had been running and undressing, undressing and running, [came] bounding into the water. . . . He was naked, naked as a tree in winter, but a halo was about his head, and he shone like a saint. He gave a strong pull, and a long drag, and a bully heave at the correspondent's hand. The correspondent, schooled in the minor formulae, said: 'Thanks, old man.'"

The oiler, of course, does not have the luck to be rescued by a wave or anything else, and the naked saint is powerless to help him. As the three survivors are given a "warm and generous" welcome by the people gathering around them, "a still and dripping shape was carried slowly up the beach, and the land's welcome for it could only be the different and sinister hospitality of the grave."

The story ends with a twelve-hour leap from morning into darkness.

> When it came night, the white waves paced to and fro in the moonlight, and the wind brought the sound of the great sea's voice to the men on shore, and they felt that they could then be interpreters.

Interpreters of the elements. Interpreters of the dividing line between coherence and a blur. Latter-day oracles reading the entrails of the world.

Earth, air, fire, and water. A poet of extreme situations, Crane was also a dedicated student of the four classical elements, and the primal, even primitive force of his best work springs from his attunement to the natural order (and chaos) of *how things are*. He does not invent, he observes, and in passage after passage of his stories, novels, and sketches we see the elements as few other writers have been able to present them. Think *earth*, for example, and suddenly you will see the landscapes described in *The Red Badge of Courage*, the southwest Texas desert described in "A Man and

Some Others," the fields of withered corn in "Nebraska's Bitter Fight for Life." Think *air*, and all at once you are seeing his manifold depictions of light, clouds, wind, snow, and rain, the blizzards in "The Blue Hotel" and "The Men in the Storm," the slant of the sun on the gleaming rifles in "An Episode of War," and the precision of this nuanced effect of light momentarily seen by the correspondent as he rows through the darkness in "The Open Boat": "Southward, some one had evidently built a watch-fire on the beach. It was too low and too far to be seen, but it made a shimmering, roseate reflection upon the bluff [in] back of it, and this could be discerned from the boat." Think *fire*, and there you are looking at the tenement fire in the New York sketch he wrote for Edward Marshall in 1894, the fire of exploding chemicals that burns off a man's face in *The Monster*, and the fire he saw in a dream toward the end of his life and transformed into "Manacled," a story about a fire that breaks out in a theater with a man trapped on the stage inside. Extreme situations. Human situations embedded in the surround of a specific natural environment, and because Crane had been blessed with an uncommon gift for observation—along with an equally uncommon gift for transcribing his observations into words—he gives tangibility to what otherwise would be mere abstractions, a ground for the reader to stand on and enter those extreme situations as lived experiences.

But we are talking about "The Open Boat" now, and the element under discussion is water, the water Crane nearly drowned in as a little boy when he waded out too far in the Raritan River, the ocean off the sands of Asbury Park that he studied obsessively throughout his teens and early twenties, the shipwrecks recounted in "Ghosts of the Jersey Coast" (1894), the specter-woman who prowled the beach at night long after she was dead, mourning her lover who had drowned in a shipwreck in 1815 ("The Ghostly Sphinx of Metedeconk," 1895), and the enormous, abandoned log raft (ten thousand tons and six hundred feet long) drifting aimlessly across oceans in the tall tale from 1896, "Six Years Afloat," and then, after the sinking of the *Commodore*, the enduring pain of Billy Higgins's death and the image of the seven drowned men that went on tormenting him for the rest of his life, and even as he was dying at the Villa Eberhardt in the Black Forest, Cora wrote that "he lives over everything in dreams & talks aloud constantly. It is too awful to hear him try to change places in the *'open boat'*!"

It was the most important experience of his life, and not only did it change him, it changed his work as well. The story he wrote about it marks a turning point in his progress as a writer, and when he wasn't scrambling to dig his way out of debt or covering wars as a battlefield correspondent, Crane continued to travel down the new road that had opened before him. God knows how far he would have gone if he had managed to live.

5

As promised, he returned to Jacksonville and started looking for another boat to take him to Cuba. More than anything else at this point, he seems to have wanted war, a real war, not just some imagined facsimile of it, and if he couldn't find it in Cuba, he would go looking for it elsewhere. For now, that compulsion had become even more important to him than his work as a writer—which is another one of the things that sets Crane apart from most other writers, both then and now.

He was in a curious spot. Over the past several months, one battering had followed another, a succession of blows that had spun him around so often it was a wonder he wasn't lying out cold on the mat. The Dora Clark Affair and his expulsion from New York; the ditching of Amy Leslie and the complicated romance now brewing with Cora Taylor; shipwreck, the open boat, and his near death in the Atlantic surf. After such a persistent, rapid-fire pounding, most people would want to withdraw for a while and contemplate their next step. Crane did just the opposite. It is true that he needed money, and therefore was in need of work, but there were a dozen other ways he could have earned money besides going off to war.

He was restless, he had always been restless, and whenever he tried to settle down somewhere, he would again fall victim to what Baudelaire termed *la grande maladie de l'horreur du domicile*, which can be loosely translated as "the great illness caused by a horror of home." Few men and even fewer women are afflicted by this disease, but those who carry the bug feel an innate revulsion against the stifling comforts and complacencies of domestic life and want nothing more than to blow down the walls and be gone. The horror can produce many different kinds of rebellion—from the basest criminality to the most exalted idealism—but in all cases it gives birth to an adventurer, a young person who abandons the safety of the warm fire and the assurance of three meals a day and instead chooses to court risk, danger, and the uncertain outcome. Crane gambled at cards because he loved not knowing whether he would win or lose. Nor did he care a jot for comfort. The hard ground suited him just as well as a bed, and when the wind rose and the rain fell and the chill crept into his bones, that only made it more interesting. He had been that way ever since he was a boy, and now that he had passed the threshold into early manhood, he knew that he was going to die young. All the more reason not to play it safe—along with the added burden of having to cram in as much as he could in the shortest time possible. After the public bashing in the New York press, Garland had urged him to retreat to the country and begin work on a long novel. A tempting thought, perhaps, but how could Crane sit still when he was burning to be gone? So off he went to Florida and nearly drowned, and from that gruesome adventure he wrote what was probably his best story. Was it worth it? Again, there is no point in asking the question, not only because it has no answer but because it has no meaning. Now the page had been turned, and the boy had chosen to begin the next chapter with war. We can examine his motives long past our bedtime and on into tomorrow morning, but whatever complex reasons we might unearth during our discussion, it will all come down to this in the end: because he wanted to.

From *Roads of Adventure* (1922) by Ralph D. Paine:

> Two men were dining in another curtained alcove adjoining, and the voice of one sounded vaguely familiar. It was not identified, however, until he began to read aloud to his companion something which was evidently in manuscript. He stopped reading to say:
>
> "Listen, Ed, I want to have this *right*, from your point of view. How does it sound so far?"
>
> "You've got it, Steve," said the other man. "That is just how it happened, and how we felt. Read me some more of it."
>
> [After "Steve" has finished reading another section of the story:]
>
> A silence in the alcove and Captain Edward Murphy commented:
>
> "The *Commodore* was a rotten old basket of junk, Steve, but I guess I did feel something like that when she went under. How do you wind it up, when poor old Billie was floating face down and all those people came running down to pull us out of the breakers?"
>
> [After "Steve" has read the conclusion of the story:]
>
> "Do you like it or not, Ed?" asked Stephen Crane.
>
> "It's good, Steve. Poor old Billie! Too bad he had to drown. He was a damn fine oiler."
>
> When there came a lull in their talk, Paine and McCready pushed the curtain aside and made a party of it. Here were four of us, all in the same boat, as one might say, foregathered by a singular chance, and our combined experiences embraced all the vicissitudes of filibustering. . . .

Young Captain Murphy was a man without a ship, but he hoped to get another one and play the game again.

Stephen Crane had never been robust and there was not much flesh on his bones, at best. Sallow and haggard, he looked too fragile to have endured his battle for survival with the furious sea, but his zest for adventure was unshaken. His thin face, mobile and very expressive, brightened when he talked of attempting another voyage. His indifference to danger was that of a fatalist.

That encounter took place in a Jacksonville café sometime after Crane's return on February tenth, and for the next several weeks he searched for another boat to smuggle him into Cuba. The sinking of the *Commodore* had tightened the U.S. blockade, however, and filibuster traffic had all but stopped. For a time, there seemed to be a chance that Crane and Charles Michelson might be able to use Hearst's yacht, the *Buccaneer*, to make the crossing, but that plan fizzled. Looking for another solution, he and Michelson (along with Captain Murphy) headed farther south to the swamplands outside Daytona, but nothing came of that long shot either. Strapped for funds, Crane sent an urgent telegram to Hitchcock on February twenty-fourth—"Wire here Heinemans payment little regiment or maggies very important"—and that same day Reynolds submitted "The Open Boat" to *Scribner's Magazine*, which promptly accepted it with an offer of three hundred dollars. (Reynolds had been hoping for more, but *Scribner's* refused to go any higher, and he accepted the terms on March ninth.) Other than two small items, no traces of anything Crane might have written during his month in Florida have come down to us. The first is an inscription in a copy of *Maggie* that he gave to the madam of a Jacksonville brothel, Lyda de Camp—"To Lyda / From her friend / Stephen Crane"—and the second is a brief letter he wrote to his brother William on March eleventh announcing a change in his plans:

My dear Will: I suppose you have again felt assured that I was the worst correspondent in the world but really I have been for over a month among the swamps further south wading miserably to and fro in an attempt to avoid our derned U.S. navy. And it cant be done. I am through trying. I have changed all my plans and am going to Crete. I expect to sail from NY one week from next Saturday. Expect me P.J. on Thursday. Give my love to all and assure them of my remembrances.

Needless to say, a month in the swamps was an exaggeration, as were most of the things Crane tended to write to his big brother Will, the substitute father he had been trying to impress ever since he was in knee pants. Not a month in the swamps, then, but a month in Florida, most of which he spent in Jacksonville, and mostly what he did in Jacksonville was see Cora. The romance seems to have caught fire then, and once they became a couple, it wasn't long before they were talking about marriage. With Cora still trapped in her dead marriage to the absent Stewart, however, it was no more than talk at that point. She wrote to her brother-in-law in India, Colonel Norman Robert Stewart, asking for his help in persuading her husband to grant her a divorce, but before she received an answer, the situation took another turn. Cuba was now out of the picture, and if Crane meant to find his war, he would have to cross the Atlantic and go to Europe, where a large-scale confrontation between the Greeks and the Turks was about to begin. Cora understood that there would be no stopping him, but nothing could stop Cora either, and within a day or two a plan had crystallized: they would travel to Greece together. More than that, he would fix her up with a job once they made it to Athens, and rather than sit around in hotels and cafés while he was off at the front reporting on battles, Cora would become Imogene Carter, America's first woman war correspondent. The transformation was so sudden and so radical that it defies understanding. A thirty-one-year-old twice-married woman, a professional mistress since the age of seventeen, a person so luxurious in her habits that she changed the color of the seat-cushion covers in her carriage according to what color dress she was wearing that day, now the owner of a thriving nightclub operation in Florida's choicest resort town, she was willing to give up everything and run away with a boy she had known for only two months. Nor did she even hesitate, hightailing it out of Jacksonville so fast that she left a mountain of unpaid bills behind her, which resulted in a warrant for nonpayment of debts and the seizure of the furniture from the Hotel de Dreme by the local sheriff. *La grande maladie de l'horreur du domicile.* It turned out that she suffered from the disease, too, and when it came to the spirit of daring and adventure, Cora was fully the equal of her mouse.

They took the train to New York, and in the five or six days they were there, Crane went about the business of preparing for the trip. If he encountered no trouble from the police, it was probably because he was dressed more smartly than usual and they failed to recognize him when he passed by. Or else he got lucky. Or else (more probable) they simply didn't know he was back in town.

He signed on with Hearst to cover the war for the *Journal* and then negotiated a separate contract with the McClure syndicate to furnish occasional longer articles about the war ("letters") for the Sunday editions of various America papers as well as the *Westminster Gazette* of London. The recent telegram to Hitchcock shows that Crane was receiving money from his English publisher, a sign that he had smartened up and was now negotiating better contracts for himself, but he still wasn't smart enough, for after making the newspaper agreement with the McClure syndicate, he then committed a colossal blunder, blindly falling into another one of McClure's traps, as if his past dealings with the man had taught him nothing. Because Crane was still wanting for cash, and because it was difficult for him to imagine the long-term consequences of short-term expedients, he made a second contract that granted McClure first option on serial publication of upcoming, as yet unwritten short stories as well as first option on his next book, which evolved into a collection entitled *The Open Boat and Other Tales of Adventure* (1898). For those rights, McClure gave him an immediate cash loan of six or seven hundred dollars. It was an absurd move on Crane's part—to accept the money as a loan rather than as an advance against future royalties—for now he would be in thrall to McClure, who could hold on to new stories as collateral against the loan and, if he decided not to publish them, effectively block the stories from being published anywhere else. This bungled transaction was probably the stupidest thing Crane ever did, and it put him in a spot no less dangerous than the one he had faced on New Year's Eve when he'd set foot on the doomed *Commodore*, that "rotten old basket of junk." Even more dangerous, as it turned out, since the loan from McClure pushed his finances permanently underwater, and from then on Crane lived as a drowning man, struggling for air until the day he died.

Not only did he owe McClure money, he was expected to start paying it back at once, and so even while he was still in New York, Crane began writing a story for him, which turned out to be the quite good but not exceptionally good "Flanagan and His Short Filibustering Adventure," which kept him so busy up to the time of his departure that he had to cancel his farewell visit to Port Jervis. Edmund scampered down from Hartwood and saw him off at the pier, but William couldn't make it, nor could any of the others.

Sometime that week, he also managed to go out to dinner with Linson, who had been abroad until recently working as an illustrator for *Scribner's Magazine* at the first modern Olympic Games in Athens, the very place where Crane would be going at the end of the week. The two friends had been out of touch for a year, and when Crane unexpectedly turned up at the old loft, he was given "a riotous welcome," Linson remembers, but this was "a new Stephen . . . a rather dandified Steve. His hair was precisely brushed, his lip covering was much more than a mere shading, a well-fitting suit showed a trim, well-cut figure. . . . Yes, another Stephen." The new clothes and the new look that had made him invisible to the police, perhaps, which no doubt was the result of Cora's influence on him, for when a man falls in love with a fashionable, well-dressed woman, he no longer wants go to around looking like a slob.

Once they settled in and started to talk, however, Linson discovered that it was "the same Steve, after all." Forty or fifty years after the fact, he quotes Crane as having said, "Willie Hearst is sending me for the war. What I'll do among those Dagoes I don't know. What are they like, CK? How did you chin their lingo?" Salty, slang-infected speech, and while it might not be exactly what Crane said that day, it seems to provide a fair sample of how he spoke to his friends.* More than anything else, Linson was impressed by Crane's enthusiasm for the job ahead. "The excitement of it all was upon him. It was to be actual war, and his only fear was that it might fizzle out before he could arrive."

They went to a restaurant at Fourth Avenue and Twenty-third Street, where they talked about old times and old friends, and eventually, "with a reserve characteristic of him when speaking of women," Crane got around to telling Linson about the woman he wanted to marry, but "touching so lightly on the story of their meeting in Jacksonville that no memory of it remains." Not wanting to shock his conservative friend, Crane withheld the woman's name and avoided mentioning her past, but even though he intended to marry her in England, he said, her presence on the steamer was bound to provoke gossip (because of his reputation) and "the weasels would draw blood anyhow." Unfazed, Linson encouraged him to hold fast and marry her as soon as he could.

They never saw each other again after that night. A good-bye dinner had been turned into a farewell dinner, but neither one of them was aware of it at the time. Seven pages later, Linson concludes his touching little book with a memory of that night:

---

* In a short, humorous article written some months later, Crane comments: "Good slang is subtle and elusive. If there is a quick equivalent for a phrase it is not good slang, because good slang comes to fill a vacancy."

As I last saw him, he was still a boy of twenty-five, full of the adventure ahead. I see a pair of serene blue eyes and a quiet smile, always as in a picture that mellows with the passing of the years. The sound of his voice comes to me, and the quick turn of his body, but it is the smile that lingers.

The Cunard liner *Etruria* left New York on Saturday, March twentieth, with Crane in one cabin and Cora in another. The bold adventurer was also a nervous prig when it came to social matters, and he kept up appearances by keeping his love life a secret from the other passengers. In all probability, he spent the better part of the weeklong crossing to Liverpool playing poker in the lounge, and in all probability Cora went along with the ruse, which continued after they reached London on Monday, March twenty-ninth, where she was both with him and not with him as Crane ventured out into public alone.

The visit lasted just three days, but he was given a warm welcome as "the one young writer of genius America possesses" (London *Daily Chronicle*), and after he left town on April first Arthur Waugh summed up the impression he had made in a neat little paragraph for the *Critic* (April 17):

> Mr. Stephen Crane has flitted through London this week on his way to the scene of insurrections in Crete, but his visit was of the briefest. Indeed, it was characterized by extreme and refreshing modesty, being conspicuously free of the tendency to self-advertisement which is so often characteristic of the Novelist's Progress. . . . Within a few hours of his arrival, he naturally made his first calling-place the house of his publisher, Mr. Heinemann, who has worked so hard to push his books in this country. He seems much pleased with the reception of his work in England, and jokingly remarked that he was off to Crete because having written so much about war, he thought it high time he should see a little fighting. Which proves him a man of humor—an excellent thing in letters.

Besides meeting his British publisher in London, Crane also met his American rival, double, and antithesis, the novelist and war correspondent Richard Harding Davis (1864–1916), an immense figure back then who continued to be a cultural reference more than a generation after his death. In Sinclair Lewis's novel *Dodsworth* (1929), his name is evoked as an example of boldness and manly virtue: "When I graduated, I thought I'd be a civil engineer and see the Brazil jungle and China and all over. Regular Richard Harding Davis stuff!" In Alfred Hitchcock's film *For-*

eign Correspondent (1940), the following conversation takes place after a newspaper editor (Harry Davenport) hires crime reporter Johnny Jones (Joel McCrea) as his new foreign correspondent. A third man, Mr. Fisher (Herbert Marshall), is in the office with them.

> *Davenport*: Jones . . . I don't like that name. It's going to handicap you, young man. Wait a minute. I've got some sort of name here. Yes, Haverstock. Huntley Haverstock. (*To Marshall*) It sounds a little more important, don't you think?
> *Marshall*: Oh yes, very dashing.
> *Davenport*: Sounds better than Richard Harding Davis.
> *Marshall*: Richard Harding Davis. Why can't you use that?
> *Davenport*: Oh, we can't do that. That's the name of one of our greatest war correspondents forty years ago.

The son of novelist Rebecca Harding Davis and journalist Lemuel Clark Davis of the *Philadelphia Public Ledger*, R.H.D. was the *beau ideal* of the age, so handsome that he served as the model for illustrator Charles Dana Gibson's "Gibson man," the escort of the famous "Gibson girl" of the shirt-waist advertisements. The combination of Davis the man and Davis the image is credited with having established the clean-shaven look among American men that became dominant in the twentieth century and has largely endured into the twenty-first. But R.H.D. had talent as well, not only as an intrepid, risk-taking reporter but as a successful writer of plays and light, entertaining fiction. At the end of his review of *Maggie* in *Arena*, Garland contrasted the socialite world depicted in Davis's *Van Bibber and Others* (1892)—a popular hit—to the slum world of Crane's book. "'Maggie' should be put beside 'Van Bibber' to see the extremes of New York as stated by two young men. Mr. Crane need not fear comparisons as far as *technique* goes, and Mr. Davis will need to step forward right briskly or he may be overtaken by a man who impresses the reader with a sense of almost unlimited resource." From the very start, Crane and Davis had been put in a sort of competition, and with the older Davis already established as a top-rank reporter and world traveler, Crane was perceived as the dark-horse outsider in the race. He didn't like it, nor did he like the thought of Davis or what he seemed to represent, and the normally live-and-let-live S.C. rankled at the mere mention of R.H.D.'s name. In a letter to Nellie Crouse, he took a swipe at Davis by calling him a "stuffed parrot" with "the intelligence of the average saw-log," and even after they had met and served as correspondents together in Greece, he dismissed him as a "fool" in a letter to his brother

William (10/29/97). Davis's opinion of Crane was more nuanced. He was an admirer of *Red Badge*, which he considered to be "the last word, as far as battles and fighting is concerned," and when he discovered that he and Crane both happened to be in London on their way to Greece, he hosted a formal luncheon for him at the Savoy hotel. Among the invited guests were J. M. Barrie (seven years before *Peter Pan*), Anthony Hope (author of *The Prisoner of Zenda*), and Harold Frederic, the American novelist and London correspondent for the *New York Times* who had written the glowing article about *Red Badge* and would become one of Crane's closest friends during the years he lived in England. After the luncheon, Davis wrote to his mother that he had found Crane to be "very modest sturdy and shy. Quite unlike I had imagined." But that didn't prevent him from making some snide comments about Cora when he saw her at the London train station the next day, dismissing Crane's companion as "a bi-roxide blonde who seemed to be attending to his luggage for him and whom I did not meet." A month or so later, while Davis was at work during the thick of the war, he wrote to his mother again: "I left Athens with John Bass [of the *Journal*] and Crane accompanied by a Lady Stuart [*sic*] who has run away from her husband to follow Crane. She is a commonplace dull woman old enough to have been his mother and with dyed yellow hair. He seems a genius with no responsibilities of any sort to anyone." Needless to say, Cora's hair was not dyed, she was not old enough to be Crane's mother, and she was neither commonplace nor dull. As Gilkes comments in her biography of Cora: "While Stephen considered Davis an egotistical fool, the dandified idol of college youth deemed the author of *Maggie* and the Bowery tales a gifted but unwashed lunatic, a boor with suicidal proclivities and unfortunate leanings toward low associations. Each however recognized in the other a core of professional integrity." A trifle exaggerated, perhaps, but this was only the beginning of the story between Crane and Davis, and when they met up again in Cuba the following year, things took a far more interesting turn . . .

From London to Dover, from Dover to Paris, from Paris to Marseille, and then five days in the Mediterranean aboard the *Guadiana* until Crane and Cora arrived at Piraeus, the port of Athens.

6

IN THE BIG PICTURE, THERE WAS THE EVER-PRESENT FEAR THAT WAR would break out among the major European countries. The fear was grounded in historical fact (the Hundred Years' War, the Thirty Years' War, the Napoleonic Wars), and a loose alliance of those countries—England, France, Germany, Italy, Russia, and Austria-Hungary, alternatively known as the Great Powers or the Concert of Europe—kept a close watch on the continent in order to ward off potential conflicts before they got out of hand. The troubled peace held for decades, but just seventeen years after Crane found his first little war, Archduke Ferdinand was assassinated by a Serbian nationalist and the universal bloodbath of the Great War began.

In the smaller picture, the picture that Crane and Cora entered in early April, there was the presence of the Ottoman Empire in Greece, a large force that had gradually overwhelmed a smaller force and claimed parts of its neighbor's territory as its own. The point of greatest tension was on the island of Crete, where the Greek Christian community (eighty percent of the population) was ruled by its Muslim conquerors. Earlier rebellions had been suppressed, but after the latest one had started in 1896, Greece began taking an active role in arming the rebels, and in February 1897 it sent in forces to invade the island, declaring that Crete was henceforth to be united with Greece. Afraid that this would spark greater disturbances throughout the Balkans, the Powers sent in a massive fleet of warships to blockade the island and prevent it from receiving further assistance.

Turkey officially declared war on April seventeenth, and while the Greeks were supported by most of the foreign press and countless young men from European countries followed Lord Byron's example by volunteering to take part in the heroic cause (a two-thousand-man brigade of Italian "Redshirts" was led by one of Garibaldi's sons), the plain fact was that the Greeks were outnumbered, outmaneuvered, and ill-equipped to hold their own against the Ottoman forces, who were mostly under the command of experienced German generals. One hundred and twenty thousand men with modern weapons against seventy-five thousand men with old-fashioned, single-shot rifles, and yet the Greeks fought hard and well, routing the Turks in several battles, and if not for the waffling of the Danish-born Greek king George I, who had been put on his throne in 1863 by the same Powers who were now blockading Crete, the double-minded king who appointed his son, Crown Prince Constantine, as commander of the Greek forces, a young man who knew nothing about military tactics or strategy and consistently ordered his army to retreat when it was on the verge of winning crucial victories, the war surely would have lasted longer than it did. As it turned out, the whole thing ended after one month. For the Greeks, the humiliation of that Thirty Days' War lived on in memory as Black '97—or, even more bluntly, as the Unfortunate War.

Nevertheless, those weeks amounted to a small lifetime for Crane, an immersion course in the science and savagery of his personal obsession. Taking on the job of war correspondent had merely been an excuse to get close to war and see it with his own eyes, to discover if he had imagined it correctly in his work (he had, but it was only after witnessing his first major battle that he knew that he had), and once he put those lingering doubts behind him, he moved on to the more important task of assimilating what he had learned and progressing to a deeper understanding of the catastrophic human consequences of war—not in the disembodied ether of words but as flesh-and-blood actuality. At first, however, the excitement was too much for him, and the prospect of what he was about to see blinded him to what he had already learned for himself, the hard facts he had already confronted in his own imagination, and he arrived in Greece with an empty head and a pounding heart, as if he were three years old again and sitting on the floor with his army of buttons.

He began by writing a letter to his brother from Athens on April tenth, an absurdly childish letter that dwarfs all his other attempts to impress Judge Will, the exemplar of bourgeois rectitude and defender of the family's name. "I expect to get a position on the staff of the Crown Prince," he writes. "Won't that be great? I am so happy over it I can hardly breathe. I shall try—I shall try like the blazes to get a decoration out of the thing. . . . The reputation of my poor old books had reached a few of the blooming Greeks and that is what has done the Crown Prince business for me. . . . They say I've got a sure thing."

Who is *they*, and what kind of nonsense had they been feeding him? Crane had no military experience, he spoke not a word of Greek, and even if the crown prince had hired him, it would have been against the law for him to serve in a foreign army. This is Crane regressing into pure fantasy, both ignorant and contemptuous of the country he is in, and so naïve about the reality of war that he sounds even more stupid than Henry Fleming in the early days after his enlistment in the Union army. A medal. That is all Crane seems to want—a medal to prove to his big brother that the disgraced bohemian outcast was at heart a military hero. After all that Crane had written about war in the past, it is shocking to hear him spout such inane drivel—almost incomprehensible.

Three weeks later, in a dispatch entitled "Greek War Correspondents," he alludes to himself as "the wild ass of the desert who wanted a decoration." It was a long distance to travel in such a short time, but his education was well underway by then, and not only had he returned to his senses, he was no longer the person he had been when he arrived.*

For the first two weeks after war was declared, Crane tended to be in the wrong place at the wrong time and continued to miss out on the heavy fighting. Rapid excursions to Epirus and Thessaly with Cora had revealed only the last stages of dwindling minor skirmishes, and a couple of short articles he composed in Athens about the mood of the Greek people had misread the intensity of popular support for the war, which was less fervent than he supposed it to be. As Davis peevishly commented in a letter to his mother on April twenty-eighth: "He has not seen as

---

* Cora was duly engaged by the *Journal* as woman war correspondent Imogene Carter, and she was at Crane's side nearly every moment throughout their stay in Greece. She wrote just three short dispatches, however, and the best and longest of them, "War Seen Through a Woman's Eyes" (April 26), clearly shows the mark of heavy rewriting by Crane. Even better than that one, though, is the rough draft of an unfinished article written entirely in her own hand, which tells of her adventures during the one night she and Crane spent apart, when she slept on a billiard table in an empty coffeehouse. "My maid who grumbled constantly at everything and who had cried over our dinner of black bread (which was very good and sweet) and cheese, now flatly rebelled—and I paid her and sent her to the diligence by which she returned to Lamia—and so I was alone, the only woman in Pharsala or within many miles of it." Such was Cora's brave, independent spirit, and if she didn't pan out as a journalist, the diary she kept during the war is an invaluable source for tracking their day-to-day movements and activities together. In another dispatch she wrote: "I spent most of the time with the Second Battery of mountain howitzers. . . . Shells screamed at me as I went toward the station, and I had one narrow squeak. . . . The soldiers were amazed at the presence of a woman during the fighting." Neither a burden nor someone just tagging along for the ride, she was a full and equal participant in the hardships and dangers of covering the Greco-Turkish War. And how telling it is that she found the black bread *very good and sweet*.

On May nineteenth, the day before the war ended, Crane's friend and fellow correspondent Sylvester Scovel had this to say about Cora in a letter to his wife, Frances:

"Stephen Crane is here with Mrs. Stewart. I was afraid that she would ruin him, but really her influence has, so far, been the reverse. He has done such good work since that his publishers and others are increasing their offers for future work.

"She went to the front with him; was under artillery fire at Velestino, and was the last non-combatant to leave the place after the battle.

"But poor woman, how will it end. She urges him along, but even if he wished to, he cant marry her, as her husband Sir Donald Stewart, son of the British Commander in Chief of India will not divorce her.

"Stephen was very glad to see me and, I to see him. He is true steel. They took my boat off my hands, and went to the front day before yesterday.

"I don't know when I shall see them again. If you were here it would be embarrassing if they were here too. Lady Stewart is received by some of the most prominent people and even the Queen may receive her. How's that for the Greeks who are said to be the only moral people in this part of Europe?"

much as I have for several reasons but then when a man can describe battles as well as he can without seeing them why should he care."

All that changed on April thirtieth, when Crane and Cora, accompanied by *Journal* chief Bass and friend-foe Davis—who was reporting for the *Times* of London—left Athens by steamer at nine in the morning and headed for Thessaly, where a new round of fighting had broken out. By noon the next day, they had stopped at Chalkis, where they transferred to another steamer, which deposited them on the dock at Stylis at six P.M. From there they rode by carriage to Lamia, which took another six hours, but even though they arrived at midnight, they somehow found a place to sleep. Cora's diary cryptically notes: "Bunked on Floor wierd [*sic*] Hotel—Café—Soldiers." At seven the next morning, they left by carriage for Domokos, which entailed ten more hours of travel on roads filled with mobs of Greek civilians running away from the advancing Turkish army—the first such mobs Crane had encountered, which provided him with another crucial lesson in his education about the consequences of war. After a stopover of two hours, the party drove to Pharsala, where Cora spent the night on her own—as recounted in her unfinished article—sleeping on the billiard table in the shuttered café under the protection of the sympathetic owner, who stood at the door with a rifle to prevent any soldiers from breaking in. Armed with a letter from the United States minister to Greece, she was hoping to be granted an interview with the crown prince at army headquarters the next day. Meanwhile, the others were stopped by sentries on the outskirts of town and decided to split up. Bass and Davis headed for Velestino; Crane and some other correspondents went to nearby Volo. The next morning, May third, Cora sat and waited at army headquarters, only to learn that the crown prince was about to make another one of his sudden retreats, so she left Pharsala and joined Crane in Volo, which he would later describe as "a beautiful town, a summer resort in time of peace for wealthy Greeks," but this was a time of war, and the harbor below the seaside village was crammed with English, Italian, and French battleships from the Concert fleet. The action was five miles off in Velestino, where three attacks by the Turkish army on three different days had failed to budge the Greek forces under the command of Colonel Constantine Smolenski, and the next day, May fourth, the Turks launched a full-scale, all-out offensive. This was the big battle Crane had wanted to see, the biggest, most decisive battle of the war, but as luck would have it, he was in no shape to go. He had come down with a case of dysentery, the secret curse and consequence of all wars, and was trapped in his room for the entire day. Cora's diary says: "mouse ill—8 P.M."

Bad luck, but there was good luck as well, and after the Greeks held off the superior Turkish forces once again, the two sides prepared to throw themselves into another round of fighting the next day. When Crane woke on the morning of the fifth, he was well enough to climb out of bed, well enough to stand, well enough to totter off to the killing ground in Velestino. He arrived at noon, and when other correspondents asked where he had been the day before, he told them he had been suffering from a toothache. After that, in the words of John Bass, he walked up "the steep hill to where the Greek mountain battery, enveloped in smoke, was dropping shells among the black lines of Turkish infantry in the plain below." Then Crane sat down on an ammunition box, lit a cigarette, and settled in to watch his first real battle.

He couldn't help himself. He knew he had come to a place of bloodshed and slaughter, but at the same time this was the long-anticipated moment of truth for him, and in the first moments of his first actual combat, the thrill of what he was seeing overwhelmed all the rest.

> The roll of musketry was tremendous. From a distance it was like tearing a cloth; nearer, it sounded like rain on a tin roof and close up it was just a long crash after crash. It was a beautiful sound—beautiful as I had ever dreamed. It was more impressive than the roar of Niagara and finer than thunder or avalanche—because it had the wonder of human tragedy in it. It was the most beautiful sound of my experience, barring no symphony. The crash of it was ideal.
>
> That is one point of view. Another might be taken from the men who died there.

A beautiful sound, he says, the most beautiful sound in the world, but what he is really talking about is an emotional sound, a sound so stirring and so thunderous that it reverberates through his entire body and nearly deafens him, a roar from the heavens that comes crashing down with a message of ultimate things, and if it is beautiful to him, it is only because it has "the wonder of human tragedy in it." War, then, as the purest expression of the dark inner workings of human life, the most extreme example of what is true about all human life at all times: that life is lived face-to-face and nose to nose with death—which is the bedrock stance underpinning all of Crane's best work.

The thrill passes, however. After the exultant, liberating crash of the guns of war, Crane comes back to earth and looks at the dead, nods to the dead as if apologizing for his effusive response to the guns that have killed them, and for the remainder of his first battle piece as a war correspondent, the four-and-a-half-page "Stephen Crane at Velestino," he confines himself to a meticulous account of the action, impressed by how well the Greek troops push back against the squadrons of charging Turks, proving themselves to be "good fighters, long fighters, stayers," but the battle ends with another one of the crown prince's inexplicable retreats—an order so devastating to the brilliant colonel commanding the army that Crane writes, in the most memorable sentence of the article: "They say Smolenski wept."

Bass was with him that day, and in an article he wrote for the *Journal*, "How Novelist Crane Acts on the Battlefield" (published May 23), he follows Crane up the hill, watches him plant himself on the ammunition box "amid a shower of shells," then light a cigarette and settle in to watch the war. Crane's conduct, as one would imagine from his previous conduct on the sinking *Commodore*, was calm throughout, and however excited he might have been at hearing the sound of the guns, none of it showed on his face or in the movements of his body.

> Stephen Crane did not appear surprised, but watched with a quiet expression the quick work of the artillerymen as they loaded, fired and jumped to replace the small cannon overturned by the recoil.
>
> I was curious to know what was passing through his mind, and said:
>
> "Crane, what impresses you most in this affair?"
>
> The author of The Red Badge of Courage lighted another cigarette, pushed back his long hair out of his eyes with his hat and answered quietly:
>
> "Between two great armies battling against each other the interesting thing is the mental attitude of the men. The Greeks I can see and understand, but the Turks seem unreal. They are shadows on the plain—vague figures in black, indications of a mysterious force."
>
> By this time the Greek army was in full retreat.
>
> As the last mountain gun was loaded on the mules Stephen Crane quietly walked down the hill. The Turkish artillery had drawn nearer, and amid the singing bullets and smashing shells the novelist had stopped, picked up a fat waddling puppy and immediately christened it Velestino, the Journal dog.*

---

* That Bass decided to write this article shows the enormous status Crane had achieved by then—a young man so famous that his own bureau chief thought it would interest the public to read about him watching Crane watch his first battle. But such was Crane's position in America that for every person who admired him, there was another who didn't, and the attacks that had begun with his first book of poems only doubled and tripled as time went

Under heavy shelling, Crane and Cora managed to catch the last train back to Volo, which was where he wrote his article, but because of the retreat at Velestino, Volo would soon be falling as well, and the dispatch concludes with an ominous certainty: "I send this from Volo and before you print it the Turks will be here." They were almost there already, and so Crane and Cora took off again, fleeing Volo on the day he sent in his article (May 10) and heading by ship to Chalkis. He reported on the experience in another dispatch he wrote the next day, a blistering piece that the *Journal* ran under the headline "The Blue Badge of Cowardice," which was his first account of the civilian victims of war.

"So the enemy withdrew," he writes, "and the Turks came on. The Greeks knew how disastrous this retreat must be. They knew Volo must be occupied by the enemy, and they guessed more might fall because of the incomprehensible order of the King's son." The beautiful town of Volo was being evacuated, and "every available ship in the harbor was employed to transport fugitives. . . . Fifteen hundred were on the *Hydra* alone. The condition of these people was pitiable in the extreme. Many of them were original refugees from Larissa and other northern points, who, flying before the march of the Turks, came to Volo as a place of certain harbor. Now they are obliged to flee even from there."

Both demoralized and indignant, the young man who had come to witness war and had rejoiced at the sound of artillery fire on the plain at Velestino now says:

> The scenes on the transports and merchant ships make one tired of war. Women and children are positively in heaps on the decks. They have no food, and they will be landed where they can.
>
> I asked one of the officers how they expected to feed the people. He answered that they did not expect to feed them—that they could not feed them.
>
> I went with a great crowd to Oreos. The town consists of six houses already crowded. The refugees came ashore carrying their household

---

on. Now that he was in Greece reporting on the war (and doing an excellent job of it), his detractors couldn't resist going after him again. First published in the *Lewiston Evening Journal* from Maine and then reprinted by the demolition experts at the *New York Tribune*, this "poem" is one example: "I have seen a battle. / I find it very like what / I wrote up before. / I congratulate myself that / I ever saw a battle. / I am pleased with the sound of war. / I think it is beautiful. / I thought it would be. / I am sure of my nose for battle. / I did not see any war correspondents while / I was watching the battle except / I." The unrelenting nastiness he was subjected to in his own country was one of the reasons (among several) why Crane moved to England after the war.

Studio photograph of Crane dressed as war correspondent, Athens,
spring 1897. (COURTESY OF THE UNIVERSITY OF VIRGINIA)

goods. They camped on the fields by great bonfires. These peasant women
are patient, suffering in curious silence, while the babies wail on all sides.

This is war—but it is another picture from that we got at the front.

The Greek naval officers, with their eyes full of tears, swore to me
the Turks would pay for all this misery. But the Turks probably will not;
nobody pays for these things in war.

Eight thousand people at least fled from Volo. Their plight makes a
man hate himself for being well fed and having a place to go.

The two correspondents wound up in Athens again, exhausted and in
need of rest, but they stayed for only a short time. Although the chronol-

Cora dressed as female war correspondent "Imogene Carter," Athens,
spring 1897. (COURTESY OF SYRACUSE UNIVERSITY)

ogy is not quite certain, it must have been during this momentary pause
that Crane sat down and wrote his fullest, deepest, most probing account
of the war, "A Fragment of Velestino," which revisits the battle and elaborates on many of the incidents and details that were hastily mentioned in

the initial report. As opposed to the article for Hearst, which covers just four and a half pages, this one extends over seventeen and can be read as a work of literature, a nonfiction version of *The Red Badge of Courage* that resembles the novel in tone and method but differs from it by telling a story that has no plot or human protagonist, for in this version the central character is the war itself, and rather than try to make sense of the war and shape it into a coherent narrative, Crane presents us with an assemblage of fractured pieces, a collage. Some examples:

Behind him was the noise of battle, the roar and rumble of an enormous factory. This was the product. This was the product, not so well finished as some, but sufficient to express the plan of the machine. This wounded soldier explained the distant roar. He defined it. This—this and worse—was what was going on. This explained the meaning of all that racket. Gazing at this soldier with his awful face, one felt a new respect for the din.

The huts of the peasants, made from stone-like cobbles, were not closed and barred, because they seemed never to have had doors, but the interiors were mere dark vacancies. It was a deserted village. One walked the streets wondering of the life that here had been, and if it would ever return—could it ever return. It is a human thing to think of a community that has been, and here was one with all its important loves, hates, friendships; all its games, spites, its wonderful complexity of relation and intercourse, suddenly smitten by the sledge of chance and rendered nothing—nothing but a few vacant houses. The chance-comer notes then that some villager had carefully repaired his front gate, and the chance-comer's sense of the futility of repairing that front gate causes him to know more of life for a moment than he had ever known before.

You can repeat to yourself, if you like, the various stated causes of the war, and mouth them over and try to apply them to the situation, but they will fail to answer your vague interrogation. The mind returns to the wonder of why so many people will put themselves to the most incredible labor and inconvenience and danger for the sake of this—this ending of a few lives like yours, or a little better or a little worse.

A soldier in the trenches suddenly screamed and clasped his hands to his eyes as if he had been struck blind. He rolled to the bottom of the trench, his body turning twice. A comrade, dazed, whistling through his teeth, reached in his pocket and drew out a hunk of bread and a hand-kerchief. It appeared that he was going to feed this corpse. But he took the handkerchief and pressed it on the wound and then looked about him helplessly. He still held the bread in his other hand, because he could not lay it down in the dirt of the trench.

To the rear lay a dead horse, and a number of blood-red poppies, mirac-ulously preserved from the countless feet, bloomed near it. Continually there was in the air a noise as if someone had thrown an empty beer-bottle with marvellous speed at you.

The volleys were rattling and crackling from one end of the hill to the other. Sometimes the pattering of individual firing swelled suddenly to one long beautiful crash that had something in it of the fall of a giant pine amid his brethren of the mountain side. It was the thunder of a monstrous breaker against the hard rocks.

The captain of the battery . . . sent a man to the rear for another pair of field-glasses. His first pair had suffered a rifle-ball wound. The man mistook the order, and he came back with a bottle of wine.

The bullet that came there struck him [the lieutenant] in the throat—squarely in the throat. He fell like a flash—as if someone had knocked his heels from under him from behind. On the ground his arms made one long stiff and shivery gesture, and then he lay still. For a moment his men had a clear case of rattle, simply rattle. It was as when the cap-tain is washed off the bridge at sea during a storm. There are two things lost—the captain, and what the captain knows about managing ships in storms.

The Turks did not come like a flood, nor did the Greeks stand like ada-mant. It was simply a shifting, changing, bitter, furious struggle, where one could not place odds nor know where to run.

Twenty moments of uproar elapsed, and then there were no Turks in front save a great number of dead ones, and none of these lay close enough to see that the fez was red. There was no indication of posture, no expression, no human character—just some small dark blots on a green field. It was the same suggestion always—a battle with the unde-fined, with phantoms.*

Crane and Cora left Athens again on the seventeenth and headed for Domokos on the *World*'s dispatch boat, which had been lent to them by Scovel. Another major battle was anticipated there, but by the time they arrived the crown prince had withdrawn his troops and sent them to Ther-mopylae in another one of the commander's self-sabotaging retreats. The next day and the days that followed were among the worst they encountered during the war, and the events that occurred on the trip back to Athens are recorded in Crane's grimmest dispatch, which was cabled to New York from Athens on the twenty-second (forty-eight hours after the armistice was declared) and published in the *Journal* under the title "Stephen Crane Tells of War's Horrors." The piece was composed on board a transport ship, the *St. Marina*, which left Chalkis on May eighteenth, and although it cov-ers just three and a half pages, it is packed with incident. By now, whatever delusions Crane might have harbored about war when he arrived in Greece have been utterly destroyed.

We are carrying the wounded away from Domokos. There are eight hundred bullet-torn men aboard, some of them dead. This steamer was formerly used for transporting sheep, but it was taken by the Govern-ment for ambulance purposes. It is not a nice place for a well man, but war takes the finical quality out of its victims, and the soldiers do not complain. The ship is not large enough for its dreadful freight. But the men must be moved, and so 800 bleeding soldiers are jammed together

---

* "A Fragment of Velestino" was published as one of Crane's "letters" for the *Westminster Gazette*, but the first installment did not turn up in print until June third, well after the end of the war. The editors explained in a prefatory note: "Mr. Stephen Crane's letters have by some accident been considerably delayed in transmission, but we make no apology for pub-lishing them three weeks after the events to which they relate, since their literary interest, as impressions of the battlefield, are in no way diminished by the lapse of time." That literary judgment still stands more than a century later, but the communication problems the *Gazette* refers to were common during the war, and travel was likewise beset with myriad difficulties. As Crane remarked in his one lighthearted report from Greece ("The Dogs of War"—which chronicles the adventures of the small puppy he found on the battlefield): "Volo is, ordi-narily, 300,000 miles from Athens. In time of war, it is the square of 300,000. Every route is impossible. All the steamers are on war business. All the carriages have vanished. There are no horses. It requires more energy to travel now in Greece than it does to do a three months' campaign."

in an insufferably hot hole, the light in which is so faint that we cannot distinguish the living from the dead. . . .

Near the hatch where I can see them is a man shot through the mouth. The bullet passed through both cheeks. He is asleep with his head pillowed on the bosom of a dead comrade. He had been awake for days, doubtless, marching on bread and water, to be finally wounded at Domokos and taken aboard this steamer. He is too weary to mind either his wound or his awful pillow. There is a breeze on the gulf and the ship is rolling, heaving one wounded man against the other.

Along with its cargo of dead and wounded soldiers, the ship now begins taking on women and children who are fleeing their towns in advance of the Turkish assault. "This is Wednesday, I think," Crane writes. "We are at Stylidia." There the same panic he witnessed among the citizens of Volo is being played out again. He uses the *Journal*'s dispatch boat to help retrieve the supplies from the field hospital there, and

while the medicines were being put aboard I went ashore, where the last few women and children crowded the quay.

One long line of dust marked the road across the green plain where Smolenski marched away. And the people stared at this and then at the great mountains in back of the town, whence the Turks were coming. All the household goods of the city were piled on the pier. . . .

With our departure Stylidia became as silent as a city of the dead. Its next inhabitants will be Turkish soldiers. The steamer and the schooner carried 183 people to safety, where the warships rode at anchor opposite Thermopylae. The women and the children were drenched when we landed them in the small boats. . . . There were about thirty women with babies in their arms among the fugitives. The poor babies wailed and the mothers groaned. There were a lot of little girls, however, who sat quietly, not understanding what was the matter.

The refugees generally seemed dazed. The old women particularly. Uprooted from the spot they had lived so long, they kept their red eyes turned toward the shore as they sat on their rough bundles of clothes and blankets.

After the boat returns to the hospital one more time to evacuate the Red Cross nurses and the last of the wounded men, Crane closes off his dispatch by turning his attention to one particular soldier.

The last boat had left the shore when a soldier came and said something to the interpreter, who shook his head negatively. The soldier turned quietly away.

On board the steamer your correspondent idly asked the interpreter what the soldier had said, and he answered that the soldier had asked for transportation to Chalkis on the ground that he was sick. The interpreter thought the man too well to go on a boat containing wounded men.

We sent ashore and after some trouble found the soldier. He was ill with fever, was shot through the calf of the leg and his knees were raw from kneeling in the trenches. We added him to our list of wounded men and then steamed away for Chalkis.

There is more of this sort of thing in war than glory and heroic death, flags, banners, shouting and victory.

He has come to the limit of what he can bear, and writing in nearly invisible prose, he has been reduced to talking in whispers. There were several more articles to be written before he left Greece, and one by one he wrote them, but his education could go no further than this. A long, arduous haul that lasted close to two months, Crane's rush into war had bogged down in the mud of lived reality, and what he learned in the end was what he had already known before he ever got there. The only difference—but it was a large difference—was that now he had seen it with his own eyes.

During the brief lull in Athens earlier that month, he and Cora and Bass had gone to a photographer's studio together to sit for formal portraits dressed in the war correspondent's getup of the period, most likely borrowed for the occasion, and when they returned to Athens on the steamer from Chalkis, the finished prints were ready. No picture of Crane presents a more dashing, impressive image of him than this one. Perched on a pile of studio rocks with his legs crossed, he is wearing a broad-brimmed hat, a high-collared tunic with a strap across his chest that holds the leather pouch hanging at his side, and tall leather boots. His gaze is steady, even piercing, his mustache is more robust than in earlier photos, and with a cigarette wedged between his right thumb and forefinger, he comes across as a lean and hungry man of action. Cora is sitting on the same pile of rocks and wearing a female version of the same costume, with a smaller hat fixed on her head, a dark blouse with billowing sleeves, a broad woolen skirt, and two leather straps crisscrossing her chest, with a canteen and a purse attached to them. She is pudgy but trim, clearly at home in herself, and with her left hand poised on her left hip, she seems comfortable in her new role as woman war correspondent. On the twenty-second, she offered one of these prints to Crane with a jocular, chummy inscription: To me old pal Stevie / with best wishes—/ "Imogene Carter."

They left Athens sometime during the last week of May and headed for Paris. Along with Velestino the *Journal* dog, they were accompanied by a pair of Greek twins named Ptolemy, whom they had hired as servants. They lingered in Paris for close to two weeks, during which the puppy chewed up the hotel room curtains and carpet one evening when he was left alone (it cost them a small fortune to cover the damages), and then, instead of returning to the United States, they crossed the Channel and moved to England as Mr. and Mrs. Stephen Crane.

7

THERE WERE COMPELLING REASONS NOT TO GO BACK TO AMERICA. IN the first place, where and how and under what conditions could they have lived there? New York was out of the question, and now that the ex-proprietor of the Hotel de Dreme had run away from her debts in Jacksonville, Florida had become forbidden territory as well. When Colonel Stewart wrote to Cora and announced that in spite of his best efforts his brother was still unwilling to divorce her, she and Crane were blocked from marrying each other, so even if they had wanted to live a quiet life in Port Jervis (which they didn't), that no longer would have been possible. As an unmarried couple bunking together under the same roof in a small provincial town, they would have brought scandal and humiliation to the Crane family, and the errant little brother had already inflicted enough unpleasantness on them with his recent troubles in New York. England, on the other hand, was less rigid in its attitudes toward marriage, and the people there tended not to stick their noses into other people's private business. Their new friend and supporter Harold Frederic had left America for England thirteen years earlier, and not only was he married and the father of four children, he maintained a second household with another woman and was the father of three more children with her. Compared to Frederic's arrangement, the plan to present themselves in public as man and wife seemed relatively simple.

Nevertheless, there were complications. Cora was married to an Englishman, she had lived in London at her father-in-law's town house from 1889 to 1892, and as her brother-in-law advised her in his letter about Stewart's rejection of divorce, if she married Crane or attempted to pass herself off as Mrs. Crane, "you ought to be very careful of your secret for a very large circle of your friends must only know you as Mrs. Stewart." They would have to be careful, then, but the fact was that Cora would no longer be traveling among her old friends. She would be making new friends with the man she would now be calling her husband, and hard as it was for that husband to turn his back on America, there were extenuating circumstances, and now that he had become "the most thoroughly abused writing man between the Atlantic and the Pacific," perhaps living in England would bring some measure of relief to him. Crossing the Channel and settling into a house in Oxted, Surrey, was not a temporary solution but a radical overhaul of how they lived and how they meant to go on living from now on. The Cranes had opted for exile.

Harold Frederic opened the door for them and took charge of their transition to English life. As a transplanted American himself, he had already experienced what they were going through now, and not only did he guide them to the place where he thought they should live, he found them a house as well—which happened to be eight miles down the road from the house he shared with his companion, the American-born Kate Lyon, and their three illegitimate children. A large man with a blustery, outspoken, good-hearted manner, Frederic was fifteen years older than Crane, and after the long article he had written about *Red Badge* for the *New York Times* (in which he had called the novel "extraordinary," "one of the deathless books"), the younger man was already predisposed to regard him as a friend. After their first meeting in London, the friendship tightened, no doubt because they discovered that they shared similar backgrounds and had followed parallel roads to arrive at the place where they found themselves now. A child of the Mohawk Valley, Frederic had been raised by strict Methodist parents in Utica, New York. He had been a journalist since his late teens, had edited newspapers in both Utica and Albany, and since coming to England to work for the *Times*, he had published five novels. The most recent one, *The Damnation of Theron Ware*, was a dark, realistic account of the undoing and fall of a Methodist minister and had been number five on the American bestseller list for 1896 (three notches above *Red Badge*). One man was louder, bigger, and older than the other, but both were novelists who also worked as journalists—and both were living with women in unconventional domestic situations—which was why Frederic steered the Cranes to Surrey, an outpost for renegades from the restrictive codes of Victorian England, just twenty-two miles south of London. Its inhabitants included members of the Fabian Society and a substantial brigade of writers, among them Ford Hueffer (later Ford Madox Ford), the critic Edward Garnett and his wife, the renowned translator Constance Garnett, and the Scottish-Canadian novelist Robert Barr, all of whom became friends of the Cranes'. Henry James lived a bit farther to the south at Lamb House in Rye, and Joseph Conrad was two counties over in Essex. They, too, became good friends, James with avuncular benevolence toward his young compatriot and Conrad as Crane's first and most intimate literary brother. America was a million miles away.

The couple moved into their rented house sometime around the middle of June. An unimaginative brick-and-tile suburban structure with the grandiose name of Ravensbrook Villa, it was situated in a damp hollow at the bottom of a hill, hardly a good place for a person with weak lungs, but it proved to be an excellent place to write, and in the ten months they lived there Crane caught fire again. In a burst similar to the conflagration of 1894, he produced a fifty-seven-page novella and stories of twelve, twenty-one, and thirty pages that are as good if not better than anything he had written so far—*The Monster*, "The Bride Comes to Yellow Sky," "Death and the Child," and "The Blue Hotel"—and even the money-work he did during those months yielded some of his best newspaper and magazine sketches: "London Impressions," "Irish Notes," and "The Scotch Express," which record his discovery of the landscapes of his new life on the rain-soaked islands of the North Atlantic. There would be no more sketches after that. Whatever journalism he did in his last three years was largely confined to battle reports from Cuba during the Spanish-American War, and while he still had many good stories left in him, none of them would ever attain the pinnacle he had touched at Ravensbrook. It was a remarkable period, then, and the most remarkable thing about it was that Crane wrote his masterpieces under conditions of ever-mounting duress.

Not long after they moved in, he sat down and made a list of all the stories he had written, both published and unpublished, noting the places where he had deposited them back in America along with the word count of each one. He was assessing his financial prospects, weighing whether he and Cora would have enough to make a go of it in England, and within days he sent off a letter to his brother Edmund, asking him to forward the manuscripts of two of his Mexico City stories, "The Wise Men" and "The Five White Mice," which he had left behind in his desk at Hartwood. He gave the offices of William Heinemann in London as his return address, and from then on for the full ten months he was in

Oxted, he continued to mask his whereabouts behind his publisher's place of business and never told either one of his brothers where he was actually living. Nor did he ever breathe a word to them about Cora.

By late June, he had started writing *The Monster*.

By then, whatever money Cora had taken with her from Jacksonville was probably gone, and after two weeks in Paris, one can assume that Crane had saved practically nothing from his war reporting. To cut down on expenses, they arranged for one of the Ptolemy brothers to work for their neighbor Edward R. Pease, the secretary of the Fabian Society, who lived with his family in the adjoining town of Limpsfield. Crane advertised Constantin Ptolemy as "a butler in shirt sleeves," and while Mrs. Pease judged his buttling skills lax, he was a tremendous hit with her young sons. The Cranes held on to the other twin, Adoni, to help with the household duties at Ravensbrook, but S.C. soon fell into the habit of dashing over to the house in Limpsfield to be shaved by Constantin, an expert barber who had performed that service for him in Greece. The otherwise amiable secretary of the Fabians looked down on these razor sessions as an aris- tocratic pretense. As a good socialist, he believed that right-thinking men should shave themselves.

The twenty-one-year-old kid who had slept on coal boxes and walked around with holes in his shoes as a struggling writer in New York now had a personal barber, a servant, a pet dog, a rented villa, and a wife who not only adored him but looked upon him as the most brilliant literary man in the English-speaking world. One wonders what he thought about all this and how hard or easy it was for him to adjust to his new circumstances— assuming he ever did. By every outward indication, he seemed to be happy where he was, but the *grande maladie* was an incurable ailment that could never be fully purged from his system, and even as he issued forth some of the best work of his life, he would lapse into daydreams about running off to cover wars in the Sudan, South Africa, and India or, like his friend Scovel, taking the long trek to gold rush country in the Klondike, which had become a Canadian madhouse swarming with tens of thousands of pros- pectors. He never went to any of those places, but even as he sat in England and continued writing his stories, they never stopped dancing in his head.

Things were going to be tight, but perhaps they could muddle through, after all, as long as Crane kept producing sellable work at rates high enough for them to live on. The house had come with no more than a few random bits of furniture, however, which meant they had to furnish the place themselves, and because there wasn't enough ready cash on hand, they bought what they needed on credit. As the empty rooms gradually became less empty, Crane wrote, Adoni did the heavy lifting, and Cora, as she put it in an October letter to Scovel, was "chief-house-maid, house-keeper, etc. but I like it and we are happy—very happy." She was also an excellent cook and baker, lauded by teatime visitors for her southern hot biscuits and American doughnuts (James was a fiend for the doughnuts), and with so many new friends in the area and others arriving from London and abroad, they entertained quite often, another thing Cora excelled at (Edmund Gosse called her "very vivid and agreeable"), but serving food to guests and filling their glasses with wine cost money, too, and in an effort to generate a small stream of steady income, Crane and Cora decided to resurrect Imogene Carter as a fashion-society-gossip writer with a Sunday column called "European Letters" for female readers of American newspapers. They managed to crank out ten of them, most of which were published in the *New York Press* (thanks to Curtis Brown), splitting the duties between them as Cora wrote about fashion and Crane about social matters, and even though Crane disparaged the Letters as "rotten bad" and said they took no more than twenty minutes to do (surely an exaggeration, since each one covers several pages), there are a few charming passages mixed in among the blather about the king of Siam's visit to England and Sarah Bernhardt's treatment of her hair. It wasn't enough to sustain their interest, however, and as with so many other get-poor-quick schemes over the centuries, it died a natural death.

The first of Crane's British reports was the eight-part "London Impressions," which was published in three installments by the British *Saturday Review*. Whimsical in tone, it perversely avoids fulfilling any of the promises offered by the title, and instead of giving the reader an American traveler's initial response to vast, majestic London, Crane reduces the scope of his observations to what he can see through the side window of his cab after he leaves the train station on a dark, foggy night. It is the same narrow focus he employed in "The Broken-Down Van" five years earlier, and once again, as in so many of his other works between that time and now, his primary interest is point of view, the subjectivity of human perception when confronted with the fragmented spectacle of the so-called objective world. Not Einstein or Niels Bohr, perhaps, but the Cranian Theory of Relativity.

> The cab finally rolled out of the gas-lit vault into a vast expanse of gloom. This changed to the shadowy lines of a street that was like a passage in a monstrous cave. The lamps winking here and there resembled

the little gleams at the caps of the miners. They were not very competent illuminations at best, merely being little pale flares of gas that at their most heroic periods could only display one fact concerning this tunnel—the fact of general direction. But at any rate I should have liked to have observed the dejection of a search-light if it had been called upon to attempt to bore through this atmosphere. In it each man sat in his own little cylinder of vision, so to speak. It was not so small as a sentry-box nor so large as a circus-tent, but the walls were opaque, and what was passing beyond the dimensions of the cylinder no man knew.

With so little to see, he begins to concentrate on sounds, noting that the wheels of the carriages are encased in rubber and produce a whirring noise reminiscent of bicycles and that because the horses' hoofs are padded, they do not make the "wild clatter" he was expecting to hear. In contrast to loud, deafening New York, where one would suppose "each citizen is obliged by statute to provide himself with a pair of cymbals and a drum" to create as much noise as possible,

this London moved with the decorum and caution of an undertaker. There was a silence and yet there was no silence. There was a low drone, perhaps, a humming contributed inevitably by closely gathered thousands and yet on second thoughts it was to me a silence. I had perched my ears for the note of London, the sound made by the existence of five million people in one place. I had imagined something deep, vastly deep, a bass from a mythical organ; but I found, as far as I was concerned, only a silence.

A silence, which is soon followed by a surprise. The cab-horse has been moving along at a "sharp trot," but when they come to the top of an incline and the rainy street glistens before them as if covered in ice, Crane suspects there is going to be

a tumble. In an accident of such kind a hansom becomes . . . a cannon in which a man finds that he has paid shillings for the privilege of serving as a projectile. I was making a rapid calculation of the arc that I would describe in my flight, when the horse met his crisis with a masterly device that I could not have imagined. He tranquilly braced his four feet like a bundle of stakes, and then, with a gentle gaiety of demeanor, he slid gracefully to the bottom of the hill as if he had been a toboggan.

When the incline ended he caught his gait again with great dexterity, and went pattering off through another tunnel.

At first, Crane thinks the cab-horse must have invented this move and is the only animal in London capable of performing it, but when the cab

arrived at a place where some dipping streets met, and the flaming front of a music-hall temporarily widened my cylinder, behold, there were many cabs, and as the moment of necessity came, the horses were all skaters. They were gliding in all directions. It might have been a rink. A great omnibus was hailed by a hand from under an umbrella on the sidewalk, and the dignified horses bidden to halt from their trot did not waste time in wild and unseemly spasms. They, too, braced their legs and slid gravely to the end of their momentum.

It was not the feat, but it was the word, which had at this time the power to conjure memories of skating parties on moonlit lakes, with laughter ringing over the ice, and a great red bonfire on the shore among the hemlocks.

The word "rink" summons up another place and another time to him, and even though Crane is writing about London (sort of), what he is really thinking about is America and his childhood in Port Jervis, which is another way of saying that he was thinking about the novella he was writing then, *The Monster*, which is set in an imaginary version of Port Jervis, a place that continued to live in him and was never far from his thoughts, even though it was a million miles away. New York City and Asbury Park would vanish for him as memory points in his fiction, but not the little town at the convergence of the Delaware and Neversink Rivers.

It was clear that he had no great interest in writing about London, but he forged on in a meandering, humorous sort of way through five more sections after that crisp opening, but having just returned from Greece, where he had seen men killed in battle and had shared space on a transport ship with dozens of dead and dying soldiers, it must have been a comfort to be in drowsy, peacetime England musing about his beloved horses as a ballet company on ice skates—at least for now, and at least for the few extra dollars it earned him.

Death came knocking again soon enough, and when he received word that Edmund's two-and-a-half-year-old son had died, the news was so paralyzing that he could scarcely bring himself to respond. "I have not written," he told his brother in a letter dated July twenty-second, "because this is a most difficult letter to write. I don't know what to say to you. I can't say the conventional thing and yet there are so few phrases which I could use to express to you how I feel about the death of brave bold little Bill. Good old Bill and the way he used to smoke my pipes!" For once, words had failed him. Surely he meant well and understood how deeply his brother and sister-in-law were suffering, but by saying so little and avoiding "the conventional thing," the letter comes across as feeble and inadequate—not callous, exactly, but remote. Perhaps Edmund understood his reticence and did not expect him to say anything more than that. Or else he forgave him—or else he was too distracted by the boy's death to notice what his brother had written.

Ten days later, when Velestino the *Journal* dog died of distemper, Crane showed far less reserve in his August first letter to Scovel (page 30), who had bought a collar for the puppy in Greece and could be counted on to sympathize with what his fellow correspondents had gone through to save the dog's life.

One sorrow that was too large for words; another sorrow that was immediately translated into words. There is no conclusion to be drawn from this, but the disparity is worth pondering. "My dear Harry: Old friends never write to each other. That is almost a law but tonight Cora and I want to speak to you because you are the only one who will understand. Velestino has just died—not two hours ago." After the letter ends, there is a postscript: "If any of those pictures taken of him on the boat are at hand send them to us."

Then, on the nineteenth of August, there was the accident.

It was Harold Frederic's birthday, and the Cranes hired a carriage to drive them to the party that Kate Lyon had planned for the occasion. Someone hadn't been paying attention, however, and the horse pulling the carriage was badly harnessed. At some point during the eight-mile trip to Kenley that afternoon, the horse bolted from its leather straps, the carriage overturned, and both Crane and Cora were severely banged up when they hit the ground with the tumbling carriage. A broken nose and an injured knee for him, bruises, bumps, and lacerations for her—a rough fall that left the two of them aching for weeks afterward. In her October letter to Scovel, who had left Europe by then to report on the Klondike gold rush for the *World*, Cora wrote, "We were almost killed in a carriage accident in Aug. . . . It was on Harold's birthday and we were going to luncheon party at his place—you can imagine our arriving covered with dust and blood. They, dear people, took us in and cured us and then carted us off to Ireland where we had a delightful three weeks in the wilds—"

That was how the Cranes landed in Ireland—by invitation from Frederic, who happened to be an outspoken defender of Irish home rule and a friend of Charles Parnell's, which had prompted one of his well-heeled admirers to offer him the use of a large house in the village of Ahakista on Dunmanus Bay. If the mending couple took the long way around to get there, it was because Crane had entered into another contract with McClure, in this case to write a report about the experience of traveling from London to Glasgow on the Scotch Express, and so the first leg of their trip to Ireland took them to Scotland—accompanied by illustrator William L. Sonntag Jr., who would be responsible for providing the window dressing to Crane's words.

No assignment could have sounded duller than this one, which in contemporary terms would have been the equivalent of being asked to cover the ho-hum trip from Boston to Washington on the Amtrak Acela. And not just in a few paragraphs but stretched out over five thousand words, or twelve tightly printed book pages. A question immediately springs to mind: How could anyone possibly write so much about so little without putting the reader to sleep? We therefore tiptoe into the article warily, girding ourselves against our low expectations, but after some introductory remarks about the imposing, rather bombastic architecture of Euston Station, the streams of travelers descending from hansom cabs outside the building and the activities of the porters inside it, we begin to understand that this is the prelude to a documentary film about the elaborate process of transporting hundreds of people from one distant city to another. It is not the story of a travel writer's trip to Glasgow, it is the story of the train, the charging steel monster known as the Scotch Express, and not once from beginning to end does Crane use the word *I*. Nor do we see him board the train or see him sitting in his compartment as the train heads for Scotland, moving "from the home of one accent to the home of another accent . . . from manner to manner, from habit to habit." As he was in most of his earlier New York sketches, Crane is invisible. Even more radically, however, all the other passengers are invisible here as well. The train is the protagonist, and the only people we see on the train are the man who is driving it and the man who feeds the fire that propels it forward.

As he moves forward himself, Crane turns the dull premise of his feature article into a stirring meditation on the interdependence of man and machine, and through close observation and unflagging curiosity, the ride north at an average speed of 49.9 miles per hour becomes as gripping as a voyage to another planet. Not just because it is so well done but because, underneath the phenomenological exactitude of Crane's remarks, he is also mapping out a philosophical position about the nature of human dignity.

At its heart, "The Scotch Express" is an examination of the vast human network involved in the successful functioning of a railway system—and, by extension, the functioning of any human enterprise that affects large numbers of people. Two principles must be at work simultaneously: a spirit of cooperation (trust in others) and a spirit of personal responsibility as well (trust in oneself). That was the lesson Crane had learned on the open boat, and now, taking his knowledge one step further, he applies it to the workings of the Scotch Express. Everyone is a part of it, and everyone has a job to do, from the cab drivers and porters at the station to the guard in the blue uniform who goes about the business of closing the doors of the train with "the importance of a ceremony" to the workers who operate the signal box as they prepare for the train's departure.

> This high signal house contains many levers standing in thick shining ranks. It perfectly resembles an organ in some great church if it were not that these rows of numbered and indexed handles typify something more acutely human than does a keyboard. It requires four men to play this organ-like thing and the strains never cease. Night and day, day and night, these four men are walking to and fro, from this lever to that lever, and under their hands the great machine raises its endless hymn of a world at work, the fall and rise of signals and the clicking swing of the switches.

When the vermilion engine is coupled to the cars behind it, the train begins its slow exit from the station, sputtering at first as it builds up steam, and before long it is passing through the London suburbs, "a monotony . . . of carefully-made walls of stone or brick," until it climbs to the top of a hill and advances into open country, where the train accelerates and begins its rush "through pictures of red habitations of men on a green earth." An echo of Blake's green and pleasant land, perhaps, and soon enough "the vermilion engine [is] . . . flying like the wind."

Few people today know how it feels to travel in a horse-drawn carriage, but millions of Americans still ride trains, especially along the thickly settled East Coast, and the sensations described by Crane as he sped toward Glasgow more than one hundred years ago are strikingly familiar to us in the twenty-first century. For example, on blasting through a small station where the express will not be stopping: "It was something of a triumphal procession conducted at thrilling speed. Perhaps there was a curve of infinite grace, a sudden hollow explosive effect made by the passing of a signal box that was close to the track, and then the deadly lunge to shave the edge of the long platform." Or on entering a tunnel: "Suddenly one knew that the train was shooting toward a black mouth in the hills. It swiftly yawned wider and then in a moment the engine dove in a place habitant with every demon of wind and noise. The speed had not been checked and the uproar was so great that in effect one was simply standing at the centre of a vast black-walled sphere. The tubular construction which one's reason proclaimed, had no meaning at all. It was a black sphere alive with shrieks." Or on passing a slow-moving train: "In the distance a goods train whooping smokily for the north of England on one of the four tracks. The over-taking of such a train was a thing of magnificent nothing for the long-strided engine and as the flying express passed its weaker brother, one heard one or two feeble and immature puffs from the other engine, saw the fireman wave his hand to the luckier fellow, saw a string of foolish clanking flat-cars, their freights covered with tarpaulins, and the train was lost to the rear."

Thrilling speed. The magnificent monster is responsible for this whirl of shifting, novel sensations, and if it is moving along at an average speed of fifty miles an hour, there will be moments when it hits sixty or even sixty-five, turning it into a rocket of pure strength in that world without cars or planes. That such a monster can exist is the work of thousands, and that the monster can reach Glasgow safely and on schedule hinges on the rail company's deft deployment of its scattered, far-flung army. In the end, however, it all comes down to the work of one man, and the full weight of the enterprise sits on his shoulders. If he fails to perform his job, everything else will be meaningless, and the work of all the others will go for naught.

It takes a while, but several pages into the article the reader finally catches on that Crane is riding up front in the cab with the man who is steering the train. For all the vivid commentary he has offered about the physical and emotional effects of riding the monster, it is this man who dominates Crane's thoughts, and in the end, as much as the train itself, this nameless employee of the London and North Western Railway is the true subject of "The Scotch Express."

> This driver was worth contemplation. He was simply a quiet middle-aged man, bearded and with the little wrinkles of habitual geniality and kindliness spreading from the eyes toward the temple, who stood at his post always gazing out through his round window while from time to time his hands went from here to there over his levers. He seldom changed either attitude or expression. There surely is no engine-driver who does

not feel the beauty of the business but the emotion lies deep and, mainly, inarticulate as it does in the mind of a man who has experienced a good and beautiful wife for many years. The driver's face displayed nothing but the cool sanity of a man whose thought was buried intelligently in his business. If there was any fierce drama in it there was no sign upon him. He was so lost in dreams of speed and signals and steam that one speculated if the wonder of his tempestuous charge and its career over England touched him, this impassive rider of a fiery thing.

It should be a well-known fact that, all over the world, the engine-driver is the finest type of man that is grown. He is the pick of the earth. He is altogether more worthy than the soldier and better than the men who move on the sea in ships. He is not paid too much, nor do his glories weight his brow, but for outright performance carried on constantly, coolly, and without elation by a temperate, honest, clean-minded man he is the further point. And so the lone human at his station in a cab, guarding money, lives, and the honor of the road, is a beautiful sight. The whole thing is aesthetic.

What Crane is setting forth here is the description of an exemplary life. His admiration for the British train man is similar to the feelings he expressed for Billy Higgins and Edward Murphy of the *Commodore* and explains why he had no interest in interviewing the king or the crown prince when he was covering the war in Greece and chose instead to write an article about his conversations with six common foot soldiers. Do your job without fuss or fanfare, keep your head down and carry on because you have to carry on, remember that you are responsible to yourself and to others even if the others have no idea who you are—and don't flinch. That was the path to honor, Crane felt, and as his thinking gradually matured, he had begun to formulate a personal credo of how the worthy life should be lived. "The Open Boat" had been the first step; this was the second.

"The Scotch Express" is a magazine article about a long-distance train ride from London to Glasgow, just one of many occasional pieces crammed into the immense, seven-hundred-and-fifty-page eighth volume of Crane's *Works*, which gathers together all his sketches and non-war journalism. It is little known and has seldom been reprinted in anthologies, but beyond its literary merit, it shines a light on the evolution of Crane's late work, that last frantic stretch when his engagement with the world flung him into broader and broader human territory and his optimism and pessimism both deepened. By *late*, of course, I am referring not to clock time or calendar time but to the things he wrote after his twenty-fifth birthday.

From Glasgow, Crane and Cora took the River Clyde steamer to Queenstown, now known as Cobh, and began their Irish holiday with the Frederics. By all accounts, the two couples had a splendid time living together in their large shared house, and as the pains from the carriage mishap receded, spirits rose, energy returned, and the earth spun around on its axis twenty-one more times. By September ninth, Crane had finished *The Monster*, and for the rest of the visit he explored the towns and coastal villages along the southern tip of Ireland, keeping his eyes and ears open as he prepared himself to churn out more words for the sake of home, food, and survival.

The "Irish Notes" consists of five short micro-sketches that add up to just sixteen pages in all, but each one is sharp, vigorously written, and assured. The small island had been home ground to a large swath of New York's population for the past fifty years, and Crane seems to have been particularly intent on getting a feel for the ancestral motherland, which he strides into with more enthusiasm than he showed for any of the other new places he visited in the past: Hot Springs, for example, or Galveston, or even Mexico. By now, he had had a small taste of living in England, the empire that had ruled over Ireland for the past four hundred years, and because Crane distrusted power and instinctively tended to side with the underdog, he was sympathetic to the Irish before he ever set foot on Irish soil. A puzzling stance for someone who had mostly treated the transplanted Irish of New York as a pack of brawling drunks in his early fiction, but perhaps the young man was becoming wise in his old age.

The first of the sketches, "Queenstown," is not only sharp but bursting with humor, and as Crane leaves the boat in a pelting downpour, he remarks:

> Cork was weeping like a widow. The rain would have gone through any top-coat but a sentry-box. The passengers looked like specimens of a new kind of sponge as they separated to gloomy ways. From the dock to a railway station and thence to a hotel in Queenstown, the path of the traveller was lined with men not schooled merely in formulae; car-drivers, porters and guards who could apparently rise beyond a law and understand a joke, a poem or even an idiosyncrasy. The difference from

England did not here exist in a conformation nor yet in the color of the turf. It existed in the gleam of a man's eye.

This is the first comparison he makes between the Irish and the English, the contrast between the flexibility of mind and temperament he perceives in the one and the somber, by-the-book rigidity displayed in the other, which turns up again at the end of the article. Expressing his admiration for the Irishman's "straight-out face-to-face courage of speech," he imagines him the sort of person who "would attempt forty games of chess at one time and play them all passably well," which is immediately followed by the concluding paragraph:

> The rain disclosed the bay at last, and from the hill one could look down upon the broad deck of the *Howe*. Against the slate-colored waters shone the white pennant of the English navy, emblem of the man who can play one game at a time.

In the next piece, "Ballydehob" (a small village on Roaringwater Bay), he comes at the subject yet again, but the playfulness is gone this time as he evokes the ancient antagonisms that have trapped the conquerors and the conquered in a state of obdurate animosity toward each other for more than a dozen generations.

> Nobody lives here that has any money. The average English tradesman with his back-breaking respect for this class, his reflex contempt for that class, his reverence for the tin gods, could here be a commercial lord and bully the people in one or two ways, until they were thrown back upon the defence which is always near them, the ability to cut his skin into strips with a wit that would be a foreign tongue to him. For amid his wrongs and rights and his failures, his colossal failures, the Irishman retains this delicate blade for his enemies, for his friends, for himself, the ancestral dagger of fast sharp speaking from fast sharp seeing—an inheritance which could move the world. And the Royal Irish Constabulary fished for trout in the adjacent streams.

That Royal Irish Constabulary gives the next piece its title, and lest there be any confusion, Crane is not referring to Irish policemen but to the British forces stationed in Ireland who watch over the so-called disturbed districts for signs of political trouble as they go about their business as officers of the law. "One cannot look Ireland straight in the face without seeing a great many constables," Crane writes, and the garrisons are everywhere, even in such minuscule localities as Ballydehob, housing contingents of four to ten men for populations of just two or three hundred in what S.C. correctly describes as "an absolute military occupation." Still, he can't help feeling a certain pity for these young men, who are so thoroughly shunned by the inhabitants that they live in an isolation comparable to that of lighthouse keepers "at a bitter end of land in a remote sea." They are not even granted the small courtesy of a nod or a mumbled hello, and when no one deigns to look at you, you become invisible. "All through the South of Ireland one sees the peasant turn his eyes pretentiously to the side of the road at the passing of the constable. It seemed to be perfectly understood . . . there was a line drawn so sternly that it reared like a fence." And heaven help the girl who is caught flirting with one of those Englishmen—she will be ostracized or punished for it—and so to fill the vacant hours of their lonely lives, the members of the Royal Irish Constabulary fish for trout.

Crane drops the British after that. He has begun to acclimate himself, and the more fully he takes part in Irish life, the more he is able to see of it—to see *into* it—and savor its contradictions, for there is something about Ireland that resembles Crane himself, a continual shifting between gloom and brightness that he finally manages to capture in the fourth piece, "A Fishing Village." A small puff of prose that lasts for just three and a half pages, it is set on an important day in the life of the town—the day of "the first respectable catch of the year"—and begins with "a little shriveled man, overcome by a profound melancholy, fish[ing] hopelessly from the end of the pier." This is Mickey, disenchanted old-timer and remnant of a forgotten world, and when a young man in a blue jersey comes sculling up to him in a dinghy, his boat filled with "three round baskets heaped high with mackerel," Mickey looks over the catch, shakes "his head mournfully," and says, "Aw, now, Denny. This would not be a very good kill." The young man snorts and replies, "This will be th' bist kill th' year, Mickey. Go along now."

The conversation meanders on for a while, with Mickey lamenting the glory days when the fish were plentiful and "runnin' sthrong in these wathers," but no more, he says, no more, "A-ll go-o-ne now!" as young Denny puts his baskets into "the hands of five incompetent but jovial little boys to carry to a waiting donkey cart."

After another paragraph in which he pauses to reflect on the differences in character between Denny and Mickey, Crane turns his attention back to the donkey cart, which leads to an extraordinary scene of all-out communal effort and coordination as the entire village takes part in preparing the fish for market, a collective enterprise similar to the one carried out by the railway company in "The Scotch Express," but the scale is smaller and far more intimate here, and for the new Crane, the man who was reborn during the thirty hours he spent in the open boat—"the best experience of his life"—what he saw in that small Irish village on that particular day in mid-September 1897 is the closest he ever comes in any of his work to presenting a vision of terrestrial paradise.

> The donkey with his cartload of gleaming fish, and escorted by the whooping and laughing boys, galloped along the quay and up a street of the village until he was turned off at the gravelly strand, at the point where the color of the brook was changing. Here twenty people of both sexes and all ages were preparing the fish for the market. The mackerel, beautiful as fire-etched salvers, first were passed to a long table, around which worked as many women as could have elbow room. Each one could clean a fish with two motions of the knife. Then the washers, men who stood over the troughs filled with running water from the brook, soused the fish until the outlet became a sinister element that in an instant changed the brook from a happy thing of the gorse and heather of the hills to an evil stream, sullen and reddened. After being washed, the fish were carried to a group of girls with knives, who made the cuts that enabled each fish to flatten out in the manner known at the breakfast table. And after the girls came the men and boys, who rubbed each fish thoroughly with great handfuls of coarse salt, which was whiter than snow, and shone in the daylight from a multitude of gleaming points, diamond-like. Last came the packers, drilled in the art of getting neither too few nor too many mackerel into the barrel, sprinkling constantly prodigal layers of the brilliant salt. There were many intermediate corps of boys and girls carrying fish from point to point, and sometimes building them into stacks convenient to the hands of the more important laborers.
>
> A vast tree hung its branches over the place. The leaves made a shadow that was religious in its effect, as if the spot was a chapel consecrated to labor.

Meanwhile, old sourpuss Mickey is still at the end of the pier, fishing with the same hopelessness and futility as before. "Bad luck to thim," he says to himself, and when the sky darkens and the ache of rheumatism crawls back into his bones, he stands up and reels in his line. "The waves were lashing the stones. He moved off toward the intense darkness of the village streets."

Crane follows him into those streets and wraps up his five-part "Irish Notes" with "An Old Man Goes Wooing," a little story about Mickey's search for a bottle of stout in a pub crowded with a gang of noisy pig buyers who are being served dinner by a brawny, formidable young woman named Nora. The subdued Mickey waits for her as she rushes about hauling gigantic platters of meat to the boisterous pig men, and when he finally gets her attention and places his order, she is reluctant to serve him because she doubts he can pay for the bottle, but after he reaches into his pocket and digs out the two coppers required to complete the transaction, she gives him his stout, "stupefied." He wanders off to a table, drinks his brown, foamy drink, and then dozes off with his face resting on his arms. Some time passes. When Nora looks up from behind the bar and sees that he has fallen asleep, she marches over to the table, yanks him from his chair, drags him across the floor, and pushes him out into the night.

Crane is Mickey. Crane is the village. Or else he is neither one nor the other and stands between the two, looking in both directions at the same time.

In the midst of these fruitful discoveries and pleasant days on the coast of Ireland, Crane wrote his last letter to Amy Leslie on September twelfth. Twice in April he had sent her money from Athens—a hundred dollars on the eighteenth; twenty-five pounds via Hawkins on the twenty-seventh (the equivalent of one hundred and twenty-five dollars)—but in neither instance had she received it. The first letter had gone astray because Amy had moved without telling him and he had sent the money to the old address, and the second letter arrived in New York about a month after the final bits of the original five hundred had been disbursed (leaving Hawkins four dollars in the hole), and having fulfilled the promise he had made to his friend, the weary, fed-up Hawkins had washed his hands of the business and returned the money to Crane. Crane still seemed to know nothing about Hawkins's decision and even less about the missing hundred. He mentioned it in the letter he wrote to Amy from Ireland, but his principal reason for contacting her was to dispel any rumors she might have heard about his involvement with another woman. Word of Cora must have reached her somehow, and while no trace of her letter exists, his own letter confirms that she wrote to him about it, and just as she had lied to him about any number of things

in the past, he now lied to her about this. It wasn't that he had any interest
in reviving his affair with her. That was over and done with as far as he was
concerned, but fearing the storm of trouble she was bound to stir up if he
told her the truth, he took the easy way out and lied.

My dear Amy: I am sorry to have you write to me in the way that you did
because I will always be willing to do anything in the world for you to help
you and see that you do not suffer. I never intended to treat you badly and
if I did appear to do so, it was more by fate or chance than from any desire
of mine. You do not say anything about receiving the $100. I sent you from
Greece. . . . Did you get it? Let me know through Heineman. I am over
here in the south of Ireland getting well from a carriage accident. It will
be sometime before I get well. I had to leave off work and borrow some
money to come here. I was doing very decently in London and would have
sent you more money before now if it were not for the accident. As soon
as I can I will send some to you if only it is a little at a time.

You know better than to believe those lies about me. You know full
well what kind of man I am. As soon as I get home I shall want to know
who told you them.

Keep heart, Amy. Trust me and it will all turn out right. Go and see
Willis and let him always know your address. When you write and tell
me that he is still in town and that you got that hundred all right I will
rake up more. Dont think too badly of me, dear. Wait, have patience and
I will see you through straight. Dont believe anything you hear of me
and dont doubt my faith and my honesty.

Yours as ever

C.

He couldn't have known how damaging this letter would be for him,
the chain reaction of events and counter-events that would follow from
his innocent mention of the hundred dollars—the one honest statement in
the entire letter. Suspecting mischief of some kind, Amy wrote to Hawkins
to ask about the missing bank check, and when he didn't answer her letter,
she jumped to the erroneous conclusion that he had been embezzling the
funds meant for her, which led her to engage the services of lawyer George
D. Mabon, who banged his rainmaker's drum and brought down the deluge
of legal entanglements, public embarrassments, and frozen royalties that
would dog Crane until February of the new year.

For now, however, it was still the old year, and as far as Crane could
tell, he had done nothing more than write a defensive, mostly untruthful

letter to his ex-lover, hardly the worst crime ever committed by a man or a woman trying to shake free of a dead affair. Just three days before that, he had finished *The Monster*, one of his darkest, most bitter works, and sometime during that same month, September, he also finished his most successful comic story, "The Bride Comes to Yellow Sky," a brisk showdown-farce in which past squares off against present in the dust of a mythological Texas town. The stories are so different, it scarcely seems credible that they were written by the same man—but look more closely, and before long it becomes apparent that the gloom and the brightness have emerged from a common source and that both stories are asking the same fundamental question: Where are we?

8

THE MONSTER.

Whilom: an old, no longer used word meaning *of old, once, formerly, once upon a time*. It comes up often in Spenser's *Faerie Queene* and other English poems from earlier centuries, but it was also embedded in Crane family lore as a word used by S.C.'s maternal grandfather and his four brothers for the fife-and-drum ensemble they created under the name of the "Whilom drum corps," a group that went on performing together for more than twenty years, right up into Crane's early childhood. A crucial part of that childhood was spent in Port Jervis, which in *The Monster* is transformed into Whilomville, and in the novella one of the principal characters is a little boy no older than Crane was at the time he moved there, Jimmie Trescott, the son of Dr. Trescott, the employer of Henry Johnson, the black hostler who rushes into the Trescotts' burning house to save Jimmie and whose face is burned off in the fire.

Not only is *The Monster* set in the town of Whilomville, it is the story of Whilomville, which could be any little town of nine or ten thousand people in the northern part of the United States, and although the faceless Henry Johnson is looked upon as a monster by both the white and the black citizens of Whilomville, the real monster in the story is the town itself.

Port Jervis/Whilomville was the place where the young Crane had seen the defective cannon go off at the town's Fourth of July celebration in 1879, killing one black veteran of the Civil War and maiming another, whose face was grotesquely disfigured for the rest of his life. An intelligent little boy surely would have grasped the tragic implications of the event. Two black men who had fought in the Union army to free their fellow black

Crane in his study at Ravensbrook, 1897 or 1898.
The blanket and spurs mounted on the wall are souvenirs from his trip to Mexico.
(COURTESY OF THE UNIVERSITY OF VIRGINIA)

Americans from the horrors of human bondage had been blasted apart by one of the cannons that had helped them achieve that liberation—on the very day when people across the country were celebrating the one hundred and third anniversary of America's liberation from the British. And then, after Crane was no longer a boy, there had been the lynching of black man Robert Lewis on that same public square in early June 1892, the drunken, chanting mob of two thousand men that Crane's brother had elbowed his way into in an unsuccessful attempt to stop the murder, which took place not more than a stone's throw from the church where Crane's father had preached his sermons and his parents had established two schools for black people in the 1880s. All those personal memories lurked behind *The Monster*, but the present factored into it as well, the bleak 1890s, the grimmest decade for black Americans since the end of the Civil War, and with the broken promises of Reconstruction all but forgotten now by whites across the North, the *Plessy v. Ferguson* decision by the Supreme Court in 1896 had turned the Union victory into a sinister joke. Slavery was dead, but a new version of slavery had been born, and thirty years after the fighting had stopped, the South had won.

Another presence in Crane's childhood was an engraving that hung in the family house, a black-and-white reproduction of an 1848 painting by T. H. Matteson entitled *The First Prayer in Congress*. The earlier Stephen

Crane from the eighteenth century is one of the figures represented in the picture, and because the parents of our Stephen Crane had told him that his namesake had spoken the opening prayer to the Continental Congress that day and had been one of the signers of the Declaration of Independence (not true, but little S.C. didn't know that), Crane felt that his family had played a fundamental role in the founding of the republic—an understandable point of pride. In *The Monster*, a similar historical engraving hangs in the Trescott house, *The Signing of the Declaration*, and it is one of the first things destroyed by the fire, the only object that Crane singles out from the mass of burning wreckage on the ground floor. "In the hall a lick of flame had found the cord that supported 'Signing of the Declaration.' The engraving slumped down suddenly at one end, and then dropped to the floor, where it burst with the sound of a bomb." A moment later, Johnson rushes upstairs to find Jimmie, who is asleep in his bedroom. All men are created equal, the document tells us, but as George Orwell has also told us, some men are more equal than others, and as one of those others, it is Johnson who is called upon to preserve the union of the Trescott family. The knife of Crane's skepticism and irony had never cut more deeply.

He was boiling, and the source of that anger was not just the flaws and hypocrisies of America's founding documents or the exclusion of black men and women from the freedoms granted to white Americans, it was all forms of hypocrisy and exclusion, the full gamut of insults that society can use to torment and isolate the individual. A number of those insults had been directed at Crane himself over the years, and even as a white man who had benefited from the freedoms granted to him by white-controlled America, he had been kicked around, at times kicked out, and now he was kicking back. Kicked out by the *New York Tribune* as a twenty-year-old beginner for a misunderstood, widely condemned article, and now, five years down the road, he calls the town's morning paper in his Whilomville story the *Tribune*, which bungles its account of the fire by declaring Johnson to be dead when in fact he is alive. Kicked around by the New York press after the Dora Clark Affair and eventually kicked out of the city, a pariah to the police, the future president, and everyone in the tristate area but his closest friends—the same sort of banishment suffered by Dr. Trescott in the story, who is condemned by the town for having created the black monster Henry Johnson by nursing him back from the dead out of gratitude for saving his son's life. Kicked around by the *Tribune* and dozens of other scornful, envious, carping voices every time he published a book or dared to breathe in public, and now he had kicked himself out of America because he had chosen to live with a woman who would have been rejected by his own family. Rage against the religion of his parents and the smug, life-denying Methodism of the Peck clan had unleashed the poems of *The Black Riders*, and now a similar rage against a multitude of other things had brought forth *The Monster*.

In both books, it is a rage controlled by the demands of art, and as with the language of *The Black Riders*—stripped down, elemental, utterly dissimilar to the prose Crane was writing at the time—the narrative structure of *The Monster* breaks from the method Crane had employed in his earlier works and is the first of his novels/novellas to be told from multiple points of view. The splintering of perspectives is essential here, since the protagonist of the story is not one person but an entire community, an agglomeration of many people both named and unnamed, and if the Trescotts and Henry Johnson are the core characters, what happens around that core is just as vital to Crane as what happens inside it. Fifty-seven pages split up into twenty-four brief chapters, the same pattern as in his other works, but the way things jump from chapter to chapter in this one is different, and beyond the shifting tones of the material within the chapters (women in kitchens, men in barbershops), there is the overall movement of the book, which divides into two distinct halves, before the fire and after the fire: the town as it was, and then the town that emerges after the monster is born.

The first chapter opens with Jimmie Trescott pretending to be engine Number 36 as it speeds along the tracks between Syracuse and Rochester. He is playing near the flower garden at the side of his family's house; a short distance away, his father is mowing the lawn in the backyard. Caught up in his game, Jimmie runs along the curve of the flower bed pulling his cart behind him, and before he can register what has happened, a wheel of the cart has hopped over the edge and cut down a peony. Jimmie is mortified. Destroying flowers is forbidden, and when he takes hold of the broken-stemmed peony and tries to prop it up again, it droops limply in his hand. "Jim could do no reparation." Trouble is bound to follow, dire, as yet unimaginable punishments, but Jimmie is a boy with a conscience, and so he manfully walks toward his father to explain what he has done. The words refuse to come out of his mouth, however, and the best he can do is point and say, "There." Not once, not twice, but again and again, and when his father still can't grasp what he is trying to tell him, they walk over to the flower bed together, with the terrified boy lagging farther and farther behind by slow, steady, increments, which leaves it up to the father to discover the problem on his own. He does, but rather than scold his son or thrash the boy in a fit of anger—the automatic response of Maggie's father toward the other Jimmie in the other book—Dr. Trescott calmly asks his little Jim how it happened, and when the boy comes clean and gives him an honest answer about "playin' train," the father reflects for a moment before coming to his decision.

> "Well, Jimmie," he said slowly, "I guess you had better not play train any more to-day. Do you think you had better?"
>
> "No, sir," said Jimmie.
>
> During the delivery of the judgment the child had not faced his father, and afterward he went away, with his head lowered, shuffling his feet.

What Crane is presenting here is a middle-class nirvana of green lawns and one-family houses in which tolerant fathers treat their earnest, respectful sons with justice and compassion. In *Maggie*, violence and brutality are the norm, but in small-town Whilomville the trampling of a flower is a calamitous event. This is an early version of the idealized America that would later be depicted in the Andy Hardy films of the 1930s and television shows such as *Leave It to Beaver* and *Father Knows Best* two decades later, a land of democratic white people with good marriages and good jobs and good, solid hearts. A black person occasionally shows up at the periphery of the action, in almost all cases a large, smiling woman who works as the cook or the maid for her gentle white employers. Her name is Beulah or Ethel, but in fact it is always Aunt Jemima, and because this woman knows her place, she is a well-liked person and an essential part of the household. Once in a blue moon, however, the black person who works for the white family is a man.

Such a man is Henry Johnson, who is no Uncle Tom but must pretend to be one in order to hold his job and convince the world that he knows his place. His life is a perfect embodiment of the dilemma W. E. B. Du Bois describes as "double consciousness" in *The Souls of Black Folks* (published just six years after Crane wrote *The Monster*)—the reflexive psychological response that became a necessary survival mechanism for threatened black people as Jim Crow segregation laws spread across the South. The laws weren't as constraining in the North, but the invisible barriers between white and black were almost as solid, and Johnson toes the line with a grin on his face and the good fortune of not having to dissemble about his affection for the doctor and his little boy, which happens to be real. His job also happens to be a good one, and it comes with an apartment above the stable where he works as the groom of the doctor's horse, the cleaner, polisher, and repairman of the doctor's carriage, and the chauffeur who escorts the doctor on his long rounds of visiting patients in Whilomville and the countryside beyond. He performs his duties well and, like his female counterparts in other stories, has become an essential figure in the household, but once his job is done for the day, the humble worker known as Henry transforms himself into the elegant, strutting Mr. Johnson, "a light, a weight, and an eminence in the suburb of the town, where lived the larger number of the negroes." In the second and third chapters, Crane sketches out the two conflicting versions of this split-in-half double man, and that is the last we see of him before he rushes into the burning house and the story of the monster begins.

After the murder of the peony and the talk with his father, the downcast little Jim heads to the stable to find refuge with Henry, who is both hero and saint to him as well as a sympathetic counselor in all things pertaining to the laws of proper conduct, which Jimmie tends to break more often than he should. "These two were pals," Crane writes, and as he delves into the intricacies of their friendship in the second chapter, he pauses over the clever tactics Henry has devised for cheering up the boy whenever he has been rebuked: recounting his own misdeeds, for example, as when "he had forgotten to put the hitch-strap in the back of the buggy . . . and had been reprimanded by the doctor," or distracting him by allowing "the child to enjoy the felicity of squeezing the sponge over a buggy-wheel," or sometimes reversing course and bullying him into contrition "by preaching . . . the precepts of the doctor's creed, and pointing out to Jimmie all his abominations," which Jimmie endures "with humility." The boy's admiration for him is a source of "great joy" to Henry, and "on all points of conduct as related to the doctor, who was the moon, they were in complete but unexpressed understanding." That unspoken bond has made them pals, and though one is a boy and the other is a grown-up, they are both underlings, the boy by virtue of his being a boy and the grown-up by virtue of his position as a hired hand, which makes the bond between them especially strong, so strong that Henry will rush into the burning house that evening and risk his life to save little Jim.

Before that happens, however, there is the transformation of Henry into Mr. Johnson. After he has eaten his supper in the kitchen, he returns to his loft above the stable, sheds his work clothes, cleans himself with all the care of a lady at court or a priest preparing himself for a major event at his church, dons the clothes he wears in his other life, and saunters forth into the pleasant evening air.

It was not altogether a matter of the lavender trousers, nor yet the straw hat with its bright silk band. The change was somewhere far in the interior of Henry. But there was no cake-walk hyperbole in it. He was simply a quiet, well-bred gentleman of position, wealth, and other necessary achievements out for an evening stroll, and he had never washed a wagon in his life.

It is a warm Saturday night, and the streets of the town are filling up with pedestrians. A crowd has gathered in front of the post office to wait for the arrival of the evening mail, others are preparing to attend the performance of a play at "the little theatre, which was a varnish and red-plush miniature of one of the famous New York theatres," and groups of young men have clustered on street corners to watch the crowd and toss off witless, acerbic comments about everyone who passes by. The electric streetcars are gonging, the gas lamps are glowing, the electric lamps are shining, and through it all strides the dapper Mr. Johnson, and even when the white boys begin to taunt him with some vaguely insulting remarks, he will not let their words break his stride. "Hello, Henry! Going to walk for a cake tonight?" "Ain't he smooth?" "Throw out your chest a little more."

Henry was not ruffled in any way by these quiet admonitions and compliments. In reply he laughed a supremely good-natured, chuckling laugh, which nevertheless expressed an underground complacency of superior metal.

Young Griscom, the lawyer, was just emerging from Reifsnyder's barber shop, rubbing his chin contentedly. On the steps he dropped his hand and looked with wide eyes into the crowd. Suddenly he bolted back into the shop. "Wow!" he cried to the parliament; "you ought to see the coon that's coming!"

It was a word that tripped off the tongue easily back then, a standard, par-for-the-course word that would not have offended anyone in the barbershop or anywhere else in the white North, and Crane, who knew how Americans talked, most definitely knows what he is doing here. When Reifsnyder is told that the man who passed by was Henry Johnson, the incredulous barber says (in his German-accented English), "I bait you money that vas not Henry Johnson! Henry Johnson! Rats! That man vas a Pullman-car porter or something. How could that be Henry Johnson?"

Crane adds that Johnson is perfectly aware of the commotion he arouses on his jaunts through the town and that he takes pleasure in it, even exults in it by laughing at the fools who make fun of him. A subtle, potentially dangerous tactic for a black man in a white neighborhood, but if the humble Henry bows his head at work, Mr. Johnson in the lavender trousers bows to no one. He laughs—and then strides on as the lawyer and the barber gawk in astonishment.

The stroll through downtown Whilomville ends when Johnson turns off the main street and heads for the "tumble-down houses" of Watermelon Alley, the black part of town, where he visits the current object of his affections, Belle Farragut, and her fat, welcoming mother. They settle in for a polite, three-way conversation that lasts "until a late hour," and after Johnson leaves, Belle exclaims to Mrs. Farragut, "Oh, ma, isn't he divine?"

What is surprising about this chapter, which must have been a difficult one to write, is that for someone with Crane's prejudices and limitations in regard to the Other, it almost works. There are some slips along the way, moments that verge on caricature or fall into the stereotypes of the period ("The saffron Miss Belle Farragut," for example), but Crane is attempting the nearly impossible in trying to see the world through a black man's eyes—almost unheard-of for a white American novelist in the 1890s—and that he manages to make most of it credible and at times even moving is a testament to the sincerity of his effort and the moral imperative that drove him to write this chapter and everything else in the book.

The narrative opens up after that as Crane turns his attention to the Saturday night activities in town, the band concert in the little park, the young men who routinely scorn the concerts but never fail to show up because of the girls, the girls and young men walking around in twos and threes and eyeing one another but seldom daring to open their mouths, the little boys darting helter-skelter through the crowd, the band playing a waltz and one of the young men wisecracking that it sounds like "the new engines on the hill pumping water into the reservoir," the evening mail arriving from New York and Rochester and the post office crowd now mingling with the crowd at the bandstand, a policeman chasing "a gang of obstreperous little boys" who jeer at him from a distance, and then, suddenly, "there arose from afar the great hoarse roar of a factory whistle," and the bandmaster, who has just raised his hand to conduct his musicians in a popular march, drops his hand slowly to his knee. The first alarm has sounded.

More alarms follow, and the people in the crowd speculate about which fire station they are coming from, Number One or Number Two, and as the fifth chapter begins, Crane slices up the story into small, self-contained vignettes of this firefighter here and that firefighter there, bouncing among them as they ready themselves to attack the fire and a small boy named Willie pleads with his mother to let him go out and watch the fun. Men rush down the avenue shouting, and the bell of the Methodist church (Crane's father's church) begins to ring out with "a solemn and terrible voice, speaking from the clouds."

By chapter VI we understand that the focus of attention is the Trescotts' Queen Anne house on a quiet block in one of the town's quietest neighborhoods. Nothing seems to be happening at first. The dog from the Hannigan place next door comes over and prowls around the front lawn, pawing the grass and growling at no one in particular; one of Johnson's friends, Peter Washington, pauses in front of the house, but when he sees no light in the windows of the loft above the stable, he walks on. A wisp of smoke escapes from a window at the end of the house and curls around the branches of a cherry tree. Another wisp emerges, then several wisps, and before long "the window brightened as if the four panes of it had been stained with blood and a quick ear might have been led to imagine the fire-imps calling and calling, clan joining clan, gathering to the colors."

At this point, the blaze behind the window is still not visible from the street, but already Crane is evoking fire as an instrument of war, and when the windowpanes burst and crash to the ground and other windows begin turning red as well, he pushes the trope a bit further and reveals what kind of war he is thinking about: "This outbreak had been well planned, as if by professional revolutionists."

After that, a dozen different things happen at once, but the essential things are that Hannigan, the neighbor, finally manages to convince Mrs. Trescott that her house is on fire by shouting up to her as she stands at a second-floor window and that just as Hannigan kicks off the lock on the front door and is about to enter the house Henry Johnson, after running along the pavement "with an almost fabulous speed," shows up at the house as well. Dr. Trescott is out on a call, the fire brigade has not yet arrived, and these two men are the only ones in a position to do anything about rescuing the boy and his mother.

The instant after Johnson enters the house, *The Signing of the Declaration* drops to the floor and explodes "with the sound of a bomb." This is the third reference to war in the trim, two-page chapter, and if Crane is referring to the war that began with the Declaration of Independence, which seems all but certain by now, exactly how or why or to what purpose is still not clear.

Mrs. Trescott is standing at the top of the stairs, waving her arms

in distress, and when Johnson goes up, she screams—"in Henry's face"—
"Jimmie! Save Jimmie!" Johnson goes past her and plunges on through the
halls and rooms upstairs, but Hannigan, who has followed him up, grabs "the
arm of the maniacal woman" and, "his face black with rage," bellows at her
that she must come down. Half out of her mind, she screams back at him:
"Jimmie! Jimmie! Save Jimmie!" Not bothering to waste his breath on words,
Hannigan drags her down the stairs and takes her outside, which leaves
Johnson as the only one still in the house, the one person in the world who
can do anything for the boy, and it is precisely then that the factory whistle
roars in the distance and the bandleader drops his arm, events Crane has
already described in an earlier chapter, and now that the scrambled sequence
has been unscrambled, we have caught up to the present again. It is an effective narrative device, and by showing the consequences before the cause (the
fire panic first, then the fire), Crane has amplified the horror of the situation.
We already know there is going to be a fire, a fire big enough to set off factory whistles and church bells and drive the whole town into the streets, and
when the first wisp of smoke slithers out of the Trescotts' window, we
know where the fire has struck. The good people we have been following
since the first page of the story are the victims. And because the consequences are already known, we know how badly they are going to suffer.

By the time Johnson reaches the second floor, the anticipated tragedy
has already been put in motion, and given what Crane has prepared us for,
it seems inevitable that Johnson will die. Stumbling his way through the
smoke in the corridors, he tries to orient himself by sliding his hands along
the walls, but they are too hot to touch. "The paper was crimpling, and
he expected at any moment to have a flame burst from under his hands."
For all that, he eventually manages to find Jimmie's door, and when he
steps inside the room, it is mercifully free of smoke. He gathers up the
frightened boy in a blanket and carries him out, as if he were involved in
some kind of kidnapping operation, and as the bawling little Jim cries for
his mother ("Mam-ma! Mam-ma!"), Johnson reaches the top of the stairs
again. "Through the smoke that rolled to him he could see that the lower
hall was all ablaze." He lets out a howl and backs off, retreating into the
upstairs corridor, and then, unexpectedly, Crane veers sharply onto another
track of thought: "From the way of him then, he had given up almost all
idea of escaping from the burning house, and with it the desire. He was
submitting, submitting because of his fathers, bending his mind in a most
perfect slavery to this conflagration."

There are some odd moments in Crane's work, but these last two sentences are downright bizarre. A man is fighting for his life, and suddenly he

is no longer fighting but giving up, relinquishing his will to the force of the fire because . . . because his father and grandfather and great-grandfather were slaves, and therefore he himself . . . is still a slave.

In the context of what is happening in the story at this point, it is a curious turn. A black man trapped in a burning house with a white child in his arms has concluded there is no way out and is ready to die in the flames. Those are the physical and psychological facts. Metaphorically, however, Crane has already established that the fire is a reenactment of the American Revolution. The fire-imps have called out to the people, clan has joined clan (colony has joined colony), they have all gathered to the colors (the flag of freedom), and now, having mapped out their "well planned" strategy, the soldiers are fighting with the skill of professional revolutionaries. Crane then adds another element to the metaphorical mix by bringing in the Declaration of Independence, the call to arms that went through several highly contested drafts before it was approved by the members of the Continental Congress, one of whom was a New Jersey delegate named Stephen Crane. Among the sentences that were eliminated in the final version were these two accusations against the British king:

1. "He has waged war against human Nature itself, violating its most sacred Rights of Life and Liberty in the Persons of a distant People who never offended him, captivating and carrying them into slavery in another Hemisphere, or to incur miserable Death in their Transportation thither."
2. "He has prostituted his Negative for Suppressing every legislative Attempt to prohibit or restrain an execrable Commerce, determined to keep open a Market where men should be bought and sold."

These statements were dropped in a compromise with the pro-slavery South in order to unify the colonies and strengthen the chances of defeating the British. In doing so, the most important idea of the Declaration— that all men are created equal—was fatally damaged by transforming the word "all" into "some" or "most" and excluding the black slave population from the ranks of humanity. Black people were the sacrifice that propelled the Revolution forward and led to the founding of a new nation, "conceived in Liberty, and dedicated to the proposition that all men are created equal," as the American president declared four score and seven years later, which happened to be the same year in which the action of *The Red Badge of Courage* is set. Now, in the symbolic fire that stands for the Revolution in the book Crane wrote during the early months of Jim Crow, Henry

Johnson, the descendant of black American slaves, will become the reincarnated symbol of that black sacrifice. As with his ancestors, the cost of martyrdom will not be death, pure and simple, but a symbolic death that robs him of his humanity and turns him into a faceless idiot, shunned, feared, and hated by the righteous citizens of the American anywhere called Whilomville.

Just when he is about to give himself up to the flames, Johnson remembers that there is a small back staircase leading from a bedroom to a downstairs apartment, which the doctor has converted into a private laboratory. The outer door of the lab opens onto the yard, and if Johnson can make his way across the lab and get to that door, he and Jimmie will be free. It is his only chance, the last chance he will have, and with this narrow avenue of hope suddenly before him, he goes down, still carrying the limp and silent boy in his arms. Johnson, who had not been afraid to die when there was no escape, is now scared to death. When he opens the door to the lab, what he had imagined would be a safe zone leading to the yard beyond has been transformed into a hallucinatory obstacle course, which Crane presents in lavish nightmare imagery as a realm of "burning flowers," and from those brilliant flames comes a stench that seems "to be alive with hatred, envy, and malice." The chemicals in the doctor's laboratory have ignited, and "flowers of violet, crimson, green, blue, orange, and purple were blooming everywhere . . . through clouds of heaving, turning, deadly smoke."

As Johnson pauses at the threshold, he lets out "a negro wail that had in it the sadness of the swamps"—a last, stinging allusion to the crime of black enslavement—and then he goes into that many-colored hell and is promptly attacked. An orange flame leaps "like a panther" onto his lavender trousers and bites "deeply" into his leg. An instant later, there is an explosion in another part of the room. The panther is gone, "and suddenly before him there reared a delicate, trembling shape like a fairy lady. With a quiet smile she blocked his path and doomed him and Jimmie." Like a figure in an allegorical poem from the fourteenth century, the sapphire woman is Lady Death, a being of pure flame whose mission is to destroy, and now, taking on yet another form, she becomes "swifter than eagles" as she swoops down and catches Johnson in her talons before he can run past her. Crane's language has become so extravagant that the thwarted escape through the lab resembles the stuff of fever dreams, but assuming he has not lost track of his original purpose—to equate the fire with the American Revolution—then the sapphire lady is also Lady Liberty, devouring her human sacrifice for the good of the cause she represents. The war has entered its final stage in the lab, and so it would seem that Johnson must and most certainly will die in this last battle.

No paragraphs in Crane's work are wilder or stranger than these, and nowhere are his intentions more obscure. What to make of the sudden reference to eagles, for example? Is it a conscious invocation of America's symbolic bird or simply a useful metaphor for high-speed movement? Is Crane in control of his imagery, or has the imagery taken control of him? A little of both, perhaps, but if he has set out to create a sensation of chaos and mortal fear, he has accomplished his goal, for by now the reader's mind is spinning.

Burned by the talon attack from the sapphire lady, Johnson staggers forward into the lab, "twisting this way and that," and then, as he falls down, Jimmie flies out of his arms. The boy, still wrapped in the blanket, rolls across the floor until the bundle comes to a stop against the outer wall—directly under a window. The yard is on the other side of the window, freedom is just inches away, but the limp and silent boy does not stir. Johnson, who has landed on his back, is out cold. He can do nothing more for Jimmie. Nor can Jimmie do anything for himself.

> Johnson had fallen with his head at the base of an old-fashioned desk. There was a row of jars upon the top of the desk. For the most part, they were silent amid this rioting, but there was one which seemed to hold a scintillant and writhing serpent.
>
> Suddenly the glass splintered, and a ruby-red snakelike thing poured its thick length out upon the top of the old desk. It coiled and hesitated, and then began to swim a languorous way down the mahogany slant. At the angle it waved its sizzling molten head to and fro over the closed eyes of the man beneath it. Then, in a moment, with mystic impulse, it moved again, and the red snake flowed directly down into Johnson's upturned face.

As the fiery acid continues to drip onto Johnson's face, the chapter ends, and Crane turns his attention elsewhere: to the arriving fire trucks, to the commotion in the streets, to the bells sounding in schoolhouses and churches, and at last to Dr. Trescott, who has returned from treating his patient and is now in front of the burning house. His wife is on the lawn, shouting, "Jimmie! Save Jimmie!" and when the doctor asks her where, she points to the second floor and says, "Up—up—up." Hannigan begins shouting as well, warning the doctor that he can't go in through the front, so

Trescott decides to use the back staircase that leads from the laboratory to the second floor. When he discovers that the door between the lawn and the lab is bolted shut, he kicks off the lock and tries to enter. The smoke pushes him back, but then, "bending low, he stepped into the garden of burning flowers. On the floor his stinging eyes could make out a form in a smoldering blanket near the window." Trescott picks up his son and carries him outside, where he is met by a small army of men and boys, "the leaders in the great charge the town was making," and within moments they have "seized him and his burden and overpowered him in wet blankets and water." Hannigan then appears on the lawn, *howling*: "Johnson is in there yet! Henry Johnson is in there yet! He went in after the kid! Johnson is in there yet!" Without pausing to think, Trescott starts to go back in to look for Johnson, angrily pushing away the others as they try to stop him from reentering the house, but before he can break free of them, they learn that someone else has already done the job.

> A young man who was a brakemen on the railway, and lived in one of the rear streets near the Trescotts, had gone into the laboratory and brought forth a thing which he laid on the grass.

The mysterious brakeman is never mentioned again. He comes and goes in this one sentence, but the unnamed shadow who carries out "the thing" and deposits it on the lawn could be yet one more ghost from Crane's past: his brother Luther, who worked as a flagman and brakeman on the Erie railroad and was crushed to death in his early twenties when he fell under the wheels of a moving train. The dead coming to the rescue of the nearly dead.

And the boy who earlier that day had destroyed a flower—for which he could "do no reparation"—has been rescued from death in a garden of burning flowers that smell of "hatred, envy, and malice." His father has carried him out, but it was Johnson who carried him down, and at this point in the story it still seems certain that Johnson will die.

Before the second half of *The Monster* begins, there is a small bridge that connects the first half of the book to what follows.

The town is buzzing with rumors, conflicting stories, gossip. Young boys watching the fire trucks gather in front of the house and argue passionately about whether Number Three or Number Two or Number Four or Number Five or Number One is doing the best job as the adults in the crowd speak in hushed voices as word spreads that Jimmie Trescott and Henry Johnson have "burned to death, and Dr. Trescott himself [has] been most savagely hurt," or that all three of them are dead, or that what really happened was that the kid had the measles "or somethin', and this coon—Johnson—was a-settin' up with 'im, and Johnson got sleepy or somethin' and upset the lamp," and when the doctor came running up from his office, he burned to death along with the two others. Meanwhile, "the bells of the town were clashing unceasingly."

The town has become a character in the story, a chorus of unidentified voices expressing the thoughts and feelings of Whilomville, and only a few of the residents will be given names to distinguish them from that mass of anonymous people as the novella spins forward. One of them is old Judge Denning Hagenthorpe, and when it is "publically learned that the doctor and his son and the negro were still alive," the three of them are carried on stretchers to the judge's house across the street. Six of the ten doctors in Whilomville come over to examine the patients, and they conclude that the doctor's burns are not "vitally important" and that while the boy "would possibly be scarred badly," his life is not in danger. The prospects for the third patient, however, are beyond hope. "As for the negro Henry Johnson, he could not live. His body was frightfully seared, but more than that, he now had no face. His face had simply been burned away."

The next morning, as the revitalized doctor tends to Johnson's bandages at the judge's house, the *Tribune* releases its false report of Johnson's death. The article contains an interview with Hannigan, who praises the dead man's courage during the fire, and there is an accompanying editorial "built from all the best words in the vocabulary of the staff." Crane's sarcasm mounts as he describes the reaction from the good people of Whilomville: "The town halted in its accustomed road of thought, and turned a reverent attention to the memory of the hostler," regretting that they "had not known enough to give him a hand ... when he was alive." And then there are the little boys of Whilomville, who now revere Johnson as a saint and look back in revulsion whenever they recall "the odious couplet" they used to chant whenever they saw him on the street: "Nigger nigger, never die, / Black face and shiny eye." In the last sentence of chapter X, we are also told that "Miss Belle Farragut, of No. 7 Watermelon Alley," was engaged to be married to "Mr. Henry Johnson." The *Mr.* is a fine little touch—just one of the many advantages of being dead.

Meanwhile, the undead Johnson hangs on in a state of unbroken agony, a burn victim confined to his bed on the second floor of the judge's house, his skull and missing face wrapped in white bandages through which only one thing appears, an eye—a single, unblinking eye. Some days pass, how many is not made clear, but four paragraphs into the eleventh chapter, when the rapidly improving Jimmie leaves the judge's house with his mother to visit his grandparents in Connecticut, the second part of the book begins.

The doctor stays behind, ostensibly to "take care of his patients," but the more compelling reason is to watch over Johnson "in the long nights and days of his vigil." Trescott goes on living, eating, and sleeping at the judge's Ontario Street mansion, a temporary member of the household, which normally consists of just two people: the retired bachelor Hagenthorpe, whose favorite possession is his ivory-headed cane, and his unmarried sister, whose principal job is to make sure he doesn't lose the cane. From now on, as the story splinters into a succession of small, contiguous story-fragments, the central point of the narrative vortex moves away from Johnson to Trescott—and the quiet war the doctor wages with the town to defend the scorched human thing that was once Johnson. The terms of that war—and the moral dilemma it poses—are delineated in a conversation between the doctor and the judge at dinner one night, and their words continue to hover over everything that happens until the last sentence of the book.

The judge is the first to speak. "No one wants to advance such ideas," he says, "but somehow I think that poor fellow ought to die." The doctor is not offended by the statement; in fact, the idea has also occurred to him. His response is a neutral one: "Who knows?" The judge, retreating "to the cold manner of the bench," begins to elaborate:

> "Perhaps we may not talk with propriety of this kind of action, but I am induced to say that you are performing a questionable charity in preserving this negro's life. As near as I can understand, he will hereafter be a monster, a perfect monster, and probably with an affected brain. No man can observe you as I have observed you and not know that it was a matter of conscience with you, but I am afraid, my friend, that it is one of the blunders of virtue."

The doctor understands. He has been through this argument with himself a dozen times already, and he is both exhausted by it and deeply torn. His answer to the judge is the counterargument: "He saved my son's life."

"'Yes,' said the judge swiftly—'yes, I know!'"

The agitated Trescott goes on: "And what am I to do? What am I to do? He gave himself for—for Jimmie. What am I to do for him?"

The judge is momentarily silenced. He lowers his eyes, picks at the cucumbers on his plate, and finally looks up again and says: "He will be your creation, you understand. He is purely your creation. Nature has very evidently given him up. He is dead. You are restoring him to life. You are making him, and he will be a monster, with no mind."

Trescott's answer, delivered *in sudden, polite fury*, is both incontestable and a sign of pure exasperation: "He will be what you like, judge. He will be anything, but, by God! he saved my boy."

An emotional outburst—which inspires an equally emotional response: "Trescott! Trescott! Don't I know?"

Two intelligent men are sitting at a table, honestly grappling with a problem that has no neat solution, but the pragmatic judge is incapable of recognizing the full scope of the problem, and when the doctor comes back at him a bit later with the one all-important question the judge has failed to consider—"Well, what would you do? Would you kill him?"—the judge backs off. "Trescott, you fool," he says, *gently.* The adverb is crucial, for Hagenthorpe has understood, finally, that the position he has been advancing is in fact a call to murder, and doctors are not in the business of murdering their patients; their job is to keep them alive. "It is hard for a man to know what to do," the judge says. Trescott agrees. He is not impervious to what the judge has been trying to tell him, but the judge is wrong, and he knows that he is wrong, even if his argument makes sense. Such is the power of this critical scene. Once again, Crane is walking along the dividing line between coherence and a blur, the uncertain, ambivalent zone in which objects lose their definition in space and can no longer be identified as this thing or that thing with any assurance. The empirical categories have broken down. In the first part of *The Monster*, Crane has already shown how this ambivalence can be applied to countries as well—a land of the free in which all are not free, a land of equals in which all are not equal—and in the second part he uses it to examine the question of morals. The conundrum of *what to do* is presented in the conversation between the doctor and the judge, which comes to an end, fittingly, with the judge repeating the words *It is hard for a man to know what to do.* After that, Crane lifts his dividing line off the ground and turns it into a high wire. He puts the doctor on the wire, and in the thirteen chapters that follow, we watch him walk on it, step by precarious step, waiting for him to fall.

Time passes between the end of the dinner and the beginning of the next scene, enough time for Johnson to have recovered sufficiently to stand on his own feet and totter forward without help. Late one night, Trescott returns from seeing his last patient, escorts Johnson out of the judge's house, and hustles him off in a carriage to another part of town—the black part of town, where the doctor will be paying for his new lodgings with the family of Johnson's old friend Alek Williams. If the plan succeeds, Trescott will be able to carry on with his own affairs (providing for his family, attending to his medical practice) and at the same time be close enough to keep a constant watch on his patient.

The burned man is covered from head to heels in "an old-fashioned ulster." Not only does Crane not want to distract the reader by describing the gruesome damage inflicted on Johnson's body, he says nothing about the condition of Johnson's face. One assumes that the bandages have come off, but not then nor at any subsequent moment in the story does Crane attempt to describe the face of a man who has no face. Other characters will see it, of course, and all of them will be horrified when they do, but his readers are left to imagine it for themselves.

Two important things are revealed in this chapter, although neither one of them is explicitly told. During the carriage ride across town, Crane quickly establishes that Johnson can still talk—a happy surprise—but then, as we listen to him laugh and respond to the doctor's comments, it soon becomes clear that he is no longer right in the head. The fire has damaged his brain, and he now has the mental capacity of an idiot. A jovial one, it would seem, but as the judge had predicted earlier, he can no longer follow what people are saying to him or form a single coherent thought. The second thing concerns the doctor. Until now, he has been presented as a noble figure, a worthy man of principle who has assumed his moral obligation with uncommon grace and tenacity, but after he pulls the carriage into the Williamses' yard, we learn the darker truth about him: he is under immense pressure, the weight of his decision to stand by Johnson and protect him has strained his inner resources, and he is ready to snap. Alek Williams, the husband of Mary and the father of six children, comes out to welcome the doctor and greet his friend Henry, but when Johnson steps into the light,

> Williams gasped for a second, and then yelled the yell of a man stabbed in the heart.
>
> For a fraction of a moment Trescott seemed to be looking for epithets. Then he roared: "You old black chump! You old black—Shut up! Shut up! Do you hear?"
>
> Williams obeyed instantly in the matter of his screams, but he continued in a lower voice: "Ma Lode amassy! Who'd ever think? Ma Lode amassy!"

Trescott spoke again in the manner of a commander of a battalion. "Alek!"

The old negro again surrendered, but to himself he repeated in a whisper, "Ma Lode!" He was aghast and trembling.

The doctor's outburst destroys the illusion that we are about to settle in for a comforting, sentimental drama of a heroic white doctor who stands up to defend the rights of a cruelly treated black servant, with a chorus of exquisitely sung Negro spirituals swelling in the wings. Trescott is a flawed and conflicted man, a real person. Johnson is a lump of human wreckage. Alek Williams is a fool, and his six little children, who jump behind the stove after they catch their first glimpse of the monster, are six frightened children.

Following a somewhat rambling chapter in which Williams renegotiates his weekly stipend with the judge (his family is terrorized by Johnson and he wants more), the narrative moves along swiftly, jumping from one part of town to another in a succession of harsh cinematic cuts, thrusting the reader into each self-contained episode as a fully elaborated portrait of this or that sliver of Whilomville life. In Reifsnyder's barbershop, four men discuss and disagree about whether Trescott was right or wrong to save Johnson's life. One of them mentions that a grocery-van driver named Johnnie Bernard saw "a terrible thing" in front of Alek Williams's shanty and couldn't eat for the next two days, which leads the men to wander off into morbid speculations about the doctor's burden and "how it feels to be without a face." When Williams returns home triumphantly after persuading the judge to lift his salary from five to six dollars a week, he and his wife tiptoe cautiously into Johnson's silent room and discover that their boarder has escaped. The action then shifts abruptly to a house in a white middle-class neighborhood. A little girl named Theresa Page is giving a party. After a long series of arguments with her mother, her father finally stepped in and said, "Oh, let her have it," and now the party is underway, with ten little boys and nine little girls sitting "primly" at the dining room table as Theresa and her mother serve them slices from the five different cakes her mother has prepared for the occasion, along with ice cream and "a vast amount of lemonade." In no time at all, we are deep in the world of children's games and the divisions that separate the girl faction from the boy faction. After the cake, two of the girls sit down on a sofa with their backs to the window, "beaming lovingly upon each other" in order to snub the boys, and when one of them hears a rustling at the window, she turns around to see what it is. An instant later, she is screaming and covering her face with her hands. The others look, but whatever was there a moment ago is now gone, and even after some of the boys pluck up their courage and venture out into the darkness, they still find nothing. The shuddering, weeping girl insists on going home, but once she gets there, "She was not coherent even to her mother. Was it a man? She didn't know. It was simply a thing, a dreadful thing."

Back on the Farraguts' rickety porch at No. 7 Watermelon Alley, Belle, her young brother, Sim, and their obese mother are "howl[ing] gossip" to their neighbors, who are likewise planted on their own rickety porches, when an "it" appears before them and makes "a low and sweeping bow." This is the monster, a thing that strikes such terror in them that they immediately start scrambling back into the house. The "blubbering" Belle, too weak in the knees to stand, is reduced to crawling on all fours. And still, as a baby cries in one house and a marital spat erupts in another, the polite and "genial monster" continues to bow. "It" says: "Don't make no botheration 'bout me, Miss Fa'gut. . . . No, 'deed. I gwine ax you to go to er daince with me, Miss Fa'gut. I ax you if I can have the magnifer-cent gratitude of you' company on that 'casion, Miss Fa'gut." Belle finally manages to get into the house, but the monster follows her in, removes its hat, and repeats its courtly, well-mannered request. The panicked girl says nothing, and as she throws herself onto the floor, the monster sits "on the edge of [a] chair gabbing courteous invitations, and holding the old hat daintily to its stomach." In the meantime, Mrs. Farragut runs out of the house through the back door, and in spite of her "enormous weight," she manages to climb over a tall wooden fence in the yard. Terror mixed with slapstick, with a dash of racial condescension thrown into the pot as well (*black people can be so silly*), but the scene confirms that the mentally impaired Johnson is a peaceful, unaggressive soul and has no intention of frightening or harming anyone. It is also the last time we hear him talk. From now on, he will only hum to himself—softly.

The Trescotts' house is in the final stages of rebuilding. As the doctor sits at the desk in his refurbished laboratory, the police chief is telling him that Johnson was found "shambling around the streets" early that morning, but where he spent the night is a mystery. For now, the police have "jugged him" for his own protection, but as he has done nothing wrong and cannot be charged with any crime, they are planning to let him go, to which the doctor says: "I'll come down and get him." The chief continues:

> "Must say he had a fine career while he was out. First thing he did was to break up a children's party at Page's. Then he went to Watermelon Alley. Whoo! He stampeded the whole outfit. Men, women, and children running pell-mell, and yelling. They say one old woman broke her leg, or

something, shinning over a fence. Then he went right out on the main street, and an Irish girl threw a fit, and there was a sort of a riot. He began to run, and a big crowd chased him, firing rocks. But he gave them the slip somehow down there by the foundry and in the railway yard. We looked for him all night, but couldn't find him."

"Was he hurt any? Did anybody hit him with a stone?"

"Guess there isn't much of him to hurt any more, is there? Guess he's been hurt up to the limit. No. They never touched him. Of course nobody really wanted to hit him, but you know how a crowd gets. It's like—it's like—"

"Yes, I know."

The doctor is in a fix. Beyond the disturbing news that Johnson has been pelted with stones, and beyond the fear that he might run into another, more hostile crowd in the future (*you know how it can get with them*), there is the failure of the plan to house Johnson with Alek Williams, which has turned everything upside down and put Trescott back at zero, still looking at the same problem he thought he had already solved: What to do? But there is more, an entire bucketload of more. The chief starts talking about the little girl who was scared at the party—Jake Winter's daughter—who turns out to be "pretty sick, they say." Trescott is surprised. He is the Winters' family doctor, and if the girl is sick, the parents would have called him. "Well—you know," the chief says, "Winter is—well, Winter has gone clean crazy over this business. He wanted—he wanted to have you arrested." The doctor has no idea what he is talking about. "Have me arrested? The idiot! What in the name of wonder would he have me arrested for?"

"Oh, it's a lot of chin about your having no right to allow this—this—this man to be at large. But I told him to tend to his own business. Only I thought I'd better let you know. And I might as well say right now, doctor, that there is a good deal of talk about this thing. If I were you, I'd come to the jail pretty late at night, because there is likely to be a crowd around the door, and I'd bring a—er—mask, or some kind of veil, anyhow."

A crowd gathered outside a jail suggests a mob, and *mob* under these circumstances suggests the possibility of a lynching. The threat of violence is suddenly in the air, and with the incensed Jake Winter clamoring for the doctor's arrest, poor Henry Johnson is not the only person in danger. If a monster is at large, then surely the creator of the monster is the guilty one in the affair, for Trescott has unleashed a contagion into the bloodstream of Whilomville, and, as the sympathetic chief has warned the doctor, Winter is not the only one pointing a finger at him. *The whole town is talking about it.*

Cut to another chapter, and no sooner do we land in Martha Goodwin's kitchen than we hear what that talk is saying. "A woman of great mind," the ferocious Martha is one of Crane's most vivid satirical inventions, and she serves as his partially demented, truth-telling Cassandra, "the most savage critic in town." In this chapter, she is merely introduced, but three chapters later, when she swings into action, we get to see what she is made of. For starters, however, there is this:

> She had adamantine opinions about the situation in Armenia, the condition of women in China, the flirtation between Mrs. Minster of Niagara Avenue and young Griscom, the conflict in the Bible class of the Baptist Sunday-school, the duty of the United States toward the Cuban insurgents, and many other colossal matters. Her fullest experience of violence was gained on an occasion when she had seen a hound clubbed, but in the plan which she had made for the reform of the world she advocated drastic measures. For instance, she contended that all the Turks should be pushed into the sea and drowned, and that Mrs. Minster and young Griscom should be hanged side by side on twin gallows. In fact, this woman of peace, who had seen only peace, argued constantly for a creed of illimitable ferocity. She was invulnerable on these questions, because eventually she overrode all opponents with a sniff. This sniff was an active force. It was to her antagonists like a bang over the head, and none was known to recover from this expression of exalted contempt. It left them windless and conquered. They never again came forward as candidates for suppression. And Martha walked her kitchen with a stern brow, an invincible being like Napoleon.

That day, one of Martha's acolytes rushes in to share the latest news with her. "Henry Johnson got away from where they was keeping him," Carrie Dungen says, "and came to town last night, and scared everybody almost to death." Martha lets out an emphatic "Well!"—which carries the force of a triumphant "I told you so!"—and then says: "This, my prophecy, has come to pass." Carrie Dungen rattles on about little Sadie Winter and how sick she is and how her father is trying to get Dr. Trescott arrested and how there is a crowd around the jail "all the time." At that point, Martha's sister, "a shivery little woman" named Kate, abandons the novel she has been reading upstairs and enters the kitchen to put in her own two cents.

> "Serves him right if he was to lose all his patients," she said suddenly, in blood-thirsty tones. She snipped her words out as if her lips were scissors.
>
> "Well, he's likely to," shouted Carrie Dungen. "Don't a lot of people say that they won't have him anymore? If you're sick and nervous, Doctor Trescott would scare the life out of you, wouldn't he? He would me. I'd keep thinking."
>
> Martha, stalking to and fro . . . surveyed the two other women with a contemplative frown.

Each shift of setting is accompanied by a shift in tone, but through it all Crane continues to advance his story and provide new information, for now we have learned (if Carrie Dungen's information is correct) that Winter isn't the only patient who has abandoned Dr. Trescott. And even if what she has said isn't true, this is the gossip spreading through the town, and as long as there are enough people willing to believe it, gossip is always true.

Jimmie and his mother have returned from Connecticut. Nothing is said about his physical condition, and in this novella of large temporal gaps and immense authorial silences, one can only assume that the boy's skin has healed and he will carry no permanent scars. After the lushly detailed prose in the first half of *The Monster*, the prose in the rapidly moving second half is pared down to skeletal thinness to enhance the speed of the storytelling. There are a few pauses for breath (the passage about Martha Goodwin, for example), but for the most part Crane is rushing forward to create an effect of simultaneity (Carrie Dungen is talking to Martha Goodwin at the same time the police chief is talking to Trescott), and rather than put in the things that have always captured his attention (light passing through the branches of a tree, a thought passing through a character's head), he leaves out as much as he possibly can. The scope of his material has widened—taking in a greater number of characters than ever before, people from all classes and all parts of town, a microcosm of all society—but his method has narrowed to the most stringent form of minimalism: to say the most he can in the fewest words he can. It is a method he applied only to the second half of *The Monster*. To do what he was hoping to do, he felt that the nature of these chapters demanded it, but in other stories still to come he would use other methods to fit the demands of those works. Crane never stopped experimenting. For now, he had become a minimalist, but in the end it was just one more instrument to be used when necessary, another monkey wrench added to his writer's bag of tools.

> After his return from Connecticut, little Jimmie was at first much afraid of the monster who lived in the room over the carriage-house. He could not identify it in any way. Gradually, however, his fear dwindled under the influence of a weird fascination. He sidled into closer and closer relations with it.
>
> One time the monster was seated on a box behind the stable basking in the rays of the afternoon sun. A heavy crêpe veil was swathed about its head.

Johnson is back in his old room, then, and his protector has followed the police chief's advice and covered the monster's head with a veil. And there is Jimmie with a large gang of his friends in the yard, showing off the freak of the Trescott household to the assembly of gaping, frightened boys. A chilling scene unfolds in which young Jim presides as master of ceremonies over a game of dare and bravado that will turn him into "the hero of the mob." When challenged to touch the thing sitting on the box, "he went to the monster and laid his hand delicately on its shoulder. 'Hello, Henry,' he said, in a voice that trembled a trifle. The monster was crooning a weird line of negro melody that was scarcely more than a thread of sound, and it paid no heed to the boy." Turning in triumph, Jimmie then dares the boy who dared him to perform the same exploit, and on it goes until Mrs. Hannigan in the next yard notices that her son Eddie is standing with the others and screeches at him, "as if she was being murdered," to come home "this minute!" Dr. Trescott returns a bit later and promptly sends the whole lot of them packing. The next morning, he sits down to have a talk with his boy. When Jimmie explains what he and the others had been doing,

> Trescott groaned deeply. His countenance was so clouded in sorrow that the lad, bewildered by the mystery of it, burst suddenly forth in dismal lamentations. "There, there. Don't cry, Jim," said Trescott, going round the desk. "Only—" He sat in a great leather reading-chair, and took the boy on his knee. "Only I want to explain to you—"

What he says, of course, is not given, but the reader has no trouble filling in the blanks.

A fellow doctor in town has been called away to care for his dying sister and asks Trescott to fill in for him while he is gone. Trescott is glad to accommodate him, and the next morning, armed with a file of medical histories from Dr. Moser, he goes to the first name on the list. It happens to be Winter, but somehow—strangely—this does not strike Trescott as "an important fact." One asks why. The Winters have dismissed him as their doctor, and Trescott has been told that Jake Winter has gone so far as to demand his arrest. Are those not important facts, and shouldn't Trescott feel somewhat wary about going to their house? Too naïve for his own good, he has failed to understand how thoroughly Winter and others in town have turned against him. He rings the bell, and when Mrs. Winter opens the door, he says good morning to her—*cheerfully*. He explains that he is filling in for Dr. Moser, and the flummoxed woman looks at him "in stony surprise." As she rushes off to find her husband, Trescott enters the house and goes into the sitting room. Winter appears at the doorway and bluntly asks, "What do you want?" "What do I want?" Trescott replies. "What do I want?"—and suddenly he understands, at long last, what kind of situation he is in. Pushing home the point in the most dramatic terms, Crane adds: "He had heard an utterly new challenge in the night of the jungle."

"'Yes, that's what I want to know,' snapped Winter. 'What do you want?'"

Trying to stay calm, Trescott looks over the notes he has been given and says that the little girl's case looks "a trifle serious." He advises Winter to consult another doctor and then transcribes Moser's remarks into his notebook. As he starts to leave, he tears out the page and hands it to Winter, but Winter shrinks back and the page flutters to the floor.

> "Good morning," said Trescott from the hall. This placid retreat seemed to suddenly arouse Winter to ferocity. It was as if he had then recalled all the truths which he had formulated to hurl at Trescott. So he followed him into the hall, and down the hall to the door, and through the door to the porch, barking in fiery rage from a respectful distance. As Trescott imperturbably turned the mare's head down the road, Winter stood on the porch, still yelping. He was like a little dog.

Back in Martha Goodwin's kitchen, Carrie Dungen is bursting with news. Everyone knows about the "awful scene" that took place this morning and how Jake Winter told Dr. Trescott "just what he thought of him." Mrs. Howarth (a wink to Cora) "heard it through her front blinds" and "it's all over town now," the *it* being that Winter told the doctor that Sadie hasn't been well since the night Henry Johnson scared her at the party and that he holds the doctor responsible and how dare he "cross his threshold—and—and—and—" But no, Martha says, interrupting the conversation between Carrie and her sister, Sadie isn't the least bit sick and has been going to school "almost the whole time." When the others refuse to accept this, "Martha wheeled from the sink. She held an iron spoon, and it seemed as if she was about to attack them. 'Sadie Winter has passed here many a morning since then carrying her school-bag. Where was she going? To a wedding?'" Furthermore—delivered in a loud voice: "If I had been Doctor Trescott, I'd have knocked that miserable Jake Winter's head off."

Carrie regroups, and "gaining support and sympathy from Kate's smile," boldly comes back at Martha:

> "I don't see how anybody can be blamed for getting angry when their little girl gets almost scared to death and gets sick from it, and all that. Besides, everybody says—"
>
> "Oh, I don't care what everybody says," said Martha.
>
> "Well, you can't go against the whole town," answered Carrie, in sudden sharp defiance.
>
> "No, Martha, you can't go against the whole town," piped Kate, following her leader rapidly.
>
> "'The whole town,'" cried Martha. I'd like to know what you call 'the whole town.' Do you call these silly people who are scared of Henry Johnson 'the whole town'?"

But . . . but, Carrie replies, Henry Johnson *is* scary, and "Everybody's afraid of him." Martha contemptuously asks her how she can know that when she hasn't even seen him herself, and Carrie's only defense is to fall back on her familiar line of reasoning: "Everybody says so."

And then, suddenly switching to another topic, she adds—just in case Martha hasn't heard—that the Hannigans are selling their house and moving to another part of town.

"'On account of him?' demanded Martha."

Yes, on account of him.

Autumn. The maple trees of Whilomville have turned crimson and yellow, and as the little boys watch the leaves fall to the ground, they "dream of the near time when they could heap bushels in the streets and burn them during the abrupt evenings." Judge Hagenthorpe and three of the town's most "active and influential citizens" are walking down Niagara Avenue together to pay a call on Dr. Trescott. The delegation is led by a man with the peculiar name of John Twelve, the wholesale grocer, who is worth four hundred thousand dollars "and reported to be worth over a million." Chapter 12 of the Book of John begins with several pointed references to the resurrection of Lazarus, the most astounding of the miracles performed by Jesus. Dr. Trescott has pulled off a similar miracle in bringing Henry Johnson back from the dead, and while Crane is not comparing the doctor to Jesus, both have defied the laws of nature and are cast under suspicion because of it. (Hagenthorpe at the dinner: "Nature has very evidently given him up. He is dead. You are restoring him to life.") In John, the miracle draws an army of new followers to Jesus, but it is also the act that inspires the Pharisees and numerous others to turn against him, and when Jesus enters Jerusalem on what is now called Palm Sunday, the story everyone knows inches toward its climax. In his role as doctor, Trescott has followed his Christian duty by healing a wounded man through the rigorous protocols of medical science, but in doing so he has also created a monster, a thing that has infected Whilomville with a new strain of disease—an epidemic of fear—and unless that thing is removed from their midst, the town will spin further and further out of control. The four distinguished men who call on Trescott are representatives of the status quo, and they have taken it upon themselves to solve the problem. They are exceedingly gracious and sympathetic toward the doctor, but while they pretend to admire what he is doing and claim to have his best interests at heart, they are practical men, hypocritical men, and won't think twice about abandoning any ethical principles they might possess or think they possess to restore order to the town.

As John Twelve begins to speak, Trescott turns his eyes toward the judge, hoping for a small sign of support, but the old man is resting his chin on his cane and refuses to look in his direction. They all like him, Twelve says to the doctor, but they're afraid he will ruin himself if he carries on like this much longer. He isn't ruining himself, Trescott says. All right, Twelve concedes, but he is doing himself a great deal of harm. "You have changed from the leading doctor of the town to about the last one. It is mainly because there are always a large number of people who are very thoughtless fools, of course, but then that doesn't change the condition." Another man, nameless, blurts out: "It's the women." They all ignore him, and Twelve continues: "Even if there are a lot of fools in the world, we can't see any reason why you should ruin yourself opposing them. You can't teach them anything, you know." With a weary smile, Trescott says he's not trying to teach them anything, but when he starts to explain himself, the words come out as an incoherent stammer: "I—it is a matter of—well—" Again the nameless man blurts out, "It's the women," and again the others ignore him. Twelve proposes that they "get Johnson a place somewhere ... up in the valley," but Trescott cuts him off and says that no one can care for him as well as he does. Thrown by this, Twelve begins to talk about the "little no-good farm" he was planning to give Henry, and after a few moments, he, too, begins to stammer. "And if you—and if you—if you—through your house burning down, or anything—why, all the boys were prepared to take him right off your hands, and—and—" The penultimate chapter ends in a standoff. Trescott won't budge, and the others have run out of ideas.

> Trescott arose and went to the window. He turned his back upon them. They sat waiting in silence. When he returned he kept his face in the shadow. "No, John Twelve," he said, "it can't be done."
>
> There was another stillness. Suddenly a man stirred on his chair.
>
> "Well, then, a public institution—" he began.
>
> "No," said Trescott; "public institutions are all very good, but he is not going to one."
>
> In the background of the group old Judge Hagenthorpe was thought-fully smoothing the polished ivory head of his cane.

Another jump forward in time. It is winter, and as Trescott returns home one evening, he "stamped the snow from his feet and shook the flakes from his shoulders." He enters the house, and when he walks into the sitting room, he finds Jimmie alone there, "reading painfully in a large book concerning giraffes and tigers and crocodiles." The doctor asks the boy where his mother is, but Jimmie isn't sure. Probably upstairs, he says.

Trescott goes to the foot of the stairs and calls out to her, but no one answers. He goes up, enters a small, dimly lit drawing room, and sees his wife "curled in an armchair." He asks if she heard him calling to her, but again she doesn't answer, and as he bends down over the chair to see what's wrong, he hears her "trying to smother a sob in the cushion." Alarmed, he asks her why she is crying, but the response she gives is not a response so much as an evasion: "I've got a headache, a dreadful head-ache, Ned."

> He pulled a chair close to hers. Later, as he cast his eye over the zone of light shed by the dull red panes, he saw that a low table had been drawn

close to the stove, and that it was burdened with many small cups and plates of uncut tea-cake. He remembered that the day was Wednesday, and that his wife received on Wednesdays.

"Who was here to-day, Gracie?" he asked.

From his shoulder there came a mumble, "Mrs. Twelve."

"Was she—um," he said. "Why—didn't Anna Hagenthorpe come over?"

The mumble from his shoulder continued. "She wasn't well enough."

Glancing down at the cups, Trescott mechanically counted them. There were fifteen of them. "There, there," he said. "Don't cry, Grace. Don't cry."

The wind was whining around the house and the snow beat aslant upon the windows. Sometimes the coal in the stove settled with a crumbling sound and the four panes of mica flushed a sudden new crimson. As he sat holding her head on his shoulder, Trescott found himself occasionally trying to count the cups. There were fifteen of them.

It is a supremely quiet and restrained ending, a subdued whimper that nevertheless carries the full, annihilating force of the bang the reader might have been expecting, for this is the way the world ends, and with this small scene in the dimly lit second-floor room, it has most definitely come to an end. The Trescotts have been pushed out. They no longer have a place in the town where they have lived and thrived for years, secure in their assumptions about what their community represents, and now that those assumptions have proven to be false, where are they? They are here and yet not here, trapped in a singular form of exile that has condemned them to live as internal émigrés in their own corner of the world, in the very rooms of their own house, and the hidden, implied tragedy of the story is that they will be stuck in this in-between no-place forever. Where could they possibly go? The doctor has pledged himself to watch over the monster for as long as he lives, and nothing will ever sway him from that commitment. Henry Johnson has become a part of who he is now, and wherever he goes, Johnson will go, too. If they tried to start again in another place, it would only turn out to be another Whilomville.

In this book of small, exploding fragments, religion is never so much as even mentioned. Church bells ring, but no one is seen in the churches, no one invokes the name of God, and no minister or priest has any role to play in the community. By introducing a character named John Twelve, however, Crane is all but begging the reader to open the Book of John and reread the twelfth chapter. We know how conflicted he was about the religion of his parents and the Christian soldiers of the Whilom drum corps, but Crane knew his Bible well, so well that his prose often carries the rhythms of the King James version deep inside its music, and now that he has alluded to the Book of John in the figure of John Twelve, I wonder if he wasn't thinking about another verse from another book when John Twelve says to Trescott that he has "changed from the leading doctor in the town to about the last one," which seems to echo the well-known verse from chapter 20 of the Book of Matthew: "So the last shall be first, and the first last: for many be called, but few chosen." Has Trescott been called, and if so, has he been chosen? And if he has been chosen—chosen for what? There is only one plausible answer that comes to mind: for martyrdom. "No, John Twelve," he says, "it can't be done." And with those words he aligns himself with the martyred Henry Johnson against the white men who control the town and becomes a martyr himself. The black man and the white man will henceforth share the same destiny.

God bless America, and long may it wave.

9

THE BRIDE COMES TO YELLOW SKY.

A tragedy followed by a comedy. A shift in tone as drastic as a jump from *King Lear* to *As You Like It*, but for all the differences between them, both works are the product of the same imagination, and each one is generated by a series of intractable human conflicts. I mention Shakespeare not to compare him to Crane but because he is the purest example of a writer with a mind large enough and flexible enough to understand that every human being is a collection of many beings and that if I weep today and curse the day I was born, tomorrow I could spring out of bed asking myself what I want for breakfast—scrambled, over easy, or hard-boiled. The line that separates tragedy from comedy is thin, and in Shakespeare's plays the only difference between the two is what happens in the final act. In *Lear*, half the characters are lying dead on the stage. In *As You Like It*, everyone gets married and lives happily ever after. With Crane's comedy, the twist is that the story begins with a marriage and plays out in reverse, and even if no one dies at the end, there is plenty of human conflict along the way— enough to keep the reader guessing until the last moment.

Both *The Monster* and "The Bride Comes to Yellow Sky" are studies in spiritual dislocation. Each one is set in a rural backwater—a small town in New York State and a microscopic Texas village just north of the Rio Grande—and as each place is transformed from something familiar and solid into something alien and incomprehensible, the central characters are forced to cope with the altered reality that has sprung up around them. In *The Monster*, chance is the agent of disruption (a fire), whereas in Crane's Western, time is the destabilizing force that upends the old traditions and ultimately destroys them. The novella ends in devastation. The story comes to a stop with a brief, resonant guffaw.

Jack Potter, the veteran marshal of Yellow Sky, has gone off to San Antonio and found himself a bride, and as the story opens the newly-weds are sitting on a train and barreling toward the marshal's hometown, which is due west from their starting point, but "a glance from the window seemed . . . to prove that the plains of Texas were pouring eastward." A common misperception, often experienced on trains, and by slipping it into the first sentence, Crane is subtly announcing the premise that will drive his little work forward: the East has moved in on the West, and the days of the wild frontier are done. He had been thinking about this ever since his travels through Texas two and a half years earlier, and now he was going to bring it to life by showing what happens when the march of civilization runs into its last, ornery holdout and wins a gunfight without firing a gun.

Potter and his new wife are a pair of middle-aged innocents on a once-in-a-lifetime journey, and they are decked out in new clothes that are as strange to them as the fact that they are now married. The sunburned, windburned Potter looks down "respectfully" at his black suit and sits there "with a hand on each knee, like a man waiting in a barber shop." His bride, who is neither pretty nor "very young," is embarrassed by her unaccustomed finery and blushes whenever one of the other passengers looks at her. But they are both happy, "very happy," and fairly stunned by the "dazzling fittings of the coach"—the plush green velvet, the shining brass and silver, the gleaming polished wood. However awkward or intimidated they might feel, Potter is determined to make the most of this once-in-a-lifetime opportunity. A bit later, they will go to the dining car, he says, and have the "finest meal in the world." It costs a dollar, he adds, to emphasize how excellent the food will be, and when his timid bride says, "That's too much—for us—ain't it, Jack?," the marshal "bravely" replies: "Not this trip, anyhow. We're going to go the whole thing."

In *The Monster*, Reifsnyder the barber makes a passing reference to Pullman car porters, the all-black contingent of railway employees that was formed in the late 1860s when George Pullman began hiring ex-slaves to serve the white passengers who rode in his newly invented sleeping cars. In the thirty years since then, the porters had established a reputation for elegance, efficiency, and impeccable decorum—the American version of the British valet for long-distance train travelers. No matter how rudely or condescendingly they were treated, the porters could never let down their guard, which made them the most doubled of all the split-in-two black men trapped in Du Bois's no-man's-land of "double consciousness." Writing just three years after the bloody Pullman Strike of 1894, and perhaps wanting to provide a comic antidote to the poisonous black-white relations depicted in *The Monster*, Crane plants one of these gentlemanly porters on the train to Yellow Sky, and it is through him that we come to understand the full depth of the couple's naïveté and unworldliness.

> To the minds of the pair, their surroundings reflected the glory of their marriage that morning in San Antonio. This was the environment of their new estate, and the man's face in particular beamed with an elation that made him appear ridiculous to the negro porter. This individual at times surveyed them from afar with an amused and superior grin. On other occasions he bullied them with skill that did not make it exactly plain to them that they were being bullied. He subtly used all the manners of the most unconquerable kind of snobbery. He oppressed them, but of this oppression they had small knowledge, and they speedily forgot that infrequently a number of travelers covered them with stares of derisive enjoyment. Historically there was supposed to be something infinitely humorous in their situation.

Historically. Another one of Crane's odd word choices, but nevertheless apt and fully congruent with his deeper purpose. History in this case refers not only to the situation on the train but to the history of Yellow Sky, and in that town Potter is a "man known, liked, and feared in his corner, a prominent person," and as the train approaches its destination, the marshal is feeling more and more unsettled by what he has done—slinking off to San Antonio to get married "without consulting Yellow Sky"—and by shirking his duty toward his friends, or at least what he perceives to be his duty, he is committing "an extraordinary crime." He knows that people in Yellow Sky marry one another "as it pleased them in accordance with a general custom," but Potter is different from the others because he is the lawman of the town. He holds himself to a higher standard, and therefore "his deed weighed upon him like a leaden slab."

A strange form of self-punishment, it would seem, but perhaps a bit less strange when one considers that Potter's guilt is the same guilt Crane was feeling when he began work on the story. He had just moved to England

and set up house with Cora, where they were living as man and wife, but he had kept the marriage hidden from his family in America and would go on hiding it for close to a year and a half, too embarrassed by the nature of that marriage to tell them the truth. In Potter's case, there is no ocean to protect him from discovery, and the news is bound to get out quickly once he returns, but still, hoping to defer the moment of reckoning as long as he can, he plans to use "all the devices of speed and plains-craft in making the journey from the station to his house." The train pulls into Yellow Sky. "With all his airy superiority gone," the porter brushes off the marshal's new clothes, and Crane adds one more detail to underscore the lawman's discomfort with the posh world of big-city refinement: "Potter fumbled out a coin and gave it to the porter as he had seen others do. It was a heavy and muscle-bound business, as that of a man shoeing his first horse." Bags in hand, Potter and his bride scurry away from the station, not even pausing to talk to the station agent, who is running toward them and waving his arms as he sprints along the platform. Potter assumes that the man wants to congratulate him on his marriage, but in fact the agent knows nothing about it. He is trying to warn the marshal that Scratchy Wilson is back in town, all boozed up and itching for a fight. The reader doesn't know that yet, however—and neither does Potter, who is walking home with his bride on his arm, praying that no one will see them.

The second part of the four-part story begins with a small chronological displacement—similar to the one in *The Monster* when the fire alarms ring out before the fire has been seen, but this time the jump is backward rather than forward, and there we are in the Weary Gentleman saloon, precisely twenty-one minutes before the California Express makes its stop at Yellow Sky. It is a purely functional scene, inserted to provide the necessary background about badman Scratchy Wilson and his ongoing, yearslong battle with lawman Jack Potter, but Crane is so fully in command of his subject here, and taking such pleasure in the multiple ironies oozing from his sentences, that it hardly makes a difference. From the dog lying in front of the saloon door—"His head was on his paws, and he glanced drowsily here and there with the constant vigilance of a dog that is kicked on occasion"—to the man at the bar saying, "There'll be some shootin'— some good shootin'," Crane is both parodying the dime-novel Westerns of his boyhood and embracing their conventions in order to advance his ideas about the mutating realities of contemporary America. He also uses the classic device of putting a newcomer in the midst of the Weary Gentleman regulars so they will have to explain to him (and us) why the barkeeper decides to bolt the doors of the saloon. "It means, my friend," someone answers in response to the stranger's question, "that for the next two hours this town won't be a health resort." It is all so transparent, and so playfully executed, that one would have to be half dead not to find it funny. Scratchy Wilson, we are told, is the last one left from the gang of outlaws "that used to hang out along the river here," and even though he "wouldn't hurt a fly" when sober, "he's a terror when he's drunk." They all know that Jack Potter is out of town and fervently wish he were here today: "He shot Wilson up once—in the leg—and he would sail in here and pull out the kinks in this thing." Without Potter, those kinks mean trouble, for "this here Scratchy Wilson is a wonder with a gun—a perfect wonder." A few moments after that, they hear a shot fired in the distance, "followed by three wild howls."

The gunman is approaching the saloon, and as Crane cuts outside to begin the third chapter, he presents us with a singular display of sartorial weirdness: "A man in a maroon-colored shirt . . . made, principally, by some Jewish women on the east side of New York. . . . And his boots had red tops with gilded imprints, of the kind beloved in winter by little sledding boys on the hillsides of New England."

The rugged outlaw turns out to be a dandy, a clownish fop, a Beau Brummell of the plains. From one sentence to the next, the dime-novel talk in the saloon has given way to satire, and beyond the blindsiding wit of the passage, it is wholly on point. The East has infiltrated the West so thoroughly by now that even the most notorious Texas bandit struts around town in a shirt made by small Jewish hands in a New York sweatshop, and his tough-guy feet are shod in a pair of quaint, ornamented cold-weather boots—shipped straight from the snowy mountaintops of Vermont. Not such a fearsome character, after all, but something of a fool, a man who has become so ridiculous that he deserves to be laughed at or, even worse, pitied.

Wilson, however, has no idea that he is ridiculous. In his own eyes, he is still the baddest cuss this side of tomorrow, and as he wanders drunkenly through the empty streets of Yellow Sky with "a long, heavy, blue-black revolver" in each hand, his loud, full-throated yells fly over the roofs and are answered by no one. The entire population is cowering indoors, and "it was as if the surrounding stillness formed the arch of a tomb over him." With that one word, *tomb*, Crane is signaling the end of Scratchy and the bygone world that made him. The old West is dead, the twentieth century is just over the horizon, but Scratchy still hasn't received the news. He doesn't understand that he is little more than a ghost now, and yet—here's the rub—with a long, blue-black revolver firmly clenched in each hand, even a ghost can be dangerous.

He wants to fight someone. He is desperate to fight someone, but for all his threats and shouting, no one answers his challenge. Drifting toward the Weary Gentleman saloon, he sees the dog lying in front and points his revolver at it, "humorously." The dog jumps up and starts to walk away, but when Scratchy lets out another one of his full-throated yells, the dog breaks into a gallop. Scratchy fires a shot and misses. The dog "screams" and charges off in another direction. Another shot, another miss. Scratchy laughs. Hard to tell if he was aiming to kill or just having fun. He knocks on the door of the saloon demanding a drink, and when the door remains shut, this "wonder with a gun" picks up a piece of paper, nails it to the building with a knife, walks across the street to shoot at it from a respectable distance, and misses by half an inch. Quite good, but not as good as advertised. He swears and walks off. One sentence later, he shoots out the windows of his best friend's house. Crane remarks: "The man was playing with the town. It was a toy for him." Still looking for a fight, growing more and more frustrated that he hasn't found anyone to fight, he begins thinking about Jack Potter and wonders if his "ancient antagonist" would be willing to have a go at it, but when he walks over to Potter's adobe house, no one is there. The chapter ends with Scratchy standing out front and cursing the house, which stares back at him "as might a great stone god."

The train has arrived by now, and Potter and his bride are walking toward the house. "Next corner, dear," the marshal says, and once they turn the corner, they find themselves "face to face with a man in a maroon-colored shirt." A gun comes out of its holster, and suddenly it is pointing "at the bridegroom's chest." The showdown plays out as follows:

> The two men faced each other at a distance of three paces. He of the revolver smiled with a new and quiet ferocity. "Tried to sneak up on me," he said. "Tried to sneak up on me!" His eyes grew more baleful. As Potter made a slight movement, the man thrust his revolver venomously forward. "No, don't you do it, Jack Potter. Don't you move a finger toward a gun just yet. Don't you move an eyelash. The time has come for me to settle with you, and I'm goin' to do it my own way and loaf along with no interferin'. So if you don't want a gun bent on you, just mind what I tell you."
>
> Potter looked at his enemy. "I ain't got a gun on me, Scratchy," he said. "Honest, I ain't." He was stiffening and steadying, but yet somewhere at the back of his mind a vision of the Pullman floated, the sea-green figured velvet, the shining brass, silver, and glass, the wood that gleamed as darkly brilliant as the surface of a pool of oil—all the glory of the

marriage, the environment of the new estate. "You know I fight when it comes to fighting, Scratchy Wilson, but I ain't got a gun on me. You'll have to do all the shootin' yourself."

His enemy's face went livid. He stepped forward and lashed his weapon to and fro before Potter's chest. "Don't you tell me you ain't got no gun on you, you whelp. Don't tell me no lie like that. There ain't a man in Texas ever seen you without no gun. Don't take me for no kid." His eyes blazed with light, and his throat worked like a pump.

"I ain't takin' you for no kid," answered Potter. His heels had not moved an inch backward. "I'm taking you for a——fool. I tell you I ain't got no gun, and I ain't. If you're goin' to shoot me up, you better begin now. You'll never get a chance like this again."

So much enforced reasoning had told on Wilson's rage. He was calmer. "If you ain't got a gun, why ain't you got a gun?" He sneered. "Been to Sunday-school?"

"I ain't got a gun because I've just come from San Anton' with my wife. I'm married," said Potter. "And if I'd thought there was going to be any galoots like you prowling around when I brought my wife home, I'd had a gun, and don't you forget it."

"Married!" said Scratchy, not at all comprehending.

"Yes, married. I'm married," said Potter distinctly.

"Married?" said Scratchy. Seemingly for the first time he saw the drooping drowning woman at the other man's side. "No!" he said. He was like a creature allowed a glimpse of another world. He moved a pace backward, and his arm with the revolver dropped to his side. "Is this—is this the lady?" he asked.

"Yes, this is the lady," answered Potter.

There was another period of silence.

"Well," said Wilson at last, slowly. "I s'pose it's all off now."

"It's all off if you say so, Scratchy. You know I didn't make trouble." Potter lifted his valise.

"Well, I 'low it's off, Jack," said Wilson. He was looking at the ground. "Married!" He was not a student of chivalry; it was merely that in the presence of this foreign condition he was a simple child of the earlier plains. He picked up his starboard revolver, and placing both weapons in their holsters, he went away. His feet made funnel-shaped tracks in the heavy sand.

A simple child of the earlier plains has been given a glimpse of another world, and as he makes his exit at the end, both mystified and defeated, the heavy sands he walks over are the sands of time, and even if he has left some tracks in that sand, a wind will blow in before long and cover them up forever.

In the end, the charm of the story lies not so much in the clash between opposing forces—past versus future, Potter versus Wilson—but in Crane's sympathy for both his protagonists and what each one represents. The anarchic gunman and the upright lawman are the two halves of Crane's doubled, divided soul—the restless boy and the maturing young man, Crane the gambler and adventurer who prowled the corners of lowlife slums and rushed headlong into wars and Crane the sober, conscientious man of principle, the hardworking writer and newly married ex-patriot who was anticipating a shared destiny with "a good and beautiful wife for many years." Crane was Scratchy Wilson, and Crane was Jack Potter, and he had just written his brightest comedy within weeks of finishing his darkest, most painful work. It was no longer a question of having to choose between one road and another road. There were two Cranes, and in that year of years, 1897, he had found a way to walk down both roads at the same time.

A couple of years later, he resurrected the two men from Yellow Sky and put them in a sequel, "Moonlight on the Snow," which was published barely a month before he died. In it, Potter has moved up from marshal to become the sheriff of the county, and as he rides into the west Texas town of War Post to stop a potential lynching, he is accompanied by his new deputy—Scratchy Wilson.

10

CORA SETTLED INTO DOMESTIC LIFE WITH HER CUSTOMARY FLAIR FOR jumping off mountains and landing on her feet. Her "new estate" as a woman married to a man who lacked the wealth of a Thompson, a Stivers, or even a Murphy was not a hardship for her as much as a challenge. A savvy observer of trends in women's fashion, she always managed to be smartly dressed for public occasions, but she invented a new and simpler style for daytime activities around the house, abandoning her elegant American footwear for a pair of Greek sandals that she'd commissioned from an Oxted shoemaker and walking around in a long, loosely flowing skirt and a puffy blouse with long sleeves and a tightly cinched bodice. It was a decidedly unconventional look for late Victorian England, and beyond the clothes there was the matter of her resplendent blond hair, which, in another break with convention, she often unpinned and wore trailing down her back, even when entertaining guests at Ravensbrook. As Gilkes notes, it was the same look that would later be perfected by Isadora Duncan—or, one might add, the flower children of the 1960s.

On quiet evenings, Crane played poker with Frederic, Barr, and other friends, but as time went on there were fewer and fewer quiet evenings. Word had gotten out that Stephen Crane was living in Oxted, and an influx of visitors began pouring into the house, all of them eager to rub shoulders with the young American star—who, of course, must have been loaded, one of the richest writers in the world. It became so overwhelming at times that Crane had to run off to London and hide out for two- and three-day stretches at Brown's Hotel on Albemarle Street in order to carry on with his work—adding one more expense to the growing list of household expenses. John Berryman neatly sums up the problem in his book:

> They came in hordes from London and America, to visit an old friend, to see the celebrity, to check up on the rumors, or to enjoy Cora's memorable cooking. They brought each other, they brought notes of introduction, they invited themselves and the Cranes invited them. Both Stephen and Cora Crane were hospitable. . . . Both were long-suffering. . . . But money was flowing out and not coming in. The house was full of guests and fruit and flowers—they would spend three or four pounds for flowers [fifteen or twenty dollars] for a dinner. . . . By the end of November they were half-crazy with guests.

A crisis was looming, and when Crane wrote to his agent Reynolds in October, the letter was more than just a business communication about fees, word counts, and contracts, it was an urgent cry for help. He begins by offering to make Reynolds his exclusive literary manager for ten percent of his earnings and then explains that the first job will be to get him "out of the ardent grasp of S.S. McClure Co." He believes he owes them five hundred dollars, but if Reynolds can negotiate a fair price for *The Monster* (twenty-one thousand words), perhaps that will wipe out the debt. No, maybe not all of it, but a good part of it in any case, and then there are the American rights for "The Bride" (forty-five hundred words), which he judges to be worth one hundred and seventy-five dollars. That story is "a daisy," he says, "and don't let them talk funny about it."

From there he moves on to the money that can be earned from newspaper work, telling Reynolds about the different fees he has been given by the *Herald* and the *World* and alerting him about a dispute he has been embroiled in with the *Journal*. "I have quite a big misunderstanding with them and can't get it pulled out straight. They say I am overdrawn. I say I am not." He has sent them his "Irish Notes"—written for the *Westminster Gazette* in England—hoping the *Journal* will publish the sketches in America, but they have not yet responded. He would be satisfied with twenty-five dollars per installment (hardly more than the cost of buying flowers for an Oxted dinner), and "if the *Journal* will explain why I am overdrawn I am the last man in the world to kick and will pay the a/c in work."

Last of all, he proposes a scheme to revive the Imogene Carter fashion and gossip column in as many newspapers as the market will bear. Promising to improve the quality and even to put his own name on the articles if that will help, he suggests that Reynolds go to Curtis Brown, "say how-how from me," and find out if he would be interested. Nothing came of it, but merely to propose such a thing proves that Crane, heralded as he was, was still prepared to roll up his sleeves and dig ditches if he had to. He signs off: "Write to me at once. Good luck to you."

Good luck. He had not yet reached the point of desperation, but he was becoming anxious, and if he didn't act now to shore up his defenses against the approaching flood, it wouldn't be long before the dam broke.

It didn't help, of course, that Mr. and Mrs. Crane were living on credit and had already piled up substantial bills from the local shops—the butcher, the greengrocer, the wine merchant—that they were in no position to pay. Not to speak of indulgences such as the foie gras and caviar they served to their mostly uninvited guests at Ravensbrook, but the world was watching, and they both felt they had to keep up appearances. Happy as they were together in their new estate, they were too much alike for either one of them to put a check on the other. More than that, they were no different in what they expected from the future, and as one day melted into another, they lived under the shared delusion that things were bound to be better tomorrow or, if not tomorrow, then the day after that.

That same month (October twenty-ninth), Crane wrote a complex, soul-searching letter to his brother William. It is one of the longest letters he wrote to anyone, and wedged in among numerous practical matters concerning the family and some scattered remarks about the places and wars he will be traveling to but never did (the Klondike, the Sudan, India), there are several paragraphs in which Crane steps back and looks at himself, assessing his current situation and what could be, perhaps, a long-range plan for the future.

> I have been in England, Ireland, Scotland, Wales, France, Turkey and Greece. I have seen Italy but never trod it. Since I have been here in England I have been in dreadfully hard luck. I have been here four

months and one month I was laid up by the carriage accident. In the working three months I have earned close to 2000 dollars but the sum actually paid in to me has been only £20.17s.3d—about 120 dollars. In consequence I have had to borrow and feel very miserable indeed. I am not sure that I am not in trouble over it.

McClures, with security of over 1000 dollars against my liability of four hundred, refuse to advance me any money. And yet they think they are going to be my American publishers.

. . . My next short thing after the novelette (The Monster) was The Bride Comes to Yellow Sky. All my friends [who] come here say it is my very best thing. I am so delighted when I am told by competent people that I have made an advance. You know they said over here in England that the Open Boat (Scribner's) was my best thing. There seem to be many Americans who want to kill, bury, and forget me purely out of unkindness and envy and—my unworthiness, if you choose. All the hard things they say of me affect me principally because I think of mine own people—you and Teddie and the families. It is nothing, bless you . . . I want you to promise to never pay any attention to it, even in your thought. It is too immaterial and foolish. Your little brother is neither braggart or a silent egotist but he knows that he is going on steadily to make his simple little place and he cant be stopped, he cant even be retarded. He is coming.

Sometimes I think you and old Ted worry about me and you may well worry! I have managed my success like a fool and a child but then it is difficult to succeed gracefully at 23. However I am learning every day. I am slowly becoming a man. My idea is to come finally to live at Port Jervis or Hartwood. I am a wanderer now and I must see enough but—afterwards—I think of P.J. and Hartwood. . . .

I am just thinking how easy it would be in my present financial extremity to cable you for a hundred dollars but then by the time this reaches you I will probably be all right again. I believe the sum I usually borrowed was fifteen dollars, wasn't it? Fifteen dollars—fifteen dollars—fifteen dollars. I can remember an interminable row of fifteen dollar requests.

He is still posing to some degree—the letter is to William, after all— but by and large these paragraphs stand as one of Crane's most honest attempts to tell the truth about himself. For the first time, the master of evasion opens up and confesses how badly he has been wounded by the continual attacks on him in America. Also for the first time, he admits that he has bungled his early success by acting like "a fool and a child." His financial situation is bleak—not for the first time—but for once he does not ask his brother for help. And then, at long last, he finally acknowledges his incurable restlessness and his intention to remain "a wanderer" until the urge for travel has left him—whenever that might be. As for the dream of returning to Port Jervis and/or Hartwood one day, it is little more than that—a dream—or else an ingratiating gesture to William or, even more likely perhaps, a fantasy inspired by a sudden burst of homesickness: nostalgia for what he already knows is a world that has been lost to him forever. Most important—and these are the most moving lines in the passage—he is "slowly becoming a man," and in spite of his struggles along the way, he has not abandoned his belief in himself and is convinced that his strongest work is still in front of him: "Your little brother is going on steadily . . . and he can't be stopped, he can't even be retarded. He is coming." Needless to say, he says nothing about Cora or where precisely he is living, but that was the hand he had chosen to play ever since he arrived in England, and there will be no need to mention it again.

Nevertheless, the hidden Cora had become Crane's hidden strength, the steady, encouraging voice that kept his confidence up and helped him forge on with his work even as the difficulties of their situation closed in around them. To be sure, that work was their sole source of income, and she knew their lives depended on his ability to keep the spout flowing, but there was more to it than just money. Cora's faith in Crane's genius was absolute. In her eyes, everything he wrote was a masterpiece, his talent surpassed that of any other living writer, and he was destined to become one of the immortals. Crane had always worked hard, again and again he had worked through difficulties in the past, but he had also wavered at times and fallen into holes of doubt and dejection over his worth as an artist. Hawker's disgust with his paintings in *The Third Violet* mirrors Crane's fits of disgust with his own work, but there had been no Cora back then, and now that she was in his life, his footing had become more secure and he was walking on firmer ground. The proof is in the quality of the work he turned out during the ten months they lived together at Ravensbrook. In the end, Crane's reputation stands on six essential works: *Maggie*, *The Red Badge of Courage*, "The Open Boat," *The Monster*, "The Bride Comes to Yellow Sky," and "The Blue Hotel." Half of them were written in the first year of their marriage.

No sooner was his Western comedy finished than Crane launched into "Death and the Child," his first stab at a fictional representation of war since his own encounter with war in Greece. Given the general movement of his work in the past nine months, one would have expected something clean and simple and down to the ground, a narrative told in short, declarative sentences with no flourishes and only the barest, most functional imagery. Instead, Crane offers up a hallucination, an onslaught of wild, metaphorical language that surges on for twenty-one delirious, simile-clogged pages of dense, cosmological allegory—a mashed-up version of *The Pilgrim's Progress* as conceived by Dante and written by Ducasse, the visionary French poet who wrote under the name of the Comte de Lautréamont and died at age twenty-four in November 1870, exactly one year before Crane was born. The Florentine cartographer who mapped out the journey from underworld to overworld and another burning boy from the late nineteenth century: European collaborators for Crane's first European story, which is set in the middle of a European war and has a cast of entirely European characters, with an Italian hero of Greek origin who is mostly addressed in French.

The story begins with a scene of chaos and horror as hundreds of peasants rush down a mountain in panicked flight. No cause is given, nothing is explained, and not once is the word *war* mentioned. "It was as if fear was a river, and this horde had simply been caught in the torrent, man tumbling over beast, beast over man, as helpless in it as the logs that fall and shoulder grindingly through the gorges of a lumber country."

This is the turmoil of hell, and once again (as in certain passages of *Maggie*) Crane, the supposedly clear-eyed, hard-nosed realist, is back in the world of Goya and Hieronymus Bosch. This is not reportage. It is a close-up view of the apocalypse.

And once again, as Crane has done so often in the past, nature looks on with supreme indifference.

> The blue bay with its pointed ships, and the white town lay below them, distant, flat, serene. There was upon this vista a peace that a bird knows when high in air it surveys the world, a great calm thing rolling noiselessly toward the end of the mystery. Here on the height one felt the existence of the universe scornfully defining the pain in ten thousand minds. The sky was an arch of stolid sapphire. Even to the mountains raising their mighty shapes from the valley, this headlong rush of the fugitives was too minute. The sea, the sky, and the hills combined in their grandeur to term this misery inconsequent.

As the frightened mass of peasants streams downward, "a young man was walking rapidly up the mountain." He looks at the horde with "agitation and pity," but at the same time the people are not fully human to him, and as he studies their faces, "they seemed to wear . . . the expressions of so many boulders rolling down the hill." In the first paragraph, the peasants were logs. Now they are stones. Living beings transformed into inanimate objects by the catastrophic circumstances of the moment.

The young man turns around and sees someone walking up the mountain behind him—a man in a lieutenant's uniform, the first little sign that the circumstance of the moment is war. He speaks to the officer in French, flapping his arms and pointing "with a dramatic finger" as he blurts out wildly, "Ah, this is too cruel, too cruel, too cruel. Is it not? I did not think it would be as bad as this. I did not think—God's mercy—I did not think at all." He explains that he is a Greek or, rather, that his father was a Greek, and he has come here not to fight but to work as a correspondent for an Italian newspaper, for in fact he is Italian and has spent his whole life in Italy, where he was a student—a student—and he has come here now because of his father, who was Greek, and therefore he loves Greece, but he did not dream—

This is Peza, Crane's ignorant, idealistic, snobbish young pilgrim who will set forth on a journey through a haunted, war-besieged landscape in search of a battle that will grant him the honor of spilling his blood for a noble cause. It is a sudden change of heart, but now that he has seen his first glimpse of war in the human boulders rolling down the hill, he feels compelled to trade in his pen for a sword and join the ranks of the fighting men. Seconds after he announces his decision to the lieutenant, Crane slyly introduces the first sounds of battle into the story. Far in the distance, Peza hears

a continuous boom of artillery fire. It was sounding in regular measures like the beating of a colossal clock—a clock that was counting the seconds in the lives of the stars, and men had time to die between the ticks. Solemn, oracular, inexorable, the great seconds tolled over the hills as if God fronted this dial rimmed by the horizon. The soldier and the correspondent found themselves silent. The latter in particular was sunk in a great mournfulness, as if he had resolved willy-nilly to swing to the bottom of the abyss where dwell secrets of this kind, and had learned beforehand that all to be met there was cruelty and hopelessness. A strap of his bright new leather leggings came unfastened, and he bowed over it slowly, impressively, as one bending over the grave of a child.

By ending the paragraph with an image of a child's grave—Peza's grave?—Crane is pointing ahead to the child in the story, an unnamed peasant boy who is the counterweight to the deluded, squeamish, highly educated correspondent turned soldier. We see the boy for the first time just two pages later, in the second part of the seven-part story, but not before the ignorant Peza has understood that "the universities had not taught him" how to adjust to a life of soldiering and that "this theatre for slaughter, built by the inscrutable needs of the earth, was an enormous affair, and . . . the accidental destruction of an individual, Peza by name, would perhaps be nothing at all."

The boy is alone on the top of a mountain, a fairy-tale child who has been abandoned by his parents in their frantic rush to escape the enemy. This is almost humanly impossible, a lapse of mindfulness so egregious that not one parent in ten million would make it, but Crane had already visited this territory as far back as 1894—in the sketch now known as "The Fire," originally published in the *New York Press* as "When Every One Is Panic Stricken." In what was undoubtedly an invented detail, he had zeroed in on a woman who runs out of the burning building with a bamboo easel in her arms but has forgotten her baby and left it inside. Now, on a hilltop in Greece, a shepherd and his wife have taken off with their flock of sheep and somehow managed to forget their little boy. Not plausible, no, but realism is not at issue here, for the child is not a real child but a central component of Crane's allegory, a creature of the natural world rather than the human world, a dream figure of unadulterated innocence.

The boy is playing on the mountaintop, ignoring the battle being fought on the flatlands below, and whenever the gunfire is loud enough to divert his attention from his game, he looks down with a "tranquillity . . . as invincible as the mountain on which he stood." To emphasize the point, Crane comes back to it two paragraphs later: "The stick in his hand was much larger than was an army corps of the distance. It was too childish for the mind of a child. He was dealing with sticks."

Meanwhile, Peza is blundering about like "a corpse walking on the bottom of the sea" or "a man groping in a cellar" as he looks for a regiment to attach himself to. Duty has called the lieutenant off in another direction, which has left Peza feeling both insulted and abandoned, but on he goes, staggering this way and that through a "vale of shells," more and more certain that this haphazard journey is in fact a march toward his own death.

He encounters many soldiers along the way, both armed and unarmed, both wounded and intact, all of them weary, dirty, disheveled, and at last he comes upon a couple of uniformed men watching over a pack of mules, the two of them sitting side by side on the grass and talking "comfortably," as if the war were no concern of theirs, that is, they have become so accustomed to war by now that they can take it calmly in their stride, and Peza is

> proud and ashamed that he was not one of them, these stupid peasants, who, throughout the world, hold potentates on their thrones, make states- men illustrious, provide generals with lasting victories, all with ignorance, indifference, or half-witted hatred, moving the world with the strength of their arms and getting their heads knocked together in the name of God, the king, or the Stock Exchange—immortal, dreaming, hopeless asses who surrender their reason to the care of a shining puppet, and persuade some toy to carry their lives in his purse. Peza mentally abased himself before them, and wished to stir them with furious kicks.

These are Peza's thoughts, but they are Crane's words, and whether they were written with the ironic detachment of an author standing back and expressing his character's opinions or were indirectly expressing Crane's own opinions *through* his character, this is one of the angriest, most mis- anthropic passages in all his work, a venomous denunciation that flies from his mouth like a great gob of spit aimed at all levels of society, the powerful and the powerless alike, the vast interconnected system of God, government, and capital that allows wars to happen and persuades the lunkheaded masses to fight in them. Buried in the middle of the story, these words illuminate the dark message that lies at the heart of "Death and the Child" and show how profoundly Crane's thinking about war had evolved since he had gone to war himself. There are no redeeming virtues in rallying men to participate in slaughter. Win or lose, the fat cats always win, and win or lose, the bottom dogs always lose. Rant against it if you will, but that is the way of the world.

Ultimately, Peza winds up with a unit preparing to defend its position from an attack by the advancing Turks, who have emerged from the black lines in the rear as "an inky mass . . . shaped like a human tongue." The uni- versity graduate, who knows the difference between a "fat, greasy" peasant and "a young student who can write sonnets and play the piano," announces to the commanding officer that he wishes, above all else, "to battle for the fatherland." The officer smiles, and because the stranger is armed only with a pistol, he points "to some dead men covered in blankets." Peza doesn't understand. He thinks the officer is "poetically referring to the danger," but no, the officer explains, he wants him to take a bandolier from one of the dead men to use for the battle ahead. Peza starts to move his hand toward the blanket covering a dead soldier, but he stops midway, unable to go on, "as if his arm had turned to plaster." Just then, the officer asks him if he has any tobacco, and the discombobulated Peza hands him his entire pouch. By way of thanks, the officer instructs one of his men to remove the bandolier for the rattled stranger, and that is the moment when Peza starts to come undone, for once he puts the long cartridge belt across his chest, "he felt that the dead man had flung his arms around him." Then another soldier hands him a rifle, "a relic of another dead man," and with "the clutch of a corpse about [Peza's] neck," the rifle becomes "as horrible as a snake that lives in a tomb." He imagines he is hearing the low voices of the two dead men "speaking to him of bloody death, mutilation," and then, inadvertently looking behind himself, he sees that the blanket has come off the face of yet another dead man. "Two liquid-like eyes were staring into his face," and suddenly the unhinged Peza feels that the dead are pulling him downward into "a chamber under the earth, where they could walk, dreadful figures, swollen and blood-marked. He was bidden; they had commanded; he was going, going, going."

He bolts to the rear, just as Henry Fleming bolted from his first test under fire, but unlike the boy in *Red Badge*, Peza does not have the luck to outrun his terror and live to see another day. He is shot, and as the other soldiers watch him flee into the distance, they think he has been "wounded somewhere in the neck, because as he ran he was tearing madly at the bandoleer, the dead man's arms."

In the last chapter, Crane returns to the mountaintop of his magic child. The boy has stopped playing now, and with the battle just at the base of the hill and the smoke rising and the noise turning into an uproar, he sits down on a stone to watch what is happening. Little by little, he begins to feel "astonished."

> Finally, without any preliminary indication, he began to weep. If the men struggling on the plain had had time and greater vision, they could have seen this strange tiny figure seated on a boulder, surveying them while the tears streamed. It was as simple as some powerful symbol.

Crane comes right out and says it here. The boy is not a boy but the embodiment of an idea, and the mountain he sits on is the same mountain that occurs again and again in the poems of *The Black Riders*, an extrusion of earth that reaches toward heaven and stands midway between the clouds and the mud below, an ideal vantage point to look down from to examine the follies of mankind. On some days, the gods laugh at what they see, and on other days they weep. Yesterday Crane laughed; today he weeps.

One could argue that the action in this paragraph is forced—and that by putting those tears in the boy's eyes Crane is pushing too hard to hammer home his meaning. Perhaps he is. But this is an allegory, after all, not a depiction of everyday events, and Crane is so forthright in his intentions, even going so far as to call the boy a symbol, that if those tears are something of a misstep, they are also a bold narrative move. The directness and simplicity of the boy's response is as pure as a line in one of Blake's stark little songs, and if read in the proper spirit, the gesture carries the sting of a divine judgment—pronounced by a silent God who does not exist to a world that in any case would refuse to listen. The boy is hungry and has started to miss his mother. Calling out to her, he goes into the empty house, which is now occupied by a "pearl-colored cow," who looks up and stares at him with her large, impassive eyes. Evening descends on the hills. Then something happens, and with that something Crane ends his nightmare treatise on the metaphysics of war:

> The child heard a rattle of loose stones on the hill-side, and facing the sound, saw a moment later a man drag himself up to the crest of the hill and fall panting. Forgetting his mother and his hunger, filled with calm interest, the child walked forward and stood over the heaving form. His eyes, too, were now large and inscrutably wise and sad, like those of the animal in the house.
>
> After a silence, he spoke inquiringly. "Are you a man?"
>
> Peza rolled over quickly and gazed up into the fearless cherubic countenance. He did not attempt to reply. He breathed as if life was about to leave his body. He was covered with dust; his face had been cut in some way, and his cheek was ribboned with blood. All the spick of his former appearance had vanished in a general dishevelment, in which he resembled a creature that had been flung to and fro, up and down, by cliffs and prairies during an earthquake. He rolled his eye glassily at the child.
>
> They remained thus until the child repeated his words. "Are you a man?"
>
> Peza gasped in the manner of a fish. Palsied, windless, and abject, he confronted the primitive courage, the sovereign child, the brother of the mountains, the sky and the sea, and he knew that the definition of his misery could be written on a wee grassblade.

II

AN ALMOST FORTY-YEAR-OLD POLISH-BORN BRITISH SUBJECT (WHO "speaks and acts like a Frenchman"—Cora) and a transplanted American on the verge of twenty-six. The first one's mother had died when he was seven, the second one's father had died when he was eight. Both of them had been brilliant, distracted, flunk-out students, and both of them had lived through repeated deaths and dislocations in childhood. The first one had attempted suicide at twenty; at twenty, the second one had told himself and others that he would die young. Later on, both of them would survive shipwrecks, and now both of them wrote books, but because the first one had started late and the second one had started early, in the eyes of the world the boy stood taller than the man. Nevertheless, it was the boy who initiated their first encounter, which took place on October 15, 1897, when Sidney Pawling, the editor who oversaw the work of both men at Heinemann's, complied with the American's request by organizing a lunch for the two writers at a restaurant in central London. It must have been a fraught moment for both of them. Each one admired the other's work, each one had found a spiritual connection with the other through that work, but writers, who are among the strangest, loneliest people on earth, rarely form deep and lasting friendships with other writers. They tend to cultivate a distant cordiality with their peers—when they aren't stabbing them in the back or being stabbed in return—and even the ones they most admire often turn out to be the most difficult ones to bear. Who knows what these two were expecting when they walked into the restaurant that afternoon, but it is almost certain that each one was girding himself against disappointment. Precisely because they respected each other and saw each other as equals, precisely because neither one had ever formed a true friendship with a respected equal. As the older one recalled twenty-six years later: "We shook hands with intense gravity and a direct stare at each other, after the manner of two children told to make friends. It was under the encouraging gaze of Sidney Pawling who, a much bigger man than either of us and possessed of a deep voice, looked like a grown-up person entertaining two strange small boys—protecting and slightly anxious as to the experiment."

With that timid, solemn handshake, Crane's friendship with Joseph Conrad began. The small strange boys and their large editor were the only ones at the table that afternoon, and once the ice had been broken, the talk flowed freely, so freely that when Pawling looked at his watch, three hours had gone by and it was four o'clock. He jumped up from the table, announced "I must

leave you two now," and hurried back to his office, but the two writers, having
no office to go to and no particular plans in mind, "went out," as Conrad later
put it, "and began to walk side by side in the manner of two tramps without
home, occupation, or care for the next night's shelter." They continued talking
as they rambled from one neighborhood to another, but mostly they were
silent, "and the only allusion we made that afternoon to our immortal works"
was an oblique remark from Conrad, "I like your General" (the most minor
of minor characters in *Red Badge*), and an equally oblique remark from Crane
about one of Conrad's equally minor characters, "I like your young man—I
can just see him." This kind of reticence is not unusual among novelists, for
contrary to what readers of novels might imagine, novelists rarely talk about
their work when they are together, especially the ones who are most deeply in
harmony. Conrad: "A stranger would have expected more, but, in a manner of
speaking, Crane and I had never been strangers. We took each other's work
for granted from the very first. . . . Henceforth mutual recognition kept to
that standard. It consisted often of an approving grunt."

They paused for a while at a dreary A.B.C. tea shop, where they concluded that while "the scheme of creation remained as obscure as ever . . .
there was still much that was interesting to expect from Gods and men,"
and with that burst of optimism they went on tramping through the
streets, "east and north and south again," moving past Piccadilly Circus
and Tottenham Court Road, when Crane suddenly—and inexplicably—
asked Conrad to tell him what he knew about Balzac and the *Comédie
Humaine*—"its contents, its scope, its plan, and its general significance,
together with a critical description of Balzac's style." It was ten o'clock in
the evening, and as they sat down to supper at Monico's, Conrad obliged
him by giving a hasty overview of Balzac's work "in the rush of hundreds
of waiters and the clatter of tons of crockery." He adds: "I wonder what
Crane made of it. He did not look bored." And then, at eleven o'clock,
they left the restaurant and parted outside on the street "with just a handshake and a good-night—no more—without making any arrangements
for meeting again, as though we had lived in the same town from childhood and were sure to run across each other the next day."

Three weeks later, Conrad sent Crane an inscribed copy of his first novel,
Almayer's Folly ("with the greatest regard and most sincere admiration"),
along with the proofs of his soon-to-be-published third novel, *The Nigger
of the "Narcissus,"* which had been appearing in installments since August in
the *New Review*, and Crane wrote back on November eleventh—with an
apology for sending the letter in care of Heinemann (he had lost Conrad's
note and address). Calling the new book "simply great," he describes the

death of Conrad's character James Wait as "too good, too terrible. I wanted to forget it at once. It caught me very hard. I felt ill over that red thread lining from the corner of the man's mouth to his chin. It was frightful with the weight of a real and present death. By such small means does the real writer flash out of the sky." He then informs Conrad that he has written to Bacheller and told him "to be valiant" in regard to this book—the first of several acts of generosity he would make on behalf of his new friend—and, as it turned out, the good-hearted Bacheller came through by arranging for the American publication of the novel with Dodd Mead & Co., which changed the title to *The Children of the Sea* (even at the height of Jim Crow racism, Conrad's original was considered too offensive). In the next paragraph, Crane invites the Conrads (Mr. and Mrs.) to come to Oxted one Sunday for lunch, any Sunday, after which they can stay on as houseguests for as long as they wish. And then a final, one-sentence paragraph before signing off: "Did not we have a good pow-wow in London?"

Conrad answered promptly on the sixteenth:

> I must write to you before I write a single word for a living to-day. I was anxious to know what you would think of the end. If I've hit *you* with the death of Jimmy I don't care if I don't hit another man. . . . When I feel depressed about it I say to myself "Crane likes the damed thing"— and am greatly consoled. What your appreciation is to me I renounce to explain. The world looks different to me now, since our long pow-wow. It was good. The memory of it is good. And now and then (human nature *is* a vile thing) I ask myself if you meant half of what you said! You must forgive me. . . . That's why one sometimes wishes to be a stone breaker. There's no doubt about breaking a stone. But there's doubt, fear—a black horror, in every page one writes. You at any rate will understand and therefore I write to you as though we had been born together before the beginning of things. For what you have done and intend to do I won't even attempt to thank you. I certainly don't know what to say, though I am perfectly certain as to what I feel.

By "intend to do," Conrad was referring to Crane's efforts to find an American publisher for his book, but as for the other matter—the invitation—it was impossible for him to accept just now, even if "it is perfectly right and proper from a ceremonial point of view that I should come to you first." His wife was seven months pregnant with their first child, and she was in no condition to travel at the moment. Instead, Conrad asked Crane to "show your condescension by coming to me first. . . . Just drop a postcard saying *I'm coming* and I shall meet the train.... I should love to have you under my roof."

Twelve days later, Crane went, covering the forty miles between his house and Conrad's in a zigzag north from Oxted to London followed by a second train east to Stanford-le-Hope in Essex for a brief solo visit of one day and one night, with an early departure the next morning. "He came, was received as an old friend, and before the end of the day conquered my wife's sympathy, as undemonstrative and sincere as his own quiet friendliness," Conrad wrote. Her name was Jessie, and she had been married to Conrad since March 1896. She was young—two years younger than Crane—a working-class girl from a large family who had been employed as a typist when she met her husband. They had two children together, and years later, in her widowhood, she published several books of her own, among them *Joseph Conrad as I Knew Him* (1926) and *Joseph Conrad and His Circle* (1935). Her first impressions of Crane:

> My husband ... had in a way prepared me for someone at once unusual and with a charm peculiarly his own. He must have been then about six and twenty, and appeared to my maternal mind very slight and delicate. He and Joseph Conrad were on the easy terms of complete understanding, I saw at once; his manner to me was slightly nervous and not a little shy. I don't remember much of the evening that followed after that dinner—I left them together and did not see him before he left early the next morning. The most lasting impression I have is of our taking our coffee, when Stephen, balancing himself on his tilted chair, discoursed gravely on the merits of his three dogs, Sponge, Flannel and Ruby.

In addition to the stories about his dogs (beloved replacements for the dead Velestino), Crane must have brought along copies of two of the stories he had written, for on December first, scarcely forty-eight hours after he left, Conrad wrote the effusive letter about "A Man and Some Others" and "The Open Boat" (page 372), showering those works with a praise that bordered on hysteria—and barely suppressed envy. "I want to swear at you, to bless you—perhaps to shoot you—but I prefer to be your friend." For all the sincerity of that friendship (there is no doubt that Conrad loved Crane), deep down in the cavern of his ego-walled writer's self—divided, doubting, often desperate—he was in competition with him as well, and five days after sending his letter to Crane, he wrote a letter to another friend, Edward Garnett, in which he expressed some reservations about the quality of the work he had just told the author was "without flaw."

I had Crane here last Sunday. We talked and smoked half the night. He is strangely hopeless about himself. I like him. The two stories are excellent. . . . His eye is very individual and his expression satisfies me artistically. He certainly is *the* impressionist and his temperament is curiously unique. His thought is concise, connected, never very deep—yet often startling. He is *the only* impressionist and *only* an impressionist. Why is he not immensely popular? With his strength, with his rapidity of action, with that amazing faculty of vision—why is he not? He has outline, he has colour, he has movement, with that he ought to go very far. But—will he? I sometimes think he won't. It is not an opinion—it is a feeling. I could not explain why he disappoints me—why my enthusiasm withers as soon as I close the book. While one reads, of course, he is not to be questioned. He is the master of the reader to the very last line—then—apparently for no reason at all—he seems to let go his hold. It is as if he has gripped you with greased fingers. His grip is strong but while you feel the pressure on your flesh you slip out from his hand— much to your own surprise. This is my stupid impression and I give it to you in confidence.

These are serious, cogently written but wrongheaded comments, and years later Conrad would retract them (in print) as he came to understand the many depths of meaning hidden under Crane's dazzling surfaces, but this letter, written to a friend and supporter of both writers, was of course not seen by Crane and therefore never stood in the way of their friendship. Just three days later, however, something else came up—in public—that potentially could have caused a rift between them, but owing to the subtle efforts each one made to protect the feelings of the other, the incident passed before any permanent damage was done. A rare instance of a friendship between two writers in which both were sensitive to the sensitivities of the other, which explains why such friendships are so rare to begin with.

The Nigger of the "Narcissus" was published on December fifth, and several of the reviews made pointed remarks about Crane's influence on Conrad. In the London *Speaker*, the novel was insultingly called "a worthy pendant to the battle-picture presented to us in *The Red Badge of Courage*," and W. L. Courtney of the *Daily Telegraph* (who had written a negative review of *Red Badge*) managed to insult both writers at the same time: "Mr. Joseph Conrad has chosen Mr. Stephen Crane for his example, and has determined to do for the sea and the sailor what his predecessor had done for war and warriors. The style, though a good deal better than Mr. Crane's, has the same jerky and spasmodic quality."

By and large, however, the Courtney review was a positive one, positive enough for Conrad to take the trouble of writing a letter of thanks to the author with "my high appreciation of your luminous and flattering notice." Strapped for money, anxious about his literary future, on the brink of becoming a father ("I hate babies," he wrote to Garnett), Conrad followed every word that was published about his work and was eager to ingratiate himself with anyone he perceived to be an ally. But when he sat down to write a Christmas/New Year's note to Crane on December twenty-fourth, he smoothly reversed his position in deference to what he imagined were Crane's hurt feelings over the review:

> ps Have you seen the Daily Tele: Article by that ass Courtney? He does not understand you—and he does not understand me either. That's a feather in our caps anyhow. It is the most *mean-minded* criticism I've read in my life. Do you think I tried to imitate you? No Sir! I may be a little fool but I know better than to try to imitate the inimitable. But here it is. Courtney says it: You are a lost sinner and you have led me astray. If it was true I would well be content to follow you but it isn't true and the perfidious ass tried to damage us both. Three cheers for the Press!*

For his part, Crane had already responded to the insult before he received that P.S. to the Christmas letter. Understanding how humiliated and angry Conrad must have felt to be charged with imitating his work, he immediately dropped whatever he was doing and made one of his infrequent excursions into the land of literary criticism—purely as a gesture to support his friend—which he sent off to Reynolds on December twentieth, four days before Conrad confirmed how angry he was in the letter, which of course was essentially a feigned anger intended to spare Crane's feelings. What a delicate dance this was, with each one bending over backward to stand by the other—but so discreetly that neither one of them fully

---

* In spite of Conrad's protests, there are clear signs of Crane's influence on that early phase of J.C.'s work, mostly through *Red Badge* and primarily on the 1897 novel and *Lord Jim* (1900). Berryman mentions this casually in his book, as if it were a foregone conclusion, but a number of scholars have looked into the question more deeply and have come up with compelling evidence to support the argument. It is not a matter of imitation, of course, but of influence—the impact Crane's work had on Conrad's thinking about his own work as well as the impact their friendship had on his life. For a particularly good article on this subject, see Nina Galen's "Stephen Crane as the Source for Conrad's Jim" (*Nineteenth-Century Fiction* 38, no. 1 [June 1983]).

understood what the other was doing. Crane's article, "Concerning the English 'Academy,'" took on the subject of "a well-known critical journal, the *Academy* ... [which] offered a prize of one hundred guineas to the book of signal merit published in the year of 1897, and a prize of fifty guineas for the next best book." The awards had been given to two poets whose names have vanished so thoroughly that I will not bother to mention them now. Crane writes:

> Many people suggested that the prizes should be given to Mr. Henry James for his *What Maisie Knew*, and to Mr. Joseph Conrad for his *The Nigger of the "Narcissus"*—a rendering which would have made a genial beginning for an English Academy of letters, since Mr. James is an American and Mr. Conrad was born in Poland. Mr. James's book is alive with all the art which is at the command of that great workman, and as for the new man, Conrad, his novel is a marvel of fine descriptive writing. It is unquestionably the best story of the sea written by a man now alive, and as a matter of fact, one would have to make an extensive search among the tombs before he who has done better could be found. As for the ruck of writers who make the sea their literary domain, Conrad seems in effect simply to warn them off the premises, and tell them to remain silent. He comes nearer to an ownership of the mysterious life on the ocean than anybody who has written in this century.
>
> Mr. Conrad was stoutly pressed for the prize, but the editors of the *Academy* judged the book to be "too slight and episodic," although they considered it "a remarkable imaginative feat marked by striking literary power." If one wanted to pause and quibble, one would instantly protest against their use of the word episodic, which as a critical epithet is absolutely and flagrantly worthless.

This is not literary criticism so much as an extended, enthusiastic blurb, but that was all Crane was hoping to accomplish with these paragraphs—to show Conrad what he felt about his work—and with that exchange of indirect responses to the double insult in the London Press (J.C.'s P.S. and S.C.'s article), the small cloud that had drifted over their friendship disappeared from the sky.

Soon after, Crane was proposing that the two of them collaborate on a play, a ridiculous, far-fetched plan to drum up some cash for their starved purses. Called *The Predecessor*, the melodrama, wholly concocted by Crane, would be set in the American West and tell the story of a man who impersonates another man (who is dead) in order to win the girl's heart, but Conrad played along because it amused him to talk about it, understanding that this "dead sure thing" (Crane's words), which never got more than two inches off the ground, "was merely the expression of our affection for each other." The nature of that affection is nicely captured in a reminiscence by Garnett from 1928, years after both of his friends were dead. Although Conrad was famously prone to long fits of depression, his

> moods of gay tenderness could be quite seductive. On the few occasions that I saw him with Stephen Crane he was delightfully sunny, and bantered "poor Steve" in the gentlest, most affectionate style, while the latter sat silent, Indian-like, turning inquiring eyes under his chiseled brow, now and then jumping up suddenly and confiding some new project with intensely electric feeling. At one of these sittings Crane passionately appealed to me to support his idea that Conrad would collaborate with him in a play on the theme of a ship wrecked on an island. I knew it was hopelessly unworkable—this plan—but Crane's brilliant visualization of the scenes was so strong and infectious I had not the heart to declare my opinion. And Conrad's skeptical answers were couched in the tenderest, most reluctant tone. I can still hear the shades of Crane's poignant friendliness in his cry "Joseph!" And Conrad's delight in Crane's personality flowed in the shining warmth of his brown eyes.

They were friends, but curiously reserved and tight-lipped friends who never shared details about their lives or talked about their pasts, and yet for all those silences they were close, the closest of close friends, or perhaps brothers under the skin, each one connected to the other by what Conrad called "profound . . . similitudes in our temperaments," and so, instead of talking about themselves, they worked together on projects they both knew would never amount to anything but which allowed them to break the silence for an occasional "brotherly serio-comic interlude . . . and some of the most light-hearted moments in the clear but sober atmosphere of our intimacy."

On January 15, 1898, the Conrads' son was born. Baby Borys, soon to be known as the Boy, received a less than joyous welcome from his father. Writing to Crane on the sixteenth, he announced: "A male infant arrived yesterday and made a devil of a row. He yelled like an Apache and ever since this morning has been on the war path again. It's a ghastly nuisance." As we have seen earlier (pages 30, 118), Crane was decidedly more enthusiastic about the advent of the Boy, and when little Borys was just two days old, Jessie Conrad "was deeply moved to receive from Stephen's wife Cora a beautiful box of flowers and a warm invitation to spend a week with them in their home Ravensbrook as soon as the baby was old enough to travel."

Conrad accepted the invitation with a funny, baby-bashing letter to Cora on the twenty-fifth, apologizing that "the child is, I am sorry to say, absolutely callous to the honor awaiting him of his very first visit being to your house. I talked myself hoarse trying to explain to him the greatness of the occurrence—all in vain. I want Crane to give it his artistic bene-diction and call upon its head the spirit—the magnificent spirit that is his familiar—the genius of his work. And then when our writing days are over he who is a child to day may write good prose . . ."

The visit began on February nineteenth and lasted ten days. In addi-tion to the three Conrads and Jessie's younger sister, Dolly, the expanded household included the two Cranes, their servant Adoni Ptolemy, and Cora's American friend Charlotte Ruedy, an unmarried woman in her late thirties who had come for a visit and wound up staying at the house as Cora's companion during Crane's long absence in Cuba. (Conrad took to calling her "the good Auntie Ruedy.") Although everyone seemed to have enjoyed the visit, details about it are scant. In her short memoir of Crane, Jessie wrote that she was touched by the "royal preparations for the small person's arrival," but other than remarking that "Stephen declared that he had some distinct claim to our precious baby," she said little about the days they spent together except to describe them as "very pleasant." Conrad wrote that the visit "is commemorated by a group photograph taken by an artist summoned with his engine (regardless of expense) to Ravensbrook. Though the likenesses are not bad it is a very awful thing. Nobody looks like him or herself in it."

It is not an awful thing. Not only is it the single photograph on record in which Crane and Conrad are standing in the frame together, it pres-ents a startlingly vivid picture of seven human beings and three dogs poised in front of a brick house in the English countryside on a chilly afternoon in early 1898, a look into a past that is still so close to us that it could have been shot the day before yesterday. Even the matching caps worn by the two Cranes and Charlotte Ruedy can still be found in a store near you.

In the end, the most notable aspect of the visit is what it tells us about the growing friendship between the two writers, for it was then that Con-rad began his custom of sitting in Crane's study while the younger man went about the business of doing his day's work. We know that Crane could write just about anywhere, with any number of people present, but for the solitary, punctilious Conrad to cohabit another writer's private

The Conrads' first visit to Ravensbrook, February 1897. Conrad and his wife, Jessie, are standing on the steps. Below them to the right are Charlotte Ruedy and Cora, who is holding the infant Borys, and below them to the left are Crane (with the black dog in his arms) and Jessie Conrad's younger sister, Dolly.
(COURTESY OF THE UNIVERSITY OF VIRGINIA)

space shows an exceptional degree of comfort, companionability, and even complicity with that other. If it had happened just once, it would hardly be worth mentioning, but the scene played out again and again on all of Conrad's subsequent visits to the Crane household, particularly after S.C.'s return from Cuba. As Conrad tells it,

> Crane would . . . settle himself at the long table at which he used to write. . . . I would take a book and settle myself at the other end of the same table, with my back to him; and for two hours or so not a sound would be heard in that room. At the end of that time Crane would say

suddenly: "I can't do any more now, Joseph." He would have covered three of his large sheets with his regular, legible, perfectly controlled handwriting, with no more than half a dozen erasures—mostly single words—in the whole lot. It seemed to me always a perfect miracle in the way of mastery over material and expression.

It is unclear what Crane was working on during that visit to Ravensbrook at the end of February, but the one thing he most definitely was *not* working on was "The Blue Hotel," which had been finished two weeks before Conrad and his family came to the house. It was the last of the "perfect miracles" Crane produced there, and between the ending of the story and the beginning of the Conrads' visit, the battleship *Maine* was destroyed by an explosion in Havana Harbor, killing two hundred and sixty-one members of the crew. War was coming—and Conrad's friend would soon be going.

12

WHY ONE PLACE AND NOT ANOTHER? WHY, FOR EXAMPLE, WOULD Crane spend ten months living in England, from June 1897 to April 1898, followed by another sixteen months from early 1899 to the middle of 1900—more than two years in all—and never write a single work of fiction set anywhere in contemporary England? On the other hand, why would a relatively short trip to Nebraska, Texas, and Mexico have furnished him with the geography of more than a dozen stories, at least half of them among the best short works he ever wrote? Port Jervis gave him Whilomville, New York City gave him five years' worth of novels, stories, and sketches, but England gave him nothing, except perhaps a place in which to dream about other places, a dull, unloved refuge where his imagination was set free to roam among the territories of his past that had stirred him most deeply: small-town America, Greece in time of war, and the immense, otherworldly landscapes of the Far West.

Faulkner stayed in Mississippi to write about Mississippi, but Joyce wrote his epic about Dublin while living in Trieste, Zurich, and Paris. Kafka, who lived in Prague and never set foot outside of Europe, called his first novel *Amerika*. In it, the torch held in the right hand of the Statue of Liberty is replaced by a sword, and the last chapter takes its title from the nonexistent Nature Theatre of Oklahoma. For a writer, all places are imaginary, even the one in which he happens to live. For Crane, who wound up living in many places, only the ones that wormed their way to the bottom of his unconscious ever surfaced in his fiction. At one time those places had been real, but once he started to write about them, they were turned into geographical markers in a country of dreams.

He had been in Nebraska for just two weeks, but the pounding blizzard and subzero temperatures he experienced there had never left him, and on the morning of his departure from Essex after his first visit to Conrad, a ferocious, wind-propelled rainstorm was sweeping through the area. Conrad: "Glad to hear you haven't had your head taken off. We had here on Monday a high tide that smashed the sea-wall flooded the marshes and washed away the Rwy line. Great excitement." We know from his letter to Garnett that Conrad had found Crane to be "strangely hopeless about himself" (due to his mounting debts), and as S.C. traveled home in that late November English storm, perhaps it called up memories of the larger, much wilder storm that had crashed down on him in Nebraska. Perhaps. In any case, he began writing "The Blue Hotel" almost immediately after he returned to Oxted, a thirty-page story that he worked on with inordinate care over the next seven or eight weeks, more time than he had spent on "The Open Boat" or any of his previous two-hundred-yard dashes. Many have called it Crane's best short story. Others have called it one of the finest American short stories ever written, period.

It is also Crane's most claustrophobic and intricately devised existential puzzle, a story with few images that takes place mostly indoors and yet begins outdoors with a startling, unforgettable blast of color: a blue building planted on a flat, empty space two hundred yards from the small prairie town of Romper, Nebraska. It is called the Palace Hotel, and the owner of the establishment, an Irish immigrant named Pat Scully, had the bright idea to paint his wooden structure blue, "a light blue, a shade that is on the legs of a kind of heron, causing the bird to declare its position against any background. The Palace Hotel, then, was always screaming and howling in a way that made the dazzling winter landscape of Nebraska seem only a gray swampish hush." The hotel stands midway between the railway station and the town, and clever, enterprising Scully makes it his business to be at the station to welcome every incoming train "and work his seductions upon any man that he might see wavering, gripsack in hand."

One morning, when a snow-crusted engine dragged its long string of freight cars and its one passenger coach to the station, Scully performed the marvel of catching three men. One was a shaky, quick-eyed Swede, with a great shining cheap valise; one was a tall bronzed cowboy, who was on his way to a ranch near the Dakota line; one was a little silent man from the East, who didn't look it, and didn't announce it. Scully practically made them prisoners.... They trudged off over the creaking board sidewalks in the wake of the eager little Irishman. He wore a heavy fur cap squeezed tightly down on his head. It caused his two red ears to stick out stiffly, as if they were made of tin.

When the prisoners reach the blue hotel, Scully conducts them inside, where they enter a small room dominated by "an enormous stove, which, in the center, was humming with god-like violence." The smallness of the room comes as a surprise, and only little by little do we learn anything about the interior architecture of the hotel as the action moves temporarily to a downstairs dining room and to a couple of upstairs bedrooms, but never does Crane tell us how many floors or how many other rooms there are in the hotel, nor how many guests are staying there (just these three, as it turns out, but then again, it could be four), and although some Scully daughters make a transitory appearance to serve the midday meal, they are as silent as shadows and flit past the others unnamed and uncounted, since we are never told how many they are—whether two or six or ten. Much later, a Mrs. Scully will deliver a harsh reproach to her husband, but she speaks no more than a dozen words and then vanishes from the story. Crane, who could be as precise in his descriptions as the most exacting botanist and could have earned a good supplemental income by writing instruction manuals for the operation of complex heavy machinery, is being intentionally vague here, blurring some parts of his canvas while keeping others in sharp focus, which has the effect of suspending the reader in a state of continual uncertainty. The eeriness is augmented by Crane's reluctance to tip his hand or even suggest that he is withholding information, and while he has made a point of telling us that we are in Nebraska, as the story unfolds we begin to feel that we are in fact at the outer edge of nowhere, locked in a self-enclosed no-place that resembles the set of a reductionist theater piece from the mid-twentieth century—Sartre's *No Exit*, for example, or Beckett's *Endgame*. Or a little dinghy with four men in it drifting on the surface of a vast, menacing ocean.

The first note of discord is struck the instant the four men walk into the small front room. Scully's son Johnnie is playing a card game called High-Five with a middle-aged farmer (a guest? a neighbor? a stranger passing through?), and the two of them are quarreling for reasons that are never explained—the first touch of narrative vagueness, but also the first hint of narrative unease. The farmer is so angry that he punctuates his words by spitting tobacco juice—"with an air of great impatience and irritation"—into a box of browning sawdust behind the stove. Not bothering to ask what the trouble is about, Scully, "with a long flourish of words ... destroy[s] the game of cards" and then orders his son to carry the bags of the new guests upstairs to their rooms. The reasons for this tantrum are likewise unexplained. Is Scully embarrassed by his son's behavior in front of the new guests—or is this a long-standing problem that has triggered similar responses in the past? One way or the other, why doesn't he apologize to the farmer? Without tackling any of these questions, Crane sends Scully upstairs as well, where the jolly/not-so-jolly innkeeper leads the men to three basins filled with "the coldest water in the world." By the time the men have washed up and returned to the front room, the angry farmer has disappeared—as if he had never been there. Crane says nothing about the missing man, and because nothing is said the reader scarcely notices his absence. What is there and not there is less a matter of physical fact than what the narrator chooses to tell and not to tell. Crane tells as little as he can but as much as he has to, and by establishing a world in which certain pieces are missing, he traps us in an ambiguous story-zone where the world still seems solid enough, and yet, at the same time, is slightly off-kilter as well.

In the washing scene upstairs, Crane had already introduced the central business of the story, but in such a small and subtle manner that it, too, might have slipped by unnoticed. The cowboy and the Easterner had plunged their hands into the icy water and rubbed their faces until they were "burnished ... fiery red," but the Swede had "merely dipped his fingers gingerly and with trepidation." Before the reader can ask why he would be spooked by a simple basin of cold water, the men are already downstairs again, settling around the stove for a brief, inconsequential chat before they are called in for lunch. Scully, the cowboy, and the Easterner take part in the conversation, but the Swede says nothing. "He seemed to be occupied in making furtive estimates of each man in the room," and so great is the suspicion in his eyes that he appears to be "badly frightened."

At lunch, however, the Swede exchanges a few words with Scully. He has come here from New York, he says, where he worked as a tailor for ten years. Scully tells him that he has been living in Romper for fourteen. When the Swede replies by asking some perfunctory questions about local crops and wages, Scully answers at length, but the Swede barely listens to him. One by one, he is carefully looking at the other men, and before the first chapter ends, he finally opens up a bit and reveals—nervously, self-consciously, with false good humor—what is preying on his mind: "with a laugh and a wink, he said that some of these Western communities were very dangerous; and after his statement he straightened his legs under the table, tilted his head, and laughed again, loudly. It was plain that the demonstration had no meaning to the others. They looked at him wondering and in silence."

Again, Crane jumps quickly away from the paranoiac Swede, who will soon become the primary figure of the story, but before that there are other matters to attend to, for one thing the "turmoiling sea of snow" outside, which has turned into a full-scale blizzard and will keep everyone trapped indoors, and for another thing the mysterious farmer, who is not mentioned when the five men return to the front room but is suddenly there again when Johnnie challenges him to another round of High-Five. The farmer accepts "with a contemptuous and bitter scoff," and before long the two are quarreling again, which brings the game to an abrupt end. Again, not one word is given about what caused the argument. The farmer stands up, looks at Johnnie with "heated scorn," buttons his coat, and stalks out of the room "with fabulous dignity." Buttoning up and leaving the room—but where does he go? Not, one would assume, out into the blizzard. Upstairs? But if he is a guest at the hotel, why wasn't he in the dining room with the others when they sat down for lunch? Again, Crane says nothing about any of this. Another blur.

And yet, many pages later, in the final sentences of the story, we are forced to think back to the two unexplained quarrels between the farmer and Scully's son at the beginning—before the story had settled into focus. If we can remember that the farmer was there.

As the farmer vanishes for the last time, the other men maintain a "discreet silence," but the Swede bursts out laughing—loudly, childishly, inappropriately—which makes the four others ask themselves what in the world is ailing him, and then, and only then, does the crazy square dance begin. We are partway into the second chapter of the nine-chapter story, and everything up to this point has been mere prelude.

> A new game was formed. . . . The cowboy volunteered to become the partner of Johnnie, and they all then turned to the Swede to throw in his lot with the little Easterner. He asked some questions about the game, and learning that it wore many names, and that he had played it when it was under an alias, he accepted the invitation. He strode toward the men nervously, as if he expected to be assaulted. Finally, seated, he gazed from face to face and laughed shrilly. This laugh was so strange that the

Easterner looked up quickly, the cowboy sat intent with his mouth open, and Johnnie paused, holding the cards with still fingers.

Afterward there was a short silence. Then Johnnie said: "Well, let's get at it. Come on, now!" They pulled their chairs forward until their knees were bunched under the board. They began to play, and their interest in the game caused the others to forget the manner of the Swede.

A blizzard is roaring down on the prairie around them, and inside the hotel, four men are packed into a room so small that it isn't big enough for a table, huddled together with a square wooden board balanced on their knees, playing a game of cards that travels the country under different aliases, but not one of them is given here and consequently the reader cannot even begin to imagine what is happening. Cramped, awkward, and almost ridiculous, the four strangers are stuck together by the board on their knees, unable to move without jostling the cards and disrupting the hand. Under different circumstances, the situation could be construed as another one of Crane's silent-comedy contortionist acts, but in the half-real, half-unreal blue hotel, the scene is not funny but bizarre, suffocating, and awful, unaccountably awful.

It is only a matter of time before the Swede begins to crack. Fingers trembling on the board, he gives the proprietor's son a knowing wink and says, "I suppose there have been a good many men killed in this room." Everyone is stopped in his tracks by this lunatic idea. Johnnie asks the Swede what in the hell he is talking about, but the ex–New York tailor won't be budged and insists that they all know what he means. "Oh, maybe you think I have been to nowheres," he says. "Maybe you think I'm a tenderfoot." Johnnie doesn't give a damn about who or what he is. All he can say is that no one has ever been killed in this room, and when the cowboy asks, "What's wrong with you, mister?" the Swede begins to act as if he is "formidably menaced." He turns to the Easterner for help, but the best the little man can do is pause for a moment before responding, and after he says, "I don't understand you," the Swede panics. "Oh, I see you are all against me," he says, which soon escalates to the next level of fear—"I don't want to fight! I don't want to fight!"—which in turn leads him to the summit of self-induced terror: "I suppose I am going to be killed before I can leave this house!"

Although it was an age of remarkable advances in medicine and psychiatry (Freud's *Interpretation of Dreams* was written at the same time as "The Blue Hotel"), it is doubtful that Crane read any of the contemporary research into paranoia or psychosis, let alone ever talked to anyone about those subjects, but the condensed version of mounting delusion presented in this case is clinically accurate. If people are after you to begin with, sooner or later they will end up wanting to kill you. The offending others are not just enemies, they are a mortal threat.

Scully walks into the room, looks at the Swede's troubled face, and demands to know what is going on. "These men are going to kill me," the Swede says, which prompts Scully to turn on his son for the second time in the past two hours, but Johnnie swears he is innocent. The man must be crazy, he says, and picking up on the word, the Swede comes back with: "Yes, I'm crazy—yes. Yes, of course, I'm crazy—yes. But I know one thing.... I know I won't get out of here alive." Again, Scully asks his son if he's been bothering this man, and again the son denies it. Meanwhile, the Swede declares that he will leave the house and go away, he will go away—"Because I do not wish to be killed." In danger of losing one of his paying customers, Scully tells him to forget about going away, he is under his roof "and I will not allow any peaceable man to be troubled here." As the Swede pushes past him to go upstairs and pack his bags, Scully looks at the three others and asks—for the last time—what is going on. Nothing, say the cowboy and Johnnie, and then the Easterner (whose name is revealed to be Mr. Blanc) says what amounts to the same thing: "I didn't see anything wrong at all." Scully goes upstairs to head off the madman.

Graciously, and with every ounce of his Irish charm, he does his best to pacify the Swede and induce him to stay. Even as the man is cinching the straps on his bag and getting ready to shove off, Scully rattles on about the modern improvements that are coming to Romper—the "ilictric street-cars" that will be installed next spring, the new railroad line that will connect the town to Broken Arm (*Broken Arm!*), the four churches, "the smashin' big brick school-house," and "the big factory, too": "Why, in two years Romper'll be a met-tro-*pol*-is." It is a clever ploy. Convince the crazy man that this is not the old West of hired gunslingers and wanton murder but the new West of a dawning century, a safe place, a friendly place where men work in factories, children are educated in splendid brick buildings, and everyone worships God. The Swede, however, is unmoved. Without a single comment, he turns to Scully and asks how much he owes, but Scully doesn't want his money, he says, and refuses to accept the seventy-five cents that are offered to him. An instant later, he comes up with a new plan. Guiding his reluctant guest across the hall to his own bedroom, he shows him a picture of his little daughter, Carrie, who died when she was young, and by demonstrating how deeply he still mourns her, perhaps he will get the Swede to understand that the citizens of the new West do not

take the business of death lightly. No response. The Swede doesn't bother
to look at the picture, nor at the second picture Scully points to of his older
son, Michael, who is a prominent lawyer in Lincoln "an' doin' well," as if to
prove that Nebraska is a place where the law is both respected and obeyed.
Running out of ideas now, Scully changes his strategy, dives under the bed,
and pulls out a bottle of whiskey. "Drink," he says, as he thrusts it toward
the Swede, but after a brief flutter of temptation (suggesting a fondness
for alcohol) the Swede backs off and "cast[s] a look of horror upon Scully,"
as if he suspects he is about to be poisoned. When Scully repeats his
command—"Drink!"—the Swede lets out one of his loud, incomprehensible laughs, snatches the bottle, puts it in his mouth, and drinks, "his glance
burning with hatred upon the old man's face."

Meanwhile, with the board still balanced on their knees, the other men
have been talking downstairs, speculating about what has just happened.
When the cowboy asks what makes the Swede act the way he does, the
little man goes straight to the heart of the problem.

> "Why, he's frightened!" The Easterner knocked his pipe against the
> rim of the stove. "He's clear frightened out of his boots."
> "What at?" cried Johnnie and the cowboy together.
> The Easterner reflected over his answer.
> "What at?" cried the others again.
> "Oh, I don't know, but it seems to me this man has been reading
> dime-novels, and he thinks he's right out in the middle of it—the shoo-
> tin' and the stabbin' and all."
> "But," said the cowboy, deeply scandalized, "this ain't Wyoming, ner
> none of them places. This is Nebrasker."
> "Yes," added Johnnie, "an' why don't he wait till he gits *out West*?"
> The traveled Easterner laughed. "It isn't different there even—not in
> these days. But he thinks he's right in the middle of hell."

Crane had presented other such cases in several of his earlier works, characters who suffer from the Quixote-Bovary mania of reading bad, seductive
books that distort their judgment and alter their perceptions of the real.
Maggie Johnson, Henry Fleming, George Kelcey, and the Tenderloin pimp
Swift Doyer are all victims of the disease. A cloud of false expectation stands
between them and the world—a mist formed by the conventions of gooey
melodramas and heroic tales of war—which prevents them from seeing that
a crass, garishly costumed bartender, for example, is not a knight in shining
armor, or that the girl you have fallen in love with cannot read the thoughts

in your head just because you are in love with her. Those earlier characters gorged themselves on brain-softening works, but the Swede in "The Blue Hotel" has hardened his brain by immersing himself in the violence of cheap Westerns, and so rigid and locked-in have his false perceptions become that he has gone blind. The others see the world through a cloud, but when the New York tailor looks out at the world, he sees nothing. And not only is he blind, he is mentally ill. Like poor, crazy Quixote, he has crossed over the edge and believes he is trapped inside a book, which in this case happens to be a dime novel set "in the middle of hell."

When Scully and the Swede come downstairs together, everything is suddenly different. The whiskey has produced a lightning transformation, and the two men enter the small front room laughing, as if they were a pair of revelers coming home from a banquet. The cowering, tremulous figure who was certain he was about to be killed has now aggressively taken charge, even to the point of "bullying" Scully at one point and talking "arrogantly, profanely, angrily." When he leaves for a moment to fetch himself a glass of water, Johnnie asks his father why he doesn't "throw 'im out in the snow." The old man's answer confirms what the Easterner has already told the two others. "'Why, he's all right now,' declared Scully. 'It was only that he was from the East and he thought this was a tough place. That's all. He's all right now.'" Then comes another meal in the dining room:

> At six o'clock supper, the Swede fizzed like a fire-wheel. He sometimes seemed on the point of bursting into riotous song, and in all his madness he was encouraged by old Scully. . . . The Swede domineered the whole feast, and he gave it the appearance of a cruel bacchanal. He seemed to have grown suddenly taller; he gazed, brutally disdainful, in every face. His voice rang through the room. Once when he jabbed out harpoon-fashion with his fork to pinion a biscuit the weapon nearly impaled the hand of the Easterner which had been stretched quietly out for the same biscuit.

This is the other side of paranoia, the manic side: strike before you are struck, throw out your chest and assert yourself before they jump you or back you into a corner, and if a few shots of whiskey can buck up your courage, by all means drink them.

Afterward, when the five men have withdrawn to the small front room, the Swede badgers Johnnie and the two guests into another game of cards, and once again "they formed a square with the little board on their knees." Scully sits off to the side reading a newspaper, and with his thoughts fixed on distant matters that have nothing to do with him, suddenly he hears three terrible words: "You are cheatin'!"

Such scenes often prove that there can be little of dramatic import in environment. Any room can present a tragic front; any room can be comic. This little den was now as hideous as a torture chamber.

In other words, anything can happen anywhere, at any time and for any reason, for the stage is a neutral arena for any human story, and if one night a pair of clowns tumble onto the boards, the next night could bring Antigone or Oedipus with his mother and father or four card players overturning their makeshift table and scattering the cards across the floor, "where the boots of men trampled the fat and painted kings and queens as they gazed with their silly eyes at the war that was waging above them."

The Swede is the accuser, Johnnie is the accused, and as the Swede holds "a huge fist in front of Johnnie's face," a scuffle breaks out, with the cowboy trying to push the Swede back and Scully and the Easterner clinging to Johnnie and all of them shouting at once: "Stop now!" (Scully), "He says I cheated!" (Johnnie), "He did cheat! I saw him! I saw him—" (the Swede), "Wait a moment, can't you?" (the Easterner). A few seconds later, they all come to a sudden stop, as if pausing for breath. The Swede and Johnnie face off against each other, the first one accusing, the second one denying, and with nothing to break the deadlock of opposing certainties, the two hotheads agree to settle the matter with their fists. "We must fight," says Johnnie. "Yes, fight!" roars the Swede, and when the cowboy turns to Scully and asks him what he's going to do about it, the old man says, "I've stood this damned Swede till I'm sick. We'll let them fight."

Out they all go into the blizzard—into "the roar of the storm"—and a simple, dime-novel fistfight between two angry men is turned into a savage reckoning between elemental forces as Crane shuttles his focus back and forth between the participants and observers on the one hand and, on the other, the tumult in the air around them, a frenzy of wind so powerful that it blows away words the instant they leave a man's mouth.

No snow was falling, but great whirls and clouds of flakes, swept up from the ground by the frantic winds, were streaming southward with the speed of bullets. The covered land was blue with the sheen of an unearthly satin, and there was no other hue save where at the low black railway station—which seemed incredibly distant—one light gleamed like a tiny jewel. As the men floundered into a thigh-high drift . . . the

Swede was bawling out something. Scully went to him, put a hand on his shoulder and projected an ear. "What's that you say?" he shouted.

"I say," bawled the Swede again, "I won't stand much show against this gang. I know you'll all pitch in on me."

Scully smote him reproachfully on the arm. "Tut, man," he yelled. The wind tore the words from Scully's lips and scattered them far a-lee.

"You are all a gang of—" boomed the Swede, but the storm also seized the remainder of this sentence.

They find a protected spot near the back wall of the hotel, a V-shaped patch of frozen grass untouched by the snow, and that is where the battle will be fought—on a small island of space cut off from the larger space around them: a boxing ring, as it were, or another stage on which one more human drama can be played out. The Easterner, whose teeth are chattering as he hops "up and down like a mechanical toy," observes that the "prelude had in it a tragedy greater than the tragedy of action, and this aspect was accentuated by the long mellow cry of the blizzard, as it sped tumbling and wailing flakes into the black abyss of the south."

Scully gives the command to start. "Now!" he says, and as the two men start to pound each other in the darkness, there is "such a perplexity of flying arms that it presented no more detail than would a swiftly-revolving wheel." The cowboy yells out, "Go it, Johnnie; go it! Kill him! Kill him!" The Easterner, however, regards the monstrous, "unchangeable fighting" as an abomination and longs for it to end. The Swede knocks down Johnnie, who falls with "a sickening heaviness to the grass." As he lies there on his back, his face "bloody, pulpy," his father asks him if he can go on. "Yes, I—it— yes," he says, and with his father's help he struggles back to his feet. The Easterner begs Scully to put a stop to it, but the old man ignores him, and then the Swede closes in to deliver his knockout punch. In spite of the odds against him, Johnnie, "half-stupid from weakness . . . miraculously dodged, and his fist sent the over-balanced Swede sprawling."

The cowboy, Scully, and the Easterner burst into a cheer that was like a chorus of triumphant soldiery, but before its conclusion the Swede had scuffled agilely to his feet and come in berserk abandon at his foe. There was another perplexity of flying arms, and Johnnie's body again swung away and fell, even as a bundle might fall from a roof. The Swede instantly staggered to a little wind-waved tree and leaned upon it, breathing like an engine, while his savage and flame-lit eyes roamed from face to face as the men bent over Johnnie. There was a splendor of isolation in his situation at this time which the Easterner felt once when, lifting his eyes from the man on the ground, he beheld that mysterious and lonely figure, waiting.

The bulkier, more powerful Swede has won. Returning to his senses, Johnnie begins to weep "from shame and bodily ill," and as the tears slide down over the blood marks on his face, he says, "He was too—too—too heavy for me." Scully announces that "Johnnie is whipped," the cowboy lets out a string of "unspellable blasphemies," and the Easterner is "startled to find that they were out in a wind that seemed to come direct from the shadowed arctic floes. He heard again the wail of the snow as it was flung to its grave in the south. He knew now that all this time the cold had been sinking into him deeper and deeper, and he wondered that he had not perished. He felt indifferent to the condition of the vanquished man."

After the men go back inside, the Swede clomps upstairs to his room, and the others warm themselves by the stove in the card-strewn "torture-chamber." The women of the household sweep in to carry Johnnie off to the kitchen, where they will wash him and dress his wounds, but before they make their joint exit, Mrs. Scully lashes into her husband with an angry verbal assault: "Shame be upon you, Patrick Scully! Your own son, too. Shame be upon you!"

The triumphant Swede comes downstairs, bangs open the door with a theatrical flourish and "swagger[s]" to the middle of the room. His bag is packed, he is on his way out of the hotel, and once again he asks Scully how much he owes him, to which Scully once again says, "Nothin'." Just to make sure, the Swede asks the question again, and again Scully says, "You don't owe me nothin'."

> "Huh!" said the Swede. "I guess you're right. I guess if it was any way at all, you'd owe me somethin'. That's what I guess." He turned to the cowboy. "Kill him! Kill him! Kill him!" he mimicked, and then guffawed victoriously. "Kill him!" He was convulsed with ironical humor.
>
> But he might have been jeering at the dead. The three men were immovable and silent, staring with glassy eyes at the stove.
>
> The Swede opened the door and passed into the storm, giving one more derisive glance backward at the still group.

The story could have ended there, for that moment marks the end of the action in the blue hotel, and it would have been a perfect ending in its way, the abrupt but satisfying conclusion to a gripping piece of work, but

Crane pushes on for two more chapters, and by digging further, and then digging still further into the consequences of what he has set in motion, he transforms his already good story into a great one.

The second-to-last chapter begins:

> The Swede, tightly gripping his valise, tacked across the face of the storm as if he carried sails. He was following a line of little naked gasping trees, which he knew must mark the way of the road. His face, fresh from the pounding of Johnnie's fists, felt more pleasure than pain in the wind and the driving snow. A number of square shapes loomed upon him finally, and he knew them as the houses of the main body of the town. He found a street and made travel along it, leaning heavily upon the wind whenever, at a corner, a terrific blast caught him.
>
> He might have been in a deserted village. We picture the world as thick with conquering and elate humanity, but here, with the bugles of the tempest pealing, it was hard to imagine a peopled earth. One viewed the existence of man then as a marvel, and conceded a glamour of wonder to these lice which were caused to cling to a whirling, fire-smote, ice-locked, disease-stricken, space-lost bulb. The conceit of man was explained by this storm to be the very engine of life. One was a coxcomb not to die in it. However, the Swede found a saloon.

The closed-in, hermetic world of the blue hotel has been blasted open, and suddenly Crane has thrust us out into the howling infinite of the white tundra. He imagines an earth so hostile to life that it is devoid of people, and if human beings exist, they must be looked upon as a sort of miracle. In "The Open Boat," he compared men to mice, insignificant creatures nibbling "the sacred cheese of life," and now he goes one step farther down the chain of being and compares them to lice, parasitic vermin clinging to a frozen, fiery, plague-ridden planet careening blindly through space, which is the darkest, most despairing picture he has ever presented of humanity, and yet, what he also says in this knotted, tormented passage is that the arrogance and self-importance of man ("the conceit") is the thing that keeps him going ("the very engine of life"), and yet, shifting gears once again in the next sentence, he declares that a person would have to be a "coxcomb" (a conceited dandy, a fop, or, in contemporary parlance, a jerk) not to die in this storm, and not only does the Swede not die in it, he chances upon a saloon.

We are still in Nebraska, but at the same time Crane has shifted the perspective so drastically and taken us so far from the town of Romper that he wants us to look down on this place as if it were a mere speck in the cosmos (which it is), but because men are involved in what is about to happen, it is of the utmost importance to men, for man is the measure of all things, at least as far as men are concerned, and therefore, lice though they may be in the large cosmic picture, what happens to human beings on earth matters, matters deeply, and is not, and never will be, meaningless, for bleak as Crane's vision of mankind has become, he is not a nihilist, and what men do to one another counts, not in the cosmos at large, perhaps, but in the moral universe created by men.

The next paragraph begins with a sign of warning. A red lamp hangs over the front door of the saloon, turning the snowflakes that fall within its arc the color of blood, and as the Swede opens the door and goes in, he is still inside the dime novel being written in his head, still flush with the victory he has won in his first Western combat. He looks around and sees that the only other customers are four men drinking at a table in a far corner of the room. In a chipper, exultant mood, he walks up to the man behind the bar and, "smiling fraternally," orders some whiskey. After the bartender rings up the sale on the nickel-plated cash register, the Swede takes hold of the bottle, pours himself an extra-large glass, and drinks it down in three gulps. The bartender steals a furtive glance at the blood-marks on the Swede's face and says, "Bad night." No, not at all, the Swede says, it's good enough for him, and in fact he likes this weather, he likes it, and it suits him fine. He asks for another drink, but when he offers to buy one for the bartender, the bartender declines and instead asks the Swede how he hurt his face. The Swede proudly tells him he was in a fight and that he "thumped the soul out of a man down here at Scully's hotel." That arouses the interest of the four men at the table. One of them asks, "Who was it?" and after the Swede tells them it was Johnnie Scully and that "he'll be pretty near dead for some weeks," he asks the others if they'll join him in a drink. No thanks, says one of them, and then Crane cuts away from the Swede and turns his attention to the four men.

Two prominent local businessmen and the district attorney are gathered around the table with their friend, "a professional gambler of the kind known as 'square,'" a distinguished gentleman in his own right who is not only respected by the leading men of the town but is considered to be a "thoroughbred." It is true that he earns his living by preying upon "reckless and senile farmers who, when flush with good crops, drove into town with the pride and confidence of an ... invulnerable stupidity," but it is also true that he is married, the father of two children, and leads "an exemplary home life." Crane could not be more emphatic about the virtues of "this thieving gambler," who is also "so generous, so just, so moral, that, in a contest, he could have put to flight the consciences of nine-tenths of the citizens of Romper."

If we are in the moral universe of men, then the gambler is an ambiguous case, a person who is simultaneously both one thing and another thing, a living, breathing contradiction who undermines any clear-cut certainties about what constitutes moral behavior, since Crane has made a point of calling this person "moral," in spite of the fact that he has also called him a thief. But he is a thief only in the sense that he is cunning enough to lure dim-witted bumpkins into playing cards with him, for he plays his cards "square," on the up and up, and he walks off with their money only because he is a more skillful card player than they are. And now, in what is probably the story's most elegant turn, this gambler is about to become entangled in the life of the card-playing Swede, who has walked into the saloon to celebrate his manly, two-fisted triumph over a supposed card cheat in the supposedly lawless, dangerous West. Blood-red snow is falling in front of the saloon, and what happens now will hinge purely on the circumstances of the moment: a chance encounter between two men steeped in the business of chance.

Meanwhile, the Swede has been downing more shots of straight whiskey and is still trying to talk the bartender into having a drink with him. "Come on," he says. "Have a drink. Come on. What—no? Well, have a little one then. By gawd, I've whipped a man to-night, and I want to celebrate. I whipped him good, too. Gentlemen," he calls out to the men at the table, "have a drink?" The bartender, aghast at the Swede's presumption, emits a hasty "Ssh!" "Thanks," says one of the men at the table. "We don't want any more."

The Swede, however, will not take no for an answer. Turning aggressive now, as if he had slipped into the part of a roughneck brawler in a classic Western scene—the showdown in the saloon—he takes the second rebuff from the men at the table as a personal insult. Thrusting "out his chest like a rooster," he tells the bartender that he is a gentleman, and he wants people to drink with him, and—just watch—he *will* make them drink with him. He strides off to the table, puts his hand on the gambler's shoulder, and repeats the threat: "I asked you to drink with me." Not bothering to turn around, the gambler gives him a sidelong glance over his shoulder and replies: "My friend, I don't know you." When the Swede continues to insist, the gambler calmly asks him to remove his hand from his shoulder and mind his own business. "What?" shouts the drunken, outraged Swede. "You won't drink with me, you little dude, I'll make you then. I'll make you!"

Note that the Swede calls the gambler "a little dude." Crane has already established that the cardsharp is a small person, "a little slim man," but "dude" is a telling indicator of how profoundly the Swede has lost himself in an imaginary West created by the books he read as a tailor in New York City, for "dude" is not only a word that evokes a slick dresser but a term of derision applied by Westerners to know-nothings from the East, as in the popular tourist phenomenon known as the "dude" ranch. Because the gambler does not conform to the dime-novel image of the true Westerner, the Swede has called him a dude, that is, has misread him as someone from the East, and because he has won his fight with Johnnie, he now feels confident enough to cast himself in the role of the bullying Westerner, and by reversing the situation in his scrambled, whiskey-sodden mind, the Swede has inadvertently stumbled into dangerous territory. "Dangerous" was the word he used to describe the West over lunch at the Palace Hotel, but not then, and not even now, has it ever occurred to him that he could be an instrument of danger himself.

> The Swede had grasped the gambler frenziedly at the throat, and was dragging him from his chair. The other men sprang up. The barkeeper dashed around the corner of his bar. There was a great tumult, and then was seen a long blade in the hand of the gambler. It shot forward, and a human body, this citadel of virtue, wisdom, power, was pierced as easily as if it had been a melon. The Swede fell with a cry of supreme astonishment.
>
> The prominent merchants and the district-attorney must have at once tumbled out of the place backward. The bartender found himself hanging limply to the arm of the chair and gazing into the eyes of a murderer.
>
> "Henry," said the latter, as he wiped the knife on one of the towels that hung beneath the bar-rail, "you tell 'em where to find me. I'll be home, waiting for 'em." Then he vanished. A moment afterward the barkeeper was in the street dinning through the storm for help, and, moreover, companionship.
>
> The corpse of the Swede, alone in the saloon, had its eyes fixed upon a dreadful legend that dwelt a-top of the cash-machine. "This registers the amount of your purchase."

In the first paragraph, it is interesting to note the odd, awkwardly constructed phrase "and then was seen a long blade in the hand of the gambler." Any other writer would have put it more or less as follows: "The gambler reached into his pocket and pulled out a knife with a long blade," but again and again in all his work Crane employs the passive voice to establish what I would call an "objective view" of the visual world, the world as perceived through the neutral, all-seeing lens of a camera. It is not a tic of style but a philosophical, even moral position about how to give the most truthful account of an event in the real world. In the present case, Crane does not presume to know what the gambler is thinking. He is watching him from the outside, just as the reader is, but in other stories and novels, when he is telling something through the eyes and mind of one of his characters (Henry Fleming, for example), he abandons the passive voice and reverts to the customary order of nouns and verbs in his sentences. In this passage, he is making an additional point, however, an extremely subtle point, perhaps, but nevertheless an important one. The Swede has come to the West expecting to be killed. And now, having provoked an absurd and unnecessary fight, he has indeed been killed, and by resorting to the passive voice, Crane gives agency to the knife rather than to the gambler, as if to say, No, the Swede was not killed by a man, he was killed by his own premonition of death, his own fear, and the knife was the weapon fate took hold of to fulfill its mission. As the cash register says: You have been given what you asked for.

Also to be noted in this passage is how quickly the gambler's friends tumble out of the saloon. They are gone in a flash, barely an instant after the Swede's body hits the floor, and by absconding in this way they are performing the same backpedaling dance of self-preservation that all respectable men perform in moments of crisis, as Crane had bitterly remarked just sixteen months earlier when he had defended himself in print for stepping forward in the Dora Clark Affair—with all the brutal aftereffects that gesture had entailed. So the district attorney and the two merchants run out into the storm and wash their hands of the whole business, as if putting into practice the words the gambler delivered to the Swede not one minute before he was jumped: "My friend, I don't know you."

In the last chapter, Crane comes armed with his own knife, the invisible writer's knife that traveled with him wherever he went, and when the moment comes to use it, watch how quickly he springs.

Months have passed, and one day the Easterner rides up with a bundle of letters and newspapers for the ranch in Dakota where the cowboy has been working. It is unclear whether Mr. Blanc is employed by the ranch himself or has found a job with the local post office, but one way or the other, there is no doubt that the two men have been in regular contact since their initial meeting at the Palace Hotel in Romper. The Easterner tells the cowboy that the gambler was sentenced to three years for killing the Swede.

A light sentence, they say to each other, but then the cowboy remarks that if the bartender had done his job and cracked the Swede on the head with a bottle, there never would have been a murder. Unimpressed by that reasoning, the Easterner "tartly" replies that a thousand things could have happened, meaning that idle speculation of that sort is useless, since only one thing happened, and that was the Swede's murder. Still, the cowboy goes on musing about the what-ifs and if-thens of the situation, saying that if the Swede hadn't accused Johnnie of cheating, he would still be alive, and what a fool he was for getting so worked up over a game that was played for fun, with no money involved, which only proves how crazy he was. Ignoring these comments, the Easterner says that he feels sorry for the gambler. The cowboy does, too, he says, adding that the gambler doesn't deserve any time at all, considering the sort of person he killed, and then, and only then—in the merest flash of an instant—Crane pulls out his knife and begins to twist it around in the guts of his story, and as that story rushes to its conclusion, everything we have been led to believe about what happened suddenly collapses. The Easterner replies:

"The Swede might not have been killed if everything had been square."

"Might not have been killed?" exclaimed the cowboy. "Everythin' square? Why, when he said that Johnnie was cheatin' and acted like such a jackass? And then in the saloon he fairly walked up to git hurt?" With these arguments the cowboy browbeat the Easterner and reduced him to rage.

"You're a fool!" cried the Easterner viciously. "You're a bigger jackass than the Swede by a million majority. Now let me tell you one thing. Let me tell you something. Listen! Johnnie *was* cheating!"

"Johnnie," said the cowboy blankly. There was a minute of silence, and then he said robustly: "Why, no. The game was only for fun."

"Fun or not," said the Easterner, "Johnnie was cheating. I saw him. I know it. I saw him. And I refused to stand up and be a man. I let the Swede fight it out alone. And you—you were simply puffing around the place and wanting to fight. And then old Scully himself! We are all in on it! This poor gambler isn't even a noun. He is kind of an adverb. Every sin is the result of a collaboration. We, five of us, have collaborated in the murder of this Swede . . . you, I, Johnnie, old Scully, and that fool of an unfortunate gambler came merely as a culmination, the apex of a human movement, and gets all the punishment."

The cowboy, injured and rebellious, cried out blindly into this fog of mysterious theory. "Well, I didn't do anythin', did I?"

If we haven't forgotten the farmer by now, we will understand that he was disgusted with Johnnie for cheating at cards. If we think back to Scully's enigmatic outbursts against his son and recall how he "destroyed" the card game the boy was playing with the farmer, we will understand that he also knew that Johnnie was a cheat. And obnoxious and deranged as he was, the Swede was not imagining things when he accused Johnnie of cheating as well, which forces us to reexamine the most salient aspects of the Swede's conduct, especially after he walks out of the hotel and stumbles into the saloon. At that point, he has become the loneliest man on earth, a stranger in a forbidding, alien territory with no friends, no allies, no connection to a single person within a thousand miles of anywhere. He is desperate for companionship, so miserably in need of the smallest flicker of kindness from someone, anyone, that he begs the bartender to share a drink with him. When the bartender turns him down, he refocuses his attention on the four men gathered around the table, but they turn him down as well, and it is only then, when every person in the room has rejected his offer of friendship, that his goodwill degenerates into anger and he goes on the attack. A moment before the Swede puts his hands around his throat, the gambler says, "My friend, I don't know you." At first glance, it seems to be a rather innocuous statement from a man who is politely attempting to brush off an annoying stranger, but when we remove the statement from its original context and look at it again, it carries a different meaning. "My friend, I don't know you." For the gambler's three respectable and vanished drinking pals, it would mean one different thing—"We're not responsible, you're on your own"—but for the ultrasensitive, lunatic Swede, it would mean yet another different thing: a brief surge of hope to begin with—"My friend"—and the heart-shattering message that follows: "I don't know you." The sentence is a pure oxymoron, a sentence that says two opposite and equal things at the same time and therefore is devoid of sense. The Swede's mind snaps.

The *mysterious theory* referred to at the end is in fact everything Crane had been working toward for the past year, the gradual refinement of a position that grew out of the rough hours he had spent on the open sea with Murphy, Montgomery, and Higgins. The revelation that human beings are ultimately dependent on one another for all things that matter most in life had led him to explore both the good and the bad that follow from this unyielding premise. An active spirit of cooperation can produce marvels of human solidarity anywhere in the world, whether in a ten-foot rowboat off the coast of Florida, in a railway line carrying hundreds of passengers to their appointed destinations between England and Scotland, or in a small Irish village preparing the first catch of the season for sale at the local fish market, but a passive unity among disconnected individuals can produce nightmares, as in the depredations visited upon Henry Johnson and Dr. Trescott in small-town Whilomville or in the silent bystanders on the Nebraska plains who lack the courage to defend a brain-sick man and consequently abandon him to the hazards of storm, knifeblade, and death. "Every sin is the result of a collaboration," says the Easterner. This is the moral code Crane had worked out for himself by the time he was twenty-six, and when you look for flaws in his proposition, you are forced to conclude that there aren't any, for the idea in this sentence applies to everything, to the sins of solitary men and women and to the sins of families, schools, industries, neighborhoods, and whole countries. We are all responsible for one another, and if we fail to assume that responsibility, life on earth becomes a living hell. This was Crane's most important idea. No American writer since then has formulated anything that surpasses it.

13

"HE IS STRANGELY HOPELESS ABOUT HIMSELF," CONRAD OBSERVED IN his letter to Garnett, and the truth was that Crane had every reason to be feeling hopeless. Nothing was going according to plan, and no matter how hard he worked or how much he had to show for his efforts, he wasn't bringing in enough to sustain the household. Bad luck played some part in these difficulties, as did the punishing contract he had signed with McClure, as did the suit brought against him by Amy Leslie's lawyer that temporarily froze his American royalties, but the deeper, more general problem was that he had put himself in an impossible position and was playing a game he could not win, for the fact was that no one—not one person in the English-speaking world—could earn an adequate living as a freelance writer of short stories.

To understand what Crane was up against, consider the publishing histories of his four Oxted masterpieces. He was banking on swift and substantial payments from each of them to pull him out of his financial hole, but one by one they all ran into protracted, unexpected delays before they found their way into print. *The Monster*, completed in September 1897, spent close to a year in limbo. Initially blocked by McClure, who held on to the manuscript although he had no intention of publishing it (too controversial), the novelette was then rejected by Gilder at the *Century* (too offensive) and did not appear in the pages of *Harper's New Monthly Magazine* until August 1898. "The Bride Comes to Yellow Sky," also finished in September 1897, had to wait five months before McClure (of all people) got around to publishing it in his magazine. "Death and the Child" also languished for five months before Reynolds sold it to *Harper's Weekly*. And then there was the long comedy of mishaps and blunders surrounding "The Blue Hotel," which Crane sent off to Reynolds on February 7, 1898. For complicated reasons having to do with what stories should be added to *The Monster* to fill out a collection large enough for Harper's to publish in book form, the editors turned it down for their magazine. Reynolds then sent it out to other quality monthlies, and one by one the *Century*, *Scribner's Magazine*, and the *Atlantic Monthly* turned it down as well. It wasn't that the *Atlantic* editor was hostile to the idea, but he wanted the rights to all of Crane's Western stories for a book to be published by Houghton Mifflin (where he held a second job as acquisitions consultant), and when Reynolds informed him that the other stories had already been claimed, the editor, William Hines Page (future ambassador to Great Britain during the First World War), returned the manuscript with the peerless, numskull comment that "one stray story is hardly worth our while." Reynolds then submitted it to *Collier's Weekly*, which came back with an affirmative answer, but given the length of the story and the tall asking price (four hundred dollars), they wondered if it couldn't be trimmed down somewhat and published for a lower price, that is, if the ten thousand words couldn't be reduced to seven thousand five hundred words and the four hundred dollars to three hundred. When Reynolds presented this half-cocked (or three-quarters cocked) proposal to his client, Crane surprisingly went along with it. He was in New York by then, on his way to cover the war in Cuba, and with his mind preoccupied by other, more urgent matters, he was in no mood for haggling. He took off for Key West before Reynolds received the contract, however, and when Crane looked for the story to make the demanded cuts, he realized that he had left the manuscript in his New York hotel room. The story was found, sent to him in Florida, and when he returned the manuscript to Reynolds on May eighth, it was accompanied by a brief note: "Can't cut this. Let Colliers do it themselves. Hold money & telegraph me when payment is made." The unaltered manuscript was then mailed back to *Collier's*, but Robert Collier, the young editor in charge of the magazine, promptly misplaced it as well, and by the time he remembered that he had forgotten about it, more time had elapsed. When *Collier's* finally published "The Blue Hotel" in two installments on November twenty-sixth and December third (ten months after it was finished), not one word had been deleted or changed, but presumably they stuck to the terms of the contract and sent Reynolds a check for three hundred dollars, not four.

To understand Crane's growing distress throughout these various ordeals, we have only to look at some of the letters he wrote from England between the fall of '97 and the spring of '98. To John Phillips (managing editor of *McClure's Magazine*) in October:

> What on earth have you done with *The Monster*? ...
>   ... I have delivered to you over 25000 words but I dont see myself any better off than if I had asked you to wait until I got damned good and ready to pay. ... Now please tell me where I am at. What has happened? Did I write a story called *The Monster*? Did I deliver it to you? And what happened after that?

To Reynolds on December twentieth:

> Of course I am awfully hard up. You know of course of my Appleton royalties being attached. They knocked me silly. ...
>   Why McClure is monkeying about with The Monster I dont quite understand. It might make me come a cropper if I dont get that money directly.

To Reynolds later in December, with the manuscript of "Death and the Child" enclosed, after telling him "I wouldn't have done it if I was not broke":

> For heaven's sake raise me all the money you can and *cable* it, *cable* it sure between Xmas and New Year's. Sell "The Monster." Don't forget that— cable me some money this month.

To Reynolds on January fourteenth:

> In all the months I have been in England I have never received a cent from America which has not been borrowed. Just read that over twice! The consequences of this have lately been that I have been obliged to make arrangements here with English agents of American houses but in all cases your commission will be protected. This is the best I could do. My English expenses have chased me to the wall. Even now I am waiting for you to cable me my share of the Monster money and if there is a fluke I am lost.

To Reynolds on January thirty-first, no longer counting the number of words he is planning to write but directly translating words into dollars:

I am going to write about a thousand or twelve hundred dollars in short stuff. . . . In the meantime every hundred dollars is a boon! I enclose you a scheme for a syndicate. I am *sure* you can work it. I could work it from here if you were not my agent.

You have done bully!

P.S.: No, I'll not enclose you the syndicate scheme at present. Next week.

To Reynolds on February seventh (in a rare burst of optimism):

As you see, I am buckling down and turning out stuff like a man. If you hold your fine gait it will only be a short time before we are throwing out our chests.

There are a few odds and ends of affairs, such as the *Journal* business and so on that I wish you would get settled up. A ten pound note even fills me with awe. . . .

However, now that I am in it, I must beat it and I feel that with your help the affair will not be too serious. I will bombard you with stuff. Then, if you sell *Harper's* "The Blue Hotel," cable money instantly. I have got big matters to attend to this month. Get me through this and I am prepared to smile.

To Reynolds on March thirteenth:

I must have some money by the first of April. Will you collect the numerous small am'ts due me if possible and send to me?

Magazines, then, were an iffy source of income at best, but they were only one half of the equation, a first step in the larger plan to put the stories together into collections and publish them as books. Here, too, however, Crane discovered that he was betting on the wrong horse, for then as now story collections rarely did much in terms of sales, at least not in comparison to novels, and no matter how good or great or even magnificent his stories were, they would never bring in enough money to rescue him from his financial difficulties.

He understood that. Falsely overconfident as he could be at times, he knew that he would have to write a novel to pay off his debts and, if luck was with him and he managed to produce a hit, to sustain the extravagant life he was building with Cora. For that reason, not long after he started writing "The Blue Hotel," he abruptly put the story aside and plunged into the novel he had been thinking about for the past several months, *Active Service*, a quasi-autobiographical story about an American newspaperman in Greece during the war. In his letter to Reynolds from December twentieth, he announced that he had written twelve thousand words out of a projected seventy-five thousand and might be able to finish the book by April or May. If they could scare up a large advance for him on the strength of a synopsis, he would push forward with it, but hard as Reynolds seems to have pushed on his end, he found no takers, and so Crane put the novel aside and returned to the story. These lunging, impulsive changes of heart suggest that he was growing frantic, inching ever closer to out-and-out desperation.

What Crane probably knew, but what he probably hadn't found the courage to admit to himself, was that his star was fading. He had had his moment of glory with the accursed *Red Badge*, but sales had been dropping steadily for the past year, and with his American royalties blocked and no money to be earned from the book in England, the one thing he might have counted on was *The Third Violet*, which had received strong, encouraging reviews in the British press—as opposed to the critical drubbing it had been given in the States—but the little screenplay-novel hadn't sold terribly well and had been written off as a commercial failure. Little matter that his work of the past two years had broken new ground. Few people understood it, and those who did were either wildly enthusiastic or scared off because, as one magazine editor wrote in a staff memo about "The Blue Hotel," it was "too strong and brutal for [our] readers." And besides, all that work had consisted of stories, accursed short stories.

Still and all, when he wasn't panicking about money or scheming with Reynolds about their next move, he continued to plug away as he always had, not only on his stories for magazines and future books but on a number of occasional pieces as well, which were written for the pure pleasure of writing them and would have added no more than nickels to his depleted purse: a pair of exuberantly nutty forays into political satire, "How the Afridis Made a Ziarat" (*New York Press*, 9/19/97) and an anti-imperialist, Ubu-esque playlet, "The Blood of the Martyr" (*New York Press*, 4/3/98), as well as a generous puff about his friend Harold Frederic (*Chap-Book*, 3/15/98). In his cover letter to Reynolds about the last article, Crane wrote, "I am sending you a fifteen hundred word essay on Harold Frederic and his work. . . . I have written this at his request. . . . The price is not a particular point at this time." As with the piece he wrote about Conrad, friendship trumped the demands of manufacturing words for dollars.

More important, he was also writing poems during this period, some of

his best poems, as it turned out, many of which would be included the following year in his second published collection, *War Is Kind. The Black Riders*
had rushed out of Crane in a single, unbroken frenzy, as if a voice trapped
inside him had suddenly been unleashed, but then the poetic spout had run
dry, and the voice went still. There were no more eruptions after that, but
in the years since then he had been quietly working on new poems, two or
three dozen in all, perhaps, which were composed in more varied registers
than the "lines" written in 1894, from the angry, sarcastic "A newspaper is a
collection of half-injustices" (page 456) to the gracefully flowing "I explain
the silvered passing of a ship at night" (page 457). The new poems tended
to be longer than first ones, but not all of them, as with these two, which
remain close in spirit to the knockout pills in *The Black Riders*:

> A man said to the universe:
> "Sir, I exist!"
> "However," replied the universe,
> "The fact has not created in me
> "A sense of obligation."

Or:

> The wayfarer
> Perceiving the pathway to truth
> Was struck with astonishment.
> It was thickly grown with weeds.
> "Ha," he said,
> "I see that none has passed here
> "In a long time."
> Later he saw that each weed
> Was a singular knife.
> "Well," he mumbled at last,
> "Doubtless there are other roads."

But in lines such as "The chanting of flowers / The screams of cut trees"
or "To the maiden / The sea was a blue meadow / Alive with little froth
people," Crane enters a new zone of lyrical daring, as he does in these lines
from "The impact of a dollar upon the heart":

> The rug of an honest bear
> Under the feet of a cryptic slave

Who speaks always of baubles
Forgetting place, multitude, work and state,
Champing and mouthing of hats
Making ratful squeak of hats,
Hats.

There is also a new sensuality in these poems and a richer, more elaborated sense of the complexities and nuances of erotic desire—a sign of how
deeply schooled Crane had become in the agonies of heartbreak and lust:

Ah, God, the way your little finger moved
As you thrust a bare arm backward
And made play with your hair
And a comb, a silly gilt comb
Ah, God—that I should suffer
Because of the way a little finger moved.

Most memorable among these later poems are the title work of the
second collection, "War Is Kind," which seems to have been written in
1895, not long before the publication of *Red Badge*, and "A Man Adrift
on a Slim Spar," which was composed in England sometime in late 1897.*
Although separated by more than two years, they are structured in nearly
identical ways: each one five stanzas long, with the majority of the stanzas
ending in a short, liturgical refrain of one sentence that consists of three
one-syllable words, and as the poems build steadily from stanza to stanza,
the end refrain grows stronger and more unsettling with each repetition.
War and shipwreck. Those are the subjects of the two poems, and in them
Crane delineates a stark, remorseless theology of human abandonment in
a world without God.

Described by John Berryman as "one of the major lyrics of the century,"
the war poem is also one of the most wrenching, bewildering, ironical,
tragic, and complex pages in all of S.C.'s work:

---

* Never published in Crane's lifetime, it did not appear in print until 1929. Why it should
have been excluded from the collection is not known, but the simple answer could be that
Crane lost track of the manuscript and didn't know where to find it—not the first time he
would have lost something he had written. The fact that he sent a copy to Elbert Hubbard
confirms that Crane intended to publish it, but his follow-up letter from January 29, 1898,
asking Hubbard whether he had received the poem would suggest that the package had
gone astray, since Hubbard routinely published all the poems Crane sent him.

Do not weep, maiden, for war is kind.
Because your lover threw wild hands toward the sky
And the affrighted steed ran on alone,
Do not weep.
War is kind.

   Hoarse, booming drums of the regiment
   Little souls who thirst for fight,
   These men were born to drill and die
   The unexplained glory flies above them
   Great is the battle-god, great, and his kingdom——
   A field where a thousand corpses lie.

Do not weep, babe, for war is kind.
Because your father tumbled in the yellow trenches,
Raged at his breast, gulped and died,
Do not weep.
War is kind.

   Swift, blazing flag of the regiment
   Eagle with crest of red and gold,
   These men were born to drill and die
   Point for them the virtue of slaughter
   Make plain to them the excellence of killing
   And a field where a thousand corpses lie.

Mother whose heart hung humble as a button
On the bright splendid shroud of your son,
Do not weep.
War is kind.

The lost poem pushes beyond the shared destinies of the men in "The Open Boat" and confines itself to the fate of one man clinging desperately to a piece of broken mast (the spar) from a ship that has already foundered and sunk. The man is about to drown, and all-powerful God, who could turn the ocean into a heap of dry ashes if He willed it, does not lift a finger for him. The moment when the man is about to go under is captured in the third line of the fourth stanza as the sky suddenly vanishes ("A reeling, drunken sky and no sky")—language so compact and so severe that it resembles a blow from a tightly clenched fist. It is a terrifying poem, a poem of helplessness and panic that was written just as Crane was starting to realize that he, too, was in danger of going under, for one year after he had escaped drowning off the coast of Florida, he was drowning again on dry land in England.

> A man adrift on a slim spar
> A horizon smaller than the rim of a bottle
> Tented waves rearing lashy dark points
> The near whine of froth in circles.
>   God is cold.

> The incessant raise and swing of the sea
> And growl after growl of crest
> The sinkings, green, seething, endless
> The upheaval half-completed.
>   God is cold.

> The seas are in the hollow of the Hand;
> Oceans may be turned to a spray
> Raining down through the stars
> Because of a gesture of pity toward a babe.
> Oceans may become grey ashes,
> Die with a long moan and a roar
> Amid the tumult of the fishes
> And the cries of the ships
> Because the Hand beckons the mice.

> A horizon smaller than a doomed assassin's cap
> Inky, surging tumults
> A reeling, drunken sky and no sky
> A pale hand sliding from a polished spar.
>   God is cold.

> A puff of a coat imprisoning air.
> A face kissing the water-death
> A weary slow sway of a lost hand
> And the sea, the moving sea, the sea.
>   God is cold.

When Crane left for Cuba on April thirteenth, not only was he running away from his troubles in England, he was running toward his next adventure, which turned out to be the one that destroyed his health and ultimately killed him. It is difficult to know which impulse was stronger in him at that moment—the desire to run away or the desire to run toward—but it is certain that he had every intention of coming back. In spite of their debts and what J. C. Levenson calls their "prodigal hospitality," Crane and Cora had become a solid, harmonious couple, so tightly connected after a year of living together that he was now dictating some of his work to her and her handwriting was becoming more and more indistinguishable from his. Knowing that they were dissatisfied with their house and wanted to remove themselves farther from London, Edward Garnett took it upon himself to steer them toward another house in Sussex (where they eventually wound up living), and both of them enthusiastically embraced the idea, so much so that S.C. talked about the house to his fellow journalists in Cuba as the place he would be going back to after the war was over.

The money squeeze on the one hand, habitual restlessness on the other—both factored into his decision to go—but there was more than that, something so difficult to define that it seems to resist being put into words. *Hopeless* was the word Conrad had used in his letter to Garnett in December, and in a letter written to Crane on February fifth, he went so far as to say, "It hurts me to think you are worried. It is bad for you and bad for your art." This gets us a little closer to what I am struggling to pin down. Something was eating at Crane, some dark force had crept into him that was slowly tearing him apart, and chances are that he himself was not even aware of it, or had no words for it, or couldn't bring himself to think about it, but whatever it was, it was pushing him toward a crisis, or perhaps had already thrown him into the middle of one. I don't want to simplify matters and bluntly declare that he sensed he was dying, but given how he acted at the front in Cuba, where he seemed to be courting death by taking such outlandish risks as putting himself directly in the line of enemy fire, one suspects that he wanted to be gunned down in action and meet the death of a common foot soldier. A quick death—and not the slow death his damaged lungs were already preparing for him.

Perhaps.

In any case, once the idea took hold of him, nothing could stop him from going, and to his eternal regret, Conrad played an active part in scrounging up the funds to pay for the crossing to New York. As he dolefully recounts in his final memory piece about Crane:

The cloudy afternoon when we two went rushing all over London together, was for him the beginning of the end. The problem was to find £60 that day, before the sun set, before dinner, before the "six forty" train to Oxted, at once, that instant—lest peace be declared and the opportunity of seeing a war be missed. I had not £60 to lend him. Sixty shillings was nearer to my mark. We tried various offices but had no luck, or rather we had the usual luck of money hunting enterprises. The man was either gone out to see about a dog, or would take no interest in the Spanish-American war. In one place the man wanted to know what was the hurry? He would have liked to have forty-eight hours to think the matter over. As we came downstairs Crane's white-faced excitement frightened me. Finally it occurred to me to take him to Messrs. William Blackwood & Sons' London office. There he was received in a most friendly way. Presently I escorted him to Charing Cross where he took the train for home with the assurance that he would have the means to start "for the war" next day. That is the reason I can not to this day read his tale "The Price of the Harness" without a pang. It has done nothing more deadly than pay his debt to Messrs. Blackwood; yet now and then I feel as though that afternoon I had led him by the hand to his doom. But, indeed, I was only the blind agent of the fate that had him in her grip! Nothing could have held him back. He was ready to swim the ocean.

THE DARK SIDE
OF THE MOON

꧁꧂

I

FIVE DAYS INTO S.C.'S CROSSING FROM LIVERPOOL TO NEW YORK ON
the steamship *Germanic*, two different versions of his latest story collection were published in the United States and England, *The Open Boat
and Other Tales of Adventure* (Doubleday & McClure) and *The Open Boat and
Other Stories* (Heinemann). In addition to the title story, both books contain "A Man and Some Others," "One Dash—Horses," "Flanagan and
His Short Filibustering Adventure," "The Bride Comes to Yellow Sky,"
"The Wise Men," "Death and the Child," and "The Five White Mice,"
but these works form only the first part of the British edition—under the
heading "Minor Conflicts"—which is followed by a second part ("Midnight Sketches") that includes a number of pieces set in New York and
Asbury Park: "An Experiment in Misery," "The Men in the Storm," "The
Duel That Was Not Fought," "An Ominous Baby," "A Great Mistake,"
"An Eloquence of Grief," "The Auction," "The Pace of Youth," and "A
Detail." Whether in the long version or the short version, this gathering
represents some of the finest work Crane had done or would ever do as a
writer of stories, but the response from the press was no better or worse
than the ones he had received for his other post–*Red Badge* books: a
mixture of pro and con, of admiration and bafflement, of hearty slaps on
the back and disdainful cold shoulders. The standard split decision for
any writer worth his salt, and therefore not so bad, finally, but for a writer
who happened to be splashing around in a pool of debt, it wouldn't be

good enough to drain out more than a few drops of water. No critical response captures Crane's dilemma more acutely than an unsigned
notice that appeared in the *Athenaeum* (London) in which the reviewer
acknowledged that the stories "show evident signs of that extraordinary
ability, amounting to genius, which distinguishes all the prose of Mr.
Crane; but we doubt whether they will hit the taste of the public in this
country, as they are too sombre and too generally concerned with persons
of a somewhat uniform type of white savagery."

This failure to "hit the taste of the public" was one of the reasons why
Crane was in the middle of the Atlantic when the book was released, for
by then even the "little hit" he had been counting on back in December
would no longer have been enough to hold him in England. He needed
money, and only a job as a correspondent in the approaching war could
give it to him.

There was that, but there was also his conflicted state of mind when he
set out for Cuba, which can be seen as an abrupt abandonment of Cora
as well or, if not Cora herself, of the domesticity she represented, the settled, unbudging routine of work, home, and continual socializing. For all his
efforts to adjust to these new circumstances, his first stab at conjugal life had
lasted just ten months, and Cora would not be accompanying him as she
had the previous spring when he bolted off to the war in Greece. The days of
their joint adventuring had come to an end, and Imogene Carter (both the
fact of her and the idea of her) had been laid permanently to rest. Instead,
wife Cora would be staying put in England to grapple with the financial ruin
she and her mouse had created and—in her mind if not in his—to keep the
home fires burning. It was his decision, not hers, and she had no choice but
to go along with it. To raise any objections would have put their unsancti-
fied marriage at risk, perhaps even smashed it beyond hope of repair, and so
she acquiesced in silence. Not without some legitimate worries about their
future together, but also deeply worried about *him*. Two weeks before he left,
she expressed those anxieties in a letter to their friend Scovel:

Dear Harry: Stephen is coming on the ship that carries this letter to
America, as correspondent in the U.S. Spain row. I suppose you will see
him as doubtless Key West will be the headquarters for newspaper men.
We have thought it best for me to remain in England. I am writing to
you to ask you and your good wife—if ye be in the same town, to look
after him a little. He is rather seedy and I am anxious about him, for he
does not care to look out for himself. . . . And if he should become ill I
beg you to wire me.

That seediness and unwillingness to look out for himself, coupled with the threat of physical illness, would be borne out by Crane's disheveled appearance and reckless behavior throughout the war, and, just as Cora had feared, he became so ill at one point that he had to be evacuated from Cuba and sent for treatment at the military hospital in Old Point Comfort, Virginia, which led to a further trip all the way to the Adirondacks to consult with a lung specialist who ran a sanatorium in Saranac Lake. Writing about Crane's appearance on a dispatch boat during the early, pre-invasion period of the war, the novelist Frank Norris observed that

> The Young Personage was wearing a pair of duck trousers grimed and fouled with all manner of pitch and grease and oil. His shirt was guiltless of collar or scarf, and was unbuttoned at the throat. His hair hung in ragged fringes over his eyes, his dress-suit case was across his lap and answered him for a desk. Between his heels he held a bottle of beer against the rolling of the boat, and when he drank was royally independent of a glass. While he was composing his descriptive dispatches which some ten thousand people would read in the morning from the bulletins in New York, I wondered what the fifty thousand who have read his war novel and have held him, no doubt rightly, to be a great genius, would have said and thought could they have seen him at the moment.

Later on, after his apparent recovery in Virginia, Crane returned to active duty to report on the invasion of Puerto Rico and found himself on a dispatch boat with fellow correspondent Charles Michelson. According to his sharp-eyed friend,

> Crane on his way to war was one of the most unprepossessing figures that ever served as a nucleus for apocryphal romances; shambling, with hair too long, usually lacking a shave, dressed like any of the deck hands, hollow-cheeked, sallow, destitute of small talk, critical if not fastidious, marked with ill-health—the very antithesis of the conquering male.
>   ... There was a head-wind most of the way, and the nose of the boat was under water with every wave, and somebody discovered that by standing far forward with a tight grip on the stays the Atlantic Ocean could be turned into an acceptable shower-bath. Crane revealed the wreck of an athlete's frame—once square shoulders crowded forward by the concavity of a collapsed chest; legs like pipestems—he looked like a frayed white ribbon, seen through the veil of green as the seas washed over him.

It would come to that after just three months, and deep down Crane probably understood that he was headed for some personal catastrophe when he ran off from England—*the beginning of the end*—but at the same time he was determined to confront that end and refused to allow his wife or Conrad or anyone else to talk him out of it. His *white-faced excitement frightened me*, and as he swam across the ocean on his ten-day journey to New York, it seems that Crane was thinking as much about his American past as the immediate future awaiting him in the jungles of Cuba. He had not set foot in his own country for more than a year, and the prospect sent him reeling back into the mythological town of his childhood, Whilomville, which became the site of a new story he began sketching out somewhere in mid-ocean and then finished in the early days of the war on a dispatch boat as he and other American correspondents cruised around in hostile waters patrolled by Spanish gunboats and battleships. One asks how he managed to detach himself so thoroughly from his surroundings that he could concentrate on a story about a young boy at such a perilous time, but once we take a closer look at the story, it becomes clear that Crane—whether he knew it or not—was in fact writing about himself and his torn feelings about his current situation.

The Whilomville of "His New Mittens" is a different place from the one depicted in *The Monster*. No fires, no burnt-off flesh, no fear-crazed citizens in this version—just the placid little town where Crane had spent the first fully remembered years of his childhood, the lost paradise that was stolen from him after his father's sudden, unexpected death. It was the single most traumatizing event of his young life—the axe blow that splintered apart his world and taught him that God was a cruel and capricious force who could not, under any circumstances, be trusted.

And there he was now at twenty-six, alone in the middle of the Atlantic, a runaway steaming forward into whatever unknown thing was about to happen to him next, a situation not unlike that of the little boy in his story, who also decides to run away from home, in his case to California, which in his imagination is as far from where he lives as the dark side of the moon. Or, to put it in another context, roughly the same distance from New York State as Cuba was from Oxted.

His name is Horace, and he seems to be around eight years old (Crane's age when his father died), and he, too, is a fatherless boy, and while Crane was not an only child as Horace is, for all practical purposes he was a boy without brothers or sisters, given the vast age difference between him and his older siblings. Horace lives with his mother and maiden aunt, and although nothing is said about the father's death, the fact that the mother walks around in "widow's weeds" would suggest it was fairly recent. The result is that the boy is now trapped within a female-run household, and he feels suffocated by the nervous, hovering presences of his two captors, who have imposed so many strictures and prohibitions on him that he is continually running afoul of their laws. The parallels are not exact, but Crane, too, had begun to squirm under the constraints of his life in England, and when the pressure became too much to bear, he, too, wound up escaping to the dark side of the moon.

Nor is it an accident that the crucial event of the story hinges on the boy's desire to take part in a "battle," which was the same impulse that took hold of Crane and sent him rushing off to Cuba. For little Horace, the guns of the American and Spanish military forces have been replaced by snowballs, but a battle is a battle, and as the story begins he is walking home from school one afternoon when he comes upon a large group of his friends engaged in a snowball fight, with one half of the gang pretending to be soldiers and the other half pretending to be Indians. Horace is desperate to join in, but two impediments are standing in his way. First, his mother has instructed him to "come straight home as soon as school is out," and second, he is wearing a new pair of red mittens, and she has sternly warned him not to "get them nice new mittens all wet, either. Do you hear?" So even as Horace's friends ask him to join the battle, the boy hesitates, which prompts the other boys to mock him with a stinging taunt:

> "A-fray-ed of his mit-tens! A-fray-ed of his mit-tens!" They sang these lines to cruel and monotonous music which is as old perhaps as American childhood and which it is the privilege of the emancipated adult to completely forget. "A-fray-ed of his mit-tens!"

Rare among emancipated adults, Crane had not forgotten his American childhood, and in an impressively intricate passage that extends over the first four pages of the thirteen-page story, he delves into the hierarchies, fluctuating alliances, and psychological factors animating the snowball war as Horace gradually succumbs to the temptations of battle over obedience, responsibility, and home. Before long, his mother comes walking down the street and drags him off with her, a public humiliation that will surely lower his standing among the other boys, and then, after he stuffs the soaking-wet mittens into his pockets and claims not to know where they are, his mother reaches into the pockets, pulls out the mittens, and punishes him. Horace breaks down and cries.

He is banished to the kitchen while his mother and aunt eat their supper in the dining room, and now that Horace is alone Crane begins to travel deep into the little boy's head, embarking on a journey similar to the ones he had taken into the heads of Henry Fleming, George Kelcey, and the New York Kid: the mind in conversation with itself as it loops and spins through an incessant rush of arguments and counter-arguments, gyrating into and out of a number of conflicting thoughts as it struggles to come up with a plan of action, which in the mind of the cruelly treated young Horace will be how best to exact a fitting revenge on his oppressors.

His aunt has carried in a plate of food and left it on the chair beside him, and although Horace is sorely tempted by the pickle lying next to the cold ham and bread, he decides that he must make his stand now and, therefore, merely touches the pickle but does not dare to lift it off the plate and eat it. Because:

His heart was black with hatred. He painted in his mind scenes of deadly retribution. His mother would be taught that he was not one to endure persecution meekly, without raising an arm in his defense. And so his dreams were of a slaughter of feelings, and near the end of them his mother was pictured as coming, bowed with pain, to his feet. Weeping, she implored his charity. Would he forgive her? No; his once tender heart had been turned to stone by her injustice. He could not forgive her. She must pay the inexorable penalty.

The first item in this horrible plan was the refusal of the food. This he knew by experience would work havoc in his mother's heart. And so he grimly waited.

But suddenly it occurred to him that the first part of his revenge was in danger of failing.

His mother is taking too long, since normally she would have come into the kitchen by now to ask if he was ill, and by telling her to leave so he could "suffer in silence," he would invariably soften her heart and wriggle himself back into her good graces. As S.C. drolly comments: "He had known such maneuvering to result even in pie."

But his mother is taking too long this time, the surefire tactic isn't working, and "as the truth sank into his mind, he supremely loathed life, the world, his mother. His heart was beating back the besiegers; he was a defeated child." So much for Plan A, but no sooner is he vanquished on that front than he comes up with the far more dramatic Plan B—to slip out of the house and run away.

Note how crude and exaggerated his thoughts are throughout the business that follows and—to compare his thinking to some of Crane's previous excursions into the minds of his characters—how great the difference is between Horace's inner world and that of Henry Fleming, for example, who is not a boy but an adolescent, and the even greater difference between him and the New York Kid, who is not an adolescent but a young man, which tells us much about Crane's method and accounts for why his characters stand distinctly apart from one another as fully individuated beings. At his best, Crane doesn't write about his creations so much as inhabit them. With little Horace in "His New Mittens," he is inhabiting the mind of a boy, and as he himself deeply understood—and deeply remembered—an eight-year-old's mind is capable of just so much and no more.

> In a remote corner of the world he would become some sort of bloody-handed person driven to a life of crime by the barbarity of his mother. She should never know his fate. He would torture her for years with doubts and doubts and drive her implacably to an unrepentant grave.

He puts on his coat and cap, and off he goes, casting one backward glance at the pickle, which he is tempted to take along with him but then decides not to, for if the plate is left untouched, "his mother would feel even worse." To make matters worse for him, however, it is snowing heavily outside, and because he isn't sure whether the journey to California should begin by walking down Niagara Avenue or Hogan Street, he ducks into the woodshed to think things over and ruminate "miserably upon his martyrdom." It is frightfully cold in there, but he is somewhat comforted when he looks over at the house and sees a lamp moving "rapidly from window to window. Then the kitchen door slammed and a shawled figure [his Aunt Martha] sped toward the gate. At last he was making them feel his power." They know that he has disappeared now, and for a little while he exults in "the terror he is causing," but then he realizes that sooner or later someone will come looking for him in the woodshed.

> He knew that it would not be manful to be caught so soon. He was not positive now that he was going to remain away forever, but at any rate he was bound to inflict some more damage before showing himself to be captured. If he merely succeeded in making his mother angry, she would thrash him on sight. He must prolong the time in order to be safe. If he held out properly, he was sure of a welcome of love, even though he should drip with crimes.

Crane couldn't have known how prescient the last two sentences of this passage would turn out to be, but weirdly enough that was more or less what happened during the eight and a half months he and Cora spent apart, for even though the fighting stopped when Spain capitulated on August twelfth, Crane *prolonged the time* of his absence by sneaking back into Havana and staying there for another four months, doing such a good job of disappearing from her and nearly everyone else that many assumed he was either dead or in prison. He tortured her with his long silences (aggravated by the fact that nearly every one of the few letters he wrote to her was lost, delayed, or tossed out by the boardinghouse cleaning woman who was supposed to mail them for him), but when he was finally tracked down and funds were raised to cover his passage back to England, he boarded the ship, crossed the ocean, and contentedly resumed his life with Cora, for even though he was *dripping with crimes*, he had stayed away long enough to receive *a welcome of love*, and all was forgiven.

As for the young hero of his story, Horace reluctantly abandons the woodshed and steps back into the storm to avoid immediate capture, but by now the storm has grown into a blizzard that swings him "violently with its rough and merciless strength. Panting, stung, half-blinded with the driving flakes, he was now a waif, exiled, friendless, and poor."

No doubt, Crane was also thinking about himself when he wrote the final words of that sentence. After his failure to make a go of it in England, he was headed back to America feeling "exiled, friendless, and poor," for at that point he hadn't secured his correspondent's job and war between Spain and America would not be officially declared until the day of his arrival, and therefore nothing was certain yet, but even as he floundered in that nothing he still had hope that the situation would somehow resolve itself, as it does for little Horace in the last chapter of the story.

The boy, adrift and pummeled by the snow, blames his mother for having "thrust him into this wild storm." At the same time, in utter opposition to that surly resentment, he wants nothing more than to go back into the house and cancel the trip to California—but he won't give in, he can't give in, he must forge on and stick to the plan out of his "enigmatical childish ideal of form." He stumbles onto Niagara Avenue and finds himself looking into the brightly lit windows of Stickney's butcher shop. The butcher, who had been a close friend of Horace's father, is standing in his cluttered emporium surrounded by "rows of pigs hung head downward . . . [and] clumps of attenuated turkeys" suspended from the ceiling. One customer is inside, a woman with "a monster basket on her arm," and once she leaves the shop, Horace summons his courage and goes in himself. From then on,

the warmhearted Stickney takes over, and in a rapidly unfolding denoue-
ment the story charges on to its complex but richly satisfying conclusion
as mother and son find each other again—just as Crane and Cora would
eventually find each other again as well.

Stickney had placed his two fat hands palms downward and wide apart
on the table, in the attitude of a butcher facing a customer, but now he
straightened.

"Here," he said, "what's wrong? What's wrong, kid?"

"Nothin'," answered Horace huskily. He labored for a moment with
something in his throat, and afterward added, "O'ny—I've—I've run
away, and—"

"Run away!" shouted Stickney. "Run away from what? Who?"

"From—home," answered Horace. "I don't like it there any more. I—"
He had arranged an oration to win the sympathy of the butcher; he had
prepared a table setting forth the merits of his case in the most logical
fashion, but it was as if the wind had been knocked out of his mind. "I've
run away. I—"

Stickney reached an enormous hand over the array of beef and
firmly grappled the emigrant. Then he swung himself to Horace's side.
His face was stretched with laughter, and he playfully shook his prisoner. "Come—come—come. What dashed nonsense is this? Run away,
hey? Run away?" Whereupon the child's long-tried spirit found vent
in howls.

"Come, come," said Stickney busily. "Never mind, now, never mind.
You just come along with me. It'll be all right. I'll fix it. Never you mind."

Five minutes later the butcher, with a great ulster over his apron, was
leading the boy homeward.

At the very threshold Horace raised his last flag of pride. "No—no,"
he sobbed. "I don't want to. I don't want to go in there." He braced his
foot against the step, and made a very respectable resistance.

"Now, Horace," cried the butcher. He thrust open the door with a
bang. "Hello there!" Across the dark kitchen the door to the living room
opened and Aunt Martha appeared. "You've found him!" she screamed.

"We've come to make a call," roared the butcher.

At the entrance to the living room a silence fell upon them all. Upon
a couch Horace saw his mother lying limp, pale as death, her eyes shining with pain. There was an electric pulse before she swung a waxen
hand toward Horace. "My child," she murmured tremulously. Whereupon the sinister person addressed, with a prolonged wail of grief and

joy, ran to her with speed. "Ma—ma! Oh, ma-ma!" She was not able to speak in a known tongue as she folded him in her weak arms.

Aunt Martha turned defiantly upon the butcher because her face betrayed her. She was crying. She made a gesture half military, half feminine. "Won't you have a glass of our root-beer, Mr. Stickney? We make it ourselves."

And with that gesture from Aunt Martha—*half military, half feminine*—Crane encapsulates the tangled ambiguities of his departure from England, the decision to quit the home front and set out for the battlefront, which was finally an impossible choice for him and would have left him in a state of conflict no matter what he had chosen to do or not to do. Hence this beautiful little story, which is at once a signal of inner distress and a wish-fulfillment fantasy in which the decision to leave home comes out right in the end. The wonder is that "His New Mittens," which surpasses any episode in Twain's *Tom Sawyer* (in my opinion) and stands as one of the great short works about boyhood in American literature, should have been composed under such odd and trying circumstances, on the way to war and in the midst of war, but just as the correspondent and the oiler in "The Open Boat" *rowed . . . and then they rowed*, Crane wrote . . . and then he wrote, and wherever he was and whatever was happening around him in any given circumstance, writing was the one unwavering thing he did throughout his brief, often wavering life. If that life is worth examining now, it is only because of the work that came out of it.

2

ON APRIL TWENTY-SECOND, THE DAY AFTER HE REACHED NEW YORK, Crane landed a job with Pulitzer's *World* as part of a team of correspondents that would be working under the supervision of his friend Harry Scovel, who had been given the post of bureau chief for the paper's wartime operations in Cuba. Crane's contract supposedly called for a payment of three thousand dollars (the equivalent of around ninety thousand dollars today), which would have been enough to clear all his debts and provide adequate support of Cora during his absence. There is every chance, however, that those three thousand dollars were a fiction concocted by the business manager of the *World*, Don Carlos Seitz, who for unknown reasons had developed an intense antipathy toward Crane and eventually pushed him off the *World*'s staff. Years later, in a book from 1924 and an article from 1933, Seitz bad-mouthed Crane in print (that is, lied about him) by declaring that S.C. had produced only "one dispatch of any merit" when the truth was that he had written twenty-four, which in the same *World*'s obituary of Crane in 1900 had been lauded as "masterpieces of description," and if a person could lie about such a hard, confirmable fact, how can he be trusted not to have lied about the three thousand dollars, for if Crane had been given that money—or even part of it—why would he have written to Reynolds from a dispatch boat at the end of May (with the final version of "His New Mittens" enclosed) that he needed money? Nine days later, he again wrote to Reynolds and said that if he had managed to collect any money by now, it should be cabled to John Scott Stokes (Harold Frederic's secretary and a good friend of both Cranes) *as usual*, the implication being that Scott Stokes would then turn the funds over to Cora, fulfilling a middleman service that allowed Crane to go on hiding his marriage from all his American connections, not just his family but his New York agent as well. In other words, if he had been given all or some of the three thousand dollars, where was it, and why was he depending on income from other sources to keep Cora afloat? As it turned out, beyond the twenty pounds he gave her before he left England (from the sixty pounds he had raised with Conrad in Blackwood's London office), she received no more than the smallest amounts from him the whole time he was gone, which put her in an ever more precarious fix. The equivalent of twenty-five hundred or three thousand dollars today is not nothing, of course, but hardly enough to sustain a debt-ridden person for the better part of a year.

Another roadblock, another conundrum. As has often been the case in trying to piece together Crane's story, there is not enough solid evidence to know exactly what was going on here. Presumably, he must have received *something* from the *World*, but whatever the amount was, it has not been accounted for, which leaves us with one more blank and reduces this eight-and-a-half-month span of his life into one of the murkiest periods of all, for not only are too many facts missing but the motives behind Crane's consistently erratic behavior are so obscure as to be all but unknowable. As I see it, he was of two minds about almost everything. A part of him felt that he was going to die in the war; another part of him felt that he was indestructible. He was going back to Cora; he wasn't sure if he was going back to Cora. On some days, he was morose and withdrawn; on other days he was in high spirits, playful to the point of rambunctiousness. And how, finally, did he regard his financial responsibilities to Cora? With a mixture of concern and indifference, it would seem, given that after he signed on with the *Journal* following his departure from the *World*, he made what he thought was an arrangement with the *Journal*'s London office to send his earnings to Cora, but they failed to keep their end of the bargain and she wound up just as stranded as she had been before. Not entirely his fault, perhaps, but neither did he carry through to find out if the arrangement was working. Some concern, then, but more than a little indifference, as if he couldn't be bothered to think about it too much. As J. C. Levenson puts it in one of his introductions to Crane's *Works*: "Despite extenuating possibilities, he seems to have acted worse than on any other occasion in his life."

Then there is the mystery of his stopover in Washington and the meeting with Lily Brandon Munroe that might or might not have happened, and, if it did, whether or not Crane proposed to her again. Paul Sorrentino, the author of the most carefully researched and accurate account of Crane's life, says that he did. Others, among them Kathryn Hilt (co-author of the article about the two Amy Leslies), are not sure, contending that the second proposal could have been made earlier, on any one of three occasions between 1895 and 1897. If there was indeed no proposal in 1898, then that is the end of the story, and we can dismiss the matter from our minds. But let us assume that it did happen, that Crane did in fact propose to her when he stopped off in Washington on his way down to Florida. Which begs the question: In light of his all but official marriage to Cora, how could he have done such a thing? Because, I would argue, he was in disarray, and because, contrary to common wisdom, even if first loves almost always end, they never die, and when Crane saw Lily again, it seems perfectly plausible that he was stunned by the sight of her, overwhelmed, and without knowing what he was about to do, impulsively blurted out his proposal. Another sign of his inner distress and confusion, but heartfelt at the moment the words came out of his mouth, and then she said no, and that was that.

Whether or not this scene took place, less than a month later, as he sat on a dispatch boat "Off Havana," Crane wrote to Lily's younger sister, Dottie, the girl from 1892 who was now on the verge of womanhood, to tell her that his visit to Washington had been cut short because he had suddenly received notice "that there was to be a big fight off Havana and I was to go there instantly. I flew; I did not telegraph because I could not explain well enough by wire and returning now from Porto Rico I find my first real opportunity to write you a note. Will you forgive me?" This last sentence suggests that he had been hoping to see her in Washington—had perhaps even arranged to see her—and was sorry to have missed his chance or, perhaps, was sending her a belated apology for having broken their appointment. He goes on: "I have not changed in the least and you may be sure that the S. Crane you knew well so long ago would not seem thoughtless if he could help it." The S. Crane of long ago was the boy who had been in love with her sister Lily and, because he hasn't changed in the least, is no doubt still in love with her. Then, in the final paragraph, he adds: "I am going to England as soon as the war is over and I wish you would send me the address of your sister there [not Lily, but another Brandon sister, Stella]. My address will be Key West Hotel, Key West. Adios!"

Short as it is, this note reveals much about Crane's complex emotional state at the time. Yes, he was going back to England after the war—back to Cora—but three weeks after his visit to Washington, he was still absorbing the impact of his encounter with Lily (whether he had proposed to her or not) and, as a consequence, was also thinking about her two sisters, so much so that he seemed intent on maintaining contact with the family however he could, for even if he was destined never to see Lily again, her ghost continued to walk inside him. She was there but not there, and in spite of the intensity of his feelings for her, that attachment to his first love in no way interfered with his intention to go back to Cora. The human heart is an immense palace, after all, and there are more than enough chambers in it for someone to love two people at the same time.

In Key West, where Crane joined the enormous battalion of American journalists in the early "rocking-chair period" of the war, he was surrounded by numerous friends and acquaintances from past jobs and assignments in Asbury Park, New York, Florida, and Greece, not just Harry Scovel but Edward Marshall, Ralph Paine, Ernest McCready, Charles Michelson, and others, not to mention his old rival Richard Harding Davis, and new friends such as photographer Jimmy Hare. For better or worse, he was with the boys again—back in his element.

3

IT WAS AMERICA'S FIRST MILITARY ADVENTURE SINCE THE END OF THE Civil War, and it redefined the country's idea of itself as well as its relationship to the rest of the world, establishing the unorthodox if not unprecedented foreign policy that has persisted through the twentieth century and on into the twenty-first: a combination of idealism and pragmatism that has sent American troops abroad to fight on behalf of oppressed peoples and at the same time has opened new markets to generate new sources of wealth for the business interests of Main Street, Wall Street, and the boulevards of national and international commerce. The secretary of state at the time, John Hay, called it "a splendid little war," but it was far from little and splendid only in the sense that the fighting lasted just a few months. In the end, America's conflict with Spain led to the expulsion of the Spanish Empire from the New World and the Pacific, the appropriation of Puerto Rico and Guam, freedom for Cuba (henceforth to be under the protection of the United States, a dominance that continued until the Castro revolution of 1959), and a brutal second war in the liberated Philippines that dragged on for several years and caused the deaths of hundreds of thousands if not more than a million noncombatants, including untold numbers of women and children. For the first time in its brief life, the Republic had flexed its muscles in several far-flung places abroad, and from then on it would be regarded by the countries of Europe and Asia as a force to be reckoned with, a world power.* Within a few years, automobiles and airplanes would be filling the roads and skies of America, but it was just then, twenty months before the end of the nineteenth century, that the concept of modern America took hold. The Spanish-American War was the beginning, and it set the pattern for everything that would follow, from the victories in the First and Second World Wars to the disasters in Vietnam and Iraq—all the good and all the harm that can come from the pursuit of noble and less than noble intentions.

It wasn't that the McKinley administration was eager to rush into battle, however. The president and his cabinet secretaries were men from the Civil War generation, and they had known the horrors of combat firsthand, which had left them with a revulsion against the idea that war could be used as an instrument to advance the interests of the country. McKinley himself had taken part in the Battle of Antietam in September 1862, which in a single day had resulted in nearly twenty-three thousand dead, wounded, or missing soldiers, and his secretary of the navy, John D. Long, was equally opposed to a military confrontation with the Spanish. But there were younger men in the administration as well, among them the ex-commissioner of the New York Police Department, Theodore Roosevelt, who as assistant secretary of the navy had spent the past year and a half building up the U.S. fleet, and not only was he an advocate of war against Spain but saw in that potential conflict a positive moral good that would revive the lax, degenerating spirit of the country and help America attain its rightful (and righteous) place in the world. As he famously concluded in "The Strenuous Life," a speech delivered in Chicago on April 10, 1899: "Above all, let us shrink from no strife, moral or physical, within or without the nation . . . for it is only through strife and

---

* That same summer (1898), in an action separate from the war with Spain, the American government took possession of the Hawaiian Islands and turned them into a territory of the United States.

dangerous endeavor, that we shall ultimately win the goal of true national greatness."

Two views, two equal and opposite approaches within the same government, and until February 15, 1898, the senior generation was in control of the argument. But once the battleship *Maine* exploded in the harbor off Havana, where it had been sent to protect American lives and property after the outbreak of anti-U.S. riots by Spanish loyalists, war began to seem almost inevitable. Two hundred and sixty-one crew members out of a total of 355 had been killed, and although it is likely that the explosion was caused internally by gases from the bituminous coal that stoked the ship, word quickly spread through the pro-war American press that the Spanish were responsible, which led to the jingoistic chant that began circulating around the country: "Remember the *Maine*! To hell with Spain!" In March, McKinley demanded that the Spanish government give full independence to Cuba, but when his words were ignored, Congress passed a resolution declaring that Cuba was free, and by the third week in April America and Spain were at war.

There were a number of prominent dissenters on the home front— Twain and Howells, labor leader Samuel Gompers, former presidents Grover Cleveland and Benjamin Harrison, and the current Speaker of the House, Thomas Brackett Reed, who in the buildup to the war spoke of "land hunger" as the secret motive behind the call for military intervention—but the vast majority of Americans saw the struggle to liberate Cuba from Spain as a cause similar to America's own Revolution against the British in 1776 and backed the war, throwing themselves behind it in a surge of wholehearted patriotic zeal.

The navy was well equipped and ready to take on the task of destroying the Spanish fleet and opening the way for a land invasion by American forces, but the standing army of the United States consisted of just twenty-eight thousand men at the time—hardly a match for the two hundred and thirty thousand Spanish soldiers stationed in Cuba. Close to a hundred thousand Americans belonged to state militias, but they were weekend soldiers at best, and most of them had never taken part in drills or fired a rifle or knew the first thing about combat. Fresh recruits would be necessary, and after the sinking of the *Maine*, one hundred thousand men enlisted, a number that would swell to almost a million, but only a small fraction of them were deemed fit for active service. To bulk up the forces, volunteer regiments were hastily organized, among them the 1st U.S. Volunteer Cavalry, commanded by Colonel Leonard Wood and Lieutenant Colonel Theodore Roosevelt, the legendary unit best known as the Rough Riders.

Roosevelt, who was on the brink of forty and had not one day or even one minute of military experience, quit his job as assistant secretary of the navy to take part in the battles ahead. It was a move that transformed him into a national celebrity and made his career. One year later, he was elected governor of New York; one year after that, vice president, and then, following McKinley's assassination in September 1901, he slid into office as the twenty-sixth president of the United States, the youngest man in American history to hold that job.*

Such was the ragtag land force that had been patched together to defeat the Spanish and their support contingent of Cuban loyalist fighters (guerrillas). The Americans eventually mustered an army of two hundred thousand men (regulars and volunteers combined, most of them white but with several thousand black soldiers as well). Add that number to the fifty thousand Cuban rebels who fought beside them, and the strength of the two sides was more or less equal. Inevitably, soldiers will die in battle, but not only did the two warring armies have to defend themselves against enemy bullets, they were also prey to the ravages of malaria, yellow fever, typhoid, and the crushing, hundred-degree heat of summertime Cuba, which wound up killing far more men than were cut down in action: fifteen thousand Spanish soldiers died from disease (compared to roughly eight hundred in combat) and close to ninety percent of the twenty-five hundred American deaths were caused by those same invisible weapons. To make matters even more difficult, the American forces were burdened by the incompetence of the general in charge of the invasion, William

---

* The darlings of the American press during the war, the Rough Riders consisted of one thousand men from all parts of the country, a mix of millionaires' sons and Arizona sheriffs, cowboys, college athletes, and young intellectuals. To the general public, they embodied the finest virtues of a free democratic society—which necessarily meant, of course, that every member of the unit was white. Crane had nothing against Roosevelt's untested volunteers and even voiced his admiration for their courage in the Battle of San Juan Hill, but it irritated him that the soldiers of the regular army were mostly ignored by the journalists. In his last article for the *World* (July 20), which carried the headline "Regulars Get No Glory," he wrote, "The public wants to learn of the gallantry of Reginald Marmaduke Maurice Montmorenci Sturtevant, and for goodness sake how the poor old chappy endures that dreadful hard-tack and bacon. Whereas, the name of the regular soldier is probably Michael Nolan ... the ungodly Nolan, the sweating, swearing, overloaded, hungry, thirsty, sleepless Nolan, tearing his breeches on the barbed wire entanglements, wallowing through the muddy fords, pursuing his way through the stiletto-pointed thickets, climbing the fire-crowned hill—Nolan gets shot." Soon after the war ended, Crane turned these sentiments into his most powerful short story about the Cuban campaign, "The Price of the Harness," which Conrad described in a letter to Cora as "magnificent ... the very best thing he has done since the Red Badge."

Rufus Shafter, a sixty-three-year-old Civil War hero who weighed over three hundred pounds, suffered from gout, and was despised by both the men who served under him and the American correspondents who covered the war. According to Roosevelt: "Not since the campaign of Crassus against the Parthians has there been so criminally incompetent a General as Shafter, and not since the expedition against Walcheren has there been a grosser mismanagement than in this. The battle simply fought itself." Or, as Davis succinctly put it: "It was not on account of Shafter, but in spite of Shafter, that the hills were taken."

By contrast, the war at sea was efficiently handled by Admiral William T. Sampson, the figure Crane considered to be "the most interesting personality of the war." Early on, S.C. spent a couple of days aboard Sampson's ship, the *New York*, and though he was initially confused by Sampson's stolid, almost phlegmatic manner, he came to admire him as an exemplary leader, someone worthy of the same sort of respect he had previously given to the man at the helm of the Scotch Express—then doubled, perhaps even tripled, for this man was not in charge of a single train but an entire fleet.

Men feared him, but he never made threats; men tumbled heels over head to obey him, but he never gave a sharp order; men loved him, but he had said no word, kindly or unkindly; men cheered him and he said: "Who are they yelling for?" Men behaved badly to him and he said nothing. Men thought of glory and he thought of the management of ships. All without a sound. A noiseless campaign on his part. No bunting, no arches, no fireworks; nothing but the perfect management of a big fleet. That is a record for you. No trumpets, no cheers from the populace, just plain, pure, unsauced accomplishment. But ultimately he will reap his reward in—in what? In text-books on sea campaigns. No more. The people choose their own and they choose the kind they like. Who has a better right? Anyhow he is a great man. And when you are once started you can continue to be a great man without the help of bouquets and banquets.

Crane arrived at the Key West Hotel on April twenty-fifth or twenty-sixth, a place swarming with navy personnel and, by his count, "some two hundred and fifty newspaper correspondents," the largest contingent of journalists ever assembled to cover a war, which by most estimates translated into one writer for every 180 American combatants—but the public on the home front had an insatiable hunger for news, and so the scribblers scribbled and cranked out articles even when there was little of anything to report. For the first six and a half weeks prior to the land invasion on June tenth, the principal story was the navy's search-and-destroy mission against the Spanish fleet commanded by Admiral Pascual Cervera y Topete. The war had begun with a blockade of the Cuban coast on April twenty-second, but by May fourth, acting on intelligence that the Spanish were anchored off Puerto Rico, Sampson ordered his ships to San Juan, only to arrive just after Cervera had fled to Martinique. By May nineteenth, the Spanish had returned to the southern coast of Cuba and settled into position at Santiago Harbor. By the end of the month, they were hemmed in by an American blockade, which led to a protracted standoff that allowed the marines to land at Guantánamo on June tenth, but the final encounter between the two navies did not occur until July third, when the Americans overwhelmed the Spanish squadron as it attempted to slip through a small breach in the encircling arc of the blockade line—a pulverizing loss that marked the beginning of the end of the war.

During the six weeks prior to his landing with the marines at Guantánamo, Crane was either parked in Key West or cruising around the waters of the Atlantic and Caribbean on various dispatch boats as he and his fellow correspondents tracked the movements of the Spanish and American fleets. Under those less than comfortable conditions—mostly sprawled out flat on the floor—he completed "His New Mittens" and wrote his first ten dispatches for the *World*.

According to Paine, "The Key West Hotel was a bedlam of a place while we waited for the war to begin. And when other diversions failed, you could stroll around the corner to a resort known as the 'Eagle Bird' where a gentlemanly gambler . . . spun the roulette wheel. And there you would be most apt to find Stephen Crane, sometimes bucking the goddess of chance in contented solitude."

Solo jaunts to pursue his favorite pastime whenever he was on land, but also some close early scrapes at sea, once on the night of May nineteenth, when he was aboard the dispatch tug the *Three Friends* and it was accidentally fired upon and then sideswiped by the U.S. gunboat *Machias* (recounted in Crane's article for the *World*, "Narrow Escape of the Three Friends"), and again on May twenty-ninth, when he was on the dispatch boat *Somers N. Smith* with six other correspondents, among them Scovel and Jimmy Hare, and they were pursued about 160 miles north of Jamaica by what appeared to be a Spanish warship. The men all prepared themselves to be captured and taken prisoner, but as the ship bore down on them and came close enough to be identified, it turned out to be the American auxiliary cruiser *St. Paul*—an episode that is sharply (and humorously) detailed in Crane's account, "Chased by a Big 'Spanish Man-o'-War.'"

Like Crane, most of his fellow correspondents were still in their twenties, and they were a rowdy, hard-drinking bunch who lived in a fraternity-house atmosphere on the dispatch boats, conscientious journalists on the one hand but also adventure-seeking young men who threw themselves into the war with an almost juvenile abandon—to such an extent that a number of them (Paine, Marshall, Davis) picked up weapons and joined the American troops in the fighting. As he had been at the Delta Upsilon house in college, at the Pendennis Club on Avenue A, and in the room he shared with the husky lot of "Indians" on East Twenty-third Street, Crane was both an essential member of the group and someone who stood slightly apart from it. Paine, McCready, Michelson, Marshall, Davis, and others all wrote about their experiences with Crane during the war, and almost to a man they present a picture of a doubled being, steadfast and inconstant, fun-loving and ornery, and because he approached his work more as a novelist than as a professional reporter, not quite one of them. A nighttime excursion on the *Three Friends* to the cable station at Môle Saint-Nicolas in Haiti on May fourteenth with Paine (representing the *Philadelphia Press*), McCready (the *New York Herald*), and McCready's bureau chief, the much older Harry Brown, led to some fraught moments with armed sentinels after they landed (during which Crane continually cracked jokes) and then to a raucous blowout of rum drinking on the beach with twenty Haitian soldiers, which Crane took part in with immense relish. The commanding officer, who spoke fluent, idiomatic American English and had worked for four years as a butler in New Rochelle, New York, so amused Crane that he took to calling him Alice in Wonderland. That was the side of Crane John Northern Hilliard declared to be "always playing," but McCready also reports that one night on a dispatch boat "Stephen . . . told me repeatedly, vehemently, imperatively, loftily, sarcastically—in fact he *told* me, precisely how to write a short story, and hence how to write any story. He also told me, with equal force, variety, and even with seeming interest, that he knew I couldn't grasp the notion, and that he was wasting his time. He was right, of course, as to the last; but I *couldn't* see why he needed to be so damned *triumphant* about it."

Not quite one of them. Even among his best friends, there was a good deal of puzzlement over Crane's attitude toward his work. According to Paine, "He abominated the drudgery of grinding out news dispatches, with an eye on the cost of cable tolls. And seldom could he be coaxed to turn his hand to it. His was the soul of the artist, slowly, carefully fashioning his phrases, sensitive to the time, the place, and the mood." McCready goes one step further and flatly says that "Crane was not a newspaperman. He was an art-

ist from crown to heel, temperamental, undisciplined in the narrow sense of
the word—careless of any interest that did not match with his own private
ones, contemptuous of mere news getting or news reporting; thinking of
his *World* connection as a convenient aid rather than as one imposing sharp
and instant responsibility upon him." Jimmy Hare, the man who later stood
up for the dead Crane when Theodore Roosevelt verbally attacked him, told
his biographer, Cecil Carnes, that he found Crane to be "a charming fellow,
fond of a drink and not too fond of work. Lighting up one cigarette after
another, he confided to Jimmy his only reason for signing up with the *New
York World* had been to get a military pass, his present ambition being to do
a book about the war." That apparent indolence, which might simply have
been something detached or unfocused in Crane's manner—or perhaps
something odd or even unsettling about the impression he created—led
the man in charge of the *World* staff in Cuba, Henry N. Cary, to disparage
his employee as "a drunken, irresponsible and amusing little cuss. He kept
me busy trying to get a little work out of him, but I failed in that respect"—
which strongly echoes Seitz and his accusation that Crane wrote almost
nothing for the *World*. Then there is Davis, who reencountered Crane early
in the war on Sampson's ship and wrote to his family that Crane seemed
to be having trouble fitting in and that "I don't like him." But Davis would
change his opinion of Crane as the war advanced, and in an article published in *Harper's New Monthly Magazine* not long after the fighting had
stopped, he wrote: "The best correspondent is probably the man who by his
energy and resource . . . is able to make the public see what he saw. If that
is a good definition, Stephen Crane would seem to have distinctly won the
first place among correspondents in the late disturbance."

The charges against him were true, but what Davis says is also true. Crane
was not a pound-it-out, meet-the-deadline, scoop-hungry journalist, nor did
he ever *appear* to be working hard, but the dispatches he sent to the *World*
were written at a level many cuts above the standard battle report and still
hold up today. Some of them, however, could be awfully slow in coming, as
was the case with his account of the initial landing of the marines and the
events that occurred on the nights of June tenth and eleventh. On the morning of the twelfth, he reluctantly dictated a dry report to McCready that
told the bare facts of the story—a collaboration of sorts (since McCready
kept paring down Crane's prose) that was published the next day without a
byline—and when S.C. finally got around to telling the full story, he was no
longer on the *World*'s payroll. He wrote it in Havana in October, sent it off to
Reynolds toward the end of the month, and by the time it was published in
McClure's Magazine in February 1899, he had already gone back to England.

That piece, "Marines Signaling Under Fire at Guantanamo," tells the story of Crane hunkered down with the invading troops and the long hours he spent with the signalmen who were responsible for sending and receiving messages to and from the battleship *Marblehead*, which was currently anchored offshore, communicating with flags by day and lanterns by night. It proved to be a harrowing, immensely dangerous mission, and because Crane simply plunges into his account and starts telling what he has to tell without reference to dates or the prior circumstances that have led him to be sitting in this particular hole on this particular spot of ground in Cuba, the piece is not a traditional battle report or news dispatch and has always been classified among his short stories, even though it is a wholly factual document—a "tale after the fact" similar to "The Open Boat," but in this case just seven pages long, not thirty. On top of its many strengths, it also includes one of the strongest, most vivid sentences Crane ever wrote: "The sky was bare and blue, and hurt like brass."

He does not mention the landing itself (which he had already covered in the collaboration with McCready), nor does he explain that the purpose of the landing was to set up a coaling station for the blockading American ships, which until then had been going to Key West in order to refuel (a round-trip of eight hundred miles). Six hundred and fifty marines took part in the operation, and Crane watched it from the *Three Friends* with Paine and McCready. After the sun set, he went ashore while the other two traveled to Port Antonio, Jamaica, to wire their stories. By the morning of the eleventh, the Spanish attack on the Americans had begun to intensify, and three marines were killed. More deaths would follow over the next days and nights.

In the first paragraph of his piece, Crane establishes the setting and the fact that four signalmen were handling communications with the *Marblehead*, and then he begins to elaborate:

> It was my good fortune—at the time I considered it my bad fortune, indeed—to be with them on two of the nights when a wild storm of fighting was pealing about the hill. . . . The noise; the impenetrable darkness; the knowledge from the sound of the bullets that the enemy was on three sides of the camp; the infrequent bloody and stumbling death of some man with whom, perhaps, one had messed two hours previous; the weariness of the body, and the more terrible weakness of the mind . . . made it wonderful that at least some of the men did not come out of it with their nerves hopelessly in shreds.

What most astonishes Crane is how a man can find the composure to mount a large wooden cracker box with a flag or a lantern in his hand and perform "the regular gestures of the wig-wagging code" when he is directly in the line of enemy bullets, a clearly defined target who is almost certain to be shot and killed. It is a hard-to-imagine if not unimaginable act of blind resolution, and, as Crane adds: "To make a confession—when one of these men stood up to wave his lantern, I, lying in the trench, invariably rolled a little to the right or left, in order that, when he was shot, he would not fall on me."

And all through "this prolonged tragedy of night," there was the fretful, agonizing wait for the first signs of dawn, which seemed to come so slowly that Crane imagines it dragging on as long as it would take a man to paint "Madison Square Garden with a camel's hair brush," and then, even after the sun had come up, "it always took me . . . some hours to get my nerves combed down" and at last fall asleep in the trench with the four signalmen.

On another day in Cuzco, a day so hot that "the sky was bare and blue, and hurt like brass," a sergeant named Quick climbs to the top of the ridge, pulls out "a blue polka dot kerchief as large as a quilt," ties it to "a long, crooked stick," and then, "turning his back to the Spanish fire, began to signal to the *Dolphin.*"

> As I looked at Sergeant Quick wig-wagging there against the sky, I would not have given a tin tobacco-tag for his life. Escape for him seemed impossible. It seemed absurd to hope that he would not be hit; I only hoped that he would be hit just a little, little, in the arm, the shoulder, or the leg.
>
> I watched his face, and it was as grave and serene as that of a man writing in his own library. He was the very embodiment of tranquillity in occupation. He stood there among the animal-like babble of the Cubans, the crack of rifles, and the whirling snarl of the bullets, and wig-wagged what he had to wig-wag without heeding anything but his business. There was not a single trace of nervousness or haste. . . .
>
> I saw Quick betray only one sign of emotion. As he swung his clumsy flag to and fro, an end of it once caught on a cactus pillar, and he looked sharply over his shoulder to see what had it. He gave the flag an impatient jerk. He looked annoyed.

Remarkably, not one of the four signalmen was killed by a bullet or even grazed by a falling twig, and after the war Sergeant Quick was given the

Congressional Medal of Honor for his conduct under fire. As with his actions on the sinking *Commodore*, however, the excessively modest Crane says nothing about what he did during those gruesome days and nights and effectively erases himself from his own text, but the historical record tells us that the man in charge of the operation, Captain George F. Elliott, in a letter to his commanding officer, Lieutenant Colonel Robert Huntington, wrote that "having been notified that a Mr. Stephen Crane would be allowed to accompany the expedition, I requested him to act as an aide if one should be needed. He accepted the duty and was of material aid during the action, carrying messages to fire volleys, etc., to different company commanders."

In his generous postwar remarks about Crane, Richard Harding Davis writes:

> He tells of how the marine stood erect, staring through the dusk with half-closed eyes, and with his lips moving as he counted the answers from the war-ships, while innumerable bullets splashed the sand about him. But it never occurs to Crane that to sit at the man's feet, as he did, close enough to watch his lips move and to be able to make mental notes for a later tribute to the marine's scorn of fear, was equally deserving of praise.

Davis adds: "Crane was the coolest man, whether army officer or civilian, that I saw under fire at any time during the war. He was most annoyingly cool, with the assurance of a fatalist."

Further instances of that annoying coolness were noted by others as well, and to understand the lengths to which Crane was willing to go in his stare-down contest with Death, I offer the testimony of the following two witnesses in evidence.

Langdon Smith of the *New York Journal*:

> Crane was standing under a tree calmly rolling a cigarette . . . some leaves dropped from the trees, cut away by the bullets; two or three men dropped within a few feet. Crane is thin as a lath. If he had been two or three inches wider or thicker through, he would undoubtedly have been shot. But he calmly finished rolling his cigarette and smoked it without moving away from the spot where the bullets had suddenly become so thick.

George Lynch of the *London Chronicle* (describing an incident that bears an uncanny resemblance to the actions of Fred Collins in "A Mystery of Heroism"):

A company under fire was badly in need of water, and water was seven miles away, down hill at that. Stephen collected all the tin canteens he could find and trotted off for the refreshment. Coming wearily back, there was a sharp ping against one of the cans, and it began to leak. Stephen turned up the can and tried to stop the leak. An officer in the woods near by shouted to him.

"Come here, quick! You're in the line of fire!"

"If you've got a knife, cut a plug and bring it to me," replied the young man, and, as he spoke, bang went a bullet against another can.

"Come under cover, or you'll lose every can you've got!"

This warning had its effect. The loss of the precious fluid terrified him in a way that the danger to himself had failed to do. He finally brought the water up to the thirsty company, and then fainted through exhaustion.

Even more drastically, there are the two somewhat different accounts of the battle in which he stood up in the line of enemy fire wearing "a gleaming white raincoat," as if consciously turning himself into a neon target to be mowed down by the Spanish. From the biography of Hare by Carnes:

> Stephen Crane turned up once more. The stubborn fellow was still unwounded, still indifferent to danger, still wearing that infernal white raincoat. He saw Jimmy, came up to where he was cuddled in a ditch, and remained standing erect, staring toward the Spanish lines. Colonel Wood . . . spoke sharply to him, ordering him down. Crane ignored the command. Wood spoke again. . . . Still Crane held his statuesque pose while bullets sang by his charmed person. It was Jimmy who finally brought his friend to earth. He remembered the two Hearst reporters, Edward Marshall and James Creelman, who had recently been wounded and had thereby gained much glory and publicity for the Hearst organization. Jimmy plucked at the hem of the white raincoat.
>
> "What's the idea, Steve?" he yelled. "Did you get a wire from Pulitzer this morning reading: 'Why the hell don't *you* get wounded so we can get some notices, too?'"
>
> There was a roar of laughter from the soldiers within hearing, and Crane, blushing, got down meekly and stayed there.

In the account by Davis, he is the one who accuses Crane of showing off, not Hare, but in both versions the tactic persuades the neon man to flatten his body on the ground. S.C. might not have been afraid of Death, but if he meant to find his death as a common soldier, then to be accused

of conduct unbecoming a soldier would have been the ultimate disgrace.
He therefore did as he was told. In his memoir *Notes of an American War
Correspondent* (1910), Davis adds:

> I knew that to Crane, anything that savored of a pose was hateful, so, as
> I did not want to see him killed, I called, "You're not impressing any one
> by doing that, Crane." As I hoped he would, he instantly dropped to his
> knees. When he crawled over to where we lay, I explained, "I knew that
> would fetch you," and he grinned, and said, "Oh, was that it?"

He was in Cuba for only a month before his health broke down, but that
was the most crucial month of the war, and Crane was in the thick of it
from beginning to end, immersed in the grisly, nonstop business of mayhem and slaughter as he darted around the island from one confrontation
to the next. First, the landing with the marines at Guantánamo Bay on
June tenth, then to Cuzco with Captain Elliott on the fourteenth, then to
Santiago with Scovel on the seventeenth, where they set up the *World*'s
headquarters and then, in the afternoon, "swam two Jamaican horses
ashore from the *Triton*, found some insurgents and took a journey into
the hills." Their object was to assess the activities of the Spanish fleet
in the harbor, and at five o'clock the next morning, continually threading
their way through enemy lines, they began a twenty-five-mile trek that
included an arduous uphill climb and equally demanding downhill climb
of a two-thousand-foot mountain—from which they had a clear view
of what Crane would later call "the doomed ships"—that brought them
to the shore again, where the *Three Friends* had just left without them.
Improvising as they went along, they hitched a ride with two Cubans in a
dugout and were eventually hauled up onto the dispatch tug, which carried
them to Sampson's flagship, the *New York*, where they gave the admiral a
full report on what they had learned about the position of Cervera's fleet.*
    June 22: At dawn, six thousand troops took part in the American inva-
sion at Daiquirí under the command of Major General Joseph Wheeler
("Crane Tells the Story of the Disembarkment," the *World*, July 7).
    June 23: Crane, McCready, Edward Marshall (working for the *New*

---

* These were not the customary duties of a war correspondent but an active participation in
the war itself. Unlike some of his friends, Crane never picked up a rifle and fired at the
enemy, but he was all in behind the cause of Cuban liberation and did not consider helping
that cause to be a conflict of interest. Staunch anti-imperialist that he was—especially British imperialism—he bought into the argument that America had no territorial ambitions
in Cuba and did not question it.

York Journal), and photographer Burr McIntosh (*Leslie's Weekly*) marched to Siboney behind the Rough Riders.

June 24: Following a jungle trail from Siboney to Las Guásimas, the Rough Riders were ambushed by Cuban guerrillas armed with smokeless Mausers and suffered numerous casualties. Marshall was shot in the spine, which led to temporary paralysis, permanent disabilities, and a partial amputation of his left leg. He later wrote: "When I regained consciousness, hours after the fight had ended, one of the first faces I saw was that of Stephen Crane. The day was hot. . . . The thermometer . . . would have shown a temperature of something like 100 degrees. Yet Stephen Crane—and mind you, he was there in the interest of another newspaper—took the dispatch which I managed to write five or six miles to the coast and cabled it for me. He had to walk, for he could get no horse or mule. Then he rushed about in the heat and arranged with a number of men to bring a stretcher up from the coast and carry me back on it. He was probably as tired then as a man could be and still walk. But he trudged back from the coast to the field hospital where I was lying and saw to it that I was properly conveyed to the coast."

June 25: Crane wrote and filed his report on Las Guásimas, "Roosevelt's Rough Riders' Loss Due to a Gallant Blunder" (the *World*, June 26).

June 27: From Siboney, Crane sent off his article about the June seventeenth trek with Scovel, "Hunger Has Made Cubans Fatalists" (published in the *World* on July 7).

July 1: The day of the "white gleaming raincoat," which was also one of the most eventful days of the war. Early in the morning, the Americans advanced toward the fortifications at San Juan, just outside Santiago, and launched an assault on the village of El Caney, six miles to the northeast, where Spanish forces were entrenched. From a vantage point a couple of miles away at El Pozo, Crane and several others (among them Frederic Remington) observed the shelling of the Spanish led by Captain Allyn Capron and the attack on El Caney by General Henry Lawton's troops. At eleven o'clock, the 71st New York Volunteer Regiment met with heavy fire on the Santiago road, and in less than an hour four hundred men from the unit were killed or wounded. At one o'clock, with Lawton's troops bogged down at El Caney, Roosevelt led the Rough Riders in a charge up Kettle Hill with regular troops following close behind—which became the subject of S.C.'s longest article for the *World*, "Stephen Crane's Vivid Story of the Battle of San Juan" (published July 14). At three o'clock, Crane and Jimmy Hare arrived at Wood's entrenchment, which was under heavy Spanish fire. That was the "neon target moment" when Crane pretended not to hear Wood's order to lie down and went on standing until Hare or Davis (or perhaps both of them at different times) shamed him into joining the others in the trench. That evening, when Davis suffered a sudden, excruciating attack of sciatica, Crane and Hare held him up as the three of them walked slowly, ever so slowly, to the correspondents' camp near El Pozo. For more than a mile of their stumbling journey, the trail was under enemy fire. Davis: "Whenever I protested and refused their sacrifice and pointed out the risk they were taking they smiled as at the ravings of a naughty child, and when I lay down in the road and refused to budge unless they left me, Crane called the attention of Hare to the effect of the setting sun behind the palm-trees."

July 2: In the morning, sitting on San Juan Hill, Crane observed Lawton's troops returning from their victory at El Caney to take their positions on the San Juan Heights, which were still under attack. In the afternoon, he stopped in at the town church in El Caney, which had been transformed into a makeshift hospital where Spanish and Cuban guerrilla prisoners were being treated by American doctors. That evening, he traveled by boat to the cable station in Port Antonio, Jamaica, to wire his dispatches.

July 3: The conclusive naval battle that destroyed the Spanish fleet began while Crane was still in Jamaica, and by the time he returned to Cuba, the fighting had ended.

July 5: Crane wrote his article "Spanish Deserters Among the Refugees at El Caney" (the *World*, July 8). "One saw in this great, gaunt assemblage the true horror of war. The sick, the lame, and the blind were there. Women and men, tottering upon the verge of death, plodded doggedly onward. . . . Their air was stolid and indifferent. It was a forlorn hope at best. If this was safety, well and good. If death, what difference how it came."

July 7: Datelined "General Shafter's Headquarters," Crane's "Captured Mausers for Volunteers" (the *World*, July 17) was highly critical of the black-powder, twenty-five-year-old Springfield rifles used by the American volunteers, which continually betrayed their positions to Spanish forces hidden behind the surrounding shrubs and thickets and led to many unnecessary deaths from bullets fired by undetectable, smokeless Mausers. The piece concludes: "In war anything is justified save killing your own men through laziness or gross stupidity."

July 8: Delirious from an attack of malaria and running a high, out-of-control fever, Crane was put aboard the *City of Washington* at Siboney and shipped back to the United States for medical treatment.

He had landed in Key West just two and a half months earlier, but the events he lived through in that short span had a monumental effect on him, and they generated an abundant outflow of writing both during and after the war. The twenty-four articles for the *World* to begin with, followed by ten short stories about the Cuban campaign (among them "The Price of the Harness"), and then the extraordinary, first-person, lightly fictionalized "War Memories," a forty-two-page retelling of his experiences during the first ten weeks of the campaign—up to and including his evacuation to Old Point Comfort, Virginia—which was composed in August 1899, eight months after his return to England.

It is the strongest, most inventive piece of work he wrote during the last year of his life, and in ways he had never quite allowed himself to do earlier, he opens up and speaks to the reader directly about himself—and with the veil suddenly lifted, he manages to establish an intimate, deeply personal manner of telling, a voice of multiple, shifting tonalities that range from the somber to the buoyant and everything in between, the full Crane in all his contradictory manyness.

On the death of Assistant Surgeon John Blair Gibbs of the U.S. Navy in the early morning hours of June twelfth:

> I went in search of Gibbs, but I soon gave over an active search for the more congenial occupation of lying flat and feeling the hot hiss of bullets trying to cut my hair. For the moment I was no longer a cynic. I was a child who, in a fit of ignorance, had jumped into the vat of war. I heard somebody dying near me. He was dying hard. Hard. It took him a long time to die. He breathed as all noble machinery breathes when it is making its gallant strife against breaking, breaking. But he was going to break. He was going to break. It seemed to me, this breathing, the noise of a heroic pump which strives to subdue a mud which comes upon it in tons. The darkness was impenetrable. The man was lying in some depression within seven feet of me. Every wave, vibration, of his anguish beat upon my senses. He was long past groaning. There was only the bitter strife for air which pulsed out into the night in a clear penetrating whistle, with intervals of terrible silence in which I held my own breath in the common unconscious aspiration to help. I thought this man would never die. I wanted him to die. Ultimately he died. At the moment, the adjutant came bustling along erect amid the spitting bullets. I knew him by his voice. "Where's the doctor? There's some wounded men over there. Where's the doctor?" A man answered briskly: "Just died this minute, sir." It was as if he had said: "Just gone around the corner this minute, sir."

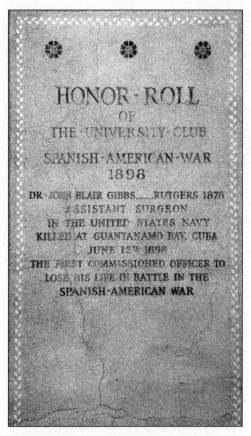

Memorial plaque to Dr. John Blair Gibbs at
the University Club, New York City.
(PHOTOGRAPH BY SPENCER OSTRANDER)

After tramping five or six miles to Siboney with Marshall's dispatch, Crane recalls how he tried to round up help for his wounded friend, an effort that began with this maddening conversation:

One of these correspondents replied . . . "Marshall? Marshall? Why, Marshall isn't in Cuba at all. He left for New York before the expedition sailed from Tampa." I said: "Beg pardon, but I remarked that Marshall was shot in the fight this morning, and have you seen any *Journal* people?" After a pause, he said: "I am sure Marshall is not down here at all. He's in New York." I said: "Pardon me, but I remarked that Marshall was shot in the fight this morning, and have you seen any *Journal* people?" He said: "No; now look here, you must have gotten two chaps mixed up somehow. Marshall isn't in Cuba at all. How could he be shot?"

I said: "Pardon me, but I remarked that Marshall was shot in the fight this morning, and have you seen any *Journal* people?" He said: "But it can't really be Marshall, you know, for the simple reason that he's not down here." I clasped my hands to my temples, gave one piercing cry to heaven and fled from his presence.

On the night of July first, when he came upon an old friend and classmate from Claverack, Reuben McNab:

Then I looked down into a miserable huddle at Bloody Bend, a huddle of hurt men, dying men, dead men. And there I saw Reuben McNab, a corporal in the 71st New York Volunteers, and with a hole through his lung. Also several holes through his clothing. "Well, they got me," he said in greeting. Usually they said that. There were no long speeches. "Well, they got me." That was sufficient. The duty of the upright, unhurt man is then difficult. I doubt if many of us learned how to speak to our own wounded. . . . "Well, they got me," said Reuben McNab. I had looked upon five hundred wounded men with stolidity, or with a conscious indifference, which filled me with amazement. But the apparition of Reuben McNab, the schoolmate lying there in the mud with a hole through his lung, awed me into stutterings, set me trembling with a sense of terrible intimacy with this war which theretofore I could have believed was a dream—almost. Twenty shot men rolled their eyes and looked at me. Only one man paid no heed. He was dying; he had no time. The bullets hummed low over them all. Death, having already struck, still insisted upon raising a venomous crest. "If you're goin' by the hospital, step in and see me," said Reuben McNab. That was all.

On visiting the makeshift hospital at El Caney:

Pushing through the throng in the plaza we came in sight of the door of the church, and here was a strange scene. The church had been turned into a hospital for Spanish wounded who had fallen into American hands. The interior of the church was too cavelike in its gloom for the eyes of the operating surgeons, so they had the altar-table carried to the doorway, where there was a bright light. Framed then in the black archway was the altar-table with the figure of a man upon it. He was naked save for a breech-clout, and so close, so clear was the ecclesiastic suggestion, that one's mind leaped to a fantasy that this thin pale figure had just been torn down from a cross. The flash of the impression was like light, and for this instant it illumined all the dark recesses of one's remotest ideas of sacrilege, ghastly and wanton. I bring this to you merely as an effect—an effect of mental light and shade, if you like; something done in thought similar to that which the French Impressionists do in color; something meaningless and at the same time overwhelming, crushing, monstrous.

On falling ill:

Very soon after this the end of the campaign came for me. I caught a fever. I am not sure to this day what kind of a fever it was. It was defined variously. I know, at any rate, that I first developed a languorous indifference to everything in the world. Then I developed a tendency to ride a horse even as a man lies on a cot. Then I—I am not sure—I think I groveled and groaned about Siboney for several days. My colleagues, Scovel and George Rhea, found me and gave me of their best, but I didn't know whether London Bridge was falling down or whether there was a war with Spain. It was all the same. What of it? Nothing of it. Everything happened, perhaps. But I cared not a jot. Life, death, dishonor—all were nothing to me. All I cared for was pickles. *Pickles* at any price! *Pickles!!*

And then, after speeding along through forty-two pages of horror, comic blunders, and head-spinning action, he comes to an abrupt halt and blows it all up:

The episode was closed. And you can depend on it that I have told you nothing at all, nothing at all, nothing at all.

The crossing to Virginia was a rough one for Crane, rough not only because of its length (five days) but also because "the only fact of the universe was that my veins burned and boiled." On top of that, the captain refused to feed him, and the army doctor on board, after one quick glance at Crane, misdiagnosed the malaria he was suffering from as yellow fever (an almost certain death sentence) and barked at him to isolate himself from the others. More than two hundred wounded soldiers were traveling on the *City of Washington*, the majority of them from the 71st New York Volunteer Regiment, and Crane spent most of the voyage lying on deck with a little rug under his body. Still, as he later wrote, "it wasn't so bad," and with most of the men in worse condition than he was, and with his long fever at last beginning to break, at mess time someone would invariably take the trouble of handing him "a tin plate of something," and so he did not starve and did not die, after all. The first thing he did when he set foot on land was to walk to the nearest soda fountain and treat himself to an ice-cream soda, something he had developed an immense and irrational craving for "somewhere in the woods between Siboney and Santiago." He asked for orange.

From the veranda of the Chamberlin Hotel, he watched the soldiers from the ship disembark as a throng of onlookers welcomed them home. Men cheered, women wept, and when the wounded were carried off to the hospital on flatcars and stretchers, Crane observed that this "dirty, ragged, emaciated, half-starved, band of cripples" hung their heads and seemed to be afflicted by something akin to stage fright. So much for the triumphs and satisfactions of war.

He stayed for about a week, perhaps a bit longer, and filed what would prove to be his last dispatches for the *World*, the long account of the Battle of San Juan and "Regulars Get No Glory." At one point, he went to Fort Monroe and outfitted himself with a fresh suit of clothes. His old clothes were in tatters by then, as Davis describes in an article for *Harper's New Monthly Magazine*: "One of the best known of the correspondents . . . was sent home, desperately ill with fever, in the same clothes he had been forced to wear for three weeks. He had forded streams in them, slept on bare ground in them, and sweated in them from the heat and from fever, and when he reached Fortress Monroe he bought himself a complete new outfit at the modest expenditure of twenty-four dollars." That correspondent was Crane, and those twenty-four dollars would soon be turned into one of the bullets used by Seitz to kill Crane's tenure at the *World*.

Meanwhile, another bullet was being manufactured in Cuba. It came off the assembly line on July sixteenth in the form of a controversial, unsigned article written for the *World* by Scovel that Seitz and the paper's New York business staff (for unfathomable reasons) convinced themselves had been written by Crane. Add in the other bullet produced when their disloyal employee trudged five or six miles through the jungle to send off the dispatch written by the injured Marshall—a correspondent for a rival paper—and suddenly there was every reason to give Crane the boot. And since he no longer worked for them, Seitz and company blithely refused to cover "the modest expenditure" of trading in a pile of rags for a new suit of clothes. It wasn't just the twenty-four dollars, you understand, it was the principle of the thing.

Scovel's article blamed the July first rout of the New York infantry division on the cowardice and incompetence of the unit's officers, a charge so grave that it set off a volley of countercharges from the *Journal* and blossomed into one of the most ferocious battles in the yearslong newspaper war between Pulitzer and Hearst. It began on July sixteenth (when Crane was still in Virginia), and the next day the valiant, hardworking Scovel, who had been in Cuba longer than any other American correspondent and had taken more risks than any of them, damaged his career as a journalist when, in one hot-headed moment during the formal surrender of Santiago, he took it upon himself to slug the corpulent, preening General Shafter in the face. Accounts differ on whether Shafter struck back, but no sooner had the scuffle broken out than Crane's friend was put under arrest and expelled from Cuba.*

From Virginia, Crane went to New York to begin negotiating an agreement with the publisher Frederick A. Stokes for a book of stories about the Cuban war and to check in with his bosses at the *World*—who promptly fired him when he turned up at the office. In his 1933 article, Seitz claims that it was one of the members of his staff, financial director John Norris, who handed Crane his walking papers and refused to give him any money for expenses. According to Seitz, after Crane's visit Norris emerged from his office "rubbing his hands gleefully. 'I have just kissed your little friend Stephen Crane goodbye,' he said with a full-face grin. 'He came here asking for another advance. Don't you think you have had enough of Mr. Pulitzer's money without earning it? I asked. Oh, very well, he said, if that's the way you look at it, by-by. So we're rid of him.'"

One wonders how much of this account was true and whether Crane actually said what Norris-via-Seitz said he said. If the incident did play out according to this version, one could also ask why Crane took his dismissal so calmly and did not speak up in his own defense. Perhaps he already knew about their diminishing faith in his work and was half-expecting to be fired when he entered the building, or else, true to form, he did not want to cause a scene, which would have let them know how hurt he was by their contemptuous attitude toward him. It sounds as if he did no more than shrug. Call it the stiff upper lip, American-style—and then *Adiós!*

He could have gone back to England at that point, but he didn't. No doubt because he didn't want to or wasn't ready to, and also because he didn't have

---

* Scovel had gone to Cuba as early as 1895 to report on the insurrection. In 1896, he was arrested by the Spanish, managed to escape, and spent a year with the rebels behind enemy lines. When he returned to Cuba in 1897, following his months in Greece during the Greco-Turkish War and his expedition to the Klondike, the Spanish arrested him again, but he was let go when the American government demanded his release. In spite of the dustup with Shafter, Scovel eventually made his way back to Cuba, settled in Havana with his wife, Frances, and continued writing for the *World* until 1902. After his resignation, he found other work in Havana and died there in 1905 at age thirty-six.

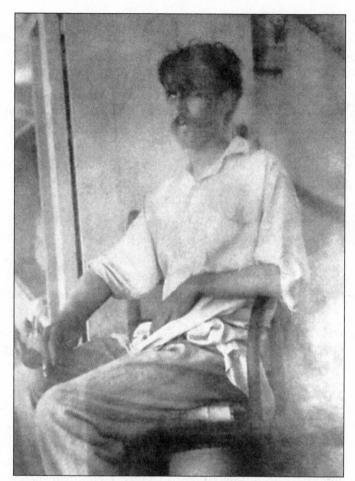

Crane aboard the Three Friends *off the coast of Cuba, 1898.*
(COURTESY OF THE UNIVERSITY OF VIRGINIA)

the money to pay for the crossing. Instead of borrowing the fare, he waved good-bye to his former employers at the *World* and walked over to the *Journal* building, where he signed on for another tour of duty with Hearst. Perhaps it made him feel a little better to switch his allegiance to Pulitzer's archrival, but who knows? What the new job meant was more war and a chance to cover the Puerto Rican campaign, but before he went south again to begin his assignment, Crane took a long detour and traveled north to consult with the lung specialist Edward Livingston Trudeau in Saranac Lake.

His recent bout with malaria must have frightened him, and even though he seemed to have recovered and pretended to be well, it is almost certain that he knew he wasn't well. Oddly enough, when Trudeau wrote to Cora in

September about the visit, he seemed distinctly untroubled by his patient's condition, whereas just one or two weeks after the checkup, Michelson would write that Crane was "hollow-cheeked," "marked by ill health," and that his body resembled "a frayed white ribbon." Even earlier than that (before the malaria), in a number of photographs taken aboard the *Three Friends*, Crane had been looking unwell, slovenly (as per Frank Norris's description), and disturbingly unlike himself. Barefoot, shaggy-haired, dressed in rumpled white pajama-clothes, and sporting a thick, drooping mustache, he comes across as a demented beachcomber or, perhaps, as a self-anointed prophet who has just spent forty days fasting in the desert, where he was struck by a bolt of lightning on the morning of the first day. Now that he had been through the shakes and deliriums of tropical fever, he must have looked even worse, and yet Dr. Trudeau calmly writes:

> Dear madam
> Your husband had a slight evidence of activity in the trouble of his lungs when he came back here this summer but it was not serious and he has improved steadily I understand since he came. I have only examined him once but he looked very well and told me he was feeling much better last time I saw him.

Among other things, this awkwardly written note tells us that Crane had come to see Trudeau on an earlier visit or visits, and *improved steadily since he came* suggests that sometime after the most recent consultation, Crane had contacted the doctor to report that he was feeling better— which might have been true but probably wasn't. Not many people lie to their doctor, at least not people who want to get well, but it would not have been beyond Crane to lie in this circumstance, for either in his lost letter to Trudeau or when they were talking to each other face-to-face, he must have asked the doctor to write to Cora and, when he did, to couch his language in the most unalarming terms possible. Otherwise, why would Trudeau have written to her, and how could he have known where to send the letter if Crane hadn't given him the address? Some have argued that Cora must have written to the doctor first and that this letter was his reply, but she wouldn't have contacted Trudeau unless Crane had already told her he had been to Saranac Lake—which amounts to more or less the same thing, since Crane would have been the instigator of the correspondence whether there was one letter or two. Above all, he wanted to protect Cora from the truth about his lungs, which was something he would continue to do even after he returned to England, and for now, as she waited for him on the other side of the ocean, the last thing he wanted was to compound her anxieties about his absence with further anxieties about his health.

Crane left New York for Pensacola, Florida, on July twenty-fifth or twenty-sixth. Spanish forces in the Puerto Rican city of Ponce surrendered to the Americans on the twenty-eighth, and promptly on the twenty-ninth Crane, Michelson, and other correspondents boarded a tug chartered by the *Journal* and set out for Puerto Rico. It was on that boat that Michelson made his observations about Crane's physical condition and general state of mind ("destitute of small talk, critical if not fastidious"), but there are other pertinent details about the things Crane said and did, as well as his interactions with the others on the boat (everyone crammed together for a week), and then, after they reached shore and landed, how he behaved in Ponce and elsewhere. Without Michelson's text, which was published as the introduction to the twelfth and final book in the first multivolume edition of Crane's work (1925–27), much of what happened during this period would be missing from the story.

It was a slow, tedious journey, according to Michelson, with "few thrills," but the water was often choppy, even rough, and most of the men on board suffered from violent attacks of seasickness. As he had shown on the *Commodore*, however, "Crane never felt a qualm." Weak lungs, yes, but a sturdy gut, and when he put his mind to it, he was still the master of the spontaneous quip. Once, when an American cruiser came close to the tug and then sharply—and indignantly—veered off after learning the nature of its business, Crane said, "Like a fat dowager duchess who had been asked by a scrubwoman where she had bought her hat." On another rough day at sea, as men were throwing up over the railing, Crane pointed out to Michelson "the convulsive jerk of their shoulders" and said that "men died with just such a spasm. . . . It was not lack of sympathy, or callousness," Michelson adds, "It was simply that motion-picture mind of his registering impressions. It was an instinct, stronger than love, pity, or fear."

These last sentences confirm why Michelson is such a valuable witness. Not just the "motion-picture mind" (a point that seems so clear in retrospect but which no one could understand during Crane's lifetime) but also the word "instinct," that is, Crane's compulsion to look at things objectively and without prejudice, to discard everyone else's opinion about the "deep bluish tint which is so widely condemned when it is put into pictures" and trust what his own eyes were seeing.

On another day, when asked by an American cruiser that was being threatened by a Spanish destroyer to run interference by making a hard turn toward the shore, the tug carried out the operation after Crane goaded the captain into doing it. Michelson: "The chaperon of our war party went to the pilot-house to learn the reason for the turn. There he found Stephen baiting the captain to run in close. Asked why he was doing it, the seaman answered fervently: "You don't think I'm going to let this damned frayed tholepin think he's got more guts than me, do you?"

As defined by the *American Heritage Dictionary*, a tholepin is "a wooden peg set in pairs in the gunwale of a boat to serve as an oarlock." In other words, the captain was comparing Crane to a wooden peg, and a frayed one at that, but soon enough, as often happens when entertainments are scarce and everyone is bored, the word stuck. It seems that Crane had mentioned that his wife was negotiating new living arrangements for them at Brede Place in Sussex, a large manor house that dated back to the fourteenth century, and suddenly he became Lord Tholepin, "a liverish British squire, with an East Indian background, and the ancestral mansion was christened Mango Chutney." Michelson contends that Crane "had more fun out of it than anybody else," although one wonders if he had any choice but to play along in those confined circumstances. In any case, the joke eventually wore thin and that was the end of it, but what this microscopic, ephemeral story tells us is that Crane was intending to go back to Cora. At least then he was, and if at other times he wasn't, the certainty displayed here as opposed to the doubt displayed at other moments only proves how torn he was about the life he wanted for himself after the war. Assuming, of course, that he would still be alive then and have something to look forward to.

Once they arrived at Ponce and went ashore, Crane did his usual vanishing act, and instead of joining the other correspondents on their excursions to the hotels and cafés, he began hanging out with "the wastrels of Ponce—drunkards, drabs, and tin-horn gamblers. They did not know a word of his language nor he a word of theirs. Moreover, this was a conquered city and he was one of the invaders. That made no difference. He was accepted into the easy brotherhood."

On the other hand, when called upon to appear in more elegant surroundings, Crane proved himself to be what Michelson terms a "social bankrupt."

The Army and Navy officers made a great deal of the literary lights. Richard Harding Davis was always the star of their parties . . . but they were intensely curious about Crane. It was hard to get him to the dinners.

Maybe he resented the contrast between himself and Davis—the latter always a full-page illustration by Gibson of a war correspondent, immaculate in a tailored uniform, his deep chest striated with service ribbons. In these gatherings, Davis glittered not only by his accoutrements but by his accomplishments. He would borrow a banjo and to its accompaniment sing "Mandalay" and other ballads, and between times carry his full share of the burden of conversation, always ready, always interesting, while Stephen, in his old campaign clothes, sat tongue-tied.

Just one month before those nights in Ponce, Crane had risked his neck to help Davis in a time of trouble, and just one month after, Davis would heap extravagant praise on the high quality of S.C.'s reportage from Cuba. But the two men never got along, perhaps because each one represented an idea of manhood so different from the other that they could never establish a middle ground between them. Crane sulked in silence as Davis hogged the attention of the crowd, no doubt wondering if the pompous oaf with the medals on his chest had any idea how ridiculous he was. The dandified hero was more tolerant, but at best he saw his little colleague as a brilliant, benighted screwup, admirable in his way, perhaps, but somehow pitiable. He probably didn't know that the silent one could play the banjo just as well as he could and had a decent tenor voice.

Puerto Rico was the aftermath, a short nineteen-day campaign during which the American troops encountered little or no resistance. The Puerto Ricans seemed more than glad to be rid of the Spanish and were cautiously hopeful that life would be better for them under the protection of the United States. The jury is still out on whether that hope was warranted, but at the time the island was in a festive mood, and so quickly did town after town surrender to the Yankee forces that Crane himself was responsible for the capture of one of them.

As usual, there are two competing versions of the story. In the first one, Crane simply walked into Juana Díaz one morning, and after he was given a warm welcome by the population, he turned his unexpected ascension to power into a high-spirited lark: Puck the prankster in all his quick-thinking, improvisatory dazzle. Gathering the men of the town into the central square, he arbitrarily divided them into two categories: "suspects" and "good fellows." The suspects were sent home, and then he appointed the good fellows as his hosts and bodyguards. "A frenzied carnival of rejoicing" followed, and the next morning, when an American colonel arrived with a regiment of eight hundred men, he told Crane that he was glad a journalist would be there to watch them take this town. "'*This* town!' said Crane in polite embarrassment. 'I'm really very sorry, Colonel, but I took this town before breakfast yesterday morning!'"

So says Richard Harding Davis, who was not in Juana Díaz and reportedly heard the story from Crane himself, but Michelson, who was there and saw what happened, gives a more complex and somewhat more subdued version of the caper. In his account, he and Crane and "a flock of correspondents" were looking for a place to eat breakfast. The new policy was that inns were supposed to serve food to "hungry officers" before anyone else, but when they arrived at Juana Díaz, there were no officers. "Then came Stephen Crane's inspiration. He rode ahead and announced that the American governor of Porto Rico was on his way and ordered breakfast for His Excellency and Staff. The most imposing member of the party, fortunately in immaculate whites, took the part of governor. He gave instructions to advise anybody who appeared that he did not wish to be disturbed during the meal. The preposterous strategy worked." When a brigadier general showed up a bit later and asked what was going on, the flustered Crane managed to lie his way out of it. "'Governor?' he said. 'Oh, I guess the people here heard us call Jack Mumford governor, he looks so much like one. There's nobody here but a bunch of newspaper correspondents.'"

Michelson's version is more plausible, but in each one the conquest of Juana Díaz shows Crane at his most boyish, his most playful, his most exuberantly silly. If he had acted that way more often in Puerto Rico, one could conclude that he was fully recovered from his tropical fever scare and the visit to the Adirondacks, but his behavior during the weeks he spent there was remarkably inconsistent. Withdrawn and quiet on the tug, withdrawn and quiet at the military dinners in Ponce, a Peter Pan extrovert in Juana Díaz, and then, as the correspondents prepared to leave the island, the tearful parting from his beloved horse (as noted on page 31), which was nothing if not a blubbering surge of sentimental excess. Not stable, then. Not steady. A mass of different moods oscillating from low to high and down to low again, and if he wasn't in any immediate danger of landing in crack-up territory, he was hovering around the outskirts, and even now, when the fighting and the war were over, the nightmares he had witnessed in Cuba continued to press in on him, and he still wasn't prepared to return to England. Instead, sometime during the third week of August, under the false pretense that he was a commercial tobacco buyer, he slipped into Havana without authorization and remained there, for reasons both obscure and more obscure, until the last week of December.

4

GOING BACK TO APRIL, BACK TO ENGLAND, AND BACK TO THE ONE who was left behind . . .

The household in Oxted now had three people in it, one half-empty bed, and three dogs. For company, Cora had the enigmatic Charlotte Ruedy (who called herself Mrs., not Miss, and about whom almost nothing is known); for help, she had the dutiful, ever-obliging Adoni Ptolemy; and beyond the perimeters of Ravensbrook, she had the moral support of Harold Frederic, Kate Lyon, Robert Barr, and Conrad, who didn't see her often but kept in touch by mail, sending her at least seven letters during Crane's absence, all of them notable for their warmth and anxious concern about her welfare. Toward the end of the year, when it became a question of finding the money to get Crane back to England, Conrad actively explored a number of possible solutions and at one point (being moneyless himself) offered to put up his own work as collateral for a potential loan. A good friend. As were the others, and for the first three or four months, all was relatively calm. She was short of funds and living on credit, of course, but out-and-out panic would not set in until later.

She didn't mope, and she didn't feel sorry for herself, and she refused to give in to the threat of loneliness. Just days after Crane's departure, she accepted an invitation from the Frederics to join them and their three young children for a return visit to the house in Ahakista on the southern coast of Ireland. As Conrad put it in a letter to her from April nineteenth:

We imagine how lonely you must have felt after Stephen's departure. The dear fellow wired me from Queenstown, just before going aboard I suppose. Jess is very concerned about you and wishes me to ask you to drop her a line on your arrival in Ireland. I think your going there would be a good thing as solitude after separation is sometimes very hard to bear.

We thought of asking you to come here at once but on receiving Stephen's wire I imagined you were all in Ireland already. However you will be more entertained and more comfortable at the Frederic's for a time and on your return to England I hope you will have the will and the courage to undertake the risky experiment of coming to us with Mrs. Ruedy. Moreover I fancy Stephen's absence won't be very prolonged and we may have the felicity of seeing you all here together. I trust you will let me know how he fares whenever you hear from him. He is not very likely to write to anyone else—if I know the man.

After spending two or three weeks with the Frederics, Cora returned to her house in Oxted and began plotting an escape from the house, from Oxted, and from all the encumbrances that had dogged her life with Crane since they had settled in England. Neither one of them had ever been happy with their suburban villa, and for some time they had been talking about moving elsewhere. A place in the country, a place more distant from London, a quiet refuge where they would be free from the continual harassment of unwanted visitors and Crane could disappear into his work. Back in March, their neighbor Garnett had told them about a house owned by a friend in Sussex, and as the critic remembered it years afterward, Crane had been so enthralled by the description of the ancient structure, "noble and gray with the passage of five hundred years," that he immediately jumped on the idea of becoming the tenant of Brede Place. With no other pressing obligations to distract her after she returned from the Irish coast, Cora buckled down to the business of making it happen.

The owner was Moreton Frewen (1853–1924), the scion of an old Sussex family endowed with enormous wealth, and his American wife, Clara, happened to be the sister of Brooklyn-born Jennie Jerome, who was the wife of another Englishman, Lord Randolph Churchill, and the mother of the twenty-four-year-old future prime minister, Winston Churchill. Frewen was something of a renegade among that august company, an adventurer who won and lost fortunes as other men win and lose at blackjack, and so incurable was his penchant for gambling on the longest of long shots that he earned the twin nicknames of "Mortal Ruin" and "the splendid pauper." His latest enterprise had been a vast, sprawling ranch in Wyoming that had been built to cash in on the western cattle boom but had generated so little profit that the scheme had gone bust. Almost inevitably, he and Crane wound up becoming fast friends. In April 1900, not two months before he died, S.C. put the finishing touch on his collection of Cuban war stories by adding a dedication to his sweet-tempered, live-and-let-live landlord, who never bothered to collect the rent and actively tried to help the Cranes whenever they fell into difficulties: *To / Moreton Frewen / this small token of things / well remembered by / his friend / Stephen Crane.*

Brede Place had been in the family for more than three hundred years, and having bought it recently from one of his brothers, Frewen was now the sole owner of the house and the one-hundred-acre property that surrounded it. Sometime in May, Cora took the first step by engaging an architect to inspect the house and report on any necessary repairs, and on June fourth she wrote to Clara Frewen explaining that

Brede Place, Sussex, in 1944. (COURTESY OF SYRACUSE UNIVERSITY)

she would have been in touch earlier but had been waiting to hear from the architect about "how much it would cost to make the house habitable." She had hoped, too, to have heard from Crane by then, but so far no word had come. Eager to keep the process moving, she decided to act on her own and made an offer to rent the place for forty pounds a year (a moot point, as it turned out, since the rent was rarely if ever paid). On the tenth, she followed up with a letter to Frewen telling him that Mr. Crane had sent her a cablegram from Jamaica and "that he is satisfied with my arrangements." With the matter settled now, she went off on a four-day driving excursion with friends and saw her future home for the first time, a pleasant jolt that prompted another letter to Frewen on the sixteenth in which she assured him that Crane "will be delighted at the idea of camping in your old house."

"Old house" hardly does justice to the tumbledown decay of Brede, a monstrosity built in the fourteenth century that had been restored twice since then—back in the fifteenth and sixteenth centuries. There was no electricity and no modern plumbing, and most of the many rooms in that immense stone hulk were in such disrepair they were not fit for anything but storing junk. On top of that, it had the further disadvantage of being a haunted house. A ghost prowled the halls at night, and there was no chance of ever getting rid of him. From *The Crane Log*:

Servants refused to spend the night in the house because of the legend that it was haunted by the spirit of its early sixteenth-century owner, Sir Goddard Oxenbridge, a warlock and an ogre who purportedly ate a child for dinner each night. According to the legend, he was executed by local children who sawed him in half with a wooden saw while he lay in an intoxicated stupor.

It made no difference to the Cranes. They both fell in love with the idea of living in their collapsed medieval ruin, and however impractical it was for them to be there, their enthusiasm for Brede Place never flagged—for the simple reason that they were not practical people. As Cora wrote to Reynolds that fall, "A man must have pure wholesome air if he wishes to succeed in art," and then, a couple of sentences later, that Crane "has . . . a wonderful home awaiting him." But it wasn't a wonderful home, and the air in that place was far from wholesome. If they had wanted wholesome air, they could have moved to some craggy perch in the Arizona desert or, if America was not an option, to the mountains of Switzerland or France. A failing, fever-ridden body will not recover its strength by living in dank, chilly rooms, and two long winters at Brede exacted a harsh toll on Crane. The house itself was not directly responsible for his death, but there is no question that it played an important role in killing him.

Perhaps the calendar had something to do with it as well. Cora went there for the first time in June, the loveliest, most welcoming month of the year. One wonders what she would have thought if she had made the trip in January.

On August twelfth, the forty-two-year-old Frederic suffered a stroke, and for the next several months Cora had additional things to worry about besides money problems and Crane's infrequent cablegrams. Her friends were in crisis, and as she stepped in to help them, the initial blow devolved into a melodrama that played out in four distinct acts, advancing from illness to death to manslaughter charges to a possible prison term for Kate Lyon. No one could have invented such a story. Only the real world is powerful enough to dream up something on this order of Weird.

Frederic was a big man who lived hard, and while not every man who drinks too much and smokes too much and maintains two separate families is a candidate for stroke—at least not when he is barely past forty—Frederic was one of the unlucky ones. And his was a bad stroke, so severe that his life was threatened. On learning the news, Cora rushed over to Homefield with Adoni Ptolemy and arranged for her servant to be lent out for as long as necessary to help with Frederic's care. Then she gathered up the three small children (ages four, five, and six) and took them back to Ravensbrook to live with her so Kate would not have to divide her energies between child care and nursing a sick man.

Frederic had been paralyzed along the right side of his body and the left side of his face, but he continued to smoke and drink in his debilitated condition, had nothing but contempt for his doctors, refused to listen to their advice, and ultimately dismissed them on September twentieth. Cora was alarmed by this impetuous move, but Kate sympathized with her husband, not just out of loyalty but because of her own lack of faith in traditional medicine, and with Frederic's wholehearted approval, they decided to handle his case by following the Christian Science precepts of nonintervention and prayer. A Christian Science healer named Mrs. Mills was called in to supervise his treatment (or nontreatment), and for a host of obvious reasons Frederic's condition continued to decline. On October sixteenth, a frantic John Scott Stokes turned up at Cora's house and explained that he had just been to Homefield and had found Frederic in miserable shape, perhaps on the point of death. He urged Cora to go there herself and try to talk Kate into summoning the doctors. Denying someone adequate medical care was a criminal offense, he told her, and he feared that Kate could be charged with manslaughter if Frederic died.

Cora went to Homefield the next morning, and after some strenuous resistance from her friend, she finally managed to persuade her to call in the doctors who had been cut loose in September. It was too little too late. In the middle of the following night, as October eighteenth was turning into the nineteenth, Frederic died when his heart gave out on him.

Two days later, an inquest concerning the cause of his death was opened by the district coroner, and in an ugly procedure that plodded on for several weeks and left Kate's reputation in a shambles, a verdict was finally delivered by the jury on November eighth to charge both her and Mrs. Mills with manslaughter—just as Scott Stokes had predicted. Both women were arrested outside the courtroom, arraigned in the local police court, and then released after posting bail in the amount of fifty pounds each. Scott Stokes and other friends pooled their money to free Kate.

She and her children went back to Ravensbrook with Cora, and two weeks later the trial began at the Croydon County Police Court. The prosecutor was Horace Avory, the same man who had helped convict Oscar Wilde on charges of sodomy and gross indecency in 1895, and along with the two doctors, the Frederics' housekeeper, Scott Stokes, and Adoni Ptolemy, Cora was one of the witnesses called on to testify. After court was adjourned for the day, a number of postponements followed, and then, in a surprising turn on December fifth, Avory asked for the charges against Kate Lyon to be dropped. Presumably, he wanted to focus his attention on Mrs. Mills, but in an even more surprising turn, the magistrates eventually dismissed the charges against both women. Still, there was one more barrier in front of them, and it wasn't until December fourteenth—four months and two days after Frederic's stroke—that the case concluded in London's Central Criminal Court (the Old Bailey) when the charges were withdrawn against Kate and dismissed against Mrs. Mills. By then, Kate Lyon had been so thoroughly beaten up in the press that she no longer had a private life. She was public property now, a fallen woman who had destroyed the marriage of an honorable man and given birth to three bastard children. For those sins, she had lost the right to show her face in decent society and now qualified as a non-person, a human smudge.

By way of response, Cora and Scott Stokes established a fund to help raise money for the support of Kate's children. Henry James and George Bernard Shaw kicked in small contributions, but Conrad, who had only eight pounds in the bank, was too strapped to offer anything. The two fundraisers forged on with mixed results, and when Cora received a letter from the wife of James Creelman (the head of the *Journal* office in London and the man who was actively *not* giving Cora the money Crane had hoped would be sent to her), the depth of the hostility toward Kate Lyon was exposed in the most naked terms. "I must say that my deep sympathy is enlisted for those little creatures brought face to face with calamity by the deliberate selfishness of their parents," Alice Creelman wrote, "and if I was certain they would not be under the corrupting influence of their mother I should gladly contribute freely to their support. As it is I must tell you frankly that I have a great scorn for Kate Lyon and the evil influence she has exerted over a morally weak man and that the only atonement possible for the crime of bringing three bastard children into the world and of wrecking the life of another woman and the lawful children, is a continuous life of sacrifice and labor to support her children without charity from strangers."

Cora's response, fired off in anger the next day, is not only a defense of Kate Lyon and her children but a document that sets forth Cora's views on Christian ethics, womanhood, female solidarity, and the pernicious harm that comes from judging others. The occasional spelling and diction errors show that it was written in the frenzy of the moment, straight off the top of her head and from deep within her gut, but it also shows who Cora was at her best—both passionate and compassionate, both tender and fierce, a woman who had thought long and hard about the big questions in life and had formed some solid, impressive answers. The letter is fairly long, but it is worth quoting more or less in full.

I thank you for your reply to my letter asking for *private* subscriptions for the support of the three youngest children of the late Harold Frederic. In justice to their mother, let me say, that she refused, absolutely, to join in a public appeal for help, thinking, as I do, such an appeal in shocking taste. Nor did she have any knowledge, until yesterday when I wrote informing her, of *this* fund for the children.

The people whom you have said "discuss this unfortunate scandal" are, naturally, not the people one would look to for help in this matter. The nasty taste that such discussion would leave in their mouths—would strike through to the organ which they use solely to pump blood—blood soured by lack of true charity—to the brain. One wonders if they think themselves christians? And how they dare set themselves up as models of virteous morality, when they have the example of Christs loving kindness to sinners, before them.

How can we judge another, we that are so full of sin and weakness? And how can any creature knowing itself mortal lose an orportunity to be charitable in the true sense? Judging not!

To me, the supreme egotism of women who never having been tempted, and so knowing nothing of the temptation of another's soul, set themselves upon their pedestals of self-conceit and concious virtue, judging their unfortunate sisters guilty alike, is the hardest thing in life. If we women who are beloved and sheltered, would help those less fortunate of our sex to help themselves (and this is not done by using a club or turning our-selves into shrews under the cover of outraged innocence) the world would be a sweeter, purer place to live in and we ourselves would be more worthy of happiness.

... These moralists swollen and distorted with the knowledge of not having, themselves, sinned a particular sin, who rush to drag a dead man's name through the mire, that they themselves, revel to hear about—to these poor souls scandal, and the throwing of mud—and stones—is meat and strong drink. They roll it on their tongues as a sweet morsel, and the wine of it is the highest exaltation they know! For those who have no charity I ask God's mercy; they are so poor a lot!

You say your surprised that I should expect anyone to help Miss Lyon with the burden of her children—my surprise is, that people can visit the sins of the parents upon those innocent babies—If self respect can come to mankind by their proving their loathing of sin, (and how can we judge the laws of God—by laws of state or those of our theological brothers?) by not helping these children to bread and shelter—let them so get what comfort they can out of the satisfaction that come with the knowledge of their own loved one's warm and fed—I have sheltered these children for five months in my own home and with my own name—and if all the world line themselves up to fight these babes, I will still shelter *them* & God will help me.

Meanwhile, running parallel to the gruesome saga of her friends, there was the deepening mystery of Crane's silence. He had sent a cablegram on September sixteenth (four days after Frederic's stroke) telling her that the Puerto Rican campaign was over and he had safely landed in Key West, and then, for the next several weeks, nothing more was heard from him. If in fact he wrote to her from his boardinghouse in Havana (a strong possibility), the Spanish-speaking person who was supposed to mail the letters for him threw them out instead. And without knowing where Crane was, Cora had no idea how to contact him.

A month went by without a single scrap of news. On September twenty-second, an article that had been published in the *Florida Times-Union* on September tenth reached Cora in England, and by the time she had absorbed the headline and taken in the first paragraph, she must have been in a full-blown panic.

STEPHEN CRANE MISSING

Stephen Crane, the novelist, also a member of the Journal staff, who entered Havana as a tobacco buyer about ten days ago, and was stopping quietly at the Hotel Pasaje, is missing, and fears for his safety are entertained by his friends. The police had been shadowing him several days before he disappeared.

It doesn't matter that the article was wrong, that it was essentially a bogus piece of conjecture inspired by the fact that Crane had left the hotel where he had been staying and moved to a less expensive boardinghouse in another part of town. With no more battles to report, the *Journal* had ambushed him by terminating his contact as a member of the regular staff, and even though he continued to write for them in Havana, he had been turned into a freelancer, paid so much per article as he turned them in, and he no longer had an expense account to cover the costs of a pricey hotel. No doubt, some of the peripheral members of his circle were unaware of this, and now that Crane had apparently disappeared, they figured he must have been snatched away by the police.

Not true, but Cora couldn't have known that, and consequently she was forced to conclude that Crane had gone missing. Desperate as she must have been, the newspaper report had given her a possible lead, and working on the assumption that Crane had been in Havana and was perhaps still there, she immediately got to work on trying to find him.

She began her search by going straight to the top, sending off a letter on September twenty-fourth to John Hay, the American secretary of state, who until recently had been the ambassador to Great Britain and was not only on friendly terms with Crane but an avid follower of his work. "Knowing you to be a personal friend of my husband, Stephen Crane," Cora began, she went on to give a brief summary of the facts as she understood them and concluded: "I am almost distracted with grief and anxiety. I am sure you will personally ask the President to instruct the American commission to demand Mr. Crane from the Havana police."

The next day, she contacted three more people, sending both a letter and a wire to the American secretary of war, Russell A. Alger, a letter to Crane's agent, Reynolds, who knew of Cora's existence by then, and a wire to William Crane, who didn't. Cora had been going along with the ruse of hide-and-pretend for a year and a half at that point, but now that the man's little brother was in danger, it was her duty to let him know about it. If he was shocked to learn that the same little brother also had a wife, that was his problem, not hers. There was a crisis to be dealt with, and it was too urgent to allow for any more hypocritical evasions. If the big brother was any kind of person, the shock of the marriage would wear off soon enough.

The communications with Alger turned out to be one of Cora's most effective moves, for not only did she give him an outline of the general situation, she specifically asked that he contact the U.S. authorities in

Havana to investigate the matter, and that put a slow, bureaucratic process in motion that wound up coming to the attention of Major General J. F. Wade, who was in charge of the evacuation of Americans from Cuba, and some weeks after Cora's initial request, the general finally got to the bottom of the story. By then, Cora had already learned that her husband was alive and had not been rotting in some Spanish dungeon, but it was Wade's intervention that induced Crane to break his long silence, and later on, toward the end of the year, the general served as the conduit through which the money was sent to bring Crane back to England.

The September twenty-fifth letter to Reynolds is another plea for help, but in this case not just in tracking down S.C.'s whereabouts but in solving the problem of Cora's rapidly increasing money troubles, which had become so extreme in the past months that they were threatening to put her life on red alert.

After rehashing the information from the Florida newspaper, she tells Reynolds that

> I am in great distress of mind as I can get no news through the Journal office here. Mr. Crane's affairs ... need his attention. I am in *great* need of money. And I fear we will lose our house ... if I cannot get money to pay some pressing debts [she had been served with summonses from the local butcher and grocer]. The Journal is behaving very shabily.... If you can collect any money due to Mr. Crane please cable it to me without delay. This being so helpless in a foreign country together with my fears for Mr. Crane are almost driving me mad. Will you use your influence with Mr. Hearst. He has no right to allow a man like Mr. Crane to be missing for over three weeks without using means to find him. And if he allows Stephen Cranes wife to be turned out of her house, while Stephen is risking his life in his service, I have told Mr. Creelman I would let every correspondent in London know about it.

Her neighbor Robert Barr (1850–1912), who had become a good friend of both Cranes since their move to Oxted, was standing at the ready, prepared to help Cora in any way he could on both fronts: finding Crane and squaring her debts. In a letter written on the twenty-seventh, he tells her that the Hearst press has wired the London office to report that Crane has been hiding out in a Havana rooming house and, according to a conversation he has had with Creelman, that it is almost certain that "at least some of your communications [have] reached Crane." Assuming this is true, he says—and he has no reason to suppose it isn't—"then I should hate to put down in black and white what I think of Stephen Crane. If he has not disappeared, and if he has been drawing money for himself, while leaving you without cash, then that article about his disappearance in the Florida paper is a put-up job, and he does not intend to return." Barr, who loved and admired Crane, who would declare in print just a few months later that he was "probably the greatest genius America has produced since Edgar Allan Poe," was so disgusted with his friend's behavior that he could barely hold back his anger, and yet, as he goes on to tell Cora, "If in these circumstances, you think it worth while to go after such a man, then there is nothing to do but consider the ways and means." He then sketches out an elaborate plan to convince the Atlantic Transport Line to grant Cora deferred payment on an ocean crossing that would allow her to reach Havana and drag Crane back to England herself. It appears that Cora entertained this possibility for a while but then backed out at the last minute, no doubt anticipating the scandal that would explode if she happened to find S.C. shacked up with another woman. It turned out to be a good decision. The ship she would have taken on October thirteenth, the SS *Mohegan*, left port on schedule and one day later struck a reef and sank.

Another episode from the endless chronicle of the *unreal real*.

She responded to a card from Reynolds by writing to him again on the twenty-ninth. Although she sounds much assuaged and refers to her "great distress" about the Florida newspaper article in the past tense, she is now aware that the agent has been in communication with her husband and asks him to let her "know if Mr. Crane gets my letters and where he is at the time this reaches you." The politeness of her request should be noted carefully, for if she could ask this favor from him, it would follow that she was almost certain Reynolds knew Crane's address, and yet she does not demand that he tell her what it is, she merely asks, and so quietly and modestly that it is hard to tell if that is what she is asking. Such restraint shows how delicate her position was just then. She was poised on a narrow balance beam, and circumstances demanded that she demonstrate the agility to walk from one end to the other without falling and breaking her neck. If she said nothing, she would fall. If she said too much and began to act as an outraged, vindictive wife, she would fall even harder. Her object was to get Crane back to England, but he wouldn't come back unless he wanted to, and because she didn't know Reynolds well enough to trust him not to reveal—and perhaps even exaggerate to S.C.—an outright demand for the address, she merely and meekly asked her simple, straightforward question and in that way kept her toes firmly planted on the beam.

She had been through a terrible scare, but now that it was over, she was back where she had been a week earlier—or almost. Crane was still silent, and she still didn't know how to contact him—but at least she knew he was somewhere in Havana, hiding out in a place so obscure that it could have been on the dark side of the moon, where *boardinghouse* was no doubt a polite term for *brothel*, just as it had been in the old Jacksonville days of Ethel Dreme.

Sometime in the first half of October, she traveled to Stanford-le-Hope with Mrs. Ruedy to visit the Conrads. Warmly received by young, sympathetic Jessie and stalwart brother-ally Conrad (who now worked with a photograph of Crane on his desk), she finally let down her defenses in that intimate, welcoming atmosphere and opened up to them. In her memoir, Jessie recalled that the visit "was marred by her very real anxiety as to [Crane's] whereabouts, and a fierce jealousy as to his possible fancy for someone he might meet. In vain I assured her of my complete conviction that Stephen was deeply attached to her, and that his thought as soon as he was able to get a letter through would be of her."

When Cora returned to Oxted, that letter (in the form of a telegram) was waiting for her. It did not contain an apology but, rather, an explanation or at least a description of what the missing man was up to in Havana: writing his head off to produce enough money to plow his way out of debt and eventually raise the funds to cover the trip back to England. Inadequate as the message might have been in human terms, in practical terms it was sufficient, at least for Cora, who, unlike most women subjected to similar ordeals of neglect, had already made up her mind to forgive Crane without a single word of reproach—as long as he was prepared to come back of his own free will. The telegram proved that he was, and for the first time in nearly two months, her heart rate slowed down to something in the general vicinity of normal.

The good news of the telegram, and then, just days afterward, the rough news of Harold Frederic's death, followed by the painful business of the inquest and trial, which rumbled along at the same time Cora was grappling with a multitude of financial dilemmas. Besides her friend Kate, money was the only issue that counted now, both finding the money to keep herself afloat until Crane returned and finding a source of money to hasten that return, a two-pronged effort that would consume most of her time throughout the fall and early winter, even as she and Scott Stokes continued their search for money to support Kate's children.

In late September, Barr looked into the matter of the threatened lawsuits from the grocer and butcher and discovered that a rumor was spreading around the village that Cora was planning to leave the country (which in fact was true—at least until she called off the trip to Havana). He suggested that she talk to those men herself and reassure them that she wasn't going anywhere. It would appear that Cora followed his advice, since she did not wind up in court, did not lose her house, and stopped referring to the problem in her letters. One danger had been removed, but when she turned to the more difficult task of generating new income for herself, she blundered into alien territory and quickly lost her way. Requests from editors were continually coming in to publish work by Crane, and rather than hold on to them until he could respond himself, Cora naïvely assumed she could act in his place. Until then, Scott Stokes had served as an informal consultant for Crane's literary business in England, but he was overwhelmed by his duties as Frederic's executor and no longer had the time. An excellent young British agent, James B. Pinker, had just started representing Crane, and although he was consistently gracious in his dealings with Cora, she often rushed in to negotiate matters he was already negotiating himself and inadvertently stepped on his toes, at one point, for example, asking a publisher for a seventy-five-pound initial advance on an unwritten novel when Pinker had already persuaded him to offer a hundred. She was hopelessly unprepared to do what she was trying to do, and the long and short of it was that the hoped-for income did not materialize.

In the end, as if acknowledging the futility of her efforts over the past several months, she wrote in her journal sometime that December: "My letters are one long inky howl!"

She had better luck enlisting various friends to help find the money to pay for Crane's trip back to England, and among those friends, no one tried harder than Conrad, who answered Cora's appeal in an October twenty-eighth letter that suggested he already had a plan in mind.

Just a word in haste to tell you I shall try to do what I can. Don't build any hopes on it. It is a *most* remote chance—but it's the only thing I can think of. What kind of trouble is Stephen in? You make me very uneasy. Are you *sure* you can bring him back. I do not doubt your influence mind! but knowing the circumstances I do not know how far it would be feasible. In Stephen's coming back to England is *salvation* there is no doubt about that.

Will he come? *Can* he come? I am utterly in the dark as to the state of affairs. . . .

Jess shall write tomorrow. I will let you know shortly (I hope) whether my plan has been of any good.

Three days later, he wrote back to tell her he had approached David Meldrum at Blackwood's (the same man who had provided the original sixty pounds for Crane's crossing to Cuba) to lend her another fifty pounds, proposing that security could be guaranteed by putting up Crane's work as collateral, or Cora's furniture (as long as she had a bill of sale to prove she owned it—which was doubtful), or, in a pinch, Conrad's own future work "for what it is worth." Two days after that, he wrote again to report on Meldrum's hedging, inconclusive response, although the Blackwood's editor had promised to approach yet another man, London publisher John Macqueen, to lend the money. Predictably enough, that man turned them down, and with Meldrum and "that wretched Macqueen" both eliminated from his list of potential benefactors, Conrad had suddenly run out of ideas. For all his efforts, he had failed to extract a single pound from anyone, but other friends were working on a solution as well, and when Scott Stokes turned to Sidney Pawling at Heinemann's, the fifty pounds suddenly and miraculously appeared. Wheels began to turn, and before long the money had been wired to General Wade in Havana. As Conrad wrote to Cora on December fourth: "It was an immense relief to hear you had been lucky in some other quarter. Do you think Stephen will be in England before Christmas? . . . Ah! but I do feel relieved."

In late December, Cora wrote to her future landlord Moreton Frewen about the preparations she had been making for the move to Brede Place. Then she added:

> The horror of the last few months is almost at an end. Mr. Crane is in New York settling up some business affairs, but sails next Saturday week.
>
> I have sent to Brede over three hundred very choice roses. One in particular which was budded by a very prominent author [Ford Madox Ford], I've had planted against the front of the house.

She was getting the place ready for her absent prince, and damn the cost of planting three hundred rosebushes in the dead of winter. Nothing could interfere with the splendor of his homecoming. They were moving into a castle, after all, and by the time they had fully settled in, the roses would be blooming again.

5

THE WAR WAS OVER, BUT UNTIL THE PEACE TREATY WAS SIGNED ON December tenth and American forces officially took control on the first day of the new year, Havana was an off-limits city. The Spanish army and administration were still there in force, Cuban rebels were barred from entering, and foreign journalists were subject to strict censorship from the local authorities, even to the point of arrest. Food was scarce, price gouging was common practice in shops, bars, groceries, and restaurants, and sanitary conditions were abysmal. In a hastily jotted-down note for an article that was never finished, Crane described the handful of Americans in Havana as "an unregenerate and abandoned collection of newspaper correspondents, cattle men, gamblers, speculators, and drummers [salesmen] who have lived practically as they pleased, without care or restraint, going—most of them—wherever interest or whim led, with no regard for yellow fever or any other terror of the tropics." Havana was a collapsed city, a not yet fully conquered city suspended between past and future as it hung on in the chaos of the present. Could there have been a more appropriate hiding place for a man similarly trapped between past and future? Havana was the capital of the present tense, and not only was Crane stuck there, he was ill, depressed, and nearly broke.

Just a few things are known about what happened to him during those four months. Beyond the work he accomplished then (the last poems for the collection *War Is Kind*, seventeen articles for the *Journal* on conditions in Havana, "The Price of the Harness," "Marines Signaling Under Fire at Guantanamo," and a pair of other stories set in Cuba), the only information comes from two reminiscences published by fellow American journalists and Crane's correspondence with Reynolds. His agent was the one person from the outside world he wrote to with any regularity, but while his letters provide details about what he was writing and when he was writing it—along with some anguished rants about how hard up he was—they tell us nothing about what Crane was thinking or feeling during what turned out to be a considerable length of time—especially considering how little time he had left.

Walter Parker of the *New Orleans Times-Democrat* was one of the two eyewitnesses who was with him in Havana during that eerie limbo phase before the Spanish pulled out and left the city. In a piece written forty-two years after the fact, Parker recounts that when Crane was still living at the Hotel Pasaje, he used to hang out next door at the correspondents' favorite watering hole, the American Bar, where the writers would begin gathering at ten in the morning and remain until ten at night "or until a riot broke out." Crane was always the last one to show up. He drank nothing but "tropical beer" (many bottles of tropical beer), "was never hurried . . . always quite reserved" and often so low on funds that the others would chip in to pay for his drinks. No one seems to have minded, however, and Parker adds how valuable Crane was to his fellow journalists because of his "Cuban revolutionary affiliations" and the respect he had won from the insurgents for his filibustering activities in late '96 and early '97. One man in particular, "an inside figure in the Cuban revolutionary movement," owed Crane his life for having rescued him from drowning just as the *Commodore* was about to sink and, according to Parker, felt so indebted to Crane that he "would kneel and kiss his hand or the hem of his coat every time they met."

The rebels were forbidden to enter Havana, but they managed to slip through anyway, and in that upside-down city where the victors were outcasts and the vanquished were still in control, the Cubans made a point of showing up at the restaurants frequented by the Spaniards, where the two groups would inevitably fall into rancorous shouting matches and hurl insults at each other across the room. That was when everyone happened to be in a tranquil mood, but there were other evenings when the words became bullets and gunshots were exchanged. On the night after a bloody melee had smashed up the Hotel Inglaterra and men had been shot, Crane and Parker found themselves in a tense situation when they were at a café talking to a Cuban officer dressed in civilian clothes and a Spanish officer invited himself to sit down at their table. An instant later, the newcomer started cursing the Cuban and his idiotic, unholy revolution, and an instant after that, the Cuban wrapped his fingers around the handle of his revolver. If Crane hadn't intervened just then, who knows if the man wouldn't have pulled it out and fired, but S.C., who could not speak Spanish, talked to the Cuban in whatever French he could muster and persuaded him to back down.

One death averted, but Parker also mentions another evening when Crane jumped in to break up a fight and things did not go so well.

The friend from the *Commodore* had invited Crane and Parker to an illegal fundraising dance for the Cuban cause, and one of Parker's colleagues from New Orleans, who had just arrived in Havana and had spent the day stupefying himself on cognac at the American Bar, was taken along "because we did not know what else to do with him."

> Down the center of the room there were two lines of chairs, back to back. Our group were assigned seats in one row. Crane's Cuban friend and his lady love, a really beautiful girl, sat in the row just back of us. Our inebriated companion kept tilting his chair which knocked against the back of the chair occupied by the lady. She complained that she was being annoyed.
>
> Up leaped the Cuban, knife in hand, and made for the offender, intending to stab him in the heart.

Crane jumped to the rescue and caught the sharp glittering blade in his right hand. The Cuban dropped to his knees and kissed the hem of Crane's coat. Crane's hand was bleeding. He wrapped it in a handkerchief and thrust it in his coat pocket. We made apologies to the lady through the Cuban and retired.

Next day we shipped the offender back to the United States. Havana was no place for him in those days.

Crane failed to show up in the morning as was his custom. His hotel door was locked and we could get no answer from him. Later we climbed over the half-wall partition and found Crane in high fever, unconscious and with a terrible wound in his hand. The Cuban procured a doctor who gave him treatment. Many days had to pass before Crane's hand was completely cured. Even then he kept his hand in his pocket most of the time as though desirous of hiding it.

He was not the same after the incident, was more reticent and less regular in his habit of joining us every morning. . . .

[Eventually,] he went into complete retirement.

A high fever, a badly infected right hand (his writing hand), and all the attendant miseries visited upon an already battered, weakened body. Not to mention the low spirits that would have followed from those things, all because that drunken fool had been allowed to attend the dance, but the "complete retirement" Parker refers to in the last sentence was not caused by those personal setbacks alone. There were practical reasons as well, and Crane went into hiding only after he had been informed that the *Journal* had pulled the plug on his expense account, a blow that turned out to be no less damaging than the knife wound in his hand.

He had come to Havana to work his way out of debt, and now he had incurred even more debts because the paper was refusing to cover his bill at the Hotel Pasaje, where he had been living for the past three weeks. It was an expensive place, one of the best hotels in Havana, and suddenly he was responsible for settling his account with money he did not have. He was still working for the *Journal*, but he was no longer on the payroll, and they were not willing to give him more than twenty dollars per article, a rock-bottom fee that was probably held back from him and deducted from what he owed the Pasaje—reducing the bill by such small increments that he must have felt he would be trapped there forever. "I positively cannot afford to write for twenty dollars a column," he complained in a letter to Reynolds, and three letters after that, on his twenty-seventh birthday: "I am working like a dog. When—oh, when—am I to have some money? If you could only witness my poverty!"

Sometime between the sixth and the eighth of September, he moved into a boardinghouse owned by Mary Horan, an Irish transplant who had been living in Havana for years. Thirteen months later, Crane would finish the last of his Cuban war stories, "This Majestic Lie," in which a character modeled on his landlady is described as "born in Ireland, bred in New York, fifteen years married to a Spanish captain, and now a widow, keeping Cuban lodgers who had no money with which to pay her." Perhaps this is an accurate account of Mary Horan's story, perhaps it isn't, but one way or the other, Crane lived in her house for more than three months, perhaps as her only boarder, perhaps not, and once his wound healed and he was able to hold a pen in his right hand again, he plunged in and started working "like a dog" as Mary Horan watched over him and made sure he remembered to eat.

Helen R. Crane, who heard about those months directly from her uncle when he stopped in New York on his way back to England, offers some interesting details about Mrs. Horan's approach to food and exercise:

> Mary did not approve of his long hours of work, and she used to go in and hover over him with a great tray of food. "I don't want to eat, please go away." "Go away, my eye, you're goin' to eat this if I have to feed it to you spoon by spoon!" And Stephen ate. It was she who made him go for a walk every night about eleven. She came into his room, pulled the chair out from under him and drove him bodily into the street.

So Crane holed up at Mary Horan's boardinghouse and he worked . . . and then he worked. Article after article for the next-to-nothing twenty dollars a shot, an outrush of new poems, and four short stories that were dispatched to Reynolds the moment they were finished. All of the stories are good, but the second one, "The Price of the Harness," which was sent off on September twenty-seventh (the same day Robert Barr wrote to Cora and vented his disgust with the silent one in Havana), is a masterpiece, a story that Conrad judged to be "magnificent" and prompted him to tell Cora, "He is maturing. He is expanding. There is more breath and more substance. . . . It is Stephen all himself—and a little more. It is the very truth of art."

In the less exalted realm of money, "The Price of the Harness" also squared Crane's debt with Blackwood's for the sixty-pound loan they had given him in April—a positive outcome for the time being, but in retrospect it was that terrible exchange between art and life that so haunted Conrad whenever he thought about the story in the years between Crane's death and his own: the pact to return the money by pulling words out of a body that had been ruined by the quest to find those words.

The title refers to the sacrifices made by the soldiers in the regular army, "the price," as Crane told Reynolds in a subsequent letter, "the men paid for wearing the military harness, Uncle Sam's military harness; and they paid blood, hunger and fever." Building on the remarks he had made about his imaginary, prototypical career soldier presented in his last article for the *World*, "Regulars Get No Glory," Crane brings his Private Jimmie Nolan to life along with three other privates, Jack Martin, Billie Grierson, and Ike Watkins, who all participate in the charge on the fortifications of San Juan, just outside Santiago. One of them will be shot in the arm, another will contract yellow fever, and two of them will be killed.

The story advances with a steady, implacable force over seventeen densely packed pages, one blunt sentence leading to the next and unfolding in a narrative that follows the four protagonists while they go about their business as common foot soldiers, digging a road up a tangled hillside, going without rations on the first night, and ultimately going into battle, all recounted with Crane's customary flair for visual and sensory details, but matter-of-factly, in a tone devoid of linguistic flourish or probing inner reflection. The men are part of a machine, and they understand their roles without questioning the dangers that lie in front of them, and once the fighting begins, "to the prut of the magazine rifles was added the under-chorus of the clicking mechanism, steady and swift as if the hand of one operator was controlling it all. It reminds one always of a loom, a great grand steel loom, clinking, clanking, plunking, plinking, to weave a woof of thin red threads, the cloth of death." The men are prepared for this, "and all the long training at the rifle ranges, all the pride of the marksman which had been so long alive in them, made them forget for the time everything but shooting. They were as deliberate and exact as so many watchmakers."

Nolan is there and happy to be there, proud to be a part of it because the regiment and the army are "his life" and he feels awed by the courage of his fellow soldiers.

> They were halfway up the beautiful sylvan slope; there was no enemy to be seen, and yet the landscape rained bullets. Somebody punched him violently in the stomach. He thought dully to lie down and rest, but instead he fell with a crash.
>
> The sparse line of men in blue shirts and dirty slouch hats swept on up the hill. He decided to shut his eyes for a moment because he felt very dreamy and peaceful. It seemed only a minute before he heard a voice say, "There he is." Grierson and Watkins had come to look for him. He searched their faces. . . .

"Nolan," said Grierson clumsily, "do you know me?"

The man on the ground smiled softly. "Of course I know you, you chowder-faced monkey. Why wouldn't I know you?"

Nolan's friends ask him where he was hit, and although he isn't entirely sure, he points to his stomach, insisting that "it ain't much," but when Grierson and Watkins lift his shirt, they understand that he has been mortally wounded.

Then follows one of the most devastating conversations in any of Crane's stories, a wrenching passage that somehow manages to convey both the horror and banality of death at the same time and in the same unwavering key. Immersed as I have been in Crane's writing over the past few years, it is this moment that comes to me first whenever I ask myself what it is about his work that draws me to it and why I find it so compelling:

> "Does it hurt, Jimmie?" said Grierson, hoarsely.
>
> "No," said Nolan, "it don't hurt any, but I feel sort of dead-to-the-world and numb all over. I don't think it's very bad."
>
> "Oh, it's all right," said Watkins.
>
> "What I need is a drink," said Nolan, grinning at them. "I'm chilly—lyin' on this damp ground."
>
> "It ain't very damp, Jimmie," said Grierson.
>
> "Well, it is damp," said Nolan, with sudden irritability. "I can feel it. I'm wet. I tell you—wet through—just from lyin' here."
>
> They answered hastily. "Yes, that's so, Jimmie. It *is* damp. That's so."
>
> "Just put your hand under my back and see how wet the ground is," he said.
>
> "No," they answered. "That's all right, Jimmie. We know it's wet."
>
> "Well, put your hand under and see," he cried, stubbornly.
>
> "Oh, never mind, Jimmie."
>
> "No," he said in a temper. "See for yourself." Grierson seemed to be afraid of Nolan's agitation, and so he slipped a hand under the prostrate man, and presently withdrew it covered with blood. "Yes," he said, hiding his hand carefully from Nolan's eyes, "you were right, Jimmie."
>
> "Of course I was," said Nolan, contentedly closing his eyes. "This hillside holds water like a swamp." After a moment he said: "Guess I ought to know. I'm flat here on it, and you fellers are standing up."

He did not know he was dying. He thought he was holding an argument on the condition of the turf.

The fifth chapter ends there, and when the final chapter begins, there has been a small temporal jump. "Cover his face," Grierson says to Watkins, but the problem is what to cover it with. They eventually decide on Nolan's hat, and after Grierson performs that grim task, neither one of them knows what to do next, although they both feel they should do *something*. "Finally Watkins said in a broken voice, 'Aw, it's a damn shame.' They moved slowly off to the firing line."

A white space follows, after which Crane launches directly into the closing scene, which takes place in a fever tent for the wounded and ill. Martin, one of the original quartet of protagonists, who has already been shot at an earlier point in the story, is one of the patients in that improvised hospital, where "a heavy odor of sickness and medicine hung in the air" and "the occasional . . . twisting of a body under a blanket was terrifying, as if dead men were moving in their graves under the sod." The men are all lying on their backs, languishing in the throes of fever, but some faint, disembodied voices are nevertheless engaged in a sort of conversation, and that is how Martin and Grierson of the Twenty-ninth Infantry learn that they both happen to be there at the same time. Grierson says:

> "What? Jack, is that you?"
> "It's a part of me. . . . Who are you?"
> "Grierson, you fat-head. I thought you were wounded."
> There was the noise of a man gulping a great drink of water, and at its conclusion Martin said, "I am."
> "Well, what you doin' in the fever place, then?"
> Martin replied with drowsy impatience, "Got the fever too."
> "Gee!" said Grierson.
> Thereafter there was silence in the fever tent save for the noises made by a man over in a corner, a kind of man always found in an American crowd, a heroic, implacable comedian and patriot, of a humor that has bitterness and ferocity and love in it, and he was wringing from the situation a grim meaning by singing the Star-Spangled Banner with all the ardor which could be procured from his fever-stricken body.
> "Billie," called Martin in a low voice, "where's Jimmie Nolan?"
> "He's dead," said Grierson.
> A triangle of raw gold light shone on a side of the tent. Somewhere in the valley an engine's bell was ringing, and it sounded of peace and home as if it hung on a cow's neck.
> "An' where's Ike Watkins?"

"Well, he ain't dead, but he got shot through the lungs. They say he ain't got much show."

Through the clouded odors of sickness and medicine rang the dauntless voice of the man in the corner:

"... Long may it wave ..."

Bitterness, ferocity, and love.

It is, as Conrad rightly observed, *magnificent*, and when Crane sent the story to Reynolds, he could scarcely contain his exuberance over what he had done. "Now this is *It*," he wrote. "If you dont touch big money for it I wonder!"

What was not touching big money were the articles he was writing for the *Journal*, but he ground them out as persistently as he could, producing a blend of reportage and commentary that resembles what we would now call op-ed columns, most of them couched in the breezy language of a jaded cosmopolitan. Not dull, precisely, but nothing to get worked up about either, except for two of them, which stand out sharply from the others. While Crane seems to have spent most of his time at Mary Horan's house wallowing in a dark emotional hole, "How They Court in Cuba" must have been written on one of his rare good days. It is a bright little comic treatise on the elaborate courtship rituals in a repressive, highly regulated society that puts up so many obstacles to marriage that it is a wonder any children ever manage to get born. "It is all barbed wire entanglements," Crane writes, and the process can drag on for so long, often stretching out over three or six or even eight years, that it generates "all the fiery excitement of being cashier in a shoe store." Still, he concludes, there is little point in worrying about any of this, for "men seek the women they love, and find them, and women wait for the men they love, and the men come, and all the circumlocution and bulwarks and clever football interference and trouble and delay and protracted agony and duennas count for nothing, count for nothing against the tides of human life, which are in Cuba or Omaha controlled by the same moon."

More in keeping with his general frame of mind, there is the somber, heartfelt "How They Leave Cuba," which discusses the evacuation of the Spanish from the city within the context of a moving scene Crane witnessed when he and a friend walked around the deck of a departing ship filled with "sick soldiers, officers, Spanish families, even some priests—all people who, by long odds, would never again set their eyes on the island of Cuba." Crane and his companion climb into a boat that will take them back to shore, and in the boat next to theirs they see a sobbing woman with a four-year-old boy in her arms. "Her eyes were fastened upon the deck of the ship, where stood an officer in the uniform of a Spanish captain of infantry. He was making no sign. He simply stood immovable, staring at the boat. Sometimes men express great emotion by merely standing still for a long time. It seemed as if he was never again going to move a muscle."

As for the person sobbing in the boat: "She was not a pretty woman and she was—old." Repellent as the idea might be to him (Crane uses the word "barbarity"), he admits that if she had been beautiful, there might have been "some consolation at least. But this to her was the end, the end of a successful love," and the man who is leaving her and going back to Spain "[is] probably her only chance at happiness."

Our attention is then directed to the woman's boatman, who is growing impatient and wants to get back to round up other fares. But Crane doesn't begin the paragraph by addressing the man's intentions. Rather, in one of the most improbable and audacious verbal surprises anywhere in the three thousand one hundred pages of his collected works, he writes: "The woman's boatman had a face like a floor." The reader necessarily will be stunned for a moment, but that is what Crane has written: "The woman's boatman had a face like a floor." And then the reader will read the sentence again, then read the sentences that follow it about the boatman's intentions and understand that a floor is a blank, a broad, expressionless blank, an impervious slab of wood or stone indifferent to anything that might happen to it and that the boatman's face is a floor because he doesn't give a damn about the woman's suffering. He spits into the water and thinks: Serves her right for taking up with a Spaniard. But Crane counters with his own thought: "The woman's heart was broken. That is the point. And that is not yet the worst of it. There is going to be a lot of it: such a hideous lot of it!" And then, in the final sentence of the piece: "But, after all—and after all—and again after all, it is human agony and human agony is not pleasant."

For once, Crane seems overwrought, and in that sudden burst of compassion for the sobbing woman, he exposes an ache that had been building within him for some time. We know about his money problems and the problem of his worsening health, but there seems to have been another problem that was tormenting him during his months in Havana as well, something connected to his love life that had embittered him and left him on the verge of hopelessness. Parker mentions a "personal shock"

Crane received toward the end of August or the beginning of September when he "found" a woman he had known "elsewhere in the world," the start of an affair or a potential affair that burned out when he discovered "a photograph of a handsome Cuban" on her mantel. This is extremely vague. If there was such a woman, she has never been identified, and given that Parker was writing *forty-two years* after the fact, it could be that he scrambled the photo incident with the photos exchanged by the two lovers in "The Clan of No-Name," a long story S.C. finished in October, or else with yet another photo that appears in one of the anguished, mostly terrible love poems Crane wrote in Havana when the narrator sees a picture of the woman he loves in another man's bedroom.

Whether Parker was right or wrong, there is no question that Crane was preoccupied by the deceits and manipulations of love in the work he was writing then. Margharita, the resplendent beauty in "The Clan of No-Name," is a two-timing gold digger who bluffs her way into a lucrative marriage—S.C.'s first femme fatale in all her seductive, irresistible glory—and, if nothing else, the bad poems attest to the fact that Crane was brooding about some unspecified love drama and suffering greatly because of it. The photograph shows up in the third stanza of "Love forgive me if I wish you grief":

> He had your picture in his room
> A scurvy traitor picture
> And he smiled
> —Merely a fat complacence
> Of men who know fine women—
> And thus I divided with him
> A part of my love.

Again and again, Crane comes back to the obsessive theme of betrayal, of being pushed out by another man and having to share his love with a contemptible rival.

> Tell me why, behind thee,
> I see always the shadow of another lover?
> Is it real
> Or is this the thrice-damned memory of a better
>   happiness?
> Plague on him if he be dead
> Plague on him if he be alive

A swinish numskull
To intrude his shade
Always between me and my peace.

It could be that Cora's past life was more of a problem for him than he had realized earlier—her affairs with other men, her two marriages, and the distasteful fact that she was still married to someone else, and now, as he pondered their own phantom marriage, perhaps the shadowy figure of ex-captain Stewart had turned into a source of humiliation for him, as this stanza from the dreadful "Intrigue" seems to suggest:

Thou art my love
And thou art the ashes of other men's love
And I bury my face in these ashes
And I love them
Woe is me.

Then again, it could be that Cora was only a part of it, just one woman among several from his life who have been joined together to form a single imaginary woman: the embodiment of all the torments he had endured over the years in the cause of love. Had he ever become entangled with anyone as duplicitous as the scheming beauty in "The Clan of No-Name"? Impossible to know, but for all his efforts to channel his feelings into those cryptic, clunky lines of self-pitying complaint, the best bit of verse he wrote in Havana was the energetic little stanza that precedes "Clan." Call it an epigraph, call it a prologue, it has both bite and music and sets the tone of the story that follows.

Unwind my riddle.
Cruel as hawks the hours fly,
Wounded men seldom come home to die,
The hard waves see an arm flung high,
Scorn hits strong because of a lie,
Yet there exists a mystic tie.
Unwind my riddle.

The riddle will never be unwound, nor will we ever know the exact nature of the crisis that kept Crane anchored in Havana for so long. There is no doubt that he produced some exceptional work while he was there, but he also wrote some uncommonly bad work, poems so far beneath his standard that one can only assume they never would have been written if he hadn't been trapped in a dark place within himself and slowly coming undone. He didn't quite get there, but never had he come so close to touching bottom.

General Wade tracked down Crane by talking to a number of American journalists posted in Havana, and his written report on October nineteenth confirmed that the missing man had "not been out of the city. After these inquiries, Mr. Crane called and expressed regret at having caused so much trouble. I do not know his business or why he had not corresponded with his family."

Nor did anyone else, not even the people who were in direct contact with him, as was the second eyewitness of his curious sojourn in Havana, Otto Carmichael, a correspondent for the *Minneapolis Times*. General Wade had asked him to deliver a message to Crane that a telegram had arrived for him from London, and when Carmichael found S.C. sitting in a café, he passed on the message. "Thanks," Crane said, and then promptly seemed to forget all about it. The next day, the general told Carmichael that a second telegram had arrived asking if the first one had been delivered, so the man from Minneapolis went back to the café, found Crane sitting in the same spot, and passed on the second message. "Say," answered the distracted S.C., "didn't you tell me something about a cablegram yesterday?" Yes, Carmichael said, and now he was back because another one had arrived asking if the first one had been delivered. "Yes, I see," Crane answered. "Using the government to find me. Anyway, I'm much obliged." "And again," Carmichael writes, "he forgot all about it." Time passed, and after they had become better acquainted, Carmichael told him that General Wade still had the telegram, but Crane shrugged it off, pretending that it was probably a bill of some sort. Not likely, but why would he tell Carmichael that he had buried himself in Havana and didn't want to be found, not even by Cora?

Carmichael's piece covers just three pages, but it gives the fullest picture of Crane during those months, and nearly every one of his remarks is pertinent, forthright, and stinging in its honesty. The fact that he published it in June 1900, only ten days after Crane's death, means that Crane was still a vivid presence for him—still alive, as it were, still breathing.

On his overall impression of the man (which sounds oddly similar to what Crane's friends from Syracuse saw in him when he was not yet twenty):

> Stephen Crane to a certainty was a Bohemian. He was absolutely worthless except for what he did. The city editor of a modern newspaper would

not have had him around the city room for a week. He was irresponsible and unmanageable. There was nothing vicious about him or even reckless; he was serenely indifferent; trifles would change him and big things would not stop him; fancy would hold him to a place and money would not move him from it.

On Crane's reputation:

I have heard many army officers say he was the bravest man they ever saw. He apparently did not think of danger. Death to him was nothing more than the next breath, or the next breakfast or sleep. Bullets were nothing to him, moving or in cartridges, except something to make copy about. This was not affected. It was the quality of the fellow. To see others suffer tore his tender heart. He was almost girlish in his sympathies. But it apparently did not bother him to be hungry himself or in pain. He never grumbled about taking his share. . . .

Crane had seen all kinds of fighting. It had a fascination for him. Danger was his dissipation. He was really grieved when he learned he had left a café just a few minutes before a noisy shooting scrape.

On his habits:

He did nothing with any regularity. He ate and slept when he could no longer do without these necessary comforts. . . . When I saw him he was doing 600 words a day. This was the only thing he did with any regularity. He was very particular about his work. He wrote somewhat slowly and was whimsical about words. He would spend a long time in trying to find what suited him. Inasmuch as he had no dictionary or books of reference, his search for words and information consisted in chewing his pencil and waiting until they came to him.

On his health:

A strong man could not help feeling sorry for Crane. He seemed on the verge of collapse for lack of strength. His arms were as thin as one who had been ill for a long time. In a dim light Crane's face was handsome to the point of being exquisitely beautiful. In the full light his face had a sick and miserable look. His drawn lips, his yellowish, haggard face, his tired eyes and generally wornout appearance combined to make a picture not particularly attractive. But he was so simple and genuine that one soon forgot all about these and could see the wan, half-pleading smile on his frank, boyish face. This little smile went for everything with Crane. It was his thanks for a light, his approval of an act, his delight over a story, his acknowledgement of distress, his pity for weakness. In fact, that sensitive little smile was always flitting about his face. . . .

To take care of his health never occurred to him. He had the Cuban fashion of drinking light drinks and coffee, but he did not indulge to excess in alcohol. This was somewhat remarkable at a time and place of excessive drinking. This was two years ago and his health then was wretched. There was no chance for him to live unless he mended his ways. It was nothing more than thoughtlessness. He simply refused to think about himself.

In September, Crane watched the Spanish authorities disinter the bones of Christopher Columbus from their grave in Havana. The man who had discovered the New World was now being expelled from the island he had conquered, and the bits of him that were left would be carried back across the ocean and reburied in Seville. More than just an acknowledgment of Spain's defeat in the war with the United States, it marked the end of a four-hundred-year chapter in world history. When the bones finally set sail for Europe on December twentieth, the American Century began.

By then, Crane was already packing his bags and preparing to leave Havana. He had hung on in Limboville for four months, but after flopping back and forth about what he wanted to do next—sending a reassuring cablegram to Cora on October ninth that all was well, then writing to Reynolds a couple of weeks later to announce that he hoped to syndicate his columns and would possibly be staying in Havana throughout the winter—he gave up, gave in, or gave out and decided to call it quits.

He left on Christmas Eve and landed in New York at five A.M. on December twenty-eighth. It would be his last visit to the city, and that afternoon, on a brief visit to McClure's offices, he ran into Hamlin Garland for the last time. That night, Garland wrote in his journal:

At McClure's I met Stephen Crane the wonderful boy whose early work I saw and advocated in 1891–2. He is just returned from Havana, and looked dingy and soaked with nicotine but appeared mentally alert and as full of odd turns of thought as ever. He strikes me now as he did in the early days as unwholesome physically—not a man of long life. He is now unusually careless in his dress and has acquired a slight

English accent in a few of his words—He was not overwhelmed with joy to see me.

He also saw his old friend Louis Senger, who later wrote, "He was sick and joked mirthlessly that they had not got him yet," as well as his brother Edmund and niece Helen R.—also for the last time—and made a last visit to Howells. From Howells to Cora on July 22, 1900:

> He came to see me last just before he sailed to England the last time, and then he showed the restlessness of the malarial fever that was preying on him; he spoke of having got it in Cuba. But even then . . . I felt his rare quality. I do not think America has produced a more distinctive and vital talent.

Wounded men seldom come home to die, but the wounded Crane was going back to England, and if that wasn't precisely his home, it was the next best thing to it—the one place in the world where he would be welcomed in without having to explain himself. As it happened, he left New York aboard the *Manitou* on New Year's Eve 1898, two years to the day since he had set foot on the doomed *Commodore*. This time, the boat did not sink.

A BRUTAL EXTINCTION

⚜

I

HE TOUCHED LAND AT GRAVESEND ON JANUARY ELEVENTH, AND AS HE marched toward his own grave over the next sixteen months, he pushed harder than he had ever pushed before, in some ways happier than he had ever been, in other ways more desperate, more frantic, and yet from start to finish he hung on for dear life and refused to let go. At the very end, when his body had burned out on him and he could no longer leave his bed, he seemed remarkably prepared for what was coming next. Days before his death, he whispered to his friend Robert Barr: "Robert, when you come to the hedge—that we all must go over—it isn't bad. You feel sleepy—and—you don't care. Just a little dreamy curiosity—which world you're really in—that's all." Hours before he lapsed into a coma on the last full day of his life, he said to Cora: "I leave here gentle, seeking to do good, firm, resolute, impregnable."

In the year that was left to him before he coughed up blood for the first time and his condition progressively worsened, he slogged through countless, ever-deepening mudholes of debt by composing more words, more pages, more published work than in any other year of his life. He traveled to Paris, Lausanne, and Ireland, he rode his two horses across the grounds of Brede Place, he went on picnics with Cora and their friends, he entertained visitors by playing his guitar and violin, he doted on his three obstreperous dogs, he attended boat regattas and garden parties, and from time to time he played handball with his writer friend Edwin Pugh, who later wrote: "His hands were miracles of strength and cleverness. He could play handball like a machine-gun. He would fire the ball at me from every conceivable angle, in that green old damp garden of his, with a sort of wild-cat fury."

He was still and ever the hell-bent athlete, but make no mistake about it: he was dying, and he knew he was dying. He had returned from his lunar voyage looking half dead, so depleted by illness that Jessie Conrad saw him as "a changed man," and within a few months he understood that the hoped-for physical recovery was not going to happen. To a man named John (possibly Scott Stokes) in mid-August: "Please have the kindness to keep your mouth shut about my health in front of Mrs. Crane hereafter. She can do nothing for me and I am too old to be nursed. It is all up with me but I will not have her scared. For some funny woman's reason, she likes me. Mind this." The following month, in a letter to George Wyndham, whose passionate endorsement of *Red Badge* had helped launch the book in England: "At present I feel like hell. . . . The truth is that Cuba libre just about liberated me from the base blue world. The clockwork is juggling badly."

What kept him going was a capacity for hard, unrelenting work and his tightening bond with Cora, his co-conspirator in the fantasy world they built for themselves after they left Oxted and moved to Brede Place in February. The mouse who had run away from his domestic responsibilities back in April was turned into a British country squire who reigned over his lands with his golden-haired consort—who now called him the Duke and in his absence had transformed the conditions of his life. But before they could begin that new life, they first had to extract themselves from the old one. The rent at Ravensbrook had gone unpaid for a year, local merchants were threatening lawsuits, and Self & Whitley's department store in London was dunning them for a long list of unpaid charges, among them the ninety-nine pounds still owed on Cora's piano. Within days of his return to England, Crane was appealing to his brother William for a five-hundred-dollar loan, even as he made excuses for not going up to see him during his stopover in New York and continued to lie about the circumstances of his marriage.

> My dear William: So I have run by you in the dark again but really my position in England was near to going to smash and I rushed to save it as soon as I could get enough money to leave Havana. Appleton's cable me that for the past 12 months my royalties amount to *thirty-five dollars*. Do you know what they mean?

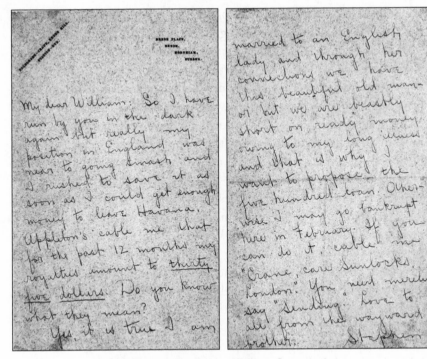

Crane's letter to his brother William, January 1899.
(COURTESY OF THE UNIVERSITY OF VIRGINIA)

Yes, it is true I am married to an English lady and through her connections we have this beautiful old manor but we are beastly short on ready money owing to my long illness and that is why I want to propose the five hundred loan. Otherwise I may go bankrupt here in February. . . . Love to all from the wayward brother.

A week later, he wrote to Reynolds:

I am still fuzzy with money troubles and last night a writ was served on me by a leading creditor. I must raise heaven and Earth between now and the middle of February. I must have every pennie that you can wrest from the enemy. . . . If I can't raise some money at once I'm going bankrupt. You know what that means. It won't do. I am going to borrow money from pretty near every body in the world and you must give me all the assistance you are able. . . . I easily see my way to paying all these people back before the end of the year. I ought to make £1500.—this year anyway. For God sake jump the game with all four feet.

The loan from William was not forthcoming, but other sources of aid charged into the breach. The ever-kind Moreton Frewen put the Cranes in touch with his solicitor, Alfred T. Plant, who took over the management of their finances and worked out arrangements to untangle the complicated messes they had created with their various creditors. To support Plant's efforts, Crane's new British agent, James B. Pinker, stepped in as the guarantor for their debts, and finally, in a temporary exchange for his Appleton royalties, the London representative of Crane's new American publisher, Frederick A. Stokes, agreed to cover the back rent on Ravensbrook. The reunited couple would not be going to the poorhouse, after all. Instead, on February nineteenth, they moved into their ancient manor house, which had more rooms in it than could be counted on the fingers of two hands. No running water, of course, toilet facilities that dated from a time before the invention of toilets, and no electric wires or gas feeds to light the rooms. Beeswax candles would have to do, but for a pair of deracinated Americans whose families had originally come from England, so much the better. They were back in the olde, olde world of their ancestors, occupants of a house that stood just eight miles from the field where the Battle of Hastings had been fought in 1066, which made them the heirs to an almost mythological past. As Cora put it in a letter to Garnett describing Crane's initial reaction to the house a month before they moved in: "Stephen is mad over the place ... [and] said that a solemn feeling of work came over him there." In other words, they would no longer be living in exile. They imagined they had come home.

What Crane found there was a haven of family life, for in addition to a number of servants and the ghostlike Mrs. Ruedy, the household now included Kate Lyon's two youngest children, five-year-old Héloïse and four-year-old Barry, Cora's much-loved little charges who had been staying with her almost nonstop since their father's stroke.* For a man who adored children as much as Crane did, this was the crowning touch of the new existence his wife had prepared for him: two kids, a capable nanny to watch over them (Lily Burke, who had been with the children for years), and a house large enough to accommodate them all. The Cranes never had children of their own, but they both had a natural gift for parenthood, and one can only imagine the pleasure the Duke must have felt as he strolled around his property holding the hands of his two surrogate offspring. Is it any accident that 1899 was the year he wrote a dozen new stories about children—all of

---

* With the blessing of their mother, of course, who was now living in London with her seven-year-old daughter, Helen.

*Barry and Héloïse, the youngest children of Harold Frederic
and Kate Lyon.* (COURTESY OF COLUMBIA UNIVERSITY)

them set in the once-upon-a-time land of Whilomville, the dream site of
his own childhood?

The Frewens' only stipulation in the rental agreement was that two of
their servants be retained at the house. Adoni Ptolemy was consequently
left behind in Surrey, where he joined his twin brother at the Pease household in Limpsfield, and the Cranes took over as the employers of William
MacVittie (known as Mack), an ancient coachman and groom with such a
full white beard that Conrad referred to him as Tolstoy, and a veteran butler
named Richard Heather. Eventually, they hired a cook as well, a Swiss-
English woman known simply as Vernall, who had worked for an American family in England for ten years and had mastered the art of American
cuisine. Along with her came her husband, Charles, known as "Chatters,"
who worked outdoors and was responsible for pumping water and carrying
it into the house. Both Mack and Vernall had a weakness for drink. Tolstoy
was such an avid tippler that the liquor cabinet eventually had to be locked,
and, according to Jessie Conrad, whenever Vernall was asked to make din-

ner for a sudden influx of visitors after eight o'clock, she would flatly refuse. Cora, "at her wit's end for the moment, would wring her hands and appeal to Stephen. He in turn would give her one glance and solemnly ring the bell. Like clockwork the old butler appeared and handed a bottle of brandy to the thirsty woman, who retired with no further comment to her kitchen, and an hour or so later a perfect dinner would be served, complete in every detail." It is worth noting that when Crane set to work on the semifictionalized "War Memories" in August, he transferred those memories to an imaginary correspondent named Vernall.

This good life had all been constructed on a foundation of bottomless sand, but the Cranes bluffed their way to respectability by maintaining a strict silence about their troubles. Not even their closest friends had any inkling of how hard up they were, and by spending more and more money they did not have, the couple affected a magnificent pose of nonchalance and well-being. When no one was looking, Crane howled forth his distress in letter after letter to his agents and publishers, but Cora was the only one who knew what they were up against, and as Crane's output increased to manic levels of hyperproduction, she took over as his correspondent by proxy, haranguing those same agents and publishers even more vociferously than he had. They were a team now, a two-person manufacturing company of words, and during the most hectic periods, when for three solid days and nights Crane would lock himself in his small study over the porch—the dampest, chilliest room in the damp stone house—he would slide each finished story or chapter or article under the door, and within hours Cora would have a clean copy typed up on their new writing machine. At other times, to relieve the discomfort of holding a pen in his hand for too many hours, he would compose his work in his head and dictate to her.

In spite of these pressures, that isn't to say they weren't happy. For the eternally hopeful Cora, this was the life she had always wanted with Crane, and whatever embarrassments they were facing just then, surely those money obstacles would be overcome in due course. For the dying man, happiness was the only human option available to him. He was not about to give in and squander his last years or months in useless self-pity. As long as he was still breathing, what would be the point in sulking or complaining about the inevitable, and the last thing he wanted was for anyone to feel sorry for him. And so he worked, and he worked, turning himself into a latter-day Sisyphus as he began pushing his rock up the mountain every morning and then watched it roll back to the bottom at night. Same thing the day after that. Same thing the day after that. As Camus puts it in his signature essay about the absurd hero, "One does not discover the absurd without being tempted to write a manual of happiness." The nineteenth-century American (1871–1900) and the twentieth-century Frenchman (1913–1960) had much in common: superbly athletic in their youth (baseball catcher, soccer goalie), early victims of TB, writers who struggled to make sense of a world in which the gods have vanished. Camus goes on: "The absurd man says yes and his effort will henceforth be unceasing." That is, by saying yes to life, one assumes the burden of endless toil and a death without meaning. Such was Crane's position in those last months before his crumbling health destroyed him. "This universe henceforth without master seems to him neither sterile nor futile," Camus writes. "One must imagine Sisyphus happy."

2

EDITH RITCHIE, KATE LYON'S NINETEEN-YEAR-OLD NIECE, LIVED with the Cranes from early July to January 1900, and she is the source of a number of delicious anecdotes that confirm the spirit of fun and nonsense that pervaded the rooms at Brede whenever the perspiring rock-pusher paused from his labors. "Who could ever forget Stephen and his whimsicalities, and Cora with her gleaming, golden hair, exquisite skin, and humorous mind?" She called them "Mr. Crane" and "Mummy Crane," and they called her "Snubby" because of her short nose. Alone among the many people who knew the Cranes during that final period, young Miss Ritchie lived on intimate terms with them and was privy to information about the day-to-day flow of their lives that was not available to anyone else. "They were darlings to me," she wrote for the *Atlantic Monthly* in 1954 (when she was in her seventies), but the excerpts that follow are not the sentimental ramblings of an old woman musing about her fondly remembered departed friends—they are vivid recollections of a time that stood out for her as one of the grand adventures of her youth.

Mr. James. All manner of people came to visit the house, among them Henry James, who, according to Ritchie, "would bicycle the seven miles over to Brede at least once a week. One day Mr. James and Stephen were having a discussion about something, and Stephen was getting the better of the argument. Suddenly Mr. James said, 'How old are you?' 'Twenty-seven,' said Stephen. 'Humph,' said Mr. James, 'prattling babe!'"

Singing dogs. The Cranes owned three dogs, but in this passage Ritchie mentions five, either through a slip of memory or because two dogs happened to be visiting the house. As told by Ritchie: "In those days, I used to sing a little and Stephen liked it. Whenever Mr. James came to call, I was made to sing for the poor man. Then Cora would say, 'Now, let's have a concert.' I would pick up the five puppies and, with three heads over one arm and two over the other, I would sing and play while five little muzzles howled in anguish. Mr. James and the Cranes would become limp with mirth."

Musical combs. "Sometimes, when there was a crowd in the house, there would be a tap on my bedroom door soon after I had gone to sleep. Cora's voice would say, 'Stephen wants some music. Slip into your dressing gown and bring your comb.' We would all troop down to the huge old kitchen.... There the party might consist of A.E.W. Mason, Joseph Conrad, Mr. and Mrs. H. G. Wells, and others. We would first raid the pantry, and then, with tissue over our combs and Stephen conducting with the toasting fork as his baton, we all would sing horribly and happily through the combs. Such foolishness amused those brilliant minds!"

Ford Madox Ford trips over his words. "When Mr. Hueffer came to Brede, he read some of his poems to us. In one, there was a line about 'birds in the treetops,' which he read 'birds in the tea trops,' and we three had much difficulty in concealing our giggles."

Animal Grab with H .G. Wells. A popular Victorian card game, the Animal Grab deck consisted of cards with pictures of animals on them, and players who drew two cards of the same animal would be obliged to imitate the sounds of the beast in question. On their way to Paris in August, the Cranes and Ritchie stopped off at Folkestone, "where we spent the night with the H. G. Wellses. That evening Mrs. Wells and I gave them some music of sorts; then we all played animal grab. I can still hear Stephen roaring like a lion, Cora twittering like a canary, and Mr. Wells barking like a dog."

Au revoir, Paris. "We met various friends in Paris and had a gay time, with lunches, dinners, theaters, cafés-chantants, and sightseeing. We had meant to stay quite a while, but suddenly we all got homesick for Brede and the dogs and decided to go home. All the time we were away, both Cora and Stephen got small pieces of candy from penny-in-the-slot machines and mailed them home to the dogs."

Ditto the Emerald Isle. "One morning in October, Stephen came down to breakfast and said, 'Edith has never been to Ireland. Let's go to Ireland.'... So we packed our bags and off we went to London.

That evening there was a big party at the Frewens', where the Cranes were lionized. Next morning we went to the station to take the boat for Ireland, but found that we had had an old timetable and that the train had gone. No matter. It was fun to have another day in London. We missed the train three days in succession. It sounds as if we were all morons. But we were just happy, carefree country bumpkins who had lost the habit of catching trains. And each day and evening was full of more parties—lunches, teas, dinners. Everyone wanted to entertain the Cranes. Finally we reached Ireland and went from Cork to Ballydehob to Skibbereen to Skull to Bantry, ending at Glengariff, staying at little country inns. . . . We were to have gone to Killarney, but again we got homesick for Brede and the dogs.

One must imagine Sisyphus happy. Ritchie's piece is more than just a catalogue of amusing, high-spirited moments, and her comments about Crane's work habits, for example, or how he and Cora behaved with each other, are indispensable to understanding the texture of their life at Brede. Beyond the descriptions of the house, with its "huge open fireplaces," its empty rooms, its large oak-paneled hall filled with "comfortable couches and chairs and pretty tables with lamps and plants and books," or the dining room with its "long refectory table and rushes on the floor from the meadow by the brook"—in lieu of unaffordable rugs—there is this confounding but revelatory statement, which proves how well the Cranes guarded the secret of their bone-crushing debts: "I never heard money discussed while I was there."

Edith Ritchie was a young woman who kept her eyes and ears open, and not only was she a member of the household for six full months, she went on two trips abroad with the Cranes (as they forked out cash for boats, hotels, restaurants, trains, theater tickets, and cafés—never flinching at a single expense, no matter how extravagant), took part in most if not all of their social activities, and sat down to meals with them once, twice, and even three times a day. If the Cranes ever talked about their finances within earshot of anyone, Ritchie would have heard what they said, but for six long months not one gasp or groan or panicked word was uttered in her presence, and the good times rolled on. Undisciplined spendthrifts, her hosts were also two of the most disciplined actors in the world.

Favorite guest. "Joseph Conrad came often to Brede, but his wife was not well at that time and I never met her. . . . I liked [him] the most of any of the Brede guests. He was charming, quiet, and courteous. I was shy and inclined to listen rather than to talk. He would discuss books with me as seriously as with his fellow writers."

Work habits. "Stephen's workroom was an austere place with a not too comfortable chair and a long table in it, bare except for his papers. When he was in a writing mood, we would all stay away from him. But sometimes he would say that he could think better if he had company, and then he would bring his work down to the hall and write while Cora and I sewed."

Preparations for the writing of "Manacled." "One day he told us that he had had a dream which he thought would make a good story. He dreamed that he was acting on the stage of some theater and in the play he was a prisoner. He had been handcuffed and his ankles were bound together. Suddenly there was a cry of 'Fire!' In his dream, all the other actors and the audience ran for the exits and forgot that he was tied up and helpless. That was his dream. He wondered, in writing about it, how long it might take him to inch his way along a corridor to an outside door. So he got Cora and me to tie his hands and his ankles together and then he spent the morning trying, over a given distance, to hop or roll or work along like an inchworm, all in deadly seriousness."

What Edith Ritchie saw—and felt. "I wish I knew how to describe the atmosphere at Brede. I have never known two people more deeply in love with one another than were Stephen and Cora. . . . Each was extremely sensitive, each protective. Cora ran the household for Stephen's comfort and happiness. She followed his every change of mood. If he wanted silence, he had silence. If he wanted company and gaiety, he had them. They were fine people, both of them. They were *good*. Always they were good. Not only were they 'good' to me. They were ethically good. They were kind. They were just. . . . I loved them both."

Others, of course, formed other opinions. The butler at Brede, Richard Heather, whom Ritchie describes as "pompous and typical, but devoted to the Cranes," was observed by Jessie Conrad to have worn that devotion as a mask, behind which he carried on a secret campaign of sabotage and insubordination. On the matter of Crane's dogs, for example, she writes, "Time after time I have seen [Stephen] raise his thin face bent low over his work and, without the least impatience, open the door for one of those spoiled animals to pass through. Then when he had almost returned to his seat he would have to repeat the performance. Sometimes, when he was too ill and languid to attend to their demands himself, he would request the old servitor . . . to do so. Many times I have observed the solemn farce,

Crane in his study at Brede Place.
(COURTESY OF THE UNIVERSITY OF VIRGINIA)

sorely tempted to interfere. The old ruffian, his face set in the most benevolent expression, would escort the dogs to the head of the stone steps and
then solemnly kick each one down the steep flight."

Nor was Crane's workroom "an austere place . . . bare except for his
papers," even if that was how Ritchie remembered it more than fifty years
after her stay at Brede. A photograph from September 1899 shows Crane
sitting at his desk with a pen or pencil in his hand, hard at work (or pretending to be at work), and the room that surrounds him is filled with
objects: at least seven framed pictures mounted on the wall to his right,
at the bottom of which one can see the top of a guitar jutting up from
the floor, as well as a tall bookcase directly behind him. The surface of the
desk is cluttered with more objects: a mess of jumbled, finished pages, a
wine glass filled with cigarettes, boxes of matches, a porcelain jar probably
used for storing pipe tobacco, a towering lamp with a ridiculously overwrought taffeta shade, and the photograph of Cora dressed in her war
correspondent's outfit, the one she had signed *To me old pal Stevie / with*

best wishes—"Imogene Carter" / Athens / May 22/97. That Ritchie's memory failed her in this instance is neither here nor there. She was recalling a feeling, not a fact, which we all tend to do with our memories from the distant past, but the striking thing about this photograph is how different Crane looks in it from a similar one taken at Ravensbrook in 1897 or 1898. Again, Crane is sitting at his cluttered desk, pen in hand and apparently at work, this time surrounded by mementos of his trip to Texas and Mexico. At most, no more than two years had gone by since then, but in the second photograph he seems to have aged drastically. His jacket is too large for his diminishing body, and his face is no longer the face of a young man.

Another disputable point is Ritchie's assertion that "I never saw an uninvited guest. The guests who came were invited by Cora at Stephen's suggestion. I have heard her protest to him that he should have a rest after a houseful over a weekend. But he loved to have people there." This was probably both true and not true. There is no question that Crane enjoyed the company of his fellow writers—Conrad, Wells, James, Ford, Barr, and A. E. W. Mason—but just as it had been at Oxted, Brede Place often filled up with unwanted moochers and hangers-on who took advantage of their hosts' generosity and goodwill and then told malicious stories about them after they returned to London. It was partly Crane's fault for being too kind, too accommodating, too reluctant to say no to anyone, and this softheartedness often aggravated his friends. Ford, who worshipped Crane and called him "the most beautiful spirit I have ever known," described his friend's life at Brede as "a nightmare of misplaced hospitality." Conrad, no less appalled by these lowlife visitors, refers to the "secret irritation" he felt whenever he encountered them on his visits. Once, when he found the courage to tell Crane that he was too "good-natured," S.C. "gave me one of his quiet smiles, that seemed to hint so poignantly at the vanity of all things, and after a period of silence remarked: 'I am glad those Indians are gone.'"

Ritchie was no doubt too young and inexperienced to penetrate the nuances of these complex social interactions, but that in no way diminishes what she felt about the Cranes themselves or undermines the essential truth of her account. Without her, we would know nothing about the singing dogs and musical combs, not to mention the roaring, twittering, and barking animal grabbers in Folkestone. In the same way, without the testimony of another young American visitor to Brede, we would know nothing about how Crane won the Challenge Cup in Spontaneous Writing. Karl Edwin Harriman was a twenty-four-year-old American fiction writer and journalist who had been sent to England by the *Detroit Free*

Press. He came to the house to do an interview with Crane and wound up staying for several weeks, overlapping with Ritchie and almost certainly wearing out his welcome, but he is the source of a memorable little story, and while he got many things wrong in the several articles he wrote about Crane, there is no reason to question the authenticity of this one.

A summer night at Brede Place, following an afternoon of thick gray skies and gathering thunder. Crane and several of his writer friends are sitting around the kitchen table drinking scotch and soda. Conrad and Mason* are the only ones mentioned by Harriman, but he implies that there are others as well. The thunder finally explodes at nine o'clock. Crane has been talking about Harold Frederic's "adverb screen," a long list of useful adverbs that his late friend had written out on a window shade to consult while composing his novels. Mason pours himself another drink, another one of Crane's cigarettes goes out between his fingers, and the thunder cracks again. Conrad thinks it isn't a bad idea. Mason stands up and says that the only way to write is to know what you are going to do in advance—to map out everything before you begin. Crane strongly disagrees. "My belief has always been that the whole business is a matter of technique," he says. "If a man is a master of his particular technique he can write a story about anything." Mason is standing by the window as a bolt of lightning turns the dark sky white, and as he looks out at the meadow in front of him, he says to Crane: "If that is true, write a story about those hay-cocks out there. I challenge you!" "I accept," says Crane, and then the talk turns in another direction. Eventually, the party breaks up, everyone goes to bed, and the next day Crane is mysteriously absent when lunch is served, but there he is at dinnertime, walking into the room "with a roll in his hand tied with a blue ribbon." Cora laughs, since she knows what is coming. "You see," she says, "Stevie has just graduated and he's brought his diploma to show you. Haven't you, Stevie?" Crane nods, and when dinner is done and the group gathers for another evening of scotch and soda, he unties the blue ribbon and says, "I'm going to prove something to you Indians." Then he unrolls the pages and reads them a story set in the time of Cromwell, which happens to be a story set on the grounds of the house in which he is reading to them, a story in which every haycock in the meadow is hiding a Commonwealth soldier, each one waiting for a signal to attack the house as the monks inside cower in holes or disappear into the cellar. When the story is finished, Mason reaches out his hand to Crane and says, "I stand corrected."

---

* A. E. W. Mason, 1865–1948. An actor and playwright, Mason also wrote popular detective stories and was the author of *The Four Feathers*, a novel that has twice been adapted into films, one from 1939 starring Ralph Richardson and the other from 2002 starring Heath Ledger.

Conrad does nothing more than grunt—a sign of deepest approval in the private language he shares with Crane.

The story has gone missing, and chances are that it will never be found, for many believe that after Crane proved his point, he crumpled up his little work and destroyed it—no doubt by throwing it into the fireplace, blue ribbon and all.

3

IN ONE OF THE JOTTINGS FOR HER NEVER WRITTEN BIOGRAPHY OF Crane, Cora remembers the sole instance of angry discord between them. "I said to him, 'Why not write a popular novel for money something that everyone will read?' He turned on me and said: 'I will write for one man & banging his fist on writing table & that man shall be myself etc etc——'"

Crane defending his honor as an artist, stiffening his resolve and refusing to cave in to the demands of commerce, but his back was pinned to the wall during that year at Brede, and the truth was that he did cave in and try to write a novel that would conform to popular taste. He had started it in the final months of 1897 when he interrupted the writing of "The Blue Hotel" to crank out the long narrative his publishers had been urging him to write (no more accursed short stories, please), and now he returned to it in a whole-hog effort to generate a windfall that would rescue the household from bankruptcy. It turned out to be the longest novel he ever published—and also the worst, the one substantial piece of work he ever wrote that qualifies as *bad*.

The early parts of *Active Service* from 1897 are promising, but they amount to just three chapters in a thirty-one-chapter potboiler, and however brilliant the third chapter might have been, with its multifaceted look at the operations of a New York City yellow-press daily (a subject Crane knew well), the subsequent material quickly devolves into a bullshit love story–adventure story set during the Greco-Turkish War as the intrepid newsman hero, torn between a wily temptress and the beautiful, highly principled daughter of a university professor, saves the day through his resourcefulness and courage—a nonsense frolic similar to a host of MGM films from the 1930s starring Clark Gable. The book was written in a surge of rapid, unreflecting composition—between late January and the middle of May—and immediately after he finished it, Crane sent off a note to Clara Frewen:

Dear Mrs. Frewen: I am an honest man above all and—according to promise—I must confess to you that on Saturday morning at 11:15—after dismal sorrow and travail—there was born into an unsuspecting world a certain novel called "Active Service," full and complete in all its shame—79000 words—which same is now being sent forth to the world to undermine whatever reputation for excellence I may have achieved up to this time and may heaven forgive it for being so bad.

Surprisingly, the book found some enthusiastic critics and readers. Not enough to produce a windfall, perhaps, but *Active Service* nevertheless managed to do some modest business, even as other voices dismissed it as a sellout and a failure, none more cruelly (and ignorantly) than Crane's old Nebraska friend Willa Cather, who wrote that "every page is like the next morning taste of a champagne supper and is heavy with the smell of stale cigarettes. . . . It is a grave matter for a man with good health and with a bank account to have written a book so coarse and dull and charmless as *Active Service*."

Good health and a bank account. If only she had known what she was talking about . . .

The myth about Crane in the final year of his life is that he degenerated into hackwork to pay the bills and produced nothing of any value, but apart from the unfortunate and admittedly bungled *Active Service*, there is little evidence to support that idea. Yes, he was writing too much, and he was pushing himself too hard, and he was mostly working to make money to fend off the bailiffs barking at his door, but in spite of recurring bouts of malarial fever and his misdiagnosed, steadily weakening lungs, most of the things he wrote from early 1899 to early 1900 are good, often better than good, and, in at least two instances, sublimely good, as good as any of his best works from the past.

Before he returned to the bad novel, and while he was in the middle of it, and long after he had finished it, he was working on two collections of stories, both of which were completed before his final collapse in early spring 1900 and published shortly after his death in June—*Whilomville Stories* (August) and *Wounds in the Rain* (September). Not only is each one an essential title in his list of works, but both volumes contain elements that suggest a turn in a new direction, offering a tantalizing glimpse of some of the territories Crane might have explored in his future work—if he had managed to live.

"His New Mittens" wound up being published in the same book as *The Monster* and "The Blue Hotel," but that was Crane's first step back into the world of childhood since the Baby Stories of 1893. Within two weeks of his return to England he wrote another story with a child protagonist set in Whilomville (dispatched to Reynolds on January twenty-seventh), then another (January thirty-first), and still another (February seventh). From then until the fall, he composed an even dozen of them, which *Harper's Magazine* began publishing every month starting in August. As with "His New Mittens," the stories are about children but not necessarily *for* children, although it seems that the young Ernest Hemingway, who was born in 1899 and overlapped with Crane for close to a year, read the Whilomville stories or had them read to him while he was growing up in Oak Park, Illinois, which began his lifelong admiration of S.C., whose work strongly marked his own progress as a writer. Strip it to the bone was the message—and say as much as you can by saying as little as you can. Think of Dr. Trescott counting his wife's teacups at the end of *The Monster*, and then think of Krebs in "Soldier's Home" looking down at the bacon fat hardening on his plate.

None of the twelve new stories quite measures up to the first story about the little fugitive and his wet mittens, but a number of them stand out as exceptional, and all of them, even the most comical ones, lack the cloying sentimentality that mars so much writing about children. The central figure in the new cycle is Jimmie Trescott, the doctor's son from *The Monster*, but in this incarnation of Whilomville the town has been thrust back into an earlier stage of its existence. It is no longer a small, expanding city from the mid-nineties but an Arcadian village of the post–Civil War seventies or eighties, the time of Crane's own boyhood, and to show how thoroughly he has wiped the slate clean, he resurrects both an unburned Jimmie and an unburned Henry Fleming for the first of them, "Lynx-Hunting," in which the little boy takes aim at a chipmunk and inadvertently fires the bullet into a cow. Unlike most of the other stories, which are set in town and feature a cast of both boys and girls, this one is about boys in the wild, boys at play in the woods. On the second page, Crane contrasts the sharp difference between their world and the world of adults, which establishes the mental and social framework for all the stories that follow.

> They passed along a maple-lined avenue, a highway common to boys bound for that freeland of hills and woods in which they lived in some part their romance of the moment—whether it was of Indians, miners, smugglers, soldiers or outlaws. The paths were their paths and much was known to them of the secrets of the dark-green hemlock thickets, the wastes of sweet-fern and huckleberry, the cliffs of gaunt blue-stone with the sumac burning red at their feet. Each boy had, I am sure, a conviction that some day the wilderness was to give forth to them a marvelous

secret.... The grown folk seemed to regard these wastes merely as so much distance between one place and another place or as rabbit cover, or as a district to be judged according to the value of the timber....

In the meantime, [the boys] lived there, in season, lives of ringing adventure—by dint of imagination.

In town, Crane creates a closed world of recurring child characters who appear in one story after another, forming a linked collection similar to the one Sherwood Anderson put together twenty years later in *Winesburg, Ohio*. The boy half of that Whilomville world is regulated by a clearly defined pecking order, with the bossy, imaginative Willie Dalzel standing at the head as undisputed chieftain, the mischievous, ever-game Jimmie Trescott serving as an upper-level subordinate, the dim-bulbed Homer Phelps wallowing in the depths of eternal serfdom, and various spear-carriers such as the Margate twins and Dan Earl, who go along with whatever the group decides. Crane, ever alert to the dynamics of groupthink, handles the interactions among the boys with spectacular precision, whether lightheartedly (in "Making an Orator" and "A Little Pilgrim") or with more serious intentions ("Shame," "The Carriage-Lamps," and "The Trial, Execution, and Burial of Homer Phelps"). When all is said and done, however, the most effective stories are the ones in which a child from another place comes to Whilomville and disturbs the balance of that closed-off world, as Crane does to great comic effect in "The Angel Child" and "The Stove" and then, with little or no comedy at all, in the somber depictions of struggle in "The Fight" and "The City Urchin and the Chaste Villagers."

The funny ones chart the adventures of little Cora, Jimmie's cousin from New York, "the brave bandit . . . and outlaw" known as the Angel Child. Her pranks begin one summer when she arrives for a visit at the Trescott house with her indulgent, fashionable mother and absentminded painter father, and when that out-to-lunch male parent casually hands her a five-dollar bill for her birthday, the blond-haired devil swings into action. Leading an army of small local kids into a well-supplied candy shop, she foots the bill for a massive gorgefest of ice cream and cake and "chocolate mice, butter-scotch, 'ever-lastings,' chocolate cigars, taffy-on-a-stick, taffy-on-a-slate-pencil, and many semi-transparent devices resembling lions, tigers, elephants, horses, cats, dogs, cows, sheep, tables, chairs, engines (both railway and for the fighting of fire), soldiers, fine ladies, odd-looking men, clocks, watches, revolvers, rabbits, and bedsteads," and once the sated, overstuffed children are too bloated to stand up anymore, the clerk hands the Angel Child her change. Two dollars and twenty-seven cents. Shocked to discover that she has made only a partial dent in the original amount, she rallies her exhausted troops with the magic words "We must think up some way of spending more money" (how the author must have grinned when he wrote that line), and off they go to flush away the rest of the cash at Neltje's barbershop, where one by one they have their beautiful children's locks shorn off by the man with the unpronounceable name, which causes no end of grief and howling consternation among the parents of the precious victims.

That same little Cora appears in the next story as well, "The Lover and the Tell-Tale," for Jimmie has lost his heart to her and is now pining for his absent cousin, who has gone back to New York with her parents. One day during recess at school, he remains in the classroom to write a letter to his beloved: "My dear Cora I love thee with all my hart oh come bac again, bac, bac gain for I love thee best of all oh come bac again When the spring come again we'l fly and we'l fly like a brid." The act of writing that letter will drag the pipsqueak suitor into a cyclone of mayhem and trouble, but by the time Cora returns to Whilomville for the Christmas holidays, he has largely recovered from his passion—or so he thinks. The Angel has arrived in the country with what has now become her favorite possession, a toy stove, which "turned out to be an affair of cast-iron, as big as a portmanteau, and, as the stage people say, practicable." Perversely, Cora insists on having it with her at all times, and since it is too heavy for her to carry herself, her poor father, in humble obedience to her commands, lugs it around for her from room to room and floor to floor of the house. When Dr. Trescott asks why they don't simply park it in one place and let her play with it there, her mother replies, "If it makes her happy to have the stove with her, why shouldn't she have it?"

It is an altogether bizarre situation, but Jimmie is beyond caring about bizarre, and he soon falls under Cora's spell again, happily turning himself into her "accomplice," or, more accurately, the slave of her whims, for "when the mind blazed within the small body, the angel-child was pure force." On the afternoon of the grand tea party to be held at the Trescotts', the children are admonished to "behave correctly," so they carry the stove out into the garden to play with it there as the house fills up with a crowd of visiting women. Unlike the other eleven stories, in which the adults are largely absent or hovering around the edges to maintain order and dole out punishments when necessary, Jimmie's and Cora's parents are central players in "The Stove," which gives Crane the narrative license to spend two full pages delving into the custom of provincial tea parties, and soon enough he is on the attack against the strangling hypocrisies of middle-class life, the same pinched environment that drove him to act so rudely at his brother William's dinner parties in Port Jervis. Two examples:

> On the fatal afternoon, a small picked company of latent enemies would meet. There would be a fanfare of affectionate greetings during which everybody would measure to an inch the importance of what everybody else was wearing. Those who wore old dresses would wish they had not come and those who saw that, in the company, they were well-clad would be pleased or exalted or filled with the joys of cruelty. Then they had tea which was a habit and a delight with none of them, their usual beverage being coffee with milk.

Or, more specifically, on the teacups themselves:

> These collections so differed in style and the obvious amount paid for them that nobody could be happy. The poorer ones envied; the richer ones feared; the poorer ones continually striving to over-take the leaders; the leaders always with their heads turned back to hear over-taking footsteps. And none of these things here written did they know. Instead of seeing that they were very stupid they thought they were very fine. And they gave and took heart bruises—fierce deep heart bruises—under the clear impression that of such kind of rubbish was the kingdom of nice people.

Meanwhile, it has been snowing outside, and the fire in the children's stove has gone out. Their first thought is to start it up again in the stable, but Peter Washington (glancingly mentioned as a friend of Henry Johnson's in *The Monster*) is now working as the Trescotts' hostler—almost as a duplicate of Johnson—and he forbids them to rekindle that pretend-but-real thing in his combustible domain, which leaves them with no option but to carry the cast-iron toy through an open outside cellar door, down a flight of steps, and into the underbelly of the house, a warm, dry enclosure in which "two huge cylindrical furnaces were humming away." As the beams overhead bounce with "the different emotions which agitated the tea-party," Jimmie relights the stove. Casting about for something to cook, they decide to raid the Trescotts' store of turnips and feed these dirt-encrusted roots to the flames, but when Cora announces that they own a hotel and the turnips are in fact the puddings they are preparing for thousands of guests, the toy stove becomes too small for their purposes.

Jimmie begins shoveling batch after batch of turnip-puddings into one of the furnaces, and when the smell of the roasting tubers begins wafting up into the realm of the adults, the two fathers, who have been hiding out in the doctor's office to avoid the tea party, go downstairs to investigate. Once they discover what is going on, the doctor sends Jimmie upstairs and the phlegmatic painter pretends to be angry with his daughter. He takes hold of her arm in "an imitation of wrath," but after a couple of vigorous shakes, she starts screaming and he abruptly stops. "I've hurt her," he says to Trescott. The doctor thinks about it for a moment and then replies: "You've hurt her, have you? Well, hurt her again. Spank her! Spank her, confound you, man! She needs it. Here's your chance. Spank her and spank her good. Spank her!" And the girl's father does it. However ineptly he goes about the job, he does it.

The other outsider who invades the walled-off territory of Whilomville is a boy named Johnnie Hedge, who moves from Jersey City with his widowed mother and younger brother into the house next door to the Trescotts, the one formerly owned by the Hannigans, who had put it up for sale in *The Monster* when they understood that the ruined, disfigured thing that had once been Henry Johnson was living with the Trescotts again. "The Fight" begins on the day the unknowns cart in their belongings and join the Whilomville community, events Jimmie has already witnessed, and a couple of minutes after Willie Dalzel and other members of the gang come around to check out the newcomers, Johnnie Hedge makes his first appearance,

> strolling down the gravel walk which led from the front door to the gate. He was about the height and age of Jimmie Trescott but he was thick through the chest and had fat legs. His face was round and rosy and plump but his hair was curly black and his brows were naturally darkling so that he resembled both a pudding and a young bull.
>
> He approached slowly the group of older inhabitants and they had grown profoundly silent. They looked him over; he looked them over. They might have been savages observing the first white man or white men observing the first savage. The silence held steady.

Within a couple of minutes, young Dalzel is declaring to Hedge that he can "lick" him, and when the newcomer acknowledges that he is probably right, Dalzel asks if he thinks he can lick Jimmie Trescott. "Whereupon the new boy looked at Jimmie respectfully but carefully and at length said: 'I dunno.'" The others then push Jimmie forward, and knowing what he is supposed to say now, he says it: "Can you lick me?" Hedge also knows what he is supposed to say at this point and, "despite his unhappy and lonely state," he says it: "Yes." An uproar ensues. Jimmie tells Hedge to come out from the yard, but the new boy holds his ground, and for the time being there is a standoff. As Crane brilliantly puts it (and no word is more brilliant in the following paragraph than "victims"), both boys are trapped in an impossible situation, one far deeper and more complex than the standard business of a picked-upon child standing up to a bully. An entire social order is being examined here, and who punches whom and who wins and who doesn't is finally of secondary importance.

> The two victims opened wide eyes at each other. The fence separated them and so it was impossible for them to immediately engage but they seemed to understand that they were ultimately to be sacrificed to the ferocious aspirations of the other boys and each scanned the other to learn something of his spirit. They were not angry at all. They were merely two little gladiators who were being clamorously told to hurt each other. Each displayed hesitation and doubt without display-ing fear. They did not exactly understand what were their feelings and they moodily kicked the ground and made low and sullen answers to Willie Dalzel who worked like a circus-manager.

The standoff is resolved with the threat of a future confrontation when Jimmie—who has a reputation to uphold and has often bragged about how tough he is—issues an ultimatum to Hedge: "The first time I catch you out of your own yard, I'll lam the head off'n you." The gang cheers in approval, and because Hedge is now obliged to say something in his turn, he counters with this "semi-defiant sentence": "Maybe you will and maybe you won't."

The story is broken into three chapters, and what follows in the second is an excruciating retelling of events Crane must have experienced half a dozen times or more in his own childhood. Always the new boy in a new town or new neighborhood, always the outsider searching for a way to fit in, always the lone-wolf stranger forced to submit to the brutal initiation rites of the pack. When Johnnie Hedge goes to school for the first time on Monday, the "torture" of adjusting to his new environment begins. Finding himself "among new people, a new tribe," he understands that "there [are] only two fates for him": victory, which will grant him a respected position among his peers, or defeat, which will hold him in thrall "to some superior boy" and require him to back that boy in all things. But how to establish a place for himself in that world where "none knew him, understood him, felt for him. He would be surrounded for this initiative time by a horde of jackal-creatures who might turn out in the end to be little boys like himself but this last point his philosophy could not understand in its fullness." During his first days at school, Hedge is mocked for his name (because "all new names struck boys as being comic"), teased by "small and utterly obscure boys," and "suffer[s] a shower of stares and whispers and giggles as if he were a man-ape."

For his part, Jimmie goes about his business and displays no interest in fighting the new boy, but after the bold threat he delivered on the first day, the other boys in his gang are beginning to suspect he is a coward. Soon enough, he is taunted by the same sort of needling chant that was inflicted on Horace in the earlier story: "'Fraid-cat! 'Fraid-cat! 'Fraid-cat!"

A confrontation is inevitable.

On the day of the fight, a hundred boys gather in the yard after school to watch. Jimmie challenges Hedge, and the new boy has no choice but to drop his books to the ground and square off against his opponent. Crane retards the action for a few moments to offer some observations on the fighting tactics of small boys, who engage in combat "much in the manner of little bear-cubs," that is, by rushing headlong at each other and then grappling until they fall to the ground, both weeping and disheveled, rolling around "in the dust or the mud or the snow or whatever the material happened to be." Jimmie, practiced in the bear-cub rush technique, charges full tilt at Hedge, but the Jersey City boy has been schooled in another approach, and now that "some spark ha[s] touched his fighting blood . . . he begin[s] to swing his arms, to revolve them so swiftly that one might have considered him a small working model of an extra-fine patented windmill." Jimmie is momentarily confused, and before he can figure out how to parry this onslaught of flailing, whirling arms, "a small knotty fist" catches him in the eye and he goes down, defeated.

The crowd is stunned, bewildered, beside itself. "Never before had Whilomville seen such a thing," and there is the new boy standing alone, "his clenched fists at his side, his face crimson, his lips still working with the fury of battle." A slight pause as a new impulse takes hold of him, and then, giving in to the impulse, he fixes his eyes on Willie Dalzel, "the front and center of his persecutors," for it is clear to him that Jimmie Trescott is no more than an instrument of the chief's will and therefore an insignificant distraction, but to take on and defeat the big man will liberate him from any further humiliations, and so he puts the windmill into motion again, drives a punch into Dalzel's face, and the leader of the gang heads for the hills—howling, running "like a hare," vanquished.

There is more. "The Fight" gives way to a sequel, a second story entitled "The City Urchin and the Chaste Villagers," which picks up where the other one left off and plays out the drama to the end.

In the micro-world of the little boys, the chieftain's fall has thrown things into a "state resembling anarchy." The boss boy is not necessarily the strongest or the one who never loses a fight, but he must not be a person who runs away, and by dashing off after his humbling defeat, Dalzel has lost the respect of his followers. He has been dethroned, and the big shot whose commands had once been obeyed is now subjected to a barrage of "whistling and cat-calling and hooting." That does not mean, however, that the boys have transferred their allegiance to Hedge. He has disrupted the order of their tranquil kingdom, and they resent him for it. Whatever he might have accomplished with his fists, he is still not one of them.

As for Jimmie, the first victim of the windmill clobber technique, he has been absolved of all blame. If anything, his status has been enhanced by the composure and dignity he demonstrated in the face of defeat, but because of that (note the deft psychological turn) this new status only encourages him to brag about how manfully he endured the pain of Hedge's knock-out punch. Through the inner manipulations of his little-boy vanity, the vanquished one has reconfigured his defeat into a triumph. A microscopic detail, perhaps, but another telling instance of Crane's refusal to idealize his characters. Young as he is, all-American Jimmie Trescott is no less flawed and self-serving than anyone else.

As time moves on, life moves on as well, and because they live next door to each other, Jimmie and Johnnie eventually make peace and form the beginnings of a friendship. As Crane observes: "The long-drawn animosities of men have no place in the life of a boy. The boy's mind is flexible; he readjusts his position with an ease which is derived from the fact—simply—that he is not yet a man."

Meanwhile, Dalzel is plotting a comeback as the tribe drifts along without an acknowledged leader. In those days of no movies, no television, and no radio, the boys satisfy their craving for stories by reading books, and "it came to pass that a certain half-dime blood-and-thunder pamphlet had a great vogue" among them, a tale about a cabin boy on a pirate ship who rises up from his lowly beginnings to become the most ruthless and successful pirate commander of the seven seas. One afternoon, with the boys gathered in the Trescotts' backyard, Dalzel begins his subtle effort to take charge again by suggesting they play out the action of the story. He, of course, will take the part of the grown-up cabin boy himself, but they have to find someone to cast in the unglamorous role of the cabin boy when he was still just a small, badly treated boy. Abject Homer Phelps says yes, then says no, the "milky and docile" Dan Earl unexpectedly says no, and a few moments later, with Dalzel lapsing into despair, he spots Johnnie Hedge's little brother gazing at them "wistfully" from the next yard.

When he was invited to become the cabin-boy he accepted joyfully thinking that it was his initiation into the tribe. Then they proceeded to give him the rope's-end and to punch him with a realism which was not altogether painless. Directly he began to cry out. They exhorted him not to cry out, not to mind it, but still they continued to hurt him.

The rest of the story unfolds in a whirl of action, counter-action, and counter-counter-action as it careens toward a wholly unexpected ending. Summoned by his brother's cries, Johnnie Hedge comes bounding into the yard, furious, boiling, unhinged, shouting at Dalzel that he is going to whip him within an inch of his life, that he is going to tan the hide off him, "and immediately there was a mixture—an infusion of two boys that looked as if it had been done by a chemist." This time, Dalzel manages to tackle Hedge before being punched, and when the dust clears they are both on the ground with Willie sitting on top of Johnnie, but the one on the bottom refuses to give up. They tussle again, pause for a moment, and again he refuses to give up. Then again, and still he refuses. "They heaved; uttered strange words; wept; and the sun looked down at them with steady, unwinking eye." The fight is still in progress, with Dalzel holding a distinct advantage—at least for the moment—but when Peter Washington emerges from the stable, he takes stock of "the tragedy of the back garden" and rushes in to break it up. He pulls the two boys apart, and "stormy and fine in his indignation," scolds them for acting like mad dogs and tells them to stop. They don't want to stop. Again and again, they try to go after each other, and as Washington continues to keep them apart, he begins to scold Jimmie as well, accusing him of encouraging the fight, which Jimmie denies, then denies again, after which Washington orders Dalzel to leave "or I'll . . . damnearkill you," and then tells Hedge that he thought he was a boy with some sense,

"but I raikon you don't know no more'n er rabbit. You jest take an' trot erlong off home an' don' lemme catch you round yere er-fightin' or I'll break yer back." The Hedge boy moved away with dignity followed by his little brother. The latter when he had placed a sufficient distance between himself and Peter, placed his fingers at his nose and called out: "Nig-ger-r-r! Nig-ger-r-r!"

Peter Washington's resentment poured out upon Jimmie. "'Pears like you never would unnerstan' you ain't reg'lar common trash. You take an' 'sociate with an'body what done come erlong."

"Aw, go on," retorted Jimmie profanely. "Go soak your head, Pete."

Crane says nothing more, but those sentences blast into the narrative with all the force of a thunderclap, of two thunderclaps—first from the little boy's drawn-out, venomous *nig-ger-r-r*, then from Jimmie's arrogant, hotheaded dressing-down of his father's adult servant—and within fifteen seconds the sweet, pastoral world of the bygone American village is turned into one more battleground in the white-on-black war that began when the first African was put on the auction block and sold off as human chattel— way back when, before America was even a country. The little boy's epithet explains itself, but Jimmie's part in the flare-up is more subtle, for this is not the first time he has turned his anger on Peter Washington (in an earlier story, "The Carriage-Lamps," he went so far as to throw stones at him), but whatever troubles the boy has caused for himself until now, he has always backed off when confronted by adult authority. But not here. He insults the hostler in full view of the other boys, telling him to butt out of their business (*Go soak your head*), which means, in fact, that he does not recognize Washington's authority as an adult. Black men, after all, are not real men. At best, they are little more than grown-up children, and why should a white boy with red blood running though his veins bother to listen to one of *them*?

All that—speeding by in a flash—and then the story hurtles onward as the boys go out to the street and join Dalzel, the partially restored chieftain, who is loudly proclaiming victory. "I licked him! I licked him! Didn't I, now?" Before the question can be answered, out walks his adversary to call his bluff and denounce him as a liar. They argue back and forth in a tommy-gun exchange of accusations and denials, and then Hedge puts his windmill into action again and goes on the attack. The first punches miss the back-pedaling Dalzel, but soon enough another one catches him on the cheek, and suddenly the frightened boy lets out a howl. Tears are falling from his eyes as Hedge moves in to continue the assault, and with a knockout all but certain now, the other boys yell, "No, no, don't hit 'im anymore! Don't hit 'im no more!" Then Jimmie, goaded by what Crane artfully terms "a panic of bravery," calls out to the avenging windmill: "We'll all jump you if you do!" But Hedge doesn't care. He lashes back at Jimmie and the others: "I'll fix him so he won't know hisself an' if any of you kids bother with me—"

Suddenly he ceased, he trembled, he collapsed. The hand of one approaching from behind had laid hold upon his ear and it was the hand of one whom he knew.

The other lads heard a loud iron-filing voice say: "Caught ye at it again, ye brat, ye!" They saw a dreadful woman with grey hair, with a sharp red nose, with bare arms, with spectacles of such magnifying quality that her eyes shone through them like two fierce white moons. She was Johnnie Hedge's mother. Still holding Johnnie by the ear, she swung out swiftly and dexterously and succeeded in boxing the ears of two boys before the crowd regained its presence of mind and stampeded. Yes; the war for supremacy was over and the question was never again disputed. The supreme power was Mrs. Hedge.

Fortinbras to the rescue—at least for now—but what of the other days when the supreme power has her back turned and the little ruffians start pounding each other again? They are all stuck in the hard-knocks academy of childhood, with graduation day so far off in the future that it is no more conceivable to them than life on the most distant star. Childhood goes on forever. Things pass by quickly for adults, but all through those early years time is so thick and heavy that it does not move. And there are the kids, trapped in the savage arena of the Now, powerless to change anything around them except by dreaming themselves into other worlds, nonexistent places where the Now will temporarily loosen its hold on them. Childhood is therefore a serious business, and among the many virtues of Crane's Whilomville stories is how profoundly he understands the seriousness of children at play, whether it is little Cora acting out her game of a thousand turnip-puddings or Willie Dalzel and his crew attempting to rescue the punished Jimmie from home confinement by imitating the tactics of the dime-novel pirates in *The Red Captain*, in spite of the obstacle created by one of the boys, who prefers Westerns to stories about pirates and wants to imagine himself as Hold-up Harry, the Terror of the Sierras, which leads to a dispute about what sort of language they should speak while pulling off their stunt, whether to call their imprisoned friend "comrade," for example, or "pard," which turns play into a form of artistic expression, a picture of artists at work. Even more elaborately, there is Homer Phelps and his failure to understand the difference between real life and pretend life. When he is supposed to be captured during a game of Soldiers and Enemies in the woods, he doesn't want to be captured. "If you're going to play, you've got to play it right," says chief Dalzel. "It ain't no fun if you go spoilin' the whole thing this way. Can't you play it right?" Later on, when he is supposed to be tried and executed, Homer doesn't want to be tried and executed, so Jimmie Trescott steps in and takes his place. When he is shot, "Jimmie threw his hands high, tottered for a moment, and then crashed full length into the snow—into, one would think, a serious case of pneumonia. It was beautiful." When the time comes to bury the dead man, they ask Homer to assume his role again, but he doesn't seem to understand.

> "You're dead," said the chief frankly. That's what you are. We executed you, we did."
> "When?" demanded the Phelps boy with some spirit.
> "Just a little while ago. Didn't we, fellers? Hey, fellers, didn't we?"
> The trained chorus cried: "Yes, of course we did. You're dead, Homer. You can't play anymore. You're dead."
> "That wasn't me. It was Jimmie Trescott," he said in a low and bitter voice. . . .
> "No," said the chief, "it was you. We're playin' it was you, an' it *was* you. You're dead, you see."

Freud, writing in 1908: "We ought surely to look in the child for the first traces of imaginative activity. The child's best loved and most absorbing occupation is play. Perhaps we may say that every child at play behaves like an imaginative writer, in that he creates a world of his own or, more truly, he rearranges the things of his world and orders it in a new way. . . . It would be incorrect to think that he does not take this world seriously; on the contrary, he takes his play very seriously and expends a great deal of emotion on it."

Again Freud: "You will not forget that the stress laid on the writer's memories of his childhood, which perhaps seems so strange, is ultimately derived from the hypothesis that imaginative creation, like day dreaming, is a continuation of and substitute for the play of childhood."

Four of the stories from the other collection about the war in Cuba had already been completed by the time Crane returned to England, and the remaining seven were written between February and August 1899, one in Oxted and the rest at Brede. Like "The Price of the Harness" and "The Clan of No-Name," they are substantial pieces of work, all but one of them covering from fifteen to twenty pages—in addition to the much longer "War Memories." Unexpectedly, they crackle with a new tone and a new manner of telling as Crane sets aside his close phenomenological scrutiny of the world for a plunge into pure narrative. It is neither a better nor a worse place for him to have landed—simply a different one—but also a sign, I believe, of his expanding capabilities as a writer. Early on, he could not have written in this way, at least not over the length of a two-hundred-yard sprint, but now he can, and the prose in these stories is smooth, flowing, and alive with spit, vinegar, and deadpan irony, the voice of a more mature and confident artist, a man who has lived hard and seen much and has come back from his travels to tell us what he knows. Unlike his novel and shorter fictions about the Civil War, these new stories are grounded in his own experiences and memories along with the things he learned firsthand by keeping his eyes open in Cuba, just as he had kept them open while drifting off the coast of Florida in the open boat.

"Virtue in War," "This Majestic Lie," and "The Second Generation" are all excellent examples of this new narrative approach, but the first one written after Crane's return to England, which is also the most directly autobiographical of the lot, is not only another excellent example but a primer on how Crane transformed events from his own life into the stuff of fiction. "God Rest Ye, Merry Gentlemen" is a story about the American correspondents in Cuba, and a number of S.C.'s friends figure in the action under different names. Scovel becomes Walkley, Marshall becomes Tailor, McCready becomes Shackles, and the young photographer Burr McIntosh becomes Point. The *New York World* becomes the *New York Eclipse*, and bureau chief Cary becomes a man named Rogers. The story begins during the "rocking-chair period" of the war, the long weeks of doing nothing in Key West alternating with the futile excursions on dispatch boats such as the *Three Friends* and the *Somers N. Smith*, which is renamed the *Jefferson G. Johnson* (yet one more of Crane's Johnsons to go along with Maggie from his first book and Henry from *The Monster*, as if Crane wanted to announce his authorial presence by leaving his fingerprints at the scene of the crime). The story then goes on to cover the first wave of the six thousand American troops who landed at Daiquirí on June twenty-second, the trek toward Siboney on the twenty-third, and the ambush of the Rough Riders near Las Guásimas on the twenty-fourth, during which Marshall (Tailor) is shot, this time in the lung rather than the spine, a life-threatening injury that impels one of his friends and fellow correspondents to run for five miles in search of assistance. That correspondent was Crane, of course, who in the story gives himself the improbable, cockeyed name of Little Nell, "sometimes called the Blessed Damosel," a reference to Rossetti's midcentury poem but also—and more pertinently—to the Little Nell created by Charles Dickens, the most maudlin, sentimentalized female figure in all of English literature, the doomed and tragic angel whose death caused

Photo portrait of Crane by Elliott and Fry, 1899.
(COURTESY OF THE UNIVERSITY OF VIRGINIA)

tens of thousands if not hundreds of thousands of readers to collapse in uncontrollable fits of sobbing when *The Old Curiosity Shop* was published in 1841. Why would Crane want to feminize himself in his own story, and why, among all the female names at his disposal, would he choose the name of that pathetic, undersized girl, a creature born in the pages of a book? Quite simply, it seems to me, because he wanted to mock himself. A man among men in the midst of war, a tough-guy correspondent surrounded by armed killers, he assumes the identity of the frailest, least heroic person he can think of, and so he becomes a girl among men, a dainty, swooning thing in petticoats who would not last an hour or even a minute in that jungle of bullets. *Little Nell in the Land of the Giants.* A book otherwise known as *Little Stevie Goes to War.*

He mocks himself, then, but only to proclaim his singular and spectacular unimportance in the grand scheme of the Heavenly What, and by saddling his little man with the name of what amounts to a fairy-tale character, Crane transforms his stand-in into an otherworldly being not fit to cope with the dangers of this world, which seems to have been how Crane felt during much of the time he spent with the army in Cuba: *this war which theretofore I could have believed was a dream—almost.*

The *Johnson* leered and tumbled her way through the community of ships. The bombardment ceased, and some of the troop-ships edged in near the land. Soon boats black with men and towed by launches were almost lost to view in the scintillant mystery of light which appeared where the sea met the land. A disembarkation had begun. . . . They were in a sort of cove, with troopships, newspaper boats and cruisers on all sides of them, and over the water came a great hum of human voices, punctuated frequently by the clang of the engine-room gongs as the steamers manoeuvred to avoid jostling.

In reality it was the great moment—the moment for which men, ships, islands and continents had been waiting for months—but somehow it did not look it. It was very calm; a certain strip of high green rocky shore was being rapidly populated from boat after boat; that was all. Like many pre-conceived moments, it refused to be supreme. But nothing lessened Little Nell's frenzy. He knew that the army was landing—he could see it; and little did he care if the great moment did not look its part—it was his virtue as a correspondent to recognize the great moment in any disguise. The *Johnson* lowered a boat for him and he dropped into it swiftly, forgetting everything. However, the mate, a bearded philanthropist, flung after him a mackintosh and a bottle of whisky. Little Nell's face was turned toward those other boats filled with men, all eyes upon the placid, gentle, noiseless shore. Little Nell saw many soldiers seated stiffly beside upright rifle barrels, their blue breasts crossed with white shelter-tent and blanket-rolls. Launches screeched; jack-tars pushed or pulled with their boathooks; a beach was alive with working soldiers, some of them stark naked. Little Nell's boat touched the shore amid a babble of tongues, dominated at that time by a single stern voice which was repeating: "Fall in, B Company!"

He took his mackintosh and his bottle of whisky and invaded Cuba . . .

The crown jewel of the book, however, is "War Memories," which is not a story so much as a lightly fictionalized memoir told in a series of discontinuous fragments. Unlike the other works in the collection, this one came about more or less by chance and never would have been written if Crane hadn't been asked to come up with a story or an article by someone close to good friends of his. He therefore did it as a favor to them, even though he did not expect to be paid for his work. These people were the Frewens, the owners of Brede Place, and through her connection with Clara Frewen, Cora became an honorary member of an organization called the Society of American Women in London. When she attended one of the club's monthly meetings on July third (1899), she was introduced to Mrs. Frewen's sister Lady Randolph Churchill, who happened to be the founder and editor of the recently launched quarterly publication the *Anglo-Saxon Review*. On July twenty-fourth, Lady Churchill wrote to Crane asking him to contribute something for the second issue: "If you could give me an article or perhaps your experiences in Crete or Cuba—of 6000 to 10000 words I should be very grateful." Crane, who "hated to write letters" (Cora), wrote back sometime within the next ten days, and on August fourth Lady Churchill responded: "I have just received your letter & am very glad to think you will write for me. As regards the subject I think I would leave it to you. Would you like to give me a military story of say from 7000 to 10000 words, or if you do not care for fiction some reminiscence of war, or a short essay—on a congenial subject."

In the end, Crane gave her sixteen thousand words and was sent fifty pounds for his trouble—an unexpected bonus. "War Memories" is an amalgam of previously untold anecdotes and stories patched together with stray sentences and paragraphs from articles he had written in Cuba (those ephemeral bits of paper used for wrapping fish—which no one in England had read), and while the result is far from a perfect piece of writing, the good passages have such energy and such a grand sense of freedom that one senses a possible explosion in the not too distant future. That explains why I consider it to be the strongest work Crane produced in the last year of his life—not so much for what it is but for what it suggests about what he might have done in the first two or three or four decades of the twentieth century.

When an artist dies at such a young age, it is impossible not to wonder what kind of work that artist would have done later in life. What novels would Emily Brontë have written if she had lived past thirty? What songs and symphonies would Schubert have composed if he had lived past thirty-one? Where would Keats have gone as a poet if he had lived past twenty-five? Every early death leaves an inexhaustible trail of what-ifs behind it, but because things are as they are and always will be as they are, those questions cannot be answered. We can't help asking them from time to time, but to go on asking them would be pointless.

Still, in my weaker moments, I sometimes ask myself: What if Crane had understood that "War Memories" was not just a slapdash concoction written as a favor to his friends but a door that opened onto an immense new kingdom of fresh possibilities? For the first time, he had given all of himself in a single work, the darkest parts of who he was as well as the brightest and most ebullient, and if he had carried on in that multivoiced, free-flowing, improvisatory vein, he might have produced demotic wonders similar to Louis-Ferdinand Céline's *Journey to the End of the Night* from the early 1930s, or, in time, more stringent monologues similar to Beckett's *Molloy* from the late 1940s, but whatever direction he might have taken, I believe Crane would have found the ultimate expression of his talents by writing in the first person, as he does in "War Memories," and as he also does in his all-but-unknown last, unfinished novel, *The O'Ruddy*, a high-spirited picaresque set in the eighteenth century that he imagined would turn into another one of his illusory cash machines, not a great work, perhaps, but a thousand times better than the dreary *Active Service*, and what holds the book together and keeps the reader reading is the bounce in the narrator's first-person voice. Not the answer, no, but another step forward in the quest to find the answer, and then Crane died when he was smack in the middle of it, and that was that: a last unfinished work at the end of his short, unfinished life.

In July, Crane severed his connection with Reynolds and began working exclusively with his London literary agent, James B. Pinker, who also represented Conrad, James, and Galsworthy. To give Pinker a sense of what he would be handling in the months ahead, Crane sent off a brief letter on around August first, explaining that his stories were "developing in three series," which broke down into the following categories:

I. The Whilomville stories (always to Harpers.)
II. The war tales.
III. Tales of Western American life similar to "Twelve O'Clock."

It might be well to remember this. For instance if you could provisionally establish the war tales with one magazine and the western tales with another as the Whilomville yarns are fixed with Harper's, it would be very nice.

Nice or not, he plugged away on all three fronts, and when the Cuban war collection was finished, he kept the word factory going at full blast by producing two more abbreviated cycles of battle stories, Tales of the Wyoming Valley, a linked trio starring Crane's great-great-grandfather in his fight against the British and their Indian allies during the Revolutionary

War, and a group of four others set in the imaginary country of Spitzbergen, whose army is locked in an all-out struggle with the forces from
neighboring Rostina. Among the Spitzbergen officers are a Colonel
Sponge (named after S.C.'s favorite dog) and a General Ritchie (a nod
to young Edith), but apart from those private jokes, the stories are grim,
violent, and often chilling. Meanwhile, category number three on Crane's
list included the aforementioned "Twelve O'Clock" along with "A Poker
Game" and "Moonlight on the Snow," the story in which Jack Potter and
Scratchy Wilson make their last appearance together as they ride into the
town of War Post as sheriff and deputy—a decent effort in its way, but no
match for the comic asperities of "The Bride Comes to Yellow Sky."

Beyond those stories, there was the bigger project to write a novel about
the Revolutionary War (in which the earlier Stephen Crane was to have
been a character), but after tinkering with it for several months he let
it drop, mostly because there weren't enough books available to him in
England to carry on with the research the novel would have required. So
he buckled down to work on *The O'Ruddy* instead, and at some point in
this frenzy of writing and more writing and still more writing he managed
to compose his last great work—a tiny blip of just a few pages that he sent
off to Pinker on November fourth with the words "I am enclosing a double
extra special good thing." It turns out he was right.

"The Upturned Face" is Crane's last word on the futility of war, but it is
also a cold, hard look at his own imminent death—as if those two things
were in fact one thing, the same thing. Cooked down to the barest residue
of what to tell and how to tell it, the story moves along in little spasms of
dread as two soldiers go about the job of burying an officer who has been
shot and killed in battle, even as that battle continues to send bullets snap-
ping toward them, posing the continual threat that they themselves will be
shot and killed before they can finish their work. Timothy Lean is a first
lieutenant in the Spitzbergen army, a figure who has already played a prominent role in two of the earlier stories, and he and his adjutant are looking
down at the chalk-blue face of "old Bill," who is lying on the ground at
their feet. Lean orders two of the men from the firing line to come over
and start digging the grave. "Dig here," he says, and the frightened men get
to work, one with a pick, one with a shovel. Before long, the adjutant says,
"I suppose we'd better search his clothes . . . for things." Lean nods, but for
several seconds he does nothing, unable to turn his eyes from the corpse.
At last, "he dropped to his knees and approached his hands to the body of
the dead officer. But his hands wavered over the buttons of the tunic. The
first button was brick-red with drying blood, and he did not seem to dare

to touch it." Eventually, he wills himself to touch what must be touched, and then, after retrieving "a watch, a whistle, a pipe, a tobacco pouch, a handkerchief, a little case of cards and papers," he stands up with a "ghastly face" and looks at the adjutant in silence. Moments after that, the grave is finished. "It was not a masterpiece—poor little shallow thing. Lean and the adjutant again looked at each other in a curious silent communication." Suddenly, the adjutant begins to laugh, a weird laugh of frayed nerves and disintegrating composure, a man on edge. As if cracking a joke—a bad but perhaps necessary joke—he says to Lean, "I suppose we had best tumble him in." Not wanting to touch the corpse, they take hold of the dead man by grabbing his clothes. "They tugged away; the corpse lifted, heaved, toppled, flopped into the grave." The adjutant asks the lieutenant if "he knows the service," but Lean says they don't begin the prayers until after the grave has been filled in. "'Don't they?' said the adjutant, shocked that he had made the mistake. 'Oh well,' he cried suddenly, 'let us . . . let us say something while . . . he can hear us.'" A peculiar, disconcerting thought, but Lean unexpectedly says, "All right" and then asks the adjutant if *he* knows the service. Not one word of it, the other replies. Lean thinks that perhaps he can remember a few lines, and after calling the two privates to attention, he mumbles out some words as the Rostina sharpshooters continue to fire at them: "*O, Father, our friend has sunk into the deep waters of death*," etc., unintentionally reciting the burial service for the dead at sea. He blunders on with some more phrases and then stops, unable to go any further, but the adjutant steps in and prompts him with another line, and then another that ends with the word *Mercy*. "*O, God have mercy*," the adjutant says, "*O, God have mercy*," Lean says, "*Mercy*," says the adjutant, "*Mercy*," says Lean. "And then he was moved by some new violence of feeling, for he turned suddenly upon his two men and tigerishly said, 'Throw the dirt in.'" A last sentence follows before the end of the first chapter: "The fire of the Rostina sharpshooters was accurate and continuous."

The brief final chapter: One of the privates scoops a load of dirt onto the blade of the shovel, holds it above the corpse, hesitates, looks down at the chalk-blue face looking up from the bottom of the hole, and then empties the shovel onto the dead man's feet. The lieutenant is immensely consoled: he had been expecting the first load of dirt to land on the face. "There was a great point gained there—ha, ha!—the first shovelful had been emptied on the feet. How satisfactory!" A moment later, the man with the shovel is hit in the arm by a bullet. Lean tells him to go to the rear, then tells the other man to "get under cover" as well. He will finish the job himself.

Timothy Lean filled the shovel, hesitated, and then in a movement which was like a gesture of abhorrence, he flung the dirt into the grave and as it landed it made a sound—plop. Lean paused and mopped his brow—a tired laborer.

"Perhaps we have been wrong," said the adjutant. His glance wavered stupidly. "It might have been better if we hadn't buried him just at this time. Of course, if we advance to-morrow, the body would have been—"

"Damn you," said Lean. "Shut your mouth." He was not a senior officer.

He again filled the shovel and flung in the earth. Always the earth made that sound—plop. For a space Lean worked frantically like a man working himself out of danger.

Soon there was nothing to be seen but the chalk-blue face. Lean filled the shovel. . . . "Good God," he cried to the adjutant. "Why didn't you turn him somehow when you put him in? This———" Then Lean began to stutter.

The adjutant understood. He was pale to the lips. "Go on, man," he cried, beseechingly, almost in a shout. . . . Lean swung back the shovel; it went forward in a pendulum curve. When the earth landed it made a sound—plop.

4

THEY ALL LIVED WITHIN SHOUTING DISTANCE OF ONE ANOTHER IN the same neck of the woods. They all had independent friendships and rivalries between and among themselves that had started before and would go on long after the years in question, but for the short time Crane occupied his houses in Oxted and Brede, all four of those men were devoted to him. Ford was two years younger than Crane, but he had published his first novel at nineteen and was firmly entrenched in the literary world when the two met in 1897. Wells, five years older than Crane, had already published his best-known science fiction novels by the time S.C. returned from Cuba and their casual association evolved into a warm friendship. Wells published a hundred books in his long life, but those early novels— *The Time Machine* (1895), *The Island of Dr. Moreau* (1896), *The Invisible Man* (1897), and *The War of the Worlds* (1898)—have continued to be his most widely read and influential works. As for Conrad, the time of his brother bond with Crane was the moment when he cracked through the wall of his uncertainties and sweated and struggled his way into completing two of his most lasting works. *Heart of Darkness* appeared in the February issue of *Blackwood's Magazine*, less than a month after Crane's return to England. To S.C. on January 13, 1899 (just two days after), J.C. wrote, "I am coming to see you directly I finish a rotten thing I am writing for B'wood. It is rotten—and I can't help it. All I write is rotten now. I am pretty well decayed myself. I ought to be taken out and flung into a dusthole—along with the dead cats—by heavens! Well. Enough. I don't want to bore you into a faint in your first week in merry England." After *Heart* was thrown out with the dead cats, Conrad returned to suffering his way to the end of *Lord Jim* (arguably his best novel) and finally began publishing it in *Blackwood's* that October. Meanwhile, at Lamb House in Rye, old man James, who was all of fifty-four, -five, and -six, published *What Maisie Knew* and *The Spoils of Poynton* in 1897, *In the Cage* and *The Turn of the Screw* in 1898, and *The Awkward Age* in 1899. Crane was working hard, but so were his four friends. Their little patch of England was ablaze with words, and the wonder of it is that most of those words are still read today.

Ford was a rascal, a snob, and an unstable nuisance at times, but he was smart and passionate about books, a perceptive judge of talent, and Crane liked him. "You are wrong about Heuffer," he wrote to a friend in mid-August. "I admit he is patronizing. He patronized his family. He patronizes Conrad. He will end up patronizing God who will have to get used to it and they will be friends." Hueffer changed his name to Ford after World War I, but under one name or the other he wound up publishing more than thirty novels (three of them in less than happy, unsuccessful collaborations with Conrad), as well as numerous books of nonfiction and memoir. Beyond his one certifiable masterpiece, *The Good Soldier* (1915), and the almost as important *Parade's End* tetrology from the 1920s, his greatest contribution to literature lay in his efforts to promote the work of others, principally in the two magazines he founded at different stages of his career: the *English Review* in 1908 (which published contributions from Conrad, a young Robert Frost, and an even younger T. S. Eliot) and the Paris-based *transatlantic review* in 1924 (James Joyce, Djuna Barnes, Gertrude Stein, and Ernest Hemingway's first short stories). In various articles and books of reminiscence, Ford presents such a fanciful, distorted, and exaggerated picture of Crane that his remarks are next to worthless, but Ford also seems to have been the only person close enough to both S.C. and Henry James to have some idea of what the two men thought of each other, and distorted as those memories might be as well, they do not come off as out-and-out fabrications.

> That James had a very great admiration for Crane I know. He constantly alluded to Crane as "that genius," and I have heard him say over and over again, "he had great, great genius," always repeating the word "great" twice and emphasizing the second "great" as if he were italicizing it in writing. Crane, of course, shocked the old man, but he was just a naughty boy who, on purpose, delighted to shock his uncle. . . .
>
> Early in their relationship Crane, I think, was pained by the thought that James did not take him or his work very seriously, and I remember having quite frequently assured him that James did take his work at least very seriously indeed. And so did Crane take the work of James. He used at first to talk of James and even to write of him in letters as "the old man," but one day he astonished me by talking of some one whom I didn't immediately identify, as "the master." When I asked him whom he meant he turned on me with a look almost of contempt, and said with deep agitation, "Why, the old man, of course. He's the master of us all! Don't you know *that*?"

What we know from other sources is that while the young man and the "old man" were not close, they saw each other with a certain regularity and that while Crane did indeed "shock" James from time to time with his unorthodox manner of dress (riding breeches and boots on formal visits to Lamb House) and his bohemian disregard of social niceties, they remained on friendly terms throughout Crane's tenure at Brede. An occasional shock, perhaps, but how to forget the master going limp with mirth at the sight of young Edith and the five singing dogs? And there was James again on the afternoon of August twenty-third at the fundraising party for the District Nursing Association in the rectory garden of the Brede village church. Cora was in charge of a booth that sold knickknacks and potted plants; Crane, dressed in white flannels and a straw hat, made himself useful by carrying the plants to the waiting carriages of the women who had bought them; and dark-haired Edith Ritchie was installed as a gypsy fortune-teller "in a little summer-house, with a table in front of me. On it were a lot of envelopes filled with sugar and spices which I sold as love potions to the 'local yokels,' as Stephen called them. Henry James insisted upon sitting there with me all afternoon, adding much to my confusion." That same afternoon, James was

Henry James at the Brede village church garden party, August 23, 1899.
(COURTESY OF COLUMBIA UNIVERSITY)

captured in a photograph with the remnant of a half-eaten doughnut in his hand, one of the many dozens Vernall had prepared at Brede Place using Cora's time-tested American recipe. Unfortunately, the shutter clicked at precisely the wrong moment. James's eyes are shut, his mouth is partly open, his fingers resemble claws. After the picture was sent to him, he wrote back to Cora with good-natured embarrassment: "All thanks for the strange images, which I never expected to behold. They form a precious memento of a romantic hour. But no, surely, it can't be any doughnut of yours that is making me make such a gruesome grimace. I look as if I had swallowed a wasp, or a penny toy. And I tried to look so beautiful. I tried too hard doubtless. But don't show it to anyone as H.J. trying."

Several months later, when the skies darkened and Crane's health began to collapse, James's initial worry spun downward into a prolonged and progressively more acute anguish. "While Crane was on his deathbed at Brede," Ford wrote, "James's condition was really pitiable. He would drive

Crane at the garden party in the rectory of the Brede village church,
August 23, 1899. (COURTESY OF SYRACUSE UNIVERSITY)

over two and three times a day to consult as to what he could *do* for the dying boy." In a later work, Ford added: "He suffered infinitely. . . . I would walk with him for hours over the marsh trying to divert his thoughts. But he would talk on and on." The passage concludes: "He was not himself for many days after Crane's death."

After Crane left Brede for the sanatorium in the Black Forest on May 15, 1900, James lost touch with him and no longer had any news about the minute-to-minute details of his condition. When he finally learned how badly things were going—and how alarming that condition had become—he sent Cora a check for fifty pounds and an accompanying letter. "It is a shock to me that Crane is less well—I was full of hope, & had been, in that hope, assuming that a good effect had come to him from his move: cheerful theories much disconcerted! I think of him with more sympathy and sorrow than I can say. I wish I could express this to him more closely & personally." Regarding the fifty pounds, he urged Cora to "dedicate it to whatever service it may best render my stricken young friend. It meagerly represents my tender benediction to him. I write in haste—to catch the post. I needn't tell you how glad I shall be of any news that you are able to send me. I wish you all courage & as much hope as possible, & I am yours and his, in deep participation."

The letter was sent from England on June fifth—the day Crane died.

H. G. Wells barking like a dog as he and his wife sat around a table with the Cranes for an Animal Grab showdown, but also this whimsical bit of cross-cultural misapprehension from Curtis Brown—by way of Crane himself. "Stephen's story of sweet corn must be told," Brown begins, and then he goes on to tell it:

> H. G. Wells and his wife, who were then neighbors, had heard talk of the delights of American corn, and wished to grow some of their own; and were given some kernels for planting. According to Crane, he inquired, at a proper season later, how the corn had fared.
> "Very well," said H.G. "We quite enjoyed it."
> "How did you cook it?"
> "Cook it! We didn't cook it. We cut it when it was six inches high, and ate it for salad. Wasn't that right?"

They were friends for only a year, and few traces of that friendship have survived anywhere but in a smattering of letters and in what Wells wrote about Crane at various times in his subsequent work, beginning with the important essay he published just two months after S.C.'s death, "Stephen Crane from an English Standpoint." However little is known about their personal relations, one certain fact is that Wells happened to be at Brede Place on the night of Crane's first lung hemorrhage and that he was the person who jumped onto a bicycle and rode seven miles in an icy December drizzle to fetch a doctor in Rye and conduct him back to the house. Wells had suffered from lung troubles himself in his early twenties, and as time went on Cora brought him into the small circle of confidants with whom she shared details about the ups and downs of her husband's worsening condition. During a nine-day pause in Dover on the way to Badenweiler in the Black Forest, Crane was visited by some of his closest friends for what turned out to be their final encounters with him. "I saw him for the last time hardly more than seven weeks ago," Wells wrote in his essay. "He was thin and gaunt and wasted, too weak for more than a remembered jest and a greeting and good wishes. It did not seem to me in any way credible that he would reach his refuge in the Black Forest only to die at journey's end. It will be a long time yet before I can fully realize that he is no longer a contemporary of mine."

After that, Wells begins to probe the inner workings of Crane's fiction, fascinated above all by the stringencies of method found "in the persistent selection of essential elements of an impression, in the ruthless exclusion of mere information, in the direct vigor with which the selected points are made." Moving on to a discussion of several individual works starting with *Red Badge*, he follows with a word about the unfair neglect of *Maggie* and *George's Mother*, which are "absolutely essential to a just understanding of Crane," and then looks into "The Open Boat," which to his mind is "beyond all question, the crown of all his work." As he heads toward the conclusion of the eight-page article, Wells comes up with a singularly astute formulation about the nature of this work, which is so dead on target, it seems to me, that it continues to stand as one of the best descriptions of Crane anyone has written: "In style, in method and in all that is distinctly *not* found in his books, he is sharply defined, the expression in literary art of certain enormous repudiations." *Enormous repudiations.* Wells, who was a writer with a drastically different approach to the world from Crane's and who wrote in an altogether different manner, gets it exactly right. Crane has cleared the literary ground for all who will come after him and is "the first expression of the opening mind of a new period."

Fifteen years later, in the satirical novel *Boon*, Wells expressed himself even more bluntly through the words of his central character, who at one point declares, "Stephen Crane—the best writer of English for the last half-century."

After Crane returned to England, his friendship with Conrad picked up precisely where it had left off in the spring. On his second day back, he sent off two wires to his not so distant neighbor—the first to announce that he had arrived safely, the second to congratulate him on winning a fifty-guinea prize for his collection of stories *Tales of Unrest*. "I am more glad than I can say to hear of you being here at last," Conrad began his letter from January thirteenth. "I long to hear your news. And let me tell you at once that the *Harness* is the best bit of work you've done (for its size) since the *Red Badge*. There is a mellowness in the vigor of the story that simply delighted me. . . . More power to your pen. I feel a new man since this morning's wire. It was good of you to think of me at once. I intended to wire myself today inquiring. Well that's over now. I know where to locate you when I think of you—which is often—very. . . . You must be full of stuff. . . . I know whatever it is will be *good*. It will be great!"

Conrad's visits resumed, and once the weather turned warm, the entire family descended on Brede for a visit that lasted more than two weeks, during which the fifteen-month-old Borys walked on his own for the first time as Crane and Conrad looked down on the lawn through the window in Crane's study. Mad for the little boy, S.C. presented him with a dog (*A boy must have a dog!*), but he was never able to fulfill his promise of teaching him how to ride. Later that summer, Crane and Conrad went in as partners and bought a twenty-two-foot sailboat from one of Conrad's friends. The boat was to be docked for six months a year in Rye (near the Cranes) and six months in Folkstone (near the Conrads), and each couple was to pay half. Not surprisingly, the Cranes were slow in coming up with their share. "I am so sorry Stephen worried about the payment," Conrad wrote to Cora on August twenty-seventh. "Thanks ever so much for the cheque."

In another letter from early September, Conrad playfully addressed Crane as "Dear Old Pard," a sign of how deeply he cared about his American friend and how fully he was willing to participate in Crane's passion for the West. It is hard not to smile at the thought of the Polish-born Conrad using that folksy cowboy expression, and whatever matter he is referring to in the opening sentences, the goodwill behind them is unmistakable: "Right. Bully for you. You are the greatest of the boys—and you are as good as I want you so you needn't trouble to apologize." For the delay in sending his share for the boat, perhaps, although it could have been something else, but Conrad quickly moves on to the central purpose of the letter:

> Could you come? You would make me happy. And will you pardon me for not coming to you. Dear Stephen I am like a damned paralyzed mud turtle. I can't move. I can't write. I can't do anything. But I can be wretched, and, by God! I am!
>
> Jess sends her love to the whole house. Give my affectionate regards and compliments. Let me know *the day before* when you are coming. You are a dear old chap.

Jessie Conrad informs us that Crane was "a frequent visitor" at Pent Farm, the house she and her family had moved to after S.C.'s departure for the war, but this time he didn't go, in spite of Conrad's urgent, almost desperate appeal. He was too busy pushing his rock up the mountain to spare the time for a visit, even as guests continued to pour into the house and he again ran off to Brown's Hotel in London to carry on with his work. Swamped as Crane was during those overcharged months before his final collapse, Conrad was always present in his thoughts, and that held true until the very end.

I can't do any more now, Joseph.

In the last letter Crane ever wrote, on the last day he spent at Brede before traveling to Dover on the death trip into the Black Forest, he barely said a word about himself. Instead, he was thinking about the tough spot his friend was in and searching for a way to help him out of it.

Dear Bennett:

Mrs. Crane writes this at my dictation. We are starting for Dover in the morning. My condition is probably known to you. The wine arrived. Many thanks. I want to say something about the Civil List. As I under-stand it, the fact of having been born outside England does not exclude a man from being taken care of. I have Conrad very much on my mind just now. Garnett does not think it likely that his writing will ever be popular outside the ring of men who write. He is poor and a gentleman and proud. His wife is not strong and they have a kid. If Garnett should ask you to help pull wires for a place on the Civil List for Conrad please do me the last favor of talking about it to that relative of yours who has something to say about these things. I am sure you will.

Yours,

S.C.

5

LIFE AT BREDE BUMPED ALONG BY FITS AND STARTS AS THE CRANES continued to perform their sloppy, improvised duo act, which somehow held together until the end of the year. There were numerous small and large headaches in 1899, but no major catastrophes, and nothing more serious than the standard problems that would have come up in any house-hold as chaotic as theirs. A fire accidentally started in Crane's study by the drunken servant Mack. A thirty-five-shilling fine for failing to procure licenses for the dogs. Or a dispute with a neighboring sheep farmer about those same dogs, who were allowed to roam free and had taken to killing the man's sheep. Jessie Conrad:

One day when we were returning from a long drive (we had been absent for two days) we all gasped and held our noses as soon as the horses turned into the drive.

A sheep's carcass hung from each of the four or five biggest trees bordering the drive in the park. Stephen's face turned deathly pale with anger while he muttered curses under his breath. The horses shied violently at the ghastly objects swinging on a level with their heads. Next morning when I went out the carcasses had all disappeared, and I never heard that Stephen did more than roundly curse the shepherd.

More headaches followed. Not long after the genial specter known as Mrs. Ruedy took herself back to Ohio in early June, another visitor showed up from America—Crane's niece Helen, the oldest of William's five daughters—who had been shipped to England in exchange for the five-hundred-dollar loan the wayward brother had finally wheedled out of the tightwad brother after months of polite but persistent badgering.* On March sixteenth, Crane had written, "In the spring, when all England is green and flowering how would you like to send Helen to us?" and by the end of the month William had sent the money. Crane couldn't have known what he was getting himself into. In the past, Helen had been his favorite niece, a pleasant little girl with a precocious gift for drawing, but now she had turned into an angry, troubled eighteen-year-old girl-woman, and her harsh skinflint father, who had been embroiled in countless discipline battles with her over the past couple of years, was more than happy to dump the problem into his little brother's lap.

Cora took charge, and for the first little while William reciprocated with some longish letters to her about Helen—addressing his new sister-in-law as "My dear Cora" and signing off "affectionately" or "your affectionate brother"—and also made nice with his own brother by offering to send him unobtainable American goodies such as maple syrup and canned corn. Clumsy gestures, perhaps, but an earnest effort to show his gratitude to them, or so it seemed at the time. The judge was especially worried about the "undesirable people" his daughter tended to associate with in Port Jervis ("she is at an age now where she cannot afford to be too democratic"), but he did not get around to sharing those worries with his brother until Helen was already on the ship to England. Not long after her arrival, the Cranes were introduced to Kate Lyon's sister and nineteen-year-old niece Edith, and because the two nieces seemed to hit it off, the Duke and his lady promptly invited the well-mannered, wholly desirable young Miss Ritchie to camp out at Brede with them and serve as a sort of

---

* Not to be confused with Wilbur's daughter Helen R., whose 1934 reminiscence of her uncle has been quoted several times in these pages. Helen R. was born eight years after William's Helen and added the initial to her name to distinguish herself from her older cousin.

unofficial companion to Helen. In her 1954 article about the months she spent there, Ritchie skirts the issue of Helen's conduct with the evasive remark that "Helen was sophisticated in some ways, childish in others, and Stephen thought she needed more education." The truth was that Stephen wanted to banish her from the house for stealing. What she stole, or why she stole, or how she was found out are three more blanks in the story, but after complex negotiations with William (who was scandalized by the incident and fully backed their plan), Helen was sent abroad in September to further her education at the Rosemont-Dézaley School in Lausanne, Switzerland, the same finishing school Ritchie had graduated from that spring. Crane took her there himself, and when Helen's larcenous habits continued with various unpaid loans from her classmates and a preposterous scheme to extort money from the headmistress by convincing her it was a loan for her uncle Stephen, life in Lausanne became so ugly for her that she quit the school on the last day of March 1900, well before the term was over. With nowhere else to put her, the Cranes buried the hatchet and reinstalled Helen at Brede. She stayed on with them for another two months, accompanying her aunt and uncle to Dover, Calais, and Baden-weiler, the only person from the family who was with them at the end, but for all the things she must have said and done while she was in those places, not one word or action has been recorded in any of the chronicles of Crane's life. A shadow who was there but not fully there, the silent niece went back to America with Cora and her uncle's body, attended the funeral in Manhattan, and then slipped off into the shadows again. She was apparently married twice (circumstances unknown) and committed suicide in 1922 at age forty or forty-one.

Dead sheep, accidental fires, and a damaged girl who was sent away and brought back, but the principal headache of 1899 was money, the same headache that had started in S.C.'s earliest days as a writer and was now intensifying into a full-bore migraine, which brings with it the pain of a nail that is hammered continuously through the side of your skull and deep into the folds of your brain. For want of a miracle cure, the challenge was one of stark necessity: How to earn enough by writing enough to become solvent enough to pull the nail out of your head? Pinker was the man Crane had entrusted to perform the operation, the inordinately kind, hardworking agent who floated out cash for stories not yet written, for projects not yet conceived, and in the frenzy of composition that followed in the months they worked together, Pinker was inundated by so many thousands of words to sell here and sell there that he often struggled to keep up with the flow. Crane was expecting to become rich, or at least to get on top of his debts, but as the squandering of nonexistent money continued to increase, his debts increased as well, and he found himself worse off than when he had started. Hence the migraine—and the everlasting nail embedded in his skull.

To Pinker on August sixth, in a typical letter from those months:

> I am mailing you at this time a whacking good Whilomville story—4000 words—and I am agitatedly wiring you at the same time. You are possibly able to forgive me by this time for the way I put upon you. I must have altogether within the next ten days £150—no less, as the Irish say. But, by the same token, I am going to earn it—mainly, in Whilomville Stories for they are sure and quick money. £40 of my £150 have I done yesterday and today, but for all your gods, help me or I perish.

The concluding paragraph of a letter mailed to Pinker the next week:

> If you can stick to your end, all will go finely and I will bombard you so hard with ms that you will think you are living in Paris during the siege.

Cora to Pinker on August thirty-first:

> In the mean time he is going to run very short. He has a wine dealer who threatens to serve papers *tomorrow*, if his bill for £35 is not paid at once. . . .
>
> This has nothing to do with my former request for £20—to enable Mr. Crane to take a few days holiday [to accompany his niece to Lausanne]. . . . The wine man must be satisfied and Mr. Crane must have a change or I fear he will break down & we cant have that.

Cora to Pinker on September thirtieth:

> I am so glad you wrote to him *not* to go to the Transvaal. His health is not fit for it. He had a return of Cuban fever while we were in Paris and he is in no physical condition to stand a campaign no matter how short it may be. . . .
>
> P.S. Please don't let Mr. Crane know I've said a word against the Transvaal.*

---

* A tentative plan by Crane to leave England again to cover the Second Boer War. Nothing came of it. Similar plans to report from St. Helena and Gibraltar also came to nothing.

After a bitter contretemps with Stokes, his new American publisher, Crane received some words of advice from Robert Barr:

> You are all right when you stick to the pen, and are apt to be all wrong when you meddle in business. . . .
>
> You have got things on exactly the right basis now, in leaving Pinker to deal with editors and publishers. Write, write, write, anything but business letters.

After receiving a panicked communication from Cora begging for more money, Pinker responded directly to Crane on October twenty-fourth. It was the first and only time the besieged, put-upon agent expressed the smallest sign of irritation.

> I confess that you are becoming most alarming. You telegraphed on Friday for £20; Mrs. Crane, on Monday, makes it £50; today comes your letter making it £150, and I very much fear that your agent must be a millionaire if he is to satisfy your necessities a week hence, at this rate. Seriously, you pinch me rather tightly. Mrs. Crane says I have "probably advanced money to Mr. Crane that I have not myself yet collected." As a matter of fact, this sum, at present, is £230. I mention this to impress you less with an obligation to me than to yourself. There is a risk of spoiling the market if we have to dump too many short stories on it at once. . . .
>
> . . . I will do my best to try and manage *something* during the next ten days or a fortnight.

Cora shot back with a semi-delusional harangue on the twenty-sixth. The fourth paragraph:

> Now Mr. Pinker, how could you say to Mr. Crane not to dump too many short stories upon the market for fear of spoiling it? This is a fatal thing to say to a writing man. Particularly to Stephen Crane. And how can you think so with an utterly unspoiled and vast American market? Harpers and the Saturday Evening Post and one story to McClures are the only things sold in America *now* and you could sell a thousand short stories of Mr. Crane there if you had them.

That was the worst it ever got. Two days later, Cora wrote Pinker a subdued, perfectly cordial letter, and just five days after that, Crane sent him the "double extra special good thing," which was the last great story he ever wrote, "The Upturned Face."

Pinker continued to stand solidly behind them, and the couple forged on, smiling, always smiling through their troubles, even as their duet of mutual pretend inched toward the final moments of the fourth act.

One must imagine Sisyphus happy.

There was going to be a party. There had to be a party because Edith Ritchie was going away, and how could they let her go without a proper sendoff? "For a long time my family had been clamoring for me to come home," she remembered, "but the Cranes would say they needed me— they would be all alone (alone! with endless guests) in the country, miles from anywhere. Finally, Christmas was in the offing and I *must* go home. 'No,' said Stephen. 'Let's have a real party. We'll have all your family here and your friends and our friends. It will be your party. We'll have a ball and a play.'"

The party would be a three-day, end-of-the-century bash with as many guests as possible, all of them to be housed at Brede for the duration, and the play would be something called *The Ghost*, a collaborative farce engineered by the Cranes with contributions (if only a line or a word) from Henry James, Joseph Conrad, H. G. Wells, Robert Barr, A. E. W. Mason, Edwin Pugh, George Gissing, Rider Haggard, and H. B. Marriott Watson, with musical numbers stolen from the comic operas of Gilbert and Sullivan. The ghost, of course, was Sir Goddard Oxenbridge, the child-eating nobleman who had once ruled over the house where the guests would be gathered.

It was Crane's last prank. He had just finished "The Upturned Face" and was about to launch into a series of articles about the Boer War (about which he had strong opinions) but in the same way he had interrupted the writing of *George's Mother* to whip up the japeries of the *Pike County Puzzle*, he now turned his head in the opposite direction to become the guiding spirit and master of ceremonies for a Carnival of Craziness.

A dying Puck pulls on his boots for a last romp in the woods.

Or, to put it another way: Back against the prison-yard wall, a condemned man looks at the firing squad lined up against him, calmly smokes his last cigarette, and then, rejecting the blindfold they offer him, laughs at his executioners as they lift their rifles and take aim.

There is no doubt that our hero did some dumb things in his short and reckless life, but throwing that party was not one of them. The only problem was that he had miscalculated the distance between the conception of the plan and its execution. Crane's body was giving out on him more quickly than he had thought it would, and when the big moment finally rolled around just after Christmas, three days and three nights of non-stop merriment proved to be more than his system could handle.

Ritchie:

> Cora and I worked like dogs before the party—sending out invitations, hiring extra servants from London. The play had to be written out and typed, each of us typing with two fingers. Music had to be copied and new words written for each song. I painted the scenery: the huge fireplace in the hall was the backdrop. Guest rooms had to be arranged for married couples. Erstwhile big empty rooms fixed up as dormitories, one for men, one for women. An orchestra had to be engaged, cots hired from a local hospital. Cora got the village blacksmith to make dozens of iron brackets, each holding two candles, to hang around the oak-paneled walls of the hall. We made long ropes of holly and greenery and festooned them around the walls. We wrote on cards who-should-take-in-whom to dinner every evening, and put them near each guest's bed.
>
> The cast came a day before the other guests. After a sketchy performance at home, we gave a trial performance of "The Ghost" that afternoon in the village schoolhouse for the school children. When the other guests arrived the next day, we numbered about fifty. We had the real performance that night.

The Conrads and the Wellses were among the fifty, but Mason was the only co-author who took part in the performance. As an experienced actor, he held center stage as the Ghost, and in spite of the harsh winter weather, the auditorium in the Brede village schoolhouse was nearly full. Among the many lines delivered to the audience were Conrad's "This is a jolly cold world," Gissing's "He died of an indignity caught in running after his hat down Piccadilly," and Pugh's "A bird in the hand may be worth two in the bush, but the birds in the bush don't think so." The orchestra mentioned by Ritchie must have been hired to perform at the ball only, since a local paper mentions that "the songs, most of which were encored, were tastefully accompanied on the piano by Mrs. H. G. Wells" and then adds: "At the close of the performance . . . the audience sang, 'For they are jolly good people,' the original word being changed in consideration of the ladies among those acting." Another paper remarked, "The inhabitants of Brede have every reason to be thankful to Mr. and Mrs. Stephen Crane, of Brede Place, for providing them with such a treat. . . . No other charge was made for admission, the whole of the expenses being defrayed by Mr. Stephen Crane, including an addition to the stage, which he has since presented to the School."

Truckloads of money must have been spent to pull off that seventy-two-hour extravaganza—the hired servants, the hired musicians, the rented beds, the dinners for fifty, the breakfasts for fifty—but that was what Puck had asked for, and that was what Puck's wife gave him, and for the first two days and nights he seems to have been in reasonably good form, holding his own, in any case, but then there was the ball on December twenty-ninth, the last late-night frolic, and as the evening dragged on with waltzes, qua-drilles, and an old-fashioned American square dance, with the orchestra clanging out its numbers and Wells romping around the hall on a broom-stick horse, the host began to withdraw into a sullen, edgy silence. In an effort to break his foul mood and force himself back into the spirit of the party, he offered to teach some of his British guests how to play poker, but the men kept talking about other things as he tried to explain the rules, and he finally stood up and said, "In any decent saloon in America, you'd be shot for talking like that at poker." Then he stomped off.

Wells: "He was profoundly weary and ill, if I had been wise enough to see it, but I thought him sulky and reserved. He was essentially the helpless artist; he wasn't the master of his party; he wasn't the master of his home; his life was altogether out of control; he was being carried along."

Perhaps. But the first point was surely correct. Crane was profoundly weary and ill, and late that night, after the musicians had gone home, as he sat downstairs plucking at his guitar, he suddenly passed out. His head fell against the shoulder of the person sitting beside him, and seconds after that blood was pouring from his mouth.

When he regained consciousness, his first thought was to hide what had happened from Cora. She was already upstairs in bed, but someone must have woken her, and no sooner did she come down than Wells was on a bicycle, pedaling through the rain to fetch a doctor.

Not all hemorrhages are fatal. This one turned out to have been a warning, a sign of the troubles that lay ahead, but for the time being the doctor was cautiously optimistic, and by January second Crane was writing a letter to Moreton Frewen's son about *The Ghost* ("a mere idle string of rubbish made to entertain the villagers") and Cora was writing to Pinker that "Mr. Crane is ill again—in bed but is still keeping at his work."

Before he was called away on other business, his current business was

The last photograph of Crane, sitting with his dog Sponge at Brede Place. Taken by Cora, 1900. (COURTESY OF THE UNIVERSITY OF VIRGINIA)

the same as it had always been, and to the degree that he was up to it, he kept on writing. *The O'Ruddy* had taken shape by then and was already out of the starting block (a letter from Pinker on January fifteenth confirmed that he had just received the third and fourth chapters), and wedged in among the political articles and short stories Crane knocked out in the early part of the year, he was also working on a nonfiction money project that Pinker had lined up for him with *Lippincott's Magazine* in America, which entailed writing a series of long articles under the heading "Great Battles of the World." Crane had no time to do the research himself, so the job was handed over to Kate Lyon, who was living in London with her daughter and in need of work. As much out of gratitude to her friends as for the work itself, she passed her days at the British Museum compiling extensive notes on bygone military engagements at New Orleans, Badajoz, Plevna, Solferino, and the Burkersdorf Heights, which Crane would edit and put into final form, but as time went on and the task became too much for him, Lyon wrote the final versions herself. Parallel to all that, and on top of all her other responsibilities, Cora was working with a young engineer named Frederick Bowen on an invention she had been tinkering with since her return from the Greco-Turkish War: a filter for army canteens that would actually work. Other filters had been manufactured before, and every one of them had proved ineffective, but by all accounts Cora's device did what it was supposed to do in all circumstances. If she had been able to carry through with it, perhaps the invention would have brought in enough ready cash to pull out the nail, but time was running short by then, and she never pursued it beyond the earliest stages of the process.

Meanwhile, their money woes continued, as dire and pressing as ever, which leads one to pause for a moment and begin to ask how two such intelligent people could have found themselves—again and again—in the same stupid fix. Most Crane biographers have tended to jump on Cora and hold her responsible, but the couple's overspending was clearly a two-person operation, and Crane was no less guilty than she was. He couldn't help himself. His improvidence was more than just a compulsion or an addiction or a mysterious character flaw, it sat at the very heart of his character and defined who he was. Crane was a gambler, which meant that he felt happiest and most fully alive only when taking risks. The same impulse that had driven him out into a snowstorm in a thin, threadbare jacket to find the story he was looking for, that had compelled him to rush off to wars and expose himself to enemy fire, that had made him the only man in the room willing to jump into a knife fight to stop one man from killing another was also what made it necessary for him to push himself into debt on the home front. Ordinary life, which he understood as well as any slippers-and-pipe office worker, was deeply boring to him, not only because he found it dull and complacent and hypocritical but because it made him feel dead. Overspending put him in danger of losing everything, and how much better it felt to be clinging to the edge of a cliff by his fingernails than to be sitting in a soft chair by a warm, cozy fire. As Otto Carmichael keenly noted after he had spent some time with Crane in Havana: "Danger was his dissipation." And with Cora dangling beside him as they clung to that same perilous cliff, no amount of danger could ever be too much. It's not that he always liked it, and it's not that he didn't suffer because of it, but he needed the cliff in the same way a poker player needs to bet his entire night's winnings on a single turn of a card. And then, unexpectedly, he began coughing up blood.

Ernest B. Skinner, the country doctor who examined Crane on the night of the party, concluded that the damage to the lung had not been severe enough to cause undue alarm. He recommended a period of sustained rest, the standard method of treatment for supposedly mild cases of tuberculosis. Thomas J. Maclagen, the eminent specialist from London who was brought in to look at Crane three months later, recommended a similar course of action. What both of those men failed to understand was that Crane's physical breakdown was being caused by more than just the damage to his lungs. The recurring bouts of Cuban fever were also undermining his strength, and when Crane developed an abscess in his rectum—an anal fistula too deeply embedded to be removed—he suffered greatly, which further undermined his strength. Sitting on a horse was too painful for him now, and the simple act of defecation must have been excruciating. Crane's body was under assault on three fronts, each ailment weakening his resistance to fight the other two, but the doctors continued to focus their attention on his lungs. TB was the scourge of the era, and the immensity of that illness blinded them to Crane's other problems. A leaking roof can cause considerable damage to a house, but if the walls are already buckling and the foundation is already sinking into the ground, it is only a matter of time before the house collapses.

On February second, a luncheon was given in Crane's honor by a wealthy book collector from Hastings. Eleven days after S.C.'s death, a local reporter who had been at the gathering recalled the impression he had made on her that afternoon:

> Already months ago . . . it was easy to see that Stephen Crane's years, if not months, were numbered. In February last I met him at the house of a friend—bibliophile, ornithologist, and amateur artist—living in Hastings. Painful was the contrast between the young author of "The Red Badge of Courage" and the other guests, all of whom were in good health and spirits. Poor Stephen Crane had that white, worn-out, restless look betokening complete nervous exhaustion. He took no tea and did not join in general conversation, but moved about uneasily as if in search of something he could not find.

The next crisis occurred at the end of March. Helen was about to board a train from Lausanne to Paris, and with Crane too occupied with his work to leave his study at Brede, Cora set out on her own to meet the renegade dropout. Her plan was to linger in Paris for a few days and shop for clothes before returning to England. On the thirty-first, within hours of Cora's departure, Crane sent Pinker the twenty-fourth and twenty-fifth chapters of *The O'Ruddy* (the last ones he wrote) along with a request to wire Cora twenty pounds, fearing that "the poor things may be left high and dry in

Paris." Not long after finishing the letter, he suffered the first of two massive hemorrhages, both of them far stronger than the last one. Again, he didn't want Cora to know what had happened, but defying the instructions she was given, Vernall eventually sent a telegram to Paris on April third. Cora came rushing back, and from then until the fifth of June the dimensions of their world grew smaller and smaller until that world was gone.

Maclagen was brought in at the suggestion of someone at the American embassy, who told Cora he was the best lung man in London, but after traveling to Brede and charging fifty pounds for the consultation, the doctor's advice was to hold on and see how things developed. Cora took this as encouraging news, but after having written a check for funds she did not have, she then had to scramble with Pinker to get fifty pounds into her bank account before the check bounced. So it went throughout the month of April and the first part of May.

William to Cora on April seventh: "We are greatly alarmed and grieved over Stephen's condition. We await further news with anxiety." And then: "I fear I cannot help you with money at present. My bank account is very much depleted."

Cora to Clara Frewen on April eleventh: "We moved my husband on Monday night downstairs in the oak room. He seems to get weaker every day and my anxiety is very great. There has been no return of hemorrhage but he suffers so greatly from the abscess, which is too deep-seated to open from the outside while he is in such a weak state. We are in hopes to get him out in the sunshine on warm days."

Cora to Pinker on April eleventh: "He had a quiet day and night with no hemorrhage, and takes his nourishment well. His illness will be a long one and I shall be under great expense.... Now Mr. Pinker, It was a matter of life & death to have the Specialist down. I could not leave any stone unturned. *You* might have not gone to office on Saturday or Friday. I had to write to Lippincott at the same time I wrote to you. One cannot stand on ceremony at such a moment, and indeed I was almost distracted. Pray forgive any seeming lack of courtesy to yourself."

William to his brother on April thirteenth: "There is in our morning paper every day a London dispatch, giving the latest news from you. We find this unsatisfactory, and are anxiously awaiting for letters."

Cora to Wells on April fifteenth: "There has been no hemorrhage now since Monday last. The doctors say that if he pulls through until next Thursday—ten days—that he will be out of danger. Then the future plans will have to be made. I fear that we shall have to give up Brede Place & go to a more bracing place, on the sea."

Cora to Wells on April twenty-fifth: "Stephen is not up to letter writing so I am answering your very cheerful letter to him. I am so anxious about him. The lung trouble seems over! The doctor today, after an examination, said that the right lung was entirely unaffected. The trouble is that this dreadful abscess which seems to open from time to time in the bowels—or rectum, makes him suffer the most awful agony. And it takes away his strength in an alarming fashion. The abscess seems to have upset the bowels too. So he is very weak. Then the *fever* (Cuban fever) comes for an hour or two each day. The chills seems to have stopped the past week. And he hopes within three or four weeks to go on a sea voyage. Write to him when you can. Sick people have fancies that their friends neglect them, and wonder at small number of letters, etc. Of course, I have up to date read all letters first and there are many which I think best he should not see—you understand."

Maclagen to Cora on May second: "I am very sorry to have so bad a report of Mr. Crane. He has shown such good rallying powers in the past that one would not readily take a hopeless view of the case. Should you feel that you would like me to see him again you have only to telegraph and I will arrange to go."

Cora to Pinker on May fifth: "The doctors say that for Mr. Crane to recover he *must* get out of England. The *Black Forest* first. Now this means, an expensive move within the week. Can you manage an advance in some way? Mr. Crane is no worse & the right lung holds out only, this change must be made without delay. We will go to some small Inn in the Black Forrest. & rent Brede Place as it stands. I shall have to take a nurse & the doctor will go with us. Its a *very* expensive Journey but its a matter of life or death and it must be done. Please advise me. Can you cable Stokes to advance or get Metheun to advance or How about Serial? Please reply at once. This climate seems simply death to lung Trouble."

Alfred T. Plant (Moreton Frewen's solicitor) to Cora on May seventh, explaining his client's intention to cover all of the Cranes' debts: "I am in receipt of your letter of the 5*th* inst. and can only say that it was at Mr. Frewen's express wish that I asked for the list of debts as he was most anxious that this trouble should be, if possible, removed. . . . I believe he has written direct to Dr. Skinner & am certain he is doing all in his power to help you."

William to Cora on May tenth: "I have received your telegram and also a letter from Dr. Skinner. We are grieving over the situation, but I really cannot send money, in any amount to make it worth while, at present. It has been years since I have been so hardly pressed as I am now." Followed by: "It looks as if it might be best for Helen to come home."

Conrad to Cora on May tenth:

Your letter distresses me beyond measure and confirms my fears as to
your material situation. It has been the object of my anxiety and of many
sad thoughts. You may imagine that had it been in my power to render
you any sort of service I would not have waited for any sort of appeal.
I've kept quiet because I feel myself powerless. I am a man without connections, without influence and without means. The daily subsistence is
a matter of anxious thought for me. What *can* I do? I am already in debt
to my two publishers, in arrears with my work, and know no one who
could be of the slightest use. It is not even in my power to jeopardize my
own future to serve you. If it had been, such is my affection for Stephen
and my admiration for his genius, that I would so do without hesitation,
to save him. But my future, such as it is, is already pawned. You can't
imagine how much I suffer in writing this to you. I have been almost distracted since I had your letter. Won't Stephen's relations come forward?
    Pardon me for not saying more. I feel too unhappy.

It was a pointless, difficult journey, but the doctors had said it was Crane's
only chance, and even though Cora must have understood how remote
that chance was, she scraped together every penny she could from every
source available to her, most vitally from Moreton Frewen and Lady Randolph Churchill, who solicited funds on her behalf, and left Brede on May
fifteenth with her dying husband, Dr. Skinner, two nurses, niece Helen,
the servant Richard Heather, and the dog Sponge. Crane was carried on a
stretcher to Rye, where he was put in an invalid carriage and conveyed to
Dover with the rest of the party. Cora had booked rooms for them at the
Lord Warden Hotel, overlooking the English Channel, but the waters were
rough that week, too rough to hazard the crossing to Calais, and so they
stayed on longer than expected, nine days in all, during which Cora often
skipped meals to keep them within the boundaries of their narrow budget.
    Conrad came on the sixteenth, Wells on the seventeenth, and Barr on
the nineteenth. "There was a thin thread of hope that he might recover,"
Barr recalled, "but to me he looked like a man already dead. When he
spoke, or rather, whispered, there was all the accustomed humor in his
sayings. I said to him that I would go over to the Schwarzwald in a few
weeks, when he was getting better, and that we would take some conva-
lescent rambles together. As his wife was listening he said faintly, 'I'll look
forward to that,' but he smiled at me, and winked slowly, as much as to say,
'You damned humbug, you know I'll take no more rambles in this world.'"

Wells wanted to see Crane again on the twenty-first, but that was the day the party was planning to leave for the continent, and Cora wrote to him on the twentieth that "Nurses think best for Stephen not to see anyone before starting. Best for him to be quite alone tomorrow, so I must ask you not to come & I *am* sorry." The trip was delayed, however, and then delayed again, which allowed Conrad to come back for another visit on the twenty-third, the day before they finally left. A matter of pure happenstance, but it seems fitting that he should have been the last friend to see Crane alive.

Nineteen years later he wrote:

I saw Stephen Crane a few days after his arrival in London. I saw him for the last time on his last day in England. It was in Dover, in a big hotel, in a bedroom with a large window looking on to the sea. He had been very ill and Mrs. Crane was taking him to some place in Germany, but one glance at the wasted face was enough to tell me that it was the most forlorn of all hopes. The last words he breathed out to me were: "I am tired. Give my love to your wife and child." When I stopped at the door for another look I saw that he had turned his head on the pillow and was staring wistfully out the window at the sails of a cutter yacht that glided slowly across the frame, like a dim shadow against the grey sky.

Jessie Conrad provided a bit more about the events of that last day in her article from 1926:

Conrad told me afterward how he had sat talking to the sick man, who was able to answer only by signs and by a few panting words scarcely above a whisper. That parting glimpse of Stephen lying on the bed with his wonderful eyes fixed on the ships that showed through his open window, the feeble voice, and the stretcher on which he made this final journey, made a deep and lasting impression on my husband's mind. I recall his words when he rejoined me in the hotel . . . "It is the end, Jess. He knows it is all useless. He goes only to please Cora, and would rather have died at home!"

The crossing to Calais on the twenty-fourth, a pause for two or three days at a hotel in Basel, and then on to Badenweiler at the edge of the Black Forest by the twenty-eighth, the last stop on their useless, exhausting, expensive journey to nowhere. They moved into a large house at Luisenstrasse 44, also known as the Villa Eberhardt because the man who owned it was named Eberhardt. The doctor in charge of the case was Albert Fraenkel. With nothing else to do until he died, Crane filled the empty hours by dictating random passages and fragmentary episodes of *The O'Ruddy* to Cora, who was steadily crumbling to pieces herself. Five days of nothing, and then more nothing until she wrote a pair of letters to Frewen on June third, a short one about looking for investors to back her canteen filter, and a long one that concludes: "It is dreadful to *have* to think or write that if God takes my husband from me I shall not know what to do. What shall I do! I can't write more about it."

The letter begins with the belated, agonizing recognition that God will indeed be taking her husband from her, and from then on it rambles haphazardly from the doctor's irritation with the British diagnosis to finding someone to finish the unfinished novel to the cost of everything from lodging to food to medical care to the laundry, since "sometimes Mr. Crane's bed is changed three times a day": "I've only sad news to write you. There seems little hope of cure. The fever seems the thing that cannot be conquered. It is not due alone to the lung but is the remains of the yellow fever and the Cuban fever." Later on she adds: "My husbands brain is never at rest. He lives over everything in dreams & talks aloud constantly. It is too awful to hear him try to change places in the '*open boat*'! I nearly went mad yesterday & the nurse gave me some drug which made me sleep for hours, so I'm fresh again for today. He worries so about his debts and about our not being able to live here. So I told him yesterday that I had £300—cash & since then he has been satisfied. I think it is really worry about my future. so I do everything possible to ease his poor tired mind."

. . . if God takes my husband from me I shall not know what to do. What shall I do!

At some point on the fourth, Crane had his last lucid moment and whispered to Cora, "I leave here gentle, seeking to do good, firm, resolute, impregnable." After she left the room, he dissolved into a twilight of pain and semiconscious delirium. The doctor injected him with morphine, and by three o'clock in the morning he was dead.

The story ends with these anguished, incoherent scribbles written by Cora sometime on the fifth:

Write to D' Skinner about Morphine—
  —"That's what strayed him"—
  "You can cut them she cant."

"Little Butcher, I will tell Skinner how he came to Bali and stole me"—

To nurse: "Did you know D' Bruce never heard of him?" Dr called

June 4th 8 P.M.—Gave morphine injection—went at once to heart, I could see by muscular contraction Dr. saw too, tried to give camphor injection to revive action of heart. Dr said next day: "Can you forgive me?" What did he mean? don't dare to think.

And then, in a letter to Cora on June seventh, this howl from Henry James after learning the news of Crane's death: "What a brutal, needless extinction—what an unmitigated unredeemed catastrophe! I think of him with such a sense of possibilities and powers!"

6

EMBALMED IN FREIBURG AND THEN CARRIED BY TRAIN, BOAT, AND another train to London, the corpse was delivered to a mortuary at 82 Baker Street, which stood almost directly across from 221b, the address of the nonexistent house where the imaginary detective Sherlock Holmes supposedly lived and worked. The man who had invented him, Arthur Conan Doyle, who had known and admired Crane, told a journalist that of all the new American writers, his young friend was the only one who had "the touch of genius." In the days and weeks that followed, dozens of other writers on both sides of the Atlantic offered their comments as well. Because of his fame, and because he had left this "base blue world" so much earlier than anyone could reasonably have expected, his death was front-page news in every town and city across America and Britain. Some of the obituaries were generous, some were neutral, and some were hostile (the *New York Tribune* pounced on him again), but all of them were featured prominently and carried large headlines. Then came the articles by friends and colleagues, beginning with Edward Marshall's "Loss of Stephen Crane—A Real Misfortune to All of Us" on June tenth, followed in the ensuing months by critical assessments of his work, none more valuable than the essay by Wells, who apologized to Cora for not having the heart to show up at the mortuary to view Crane's body. "These things . . . affect me so darkly," he wrote. "I should have found so little comfort & so much distress in this encounter and I have the memory of him in still comfort before that open window & the sea so vividly in my mind, that I do not care to disturb & weaken it by meeting something that was no longer him."

Other friends did not share those qualms, and for the better part of a week they tramped in to have a last look at Crane, whose dead face was visible through a glass window that had been cut into the lid of the coffin. Among those who turned up were Joseph and Jessie Conrad and Curtis Brown. The undertaker's shop was a small, tawdry place, Brown remembered, and when the woman in charge finally understood why he was there, she brightened and said, "Outside, under the archway."

I went out, and through the adjoining archway into a large, square stable-yard, surrounded on three sides by covered bays, and with carts piled up in the middle. There were horses in two or three of the bays; but the rest were empty, except one and there was a coffin on trestles, with the face of my old friend exposed through the glass. He looked as if he had suffered greatly. There was no one else about. I stayed for a time, thinking over our talks together; and then walked slowly away, with a heavy heart.

Grim as that London death parlor must have been, with Crane's coffin shoved into an empty horse stall somewhere out in the backyard, the American funeral was even worse. Crane had told Cora that he wanted to be buried next to his parents in the family plot at Evergreen Cemetery in Hillside, New Jersey, and with William attending to the arrangements for the service at a church in lower Manhattan, Cora left England on June seventeenth with her husband's body, her husband's niece Helen, Sponge, and another dog from Brede named Powder Puff. They arrived in New York on the twenty-seventh, in the middle of an early summer heat wave, and went to the funeral the next morning. Townley was drying out at the Binghamton Asylum for the Chronic Insane, but all of Crane's other siblings were there—Wilbur, Edmund, Mary Helen, George, and William—as well as other members of the Crane family. Among the pallbearers were Ripley Hitchcock, Willis Brooks Hawkins, and John Kendrick Bangs from *Harper's*, but there was no Howells, no Bacheller, no Linson, no Senger, no Indians from the Art Students League building, no young cohort from Crane's past. To preside over the gathering and deliver the sermon, William had chosen Reverend James M. Buckley from Newark, the current editor of the *Christian Advocate*, a onetime friend of Reverend Crane's and a sanctimonious windbag who had little or no idea who Stephen Crane was. He spoke solemnly and at length about the religious zeal of Crane's father and maternal grandfather, bemoaned the tragedy of dying in a foreign land, and compared the dead author to Shelley, "a meteor that glows brightly in the sky and then sinks to rest." To top it off,

The Crane family monument, Evergreen Cemetery, Hillside, New Jersey.
The names and dates of Crane's parents are on the front of the stone.
Crane and his brother Townley are commemorated on one of the sides
and three of their siblings on the other side: George, Wilbur, and Mary Helen.
(PHOTOGRAPH BY SPENCER OSTRANDER)

he ended his eulogy by criticizing Crane's early work for having indulged in too much "word-painting," although in recent years he seemed to have recognized his error and had written some less objectionable works.

Various members of the press had been assigned to cover the event, among them a twenty-year-old Wallace Stevens, fresh out of Harvard and temporarily working as a journalist before going on to law school. Just eight years younger than Crane, the future prince of twentieth-century American poetry returned to his Greenwich Village apartment that afternoon and wrote in his journal:

> This morning I went to the funeral of Stephen Crane at the Central Metropolitan Temple on Seventh Avenue near Fourteenth Street. The church is a small one and was about third full. Most of the people were of the lower classes and had dropped in apparently to pass away the time. There was a sprinkling of men and women who looked literary, but they were a wretched, rag tag, and bob-tail. I recognized John Kendrick Bangs. The

Plaque marking the site of Crane's grave, Evergreen Cemetery, Hillside, New Jersey.
The words read: "Stephen Crane—Author—1871–1900."

whole thing was frightful. The prayers were perfunctory, the choir was worse than perfunctory with the exception of its hymn "Nearer My God to Thee" which is the only appropriate hymn for funerals I ever heard. The address was absurd. The man kept me tittering from the time he began till the time he ended. He spoke of Gladstone + Goethe. Then—on the line of premature death—he dragged in Shelley; and speaking of the dead man's later work he referred to Hawthorne. Finally came the Judgement Day—and all this with most delicate, sweet, and bursal gestures—when the earth and the sea shall give up their dead. A few of the figures to appear that day flashed through my head—and poor Crane looked ridiculous among them. But he lived a brave, aspiring, hard-working life. Certainly he deserved something better than this absolutely commonplace, bare, silly service I have just come from. As the hearse rattled up the street over the cobbles, in the stifling heat of the sun, with not a single person paying the least attention to it and with only four or five carriages behind it at a distance I realized much that I had doubtingly suspected before—There are few hero-worshippers.

Therefore, few heroes.

Cora remained in America for the next three weeks, mostly with her new relatives in Port Jervis and the surrounding countryside, taking walks and swapping stories with her young nieces, who fell for her as all children did whenever she was around, seemed to hit it off especially well with Edmund, who gave her his brother's old scrapbooks, not so well with her sisters-in-law (who probably didn't know what to make of her), and did her best to establish cordial relations with William. Getting along with him was crucial, since they were both involved in the will Crane had drawn up with solicitor Plant at the end of April, which had named William as his American executor and Cora ("my dear wife Cora Howorth Crane") as the beneficiary of all his present and future literary earnings. She therefore had certain financial expectations, and with *Wounds in the Rain, Whilomville Stories*, and *Great Battles of the World* all on the brink of publication, not to mention the royalties from earlier books that were still trickling in, she had every reason not to worry about her immediate future. But William was too clever for her, and little by little, through one legal manipulation after another, he gradually pushed her out. His little brother still owed him money, he argued. All those loans he had sprung for over the years had not been paid back, and now that Cora was responsible for squaring the account, whatever royalties that came in would go to the estate, not to her—until such time that all past debts had been settled, which, needless to say, would be never. All legal and aboveboard, but by any ethical or moral or Reverend Buckley standard, repulsive.

One is reminded of the old Aesop fable about the ant and the grasshopper. The ant (William) spends the summer hard at work preparing for the winter ahead while the grasshopper (Crane) prances around all summer singing his songs and neglecting to think about the future. Winter comes, and when the shivering, starving grasshopper shows up at the ant's door and begs for food, the ant tells him, Sorry, friend, but why should I give you anything? You frittered away the summer on idle amusements while I was in here working my head off, and now you expect me to pay for your mistakes? Too bad, but fair is fair, and I'm not going to do it. So he slams the door on the grasshopper and lets him die in the cold.

William, who had once risked his life to save a black man from lynching, had turned into Uriah Heep. It sounds harsh, perhaps, but what else is one to make of a man whose one published book (1910) bore the title *A Scientific Currency?*

Cora returned to England and floundered around for the better part of a year, trying to make a go of it as a freelance writer. In spite of help and encouragement from the Frewens and Curtis Brown, the results were paltry. Stokes was unwilling to advance any money on her proposed biography of Crane, and although she managed to complete and sell one or two of S.C.'s unfinished stories and to publish a few short pieces of her own, she eventually called it quits and returned to America. For a time, she holed up in rural Kentucky at the house of a woman named Lyda Brotherton, a distant relative of Kate Lyon's, but with her money beginning to run out and her future turning into a brick wall, she left Kentucky, leapfrogged into the past, and resumed the life she had led as Cora Taylor.

"The least boring author's mate in American literary history," as A. J. Liebling described her in 1961, Cora had been with Crane for just three and a half years, and now, after a year of mourning, she had to find a way to go on without him. Returning to Jacksonville might not have been the wisest decision, but the success she had found there in the mid-nineties was the only thing she had ever done on her own that made any sense, and surely it was a better way to spend her life than staring at a brick wall.

To invoke the Book of John again, as Crane does at the end of *The Monster*: He that is without, etc., . . . let him first cast, etc., . . . at her.

It took some time to renew old acquaintances and reestablish contact with the wealthiest and most powerful of her former clients, but once the money wheels had been sufficiently greased to put the business in operation, she found herself presiding over a freshly built establishment at the junction of Davis and Ward Streets that she named "The Court." Two stories tall and wrapping around the corner of the block, it was an out-and-out whorehouse this time, with girls living on the premises and hard liquor added to the drinks menu, but the new sporting club was far more elegant than the Hotel de Dreme had ever been: a full-scale, state-of-the-art pleasure palace for well-heeled men looking for diversion, relaxation, and young female bodies.

The business thrived, and within a couple of years Cora had become a woman of substance and property, but little by little, even as she was preparing to open an annex to the Court in a seaside town twenty miles east of Jacksonville, her inner bearings began to wobble, and her life veered slowly into the Land of Strange. The results were catastrophic.

In the summer of 1905, three months in advance of her husband Stewart's death (which she didn't learn about until 1907), Cora entered into a ridiculous marriage with a twenty-five-year-old no one named Hammond P. McNeil, a clerk for the wholesale liquor merchant who provided the Court with its booze. A strapping, unbalanced boy from a supposedly good family in Waycross, Georgia, McNeil drank, became violent when drunk, and when not drunk was stupid. Just months after the wedding, the marriage had fallen apart, but for unknown reasons they stayed married, and on the last day of May 1907, convinced that Cora was having an affair with nineteen-year-old Harry Parker, her maid's boyfriend, McNeil fired four shots into Parker's body and killed him. He pleaded self-defense

Cora's grave, Evergreen Cemetery, Jacksonville, Florida.
(PHOTOGRAPH BY ELIZABETH FRIEDMANN)

at the trial in December and was acquitted. A little more than a year after that, on another psychotic bender, he bloodied Cora so badly in a domestic brawl that she finally sued for divorce. McNeil vanished from her life, but the fearful symmetry continued: Four years after he married again, McNeil's second wife shot and killed *him*.

By 1910, burned out and living in semi-retirement at her house in Pablo Beach, the now vastly overweight Cora had already suffered a first, mild stroke. On September fourth, a warm Sunday afternoon with dozens of motorcars traveling up and down the beach outside, Cora was parked somewhere in her living room, doing whatever it was she happened to be doing that day. When she looked out the window and saw that one of the cars had hit a soft spot and was bogged down in the sand, she went outside to help. Others were already helping by then, and so she joined in and started pushing with them. It took some time, but eventually, after much exertion in the hot Florida sun, they maneuvered the car back onto solid ground. Worn out and feeling somewhat dizzy, Cora walked back into the house. Considering all she had been through in the years since she had struck out on her own, it was a remarkably peaceful exit. She lay down on the couch, closed her eyes, and never opened them again. The *Evening Metropolis* of September fifth reported the cause of death as "hemorrhage of the brain."

She was forty-five years old. Ten years earlier, Crane had been buried in Evergreen Cemetery in Hillside, New Jersey, and now Cora's body was put into a grave in another Evergreen Cemetery, nine hundred miles away in Jacksonville, Florida. Make of that what you will. Her headstone reads: CORA E. CRANE / 1868–1910. There is no mystery as to why she had wanted to be remembered as Mrs. Crane, but neither is there a mystery to the puzzle of how a forty-five-year-old woman could have been buried at forty-two. She had been shaving off those three years for decades, and now that her life had stopped, she would be able to prolong the ruse forever. A last little show of vanity before she disappeared into the next world.

7

NEWARK. PORT JERVIS. ASBURY PARK. SYRACUSE. LAKE VIEW. SULLIvan County. New York City. Hartwood. Nebraska. Texas. Mexico. Jacksonville. Greece. Oxted. Key West. Cuba. Puerto Rico. Brede. Badenweiler. Hillside.

From The Men in the Storm to An Ominous Baby. From Maggie to The Pace of Youth to The Monster. From Mr. Binks to The Third Violet to The Blue Hotel. From a Pennsylvania coal mine to the electric chair at Sing Sing. From The Red Badge of Courage to The Bride Comes to Yellow Sky. From A Duel Between an Alarm Clock and a Suicidal Purpose to The City Urchin and the Chaste Villagers. From The Black Riders to War Is Kind to A Man Adrift on a Slim Spar. From One Dash—Horses to A Man and Some Others to The Five White Mice. From An Episode of War to The Price of the Harness to The Upturned Face. An Experiment in Misery. The Open Boat. War Memories.

If the people on this veranda ever lower their eyes from the wide river and gaze at these tombstones they probably find that they can just make out the inscriptions at the distance and just can't make them out at the distance. They encounter the dividing line between coherence and a blur.

Senger, Wheeler, Lawrence. Linson and the husky lot. Hawkins. Hubbard. Button and Barr. Frederic. Bacheller, Marshall, Scovel, Davis, and Hare. Billy Higgins. Captain Murphy. McClure . . . Hearst . . . Pulitzer.

Dora Clark. Charles Becker. Theodore Roosevelt.

This poor gambler isn't even a noun. He is kind of an adverb. Every sin is the result of a collaboration. We, five of us, have collaborated in the murder of this Swede.

Lily Brandon Munroe, Nellie Crouse, and Amy Leslie.

Cora Howorth Murphy Stewart Taylor Crane McNeil.

Yes—no. I don't know.

Garland and Howells. James, Wells, and Conrad. They were all older than he was, and each man outlived him by many years.

Sisyphus.

He was no one, then he was someone. He was adored by many, despised by many, and then he disappeared. He was forgotten. He was remembered. He was forgotten again. He was remembered again, and now, as I write the last sentences of this book in the early days of 2020, his books are being forgotten again. It is a dark time for America, a dark time everywhere, and with so much happening to erode our certainties about who we are and where we are going next, perhaps the moment has come to dig the burning boy out of his grave and start remembering him again. The prose still crackles, the eye still cuts, the work still stings. Does any of this matter to us anymore? If it does, and one can only hope that it does, attention must be paid.

It is as if the wounded man's hand is upon the curtain which hangs before the revelations of all existence, the meaning of ants, potentates, wars, cities, sunshine, snow, a feather dropped from a bird's wing, and the power of it sheds radiance upon a bloody form, and makes the other men understand sometimes that they are little.

October 2017–February 2020

NOTES

Abbreviations

Berryman John Berryman, *Stephen Crane* (Sloane, 1950; reprint: Meridian Books, 1962)

C The Correspondence of Stephen Crane, ed. Stanley Wertheim and Paul Sorrentino, 2 vols. (Columbia University Press, 1988)

Conrad Joseph Conrad, Introduction to Thomas Beer, *Stephen Crane: A Study in American Letters* (Knopf, 1923)

Encyclopedia Stanley Wertheim, *A Stephen Crane Encyclopedia* (Greenwood Press, 1997)

Fryckstedt Olov W. Fryckstedt, "Stephen Crane in the Tenderloin" (*Studia Neophilologica* 34 [1962]: 135–63)

Gilkes Lillian Gilkes, *Cora Crane: A Biography of Mrs. Stephen Crane* (Indiana University Press, 1960)

Linson Corwin K. Linson, *My Stephen Crane*, ed. Edwin H. Cady (Syracuse University Press, 1958)

LOF Paul Sorrentino, *Stephen Crane: A Life of Fire* (Harvard University Press, 2014)

Log Stanley Wertheim and Paul Sorrentino, *The Crane Log: A Documentary Life of Stephen Crane 1871–1900* (G. K. Hall, 1994)

SCR Stephen Crane Remembered, ed. Paul Sorrentino (University of Alabama Press, 2006)

Stallman R. W. Stallman, *Stephen Crane: A Biography* (George Braziller, 1968)

Stallman and Gilkes *Stephen Crane: Letters*, ed. R. W. Stallman and Lillian Gilkes (New York University Press, 1960)

Stallman and Hagemann *The New York City Sketches of Stephen Crane and Related Pieces*, ed. R. W. Stallman and E. R. Hagemann (New York University Press, 1966)

Weatherford *Stephen Crane: The Critical Heritage*, ed. Richard M. Weatherford (Routledge and Kegan Paul, 1973)

Works The Works of Stephen Crane, ed. Fredson Bowers, 10 vols. (University Press of Virginia, 1969–1976)

Unless otherwise noted, all quotations of Crane's work are from the one-volume Library of America edition, *Crane: Prose and Poetry*, selected by J. C. Levenson (1984). For the sake of economy, the page references do not appear in the Notes.

Stevie

13 **The family is founded** *C*, 227.

13 **I am not much versed** *C*, 165–67.

16 **His mother's memory** Helen R. Crane, "My Uncle, Stephen Crane," *American Mercury* 31 (January 1934). Subsequent quotations of Helen R. Crane derive from this source. *SCR*, 43–50.

19 **My dear Stephen** *C*, 590.

22 **One day when 2½** *Works* 10:343.

22 **There was a smooth, sandy bar** Edmund B. Crane, "Notes on the Life of Stephen Crane by His Brother, Edmund B. Crane" (Thomas Beer Papers, Yale University Archives). Subsequent quotations of Edmund Crane are from this source. *SCR*, 11–15.

22 **a vigorous lad** Mrs. George Crane, "Stephen Crane's Boyhood," *New York World*, June 10, 1900. SCR, 16.

22 **greatest play as infant boy** *Works* 10:345.

24 **Stephen's most marked characteristic** Wilbur F. Crane, "Reminiscences of Stephen Crane," *Binghamton Chronicle*, December 15, 1900. Subsequent quotations of Wilbur Crane are from this source. *SCR*, 17–19.

24 **he thought his indifference** Letter from Frank W. Noxon to Corwin Knapp Linson, April 14, 1930 (Stephen Crane Collection, Syracuse University Libraries). *SCR*, 76.

25   **That was my first meeting** Post Wheeler and
Hallie E. Rives, *Dome of Many-Colored Glass*
(Doubleday, 1955). Subsequent quotations of
Wheeler are from this source. *SCR*, 23–29.

28   **his mother was small** *Log*, 31–32.

28   **I'D RATHER HAVE—**Works 10:73.

30   **For eleven days we fought** *C*, 295–96.

30   **he must have a dog** Jessie Conrad, "Recollections of Stephen Crane," *Bookman* 63 (April
1926). Unless otherwise noted, quotations of
Jessie Conrad derive from this source. *SCR*,
251–56.

30   **What can be finer** *C*,127.

30   **never appeared so happy** Joseph Conrad,
"Stephen Crane: A Note Without Dates,"
London Mercury 1 (December 1919). *SCR*, 250.

30   **My idea of happiness** *C*, 167.

31   **His horse was always** Charles Michelson,
Introduction to *The Open Boat and Other
Tales of Adventure* (1927); vol. 12 of *The Work
of Stephen Crane*, ed. Wilson Follet (Knopf,
1925–27). Subsequent quotations of Michelson are from this source. Excerpted in *SCR*,
215–21.

31   **How the Donkey Lifted the Hills** *Works*
8:91–94.

32   **secured a heavy buckskin glove** Abraham
Lincoln Travis, "Recollections of Stephen
Crane" (Alumni Folder, Special Collections,
Syracuse University). *SCR*, 61–62.

32   **very quick and active** Mansfield J. French,
"Stephen Crane, Ball Player," *Syracuse
Alumni News* (January 1934). *SCR*, 77–79.

32   **He was the best player** Clarence Loomis
Peaslee, "Stephen Crane's College Days,"
Monthly Illustrator and Home and Country 13
(August 1896). *SCR*, 84–87.

34   **smoked cigars incessantly** From the first of
two short reminiscences by Nelson Greene
sent to Crane scholar Melvin H. Schoberlin
on September 4 and October 3, 1947. Subsequent quotations of Greene derive from
these texts (Stephen Crane Collection, Syracuse University Libraries). *SCR*, 125–33.

34   **My mother . . . was always glad** Edna
Crane Sidbury, "My Uncle, Stephen Crane,
as I Knew Him," *Literary Digest International Book Review* 4 (1926). Subsequent
quotations of Crane Sidbury are from this
source. *SCR*, 50–56.

34   **Uncle Jake and the Bell-Handle** *Works* 8:3–7.

37   **Students . . . roamed** Harvey Wickham,
"Stephen Crane at College," *American Mercury* 7 (March 1926). *SCR*, 63.

38   **My dear Miss Allen** *C*, 212.

39   **'Steve' was my hero** Undated letter from
Armistead Borland to Schoberlin. *Log*,
44–45.

41   WORKERS AT OCEAN GROVE *Works* 8:533–34.

42   THRONGS AT ASBURY PARK *Works* 8:537–38.

42   THE BABIES ON PARADE *Works* 8:539–40.

42   ASBURY PARK *Works* 8:541–43.

42   ASBURY PARK'S BIG BOARDWALK *Works* 8:533–34.

44   **Sophomore gangsters** Ernest G. Smith,
"Comments and Queries," *Lafayette Alumnus*
2 (February 1932). *SCR*, 71.

45   **As for myself, I went** *C*, 166–67.

45   **I did little work** *C*, 99.

46   GREAT BUGS IN ONONDAGA *Works* 8:578–80.

48   **He soon proved himself to be** Clarence N.
Goodwin to Crane scholar Max J. Herzberg
in a letter, November 3, 1921 (Stephen Crane
Collection, Newark Public Library). *SCR*,
79–80.

48   **Having thus promptly and fearlessly**
Frederic M. Lawrence, "The Real Stephen
Crane," typescript, 25 pages (Newark Public
Library). Written at various intervals in the
1920s. Subsequent quotations of Lawrence
are from this source. *SCR*, 110–23.

The Pace of Youth

53   **began the war with no talent** *C*, 97.

54   **clever school in literature** *C*, 63.

54   **They were fantastic and impressionistic**
Willis Fletcher Johnson, "The Launching of
Stephen Crane," *Literary Digest and Inter-
national Book Review* 4 (1926) Subsequent
quotations of Johnson are from this source.
SCR, 38–43.

56   **The Way in Sullivan County** *Works* 8:220–22.

58   **An Explosion of Seven Babies** *Works* 8:267–68.

58   **The Cry of a Huckleberry Pudding** *Works*
8:254–59.

59   **Not Much of a Hero** *Works* 8:211–15.

61   **Shortly after dusk** *Log*, 66.

61   **Mrs. Crane attended** *Log*, 66.

63   **So you lack females** *C*, 44.

64   **"Yer see," said little Alstrumpt** *Log*, 70.

67   **the body was going up** *Log*, 73.

69   **not a handsome man** *Log*, 74.

70   **The Captain** *Works* 8:10–14.

71   **My daughter does not speak French** *LOF*, 94.

71   **you can't find preaching** Linson, 18.

72   **Dearest L.B.** *C*, 55.

74   **Your face is a torturing thing** *C*, 57–58.

75   **My career has been** *C*, 62–64.

76   **Are you coming north** *C*, 112.

79   **Somehow I can't get down** Arthur Oliver,
"Jersey Memories—Stephen Crane," *Pro-*

ceedings of the New Jersey Historical Society
(1931). Subsequent quotations of Oliver are
from this source. *SCR*, 30–36.

82 **uncalled-for and un-American** *Log*, 78.

83 **a bit of random correspondence** *Log*, 78.

83 **slanderous** *Log*, 79–80.

84 **What did you expect** Hamlin Garland,
Roadside Meetings (Macmillan, 1930). Unless
otherwise noted, all subsequent quotations of
Garland derive from this text. *SCR*, 91–102.

84 **was the man who beat me** *LOF*, 101.

105 **Some Hints for Play-Makers** *Works* 8:42–47.

105 **As an irresponsible artistic** *C*, 69.

107 **Commonest name I could think of** Linson,
21.

109 **It is inevitable that you** *C*, 53.

110 **Why Did the Young Clerk Swear?** *Works*
8:33–38.

111 **thrumming chords** Linson, 27.

111 **Cheese it, for God's sake!** *Log*, 86, 88.

113 **the deepest interest** *C*, 49–51.

114 **I sent you a small book** *C*, 51.

114 **but from the glance** *C*, 52.

115 **talking about his work** Stallman and Gilkes, 306.

115 **By a far window** Linson, 28.

116 **slumberous corridors** "The Art Students'
League Building" (in the Library of America edition, 567–68).

116 **the most truthful and unhackneyed**
Weatherford, 37–38.

117 **Modern American literature** Weatherford,
326–31.

117 **Hamlin Garland was the first** *C*, 55.

117 **My first great disappointment** *C*, 232.

118 **I never heard him laugh** Conrad, 20.

121 **Have you finished the "Ominous Baby"** *C*,
56.

121 **The little chap** *Log*, 106.

126 **is one of the perfectly imagined** Berryman,
69.

127 **On his return in October** Letter from
Frederick C. Gordon to Thomas Beer, May
25, 1923 (Thomas Beer Papers, Yale University Archives). Subsequent quotations of
Gordon are from this source. *SCR*, 138–40.

128 **My brother, Edmund** William Howe Crane
to Thomas Beer, November 21, 1922 (Thomas
Beer Papers, Yale University Archives). *Log*,
81.

128 **The Darkest Hour in the Life of Stephen
Crane** R. G. Vosburgh, *Criterion* (1901).
Subsequent quotations of Vosburgh are
from this source. *SCR*, 133–36.

129 **I have not been up to see you** *C*, 65.

129 **If I had a new suit** Linson, 3, 8.

130 **Ah, haggard purse** *Works* 10:74.

131 **I deliberately started out** Letter from Louis
C. Senger to Hamlin Garland, October 9,
1900. Stallman and Gilkes, 319.

132 **thin—almost cadaverous** Edward Marshall,
"Loss of Stephen Crane—A Real Misfortune to All of Us," *New York Herald*, June 10,
1900. Unless otherwise noted, subsequent
quotations of Marshall derive from this text.
SCR, 226–27.

133 **Crane shed his long rain ulster** Linson, 2.

133 **I wonder that some** Linson, 37.

135 **The greatest damage** *Log*, 93.

136 **That is great!** Letter from David Ericson
to Ames W. Williams, November 4, 1942
(Tweed Museum of Art, University of Minnesota, Duluth). *SCR*, 136–38.

136 **It is beyond me** *C*, 57.

136 **There is another whom** *Log*, 99.

137 **There is unquestionable truth** *Log*, 100.

137 **I've moved now** *C*, 65.

139 **He brought with him a bundle** Irving Bacheller, *Coming Up the Road* (Bobbs-Merrill,
1928). Unless otherwise noted, subsequent
quotations of Bacheller derive from this text.
SCR,149–50.

139 **much smaller and to my mind** *C*, 81.

139 **Beg, borrow or steal** *C*, 80.

140 **My dear friend** *C*, 79.

141 **and on emerging, met Stephen** Curtis
Brown, *Contacts* (Casell, 1935). Subsequent
quotations of Brown are from this source.
SCR, 140–42.

141 **If Mr. Crane is careful** *Log*, 117.

142 **promised himself to burn the novel** Willis Brooks Hawkins published three short
pieces about Crane in his "All in a Lifetime" newspaper column in the 1920s: "The
Genius of Stephen Crane," "Stephen Crane
Struggles," and "Stephen Crane Flinches."
In the second one he writes: "He afterward
assured me he would have burned the manuscript." Unless otherwise noted, subsequent
quotations of Hawkins derive from these
texts. *SCR*, 165–69.

142 **At the end of February** Linson, 58.

146 **slept like a healthy baby** Untitled reminiscence sent by William Waring Carroll to
Thomas Beer, March 20, 1924 (Thomas Beer
Papers, Yale University Archives). *SCR*,
144–46.

147 **It was a fearful day** Linson, 59.

147 **Two men stood regarding** *Works* 8:304.

154 **Sailing Day Scenes** *Works* 8:302–5.

157   **Heard on the Street Election Night** *Works* 8:333–37.

194   **One cannot go down in the mines** This paragraph and the three that follow are in *Works* 8:607–8.

195   **The birds didn't want** Linson, 70.

196   **They came, and I wrote them** Linson, 49–50.

197   **Tell me not in joyous numbers** Daniel Hoffman, *The Poetry of Stephen Crane* (Columbia University Press, 1957), 41. Hoffman adds that the lines are on a "random sheet in the Columbia Stephen Crane Collection . . . half covered with doodles." Crane turns Longfellow's "mournful numbers" into "joyous numbers" but keeps "We can make our lives sublime" intact.

197   **Crane is the most important** Berryman, 169.

198   **pointed to a pinned-up squib** Linson, 51–52.

199   **these things are too orphic** *C*, 75.

200   **Mr. Howells took from his shelves** *Bookman* (April 1901). Weatherford, 80–81.

200   **the Aubrey Beardsley of poetry** Henry Thurston Peck, *Bookman* (April 1901). Weatherford, 67.

203   **rather die than do it** Cited in Linson, 56.

203   **Mr. Barry read the poems** *Log*, 71.

203   **the glowing report** Linson, 56.

204   **A Night at the Millionaire's Club** *Works* 8:280–83.

207   **A Christmas Dinner Won in Battle** *Works* 8:82–88.

207   **Dollars damn me** *The Letters of Herman Melville*, ed. Merrell R. Davis and William H. Gilman (Yale University Press, 1960), 128.

209   **talk reveals, it lightens** Linson, 73.

210   **a certain William B. Kelsey** *LOF*, 141.

223   **Steve was happy there** Linson, 75–76.

223   **a photograph, a funny poem** *LOF*, 143.

223   *Pike County Puzzle* *Works* 8:608–35.

224   **The "Puzzle"** *Log*, 112.

225   **I would like to hear from you** *C*, 72.

226   **We disagree on a multitude** *C*, 73–74.

228   **Greed Rampant** *Works* 8:7–10.

229   **I would like to know** *C*, 245.

229   **intelligent appearance** Quoted in *LOF*, 413n14. The translation of Cahan has been slightly emended.

230   **Tales of the Wyoming Valley** "The Battle of Forty Fort," "The Surrender of Forty-Fort," and "'Ol' Bennet' and the Indians." *Works* 8:137–54.

230   **butchers . . . idiotic murderers** Richard White, *The Republic for Which It Stands: The United States During Reconstruction and the Gilded Age, 1865–1896* (Oxford University Press, 2017), 646–47. Howells's remarks were originally published in "Editor's Study," *Harper's New Monthly Magazine*, January 1891.

231   **The first one was played** "Harvard University Against the Carlisle Indians." *Works* 8:669–73.

231   **Kill the Indian** Quoted by Princeton history professor Tera W. Hunter in "The Long History of Child-Snatching," *New York Times* op-ed piece, June 3, 2018.

234   STEPHEN CRANE IN MINETTA LANE *Works* 8:399–406.

236   **It was a woman!** *C*, 212–13.

236   **a young woman named Grace Hall** *LOF*, 137.

237   **had a hankering after the women** Letter from John Northern Hilliard to Thomas Beer, February 1, 1922. Unless otherwise noted, subsequent quotations of Hilliard derive from this source. *SCR*, 162–63.

238   **My impression is that the building** Harry B. Smith, *First Nights and First Editions* (Little, Brown, 1931). *SCR*, 164–65.

238   **bent upon the pavement** Robert H. Davis, Introduction to *Tales of Two Wars* (1925), in vol. 2 of *The Work of Stephen Crane*, ed. Wilson Follett (Knopf, 1925–27), ix–xxiv. Excerpted in *SCR*, 154–55.

240   **Against the window** Linson, 2.

241   **Fate sets its stamp** *Works* 10:344.

243   **It was impossible at any time** Linson, 108, 110.

246   **Dear Stevie** and **Good heavens!** *C*, 85.

246   **Dear Mr. Hitchcock: I have not** *C*, 217.

247   **the spunkiest fellow out** *New York Press*, January 5, 1897. *Log*, 238.

248   **Dear Mr. Hitchcock: Of course eccentric** *C*, 213.

249   **My dear Miss Hill** *C*, 208–9.

250   **Great heavens! What a green voice!** *Log*, 188.

250   **an early case of tuberculosis** As Sorrentino speculates in *LOF*, 165.

251   **I can't wait ten years** Willa Cather (writing under the name Henry Nicklemann), "When I Knew Stephen Crane," *Library* (Pittsburgh) vol. 1 (June 23, 1900). Unless otherwise noted, further quotations of Cather derive from this source. *SCR*, 173–78.

251   **Dear Budge** *C*, 96.

251   **Stephen Crane, representing** *Log*, 124–25.

255   **As far as myself** *C*, 97 (the only paragraph of the letter published in Pease's article).

255   **I had to build up** *C*, 99.

256   **If legend is to be believed** The story comes

from Edith Lewis, Cather's longtime friend and companion. *SCR*, 342n4.

258 **Garnett on Crane** *Academy*, December 17, 1898. Weatherford, 225–29.

260 **Mon ami Linson** *C*, 98.

261 **I have always believed** *C*, 128.

261 **a great number of small corrections** *C*, 100.

262 **To my honor** *Log*, 128.

262 **The quiet demeanor** *Log*, 130.

263 **five months after his death** "Galveston, Texas, 1895," *Westminster Gazette*, November 6, 1900.

263 **a most intolerable duffer** *C*, 101.

264 **The last glimpse** Frank H. Bushick, *Glamorous Days: In Old San Antonio* (Naylor, 1934). Cited in Linda H. Davis, *Badge of Courage: The Life of Stephen Crane* (Houghton Mifflin, 1998).

265 **the lazy, alcoholic, gambling life** Berryman, 112.

265 **The bull-fighters** "The City of Mexico," *Works* 8:429–32.

266 **Out from behind** "The Viga Canal," *Works* 8:432–35.

266 **The burro, born in slavery** "Stephen Crane in Mexico I," *Works* 8:438–44.

266 **On money and prices** "Free Silver Down in Mexico," *Works* 8:444–46.

266 **On pulque** "A Jug of Pulque Is Heavy," *Works* 8:356–59.

271 **I am engaged at last** *C*, 123.

271 **I did hear about** Written by Edna F. Crane, one of Edmund's daughters. A photocopy of the letter was given to the author by Paul Sorrentino.

271 **Just as abruptly** Linson, 87.

273 **There is not a line of poetry** *Chicago Daily Inter-Ocean*, May 11, 1895. *Log*, 132.

273 **because I am not in very good health** *C*, 104.

273 **Captain Kidd . . . Washington** *LOF*, 161.

273 **The shanty on the roof** Irving Bacheller, "Authors' Associations," *Manuscript* 1 (1901). *Log*, 132–33.

274 **I remember perfectly** Amy Lowell, Introduction to *The Black Riders and Other Lines*, vol. 6 of *The Work of Stephen Crane*, ed. Wilson Follett (Knopf, 1926).

275 **I see they have been pounding** *C*, 111.

275 **In their futility and affectation** Weatherford, 66.

275 **Is this poetry?** Weatherford, 67.

275 **vigorous earnestness** Weatherford, 68.

275 **a true poet** Weatherford, 63, 65.

276 **I saw a meter measuring gas** *Log*, 139.

277 **The one thing that deeply pleases me** *C*, 195.

278 **It is not in any sense** *C*, 171.

278 **It is good that you like** *C*, 180.

283 **As a matter of fact** *C*, 116.

283 **grotesque tales** *C*, 111.

284 **I am cruising around** *C*, 118.

284 **Dear Willis: It's dramatic criticism** *C*, 121.

284 **Dear old man** *C*, 122.

285 **Mr. Stephen Crane, the author** Weatherford, 108.

285 **has now attempted** Weatherford, 91.

286 **interest which you have shown** *C*, 115.

286 **Your New Year's greeting** *C*, 188–89.

286 **a chromatic nightmare** *Log*, 143.

286 **a vicious satire** Weatherford, 140–41.

286 **The *New York Times*** Weatherford, 89.

287 **Sydney Brooks** Weatherford, 101.

287 **this mysteriously unknown youth** Weatherford, 115, 116.

288 **I had just become well habituated** *C*, 192.

289 **My dear Willis: There are none** *C*, 189.

289 **Dear Mr. Hitchcock: I fear that when** *C*, 191.

290 **I lost my temper** *C*, 145.

291 **My dear Willis: The brown October** *C*, 127.

292 **the story is working out** *C*, 128.

292 **I am working out-of-sight** *C*, 134.

292 **The novel is one-third completed** *C*, 136.

292 **The novel is exactly half finished** *C*, 140.

292 **The new novel is two-thirds done** *C*, 144.

292 **I have been frantically hustling** *C*, 148.

292 **Thank you for your kind words** *C*, 161.

293 **I think it is well** *C*, 204.

293 **Before "The Red Badge"** *C*, 230. To *Demorest's Family Magazine*, May 1896.

327 **a weak sister** The comments from Buffalo, New York, Brooklyn, Springfield, and Providence are all cited in *Log*, 255, 258.

327 ***Godey's Magazine*** Weatherford, 214–15.

329 **The dinner scheme** *C*, 175.

330 **a magazine of that kind** *LOF*, 178–81.

330 **might as easily have been green** *C*, 110n1.

330 **trusting you will not** *C*, 109.

331 **It was difficult for the world** Amy Lowell, Introduction to *The Black Riders and Other Lines*, xxii, xxvi.

331 **Recognizing in yourself** *C*, 137.

331 **you may answer** *C*, 138–39.

332 **I am a very simple person** *C*, 138.

332 **when I think I was low enough** *C*, 139–40.

332 **admire the valiant Philistines** *C*, 108.

332 **I have mapped out** *C*, 154–55.

333 **If you reach the Genesee** *C*, 156–57.

334 **that dinner, held** Claude Bragdon, *Merely Players* (Knopf, 1905). *SCR*, 169.

334 **Thursday evening** *SCR*, 168–69.

335 **Years later** *SCR*, 341–42. Cited in n257.

335 **Mr. Crane responded** *Log*, 156.

336 **the irrepressible mediocrity** *Log*, 157.

336 **the fag-end of the century** *Lotus*, March 1896. *Encyclopedia*, 165.

336 **Hubbard and Taber think** *C*, 162–63.

337 **prim, thoroughly conventional** As described in *Log*, 123.

339 **I do not suppose** *C*, 162–63.

340 **a man in Boston** *C*, 170–72.

341 **How dreadfully weary** *C*, 180–83.

341 **served as a foot soldier** *LOF*, 411n28.

342 **Your recent confession** *C*, 200–203.

343 **Dear me, how much** *C*, 207–8.

343 **The following year** *Encyclopedia*, 78.

345 **I am very glad** *C*, 196.

345 **I have dispensed with** *C*, 197.

345 **I have carefully plugged** *C*, 200.

345 **Maggie was born** *C*, 206–7.

345 **I will begin to drive Maggie** *C*, 214.

345 **the proofs make me ill** *C*, 224.

346 **I am writing a story** *C*, 175.

347 **gradually learning things** *C*, 214.

347 **You may see me back** *C*, 218.

347 **Washington pains me** *C*, 219.

348 **I think the agreement** *C*, 192.

348 **Don't go to Bacheller or McClure** *C*, 254.

348 **Reynolds (1864–1944)** *Encyclopedia*, 293.

349 **Evidently the change** *Works* 3, Introduction, xxxv.

350 **prompt sympathy** *C*, 200.

354 **He puts on paper the grossness** *Log*, 185–86.

354 **the hand of an artist** Weatherford, 42.

354 **He's a good boy** *Log*, 196.

354 **There is a curious unity** Weatherford, 47.

355 **The wonder of it** Weatherford, 48.

355 **It is of course** *C*, 295.

354 **as three young exponents** *Log*, 208.

356 **enormous room at the top** *Log*, 192.

361 **In common with** *C*, 130.

361 **would be very glad** *C*, 133.

361 **this lieutenant is** *C*, 221.

361 **his uncle Wilbur Peck** *LOF*, 39–40.

381 **How much money** *C*, 244.

381 **It is likely that Crane met** *Encyclopedia*, 278.

381 **McClure was toying** *LOF*, 197.

381 **Court opens at ten** *C*, 241.

382 **I am much obliged** *C*, 249.

383 **the remote Port Jervis Evening Gazette** The three articles are so obscure that they were still unknown when the ten-volume University Press of Virginia edition of Crane's works was released in the 1970s. Discovered by Crane scholar Joseph Katz, they were first published in Katz's 1983 article "Ste-

phen Crane: Metropolitan Correspondent," *Kentucky Review* 4, no. 3 (1983): 39–51.

385 **like a man in trouble** The lunch and Garland's comment are reported in *LOF*, 199.

386 **I've been having chuck** Edwin G. Burrows and Mike Wallace, *Gotham: A History of New York City to 1898* (Oxford University Press, 1999), 959.

386 **he built a fortune** *LOF*, 195–96.

386 **The Tenderloin is more** *Works* 8:392.

387 **a notorious hangout** *LOF*, 204.

392 **the young woman denied** Stallman and Hagemann, 220–21. The newspaper from which the article was reprinted is unidentified. It was found in a scrapbook kept by Crane and is now in the Stephen Crane Papers at Columbia University's Rare Book and Manuscript Library.

394 **I was strongly advised** Stallman and Hagemann, 224–25.

395 **Stephen Crane, novelist** Fryckstedt, 148–49.

395 **Everyone who thinks** Fryckstedt, 149.

397 **A Detail** *Works* 8:111–13.

400 **In the Tenderloin: A Duel** *Works* 8:384–87.

403 **the veriest filth** *Wave*, November 7, 1896. *Log*, 218.

405 **Yen-Hock Bill** *Works* 8:396–99.

405 **Diamonds and Diamonds** *Works* 8:114–18.

405 **The Tenderloin as It Really Is** *Works* 8:188–92.

407 **The Devil's Acre** *Works* 8:664–69.

410 **it was long considered** Mike Dash, *Satan's Circus: Murder, Vice, Police Corruption, and New York's Trial of the Century* (Rivers Press, 2008), 329.

411 **Filled with faces** F. Scott Fitzgerald, *The Great Gatsby* (Charles Scribner's Sons, 1925; reprint, Scribner, 2004), 70.

411 **On September 20, 1896** Stallman and Hagemann, 232.

411 **On October second** Fryckstedt, 151.

411 **Stevie Crane seems** Stallman and Hagemann, 231.

413 **There is not an atom** Stallman and Hagemann, 234–35.

415 **leaned against a window** Stallman and Hagemann, 236. From a partial report written before the trial had ended, *New York Journal*, October 16, 1896.

415 **the women with artificial manners** Stallman and Hagemann, 243. *New York Journal*, October 17, 1896.

415 **another woman of the streets** Stallman and Hagemann, 237. *New York Journal*, October 16, 1896.

415   **a legendary prostitute** Fryckstedt, 155, quoting *New York City Folklore*, ed. B. A. Botkin (Random House, 1956), 318–19.

420   **nothing so much** Edmund Morris, *The Rise of Theodore Roosevelt* (Ballantine, 1980), 490.

421   **a gallant gentleman** Stallman and Hagemann, 254. *New York Journal*, October 18, 1896.

421   **a man who had not violated** Stallman and Hagemann, 253. *Brooklyn Daily Eagle*, October 17, 1896.

421   **At nine o'clock** Pieced together from *Log*, 217; Stallman and Hagemann, 229; and Fryckstedt, 162.

422   **A man who possessed** Fryckstedt, 161–62.

423   **I forgot to mention** *C*, 266.

423   **Howells was apparently** Berryman, 146. The source is unnamed. Berryman's sentence reads: "'Mr. Howells was greatly distrest by the incident,' one friend recalled in 1924, 'until I put the matter before him in its true light.'"

423   **small hand** Morris, 490.

424   **You knew this fellow Crane** Cecil Carnes, *Jimmy Hare, News Photographer: Half a Century with a Camera* (Macmillan, 1940), 128–29. The full passage is reprinted in *Log*, 210–11.

425   **Garland sold his inscribed copy** *LOF*, 114.

428   **claim that she was pregnant** A note by Marlene Zara in the Ohio State University Library reads, "Mrs. Anthony told me that Hawkins told her that Amy had 'framed' Crane, saying she was pregnant, in an effort to get Crane to marry her." *C*, 262.

428   **totaling $776.50** *Log*, 218.

429   **I am broke** Hilt and Wertheim, 264.

430   **My Blessed Girl** *C*, 268–69.

430   **My dearest** *C*, 269.

431   **In case you see Amy** *C*, 267.

431   **My own Sweetheart** *C*, 270–71.

432   **My Beloved** *C*, 271.

Exile

433   **No doubt a winking nod** *Log*, 213.

434   **We are troubled occasionally** *C*, 271.

434   **The Filibustering Industry** *Works* 9:94–99.

435   **in case my journey is protracted** *C*, 267.

435   **perfectly satisfactory** *C*, 264–66.

437   **the 1920 census report** Hilt and Wertheim, 265.

437   **being closely watched** *Daily Florida Citizen*, December 2, 1896. Quoted in Linda H.

Davis, *Badge of Courage: The Life of Stephen Crane* (Houghton Mifflin, 1998), 174.

439   **Her great-grandfather** See Gilkes, 30–37, for the history of Cora's family.

440   **during a difficult pregnancy** Information on Cora's mother's death is from a conversation with Elizabeth Friedmann, who is currently at work on a new biography of Cora Crane.

440   **Sometimes I like to sit at home** A grateful salute to Elizabeth Friedmann for providing the source of this quotation as well as the two others on p. 440 and the fourth on p. 444. Robert Hitchens, "Reggie Hastings in Society: A Green Carnation," excerpted in *Current Literature* (December 1894), 543.

440   **If more allowance** Edmund Pendleton, *One Woman's Way* (Appleton, 1893), 66.

440   **I am a strange woman** W. K. Clifford, *Love-Letters of a Worldly Woman* (Harper & Brothers, 1892), 73.

440   **an all around man** *Evening World*, December 26, 1894.

444   **Whatever is too precious** Samuel Rutherford Crockett, *The Lilac Sunbonnet*, serialized in *Current Literature* (December 1894), 553.

446   **handsome, of some real refinement** Letter from Ernest W. McCready to Benjamin R. Stolper, January 22, 1934 (Stephen Crane Papers, Columbia University). Unless otherwise noted, subsequent quotations of McCready derive from this source. *SCR*, 204–12.

446   **guiding star** Gilkes, 57.

446   **The first thing my mouse** James E. Kibler Jr., "The Library of Stephen and Cora Crane," *Proof: The Yearbook of American and Bibliographic Studies*, ed. Joseph Katz (University of South Carolina Press, 1971), 221. *Log*, 226.

447   **Brevity is an element** *C*, 269.

447   **To an unnamed sweetheart** *C*, 270.

447   **By the end of 1896** Stallman, 244, on the two successful and two failed attempts by the *Commodore*.

447   **arms or sausages** *Florida Times-Union*, December 3, 1896. *LOF*, 219.

447   **Certainly I will** *Florida Times-Union*, December 3, 1896. *Log*, 220.

448   **as the representative** *Log*, 232.

448   **Are you fellows** "Stephen Crane's Own Story," *New York Press* and other papers, January 7, 1897. In the Library of America edition, 875–84.

449   **even old sailors** Stallman, 247.

449   **the water gained upon us** Stallman, 246.

449 **The dynamite was** Stallman, 247.

450 **That newspaper feller** Stallman, 248.

451 **He reminded me of George Washington**
Horatio S. Rubens, *Liberty: The Story of Cuba*
(Brewer, Warren & Putnam, 1932), 155. *Log*,
237–38.

454 **fear the worst** *C*, 274. From a clerk at the St.
James Hotel who was providing Cora with
updates on the situation.

454 **Telegram received** *C*, 274.

454 **Congratulations on plucky** *C*, 275.

454 **Come by special today** *C*, 276.

454 **They sat in a corner** "The Day That Stephen
Crane Was Shipwrecked," *Daytona Beach
News Journal*, April 22, 1962.

455 **Where's that album?** *LOF*, 225.

455 **I am unable to write** *C*, 277.

455 **a newspaper from Asbury Park** The article
from the unidentified paper is in the Syracuse University Library.

455 **Seven of the Commodore's men** *C*, 277.

455 **manly bearing** *C*, 279. From a letter written
by Hawkins on behalf of the Lantern Club.

455 **Thanks awfully old man** *C*, 278.

455 **a bright yellow halo** Gilkes, 62.

456 **so worn out** *New York Press*, January 7, 1897.
Gilkes, 62.

456 **rather slouchy** Branch Cabell and A. J.
Hanna, *The St. Johns: A Parade of Diversities*
(Farrar & Rinehart, 1943), 281. Quoted in
Linda H. Davis, *Badge of Courage*, 189.

457 **to go to Cuba** *Log*, 240.

457 **I am feeling stronger** *Log*, 240.

458 **The yearly ball** *LOF*, 234–35.

458 **looked like a man from a grave** *C*, 263.

458 **In the presence of extraordinary** Wallace
Stevens, *Opus Posthumous* (Knopf, 1957), 165.

476 *la grande maladie* Charles Baudelaire, *Mon
Coeur Mis à Nu: Journal Intime* (published
posthumously, 1887). Reprint, La Collection
Électronique de la Bibliothèque Municipale
de Lisieux, 1999.

477 *Roads of Adventure* Ralph D. Paine (Houghton Mifflin, 1922). *SCR*, 191–92.

478 **Wire here Heinemans** *C*, 280.

478 **To Lyda** *C*, 280.

478 **My dear Will** *C*, 281.

481 **a riotous welcome** and the four ensuing
paragraphs: Linson, 99, 101, 110. In the first
sentence of the final paragraph, he errone-
ously gives Crane's age as twenty-six, which
I have silently corrected.

482 **Mr. Stephen Crane** *Log*, 247.

483 **"Maggie" should be put beside** Weatherford, 58.

483 **stuffed parrot** *C*, 186.

484 **the last word** Stallman, 268.

484 **very modest sturdy and shy** *LOF*, 239.

484 **a bi-roxide blonde** Stallman, 268.

484 **I left Athens** Stallman, 268.

484 **While Stephen considered** Gilkes, 74.

486 **I expect to get a position** *C*, 285.

486 **the wild ass** *Works* 9:18.

487 **My maid who grumbled** "Imogene Carter's
Adventure at Pharsala," *Works* 9:270.

487 **He has not seen as much** *Log*, 251.

487 **I spent most of the time** "Imogene Carter's
Pen Picture of the Fighting at Velestino,"
Works 9:274.

487 **Stephen Crane is here** *Log*, 260–61.

488 **Bunked on Floor** "Manuscript Notes,"
Works 9:72.

488 **a beautiful town** "The Blue Badge of Cowardice," *Works* 9:45.

488 **mouse ill** *Log*, 253.

490 **How Novelist Crane** *Log*, 253–54.

491 **I have seen a battle** *Log*, 260.

491 **So the enemy withdrew** "The Blue Badge of
Cowardice," *Works* 9:45.

493 **A Fragment of Velestino** *Works* 9:27–44.

496 **Mr. Stephen Crane's letters** *Works* 9:49–53.

499 **you ought to be very** *LOF*, 250.

500 **the most thoroughly abused** John N. Hilliard, "Stephen Crane," *New York Times*, July
14, 1900. *LOF*, 249.

500 **three notches above** *The Chronology of American Literature*, ed. Daniel Burt (Houghton
Mifflin, 2004), 289.

502 **a butler in shirt sleeves** Stallman, 305.

503 **chief-house-maid** *C*, 300.

503 **southern hot biscuits** Gilkes, 121.

503 **very vivid and agreeable** Stallman, 303.

503 **rotten bad** *C*, 306; to Reynolds, October
1897.

505 **I have not written** *C*, 294.

506 **My dear Harry** *C*, 295.

506 **We were almost killed** *C*, 300.

507 **from London to Glasgow** "The Scotch
Express," *Works* 8:739–51. I have used the
information provided by Stanley Wertheim's
dependable *Encyclopedia* for the approximate
date of the trip on the Scotch Express as well
as the route S.C. and Cora followed between
England and Ireland, but as with so many
other events in Crane's life, both the date
and the itinerary are open to question. Writing to his brother Edmund from Ireland on
September 9, Crane says, "Next week I am
going to Scotland for McClure" (*C*, 296).
In a letter written to Reynolds sometime

in October, he says, "As for my existing contracts there are only two. I. To write an article on the engine ride from London to Glasgow for the McClures. II. To give them my next book" (*C*, 305). With three possible dates to choose from, it is impossible to know which one is correct. In the long run, however, the *when* is less important than the *what*. We know that Crane traveled from London to Glasgow on the Scotch Express sometime in August, September, or October 1897 and that he wrote about the experience in an article published in January 1899 by *McClure's Magazine* in America and *Cassell's Magazine* in England.

511 **The first of the sketches, "Queenstown"** *Works* 8:483–86.

515 **An Old Man Goes Wooing** *Works* 8:495–98.

516 **My dear Amy** *C*, 297–98.

517 **embedded in Crane family lore** *LOF*, 264–65.

518 **Another presence in Crane's** *LOF*, 266.

554 **They came in hordes** Berryman, 202–3.

554 **out of the ardent grasp** *C*, 305–6.

555 **I have been in England** *C*, 300–303.

564 **speaks and acts like a Frenchman** Written on the reverse side of a detached page bearing an inscription from Conrad to the Cranes—"with the Author's / regard." Cora's text is a summary of Conrad's life, up to and including his change of address to Pent Farm in 1899. *C*, 342n1.

564 **We shook hands** Conrad, 6. Except for passages from letters, all of Conrad's remarks in this chapter are taken from his Introduction to Thomas Beer's biography of Crane.

565 **an approving grunt** On the subject of friendship between novelists, I offer this example from my own life: a letter I wrote to one novelist friend about my long friendship with another novelist: "We communicate by emitting short grunts, reverting to a kind of shorthand language that would be incomprehensible to a stranger. As for our own work (the driving force of both our lives), we rarely even mention it." Paul Auster and J. M. Coetzee, *Here and Now: Letters 2008–2011* (Viking, 2013), 5.

565 **with the greatest regard** *C*, 309.

566 **too good, too terrible** *C*, 310.

566 **I must write to you** *C*, 312–13.

568 **I had Crane here** *The Collected Letters of Joseph Conrad*, ed. Frederick R. Karl and Lawrence Davies (Cambridge University Press, 1983), 416. *Log*, 281.

568 **would retract them** ". . . a wonderful artist in words whenever he took a pen in his hand. Then his gift came out—and it was seen to be much more than a felicity of language. His impressionism of phrase went really deeper than the surface." "Stephen Crane: A Note Without Dates." *SCR*, 250.

568 **a worthy pendant** Conrad: *The Critical Heritage*, ed. Norman Sherry (Routledge and Kegan Paul, 1973), 13.

568 **W. L. Courtney** *Daily Telegraph*, December 8, 1897. *Log*, 282.

569 **ps Have you seen** *C*, 319.

570 **Concerning the English "Academy"** *Bookman* 7 (March 1898). In the Library of America edition, 188–91.

571 **moods of gay tenderness** Edward Garnett, *Letters from Joseph Conrad* (Bobbs-Merrill, 1928), 11–12. *Log*, 281.

571 **A male infant** *C*, 328.

572 **baby-bashing letter** *C*, 330–31.

575 **Glad to hear** *C*, 315.

575 **perhaps it called up memories** J. C. Levenson suggests as much in his long and excellent Introduction to *Works* 5; see pp. xciv–xcv.

594 **one stray story** Quoted by Levenson in his Introduction to *Works* 5, p. lii.

594 **Can't cut this** *C*, 359.

595 **What on earth** *C*, 307–8.

595 **Of course I am awfully** *C*, 318.

595 **For heaven's sake** *C*, 321.

595 **In all the months** *C*, 327.

596 **I am going to write** *C*, 332–33.

596 **As you see** *C*, 336–37.

596 **I must have some money** *C*, 345.

597 **too strong and brutal** Quoted by Levenson in his Introduction to *Works* 5, p. cvii. The editor was David Meldrum, head of the London office of *Blackwood's Magazine*. After the remark about the story being "too strong and brutal" for the magazine's middle-class readers, he ends with the following: "I am sorry, for I admire the story greatly and precisely for its strength, but I couldn't take the responsibility of advising its publication. It seems to me to be one of those cases where, greatly against our will, rejection is the wise course."

597 **I am sending you** *C*, 308.

599 **one of the major** Berryman, 271.

602 **prodigal hospitality** Levenson's Introduction to *Works* 5, p. xciv.

602 **It hurts me to think** *C*, 335.

The Dark Side of the Moon

605 **show evident signs** Weatherford, 227.

605 **little hit** Crane to Reynolds, December 20, 1897: "As soon as the Open Boat volume comes out and makes its little hit as I am sure it will, I want you to drop some news of the novel here and there." *C*, 317.

605 **Dear Harry** *C*, 356–57.

606 **The Young Personage** Frank Norris, "On the Cuban Blockade." Unpublished in his lifetime; *New York Evening Post*, April 11, 1914. *Log*, 302.

613 **a book from 1924 and an article from 1933** Don Carlos Seitz, *Joseph Pulitzer: His Life and Letters* (Simon & Schuster, 1924), and "Stephen Crane: War Correspondent," *Bookman* 76 (February 1933).

614 **masterpieces of description** Stallman, 407.

614 **that he needed money** *C*, 361.

614 **he again wrote to Reynolds** *C*, 361.

615 **Despite extenuating possibilities** *Works* 5:cxi, n.97.

615 **says that he did** *LOF*, 274.

615 **are not sure** Based on conversations with Elizabeth Friedmann (11/2/2019) and Kathryn Hilt (11/4/19).

615 **that there was to be** *C*, 360.

616 **rocking-chair period** Phrase coined by Richard Harding Davis to describe the period between the declaration of war and the invasion of Cuba by American forces six weeks later.

618 **call for military intervention** Clay Risen, *The Crowded Hour: Theodore Roosevelt, the Rough Riders, and the Dawn of the American Century* (Scribner, 2019), 45. Risen goes on: "The anti-imperialists were not wrong. For all the talk about humanitarian intervention and the spread of liberty, what was just as real, but much less explicit, were concerns over markets, and investments, and the need to find new outlets for social frustration and an expanding, restless population. The same urge that had driven white Americans to massacre Indians and take their land was now appearing in the rhetoric around Cuba—except this time, it was clothed in righteousness. Many clear-eyed Americans saw this. But events would soon unfold in a way that rendered them helpless to stop it."

619 **magnificent . . . the very best thing** *C*, 396.

620 **Not since the campaign** *The Letters of Theodore Roosevelt: The Years of Preparation*, ed. Elting E. Morison (Harvard University Press, 1951), 849. Addressed to Henry Cabot Lodge. Risen, *Crowded Hour*, 215.

620 **It was not on account** Richard Harding Davis, *The Cuban and Porto Rican Campaigns* (Charles Scribner's Sons, 1898), 187. Risen, *Crowded Hour*, 215.

620 **Men feared him** "War Memories," *Works* 6:240.

621 **The Key West Hotel** Ralph D. Paine, *Roads of Adventure* (Houghton, Mifflin, 1922). *SCR*, 192.

622 **A nighttime excursion** The high-spirited lark is extensively described in Paine's book. *SCR*, 192–200.

622 **He abominated** *SCR*, 193.

623 **a charming fellow** *SCR*, 221–22.

623 **a drunken, irresponsible** Letter from Henry N. Cary to Vincent Starrett, March 30, 1922. *Log*, 321.

623 **I don't like him** *Log*, 300.

623 **The best correspondent** *SCR*, 230.

626 **having been notified** *C*, 264n1. From *Report for the Secretary of the Navy for the Year 1898* (Washington, DC: GPO, 1898).

626 **He tells of how** *SCR*, 230.

626 **Crane was standing** Arthur Brisbane, "Some Men Who Have Reported This War," *Cosmopolitan* (September 1898). *SCR*, 347n37.

627 **A company under fire** Robert Barr, "American Brains in London: The Men Who Have Succeeded," *Saturday Evening Post*, April 8, 1899. *SCR*, 348n37.

627 **a gleaming white raincoat** Carnes, *Jimmy Hare* passim. The extract is quoted in *SCR*, 223.

627 **Stephen Crane turned up** Carnes, *Jimmy Hare*. *SCR*, 224.

628 **I knew that to Crane** *SCR*, 347n37.

628 **swam two Jamaican horses** "Hunger Has Made Cubans Fatalists," *Works* 9:146–52.

628 **the doomed ships** "War Memories," *Works* 6:287.

629 **When I regained** Edward Marshall, "Stories of Stephen Crane," *San Francisco Call*, December 1900. *Log*, 318.

630 **Whenever I protested** Davis, *Notes of a War Correspondent*. *SCR*, 234.

631 **War Memories** *Works* 6:222–63.

634 **the only fact** *Works* 6:259.

634 **it wasn't so bad** *Works* 6:260.

634 **a tin plate of something** *Works* 6:260.

635 **somewhere in the woods** *Works* 6:261.

635 **dirty, ragged, emaciated** *Works* 6:263.

635 **One of the best known** Richard Harding

Davis, "Our War Correspondents in Cuba and Puerto Rico," *Harper's New Monthly Magazine* 98 (1898–99). *Log*, 328.

636 **Scovel had gone** *Encyclopedia*, 303–4.

636 **rubbing his hands** Seitz, *Joseph Pulitzer*, 1933. *Log*, 331–32.

638 **Dear madam** *C*, 370.

642 **So says** Richard Harding Davis, "How Stephen Crane Took Juana Dias," in *In Many Wars by Many War-Correspondents*, ed. George Lynch and Frederick Palmer (1904). Reprint, Sumac Press, 1976. *SCR*, 232–33.

643 **We imagine how lonely** *C*, 357.

644 **noble and gray** Edward Garnett, *Friday Nights: Literary Criticisms and Appreciations* (Jonathan Cape, 1922). *Log*, 293.

645 **how much it would cost** *Log*, 307.

645 **that he is satisfied** *C*, 362.

645 **will be delighted** *Log*, 314.

646 **Servants refused to spend** *Log*, 308.

646 **A man must have pure** *C*, 388–89.

647 **John Scott Stokes turned up** The visit by Scott Stokes and subsequent information about the inquest and trial are delineated in a chapter of Elizabeth Friedmann's work in progress, *Cora Crane: A Biography*.

648 **I must say** Cited in Friedmann's manuscript. Alice B. Creelman's letter is dated December 29, 1898 (Stephen Crane Papers, Columbia University).

649 **I thank you for your reply** *C*, 402–3.

650 STEPHEN CRANE MISSING Gilkes, 151.

651 **John Hay** Crane had asked Heinemann's to send the Hay family a copy of *The Open Boat and Other Stories* that spring. Helen Hay (a daughter) wrote him a letter of thanks and reported that her father had told her that one of the stories ("A Man and Some Others") "has added tenfold to his joy in life!" *C*, 358.

651 **Knowing you to be** *C*, 370–71.

651 **Russell A. Alger** *C*, 372.

652 **I am in great distress** *C*, 371–72.

652 **at least some** *C*, 374–75.

653 **probably the greatest genius** *Saturday Evening Post*, April 8, 1899. *Encyclopedia*, 19.

653 **struck a reef and sank** *LOF*, 315.

654 **a photograph of Crane** James Gibbons Huneker (a friend of Crane's) on his first visit to Conrad's house: "When I went to see him in England I found a photograph of Stephen Crane on his desk. The Conrads loved the American writer, who had often visited them." From Huneker's book *Steeplejack* (Charles Scribner's Sons, 1920), 2:128. *Log*, 332.

655 **My letters are one long** *Log*, 353. (Stephen Crane Papers, Columbia University.)

655 **Just a word in haste** *C*, 383–84.

656 **for what it is worth** *C*, 386.

656 **that wretched Macqueen** *C*, 396.

656 **It was an immense relief** *C*, 396.

656 **The horror of the last few** *C*, 405.

657 **an unregenerate and abandoned** *LOF*, 305–6.

657 **or until a riot broke out** This and all subsequent quotations of Walter Parker's are from a letter to H. L. Mencken, October 1940 (New York Public Library). *SCR*, 236–39.

658 **Crane and Parker found themselves** *LOF*, 306.

659 **I positively cannot** *C*, 381.

659 **I am working** *C*, 385.

660 **magnificent** *C*, 396.

661 **the price** *C*, 387.

664 **Now this is It** *C*, 373.

664 **How They Court in Cuba** *Works* 9:203–5.

664 **How They Leave Cuba** *Works* 9:199–201.

668 **had not been out** National Archives. *Log*, 347.

668 **"Thanks," Crane said** This and all subsequent quotations of Otto Carmichael's are from "Stephen Crane in Havana," *Omaha Daily Bee*, June 17, 1900; reprinted in *Prairie Schooner* 43, no. 2 (1969). *SCR*, 240–44.

670 **At McClure's I met** *Log*, 359. Not for the first time, Garland seems to have misunderstood the boy he had once championed. In a letter to Garland from October 9, 1900 (four months after Crane's death), Louis Senger wrote, "He spoke of you often, and always with a sense of blame for himself lest you think him ungrateful. He was never that." Stallman and Gilkes, 319.

671 **He was sick and joked** *Log*, 359.

671 **He came to see me last** *Log*, 306.

A Brutal Extinction

672 **Robert, when you come** *LOF*, 367.

672 **I leave here gentle** *Works* 10:343.

673 **His hands were miracles** Edwin Pugh, "Stephen Crane," *Bookman* (England) 67 (December 1924). *SCR*, 297.

673 **Please have the kindness** *C*, 504.

673 **At present I feel like hell** *C*, 515.

673 **My dear William** *C*, 416.

674 **I am still fuzzy** *C*, 418–19.

675 **Stephen is mad** *C*, 420.

677 **at her wit's end** Jessie Conrad, *Joseph Conrad and His Circle* (Dutton, 1935). *SCR*, 255.

678 **As Camus puts it** Albert Camus, *The Myth*

of Sisyphus and Other Essays, trans. Justin O'Brien (Knopf, 1955), 81, 88. Originally published in France by Gallimard, 1942.

678 **Who could ever forget** Edith Ritchie Jones, "Stephen Crane at Brede," *Atlantic Monthly*, July 1954. *SCR*, 283–93.

683 **the most beautiful spirit** Ford's remarks on Crane and Henry James here and in chapter 4 are culled from a variety of sources, all of them gathered in *SCR*, 257–67.

683 **secret irritation** Joseph Conrad, "Stephen Crane: A Note Without Dates," *SCR*, 250.

683 **gave me one of his quiet smiles** Conrad, 26.

684 **a memorable little story** Karl Edwin Harriman, "The Last Days of Stephen Crane," eight-page typescript (Syracuse University Library). *SCR*, 278–80.

685 **I said to him** *Works* 10:344.

685 *Active Service* *Works* 3:113–328.

685 **Dear Mrs. Frewen** *C*, 480–81.

686 **every page is like** Willa Cather, *Pittsburgh Leader*, November 11, 1899. *Log*, 406.

688 **Making an Orator** *Works* 7:158–64.

688 **A Little Pilgrim** *Works* 7:235–39.

688 **Shame** *Works* 7:164–73.

688 **The Stove** *Works* 7:195–207.

698 **Freud, writing in 1908** Sigmund Freud, "The Relation of the Poet to Day-Dreaming," *On Creativity and the Unconscious* (Harper & Row, 1958), 45.

698 **Again Freud** Freud, 52.

702 **If you could give me** *C*, 491.

702 **hated to write letters** *Works* 10:344.

702 **I have just received** *C*, 494.

703 *The O'Ruddy* *Works*, vol. 4. The manuscript was completed by Robert Barr and published in 1903.

703 **developing in three series** *C*, 492.

707 **I am coming to see you** *C*, 417.

707 **I admit he is** *C*, 497. There is reason to suppose that Crane's letters to Henry Sanford Bennett were in fact written by Thomas Beer in his semifictionalized 1923 biography, *Stephen Crane: A Study in American Letters* (with an introduction by Conrad). If so, Crane's remarks about Hueffer can be discounted along with the letter about Conrad quoted on page 714. According to an April 2020 letter from Paul Sorrentino to the author, after he and Stanley Wertheim finished their work on *The Correspondence of Stephen Crane* (1988), they began to have "serious doubts about the authenticity of the letters to Bennett."

708 **in a little summer-house** *SCR*, 286.

709 **All thanks for the strange** *Log*, 393.

709 **While Crane was on** *SCR*, 356–57n63. Originally published as "Stevie," *New York Evening Post Literary Review*, July 12, 1924.

710 **He suffered infinitely** *SCR*, 263. Ford Madox Ford, *Return to Yesterday* (Victor Gollancz, 1931).

710 **It is a shock** *C*, 558–59.

711 **Stephen's story of sweet corn** *SCR*, 141.

711 **I saw him for the** "Stephen Crane from an English Standpoint," *North American Review*, August 1900. Weatherford, 267–68.

712 **Stephen Crane—the best** *SCR*, 358n74.

712 **I am more glad** *C*, 417.

713 **I am so sorry** *C*, 506.

713 **Dear old Pard** *C*, 516.

714 **Dear Bennett** *C*, 651.

715 **In the spring** *C*, 456.

715 **she is at an age** *C*, 488.

716 **She was apparently** *Encyclopedia*, 71. Wertheim's short entry on Helen concludes: "In later life, she was twice married and reportedly died a suicide."

717 **I am mailing** *C*, 494.

717 **If you can stick** *C*, 498.

717 **In the mean time** *C*, 508.

717 **I am so glad** *C*, 527–28.

718 **You are all right** *C*, 531–32.

718 **I confess** *C*, 539–40.

718 **Now Mr. Pinker** *C*, 541.

720 **This is a jolly cold . . . don't think so** Stallman, 491.

720 **the songs, most of which** *Sussex Express*, January 5, 1900. *Log*, 419.

720 **The inhabitants of Brede** *South Eastern Advertiser*, January 5, 1900. *Log*, 419.

721 **He was profoundly weary** H. G. Wells, *Experiment in Autobiography* (Macmillan, 1934). *SCR*, 268.

721 **plucking at his guitar** My sources are Gilkes, *Cora Crane*, and Stallman, *Stephen Crane*, but the detail about the guitar could be apocryphal.

721 **a mere idle string** *C*, 569.

721 **Mr. Crane is ill** *C*, 572.

724 **Already months ago** *Sussex Express*, June 16, 1900. *Log*, 424.

725 **We moved my husband** *C*, 620.

725 **He had a quiet** *C*, 621–22.

725 **There is in our morning** *C*, 623.

725 **There has been** *C*, 623.

726 **Stephen is not** *C*, 632.

726 **I am very sorry** *C*, 635.

726 **The doctors say** *C*, 638.

726 **I am in receipt** *C*, 640.

726 **I have received** *C*, 644.

727 **Your letter distresses me** *C*, 643.

727 **There was a thin thread** *New York Herald*, June 21, 1900. *LOF*, 439–40.

728 **Nurses think** *C*, 649.

728 **I saw Stephen Crane** Joseph Conrad, "Stephen Crane: A Note Without Dates." *SCR*, 250–51.

729 **It is dreadful** *C*, 655–57.

729 **Write to D' Skinner** *Works* 10:343.

730 **What a brutal** *C*, 659n1.

730 **the touch of genius** James Walter Smith, "Literary Letter," *Literary Era*, July 1900. *LOF*, 340.

730 **These things** . . . Stanley Wertheim, "H. G. Wells to Cora Crane: Some Letters and Corrections," *Resources for American Literary Studies*, 1979. *Log*, 448.

731 **I went out** *Log*, 448.

731 **a meteor that glows** *New York Times*, June 29, 1900. Referred to in Elizabeth Friedmann's manuscript in progress about Cora Crane.

732 **This morning I went** *Letters of Wallace Stevens*, ed. Holly Stevens (Knopf, 1966), 42.

735 **The least boring** A. J. Liebling, "The Dollars Damned Him," *New Yorker*, August 5, 1961.

737 **hemorrhage of the brain** Cited in Elizabeth Friedmann's manuscript in progress.

ACKNOWLEDGMENTS

This book is intended as an introduction to the life and work of Stephen Crane and has been written for those who know little or nothing about him. Roughly half of it is devoted to presenting his work in all its multiple forms—novels, novellas, short stories, poems, sketches, journalism, and battle reports from two wars. In discussing those texts, I have not taken a scholarly approach and have steered clear of traditional literary criticism. What I have wanted to do is communicate something about the experience of reading Crane and *how it feels* to encounter his work for the first time—a raw and direct response to what is sitting in front of us on the page, the words themselves, and the thoughts and images those words provoke in us as we move from one sentence to the next. A writer's approach, if you will, the nuts and bolts of how it is done, and because I have assumed my readers have never read a word of Crane, I have quoted many passages at length in order to give them a full sampling of what he could do and how he went about doing it in each specific work.

The other half of the book investigates the twists and turns of Crane's short life, and for those sections I have relied heavily on the work of others, the scholars and biographers who have made it their business to delve into historical archives and extract bones from ancient tar pits to piece together the missing links of Crane's story. This work has taken generations to compile, and whatever I know about Crane comes from the efforts of the men and women who came before me. The notes at the end of *Burning Boy* are densely crowded with their names and the books and articles they have written, but two of those scholars need to be mentioned here, for the bulk of what I have written about Crane's life is a by-product of their labors: Stanley Wertheim and Paul Sorrentino. Between them, they have produced five indispensable books of biographical research about Crane over the past three decades: the jointly edited two-volume *Correspondence* (1988); the jointly assembled *Log* (1994), a five-hundred-page documentary history of

Crane's life, including letters, news reports, reviews, and background details; Wertheim's *Encyclopedia* (1997), an alphabetical listing of Crane's work by title (every book, story, poem, and article he ever published, followed by a brief or long description) and short biographies of all the people who figured prominently in his life; Sorrentino's *Stephen Crane Remembered* (2006), a compendium of sixty-two reminiscences of Crane by his family, friends, and contemporaries; and Sorrentino's *Stephen Crane: A Life of Fire* (2014), the most rigorous and accurate biography ever published about Crane—following a dozen attempts by others in the previous ninety-plus years, beginning with Thomas Beer's half-baked, semifictionalized travesty from 1923. Together, the books by Wertheim and Sorrentino form the five books of the Stephen Crane Bible, and one-half of my own book would not exist without them.

My list of thank-yous is short, but my gratitude to the ones who have helped me along the way runs deep.

Working on this book has taken me into a new, often bewildering country, and for the first time in what has now been half a century of writing and publishing, I have shared the manuscript with others before it was finished, wanting to know if the project made any sense to them and if they were still with me as the pages continued to pile up, far exceeding the bounds of what I had originally announced would be *a short book*. To those three amigos—Barbara Jones of Henry Holt in New York, Walter Donohue of Faber and Faber in London, and my longtime agent Carol Mann—thank you for reassuring me that I had not gone off the deep end.

Thanks as well to Paul Sorrentino, a stranger I reached out to in early 2018, hoping to make contact with someone in the Crane universe. Contrary to my expectations, he did not ignore my letter. Even more encouraging, he did not treat me as a barbarian novelist threatening to invade his kingdom but welcomed me in as a brother lunatic, a member of the tribe. We have become friends since then, and not only has he put me up at his house in Blacksburg, Virginia, for a long weekend of discussions about our favorite subject, he has answered questions and talked out problems with me in numerous telephone conversations and letters. For no other reason than goodwill and a shared desire to promote Crane's work, he has carefully vetted every word I have written, fifty or sixty pages at a time over the past two years, pointing out factual errors whenever I have made them and preventing me from going off track any number of times. His patience and generosity have kept me standing as I blundered my way forward, and without his help, it is hard to imagine how I could have reached the end.

He is also the person who put me in touch with Elizabeth Friedmann, who is hard at work on a new biography of Cora Crane. I called her about a year ago, and since then we have shared manuscripts, ideas, and speculations in a series of lively telephone conversations and letters that have greatly expanded my knowledge of Crane's remarkable wife and given me a new friend. It was Elizabeth Friedmann who in turn put me in touch with Kathryn Hilt, another Crane scholar, who confirmed that the murky episode I was investigating at the time was indeed murky, and I thank Elizabeth Friedmann for that as well as all the other things she has done to help improve this book.

Last of all, but in fact first of all and above all the others, deepest thanks to Siri Hustvedt, who for the past forty years has been the first and most important reader of everything I have written. People say that writers should never marry each other because . . . because it is impossible for two writers to live together under the same roof. They are wrong.

INDEX

Page numbers in *italics* refer to illustrations.

ABOUT THE AUTHOR

Paul Auster is the bestselling author of *4 3 2 1*, *Sunset Park*, *Invisible*, *The Book of Illusions*, and *The New York Trilogy*, among many other works. In 2006 he was awarded the Prince of Asturias Prize for Literature. Among his other honors are the Prix Médicis Étranger for *Leviathan*, the Independent Spirit Award for the screenplay of *Smoke*, and the Premio Napoli for *Sunset Park*. In 2012, he was the first recipient of the NYC Literary Honors in the category of fiction. He has also been a finalist for the International IMPAC Dublin Literary Award (*The Book of Illusions*), the PEN/Faulkner Award (*The Music of Chance*), the Edgar Award (*City of Glass*), and the Man Booker Prize (*4 3 2 1*). He is a member of the American Academy of Arts and Letters and a Commandeur de l'Ordre des Arts et des Lettres. His work has been translated into more than forty languages. He lives in Brooklyn, New York.